ENVIRONMENTAL PSYCHOLOGY

PRINCIPLES AND PRACTICE

SECOND EDITION

Robert Gifford
University of Victoria

Allyn and Bacon

Boston ◆ London ◆ Toronto ◆ Sydney ◆ Tokyo ◆ Singapore

Vice-President, Editor in Chief, Social Sciences: Sean W. Wakely
Editorial Assistant: Erika Stuart
Vice-President, Director of Field Marketing: Joyce Nilsen
Production Administrator: Annette Joseph
Production Coordinator: Susan Freese
Editorial-Production Service: TKM Productions
Text Designer: Denise Hoffman, Glenview Studios
Composition Buyer: Linda Cox
Manufacturing Buyer: Megan Cochran
Cover Administrator: Suzanne Harbison

Copyright © 1997, 1987 by Allyn & Bacon
A Viacom Company
160 Gould Street
Needham Heights, MA 02194

Internet: www.abacon.com
America Online: keyword:College Online

This book is printed on
recycled, acid-free paper.

Library of Congress Cataloging-in-Publication Data

Gifford, Robert.
    Environmental psychology : principles and practices / Robert
Gifford. — 2nd ed.
      p. cm.
    Includes bibliographical references and indexes.
    ISBN 0-205-18941-5
    1. Environmental psychology.   I. Title
[BF353.G54   1996]
155.9—dc20   96-13420
                                                      CIP

Printed in the United States of America

10 9 8 7 6 5 4 3 2 1   01 00 99 98 97 96

See source credits on pages 505–506, which constitute an
extension of the copyright page.

CONTENTS

PREFACE

Every author, but especially an environmental psychologist, should think twice about putting words onto processed trees and three times about producing a second version of the same book. This is, in part, why I have taken nine years to write this second edition. I feel compelled to justify my decision, so what follows describes what is new and what still seems true about this book.

As for what is new, environmental psychologists and kindred spirits have produced a large volume of research and ideas in the last decade. This recent work has produced a more mature image of person-environment transactions, an image that has moved much further toward the perspective our theoreticians have always predicted: that multifarious personal and environmental outcomes are the mediated and moderated products of multifaceted individuals engaged in many different behaviors and psychological processes as they influence and are influenced by multiform settings.

To tell this tale properly required me to invoke 2,500 studies and experiments, more than double the number cited in the first edition. I could not, in good conscience, oversimplify the news that sprung from our researchers' fertile minds. However, in response to many entreaties, I have removed the vast majority of names from the main body of the text. The names of researchers whose work, it seemed to me, clearly merited an affirmative response to the ancient student plea "Will the names be on the test?" remain in the main text. However, in keeping with the scholarly pursuits of truth and due credit, every researcher whose work is cited is credited in the References at the end of the book.

Some readers may be taken aback at the fullness with which person-environment transactions are described in these chapters. I challenged myself to see the field as completely and accurately as current research allows. Then I endeavored to integrate and synthesize the diverse and sometimes disparate results and perspectives clearly. I could not oversimplify, but I sincerely hope the explication is clear.

KEY CHANGES

Readers familiar with the first edition will notice three chapters that look different. This mainly results from a threefold split of the former Chapter 9, Thriving and Surviving at Home and in the City (a title that clearly reveals the chapter should have been split before!). The new Chapter 9, Residential Environmental Psychology, focuses on home in the sense of the primary dwelling. Chapter 10, Community Environmental Psychology, covers home in the larger sense of neighborhoods and cities. The portion in the former Chapter 9 on environmental hazards now is a prominent section of the new Chapter 13, Natural Environmental Psychology. This chapter also contains much new material on nonhazardous nature.

The inclusion of more nature material reflects my belief that environmental psychology, without losing its emphasis on buildings, has grown to include much more serious consideration of people's relations with parks, wilderness, and even the earth as a whole (see Epilogue). Environmental psychologists now count among our ranks ecopsychologists, biophiliacs, and "green" psychologists.

So this edition now contains 15 chapters. This number allows instructors to customize courses by dropping a chapter or three to reflect their own conception of essential environmental psychology. Alternatively, as I said in the Preface to the first edition, certain parts of all chapters might be omitted, such as the methods or applications sections.

WHAT REMAINS THE SAME

I still believe environmental psychology is a science, an applied science, and an art. I detect a tension between the first two of these, but it is a healthy tension. Soon, I believe, the subdisciplines of experimental environmental psychology and applied environmental psychology will be recognized, reflecting differences in the activities of environmental psychology that already exist. To flourish, both will require an artistic sensitivity in the choice of problems to study and the most appropriate methods (for sensitive interaction with research participants and clients) and in data interpretation.

Each chapter is arranged, for the most part, in the same five sections used in the first edition. In general, the topic is introduced, research methods are introduced, existing knowledge is surveyed, theories are described, and case studies provide a conclusion to each chapter. Each key term is in bold and defined in plain English and in context (rather than in a distant glossary).

ACKNOWLEDGMENTS

Only one name appears on the title page, but this book could not have been written without the help of many persons.

First, I wish once again to thank my parents, Robert and Dorothy, or alas, their spirits, wherever they roam. Their support and encouragement loom ever larger as I move through the life-cycle stages in which they offered them to me and try to emulate their selfless concern. And as in the previous edition, I thank Robert Sommer for the start he gave me before the subject environmental psychology had a name.

As for direct efforts in producing this manuscript, I am grateful to a succession of brave souls who struggled with the endless details that comprise a work like this. Sharon Ali contributed to many phases, stages, and parts of the manuscript, and I am very grateful for her many efforts. Earlier, Mike Miller, Kim Syer, and Tara Brookman were very helpful. Jo Moreland and Catherine Corey moved many cut-and-pasted bits into malleable word-processor format. Kelly Shaw helped with permissions letters. My sister, Coe Gifford, contributed excellent photographs. Jennifer Veitch and Don Hine answered questions in areas about which they know more than I do. Paul Coulson helped tidy up the ends near the finish line. Darren Douglas, Jonas Gifford, and D'Arcy Reynolds helped greatly with the indexes.

I also want to acknowledge several people at Allyn and Bacon. Thanks to Bill Barke for lunch, Susan Badger for patience, Erika Stuart for the details, and Lynda Griffiths for copyediting. My gratitude is also extended to the following survey respondents for their helpful comments: Julia Hall, Drexel University; John Morganti, State University College at Buffalo; Paul Paulus, University of Texas at Arlington; Dahrl Pedersen, Brigham Young University; and John Sparrow, State University of New York–Geneseo.

As is the lot of every writer's family, Sarah, Anna, Jonas, and Eva worked around my long hours, preoccupation, and moods. Their support and forbearance were then and are now crucial to me, and I am grateful to them.

My sincere thanks to the instructors who adopted the first edition, particularly those who have offered their views and suggestions over the years. Tory Hoff deserves special mention in this regard. Joe Lyons's secret maxim was difficult to apply, but it did work again. I encourage instructors and readers to contact me with questions, comments, or suggestions at any of the addresses below.

Robert Gifford
Department of Psychology
University of Victoria
Victoria, British Columbia
Canada V8W 3P5

E-mail: snap@uvvm.uvic.ca
Fax: 604-721-8929
Phone: 604-721-7532

CHAPTER 1

THE NATURE AND SCOPE OF ENVIRONMENTAL PSYCHOLOGY

> Perhaps one of the outstanding weaknesses of contemporary psychological theory is the relative neglect of the environment by many of the most influential theoretical viewpoints.
>
> —Isidor Chein[1]

◆ WHAT IS ENVIRONMENTAL ◆
PSYCHOLOGY?

Environmental psychology is the study of transactions between individuals and their physical settings. In these transactions, individuals change the environment and their behavior and experiences are changed by the environment. Environmental psychology includes research and practice aimed at making buildings more humane and improving our relationship with the natural environment.

As a recognized field, environmental psychology is only about 30 years old, but some social scientists have worked for decades on the issues that will be discussed in this book. In the early days of psychology, most researchers concentrated heavily on processes *within* persons rather than person-environment transactions. Yet, considering the enormous investment society makes in the construction and maintenance of the physical environment (including buildings, parks, streets, the atmosphere and bodies of water) and the enormous cost of misusing nature and natural resources, the long delay before person-environment relations received adequate attention seems almost tragic.

Fortunately, since the late 1960s, thousands of studies have dealt with the major topics represented by the chapters to follow. Much of this work has been stimulated by the recognition of environmental problems such as pollution, energy shortages, and unsuitable buildings. Other research is motivated by pure curiosity about how and why humans act and feel in their natural settings. Many mysteries remain about the intricacies of person-environment transactions, but we have begun to understand some of them.

In this chapter, the main issues and topics of environmental psychology are described. Its dual goals of discovery and application are emphasized. The origins and present status of the field are briefly discussed, along with overviews of the major theoretical approaches and some observations on research methods. Comments on the international dimensions and future prospects of environmental psychology close the chapter.

The Issues

The simple definition that opens this chapter does not convey the fascinating variety of topics that environmental psychologists study. Each of the following actual headlines alludes to a problem that will be discussed in this book:

- "Sanctuary Now Battlefield as Neighbors Fight Fence"
- "Working in an Office Is Dangerous to Your Health"
- "The Greening of Psychology"
- "Violence: A Fact of Life in Overcrowded Jails"
- "Air Pollution Threatening Pristine Alaska Wilderness"
- "Quotas Slashed in Attempt to Help Troubled Herring Fishery"
- "The Noise Pollution Toll"
- "Crazy Summer Days Goad Child Abuse"
- "Weather Stress Index Blows Ill Wind"
- "What's Wrong with High Rises?"
- "When Kids Crave Privacy"
- "Satisfying Workers a Matter of Color?"

We must be cautious about some of the claims made by the enthusiastic authors of these headlines; some exaggerate the truth. However, what *is* real and important in each case is a problem. Each problem involves not just the environment but some *transaction* between individuals and settings.

The term **environment**, in this book, means built settings, such as homes, offices, schools, and streets, and natural settings, such as national parks and wilderness areas. On the human side of the transaction, this book refers less often to the behavior of large aggregates of people (society or humankind or governments) than it does to the behavior of individuals and small groups (office workers, pedestrians, pupils, extraverts, shoppers, neighbors, hikers, dormitory residents, burglars, architects, commuters, and other everyday people; see Figures 1–1 and 1–2).

Environmental psychologists recognize the need to accomplish two related goals: to understand person-environment transactions and to use this knowledge to help solve a wide variety of problems. The subtitle of this book, *Principles and Practice,* was not chosen lightly;

FIGURE 1–1 This uncompleted building could serve as a symbol of environmental psychology's task in the built environment. It was designed 3,000 miles from its site; the architects never even met most of those who will work in it or visit it. The specific needs of its occupants could not have been adequately studied.

FIGURE 1–2 Environmental psychology investigates persons-in-relation-to-nature.

environmental psychology distinctly includes both science and application.

As individuals, of course, environmental psychologists are not superhuman: Each has only enough energy to work on a fraction of the topics described in the chapters to follow. Some feel more comfortable working on the *principles;* others feel more comfortable with the *practice.* The situation is similar to that in medicine, where some physicians go into family practice and others remain in the laboratory. Still, all environmental psychologists support the need for theory, research, *and* practice that may help to solve these and other problems.

Finding the Principles

To ease a real-world problem, one must have knowledge to apply. Two forms of knowledge are *theory* and *research findings.* Theory guides both research and practice by providing a coherent framework for understanding problematic human-environment problems. In environmental psychology, theories themselves do not provide answers to specific problems. Instead, their job is to provide a direction that may yield solutions.

Many theories are described throughout this book. The number and variety of them illustrate the youthful ferment and enthusiasm of environmental psychology. A sorting-out process among theories may eventually reduce their number, but it probably would be unwise to seek a single, all-inclusive theory. Even in working on a single problem, environmental psychologists find multiple viewpoints helpful in enabling them to see more of the problem's ramifications. The major theoretical approaches will be briefly described later in this chapter, but most theoretical discussion occurs in the chapter where a given theory is most appropriate.

The second form of knowledge that may be applied to a problem is that gained from research. This book is crammed with the findings of studies on dozens of topics. Some of you may find the book contains too many studies for your taste. Reality is complex, however, and I feel very uncomfortable telling you half a story when I am aware that researchers know more than a simplistic account would include. Even so, students sometimes are surprised that the available, published research does *not* contain answers to many questions. The research literature often cannot supply a concrete answer to a specific current problem because today's problem involves different individuals in a different place and different time than did yesterday's problem. Differences among individuals, cultures, eras, and settings often lead to different results in studies that otherwise appear similar.

Why should you read about all these previous studies, then? There are several reasons.

1. Despite what was just said, some results *do* appear time after time. Environmental psychology does not yet have a large number of established principles, but certain findings and principles have been confirmed repeatedly.

2. Previous work provides guidance for future study. On the negative side, research sometimes demonstrates that a certain idea or method is a blind alley. The main discovery may be that no one should venture in *that* direction again! On the positive side—and more typically—research provokes new questions by producing unanticipated outcomes. Future studies may then be more sophisticated: Researchers can avoid known pitfalls and be aware of important issues that were unknown to earlier researchers. If you plan to conduct research in environmental psychology someday, you will need this knowledge. Even if you do not plan to do so, you should have a realistic picture of the field that accurately depicts its current width and breadth.

3. Knowledge of past research serves to correct misconceptions about many person-environment transactions that crop up in everyday conversations. The following are only a few examples of conclusions from research that go against popular wisdom: Crowding has only a weak relation to the number of other persons around; human territoriality is not primarily associated with aggression; and there is no good evidence that pink jail cells calm down violent prisoners or that full-spectrum lighting is good for people. In each of these cases, other personal or environmental factors are more important. In fact, a basic message I hope to convey is that every person-environment transaction is governed by a multiplicity of influences. Within the normal range of human experience, it is almost never true that only one influence shapes our experience or behavior.

The Principles in Practice

While recognizing the value of theory and research, some environmental psychologists nevertheless prefer to *apply* knowledge. Instead of working in an academic setting, where most researchers work, they venture into private practice. After appropriate graduate training, they operate as consultants to public and private-sector clients. The practicing environmental psychologist, like the researcher, also makes new discoveries, but these findings are primarily intended to assist a specific client in a specific place and time rather than to establish a scientific principle.

◆ *IN SUM, environmental psychology is a young and vital discipline that genuinely requires the pursuit of both scientific principles and practical application as it seeks to ameliorate a wide variety of problems arising from person-environment transactions. Much is known, but much is still unknown, too, and this challenge of the unknown is what motivates many environmental psychologists. Practicing environmental psychologists are motivated by the conviction that they can help create more humane buildings or improve the way people interact with nature.*

◆ THE ROOTS AND EDGES ◆ OF ENVIRONMENTAL PSYCHOLOGY

The field of environmental psychology may be traced far back into the history of psychology. In some ways, it seems at first to be indistinguishable from the main core of psychology; most psychologists examine the relations between environmental stimuli and human responses. Yet, what sets environmental psychology apart is its commitment to research that subscribes to the following principles:

- It is ultimately capable of improving the built environment and the stewardship of natural resources.
- It is carried out in everyday settings (or close simulations of them).
- It considers the person and setting to be a holistic entity.
- It recognizes that individuals actively cope with and shape settings, rather than passively absorb environmental forces.
- It is often performed in conjunction with other disciplines.

Environmental psychology's historical origins may be traced almost as far back as the rest of psychology, but it has always been on the edge of psychology—in two senses.

1. Environmental psychology still is not part of the central core of psychology. It is not taught in every college, nor can it claim as many researchers as some other areas of psychology.
2. The main concern of environmental psychology— the everyday physical environment—has rarely received serious attention in psychology, as stated by the quote that opens this chapter.

Although the major processes and topics in psychology—development, cognition, learning, social relations, abnormal behavior—occur in everyday physical settings, only environmental psychology systematically investigates the settings in which these processes occur. To offer just one example, the study of learning ultimately and intimately relates to classrooms, yet few studies of learning in traditional psychology have been done in classrooms.

EGON BRUNSWIK

was probably the first person to use the term environmental psychology *in print.*

The fact that environmental psychology has deep roots within the field and is at the same time at the edge of the discipline is illustrated in the theoretical work of Egon Brunswik and Kurt Lewin, two great precursors of the field.

Egon Brunswik (1903–1955) was born in Budapest and trained in Vienna. He emigrated to the United States in the 1930s. Brunswik originally concentrated on the process of perception (discussed in Chapter 2), but his ideas have been extended far beyond that. In calling for a more detailed analysis of the way physical environment factors affect behavior, Brunswik was probably the first to use to use the term *environmental psychology*, back in 1943.[2]

Brunswik also strongly advocated **representative design**, the idea that research designs should include a much wider array of environmental stimuli than psychologists of the day typically employed. These stimuli, he said, should be more representative of the real world of the persons we are trying to understand.

Kurt Lewin (1890–1947), the other great precursor in this field, was born in Prussia and trained in Germany.

KURT LEWIN

was an inspired theorist, an inspiring teacher, and the founder of action research.

He, too, emigrated to the United States in the 1930s. His **field theory** was one of the first to give active consideration to the molar physical environment. Lewin's idea of **action research** was perhaps the first major push in psychology toward linking scientific research with real social change. Lewin's influence, through these two ideas, has been very strong in environmental psychology.

The sense in which Lewin thought of the physical environment—at least all those aspects of it that are outside a person's awareness—is revealed in his name for it: the **foreign hull**. Early on, Lewin did not accept that the foreign hull could be a part of psychology.[3] Later, he agreed that forces from the foreign hull do reach awareness and begin to affect psychological processes. He proposed that this field of inquiry be called **psychological ecology**.

Brunswik and others[4] believed, however, that the physical environment *could* affect people without their knowing. For example, the hum of a fluorescent light fixture might affect an office worker's satisfaction with work or productivity even though the office worker is unaware of the hum. Brunswik believed that if such factors really can affect us psychologically, then they must be studied systematically.

Despite their influential ideas, however, neither Brunswik nor Lewin actually performed studies that today would be called environmental psychology. Brunswik had few students, and for many years his ideas had little influence on psychology; that is one reason why his ideas, although important, have been on the edge of psychology.

Lewin, on the other hand, has had a strong influence in psychology. A dynamic and charismatic person, he inspired many students who, in turn, profoundly shaped the direction of social science. However, most of Lewin's students interpreted his ideas to mean that the *social* environment and the *perceived* environment were crucial; the actual or objective physical environment was not stressed. Thus, environmental psychology was one *edge* of Lewin's legacy. However, two of his students did take the physical environment more seriously and pursued psychological ecology, later changing the term to **ecological psychology**. These students, Roger Barker and Herbert Wright, began a large-scale research project in 1947 that studied **behavior settings**, small ecological units enclosing everyday human behavior.[5]

ROGER BARKER
*was a student of Kurt Lewin and the
founder of behavioral ecology and
behavior-setting theory.*

Behavior settings include both the social rules *and*
the physical-spatial aspects of our daily lives. The classroom, the concert hall, the restaurant, and the council
meeting are examples. Barker and his colleagues worked
hard to describe the social and physical characteristics of
these and other identifiable behavior settings for entire
towns. In reflecting on the origins of his research, Barker
later said,

> The awful truth dawned upon me that although I was
> well informed about the behavior of children when con-
> fronted with tests and experiments devised by scientific
> investigators, I knew no more than a lay person about the
> situations and conditions the towns provided their chil-
> dren and how the children behaved.[6]

Brunswik's and Lewin's ideas helped create the intellectual basis for environmental psychology, but the empirical roots of environmental psychology began much
earlier. Before 1920, psychologists had studied the effect
of noise[7] and heat[8] on work performance. A study of
where students sat in classrooms in relation to the grades
they earned was published in 1921,[9] and the famous
Hawthorne studies of light's effect on work performance
began in 1924.[10] These studies were almost atheoretical;
the researchers looked for simple, deterministic effects of
the environment on work performance.

By the 1950s, other pioneers in environmental psychology were at work even before the field had a name.
For example, Abraham Maslow and a colleague showed
in 1954 that the same photos of people were rated more
positively when the ratings were done in a beautiful
room than when they were done in an average or ugly
room, even though the aesthetics of the room was never
mentioned to the raters.[11]

In the late 1950s, Robert Sommer and Humphrey
Osmond began to systematically alter the physical elements of buildings in Saskatchewan, Canada, and to
monitor the effects of these changes on behavior.[12,13] By
rearranging furniture and redesigning wards in a geriatric hospital, they found they could increase communication among the patients. At the same time, Sommer
began his famous studies of personal space (discussed in
Chapter 5).[14] In New York, another team, headed by
William Ittelson and Harold Proshansky, read about the
Sommer and Osmond work and began to map the behavior of patients on a mental hospital ward.[15]

The first conferences specifically devoted to what
was then called **architectural psychology** were held at
the University of Utah in 1961 and 1966. Proshansky
and Ittelson went on to establish the first Ph.D. program in environmental psychology at the City University of New York (CUNY) in 1968. One marker of
environmental psychology's youth is that the first Ph.D.
in the CUNY program was earned in 1975. By contrast,
the first American Ph.D. in psychology was granted in
1861, the first in industrial-organizational psychology
in 1921, and the first in clinical psychology just after
World War I.

By the late 1960s, the first professional journals devoted to the field were established; the most prominent
of these today are the *Journal of Environmental Psychology* and *Environment and Behavior*. In 1968, the largest
environment-behavior organization, the Environmental
Design Research Association (EDRA), was formed; it
has held annual meetings since 1969. (Many other organizations, journals, and graduate schools are listed in
the Appendix.)

♦ *IN SUM, whisperings of an environmental psychology began in the 1910s, followed by a trickle of activity
through the 1950s, which grew throughout the 1960s into
a torrent by the beginning of the 1970s.*

♦ THEORIES AND APPROACHES ♦ IN BRIEF

As noted earlier, no single theory applies to all the topics
in environmental psychology. Competing theories still
jostle one another to explain person-environment
events. If the future is like the brief past, new theories

will evolve and there will be mergers, takeovers, bankruptcies, and spin-offs among the current theories.

Do not be discouraged by the existence of apparently conflicting theories. Remember the ancient story about three blind sages who encounter a being unknown to them (an elephant). One sage, grasping the animal's tail, described the being as similar to a rope. Another, holding its trunk, claimed the being was like a hose. A third, arms wrapped around a stout leg, could not believe the others were unable to realize that the being resembled a tree. Similarly, each of today's theories in environmental psychology is probably an accurate but partial explanation of human behavior in physical contexts.

Next, six major theoretical approaches will be described briefly, which should allow you to begin thinking about how the research findings you will soon be reading about fit together. One of the most important functions of a theory is to provide generalizations that give order and meaning to specific observations about person-environment relations.

Stimulation Theories

The stimulation theories conceptualize the physical environment as a source of sensory information that is crucial to our welfare.[16] This stimulation includes relatively simple stimuli such as light, color, sound, noise, heat, and cold, but also more complex stimuli such as buildings, streets, outdoor settings, and other people. In environmental psychology, the stimulus usually is not some artificial laboratory event, but information from the real world.

Two significant ways environmental stimulation can vary are in amount and in meaning. In *amount*, stimulation varies in such obvious dimensions as intensity, duration, frequency, and number of sources. *Meaning* refers to each person's integration and interpretation of the stimulus information that arrives.

One important stimulation-based theory is **adaptation-level theory**, which maintains that individuals adapt to certain levels of stimulation in certain contexts—that is, no particular amount of stimulation is good for everyone. The theory also claims that stimulation different from one's adaptation level changes one's feelings and behavior.[17]

Arousal theories are based on the assumption that the form and content of a broad range of our behavior and experience are related to how physiologically aroused we are.[18,19] **Overload theory** concentrates on the effects of too much stimulation.[20,21] Considerable research in environmental psychology originates with problems that may be viewed from an arousal or overload perspective, such as the effects of noise, heat, cold, and crowding. However, we also find ourselves in settings that offer too little stimulation. **Restricted environmental stimulation** (once called *stimulus deprivation*) causes problems for us in some circumstances, as you might expect, but in others, it yields surprisingly positive results.[22] The performance of easy cognitive tasks, for example, is improved under low stimulation conditions.[23]

Stress has also become an important theoretical concept in recent years. Environmental psychologists have extended the work of Hans Selye to help explain the behavioral and health effects that occur when environmental stimulation exceeds an individual's adaptive resources.[24,25] The stress concept has been applied in a very wide variety of everyday contexts; suspected stressors include air pollution, hospitals, offices, extreme temperatures, traffic, noise, and disasters. One can distinguish **acute stressors** (negative, intense, relatively short impacts that are in the forefront of consciousness), **ambient stressors** (negative, chronic, global environmental conditions that usually remain in the background of consciousness and seem hard to alter), and **daily hassles** (negative, nonurgent, recurrent stressors).[26]

Two basic stress models predominate: One emphasizes physiological responses, and the other emphasizes psychological responses.[27] On the physiological side, Selye first described the **general adaptation syndrome**, a pattern of bodily reactions that remains similar even when the specific source of the stress varies. The pituitary and adrenal glands respond to stressors in a particular sequence: alarm, then resistance, and then exhaustion from the cumulative effort of much resistance. The psychological side of stress emphasizes the role of cognitive appraisal—that is, our efforts to assess the seriousness of the situation and to cope with the stressor. Thus, the *meaning* of the stressor is an important factor in psychological stress.[28]

Other theorists emphasize the meaning of stimulation even more. The bestowal of meaning—together with our selection, construction, modification, and destruction of settings—is among the ways we shape the environment during our continuous series of transactions with it. The personal meanings we give to a place are essential to our *experience* of the environment.[29]

The meaning of the environment, in this sense, has been studied from the perspective of **phenomenology**, a form of careful contemplation in which one goal is to understand what a setting really means, especially to those who regularly spend time in the setting. As we become familiar with a setting, we create meaning for it. This meaning may be positive or negative in tone, similar or different from the meanings attached to it by others, weak or strong. Places without meaning affect us differently than places with meaning; we treat places without meaning differently than we treat meaningful places.

Control Theories

A second set of theories in environmental psychology focuses on control. We may adapt to a certain level of stimulation and sometimes be faced with too little or too much of it, but another obviously important consideration is how much control we actually have (or think we have or want to have) over environmental stimulation. Clearly, those who have much control over the amount and kind of stimulation that comes their way generally are better off than those who have little control. We may have considerable control in some settings, such as at home, and very little in others, such as in traffic jams.

Theories of **personal control**[30] have been developed to account for the effects of being able or unable to influence stimulation patterns. For example, the lack of control often leads to **psychological reactance**, an attempt to regain the freedom one has lost.[31] Individuals who conclude that control is difficult or impossible to regain may succumb to **learned helplessness**, the conviction that no amount of effort can succeed in overcoming an unpleasant or painful situation.[32] In everyday social transactions, we attempt to achieve personal control through several **boundary regulation mechanisms**, such as personal space and territoriality.[33]

Behavior-Setting Theory

A third major theoretical formulation is **behavior setting**, a concept based on Barker's ecological psychology, mentioned earlier.[34,35] A central tenet of behavior-setting theory is that consistent, prescribed patterns of behavior, called **programs**, are found in many places. If you walk into a barber shop, a football game, or a food store, you are likely to see recurrent activities, regularly carried out by persons holding specific roles. For example, every football game features two teams of players who run, pass, and score; officials who monitor rule violations; and fans who cheer and boo.

Variations in the actions of individuals do occur, of course, but traditional behavior-setting theorists pay less attention to psychological processes and individual differences among participants than do the stimulation and control theorists. Proponents of behavior-setting theory are impressed by the uniformity rather than the variability in the actions of those who occupy a given role, especially in contrast to the behavior of those occupying a different role. Consider, for example, the differences in behavior of players, officials, and fans in the football game. Behavior-setting theorists tend to explain person-environment relations primarily in terms of the social features of a setting, such as rules, customs, and typical activities, and its physical features.

One key concept in behavior-setting theory is the level of **staffing**.[36] For a variety of reasons, a given behavior setting may attract many or few who wish to participate in its activities. When there are too many individuals around (and the behavior setting fails to find a way to exclude extras), overstaffing results. When too few are attracted, understaffing results. You can probably recall instances of both overstaffed and understaffed behavior settings in your experiences. What were the consequences for individuals in these settings?

Allan Wicker has extended the behavior-setting concept in time.[37] Behavior settings are not static entities; they are born, they struggle, adapt, thrive, and die. (The sewing bee is almost extinct; make way for the Internet café!)

Integral Theories

A fourth group of theoreticians have searched for a model that captures the full complexity of everyday person-environment relations. I will use the term **integral theories** to characterize these approaches.

Perhaps the earliest explicit theory of environmental psychology was proposed by Isidor Chein.[38] He called it a description of the **geo-behavioral environment**; in 1954, when his proposal was published, environmental psychology as we know it did not yet exist. Chein's integral framework consisted of five major elements.

1. **Instigators:** Environmental stimuli that trigger particular behaviors[39]
2. **Goal objects and noxients:** Situations that can satisfy needs or produce pain or unpleasantness
3. **Supports and constraints:** Aspects of the physical environment that facilitate (lights, desks, roads) or restrict (fences, locks, trackless wilderness) our actions
4. **Directors:** Features of the environment that tell us what to do or where to go
5. **Global environment:** Generalized characteristics of an environment (e.g., the Arctic is harsh, jungles are wet, and high rises are made of steel and glass)

In broad terms, if you understand a person's environments in terms of Chein's five elements, you probably will be able to understand that person's behavior pretty well.

Another, simpler, form of integral theory is **interactionism** (see Figure 1–3). It represents an advance over older, simpler, deterministic theories that attributed most or all of the causes of human behavior *either* to the person *or* to the environment. Persons and environments are considered to be separate entities, but they are continually engaged in a series of interactions.

Transactionalism emphasizes that a person and an environment are part of one inclusive entity.[40] This means that neither individuals nor settings can be adequately defined without reference to the other and that activities of one necessarily influence the other.[41] We influence environments and environments influence us.

Organismic theories emphasize the dynamic interplay of social, societal, and individual factors in a mutual, complex system.[42] Behavior is viewed as part of many possible developmental equilibria that have both short-term and long-term goals (see Figure 1–4). These integral theories represent the highest, most encompassing dreams of environmental psychologists. They prob-

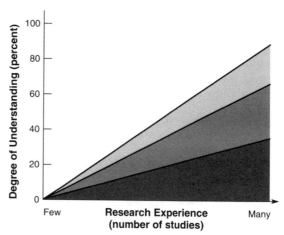

Contribution to Understanding of Person-Environment Relations

■ Person Characteristics

■ Environment Characteristics

■ Person × Environment Interactions

FIGURE 1–3 The growth of knowledge about person-environment transactions. In general, our understanding of outcomes (behaviors, cognitions, and well-being) grows with the number of quality scientific investigations. Some outcomes can be primarily explained by knowing key information about the *person*, and others primarily by knowing key information about the *setting*. Finally, some outcomes require an explanation based on knowing which kind of person is in which kind of setting—an *interaction*.

ably do describe "the way it really is." Yet, a persistent problem is a gap between their attractive themes and the reality of current research methods. Few methods have yet been developed that are capable of adequately testing integral theories. Most research design and statistical analysis methods are better geared to interactionism, the simplest form of integral theory: Person and environment are defined separately and the influence of each (plus their joint influence) is measured.

The Operant Approach

A fifth theoretical perspective is the **operant** approach.[43] This approach is based on Skinnerian principles, and its goal is to modify the behavior of individuals whose behavior is contributing to some environmental problem.

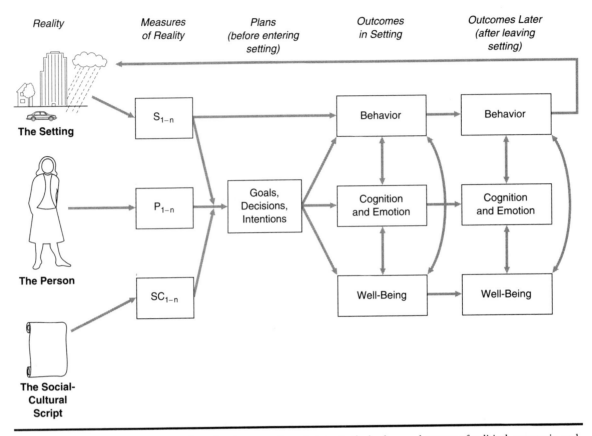

FIGURE 1–4 A comprehensive overview of environmental psychology. In the background context of political, economic, and historical factors (not shown here), a person enters an environment. The consequences for that person and environment are partially determined by social and cultural norms. The person's plans upon entering the environment (if any!) reflect these norms, as well as the person's own talents, dispositions, and past experiences. Once in the environment, transacting with it (consciously or not), the person thinks, feels, and behaves. These transactions often have important outcomes both for the person and the environment. Some outcomes are immediate; others are delayed. The twin goals of environmental psychologists are to understand these transactions and to improve outcomes for both persons and environments.

Specific problematic behaviors are identified, then appropriate positive reinforcements are delivered when individuals engage in more beneficial behavior. Some prime examples of problems that have been attacked with the operant approach are recycling, littering, and residential energy wastage.

Environment-Centered Approaches

A sixth theoretical direction, more recent than the others, might be termed the **environment-centered approaches**. These theories, without ignoring people, pay special attention to the state or quality of the environment. One such approach contrasts instrumental versus spiritual views of the environment: Should the environment be viewed as a tool for supporting human goals such as productivity or as a context in which important human values can be cultivated?[44] Another such approach contrasts person-centered theories with approaches that concentrate on preserving, conserving, and helping the natural environment,[45,46] an approach that has been called **green psychology**.

Finally, some psychologists have begun to think of our relationship to the earth in terms of an almost mystical sympathetic bond that has been suffering in recent times. These **ecopsychologists,** many of whom are clinical psychologists, think of this bond in term of ecological unconsciousness, denial, addiction, and mental health.[47]

◆ *IN SUM, theory in environmental psychology is vital, diverse, and still developing. Some theorists emphasize stimulation. The adaptation-level approach begins with the assumption that each of us becomes accustomed to a certain level of environmental stimulation. The common occurrence of too much or too little stimulation is the focus of arousal, overload, underload, and stress theories, which predict that a wide range of behaviors and experiences will be affected. A second type of theory emphasizes the importance of an individual's real, perceived, or desired control over stimulation, such as personal control, reactance, learned helplessness, and boundary regulation theories. Third, the ecological-psychology approach asserts the importance of behavior settings, naturally occurring small-scale social-physical units consisting of regular patterns of person-environment behavior. Fourth, integral approaches such as interactionism, transactionalism, and organismic theory attempt to describe the full, complex interrelationship of persons and setting. Fifth, operant approaches downplay abstract principles, adopting a direct problem-solving approach that employs behavior-modification techniques. Sixth, environment-centered theories such as green psychology and ecopsychology raise the issue of the environment's own welfare and its ability to support our welfare.*

◆ RESEARCH METHODS ◆ IN ENVIRONMENTAL PSYCHOLOGY

Environmental psychologists use a wide variety of methods in their work. Each of these methods is best described in the chapter covering the topic in which it is primarily used. This section, therefore, is not a detailed examination of research methods. But because research methods are important, descriptions and evaluations of them are found throughout the book. For those who are keen to learn many details of environmental research methods, entire books have been devoted to the topic.[48,49] I will largely confine my re-

marks to several points about research methods that I think are important.

1. Environmental psychology is a **multiple paradigm** field.[50] This means that different researchers may employ not only different methods but also entirely different kinds of techniques based on different philosophies of science. Research methods vary not just in their procedures but also in the very beliefs and values of the investigators who use them. One example is the stark contrast between the reinforcement strategies of the operant approach and the experiential strategies of the phenomenologists who study the meaning of place. Paradigms need not conflict; they may represent alternative, complementary visions of the field, or views of the same phenomena at different levels of analysis.

The word *paradigm* also means something broader than research methods; it is an overall perspective about what the field as a whole is all about. For example, one view is that environmental psychology consists of three broad paradigms.[51] The **adaptation paradigm** sees biological and psychological survival as the key process. Coping with stress and perception, cognition, and assessment of our environments all may be seen as processes whose aim is to help us survive. The **opportunity structure paradigm** considers the environment as a place for us to actively fulfill goals, as opposed to reacting to the environment's threats and demands. We plan and use the environment—or at least try to—in order to achieve whatever purposes we may have. The **sociocultural paradigm** is a recognition that environmental psychology is nested within other contexts and disciplines: History, culture, and economic and societal forces cannot be ignored as we seek to understand person-environment relations.

Environmental psychologists, despite occasional paradigm clashes, generally advocate the use of multiple methods and approaches to gain knowledge; they recognize that each method has strengths and weaknesses. Researchers cannot include all methods in any one study, so the findings of any single study must usually be treated as one bit of knowledge to be integrated with the findings of other studies before firm conclusions may be drawn.

Researchers must be very patient and cautious about drawing strong conclusions from single studies, which are likely to have one or more limitations. Responsible researchers search for patterns of results in a *series* of studies by themselves and others. Multiple methods, multiple paradigms, and multiple studies are necessary for understanding.

On the other hand, any old method will not do. Once a particular question is identified—and it is crucial to have a *clear* question or hypothesis—some research methods become much better choices than others. However, in order to select the *best* method, researchers must be aware of the many possibilities. You cannot select the best method if you have never heard of it.

2. Some methods employed by environmental psychologists are quite standard social science techniques, such as naturalistic observation and description, interviews, rating scales, laboratory experiments, and videotaping. Other methods—including some of the ways to study personal space, cognitive maps, and movement through buildings—are unique to environmental psychology.

3. A central concern of environmental psychology is **external validity**, the degree to which results of a study apply in contexts beyond the setting where they were obtained, such as the everyday world. This concern has led to a widespread suspicion of laboratory research: How sure are we that whatever occurs in a lab will occur in an everyday setting? It is important to remember that some studies (in particular, studies in which the specific purpose is to definitively test a theory) are best conducted in laboratories.

This concern with external validity naturally leads to a tendency to conduct **field studies**. Field studies are performed in the very setting where the results are to be applied, or in one as similar as possible. Of course, some studies cannot be conducted in the setting for which the results are intended. For example, research on the performance or satisfaction of employees who will work in a proposed office complex is impossible. Yet, if the research waits until the complex is built, it is too late to use the results in the design of the complex. One solution is to simulate the building before it is constructed. Sophisticated facilities have been built to simulate offices (Irvine, California), regional landscapes (Berkeley, California) and residences (Lausanne, Switzerland).

Field studies usually cannot provide critical tests of theories or reach conclusions about the causal nature of events in the setting. This is because in real settings, many influences other than those of interest to the investigator are at work and may influence the outcomes. The ideal piece of research is a **field experiment**. Such a study occurs in the real setting of interest, but the experimenter is able to randomly assign participants to different conditions and he or she controls all the major independent variables or presumed influences on behavior or well-being. In a true field experiment, researchers can claim external validity automatically because the investigation occurs in the very setting to which they wish to generalize their findings. Researchers may also draw causal conclusions because other influences have been controlled through random assignment and other features of the scientific method. Unfortunately, as you might have guessed, opportunities to conduct field experiments are quite rare. So, we must often make do with laboratory or field studies.

4. Environmental psychology accepts the idea that behavior is subject to many influences. Field studies often reveal an environment's total effect on a person, but they usually do not shed light on the way the particular aspects of the environment acted to produce the effect. If a researcher's goal is to isolate specific causes of behavior or to test a theory in a precise way—that is, principles of behavior rather than practice—the laboratory may be necessary.

Between the artificial but precise laboratory and the realistic but imprecise everyday setting lie various **quasi-experimental designs** as compromises. Among the requirements of true experiments are random assignment of subjects to conditions and experimenter control of the conditions or variables hypothesized to affect one's behavior or thinking. Quasi-experimental designs might, for example, include real classrooms but accept the limitation that the experimenter is unable to randomly assign pupils to the classrooms. Or, in a study of outdoor heat on aggression, rates of violent acts on hot versus normal days might be compared even though the investigator could not control the day's temperature. In short, quasi-experimental designs *resemble* true experimental designs, yet fail to satisfy some criteria of true experiments.

◆ *IN SUM,* *environmental psychologists recognize and accept that person-environment transactions are influenced by many different factors, which has led to multiple paradigms for studying them. A wide variety of research methods are employed—some standard in social science and others devised especially for environmental psychology. A strong preference for performing research in the everyday world means that field studies are common. Sometimes laboratories and simulated settings are necessary, but they are used primarily when a field study is not possible. True experiments are sometimes possible; they are desirable when a researcher seeks to isolate particular causes and effects. Quasi-experimental research designs are much more common.*

◆ ENVIRONMENTAL PSYCHOLOGY ◆ TODAY

In the early 1970s, environmental psychology was borne along on the first massive tide of environmentalism. But environmentalism as a political force lost some of its early naive enthusiasm and support in the 1980s, and environmental psychology suffered slightly from the defection of faddists. Its growth in academia and large organizations was somewhat muffled by the general funding problems that affect many sectors of society. However, the 1980s saw the establishment of a major new international journal in 1981, the *Journal of Environmental Psychology*, and the publication of the *Handbook of Environmental Psychology* in 1987.

In the 1990s, environmentalism has once again strengthened, and the growth of research in environmental psychology has increased. I searched a psychology computer database and found that the absolute number and proportion of articles related to environmental issues and attitudes has doubled in the mid-1990s from the low point of 1988 and 1989. The public also shows increasing interest in environmental psychology. Just mention to someone that you are taking this class, and check the reaction.

Three Levels of Inquiry

Environmental psychology is studied at three levels of analysis. At the most basic level are studies of such fundamental psychological processes as perception, cognition, and personality as they filter and structure each individual's experience of the environment. Next comes the study of our social management of space: interpersonal distancing (or personal space), territoriality, crowding, and privacy. Third, environmental psychologists concentrate on the physical setting aspects of complex but common behaviors in everyday life, such as working, learning, daily life at home and in the community, and our relationship with nature. Perhaps the most important topics in environmental psychology are its contribution to better design of the built environment and improvements in the way we manage environmental resources (energy conservation, recycling, and harvesting natural resources) (see Figure 1–5).

The whole enterprise of environmental psychology is difficult to comprehend in its entirety, even for professionals. This book is based on about 2,500 studies. Yet, this represents only a fraction of all the published work in environmental psychology. Even 2,500 studies do not provide final answers to the theoretical issues and practical problems environmental psychologists try to solve. Do not expect many simple cookbook conclusions in the pages to follow. Instead, enjoy the *diversity* of viewpoints and findings. These are still the pioneer days of environmental psychology, when most studies uncover previously unknown territory as much as they further our knowledge of the known terrain.

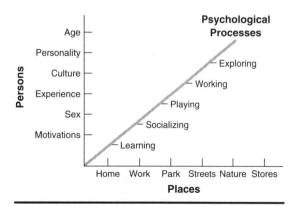

FIGURE 1–5 Environmental psychology's three dimensions: persons, processes, and places. All human activity occurs in this three-dimensional space.

International Dimensions

From its first stirrings, environmental psychology is six or seven decades old in some developed countries. In Germany, Hellpach explored the concept during the 1920s.[52] Lighting in English dwellings was studied in the 1930s,[53] but even before that, the effect of heat on tinplate workers was examined by 1919.[54]

In Japan, Tetsuro considered environment-behavior relations throughout the 1930s.[55] A strong movement has developed since then,[56] beginning with an early book on architectural psychology.[57] Research illustrating activity in Japan includes studies of how the design of religious shrines affects the feelings of pilgrims[58] and investigations of behavioral responses to disasters, such as earthquakes.[59]

In Canada, the effects of restricted environmental stimulation were first investigated in McGill University laboratories in the 1950s.[60] The first research on personal space and the first explicit use of environmental psychology to design buildings occurred in Saskatchewan in the late 1950s.[61]

Sweden has long been at the forefront of environmental psychology,[62] with particular emphasis on the visual perception of architecture.[63,64] Ecological concerns have spurred considerable research into air and noise pollution.[65,66] Cold outdoor environments have produced much work directed toward creating quality indoor environments[67] and understanding the very meaning of the environment.[68,69]

Research in environmental psychology is also widespread in eastern Europe, especially in Estonia, where one emphasis is on the design and improvement of mass housing and neighborhoods.[70] A series of regionwide conferences in 1981, 1983, and 1985 helped to establish environmental psychology as a discipline in eastern Europe.

In other countries, environmental psychology has developed more slowly. Nevertheless, small devoted groups of researchers exist in the Netherlands,[71] Israel,[72] France,[73] Australia,[74] Turkey,[75] Venezuela,[76] Italy,[77] Mexico,[78] Saudi Arabia,[79] South Africa,[80] and Finland.[81] In recent years, regular international conferences have helped to knit the worldwide community of environmental psychology.

Environmental psychologists are also at work above and below the surface of the earth, at its top and bottom, and in all sorts of extreme environments.[82] Environmental psychologists have researched the ability of submarine crews to orient themselves in their watery abodes, investigated the design of living and working quarters on space stations,[83,84] and examined environment-behavior transactions in both the Arctic and Antarctic[85] (see Figure 1–6).

◆ *IN SUM, environmental psychology has taken root in many countries as well as under the sea and above the earth. To some extent, the field has a unique character in each country because each country has distinct environmental problems and philosophies. Links among environ-*

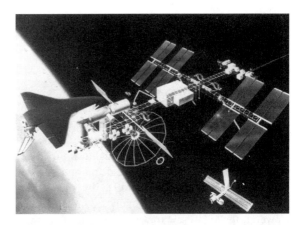

FIGURE 1–6 Environmental psychologists have studied environments to be above the atmosphere (*top:* the proposed space station) and under the sea (*bottom:* Tektite), as well as those on earth.

mental psychologists have been increasing due to more frequent international conferences and exchanges of views in prominent journals.

Future Prospects

Environmental psychology is a young and vigorous field; it will be increasingly influential as cries for a more realistic psychology are heard. Some observers see it as a blueprint for the future of psychology as a whole.[86] Already, signs of the influence of the environmental-psychology perspective may be seen in many other areas of psychology. *Environmental psychology* has been described as the leader in a revolution of relevance that is sweeping other areas such as developmental and cognitive psychology.[87] However, four formidable challenges also exist.

1. *Translate research in practice.* Translating research into practice has been a recognized difficulty since the beginning of the field. In this book, many successful applications are described. Nevertheless, each new project seems to raise its own peculiar obstacles to be overcome.

2. *Discover more appropriate research methods.* Environmental psychology has come of age in its advocacy of contextualism, or the integral approaches described earlier. But for the most part, research methods still have not been developed that can do justice to the complexity of contextualism.[88]

3. *Achieve a more coherent core.*[89] When fields of inquiry are mere collections of topics that are not linked together, they can be absorbed into other fields and disappear. Perspectives that show the wholeness and distinctiveness of environmental psychology are now appearing, but more are needed. Its boundaries are still growing and changing. A chief goal of this book is to reveal the natural coherence of environmental psychology even as it evolves.

4. *Further integrate and develop theory.* Theoretical diversity is stimulating and productive, but further integration and development of theory is necessary. More efforts like those of thinkers who have explored the relations between environmental psychology and psychophysics,[90] for example, or behavior-setting theory and the operant approach are necessary.[91] This goal is related to the third challenge; the evolution of an agreed-upon central core depends in part on the development of more comprehensive theories.

◆ **SUMMARY** ◆

Environmental psychology is a new area of psychology, but its roots go deep into the history of the discipline. It seeks understanding of person-environment transactions. Environmental psychologists solve physical setting problems, although some of them work primarily on the establishment of scientific principles while others work to improve human habitats. Several complementary but distinct paradigms are used—some contemplative, some experimental, and some consultative.

Around the world, the face of environmental psychology changes with national and regional concerns, but it retains a fundamental commitment to understanding and improving human-environment relations. Environmental psychology is at the forefront of a general movement to make psychology more relevant to everyday life. But it is still challenged to find more ways to turn knowledge into practice, to devise methods that are better able to accomplish its goals, to reach greater consensus on what constitutes its central core, and to develop more comprehensive theories reflecting and embodying that core. However, the field is vigorous and will meet these challenges.

Suggested Supplementary Readings

Altman, I., & Stokols, D. (Eds.). (1987). *Handbook of environmental psychology.* New York: Wiley.
Environment and Behavior, a journal established in 1969.
Journal of Environmental Psychology, a journal established in 1981.
Saegert, S., & Winkel, G. H. (1990). Environmental psychology. *Annual Review of Psychology, 41,* 441–447.
Stern, P. C. (1992). Psychological dimensions of global environmental change. *Annual Review of Psychology, 43,* 269–302.

2

ENVIRONMENTAL PERCEPTION AND COGNITION

We know a great deal about the perception of a one-eyed man with his head in a clamp watching glowing lights in a dark room, but surprisingly little about his perceptual abilities in a real-life situation.

—Helen Ross[1]

It was a very promising long weekend except for the fog that clung to the valley, enveloping the town. Tom had asked Jane, a woman he had recently met, to go camping in the mountains. As they made their way out of town through Friday afternoon traffic, the snail's pace made the sights along the city streets somehow more vivid. The glaring yellow motel and fast-food restaurant signs along the strip seemed larger and closer than usual.

"How far is it to the campsite?" Jane asked as they cleared town and the fog.

"Right over there," said Tom. "See that jagged peak just to the left? Guess how far it is."

"I'd say about 50 miles," said Jane. "How far is it?"

"I don't know for sure," Tom replied, "but I would guess it's closer than that, maybe 40 miles."
After they had driven through landscapes that gradually changed from dry golden grasses and green oaks to evergreen shrubs and slender pines for 60 miles, the jagged peak did look quite a bit closer, but it was still some distance away.

When they finally entered the park, Tom tried to recall where that great campsite from last year was. Jane spotted a "You are here" map just inside the gates, but they couldn't orient themselves from it. They couldn't decide whether the map was too vague to be useful or if too many exams had burned out their map-reading circuits.

Tom finally was able to conjure up a mental image of the park; he remembered that the roads were arranged in a unique system of concentric circles. Now it came back: The good site was just near that giant fir on the third ring road.

As Friday evening settled into utter peace, Tom and Jane sat on a ridge watching the sun sink into a distant range of snowy peaks. A pleasing thunder of a waterfall could be heard and a deep, dark mountain lake lay before them. The meadow wildflowers around them gathered dew and began to fold their petals.

◆   ◆   ◆

If you and I looked up and down a street, would we see the same thing? How would our thoughts about what we see differ? Environmental psychology begins with the basic psychological processes involved as we come to know our surroundings. This chapter and the next one cover several closely connected psychological processes that occur as we perceive and comprehend the built and natural environments.[2]

Environmental perception is the initial gathering of information. We primarily are visual beings,[3] but environmental perception includes the ways and means by which we collect information through all our senses. The term *environmental perception* sometimes is used more broadly to include aspects of how we appraise and assess environments, but in this chapter, it will primarily refer to the initial information-gathering phase of the process.

Our experience may suggest that perception is simple and automatic, but it is not. We are so familiar with the act of perceiving that the wondrous complexity of the process emerges only when we deliberately turn our perceptual talents back on themselves to observe what is going on as we see, hear, smell, taste, and touch the world. Perception of the everyday world is an exceedingly complicated phenomenon.

The topics in the first half of this chapter include the nature and measurement of environmental perception, what influences it, theories about how it works, and some of its applications to design and planning. In the course of this discussion, basic awareness of our immediate surroundings and perceptual adaptation are also examined.

The second half of the chapter is about **environmental cognition.** This includes spatial cognition—the manner in which we process, store, and recall informa-

tion about the locations and arrangements of places—and broader thinking about environments, beyond their spatial aspects. Through experience, for example, we develop an extensive body of knowledge about the buildings, streets, and communities around us. The topics in this section include cognitive mapping, spatial knowledge, memory for environments, and orientation in built and natural settings. Methods of investigating environmental cognition—as well as influences on it, theories about it, and its application to environmental design—are discussed.

◆ ENVIRONMENTAL PERCEPTION ◆

Distinctions and Variations

Contrasts with Traditional Perception Research. When psychologists long ago began to study perception, they quickly realized the complexity of the task facing them. Many decided that in order to learn something about the process, everyday perception would have to be simplified. One way to simplify the process is to present the perceiver with a simple stimulus. Traditional perception researchers assume that understanding the perception of simple stimuli is a useful and perhaps necessary path to understanding how the much more complex stimuli in daily life are perceived. The traditional approach also favors examining the perception process in the laboratory, where maximum control over all possible extraneous influences may be exerted.

Environmental psychologists, in contrast, embrace and even celebrate the complexity of the environmental displays they present to subjects (e.g., entire buildings and landscapes). William Ittelson, a pioneer in this area, distinguishes between the older approach, which he calls **object perception,** and the newer **environmental perception**[4,5,6] (see Figure 2–1). In object perception research, the emphasis is on the properties of simple stimuli, such as their brightness, color, depth, perceptual constancy, form, and apparent movement. In environmental perception research, the emphasis is on large-scale scenes, treated as whole entities. Much more research has been done in object perception than in environmental perception, as the chapter-opening quote from Helen Ross suggests.

The difference between the two approaches is not merely in the size and complexity of the stimulus presented; the role of the perceiver is also different. In environmental perception studies, the participants often move around in and through the scene; they are *part* of the scene. Moving through the environmental display means that the perceiver experiences it from multiple perspectives.

A third important difference from the object perception tradition is that the perceiver often is *connected* to the environmental display by a clear goal or purpose. For example, we scan a wilderness area for a clean campsite; while driving, we watch signs and lights to avoid being in an accident; we look over a restaurant for a private table; and so on.

Everyday environmental perception has many purposes, but an appropriate way to divide them is into utilitarian purposes and aesthetic purposes. Ironically, many studies of the aesthetic qualities of buildings and landscapes have been undertaken, but, at least in urban streets, most of us actually pay much more attention to utilitarian elements of the environment (e.g., businesses) than to aesthetic elements (e.g., large wall murals).[7] An important difficulty with research in environmental perception, of course, is accounting for the myriad of personal and physical influences on the perceptual process. Despite the methodological difficulties

FIGURE 2–1 Traditional perception researchers usually examine how simple displays such as the Gestalt figure *(top)* are seen. Environmental psychologists usually investigate real scenes *(bottom).*

involved, however, environmental psychologists prefer to investigate the perception of everyday scenes rather than the perception of greatly simplified stimulus displays in laboratories.

Awareness and Adaptation. The environment constantly offers many more pieces of information than any of us can possibly handle. We are always selecting for our attention a relatively small, manageable portion of the available information. We may focus intensely or minimally on environmental displays ranging in size from architectural details to vast panoramic landscapes that range in distance from very near to very distant. We may actively scrutinize the environment (e.g., when we evaluate an apartment as a possible place to rent) or be quite unaware of our surroundings (e.g., when we are daydreaming, reading, or very involved in a conversation). We may adapt or habituate to some environmental displays so that we really do not *see* them at all (e.g., a street we drive along every day) or we may be riveted to a scene by its importance or novelty (e.g., your first look at a campus where you will spend several years).

Another example of habituation is the way we adapt to the perception of air pollution. We primarily notice air pollution when it is new to us—such as when we move to a smoggy place or when there is a sudden increase in smog where we live. Basing his observations on an old principle of psychophysics called the *Weber-Fechner law,* Robert Sommer pointed out that as the amount of air pollution increases, larger and larger increments of *new* air pollution are needed before we notice that pollution is getting worse.[8] The same smokestack that would have outraged a community when it had little air pollution is barely noticed after the community becomes heavily polluted.

Our perception is not always directed toward physical settings; in fact, it is often directed toward other people or inward, toward ourselves. We sometimes pay very little attention to our physical surroundings, even when they cause us some discomfort—a state that has been called **environmental numbness.**[9] This numbness, or lack of awareness of our surroundings, often arises when more lively aspects of the world—such as the attentions of a friend, absorption in a book, or daydreaming—command our attention. Environmental numbness can cause us to overlook major problems, such as

toxins in our everyday life, or expose us to minor hazards, such as bumping into a cupboard door, or major hazards, such as oncoming traffic when we absentmindedly cross the street.

On the positive side, we are capable of greatly enhancing our awareness and appreciation of the environment. Herbert Leff has provided an elaborate description of ways we might consciously direct our perceptions and cognitions to obtain richer environmental experiences.[10] Here, very briefly, are some of Leff's exercises for getting more out of any particular scene:

- Rapidly switch your visual focus from one point in the scene to another while forming a vivid impression of each view.
- Look for views in the scene that would make personally relevant photographs.
- Imagine what it would be like to be one of the objects in the scene.
- See inanimate objects as if they were alive.

The mental gymnastics involved in these exercises can produce very positive feelings while increasing your environmental awareness.

◆ ***IN SUM,*** *environmental psychologists usually study the perception of whole, everyday scenes. In doing so, they sometimes must sacrifice a degree of experimental control, but in return, they are able to investigate the perception of real, complex settings that perceivers move through and feel connected to. Awareness and adaptation mean that perceivers select a few cues from scenes and ignore most others. Unfortunately, some cues that are ignored may be important, at least in the long run (e.g., air pollution). There are, however, ways to enhance our perception of everyday settings.*

Research Methods

How can environmental perception be studied? This question may be answered in terms of how the environment is presented to the perceiver or in terms of how we measure the perceiver's perception.

Presenting the Environment to the Perceiver. How should the environment be presented to the perceiver?

Environmental psychologists prefer to study the perception of whole, complex, everyday scenes. Ideally, this means showing real (live) scenes to subjects, which is often done. However, this is not always possible. For example, what if you want to know how people will perceive a building that has not yet been constructed or that is far away? Real scenes change—weather conditions, lighting, and many other factors—which means that if you wish to present the *same* scene to many perceivers, you cannot rely on a real, live scene.

Thus, sometimes—if necessary—photos, videos, sketches, or models of real scenes are used.[11] In fact, one specialized area of research aims to identify which method of simulating real scenes comes closest to eliciting the same responses as real scenes. A typical study might compare responses to a scenic, wild river based on video pictures plus sound, video pictures with no sound, and still photos with no sound.[12] A few very sophisticated laboratories allow a user to simulate travel through entire regions to be carried out.[13,14] Simulations do have shortcomings, such as the inability of the perceiver to be *in* the scene, but some simulations are surprisingly good at producing the same perceptual responses elicited by the real setting[15] (see Figure 2–2). Researchers now investigate which aspect of the scene (e.g., depth perception versus size versus texture) is simulated best by which type of simulation.[16] Perhaps the best overall simulation, short of a million-dollar laboratory, is a simple sequence of color slides or videotapes.[17,18,19]

Studying the Process of Perception. How can someone's perception be measured? After all, a person's perception is his or her *experience*. Because researchers do not have direct access to their subjects' experiences, per-

FIGURE 2–2 This environmental simulation laboratory at the University of California's Berkeley campus has been used to assess how different plans for the development of the region affect landscape quality in the eyes of local residents. A tiny camera at the point of the mobile apparatus at the left produces a video image on the monitor that is similar to the view that would be seen by a motorist driving through the region.

ception is usually measured indirectly. Five general methods of doing so will be discussed next.

1. The most common method of measuring perception is simply to ask perceivers what they see (or hear, smell, touch, taste). These **self-report methods** include questionnaires, interviews, checklists, and free descriptions. An obvious shortcoming of these methods is that perceivers may produce inaccurate reports of their own perceptions. They may not pay careful attention to their own perceptions of a moment ago, they may incorrectly recall or entirely forget perceptions from the past, or they may report what they think the experimenter wishes to hear. Finally, the actual perception must be filtered through language.[20] Self-report methods are, nevertheless, useful as reasonably accurate, economical ways to study environmental perception.

2. Another way of studying what perceivers in everyday situations attend to—**time sampling**—was suggested long ago by Brunswik[21] and revived later by others.[22,23] The idea is simple: Ask observers to move through a setting and to report, at certain intervals (or afterward), exactly what they are (or were) looking at. Although this is another form of self-report, it adds the idea of active, moving perception and it can be used to discover whether observers pay attention more to environmental elements that are moving or stationary, large or small, near or far, straight ahead or to one side, and so on. The participants in one study that used this method walked around a small college town.[24] The researchers found that most objects the perceivers looked at were closer than 40 meters and less than 30 degrees from straight ahead. About 40 percent of the objects perceived were moving elements, such as people or cars.

3. Infer something about perception from the perceiver's behavior. This **behavior-inference method** has been used, for example, in studies of museums and art galleries. The length of time museum visitors spend looking at a painting or a science exhibit has been used as an index of their interest in that display.

4. Environmental perception can also be studied with the **psychophysical method**. Psychophysicists discovered long ago that people can reliably adjust some physical variable (e.g., the heaviness of a weight) in direct pro-

portion to the perception of a psychological construct (e.g., the seriousness of a crime).[25] These **magnitude estimations** allow for the calculation of equations called **power functions** that express a psychological variable in terms of a known physical scale. In one example of this, subjects adjusted the brightness of a light to correspond to their perceptions of how architecturally complex different houses seemed to them.[26] In such studies, subjects often agree so much with one another that quite accurate predictions about future perceivers' responses to a scene can be made. Thus, the perception of architectural complexity (or any other psychological variable) may be expressed as a function of a physically measurable variable such as brightness.

5. In the **phenomenological approach,** which will be discussed later in more detail as a theory, the researcher usually is also the perceiver. Rather than employ many subjects, the goal is to use a single very careful observer who tries to perceive the essence of a setting in a qualitative way.

◆ *IN SUM, environmental psychologists present real settings to perceivers whenever they can, but sometimes they must use simulations. Some simulations produce very similar perceptual responses to real environments. Five general methods of studying environmental perception are self-reports, time sampling, behavior inference, psychophysical, and phenomenology. Because each method has strengths and weaknesses, multiple methods should be used whenever possible, which will allow the researcher to more fully understand environmental perception.*

Influences on Environmental Perception

Have you ever disagreed with someone about the distance to a building, the temperature in a room, or the beauty of a place? If so, you know that perceptions of the environment may differ. What accounts for these differences? Some can be attributed to personal variations among perceivers (e.g., differences associated with culture, perceptual ability, and training) and others have been explained by physical variations among environmental displays (e.g., concrete versus wood, or degree of visual complexity). Some perceptions are the result of particular *combinations* of observer and environmental display characteristics. We should remember that no single influence, by itself, determines what an observer perceives. In this book, I must describe them one at a time, but any given perception is determined by the force of many influences, each delivering its own large or small push toward shaping the overall perception.

Personal Influences. Which characteristics of observers themselves are associated with different perceptions of the environment? Obviously, variability in perceptual ability is one factor. Impaired sight or hearing produces a restricted or fuzzy image of one's surroundings. For example, veteran factory workers and rock music performers often hear less well than others.[27] But personal characteristics—such as sex, education or training, experience with a setting, and whether a person likes the setting—also affect environmental perception. It is interesting to note that men and women may perceive distances differently. In one study, men perceived distances to visible buildings as significantly less than distances to hidden buildings, but women did not perceive the distances differently.[28]

Another important difference in perception is based on education or training. Along with the basic knowledge we acquire, we seem to learn a *way of seeing* that is characteristic of our chosen professions. Civil engineers see roads and dams where only slopes, streams, and valleys exist; architects see form, light, and color where the rest of us see walls, floors, and doors. Many studies have documented differences between the environmental appraisals of design professionals and nonprofessionals, as well as between different groups of design professionals.[29,30]

Therefore, researchers began to examine the particular *ways* that architects' perceptions differ from those of others. For example, a study showed there were no differences in the perceptions of landscape architects and some other groups in the *quantitative* features of backyards (e.g., the number of different plants and activity areas), but the landscape architects differed significantly in their views of the *qualitative* features (e.g., how "defined" the landscape is).[31] To the extent such discrepancies represent differences in the original perceptions of these professionals (before the information is interpreted), and some physiological evidence suggests that they do,[32] professional education is a key personal difference in environmental perception.

One's experience with or evaluation of the setting affects environmental perception. Even small differences in familiarity can affect perception. For example, observers who had been in a room for just half an hour saw it as smaller than did those who had just entered it.[33] Buildings with which perceivers are more familiar are judged to be closer to them than are less familiar buildings.[34] Finally, individuals perceive the distance to buildings they find pleasing more accurately than they judge distances to buildings they find less pleasing.[35]

Cultural Influences. The cultural context in which individuals are raised can lead to quite different ways of seeing the world. Anthropologist Colin Turnbull, for example, has described his experiences with the Bambuti Pygmies of the Congo region.[36] These people live in dense rain forests and rarely experience vistas that extend for more than 30 meters. Once, Turnbull took his Pygmy guide out of the forest to a broad plain where a herd of buffalo could be seen several kilometers away.

The Pygmy asked, "What sort of insects are those?" Turnbull explained that they were plains buffalo—animals about twice as large as the rain forest buffalo with which Pygmies are familiar. The guide laughed and told Turnbull not to tell such stupid stories. Turnbull drove his guide closer to the herd. As the buffalo approached, they seemed to the Pygmy to be growing in size, and he was convinced that witchcraft was at work. The Pygmy's lack of experience with distance vision interfered with size constancy—our learned tendency to stabilize *perceived* size despite changes in objective distance and the size of the image on our retinas.

This is one example of what has been called the **carpentered-world hypothesis,** which attributes certain differences in perception to the striking discrepancies among the perceptual environments of various societies. Urban settings, with their high frequency of rectangular objects and straight lines, produce different perceptual experiences than uncarpentered settings, simple rural places where curved, rounded lines characterize the houses and landscape.[37]

Physical Influences. Environmental perception also depends, of course, on the scene being perceived. Obviously, the Eiffel Tower does not look like the Rocky Mountains. However, for relatively similar scenes, there is some controversy about the relative importance of person-based and environment-based influences on perception. Some emphasize the considerable processing of visual information that occurs by sensory receptors and the brain, involving both physiology and learning. This point of view is expressed in the old saying "Beauty is in the eye of the beholder." Others point to obvious physical differences in the settings being perceived. This point of view would reply, "Yes, but is anyone going to claim that an open sewer is more beautiful than a wild river?" This perspective is expressed in the title of a presentation by a well-known environmental psychologist: "The Environment Is *Not* in the Head!"[38] One resolution of this controversy is the proposition that the more scenes differ, the stronger the influence of the environment; the more scenes are similar, the greater the influence of personal factors.

Which physical features of the scene affect perception of that scene? This is a vast topic, but I will discuss a few examples: architectural features that make a room seem more enclosed, color and architectural perception, how certain natural phenomena throw off one's perception of distance or size, and what makes water look dangerous.

What makes a room look enclosed? The obvious answer is that a room appears enclosed when it has walls, floors, and ceilings, which "establish space."[39,40] However, is one of these elements more important than another? Do the elements each add to the perception, or do they work only as combinations? One study found that the presence of ceilings is three times as important as floors in establishing the perception of being enclosed, and that walls are twice as important.[41] Although walls, floors, and ceilings each make their own independent contribution to the perception, they apparently do not *combine* to enhance the perception of being enclosed.[42]

Did you ever pick out a great color from the sample chips at a paint store and then find yourself disappointed with it once you painted? This happens because, as you might suspect, colors have a different impact on us when they appear on isolated chips from when they appear on our walls.[43] The meaning of a color is different when we see it alone versus when it is combined with, say, the design of a low-income multifamily housing complex. Different designs suit different colors; the meaning of a color is not equal to the meaning of that color-plus-design.

In a fascinating book called *Behavior and Perception in Strange Environments*, Helen Ross described many perceptual illusions that occur in natural settings.[44] Fog, for example, makes us believe that features of the environment such as trees or hills are farther away and larger than they really are. The same effects occur when we view things under water, especially as the water grows murkier. The **terrestrial saucer effect** leads mountain climbers to believe that neighboring mountain peaks that are equal in altitude to their own are much higher than their own. The same effect also influences our perception of roads so that, under certain conditions, slopes that are actually uphill appear to be downhill, and vice versa.

Likewise, when we walk a path that is either uphill or downhill, we tend to overestimate its length; when the trail is winding, we tend to err about the direction it is taking us in favor of the direction of the vanishing point (the direction implied by the last point of the trail that can be seen).[45] Edward Sadalla and his associates have investigated many similar effects. For example, the estimated length of a path grows as a function of the number of turns in the path[46] and the number of intersections along the path.[47] Rectangular rooms appear larger than square rooms of equal size.[48] Distances *to* landmarks are estimated as smaller than distances *from* landmarks[49,50] (see Figure 2–3).

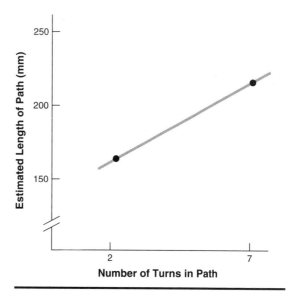

FIGURE 2–3 Distances are perceived as longer when the route has more turns in it.

People also make subjective clusters out of locations that show no particular physical pattern, and these clusterings affect our distance judgments. In particular, we seem to underestimate distances between locations within the clusters but overestimate the distances between locations in different clusters.[51]

Such effects in natural and built settings may be illusions or distortions, but they are nevertheless important. For instance, the very lives of drivers and divers are at stake in the case of the fog, road, and underwater effects. The path and room size distortions may affect perceptions of crowding, status, confinement, and other psychologically important aspects of building interiors.[52] Perceptions on city streets are also affected by the physical context. When pedestrians are subjected to more traffic noise, their perceptual fields narrow.[53] They actually look straight ahead more, missing much information from the periphery of their paths.

In the classic study of environmental context on the perception of people, the quality of room environments was shown to affect perceptions of others.[54] Perceivers were placed in messy, closetlike rooms to make their judgments (but the room's qualities were not pointed out to them) and asked to rate the well-being of people in photos. The judges in messy rooms perceived the people in the photos to be lower in well-being than the judges who perceived the photos in tidy rooms. A later study did find that this effect depends on the perceiver's expectations of the room's aesthetic qualities. If the perceiver *expects* the room to be beautiful or ugly, the results found in the original study can even be reversed.[55] So, once more, the environment affects perception, but personal factors, such as the perceiver's expectations, can also play a crucial role.

◆ *IN SUM, available evidence suggests that environmental perceptions such as length, distance, and size are largely dependent on which physical elements are in the scene and how they are arranged. But personal factors (e.g., familiarity or finding a building pleasing), culture (e.g., being raised in a carpentered world), and training (e.g., in architecture) also affect the way we see the world.*

Theories

Environmental perception, like the rest of environmental psychology, needs models, theories, and frameworks to provide a guiding, overall picture of the environment perception process and to generate testable hypotheses for research. There is no single accepted theory of environmental perception, but the following theories—or some combination of them—may someday yield a valuable, encompassing theory.

Brunswik: Probabilistic Functionalism. One influential approach to environmental perception is based on the work of Egon Brunswik, whose theory may be described best by reference to his **lens model**[56] (see Figure 2–4). Brunswik's influence on environmental psychology derives from his view that both perceiver and environment are important: "Both the organism and the environment will have to be seen as systems, each with properties of their own. . . . As much as psychology must be concerned with the texture of the organism . . . it must also be concerned with the texture of the environment" (p. 5).[57]

Brunswik maintained that the environment offers a multitude of cues; the perceiver must make sense of the most important ones to function effectively in a setting. This is why Brunswik is called a **functionalist.** Usually, only a small number of cues in a given scene are useful to the perceiver; therefore, many of them are given little attention while close attention is paid to others. Some people (infants or those cast suddenly into a new setting) may be perceptually confused because they are overwhelmed with cues and have not yet learned to sort the important from the unimportant ones.

The theory's **probabilism** refers to Brunswik's belief that no single cue is either perfectly reliable or perfectly unreliable, but rather it has a certain probability of being an accurate clue about the true nature of the environment. If, while driving, you approach a bridge, you can be quite sure it will afford you safe passage to other side, but, as a few victims of the 1989 San Francisco earthquake found, you cannot be 100 percent sure. The various perceptual errors and illusions described here mean that some cues are considerably less certain or accurate than others.

In Brunswik's theory, **ecological validity** refers to the correct probabilistic relations between the environment and each of the cues—weightings that would lead to effective perception of the setting, if they exist and if the perceiver knows them. **Cue utilization** represents the

The Setting:

The Quality to Be Judged: BEAUTY

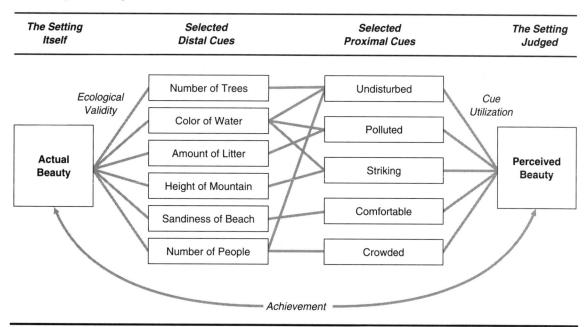

FIGURE 2-4 Brunswik's lens model applied to environmental perception. Qualities of the setting itself are not perceived directly; rather, they are manifested in **distal cues** (objectively measurable characteristics of the setting). **Proximal cues** are the observer's subjective impressions of these distal cues. Perceived beauty is based on the observer's interpretation of the proximal cues. Perceived beauty will closely approximate actual beauty (i.e., there will be high achievement) if (a) actual beauty really is manifested in distal cues (i.e., there is high ecological validity), (b) proximal cues are closely related to distal cues, and (c) proximal cues are closely related to judged beauty (i.e., observers have excellent cue utilization).

probabilistic weights given to each cue by the perceiver. (Obviously, we rarely assign these weights as a conscious process; we gradually learn what to look for in a given setting, but we usually cannot or do not do so consciously.) When a perceiver weights the cues in a manner that is similar to the way the cues are actually related to the environment, he or she has an image that allows for accurate perception of the scene. When cue utilization closely matches ecological validity, **achievement** will be high (i.e., the perceiver's reading of the environment will closely match the actual environment).

Brunswik believed that perception is an attempt to extract a *useful* image of the environment from the mass of potentially confusing cues. He viewed perceivers as active agents, intentionally seeking views of the environment that assist them as they make their way through the world.

After we have repeatedly sampled settings as "intuitive scientists," we become familiar with them. In Brunswik's terms, we have learned what the important cues are and how to use them. Perceptual problems arise in strange settings, especially those that offer patterns of cues that do not bear a resemblance to those in our familiar settings. Such problems (recall Helen Ross's climbers, divers, and drivers) may lead us to draw false conclusions about the nature of the setting. These false conclusions range in seriousness from misjudging the color of a wall to misjudging a curve on the highway under foggy conditions.

The Brunswik approach can guide research in environmental psychology aimed at identifying *which* setting cues reveal actual conditions that may not be directly visible. One such condition might be fear of crime in a residential neighborhood. For example, which (if any) of the many observable features of a residential street are highly correlated with fear of crime in residents?[58] In concrete terms, is the presence of a front yard fence a valid cue that the resident is afraid of crime? Brunswik would say that such a cue is neither perfectly valid (correlated 1.00 with fear of crime) nor perfectly invalid (correlated .00); it is somewhere between. The environmental psychologist's task is to discover just how strong the relation is between front yard fences and fear of crime. This question is represented by the left half of the lens model.

On the right side of the lens model, the Brunswik approach is to find out whether the perceiver correctly or incorrectly interprets the fence cue. The perceiver can err either by overestimating or underestimating the connection between fences and residents' fear of crime. High achievement occurs when a perceiver weights a pattern of cues (right side of the lens model) the same way they are actually weighted (left side of the lens model). To be successful, for example, a burglar must accurately "read" houses: Is the resident home? Likely to have jewels? Likely to have a good alarm system? In Chapter 6, research on this very question will be described.

Gibson: Affordances. James J. Gibson's approach to environmental perception differs from Brunswik's in that Gibson believed certain arrangements of cues give the perceiver *direct, immediate* perceptions of the environment.[59,60] Gibson felt that the world is composed of *substances* (such as clay, steel, glass) and *surfaces* (such as floors, walls, ceilings). The arrangements of these substances and surfaces (called *layouts*) provide **affordances,** or instantly detectable functions. For example, a solid horizontal surface is said to offer or afford support and rest. An extended solid horizontal surface affords locomotion, but a vertical solid surface affords mechanical contact and stops locomotion[61] (see Figure 2–5).

The perception of such affordances, Gibson maintained, does not require us to interpret sensory information, construct reality, or weight cues, as in Brunswik's theory. Gibson's perspective stands almost alone against a powerful tradition that assigns a much greater role to the processing of information after it is gathered. Other theorists point out, for example, that some images we perceive are so similar that without cognitive processes (such as recalling past experiences or attending to neighboring contextual cues), we could not be sure what we were seeing.[62]

Nevertheless, Gibson's ideas have served to help refocus attention on the environment itself, particularly on the everyday environment, as a crucial element in perception. The relevance of Gibson's ideas to environmental psychology and the design professions also lies in his insistence that perception is *not* composed of elemental building blocks of perception such as color, form, and shape.

Traditional architectural education, drawing on the traditions of visual arts such as painting and sculpture,

FIGURE 2–5 James Gibson would say that these surfaces automatically offer or afford seating and walking.

emphasizes these very building blocks as the "basis" of design. Architecture students are taught to see form and shape. Gibson argued that this is exactly what architects should *not* be taught.[63] Most of us, the users of architects' buildings, do not see form and shape when we see a place; rather, we perceive affordances—what the place can *do* for us. Obviously, then, according to Gibson, architects should be taught about the relations between surfaces and affordances. Excessive concern with form and shape occurs when architecture is seen primarily as a visual art rather than as a way to provide functional space in which people can work, live, and relax.

Berlyne: Collative Properties. Daniel Berlyne contributed important insights about environmental aesthetics[64,65] that have been extended to a broader view of environment perception and cognition. Berlyne's ideas straddle the distinction between perception and cognition, which is somewhat artificial anyway. His view was that environmental stimulation has several **collative properties**—characteristics of the stimulus that cause the perceiver to pay attention, investigate further, and compare. These collative properties include **novelty** (newness to the perceiver), **incongruity** (that something is out of place), **complexity** (a large variety of elements in the display), and "**surprisingness**" (unexpected elements).

Berlyne believed that these collative properties influence the perceiver's aesthetic judgments and desire to explore. They do so through two psychological dimensions, **hedonic tone** (beauty or pleasure) and **uncertainty arousal**. For simple laboratory stimuli and for two-dimensional displays such as paintings, these relations are fairly clear: Images of moderate complexity, novelty, incongruity, and surprise are perceived as more beautiful than are images that are either very high or very low on these collative properties.

The implications for environmental design *seem* clear, and several designers have suggested that buildings ought to be designed in accordance with these ideas. For example, some architects argued in the 1960s that modern architecture should have *more* complexity because most urban buildings were too simple in their lines— that is, below the optimum amount of complexity.[66,67] Since then, buildings have become more complex in the postmodern era.

These relations between complexity and preference may apply only to the built environment. Research in natural settings does not always support these ideas. For example, although scenes of built environments show the predicted results (moderate complexity rated highest), those of landscapes do not.[68] This does not mean that Berlyne's theory of collative properties is wrong, but it may mean that relations between beauty and the collative properties are different or less universal than Berlyne first thought. Research on collative properties other than complexity often finds, for example, a straight-line relation between the property and the rated beauty or preference rather than the curvilinear (inverted-U shaped) one predicted by Berlyne.[69]

Nevertheless, Berlyne's ideas have stimulated researchers to search for properties of environmental displays that reliably lead to certain perceptions. Joachim Wohlwill, for example, suggested some revisions to the list of collative properties—changes that make Berlyne's ideas more directly suitable to environmental perception. One such idea is the notion of **fittingness**, or how well a certain element (a house) suits a certain setting (wilderness).[70]

Berlyne's hedonic tone and uncertainty-arousal dimensions are also very similar to the core concepts (pleasure and arousal) in the work of James Russell, whose influential work on the emotion-eliciting qualities of the environment will be discussed in the next chapter.[71,72,73] Furthermore, Stephen and Rachel Kaplan's model of environmental preference, also be discussed in the next chapter, owes a debt to Berlyne's ideas.[74]

Phenomenology. The fourth and final theory of environment perception considered in this chapter is phenomenology. This theory has its roots in philosophy. Heidegger, for example, discusses *dwelling* as a process of existence through which a mere place becomes a dear home.[75] Phenomenology's value for environmental psychology has been advocated since the early 1980s.[76]

The phenomenological approach ultimately results in a self-report, but these self-reports differ in important ways from those discussed earlier.

1. The emphasis is on the perceptions of an individual, or at least one individual at a time, rather than on group averages.

2. Like Gibson but in sharp contrast to Brunswik, phenomenologists try to overcome or erase the distinction between the setting and the perceiver.

3. The researcher usually is also the perceiver, although sometimes the researcher asks other perceivers (e.g., those who live or work in the setting) to help by carefully reporting their impressions.

4. Phenomenologists try to qualitatively understand the unique and holistic meaning of a place as revealed *by the place*, rather than by resorting to external concepts or ideas.

Because of its emphasis on the uniqueness of each setting, the phenomenology of place has produced penetrating portraits of particular locations, such as homes,[77] cities,[78] and marketplaces,[79] as well as particular experiences, such as *topophilia* (emotional attachment to a place)[80] or *existential outsideness* (alienation from a place).[81] These essays on the holistic meaning of places and experiences do not readily lend themselves to textbook condensation, but you may sample them directly in books by Buttimer and Seamon,[82] Norberg-Schulz,[83] and Relph.[84]

The phenomenological approach has been accused of certain inconsistencies.[85,86] Not surprisingly, advocates of phenomenology believe these critics do not understand them or the discipline of phenomenology.[87] The critics may be judging this psychological form of phenomenology as if it were a philosophy, when its goals in this field are more practical: to gain insight into the ways that people who are in the settings view them, and to understand the meaning and relevance of a place to those who know the place best. In this way, phenomenological-environmental psychology can make valuable contributions to the design of settings by eliciting the meaning of places to those who will have to live or work in them.

It may be fair to conclude that phenomenology appeals to a different sort of researcher than experimental methods do. Even its critics agree that phenomenology is a valuable complement to the other approaches to environmental psychology in a valuable way.

◆ *IN SUM, the theories of Brunswik, Gibson, Berlyne, and environmental phenomenology have had a major impact on current thinking and research in environmental perception. Each began as a traditional (nonenvironmental) theory, but contained the necessary seed to be fruitful for environmental psychology. The theories have stimulated considerable pure research (i.e., attempting to understand how nature works while showing little concern for practice or application) into the nature of environmental perception and have been extended into the practical domains of city planning, park planning, and architecture.*

Environmental Perception and Design

What Does a Typical Building Look Like? If an old building in your community is facing the wrecking ball, you might consider trying to save it. One reason for saving heritage buildings is that they preserve the architectural character of the community. But how do you know what that character looks like, in objective terms?

Researchers in Pennsylvania wanted to discover just which architectural features comprised the central or archetypal image of buildings in a rural area.[88] They showed residents a series of drawings in which building elements such as window shape and roof slant varied. The residents judged each scene according to how typical it seemed of local farmhouses. Through these ratings, the researchers were able to identify which architectural features made a farmhouse look most like a typical farmhouse to residents of that area. In this way, environmental-perception researchers can discover the essence of architectural character for a city, town, or region. The knowledge that residents used to make their ratings was buried in their experiences; they hardly realized that their lifetime of perceiving these buildings had added up to a particular image of how a typical local farmhouse looks.

How Does a Room Look Big? In this age of expensive space, designers may often wish to make rooms look as large as possible. How might that be done? You may have heard that light-colored rooms appear larger than dark-colored rooms; this is one way to make a room look larger, but it is not the only way.

A study of lighting by Stuart Kaye shows how the type and placement of light can affect the perceived spaciousness of a room.[89] For example, when the lights illuminate only the walls, the room will look larger than when the lights illuminate the middle of the room but not the walls. The presence of windows and extra furniture also affects the perceived size of rooms: Rooms with windows look larger than those without, and those with more furniture look smaller than those with less furniture.[90]

◆ ENVIRONMENTAL COGNITION ◆

Have a little daydream. Transport yourself back to your all-time favorite place, whether it is a city, town, campground, farm, wilderness, neighborhood, school, house, street, building, beach, theme park, or room. Conjure the place up in as much colorful detail as you can, and spend a few minutes enjoying it. Can you recall how to find your way around it? What important items were there and where were they placed? What was the size of the setting and where was it located relative to other nearby places? This is environmental cognition—in part.

Distinctions and Definitions

What Is Environmental Cognition? **Environmental cognition** concerns the way we acquire, store, organize, and recall information about locations, distances, and arrangements in buildings, streets, and the great outdoors. It includes **spatial cognition**—that is, the thinking processes that help us "wayfind" (i.e., successfully navigate in an environment), estimate distances, recognize route cues, make and read maps, and generally understand the relative location in space of different places. Spatial cognition includes the concept of **cognitive maps,** which are pictorial and semantic images in our heads of how places are arranged.[91] If you look around, evidence of cognitive mapping is in advertisements, subway maps, magazines, and in every person's memory and thinking.[92]

Nonspatial Environmental Cognition. Not all environmental cognition concerns the spatial relations among environments. For example, when we think about or remember a place, with no particular reference to its relative location or distance, that is environmental cognition in the nonspatial sense. For example, researchers have examined the mental models of hazards held by everyday people,[93] such as how farmers think about droughts;[94] people's attributions about the causes of, responsibility for, and likely future disease rates following toxic spills;[95] and how we cognitively organize different kinds of restaurants.[96]

Memory is an important part of environmental cognition. One researcher tried to identify the different kinds of memory that we might have for places.[97] Others have examined how familiarity with[98] or renovations to[99] buildings affect our memory for them, or which outdoor scenes we remember after hiking.[100] These are important questions, but so far, most research has focused on spatial cognition rather than on memory for places or other forms of environmental cognition.

You Are Not a Camera. A cardinal principle of spatial cognition is that people do not process information about the environment the way cameras or computers do. Our processing, from a mechanical point of view, is full of errors. Our cognitions also differ from one person to the next. Yet, as a species, we are remarkably successful.

These deviations (from objective reality and from one another), together with our success as a species, suggest that we must entertain two ideas: First, our imperfect images must be quite useful to us, and second, spatial cognition must be determined in part by differences in our individual backgrounds. Our cognitive maps help us solve spatial problems, such as how to infer the way from one place to another when we have never directly traversed the route and where to find needed resources of all kinds, from the closest all-night grocery store to the best place to find truffles. They also simplify and facilitate communication. We absorb into these images the distinctive monuments, symbols, and arrangements of streets and we can conjure them up in order to recognize and enjoy places we have known.

Legibility. Understanding the peculiar ways that humans think about their environments may be used to design better settings. This central concept in this applied area is **legibility,** or the ease with which a setting may be recognized and organized by people. This concept was established by Kevin Lynch in his classic book *The Image of the City.*[101] Some cities, for example, are much more legible than others. What makes a city legible? Lynch suggested five elements of city images that contribute strongly to legibility (you might find it useful to think of examples of each element where you live):

1. *Paths.* The routes along which people travel (typically, roads, walkways, and public transit routes)
2. *Edges.* Nontraveled lines, such as cliffs, escarpments, or shores of rivers, lakes, or oceans
3. *Districts.* Moderate-sized areas that city residents identify as having a particular character
4. *Nodes.* Well-known points that people travel to and from, often at the junctures of important paths,

KEVIN LYNCH
*introduced key concepts
in spatial cognition.*

such as key intersections, transit terminals, and popular plazas or squares

5. *Landmarks.* Easily viewed elements, either on a grand scale (e.g., the tallest building in town) or on a smaller scale (e.g., a statue or unique storefront)

These five elements were suggested by Lynch speculatively, without much formal research. Their validity, however, has been confirmed by more experimental methods.[102,103] In these studies, the elements in maps drawn by everyday people were subjected to a sophisticated statistical technique called *cluster analysis.* Five distinct clusters of map elements emerged, and these were very similar to the elements Lynch hypothesized. These elements are important components of cognitive maps, not only at the urban scale but also at the international scale as well as the room scale.

The term *cognitive map* is so intuitively attractive that it is easy to oversimplify both its meaning and its role in our daily activities.[104,105] A cognitive map is not a folded piece of paper in the cranium; no miniature navigator sits inside our heads poring over intricacies of the map by the light of our ideas. In fact, some cognitive psychologists who favor the information-processing approach doubt that spatial knowledge is represented at all like a map in the head.[106] They feel that maps contain far too much information to be conjured up all at once. Instead, they believe we retrieve small subparts of the map one at a time when we draw maps or give directions.

Nevertheless, it is clear that we do possess large stores of information—partly pictorial, partly verbal—about the paths, edges, nodes, districts, and landmarks of the places we know. We know that the accuracy of a person's cognitive map is an essential part of the relation between the complexity of a setting and how well people find their way around in that setting.[107]

Spatial cognition research is concerned with memory for, orientation in, and knowledge about distances and locations in physical settings. The next sections will describe how and why some features of the environment are remembered while others are forgotten, the processes involved in getting lost and getting found, and how we organize (and incorrectly organize) the physical features of our homes, cities, countries, and even the world as a whole.

◆ *IN SUM, people do not acquire, store, and recall information about locations, distances, and arrangements mechanically. Yet, our ways of doing so are effective and nonrandom. The study of cognitive maps reveals some human strategies for processing environmental information. Legible places are easier to comprehend: they have clear paths and distinct edges, districts, nodes, and landmarks.*

Research Methods

Spatial cognition, like environmental perception, must be studied indirectly. The goal is to extract an accurate representation of an individual's spatial knowledge. The most common way of approaching this problem has been to ask individuals to sketch a map, construct a scale model, or estimate distances between pairs of places. Other methods of studying spatial cognition are available[108] but have not been used frequently. Some researchers have actually tested children and adults in mazes.[109] Others have created computer-simulated places in which subjects are to find their way around.[110] Perhaps the least used method in contrast to its great potential is naturalistic observation of people in the midst of wayfinding, although this is changing.[111]

We must remember, however, that none of these methods, itself, yields an individual's spatial knowledge. For example, a **sketch map** is not a cognitive map; it is a representation of what is stored in the head that is limited in its accuracy by such factors as the individual's drawing ability, stage of development, memory, and problems with translating a large place onto a small piece of paper.

Evidence on the accuracy of these methods is mixed.[112] Sometimes the methods are reliable (yield similar information from one occasion to the next or from one method to the next)[113] and sometimes they are

not.[114] **Validity** (whether the methods yield data that truly represent an individual's cognitive map) is a problem with most methods of studying spatial cognition. In a study of Northwest coast aboriginals, paper-and-pencil measures of spatial cognition bore little relation to their ability to wayfind in the real environment.[115] However, in another study, sketch maps did represent the actual movements of individuals around a setting,[116] and in a third, spatial decision making was similar, whether the experimenter used sketch maps, a computer simulation, or actual wayfinding.[117]

Methods that ask research participants for interplace distance judgments, which are then analyzed with a sophisticated statistical procedure called **multidimensional scaling,** may be more accurate than the familiar sketch maps.[118] Other researchers believe that *any* translation from cognitive distance to physical distance will be extremely difficult.[119] Given the uncertainty of these measures, the best approach may be to employ multiple measures of spatial cognition,[120] or at least to be certain the measure used really is appropriate to the particular form of spatial cognition being studied.

◆ *IN SUM, spatial cognition measurement techniques include sketch maps, model construction or manipulation, distance estimation, and naturalistic observation. Evidence for their usefulness is mixed. Once again, the best solution to the problem of imperfect methods is either to employ multiple methods, so as to gain complementary perspectives on the truth, or at least to select carefully the most appropriate method for the specific investigation that is undertaken.*[121]

Influences on Spatial Cognition

This section describes factors that affect the speed of acquiring information about the environment, the accuracy of this information, the way individuals organize the information, and the differences in ability to recall spatial information. The factors may be divided into those primarily located in the person—such as spatial ability, visual impairment, age, sex, and familiarity with the setting—and those located in the physical environment, such as a town's street arrangement (e.g., like a grid versus like a plate of spaghetti).[122]

Even shared environments are not thought about in the same way by their inhabitants. Individual differences are the key to this variability in spatial cognition.[123] The crucial questions are: *Which* individual differences affect our thinking about our everyday settings, and *How* do they affect it?

Five factors will be discussed in some detail. These are stage of life, spatial ability, familiarity with the place, sex, and cognitive biases; these factors have received the most attention from researchers. I should note that spatial cognition is also affected by many other factors that have not yet received much attention: personality,[124] intelligence,[125] self-efficacy (the conviction that one can get things done),[126] culture,[127] education,[128] emotion,[129] time pressure, risk, interest,[130] testosterone level,[131] and even which direction a person is facing when he or she thinks about place locations.[132] However, let's start with developmental changes, the first of the influences that have received considerable attention.

Stage of Life. As a toddler, you were not allowed out of the house alone. A few years later, the yard or the block was the limit. Then you got a bike—and the whole neighborhood was yours. As a teen, your horizon may have been the whole community. These expansions in a person's permissible range are accompanied by changes in general cognitive development.[133]

These changes may be described in terms of Jean Piaget's influential theory of cognitive development. Spatial cognition is viewed in this theory as one aspect of a child's more general cognitive unfolding. Early on, children are **egocentric**—they believe they are the center of the world. They perceive environments in terms of how close something in it is to them, whether they can touch it, and whether it is part of them. Infants must learn, for example, that those five small pink objects flying around near them are their own toes rather than a friendly, tasty five-headed being of independent means.

Roughly at the time of starting school, children enter a stage that allows them to adopt perspectives from viewpoints other than their own; this is sometimes called the **projective** stage. In terms of spatial cognition, children are now able to think of settings from various physical vantage points. Children at this stage are able, theoretically, to orient themselves using prominent landmarks. For example, most are able to find their way home from school.

Later, at around 11 years of age, most children are able to think in more **abstract** terms. The reflection of this change in spatial cognition is an ability to use abstract concepts such as sets of Euclidean coordinates (grid systems such as latitude and longitude) or directions such as north, south, east, and west.[134]

Research generally supports this Piagetan model of children's spatial cognition.[135] However, some believe that researchers who have limited their studies to laboratory techniques have underestimated the spatial cognitive abilities of children.[136] For example, some children as young as 12 months old can use landmarks.[137] Relatively young children can use aerial maps effectively. Some 6-year-olds can make spatial judgments that appear to require perspective taking or Euclidean abilities.[138] Children can draw a map of the route from home to school that contains much more detail that they can report when asked to tell someone about the same route.[139] In familiar settings, even children as young as age 3½ have shown Euclidean knowledge[140]—an accomplishment that Piagetans would not expect for almost another decade of life!

Thus, the spatial cognitive abilities of children have been underestimated because their spatial abilities outstrip their verbal abilities. For instance, they are able to use a map or to find their way home but they are not yet able to explain very well how they accomplished the feat.[141] Attention must therefore be paid to the most appropriate method of assessing the spatial cognitive abilities of children (see Figure 2–6).

What about the other end of the developmental spectrum? Older people say they have more difficulty finding their way around unfamiliar places.[142] Most research does indicate that spatial ability declines with advancing age,[143,144,145,146,147] but some studies have found no decline in performance with age.[148,149] Because quite a bit of research has been conducted on this topic, a fair amount is known about it, and reality is—as usual—somewhat complex.

In general, two likely broad conclusions are that (1) with age, some spatial abilities decline, others do not, and some may even improve; and (2) older individuals think about space *differently* than younger individuals. For example, elderly individuals may perform better in settings that are familiar and meaningful to them,[150] although this does not always hold either.[151] Older people

FIGURE 2-6 Children gradually learn to orient themselves in their homes, neighborhoods, and communities.

learn *new* spatial information more slowly than young people;[152] they may have greater difficulty in learning new routes, finding new routes, and remembering the layout of places.[153] Another problem is that elderly people may *believe* their performance is better when it is actually declining.[154]

These changes may be due to both behavioral and physiological changes, such as reduced mobility and sensory ability. For example, one study found no age-related performance decline in a task that required no movement through a real setting—that is, participants were asked to recall the spatial location of typed words on cards.[155] In contrast, another study found that after older and younger travelers drove a 340-kilometer route along the coast in Australia, the older travelers more frequently mislabeled landmarks.[156]

Older people in this study, however, remembered *more* districts and reported *more* details than did younger travelers. Apparently, older people rely more for their memory of the environment on features that are (1) more meaningful to them, such as buildings that are used more often or more easily; (2) are historical,[157,158] (3) are unique in architectural style,[159] and (4) incorporate landscape elements that make them feel good.[160] Researchers are now investigating which specific teaching methods will best help older people to learn new environments.[161]

Spatial Ability. You might think it is obvious that individuals with greater spatial ability would perform better on spatial cognition tasks such as wayfinding, but it is not that simple. Standard psychological tests that mea-

sure one's ability to mentally rotate objects or find objects embedded in a complex background do predict how well people learn or remember new settings, but only modestly.[162,163] This is probably because other factors come into play. Thus, natural talent in spatial cognition does not neatly translate into better real-world spatial-cognitive performance. However, this does not mean one's basic spatial ability has no impact on one's life. For example, being able to learn and remember the location and orientation of objects in space without any contextual or background information is a better predictor of whether older adults will use the goods and services in their neighborhoods than how long they have lived in the neighborhood or how mobile they are.[164]

Familiarity or Experience. Clearly, as we spend time in a setting, our spatial cognitions about it will change. The most obvious change is that our knowledge about it will grow, which means we are usually able to find our way around in it better.[165,166,167] In a study by Seymour Wapner and colleagues of new students at a university, sketch maps of the campus drawn six months apart showed significant increases not only in the amount of information but also in the differentiation and the integration of that information.[168] A study of Parisian taxi drivers confirmed that experienced drivers perform better than inexperienced drivers; they also knew to use different strategies in different parts of the city.[169]

Increasing experience does not necessarily mean that we have a more *accurate* mental map of a setting, compared to an objective or cartographic map. In a study of distance judgments in a very large building, the

SEYMOUR WAPNER
has been a leading proponent of integral theory (as discussed in Chapter 1) in environmental psychology.

more experienced people were, the more *incorrect* their maps were.[170] Researchers suggest that as we become more familiar with a setting, we change our image of it in ways that help us wayfind better. But depending on the setting, this may require that we develop an inaccurate image of it in cartographic terms.

Wayfinding is more difficult in more complex settings, but experience helps.[171] Students with at least one year's experience at another campus depicted their campus with greater configurational accuracy than students with less experience.[172] This accuracy, to be precise, may be a superiority in *relative* location of campus locations rather than a superiority in the *absolute* distances between, and locations of, places.

When we are aware that it is important to learn the spatial layout of a place, we can do so very quickly[173]— more quickly than when we are not instructed to pay attention to the environment.[174] If we simply learn the parts of a building that we need, however, our knowledge of the whole building may be weak. People who knew nothing about a specific building were asked to memorize floor plans of it. Those people were able to find their way around that building significantly better than people who had worked in the building for two years.[175]

Several variables that represent experiential differences are also related to spatial cognition. For example, drivers may acquire different and perhaps *better organized* environmental information than their passengers, even though they do not necessarily acquire *more* information.[176,177] Studies show that social class, urban versus rural residence, and husbands versus wives differ in the form and content of spatial knowledge.[178,179] But presumably, these variables indicate that individuals move through cities differently, depending on social factors

(rather than, for example, that husbands and wives are intrinsically different in this way). Poorer citizens, for instance, have quite different activity patterns in most cities than wealthier citizens; this leads them to know some places in the city better and other places less well.[180]

Sex. Several studies find differences between the sexes in the acquisition, accuracy, and organization of spatial information. When there is a difference, it is likely to favor males,[181,182,183] and women more often say they have difficulty wayfinding in new settings.[184] This difference does not always hold, though. In a Swedish study, for example, men and women either walked or were driven through an unfamiliar residential neighborhood.[185] When the participants were driven, men learned about the setting slightly faster than women, but when they walked through the setting, men and women learned equally quickly. In another study, men were more accurate than women only in locating those places that were difficult to locate.[186]

This sex difference, to the extent it holds, may reflect the different experiences that males and females are likely to have, rather than basic differences in cognitive abilities or tendencies.[187,188] Some direct evidence for this has been reported.[189] For example, boys have more experience because they are allowed to roam further; that is, they have larger **home ranges** than girls.[190,191] In adults, there is some evidence that the sexes are *not* different in ability, although men express their judgments with more confidence.[192]

Apart from differences in ability, men and women seem to have different *kinds* of spatial cognitions. Men's sketch maps may include more territory[193] and be more gridlike; women's maps tend to be more home centered.[194] When asked to give directions, men give more distance estimates ("it's about 6 miles") and cardinal directions ("west of here") than women.[195] Women may base their spatial cognition more on their experiences traveling along paths, whereas men may rely more on maplike mental representations of the city.[196]

Spatial-Cognitive Biases. People's cognitive maps do not match cartographic maps for a variety of reasons, as we have already seen. Apart from these, however, we may err in three predictable ways, which we may call the Euclidean, superordinate-scale, and segmentation biases.

In **Euclidean bias**, people think of the world as more Euclidean or gridlike than it really is. On sketch maps, many individuals draw converging streets as parallel, intersections that do not form right angles as if they did, and streets with gentle curves as straight lines.[197,198,199] When asked to point toward targets that are not visible, people make more mistakes if they are at an intersection that is not a right angle.[200] This makes cities with gridlike street patterns easier to navigate than cities with curving, radial, or nonparallel streets.

To illustrate **superordinate-scale bias**, answer the following three questions for yourself. Which is farther north: Toronto or Minneapolis? Which is farther west: Athens or Warsaw? Which is farther east: Reno or San Diego? In thinking about locations that we are not sure about, we apparently rely on superordinate groupings— that is, larger categories of which the place in question is a member.[201] Toronto is in Canada; Canada is north of the United States; Minneapolis is in the United States; therefore, Toronto must be north of Minneapolis. Athens is in Greece, which has been part of the Western alliance, and Warsaw, in Poland, was part of the Eastern bloc; therefore, Athens must be west of Warsaw. Reno, being a city in Nevada, which is a state east of California, where San Diego is located, must be east of San Diego. Each of these lines of reasoning is, of course, incorrect. Using larger categories to reason about the location of places within them sometimes leads to errors in spatial cognition.

Segmentation bias pertains to distance judgments. Mentally breaking a route into separate segments seems to alter people's distance estimates.[202] Estimates over the whole route, or from segment to segment, increase with objective distance (as they should), but distance estimates *within* segments do not increase with objective distance. It is as if we do not make reliable distance differentiations for places that are within the same segment of the route.

Physical Influences. Which features of the environment affect environmental cognition? We will consider this question first at the city scale then at the building scale.

Long ago, Kevin Lynch[203] and Donald Appleyard[204] hypothesized that regular, clear paths and highly visible

landmarks would improve cognition of cities. Research has supported this contention[205] and extended it. For example, distance judgments are more accurate in cities that have more regular traffic patterns.[206] In addition, the presence of strongly organizing features in cities— such as rivers, roads, and railroads—improve spatial cognition.

One might also expect that highly salient (prominent, conspicuous) features of a cityscape would further enhance one's processing of information about it. A study tested this idea by comparing the speed of processing and the number of errors in the reading of maps that varied both in their degree of organization and in the degree of salience of certain features.[207] As Lynch and Appleyard would predict, greater organization improved speed and reduced errors. However, salience *without* organization significantly *harmed* spatial cognition (see Figure 2–7). Apparently, salient features can enhance the cognition of settings that are clearly organized, but can confuse us when their salience is not accompanied by clear organization.

Features of a city that break up the transportation system may interfere with cognitive mapping, too. Fargo, North Dakota, has a large railroad switching yard in its center. When an overpass that linked the two sides of the switching yard was built, women's estimates of distances between places that had been separated by

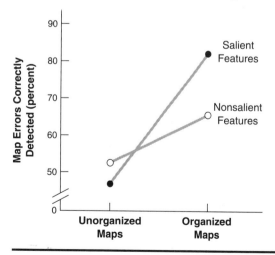

FIGURE 2–7 Accurate map reading depends on how well the map is organized and how salient, visible, or obvious features of the place are rendered on the map.

the switching yard became more accurate.[208] This presumably occurred because women tend to rely on travel experience for distance estimates; when they had to travel further around the switching yards, even the "as-the-crow-flies" distance seemed greater. When the overpass was built, their new travel experiences correctly informed them that the straight-line distance was not so great.

One controversy concerns which features of a new environment are learned first. Some hypothesize that people learn landmarks first, before elaborating paths.[209,210] Others have reached the conclusion that paths and districts are learned first, then landmarks are used for orientation.[211,212] Evidence supports both positions.[213,214] After a careful review, Gary Evans[215] concluded that both may be true, depending on the physical character of the setting in question. For example, in one study, supporting the idea that paths are learned before landmarks, the authors noted that participants were virtually forced to learn the paths first because the distance between landmarks was so great. In other places, where many salient landmarks are available, they may be learned first.

So far, we have focused on some features of cities that affect urban spatial cognition. Which features of building interiors influence spatial cognition or wayfinding in them? In general, four factors play a role in this:

• Signs and numbering systems
• Visibility of the destination and views to outdoors
• Differentiation (the distinctiveness of different parts of the building)
• Configuration (the overall layout of the building)[216]

GARY EVANS
is a major researcher in the areas of environmental cognition and environmental stress.

Thus, in general, one would expect wayfinding to be easier in buildings with clear signs and numbering systems, good visibility, greater differentiation, and simpler configuration.[217] Some research supports this. Wayfinding is easier in buildings that have simpler floor plans.[218] One study found that signs significantly increased the rate of travel through complex buildings and reduced the number of wrong turns by 50 percent and backtracking by 62 percent.[219] However, signs did not fully overcome building complexity; it was still generally easier to find one's way around in buildings with simpler floor plans.

When people are learning the layout of a building on their own, they consistently move toward the parts of the building that allow the best surveillance of the building as a whole.[220] Presumably, buildings that have no place from which the rest of the building can be scanned are more difficult to comprehend. Full understanding of a building's layout requires the development of an overall cognitive map; wayfinding that must rely merely on moving from sign to sign or landmark to landmark is limited.

For many reasons, buildings cannot always be constructed for optimal wayfinding. What can we do when the building already exists and is a virtual maze? We might improve the signage and numbering, but the other architectural dimensions (i.e., visibility, differentiation, and configuration) are not easy to change. Thus, something else we could do is to teach people how to wayfind in complex buildings. One researcher proposes that the fastest way to enhance the spatial cognition of a building is to show people sequences of slides or photos and building models.[221] The models should be simplified—showing the main elements of the building but not any distracting elements that would not help with wayfinding.

Some people actually *want* wayfinding to be awful, and are even willing to pay to get lost. In Japan and England, life-sized mazes have become a national pastime.[222] The British Tourist Authority declared 1991 the Year of the Maze, and in Japan, at least 100 commercial mazes have recently sprung up. People have been building mazes for enjoyment since the days of ancient Crete. A good maze is one that deliberately violates all four of the principles listed earlier—no signs or numbers, no visibility, no distinctive parts, and very high complexity.

Although we may like the challenge of a maze once in a while, no one likes a maze when trying to get to an appointment or a class.

Apart from wayfinding, what might make buildings cognitively stand out or be remembered better? Donald Appleyard[223] pioneered this line of research in Ciudad Guyana, a Venezuelan city that was planned from the ground up. He assessed a variety of relatively objective characteristics of buildings in Ciudad Guyana and compared them with the frequency they were recalled by residents. The better-recalled buildings were tall, freestanding, distinctive in shape, easily visible, frequently used, and had much human movement around them.

Each of these characteristics also enhanced resident recall of buildings in Orange, California.[224] However, a few characteristics were found to enhance recall only in Ciudad Guyana (such as singularity of the building's use) or only in Orange (such as building quality). This suggests, pending further research, that certain building characteristics make a stronger impact on individuals regardless of culture, but others make an impact in one culture but not others.

A quite different way of thinking about environmental cognition is this: How does the physical environment affect cognition (in general—not spatial cognition)? In an important early article, Joachim Wohlwill[225] introduced the concept of an **optimal level of stimulation** to environmental psychology, based on the **adaptation-level theory** of Harry Helson.[226] The idea is that for any given activity, one may be either over- or understimulated, leading to a decrease in satisfaction. Each of us adapts to a certain level of stimulation, which might be relatively high or low in objective terms, depending on our circumstances. As the level of stimulation we experience in a given setting moves slightly to moderately away from this adaptation level, our pleasure is hypothesized to increase: The change is stimulating, if you will pardon the choice of words. But as the level of stimulation changes further in the same direction, it becomes too much or too little stimulation to enjoy, and pleasure declines.

Thus, when a setting is too novel, complex, or fast moving for our usual adaptation level, we find it overstimulating or stressful; our pleasure, and perhaps our performance, may suffer. The same outcome may occur when we find a setting understimulating—that is, too well known, simple, slow moving, or just plain boring.

The cognitive outcomes of low-level stimulation have been studied experimentally by Peter Suedfeld and others. In one study, volunteers spent 24 hours in a dark and silent chamber.[227] Control group volunteers were confined to a small room but were allowed stimulation (a phone and any activity they chose except leaving the room). Earlier research had shown that drastic stimulus reduction can improve performance on simple cognitive tasks. Suedfeld and colleagues wanted to know the effects on complex and difficult tasks, and selected tasks that varied in both complexity and difficulty. The restricted stimulation group performed worse than the control group on complex tasks but not on difficult tasks. However, these results may depend on just what the task is. In another study, with a different kind of task, the performance of low-stimulation participants suffered with increases in both task complexity and task difficulty.[228]

◆ **IN SUM,** *spatial cognition—the way we acquire, process, store, and recall information about everyday settings—is affected by one's stage of life, familiarity or experience with the setting, spatial and perceptual ability, cognitive biases, and features of the city or building. The spatial cognition of children generally follows a sequence moving from egocentric to projective to abstract, although they may move through these stages faster than laboratory studies suggest. The spatial cognition of older people differ from those of younger adults. Where their experience is limited by lowered mobility or sensory abilities, they may perform less well. Their memories of the environment are more personalized and are, in some respects, better than those of young adults. Male-female differences in spatial cognition exist, but may largely reflect the different travel experiences of men and women. Experience in a setting*

PETER SUEDFELD

is the most important contributor to the environmental psychology of low-stimulation settings.

gives one a fuller and better organized cognitive image of it. Three common cognitive biases are to envision places as more gridlike or Euclidean than they really are, to wrongly employ larger geographical entities in placing smaller ones, and to be affected by the segments or barriers along a path.

Spatial cognition is also affected by characteristics of the place about which one is cognizing. For example, spatial cognition of urban forms is improved by clear paths and visible landmarks. Where one of these elements is more common or salient than the other, examples of it will be learned first. Some evidence suggests that visibility without organization, however, may detract from effective spatial cognition. At the architectural level, buildings that are tall, freestanding, distinctively shaped, and used often are better recalled than others. Cognition, in general, is affected by the level of stimulation we receive from the environment in comparison to the level of stimulation to which we are accustomed.

Theories

How can all this knowledge about how we comprehend everyday settings be integrated? Clearly, information flows from the physical environment to a cognitive apparatus that must ultimately be represented in the brain. Appropriately, the theoretical approaches to the puzzle of spatial cognition, to be discussed next, complement one another by originating with physical, cognitive, and physiological structures. Even better, though there is still a long way to go, some preliminary signposts indicate the direction toward unification of these approaches.

Legibility: A Physical Perspective. The seminal works of Kevin Lynch[229,230] and Donald Appleyard[231] have been extremely influential in urban planning and environmental psychology. The concept of legibility (the ease with which a place may be cognitively organized, understood, or "read" by someone) and its relations to paths, landmarks, edges, nodes, and districts have provided the basic infrastructure for hundreds of studies. The role of information processing in the head is not ignored in this approach (as we shall see at the end of this section), but the theory does begin with and emphasize the physical arrangement of space.

The principal elements of this physical perspective have already been described. The thrust of the theory is to predict that places high in legibility are easy to comprehend and use. Lynch's ideas have been studied and applied at scales ranging from buildings to entire cities (see Figure 2–8). For example, to create more legible cities, urban planners should gradually shape their communities in five ways as the city grows and redevelops.[232]

1. Place landmarks at major decision points in the road system.

FIGURE 2-8 The Empress Hotel is one of the most legible buildings in Victoria, British Columbia.

2. Keep these landmarks distinctive by maximizing their visibility; this can be accomplished by making them tall, separate from neighboring buildings, unique in architectural style, and into enclosures for activities that result in much public use of the building.
3. Primary roads should coincide with the functional boundaries of districts to reinforce edges.
4. Preserve buildings that might serve as good landmarks when a district undergoes extensive redevelopment.
5. Construct landmarks in overly homogeneous districts.

Lynch's ideas also have been applied to you-are-here maps, color-coded buildings, and transit map designs. The latter will be described here; you-are-here maps and color coding will be described later. Legibility principles have been used to design bus and subway maps that improve comprehension of transit routes. The best maps do not represent transit routes cartographically; rather, in a simplified schematic manner, they match one's experiences as one moves from point to point in a journey.[233] Maps that use color coding to enhance legibility of routes give transit riders greater accuracy and confidence, but those that try too hard to be helpful by providing off-route street details result in less accuracy and more frustration.[234]

Maps have not completely solved the problem of environmental orientation. Even experienced subway riders, when asked to take a trip from A to B, chose nonoptimal routes more than half the time.[235] The riders had difficulty with subway maps and signs; they often responded by selecting a *familiar* route rather than the *optimal* route to reach their destinations.

In a hospital outpatient department, researchers gave some women hand-held maps to use in locating numerous destinations in the building; other women in the study were given no map.[236] Those who used the hand-held maps actually took longer to locate the destinations, but they did retrace their steps less often and *believed* the map was useful in planning their trip.

Intellectual Growth and Planning: Two Cognitive Perspectives. Whereas the legibility approach originally emphasized the role of the environment in spatial cog-

nition, the intellectual growth and planning approaches originally emphasized the role of cognition in spatial cognition. However, the two approaches now are converging. The intellectual growth perspective examines the way individuals develop the capacity to comprehend space. It is concerned with the ways we develop the ability to use spatial information, such as in wayfinding, giving directions, and remembering where places are. Mainly derived from Piagetan theory, it includes the egocentric, place-oriented, and abstract-coordinates stages that children are presumed to follow.

Gary Moore has provided an extension of these ideas that serves to increase the role of the environment within this approach.[237] He believes that in each stage, not only does the individual know different things about the environment but he or she also *organizes* that knowledge differently. Moore also has suggested there are conceptual parallels between the childhood progression from stage to stage and the short-term progression that adults move through as they learn a new setting. As a **transactional-constructivist,**[238] Moore has asserted that spatial cognition cannot be understood until the transactions that occur between individuals and their settings are understood. He also believes we actively construct the world from data we have gleaned about it (as opposed to those who believe the world reveals itself to us as it is or already constructed).

One relatively simple demonstration of constructivism in children is provided by studies in which children start at a certain home base X and are taught how to get from X to three other places: A, B, and C.[239] The children are not taught how to get from A to B, from B to C, or from A to C, yet they are able to explain the spatial relations between these places. Because the children had no direct experience with the spatial relations, they must have constructed them.

Other researchers have begun to develop formal models that simulate the process by which we, for example, make our way though a new neighborhood.[240] Computer programs have been developed to model the way people gradually learn the spatial features of places.[241] Most such models assume that we create regionalized, hierarchical mental maps.[242] **Regionalization** means that we tend to create groups of locations (e.g., rooms within a large building, buildings within a large city, towns within a geographic region). **Hierarchical organization** means that we create categories within categories, such as cities within countries.

Each region may be identified with one or more landmarks, and some theories of spatial cognition focus on the ways that we use landmarks to organize space.[243] Because there is some dispute about the precise definition of a landmark,[244] it may be more accurate to say that regions tend to have cognitive **anchor points**.[245]

In everyday spatial behavior, these regionalized and hierarchical mental maps are used whenever we need to plan how to get from *A* to *B*. Of course, not all our wayfinding requires conscious planning; many trips are so familiar that we traverse them with no planning.[246] However, as we soon shall see, planning plays a key role in *some* everyday spatial behavior.

What does all this mean in practice? Many important consequences are implied for spatial cognition of both children and adults. For example, one study showed that residents' regionalizations of their neighborhoods do not necessarily correspond to the way neighborhoods are organized in the political system.[247] If the boundaries drawn by lawmakers for voting districts, school districts, or park planning are quite different from the residents' own image of the neighborhood's boundaries, confusion and conflict may ensue.

Another practical application concerns getting lost. Describing the case of a lost 3-year-old boy, researchers showed, by reconstructing the paths he took, that his wanderings were not random.[248] Depending on age, experience, and the setting, the likely paths taken by lost persons may be predicted with fair success. Others have used spatial cognition principles to help people who are severely mentally ill find their way around their communities.[249] The standard procedures used by police and other officials sometimes involve search strategies (e.g., following a strict grid pattern) that do not take these most likely paths into account. Knowledge of a child's developmental stage and the terrain may lead to more efficient search strategies. For example, lost children under age 6 are more often found in open spaces, but lost children in the 6- to 12-year-old range often seek enclosures or refuges when they get lost.

The hierarchical manner in which we organize spatial knowledge means that we construct maps at different levels (like the different magnifications on a micro-

scope) and we are able (under the right conditions) to use whichever "magnification" best suits our needs. For example, in a study, people were given a task in which they were to minimize the total distance they traveled to do a series of errands. Afterwards, they were able to recognize and select segments of their trip that were not the shortest they might have chosen in order to accomplish the overall goal of traveling the shortest *total* distance.[250]

Personal constructions of spatial relations mean that people do not always act according to cartographic reality. For example, cognitive distances are strongly related to where consumers decide to shop—more so than to objective distances, socioeconomic factors, or other demographic information about the shopper.[251] We shop according to how we *think* the world is organized more than according to how it is actually organized.

The second—but very much related—cognitive perspective involves the role of **plans and goals** in spatial cognition.[252,253,254] This perspective is concerned with the secondary or indirect use of spatial knowledge, such as when we plan a series of errands or other spatial tasks to be done in a certain order. Even the world we cognitively construct depends on the goals and plans we carry with us as we move through the world. For example, individuals who enter a room with the intention to hide something in it or redecorate it end up with quite different mental maps of the room (and different feelings about it) than individuals who enter it merely to wait.[255]

Like the constructivists, theorists in this perspective observe that we are active agents in our transactions with settings. According to Tommy Garling, we develop *action plans* to guide our behavior. Travel plans, one kind of action plan, partly determine what spatial information is acquired, how it is organized, and what infer-

TOMMY GARLING,
a leading Swedish environmental psychologist, has extensively studied environmental perception and cognition.

ences (or constructions) about settings are drawn by a person (see Figure 2–9).

The development of spatial knowledge—here is one connection to the intellectual growth perspective—is influenced by the nature of the activity in which we are engaged.[256] In everyday life, spatial activity is guided by meaningful plans and goals. In laboratory studies, the researchers' goals often replace any goals the subjects might have had. To learn more about the role of goals and planning in spatial cognition, people must be studied in their own habitats. For example, even short local trips of 20 minutes require as many as 50 wayfinding decisions: Travel planning and execution are considerable cognitive tasks.[257] When individuals have (or are given) specific goals, plans, or tasks that involve spatial relations (such as celestial navigation, going to the store as a child for your parents, or hunting for mushrooms in the woods), their spatial development may proceed more quickly than laboratory-based studies might predict.

An interesting application based on planfulness has been proposed.[258] Criminals as well as their victims have cognitive maps, like everyone else. Law enforcement might be more efficient if cognitive mapping techniques were used to identify "fear zones" in cities and the cognitive maps of criminals.[259] Cognitive maps of crime do not necessarily match official crime statistics. For example, suburbanites may incorrectly locate high levels of crime in the downtown area of cities.[260] On the other hand, researchers have helped to construct cognitive map profiles of suspects based on their apparent plans and actual patterns of crime sites. Serial rapists exhibit nonrandom spatial patterns in their crimes, suggesting that one could learn to predict where they are likely to strike next.[261]

The Hippocampus: A Physiological Perspective. Too rarely have connections between environmental psychology and the neurosciences been made, although presumably all behavior (including environmentally relevant behavior) is represented one way or another in brain physiology. The most ambitious attempt to link spatial cognition and the brain has been that of John O'Keefe and Lynn Nadel. Working originally from studies on rats, O'Keefe and Nadel proposed that the hippocampus, a seahorse-shaped part of the limbic system in the central core of the brain, is the home of the cognitive map (see Figure 2–10).[262,263]

The idea that animal behavior is guided by maps was introduced to psychology long ago by Edward Tolman, but not in such specific physiological detail.[264,265] O'Keefe and Nadel's basic and controversial idea is that (1) some neurons in the hippocampus are specifically coded for place; (2) networks of such neurons form a framework that represents, in a three-dimensional Euclidean framework, the settings known to the individual; and (3) in humans, the portion of the hippocampus in the left hemisphere houses a semantic or word-based map and the portion in the right hemisphere houses a spatial or pictorial map.

O'Keefe and Nadel's theory also postulates the existence of two systems of spatial cognition: the taxon system and the locale system. The taxon system guides the routes one takes, using guidance hypotheses and orientation hypotheses. *Guidance hypotheses* specify objects or

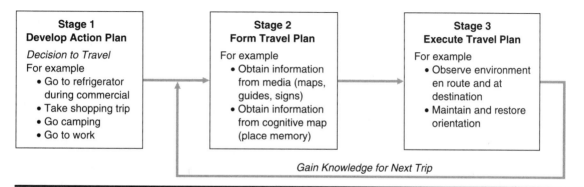

Stage 1 Develop Action Plan	Stage 2 Form Travel Plan	Stage 3 Execute Travel Plan
Decision to Travel For example • Go to refrigerator during commercial • Take shopping trip • Go camping • Go to work	For example • Obtain information from media (maps, guides, signs) • Obtain information from cognitive map (place memory)	For example • Observe environment en route and at destination • Maintain and restore orientation

Gain Knowledge for Next Trip

FIGURE 2-9 This diagram shows an information-processing model of travel and orientation.

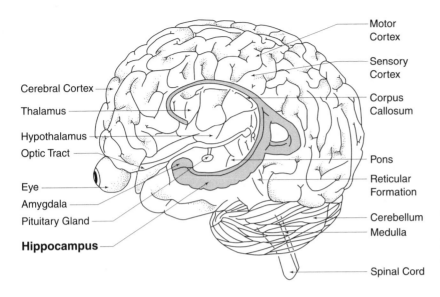

Cerebral Cortex

Thalamus

Hypothalamus

Optic Tract

Eye

Amygdala

Pituitary Gland

Hippocampus

Motor Cortex

Sensory Cortex

Corpus Callosum

Pons

Reticular Formation

Cerebellum

Medulla

Spinal Cord

FIGURE 2-10 The hippocampus may be the neurological site where much of our spatial cognition occurs.

cues in the setting that should be approached or kept at a certain distance. *Orientation hypotheses* specify how this is to be accomplished behaviorally, such as "Turn right 90 degrees." The locale system, as its name suggests, refers to places. *Place hypotheses* are constructions by the brain that organize space knowledge important to the individual. Typical place hypotheses might be "This is a dangerous place" or "That place usually supplies water."

O'Keefe and Nadel's own work is primarily with freely moving rats whose brains are monitored as they explore their settings. However, their book gathers evidence from human neuropsychology that appears to support their ideas. The potential applications of O'Keefe and Nadel's theory to humans are interesting. They speculate, for example, that language developed primarily as a way for us to express our place knowledge to others. These researchers see connections between the hippocampal model of the cognitive map and the problems experienced by patients with Korsakoff's syndrome (a pattern of cognitive deficits, including amnesia, brought on by chronic alcohol abuse). Victims of Alzheimer's disease, which affects the hippocampus as well as other regions of the brain, have difficulty using maps (among their many other problems).[266]

The hippocampus is not the only brain location related to cognitive mapping. For example, individuals with damage to the parietal region of the cortex lose the ability to draw maps of familiar places and seem to lose

their knowledge of how places they know are arranged in geographic space.[267] It is becoming clear that different parts of the brain are associated with different kinds of spatial cognition. One summary of the research concludes there are five categories of spatial cognition and these are represented in various parts of the brain.[268] This idea is presented in Table 2–1.

One notable theoretical problem has not yet been mentioned. The issue is whether spatial knowledge in humans is stored as **propositions** or as **analogies.** Simply put, the propositional approach hypothesizes that our knowledge of everyday space is stored in the brain as words. The analogical approach hypothesizes that the knowledge is stored as pictorial images. The propositional approach assumes information is stored in abstract networks of meaning, or schemata.[269] The analogical approach assumes it is stored as a model or image of the real world.[270] As often happens in psychology, the resolution of the issue may be that both forms of information storage occur.[271]

Another brain-based (but not necessarily hippocampus-based) theory of spatial cognition is the **world graph,** a representation of relations among situations encountered by the individual.[272] Each situation is said to be encoded in a neural node, but each place may be encoded in several neural nodes. The world graph model appears to explain certain classic findings in animal exploration research and, if extended to humans,

TABLE 2–1 Locations of Various Spatial-Cognition Functions in the Brain

Spatial Cognition Type	Sample Function	Brain Region
Spatial perception	Object localization	Occipital and parietal lobes
Spatial memory	Short-term memory for space	Hippocampus, thalamus
Spatial attention	Attention to space	Parietal lobe
Spatial operations	Mental rotation	Right parietal lobe
Spatial construction	Assembling parts into a whole	Parietal lobe

would presumably assist in the understanding of cognitive maps.

◆ **IN SUM,** *five theories of environmental cognition concentrate on the physical environment, cognitive, or physiological aspects of spatial cognition. The legibility approach focuses on how settings from buildings to cities should be arranged to promote easy comprehension of them by individuals who need to find their way. Two cognitive theories, the intellectual growth and planning approaches, focus on the way that children learn to comprehend the settings around them as their cognitive abilities increase and the ways in which our travel plans affect both typical and optimal wayfinding. Two physiological theories, the hippocampal and world graph approaches, examine the basis of wayfinding in the brain. The five theories complement one another because a full understanding of spatial cognition will require knowledge of the physical environment, how we think about those spaces, and the neural basis of it all.*

Environmental Cognition and Design

You-Are-Here Maps. How can environmental cognition principles be used in environmental design? You-are-here maps are one important application, although, as we shall see, many you-are-here maps fail to use the principles of environmental cognition and actually confuse people.

Many places, such as large buildings, campuses, and shopping centers, are difficult for people find their way in or around. Some of them place maps on pedestals or walls near the entrance, showing the layout of the building, complete with a little arrow saying "You are here." These maps are an attempt to make the build-

ing more legible, but in a way, they are admissions that the building is insufficiently legible on its own.

There are good and poor you-are-here maps; some succeed in improving the building's legibility, others may be worse with the map than without it (see Figure 2–11). Two general principles should be followed to make you-are-here maps effective: structure matching and orientation.[273]

Structure matching means the map should usefully reflect the layout and appearance of the setting it represents. Structure matching is improved when the following criteria are met.

- The map contains labels that resemble actual labels (such as logos) in the setting.
- The map is placed asymmetrically along the path in which it is placed, so that its viewers can easily see the relative location of the map within the setting.
- The you-are-here symbol on the map points to a little picture of the map itself and consists of an arrow pointing to exactly where the viewer is in relation to the map.

Orientation is improved when the following principles have been employed.

- The map is aligned the same way as the setting (e.g., east is east and west is west).
- The map has *forward-up equivalence* (the top of the map represents straight ahead in the actual setting).

In laboratory and field tests, these two principles have been shown to significantly improve wayfinding in buildings.[274,275,276] However, even good you-are-here maps require more cognitive effort than good signs on

FIGURE 2-11   Based on the text, is this typical you-are-here map a good one?

walls. One study found that wayfinders who used signs found their destinations faster than those who used you-are-here maps.[277] Thus, good signs, where they are possible, may be better than good you-are-here maps.

Improving Wayfinding with Color Coding. Buildings may also be made more legible through the use of color-coded paths and carefully researched numbering systems. For example, painting the floors of a campus building different colors reduces wayfinding errors and improves comprehension of the building by undergraduates.[278] In a hospital, researchers have shown that a minor detail such as how the floors below ground are numbered can seriously affect how many patients and visitors get lost on their way to an appointment.[279]

◆ SUMMARY ◆

Environmental-perception research emphasizes understanding how individuals respond to complex everyday scenes (rather than simplified stimulus presentations). Sometimes, such scenes must be simulated, as when the research goal is to understand reactions to a building that has not yet been built. Level of awareness, degree of adaptation, and necessary selectivity given the massive complexity of real scenes have major effects on what people perceive in a real scene. At times, this means that

we miss important elements of a scene, with negative consequences for health or safety. Environmental perception is not the same for everyone: Various personal and cultural differences are associated with seeing the same scene differently. Brunswik's probablistic functionalism, Gibson's theory of affordances, Berlyne's collative properties, and the phenomenologist's first-person approach all represent valuable ways to understand how people "read" the world.

Spatial cognition, a subset of environmental cognition, has mainly been studied as a human information process that does not resemble mechanical information processing but is generally effective (although certain biases do often lead to some errors). The elements of cognitive maps are studied by sketch maps, model manipulations, distance estimations, and natural observation. Cognitive maps develop along with other cognitive processes in a Piagetan manner, but one's experience with the environment can speed or slow this development. Legible cities and buildings are easier to comprehend. Reversing the usual sense of the term *environmental cognition*, different levels of stimulation affect how well we think and perform everyday tasks. Five theories of spatial cognition begin from different points of departure: the setting itself, cognitive development, and brain physiology. Obviously, these theories need not compete, but may be integrated into a complete model of spatial cognition. Someday, the physiological structures associated with spatial cognition will be fully connected with the cognitive and physical theories. The approaches we have discussed bring us closer than ever before to that eventual union of ideas.

Suggested Supplementary Readings

Brantingham, P. L., & Brantingham, P. J. (1993). Nodes, paths, and edges: Considerations on the complexity of crime and the physical environment. *Journal of Environmental Psychology, 13,* 3–28.

Buttimer, A., & Seamon, D. (Eds.). (1980). *The human experience of space and place.* London: Croom Helm.

Downs, R. M., & Stea, D. (1977). *Maps in minds: Reflections on cognitive mapping.* San Francisco: Harper & Row.

Garling, T., & Evans, G. (1991). *Environment, cognition, and action: An integrative multidisciplinary approach.* New York: Oxford.

Gauvain, M. (1993). The development of spatial thinking in everyday activity. *Developmental Review, 13,* 92–121.

Golledge, R. G. (1987). Environmental cognition. In D. Stokols & I. Altman (Eds.), *Handbook of environmental psychology.* New York: Wiley.

Kitchin, R. M. (1994). Cognitive maps: What they are and why study them? *Journal of Environmental Psychology, 14,* 1–19.

Lynch, K. (1960). *The image of the city.* Cambridge, MA: MIT Press.

Marans, R. W., & Stokols, D. (1993). *Environmental simulation: Research and policy issues.* New York: Plenum.

CHAPTER 3

ENVIRONMENTAL ATTITUDES, APPRAISALS, AND ASSESSMENTS

[Beauty] exists merely in the mind which contemplates [things]; and each mind
perceives a different beauty. One person may even perceive deformity, where
another is sensible of beauty; and every individual ought to acquiesce in his own
sentiment, without pretending to regulate those of others.

—David Hume (1757)[1]

*Tom and Jane were sitting in the coffee shop talking to friends about their camping trip. Someone
asked what the park was like.*

*"It's incredible," Jane quickly answered. Then she realized that her statement was not very in-
formative, so she tried to describe the steep valleys, granite mountains, and the alpine meadow with
its tiny shimmering lakes. Tom broke in to relate how beautiful the deep forest was to him, but Jane
looked at him with a puzzled expression.*

*"That place was creepy," she said, "I felt awful—almost trapped—and there was no sunlight."
Now it was Tom's turn to look puzzled. They didn't know each other all that well yet.*

"I grew up near heavy timber like that," he said, "and we used to spend hours playing in it. It's like being enclosed, but not like being trapped—unless you feel trapped in your own natural world," he joked.

A friend asked if they knew about the new mine planned for the park. "Whaaat?" Tom and Jane exclaimed in unison. "Don't you read the papers?" the friend asked. "Gouge Mines figures there's enough zinc in there to make a pit profitable, as long as they don't have to do too much reclamation of the land. They've offered to build a smelter near there, too, and the locals are already looking forward to jobs."

Tom and Jane looked at each other. "That's unbelievable," they said in unison.

"The government has commissioned some kind of study, though," continued the friend. "Something about assessing the impact of the mine and smelter on the scenic quality of the region. They do it by assembling a panel of observers who look at the park before development and look at simulations of what it would look like afterward."

"Where do I sign up?" asked Tom.

◆ ◆ ◆

Consider some place you know—perhaps your favorite vacation spot, or your bedroom, or your friend's mountain cottage, or whatever. Do you care about it? How would you go about describing it? Is it beautiful? Good quality? How does it make you feel? What, if anything, does it mean to you? Is it safe? To what extent, do you think, is your own assessment of the place similar to one that might be made by a panel of experts or other people who visit it? Do individuals entering a town experience "different" towns?

This chapter continues the discussion, begun in Chapter 2, of the process by which we come to know and understand the everyday physical environment. The initial gathering of information from settings—environmental perception—is followed by much cognitive interpretation of that information: the way we store, transform, organize, forget, and recall knowledge about places.

The focus here is on environmental attitudes and on two judgment processes—appraisal and assessment. **Environmental attitudes** can include any attitude related to nature or architecture, but the usual focus is on environmental concern for nature, or the amount a person cares about the state of the natural environment. Concern for certain parts of the built environment also deserves some attention.

The terms *environmental appraisal* and *environmental assessment* have been used differently by different authors,[2] but in this book, the following definitions will be employed. **Environmental appraisal** refers to an individual's personal impressions of a setting. Both environmental appraisals and assessments involve an observer and a place, but in research on appraisals, more emphasis is placed on understanding the person than understanding the place. Many different kinds of appraisals have been studied; six kinds are discussed in this chapter. **Environmental assessment** refers to the combining of ratings by several observers (experts or setting users) into a broader-based judgment of an environment. The emphasis is on investigating the environment (usually its quality or lack of quality) rather than understanding the persons who make the judgments.

◆ ENVIRONMENTAL ATTITUDES: ◆ CONCERN FOR PLACES

What Is an Environmental Attitude?

Although they might refer to many aspects of the environment, **environmental attitudes** are broadly defined here as an individual's *concern* for the physical environment as something that is worthy of protection, understanding, or enhancement. How concerned are you about the welfare of your own room, your residence, your neighborhood or city, a nearby wilderness area, or planet Earth?

Why study environmental attitudes, anyway? Although attitudes do not always translate into action, as we will soon see, they can be very useful for environmental managers such as park superintendents, fish and game officers, forestry officials, building managers, and recycling coordinators.[3] First, environmental attitudes can inform these individuals how much or little support exists for specific programs or the environment in general. Second, they can help in the setting of environmental goals (e.g., 60 percent of newspapers to be recycled within two years); such goals should neither be unrealistic, given the current support of the public, nor too easy to attain if more could be accomplished. Third, they can indicate with some accuracy what people are doing about the environment now, or at least what they *intend* to do.

Components of Environmental Attitudes. Attitudes, in general, are usually said to have three components: cognitive, affective, and conative. In terms of the environment, the **cognitive component** refers to what an individual knows or thinks about a place, including facts and opinions about it. The **affective component** refers to the emotional aspects of attitudes toward the place. The **conative component** relates to an individual's behavioral intentions toward the place.

Measurement Instruments. In order to measure environmental attitudes, reliable and valid measurement instruments are needed. Many instruments have been developed, some for specific purposes, such as ecological concern about consumer products[4] or the transportation of nuclear waste.[5] Eight measures will be discussed here.

1. The Maloney-Ward Ecology Inventory contains 45 items arranged in four subscales: affect, knowledge, verbal commitment, and actual commitment.[6,7] *Affect* relates to the affective component of attitudes; *knowledge* relates to the cognitive component. The latter two subscales represent the conative component: *Verbal commitment* measures what respondents *say* they will do for conservation; and *actual commitment* asks them to report what they have actually *done*.

2. The Weigel Environmental Concern Scale is a shorter 16-item scale without separate subscales.[8]

3. The New Environmental Paradigm (NEP) scale is a 12-item measure of agreement with a general "planet Earth" perspective,[9] although the NEP probably contains two or three subscales.[10]

4. A German scale also measures environmental concern, knowledge, and reported behavior.[11]

5. The Environmentalism Scale was created from the previous scales.[12] Its three subscales divide environmental attitudes into a different set of dimensions. *Internal environmentalism* refers to a person's beliefs about the relations between humanity and nature, and personal relevance to environmental issues. *External environmentalism* includes attitudes about issues outside the self, such as consumer goods, legislation, and economic aspects of environmental issues. *Substantive environmentalism* assesses a person's attitudes about the severity of environmental problems, pollution, deforestation, and biological extinction.

6. A scale developed in Germany assesses the degree of hopelessness about the environment that individuals feel.[13] Called "Is It Five Past Twelve Already?" the article notes that many people believe it is already too late and discusses the negative consequences when people give up hope that environmental problems can be solved. An international survey revealed that undergraduates from the former socialist countries of eastern Europe were more pessimistic about the environment than those from western Europe.[14] This environmental pessimism may have increased, but it is not exactly new. I knew an extremely bright student in the 1960s who chose not to go to graduate school because he thought the ecology was going to collapse too soon to make graduate school worthwhile.

7. The Environmental Worry Scale shifts from concern or pessimism to worry. It was developed to assess workers' anxiety about the effects of their exposure to organic solvents.[15] The health consequences of exposure to many technological hazards do not manifest themselves for many years (if at all), so many people worry. Worry may sound the same as pessimism, but the difference is that pessimism is fatalistic, whereas worry may be the proper and necessary prerequisite to galvanize exposed (and worried) persons into taking action against the hazard or their own exposure to it.

The validity of these scales is usually demonstrated by showing that individuals known to have pro-ecology attitudes (e.g., Sierra Club or Greenpeace members) have significantly higher environmental concern scores than do individuals who are not members of activist organizations. Thus, when the scales are given to individuals whose environmental attitudes are not yet known, one can be reasonably certain that a high score does, in fact, indicate pro-environment attitudes. All seven of these scales were mainly developed for adults. An eighth scale has been developed for children.

8. The Test for the Environmental Attitudes of Children (TEACH) examines agreement with five themes: the interrelationship of all life forms, ownership versus stewardship of the environment, the necessity of action to solve environmental problems, commitment to quality environments, and a sense of awe and wonder toward nature.[16]

All these scales were specifically developed to measure environmental concern, either as a whole or in components. However, some traditional psychological measurement instruments have been revised to include environmental concern. One classic scale, the Rokeach Value Survey, assesses the importance to individuals of 20 values, such as equality, a world of peace, family security, health, and so on. It has now been modified to include a 21st value: a clean environment.[17] With these instruments, we can begin to answer important questions about environmental attitudes, such as the one that follows.

How Concerned *Are* We, Anyway?

Level of Concern. Isn't *everyone* concerned about the environment these days? Judging from the media, the polls, and the general population, one might think so (see Figure 3–1). Certainly, it is no longer fashionable to be anti-environment. But privately, some people are not *that* concerned; they may be more concerned with jobs, health, or other considerations than the environment. A legitimate question is this: Just *how* concerned are people about the environment? How much has this concern changed over the years? Do environmental disasters affect the level of concern?

One large survey of U.S. college students found that concern for the environment actually declined from 1971 to 1981.[18] A different survey (of Kentucky adults) found that environmental concern increased from 1984 to 1988.[19] A study of U.S. university students published in 1993 reported that students have "strong" concern for the environment.[20] Some 60 percent believed that society spends too little on the environment. However, the study concluded that this support may be superficial; many students' enthusiasm for change declined if they believed that the adjustments they would have to make would cramp their lifestyles. Could it be that support for the environment is "strong" but not very committed?

One way to approach this question is to ask how important the environment is *compared to* other concerns. One study found that of the Rokeach Value Survey's 21 values, a clean environment was tied for fifth,

FIGURE 3–1 Recycling has become a major way for many people to express their environmental concern in concrete action.

behind freedom, family security, health, a world at peace, and tied with self-respect.[21] Another large-scale study of students found that the willingness to give up material goods to help the environment declined from 1971 to 1981 and 1990.[22] Once again, the data suggest that people are committed to the environment, but not if it means sacrificing their toys and comforts.

What do we know about environmental concern around the world? In Spain, survey results suggest that environmentalism has become a "central element" of the Spanish belief system.[23] Chinese teens rate environmental pollution and overpopulation as their *greatest* concerns, even more important than the death of a parent, fear of nuclear war, or getting a good job.[24] In Calcutta, more than 80 percent of the respondents in a large-scale survey believed that air pollution there was, or was soon to be, a major problem.[25] However, Thai students—although moderately concerned about the environment—are more concerned about economic, social, political, and educational issues.[26] Thus, in general, environmental concern is near the top of people's concerns, even if it is not always the number-one priority.

The Generality and Stability of Environmental Concern. A related issue is the generality of environmental concern, in two senses of the term. First, are we equally concerned about all sorts of environments? Some researchers have investigated how concern varies for different parts of the environment; to think that concern does not differ for different places or for different life domains would be simplistic.[27,28] As an example, we seem to have separate (and different) environmental concerns related to transportation, purchasing choices, cleanup, and the public advocacy of our concerns. However, persons who hold pro-environment attitudes in more than one domain do exist, of course, and they may be said to have a generalized environmental ethic.[29]

Second, are we equally concerned across time? When something goes wrong, concern rises. For example, after the Three Mile Island nuclear incident, concerns about nuclear energy rose until they were about equal to such central life concerns as finances, health, and social well-being.[30] A Dutch study found that concern about nuclear power went from negative before the Chernobyl nuclear incident to very negative one month

after the incident to the original level of negativity a year and a half later.[31]

Another Dutch survey found that stability of environmental concern appeared more at the group or average level than at the individual level, where more variability over time occurred.[32] Also, supporters of nuclear energy wavered in their views more so than opponents of nuclear energy. Thus, disaster increases concern, but for some people, it sinks back to pre-disaster levels in time.

Is Everyone Concerned?

Not everyone is equally concerned about the environment, as we have just seen. Many studies have reported differences in concern. Here are some findings of those studies, which will provide the flavor of differences.

Sex. Women usually (but not always)[33] report more concern about the environment.[34,35] However, there is a disturbing sex difference: Women *say* they are more upset by anti-environmental events (affect), *say* they will do more about the problems (verbal commitment), but report actually *doing* less (actual commitment) and *knowing* less about environmental problems than men.[36,37]

This pattern—that women express more concern, but men are more knowledgeable—has been confirmed in other studies.[38,39,40,41] Perhaps this is the outcome of social and school systems that discourage girls from early interests in science and the environment. This would strongly suggest that educators pay more attention to the environmental education of girls and women.

Age and Childhood Experiences. Most (but not all) research shows that younger people are more environmentally concerned than older people, at least about the general environment.[42,43,44] This finding holds even *within* the younger age range; a German study found that 12-year-olds were more concerned than 15- and 18-year-olds.[45]

There are three possible interpretations of this trend. First, it may be that as we age, we become less concerned about the environment; this a true **age effect**. However, a second possibility is that something important happened to a particular generation (e.g., Baby

Boomers) that did not happen to an older generation (e.g., children of the Great Depression). Such a **cohort effect** is not due to aging, but to events that had more impact on one age group than another. A third possibility is that the times are changing; the overall political-social climate is growing more conservative, so we *all* are less concerned about the environment than we used to be. Because we are also all older than we used to be, if this **era effect** holds true, older people seem less concerned about the environment.

In a clever study that compared concern across different ages, generations, and eras, it appears that the decline in environmental concern with age primarily is an era effect, although true age effects do appear strong for the young-adult age group.[46]

Childhood experiences may account, in part, for environmental concern. When over 200 environmental educators from around the world were surveyed, the strongest predictor of environmental concern was the amount of outdoor experience they had as children.[47]

Politics, Religion, and Social Class.
Less environmental concern has been reported for individuals with conservative political views[48,49] and with fundamentalist Christian beliefs.[50,51,52] The basis for this may be that these political and religious views are closely tied to a mastery-over-nature philosophical perspective.[53]

A number of studies suggest that environmentalists tend to be middle class or upper-middle class.[54,55] However, in a study in which occupations were counted at environmentalist group meetings, there were no more occupations from one class than another.[56] Even if environmentalism saves money in the long run, wealthier people can more easily afford the initial costs. One psychologist decided to turn this into an advantage for the environmental movement by urging his fellow psychologists to invest in companies that produce energy-saving technologies.[57]

Personality, Values, Beliefs, and Moral Development.
Individuals who are more environmentally concerned report stronger value orientations; are more people oriented, less authoritarian,[58] and more ethics oriented;[59] and have higher levels of moral development.[60] Individuals who believe their actions will make a difference[61] and who are more tolerant and understanding report

more environmental concern.[62] Among students, moral principles are better predictors of environmental actions; among community residents, tangible outcomes (such as economic rewards) are better predictors of environmental actions.[63]

Most of us favor environmentalism, but researchers have begun to make finer distinctions. For example, some people (**ecocentrics**) value nature for its own sake, whereas others (**anthropocentrics**) support environmental issues because they see nature as the fountain of human comfort, health, and quality of life.[64] Individuals who are more ecocentric express greater concern about environmental issues; people who are more anthropocentric express less concern.

Activities and Education.
Environmental concern is associated with choice of activities. For example, those who have consumptive leisure preferences, such as hunting, are less concerned.[65] People who spend more time reading newspapers are more concerned, and those who watch more TV are less concerned,[66] although adolescents who watch more science shows on TV are more concerned.[67] Women who take care of themselves (engage more in personal health care) are more concerned.[68]

Education and knowledge differences are also apparent. Business[69] and engineering[70] majors are generally less concerned. Students enrolled in a university environmental education (EE) program have significantly greater environmental knowledge, verbal commitment, and actual commitment than similar students who are not enrolled in EE.[71] Private school students are more knowledgeable than public school students.[72] Individuals with more education, in general, are more concerned about the environment.[73,74] A British study found that the best discriminator between environmentally concerned and indifferent teens was the amount of environmental knowledge about specific issues they claimed to have, although concerned teens also had more scientific knowledge than unconcerned teens.[75]

Proximity to and Threat from Problem Sites.
Although other factors do play a role, people who live further from a problem site, such as a landfill or waste disposal site, tend to be less concerned, at least about that environmental problem.[76] In a southern California study, residents who felt their health and well-being were more

threatened by environmental problems were more likely to engage in recycling, water conservation, less driving, and purchasing environmentally safer products.[77]

How to Increase Environmental Concern

Given that environmental concern is widespread, but perhaps not as deep, committed, or universal as might be desirable, how can it be increased? The broad answer is education. But just how best to educate people is not fully understood. The main approaches have been traditional classroom lectures, field trips, recruitment into activist organizations, asking for commitments, modeling desirable behaviors, and setting goals. Some newer approaches involve use of the media, simulations of environmental problems, story telling, and public events or rallies.

Environmental Education. Environmental education (EE) encompasses a broad variety of attempts to change attitudes or behavior through many different methods, all of which adopt a broad teacher/learner approach. Most research on its effectiveness has compared traditional lectures with innovative EE course materials. In a typical study, Australian fifth- and sixth-graders were placed in an EE program called Sunship Earth, and the changes in their environmental knowledge and attitudes before and afterward were compared.[78] In this study, the program managed to increase ecological knowledge but did not result in more positive environmental attitudes.

You might think the EE would, by its very nature, be effective. However, some EE programs have not worked, and some have even backfired; one managed to *reduce* students' empowerment to work on environmental issues.[79] A review of 34 published studies of EE programs found that only 14 reported positive effects.[80] Given that journals sometimes reject studies that find no effects, the real failure rate is probably even higher.

More success has been reported with an approach called Issue Investigation and Action Training (IIAT).[81,82] In IIAT, students analyze and investigate specific environmental issues and consider ways to resolve the issues. For example, compared to other seventh-graders who received standard science instruction, students in the IIAT program increased their environmental knowledge, skills, and beliefs. Another test of IIAT involved high school students in a six-day residential workshop. The outcomes for those who received instruction that was meant to raise their environmental awareness (only) was compared with the outcomes for who received awareness instruction *and* action strategies.[83] Those who received action strategy training learned more about environmental action and reported engaging in more environment-related behaviors.

Environmental education is now widespread at the college level. One study compared students in standard science courses with those in EE courses.[84] The two groups did not differ in environmental concern, but the EE students were significantly better able to defend their views with facts.

Another EE approach to increasing environmental concern advocates getting people out into nature. After some Canadian high school students went into the wilderness for a six-day experience, their environmental knowledge increased significantly.[85] When the impact of an outdoor education program at summer camp on 9- to 14-year-olds was examined, researchers found that longer programs resulted in greater changes in environmental concern. Greater changes also occurred in first-time campers than in those who had camped before.[86]

Thus, EE can increase environmental concern, but, as noted earlier, not every EE program works for every participant. One review of numerous programs produced a list of four guidelines for EE programs that should increase their power to effect change:

- Gear the program to the audience's current level of knowledge, attitude, and moral development.
- Explain both sides of the issue.
- Encourage more direct contact with nature.
- Stimulate a sense of responsibility and personal control.[87]

Based on a review of research, other writers added eight further guidelines.

- Know the action strategies.
- Employ action skills.
- Enhance environmental attitudes.
- Maintain a sense of control.
- Provide a feeling of personal responsibility.
- Know the issues.

- Encourage social norms in favor of the environment.
- Enhance environmental sensitivity.[88]

One reason that some EE programs fail, according to the same writers, is an overreliance on knowledge at the expense of the other guidelines.

Simulations. Another approach to increasing concern about the environment is to simulate environmental situations and outcomes. One college professor designed and used a simulation of local energy use and conservation.[89] Compared to other students who received a standard lecture on the same material, those who took part in the simulation showed a greater improvement in energy-conservation attitudes and greater likelihood of taking action.

Environmental Stories. Stories (as opposed to straight textbook material) may be valuable, at least for sixth- to eighth-graders. Students find stories that depict young people engaging in pro-environmental activities more interesting, and the stories manage to promote increased environmental knowledge and concern at the same time.[90] Environmental stories can be powerful mechanisms for increasing students' sense of hopefulness and power to change the world.

The Power of Images. Activist organizations such as Greenpeace have long realized the power of the media to effect environmental concern. Many distribute films of their activities and environmental problems to media outlets. On the day I am writing this, a Greenpeace film showing Russian ships dumping nuclear waste into the sea near Japan had an immediate effect: Russia announced it would stop the dumping. Nevertheless, empirical studies of how such images affect viewers' environmental concerns have been strangely lacking. However, one study examined the effect of graphic scenes, such as needles washing up on a beach, on viewers' environmental attitudes. Compared to a control group that watched architectural images, the graphic scenes produced significantly more verbal commitment and actual financial donations to a local pollution group.[91]

Organized Public Events. Finally, are public events useful in changing attitudes or are they just flashy circuses?

One researcher took the opportunity of administering an environmental concern survey six months before and six months after Earth Day in 1990.[92] Although concern was evident before Earth Day, afterwards, students showed increased acceptance that environmental problems exist, recycled more, and were more concerned about world population. Events such as Earth Day do seem to have a positive influence.

Does Concern Translate to Action?

A very important issue in environmental attitude research is whether, or to what extent, individuals follow up their attitudes with action. How many times in your own life have you heard people say they were in favor of something, or intended to do something, but never actually followed through?

Some evidence indicates that links between environmental concern and actual behavior are quite weak.[93,94] Certain studies that claim to find significant links between attitudes and behavior actually correlated attitudes with *self-reported* behavior.[95,96] Unfortunately, self-reported behavior does not always match up well with *actual* behavior. In fact, reported (or intended) behaviors and actual behaviors do not even necessarily have the same predictors.[97,98] Researchers have begun to explore how people justify the gaps between their environmental attitudes and their actual behaviors.[99]

Other environmental psychologists, however, have found that pro-environmental behaviors *do* seem to follow from pro-environmental attitudes,[100] and assert that the strength of the link between attitudes and behavior has been underestimated. They observe that studies reporting weak attitude/behavior links usually focus on only one or two environmental behaviors. Agreeing that the links between a broad attitude and any *few* behaviors might be weak, they assert that when a wider variety of behaviors is examined, the link is stronger.

One study demonstrated this by investigating the relation between attitude scores on the Environmental Concern Scale and numerous individual behaviors, such as circulating a petition, recycling, and recruiting a friend to help in an environmental action project.[101] Correlations with each of these behaviors (alone) were low, suggesting support for the weak-link position. But the correlation with an index composed of all the pro-environment behaviors was much higher, supporting the idea that pro-environment attitudes really do predict pro-environmental behavior in general. Clearly, persons who care about the environment may not engage in this or that particular pro-environment activity, but they do take part in *more* activities from the entire spectrum of pro-environment activities.

More sophisticated investigations of the attitude/behavior link examine moderators and mediators. A **moderator** is a variable that indicates for which group or under which condition the correlation is stronger or weaker. For example, one study examined the link between soil-conservation attitudes in farmers and their actual soil-conservation behavior.[102] The correlation was not very strong in general. However, the farmers' incomes moderated the relation: The attitude/behavior link was stronger for farmers with higher incomes than for those with lower incomes. Presumably, wealthier farmers could better afford to turn their attitudes into reality. Similarly, a Dutch study found that the relation between attitudes toward nuclear power and behavioral intentions toward nuclear power was stronger or weaker depending on (i.e., was moderated by) the amount of cognitive effort individuals put into forming or changing their attitudes.[103]

A **mediator** is a variable that, in a causal sequence, fits between the attitude and the behavior. The attitude changes a certain variable (the mediator), which, in turn, changes actual behavior. For example, a study of the link between environmental concern and a specific behavior (voting for a bottle-deposit law) discovered that this link was mediated by several variables, including a change in norms.[104] Thus, the conclusion is that attitudes change norms, and then the norms change behavior. If one's norms are *not* altered by one's attitude, the behavior will not change.

In another study, the goal was to predict who became involved in a struggle to preserve wetlands.[105] Activism was hypothesized to be a function of a person's personality (urbanism) and knowledge about wetlands, but not directly. The researchers proposed that personality and knowledge would influence two mediators—assessment of the problem and arousal over the problem—and that these two mediators would, in turn, predict activism. The results of the study supported this model.

Key Predictors of Responsible Behavior. Assuming, then, that environmental attitudes do predict actual behavior reasonably well if the question is properly examined, we might ask *which* attitudes are most predictive of environmentally responsible behavior. One way to answer this question is to conduct a **meta-analysis**, which is a statistical way to combine the results of many similar studies in order to reach a general conclusion. A meta-analysis of 315 studies that have examined this question found that the best predictors of responsible environmental behavior are:

• Knowledge of environmental issues
• Knowledge of action strategies
• Internal locus of control
• Verbal commitment
• Environmental concern
• A sense of personal responsibility[106]

However, not all environmental behaviors are equally influenced by the same factors. Each cluster of behaviors—say, energy conservation, anti-nuclear activism, and recycling—has its own set of significant predictors.[107,108,109] Others believe that behavioral change is much more likely to occur when social environments are restructured than when we try to change attitudes.[110] For example, these social scientists would forego a lecture on the benefits of recycling in favor of tripling the deposit on cans and bottles.

In general, the **applied behavioral analysis** approach believes that positive or negative consequences for behavior are what count. In applying B. F. Skinner's ideas to environmental problems, this approach advocates that the way to change environmental behavior may be summed up in the acronym DO-RITE, which stands for the following sequence:[111]

1. Define the target behavior to be changed.
2. Observe the target behavior.
3. Record the rate of occurrence of the behavior.
4. Intervene with a program that changes the consequences of engaging in that behavior.
5. Test the impact of the program by comparing the frequency of the behavior before and after the program.
6. Evaluate the program. Was it cost effective? Were the consequences appropriate and strong enough?

Applied behavior analysts believe that environmental messages and lectures have limited value as behavior-change agents. They believe that programs that use more modeling, hands-on involvement, how-to demonstrations, goal setting, and written commitments are more effective. One review of many behavior-intervention studies concluded that the best ways to change environment-related behavior are to obtain commitments from people, to model or demonstrate desired activities, and to persuade people to set goals.[112] Another study, however, concludes that the problem of inducing *durable* behavior change is more complex.[113]

◆ *IN SUM, environmental concern is an attitude or appraisal, one for which behavioral connections, if any, are of particular importance. Early research suggested there are poor links between environmental concern and action, but later work has shown that when action is more broadly conceived, the links are stronger. Many personal and social factors are correlated with environmental concern. Concern for the environment often ranks in the top five concerns that individuals have in their whole lives, but the amount and stability of concern varies with place and time; concern is not necessarily increasing everywhere. Applied behavior analysis provides one blueprint for increasing the frequency of pro-environmental behaviors with a more direct, consequence-based approach.*

◆ ENVIRONMENTAL APPRAISALS: ◆ PERSONAL IMPRESSIONS OF PLACES

People like some settings and dislike others. We develop strong feelings about specific places. Certain buildings have meaning for us. Some areas seem dangerous. In general, environmental appraisal refers to at least six kinds of personal impressions in addition to environmental concern: descriptions, evaluations, judgments of beauty (aesthetics), emotional reactions, meanings, and risk or safety.

The six kinds of impressions overlap to a certain extent. For example, if you consider a certain city to be beautiful, you are also likely to report that it gives you good feelings to be there and that it is a good and personally significant city. On the other hand, the different kinds of impressions do not *always* follow from one another. For example, a place may be significant to a person, but this meaning may derive from horrible experiences rather than pleasant ones. Thus, different kinds of appraisals may be correlated from time to time, but they are quite distinct conceptually.

A useful organizing framework for understanding environmental appraisals and assessments was provided by Kenneth Craik.[114] A slightly adapted version of it is presented in Table 3–1. The complexity of the process is evident in the many possibilities implied by Craik's framework. Many different kinds of **observers** may be shown **environmental displays** in many different **presentation formats** and asked to report their impressions in many different **judgment formats**, the accuracy of which may be tested by many different **validational criteria**.

Most studies select or one or two items from each column of Craik's framework, although a few investigators have systematically compared items from each of several columns within a single study to understand how they interrelate to affect perception.[115] Environmental appraisals as well as environmental assessments can be studied within this framework, depending on which elements of it are selected for study and how the resulting data are analyzed. Broad or narrow judgments of either specific settings or the environment (as a global entity) may be studied.

Evidence that a variety of personal and environmental characteristics—and interactions of them—combine to influence appraisals will be reviewed. Personal characteristics include an individual's stage of life, culture, personality, mood, and experience. The person's plans, goals, and intentions toward the setting are particularly important.[116,117] Environmental characteristics include complexity, naturalness, architectural style, contents, state of repair, and many other relatively objective features.

Descriptions: What Is There?

Environmental description has been left, for most of history, to poets and novelists. The centuries of practice have been fruitful. The most accurate and memorable descriptions of houses, mountains, trees, the sea, farms, towns, and prisons have come from the pens of the best novelists and poets. If your purpose is to produce a penetrating, unforgettable portrait of a place, commission a good writer to do the job.

TABLE 3–1 A Process Model for the Comprehension of Environmental Displays

Which Observer?	Which Environmental Display Method?	Which Appraisal?	Which Format?
User Groups: e.g., Residents Employees Students Customers	**In Person:** e.g., Walking through Driving by Aerial View	Description Evaluation Aesthetic Emotional Meaning Risk	Free (blank piece of paper) Checklist Scale Viewing Time Beliefs about Human Consequences
Experts: e.g., Facility Managers Architects Real Estate Appraisers	Slides or Photos Video or Film Models Sketches or Drawings Audios (soundscapes) No Presentation		
Special Groups: e.g., Elderly Introverts Poor Disabled			
Everyone i.e., All Observers			

If, however, your purpose is to understand how everyday people think about the settings in their daily lives, a different strategy may be necessary. In Craik's framework, it is true, one suggested method of obtaining descriptions of the environment is to ask individuals to write free descriptions of certain settings—simply give them blank pieces of paper and pens. This strategy can lead to some valuable insights (e.g., which features of the setting are written about first or at all; which themes naturally emerge from the writer's narrative). But there are difficulties, too. Some people are intimidated by a blank piece of paper; some features of the setting that are important to the writer may be inadvertently overlooked; and descriptions obtained from different writers may be difficult to compare—if comparison is a goal of the study.

For these reasons, environmental psychologists have tried to develop comprehensive, standardized sets of environmental descriptors. The free-description technique allows the researcher to discover which dimensions observers select to describe a setting. But when the purpose of the study is to discover what observers say about certain specific aspects of a setting, standardized descriptor sets offer comprehensiveness and, for many observers, easier responding.

How Many Dimensions? How many distinct dimensions, themes, or factors are needed to describe environments efficiently yet without omitting anything important? The answer, in part, is that different dimensions will emerge depending on which buildings or observers are studied and which individual items are included. Psychologists studying meaning in other areas of psychology[118] were successful in showing that three dimensions (potency, activity, and evaluation) seemed to pervade meaning across a wide variety of physical, cultural, and individual differences. Perhaps because of this, many early environmental psychologists pushed on, attempting to find the basic dimensions of architectural meaning.[119,120,121,122,123] This work produced a large variety of dimensions, some of which arose frequently; others arose only in one or two studies. Apparently, sim-

DAVID CANTER
is a leading British environmental psychologist who pioneered the study of environmental appraisals and is the managing editor of the Journal of Environmental Psychology.

ple three-factor systems that include only potency, activity, and evaluation are inadequate to characterize physical environments.

No widely accepted set of dimensions for describing all physical environments has emerged. However, a useful set of central and peripheral dimensions for describing building interiors was proposed by one team[124] (see Table 3–2). Clearly, however, these dimensions include some that are rather broad in the sense that many features of the building interior contribute to them (e.g., beauty) and others are narrow in that they primarily reflect fewer features (e.g., temperature).

The Description of Cities. Other environmental psychologists have developed similar descriptor sets for cities. Beginning with open-ended questions to a representative sample of town residents, researchers gradually evolved a short but comprehensive list of qualities or dimensions that make up the image of an urban setting.[125] These dimensions are:

- Economic potential (space for commercial or industrial growth)
- Diversity of land use (a combination of recreational, public-service, industrial, commercial, and residential lands)
- Historic significance (historic landmarks, events, boundaries, etc.)
- Fond memories (positive personal memories for residents)
- Appearance of the built environment (age, style, and type of buildings)
- Natural features (water, hills, trees, etc.)
- Movement and location (traffic, walkways, centrality of arrangements, etc.)
- Importance as an activity center (dynamism of public involvement in ceremonies, shopping, sports, public events, etc.)

These dimensions may, of course, be present or absent in any given town. They may even vary in different parts of a city. Different dimensions may be more important to residents as a whole or to particular subsets of residents. In general, however, the framework serves as a way to describe urban settings in a compact manner.

TABLE 3–2   Semantic Scales to Measure the Meaning of Designed Environments

Factors or Concepts	Primary and Alternate Scale	
1. General Evaluative	good-bad	pleasing-annoying
2. Utility Evaluative	useful-useless	friendly-hostile
3. Aesthetic Evaluative	unique-common	interesting-boring
4. Activity	active-passive	complex-simple
5. Space	cozy-roomy	private-public
6. Potency	rugged-delicate	rough-smooth
7. Tidiness	clean-dirty	tidy-messy
8. Organization	ordered-chaotic	formal-casual
9. Temperature	warm-cool	hot-cold
10. Lighting	light-dark	bright-dull

Secondary scales might include old-new, expensive-inexpensive, large-small, exciting-calming, clear-ambiguous, colorful-subdued, safe-dangerous, quiet-noisy, stuffy-drafty.

Such descriptions might be used to chart how the image of a given town changes over time or to compare cities.

Evaluations: Is It Good?

When asked for their impressions of a place, individuals very frequently include comments as to whether they like it or not. Evaluation includes appraisals such as liking, goodness, quality, and preference. What influences these evaluative appraisals?

Personal Influences. Whether a personal evaluation is positive or negative depends, in part, on the person's background. The very same everyday buildings are judged differently based on social class, sex, age, mood, and educational level.[126,127] In one pioneering study, adults were asked to express their preferences among slides depicting scenes of Alaska and Delaware.[128] The observers' preferences were predictable from such influences as their age, sex, and culture. For example, younger adults preferred the more exotic scenes. Other research shows that older children (16-year-olds) prefer more exotic or riskier landscapes than younger children (11-year-olds).[129] Thus, in general, wilder landscapes appear to be preferred more by young adults than by children or older adults. Females, at least in the Alaska-Delaware study, preferred more richly vegetated and warmer scenes.

Natives of Delaware and Alaska both preferred scenes of their native land. More recent studies also support the idea that familiar landscapes are preferred,[130,131] but this familiarity effect does not always hold. In other studies, Scots and Australians shown housing scenes from Scotland and Australia preferred scenes from the other country,[132] Japanese and American students preferred street scenes from the other country over street scenes from their own country,[133,134] and Koreans preferred Western landscapes to their own whereas Westerners preferred Korean landscapes.[135]

Whether a person is a design expert or an average resident affects preference. For example, when various possible nursing home designs were evaluated, nursing home administrators and designers favored designs that promoted social interaction (apparently believing that social interaction is desired or needed by nursing home residents). However, the residents themselves consis-

tently favored designs that enhanced their privacy.[136] Preferences among 10 possible housing designs expressed by a special neighborhood design review board showed little correlation with the preferences of the same designs expressed by residents of the neighborhood.[137]

Some studies show that architects prefer more unusual house forms and that nonarchitects prefer more typical house forms.[138] Despite (of perhaps *because of*) their training, architects not only have different preferences than nonarchitects but they also do not seem to understand what the public likes. Even when they are specifically asked to predict what nonarchitects will find desirable, architects are often unable to do so.[139] Perhaps this is because architects and nonarchitects apply different interpretational schemes to the judgment of buildings, and architects think more in terms of design issues than like/dislike when considering a building.[140]

Preference ratings will differ merely because one happens to make the ratings while thinking about one's role in the building (such as judging a house plan as a wife versus judging it without one's wife role in mind).[141] One's mental health,[142] personality,[143] and environmental sensitivity[144] affect environmental preferences. Mechanically oriented and older observers like well-lit buildings, and pro-development observers prefer big, new urban buildings.[145,146] In general, individual differences are very much related to setting preferences.

Physical Influences. Features of the setting itself also matter, of course. Would *any* individual prefer a scene showing an outlet pipe discharging reddish-orange chemicals into a river that is already full of discarded tires and dubious floating objects over a scene depicting a sunny meadow with wild flowers? Among less dramatically attractive or unattractive scenes, however, the physical elements associated with visual preference are not obvious; research is necessary to identify cues that lead viewers to prefer one scene over another.[147]

One approach, which has most often been used by Jack Nasar to study preferences for built settings, has been to investigate how specific, concrete features of an environment affect preference. For example, rooms with windows are more appealing than rooms without windows,[148] square rooms are preferred over rectangular ones,[149] and higher-than-usual ceilings are preferred.[150]

JACK NASAR
is a leading researcher in environmental aesthetics.

However, preference is not as simple as a list of features; the context should also be taken into account. For example, window preferences are affected by the size of the room they are in; specifically, we seem to prefer proportionately larger windows in smaller rooms.[151]

Studies of building facades suggest that observers prefer exteriors that express a sense of the past and that have detailed, curved, decorated, grooved, or three-dimensional surfaces that seem to provide shelter and invite touching and exploration.[152] Certain architectural styles are preferred over others,[153] although such stylistic preferences probably will change over time as fashions change.

Most observers prefer ornate, clean, open, and single-purpose (e.g., residential-use only) buildings.[154] Preferred city districts tend to have some or all of five features: naturalness, good upkeep, an ordered appearance, openness, and historical significance.[155] A related study disagreed in one respect—it found that more *enclosed* urban spaces were more pleasant, but it confirmed the value of other features and added two more: preferred urban scenes have fewer cars and more noise (from human sources, not mechanical noise).[156] As you might expect, streets with more trees and other vegetation are preferred.[157] Similar features are preferred in urban shoreline scenes.[158]

Other environmental features that are related to evaluations are more abstract. One early system proposed the following elements (among others), which clearly are more conceptual than those just mentioned: pleasantness, complexity, unity, potency, enclosedness, and originality.[159]

Berlyne's collative properties are another set of abstract qualities based on physical features. Among them are **congruity** and **contrast**. In one study, observers were

shown simulated landscapes into which various built structures had been placed through the wonders of model building and photography.[160] Landscape scenes that contained buildings judged (by previous observers) to be strongly incongruous with, and in contrast to, the landscape were strongly disliked. This may not be surprising. But would observers like buildings that are very much in context and very low on contrast, or would they prefer buildings with a moderate degree of these qualities?

Some observers preferred the latter over the dullness of buildings that blend in almost too well; other groups showed no preference. Thus, individual differences among observers may play a role in preference of scenes that are low to medium in contrast and congruity, but few observers prefer strongly contrasting, incongruous developments in landscapes (see Figure 3–2).

Three other collative properties are **complexity** (i.e., much detail and many design elements), **coherence** (the degree to which a scene appears ordered or "hangs together"), and **novelty** (the unusualness of a place's appearance). A study of urban signs found that the most pleasant streets had signs of moderate complexity and high coherence.[161] More complex high-rises were preferred over plainer ones.[162] Architecturally designed houses tend to be more novel and coherent than nonarchitect-designed houses. Both architects and nonarchitects seem to prefer novel but coherent designs,[163,164] although in one study, only architects preferred novel or atypical houses; nonarchitects preferred more typical designs.[165]

Jack Nasar's approach to specifying the physical but abstract qualities that result in positive or negative evaluations proposes that there are three kinds of relevant qualities: formal, symbolic, and schemas.[166] **Formal** qualities include the design's complexity and order. **Symbolic** quality is expressed in the style (e.g., colonial or postmodern). **Schemas** refer to the typicality of the design—is it usual or unusual? Different kinds of evaluation, Nasar has hypothesized, will be based on different qualities. For example, a *pleasant* building (to most eyes) will show orderliness, moderate complexity, and elements of familiar styles. An *exciting* building will be atypical, complex, and low in orderliness.

What about nature scenes? In a study of preferences for coastline features in British Columbia, observers

FIGURE 3-2 Does the newer building in this scene fit into the landscape or is it incongruous in its context?

(ferry passengers) preferred natural shorelines with small built structures on them over undeveloped, plain shorelines.[167] This seems to support the notion that moderate complexity, development, or contrast is preferred to very low levels of these qualities. Most people prefer woodlawn (forests with underbrush removed or treed grassy areas) over fields with taller, browner, weedy-looking plants, cultivated fields, or scrubland.[168] People prefer, in general, tranquil nature scenes.[169]

Another environment-based approach to scene preference is called **prospect-refuge theory**.[170] It proposes, based on evolutionary ideas, that people prefer environments at the edges between open areas (e.g., fields, savannahs) and closed areas (e.g., forests, jungles). The open areas provide prospect, the opportunity to see game or danger at some distance, and the closed area provides refuge, the opportunity to hide. Compared to other species, humans are not the strongest or the fastest, but we do need to eat and we do have survival instincts. Thus, prospect-refuge theory proposes that we like edge settings so we can "hit and run." In a study that asked recreationists to rate scenes varying in prospect and refuge, the most preferred scenes were those that suggested the viewer was close to a clearly defined refuge but had easy access to an open grassy meadow, which supports the theory.[171]

However, the main point of this section is that preference may be explained in terms of concrete features such as the number of windows or trees, or in more abstract concepts such as coherence, congruity, prospect, and refuge. Clearly, however, preferences are best explained by knowing something about the observer *and* something about the setting.[172] Many studies show that preferences vary with observer characteristics as well as with setting characteristics. Thus, to fully understand preference, we need to investigate both **consensus** (when virtually all observers agree on the value of a feature) and **contrast** (when some kinds of observers prefer a feature, but others do not).[173] For example, most observers may agree about which landscapes are *beautiful*, but cultural differences may influence the observers to vary in their *preferences* for one landscape over another.[174]

Perceiver-Environment Approaches. Another approach to environmental preference essentially fuses observer and environment by employing concepts that imply both. In one such approach, which draws on cognitive and evolutionary ideas, Stephen and Rachel Kaplan have developed an integrative conceptualization of environmental preference.[175,176] The Kaplans, and others,[177] believe that human preference for settings originates in the evolutionary past of our species and in the adaptive value offered by particular settings. For example, one study of landscape preference found that children prefer savannahs to other landscape types.[178] Because humans apparently originated in the African savannah, the authors suggest that the children's preference for this landscape may indicate an evolutionary basis for landscape prefer-

STEPHEN KAPLAN

has contributed much to the understanding of environmental cognition, particularly of nature scenes.

TABLE 3–3   The Kaplans' Preference Framework.

Preference for a scene is believed to be a function of the need to make sense of the scene and the need to be involved in the scene. Information may be immediately available to the observer or promised "around the corner." *Coherent* scenes allow the observer to immediately structure or organize the scene's elements. *Complex* scenes offer much information to keep the observer occupied. *Legible* scenes give the impression to observers that they will not get lost or disoriented. *Mysterious* scenes suggest to observers that they will learn more if they venture into the scene.

Availability of Information	Needs	
	Making Sense	*Involvement*
Present or Immediate	Coherence	Complexity
Future or Promised	Legibility	Mystery

ence. However, others were quick to point out the highly speculative nature of this suggestion. A simpler explanation may be that people are simply more *familiar* with local savannah-type landscapes.[179]

Because of the vast experience of humans (as a species) with natural landscapes, the Kaplans believe we are able to form preferences after very brief exposure to a new scene. They extend Gibson's idea that environments provide affordances—direct knowledge about the possibilities for orientation, safety, locomotion, and new information. Their idea is that we prefer sites that allow us to accomplish central human goals such as being safe and finding food or shelter. Other environmental psychologists have pointed out that we tend to base our preferences on what is important to us or the consequences of our choices.[180,181,182] The Kaplans call the functional qualities of environments that help people meet important goals **cognitive affordances.**

In addition to these basic needs, the Kaplans postulate that humans have a strong desire to make sense of the environment and to be involved with it. One outcome of the need to make sense of places is our construction and use of cognitive maps, as discussed in the last chapter. In general, the Kaplans believe that people prefer landscapes and interior settings that "offer promise of being involving and making sense."[183] Environments may offer this promise either immediately or for the future. When involvement and making sense are combined with immediate or future promise, a 2 × 2 matrix results, yielding four elements of preference (see Table 3–3).

In the Kaplans' preference framework, **coherence** (making sense immediately) refers to the ease with which a scene can be cognitively organized. **Complexity** (being

involved immediately) refers to the scene's capacity to keep an individual busy (occupied without becoming bored or overstimulated). **Legibility** (the promise of making sense in the future) means that the environment appears to be one that could be explored without getting lost; it is arranged in a clear manner. **Mystery** (the promise of future involvement) means that the environment suggests one could learn more, interact more, or be further occupied—if one entered it. These elements are the essence of the manner in which the Kaplans have integrated person and environment considerations in conceptualizing preference. Consider coherence. Cognitive organization is a human activity, yet some scenes are easier to organize than others. Coherence, therefore, is not *in* our heads or *in* the environment; it is in the way we appraise the environment.

For the Kaplans, preference should be predictable from coherence, legibility, complexity, and mystery, but not necessarily in simple ways. Generally, preference should increase as each of these qualities increases, but there are limits. Too much legibility in a setting might necessarily reduce mystery; the setting would be clear but it would lack interest and be boring.

Evidence on how cognitive affordances relate to preference has been mounting quickly. For example, scenes with greater mystery are often preferred more.[184,185,186,187,188,189,190,191] However, this seems more true for nature scenes (and perhaps individual buildings) than for others (e.g., urban street scenes). Perhaps mysterious scenes are preferable as long as they are not thought to be dangerous, as urban street scenes often are. More complexity also seems to be associated with greater preference, at least in zoos,[192] urban scenes,[193] and rural settings.[194] More coherence also is generally associated with greater preference.[195,196,197,198]

The Kaplans also stress the role of familiarity in preference. When a place is new, strange, or possibly dangerous to us, our preference is for more familiar places. For example, studies of woodlands scenes show that more familiar scenes are preferred over less familiar ones.[199] However, familiarity and making sense can work in opposite directions. Once we know a place so well that it is very familiar, there may be little new making sense to be done, and preference for the place may decline. We like to make sense of places, as long as the task is not overwhelming, dangerous, or complete.

Aesthetics: Is It Beautiful?

This section concentrates on the experimental social science approach to *appraisals* of beauty, which emphasize individual differences or psychological factors in the judgment of environmental beauty. The *assessment* of scenic beauty is based on finding beauty in the elements of the scene itself. It will be discussed in the second half of this chapter.

The appraisal approach takes this position: If beauty is entirely a property of the environment, then every observer would agree on how beautiful or ugly every scene is. But, obviously, some people think deserts are beautiful and others do not; some think rocky peaks, chaotic markets, undersea vistas, and skyscrapers are beautiful and others do not. For example, an Australian study found that although beauty, averaged across observers, was greatest for natural, green, open grasslands with some water and pathways, each individual observer favored scenes with different combinations of these qualities.[200]

Eventually, of course, both viewer and scene must be considered if we are to construct a complete account of environmental aesthetics. As with evaluative appraisals, researchers have begun to suggest constructs that integrate observer and scene. One such construct is

visual penetration—the visual depth of a scene. In a study of the natural beauty of Texas pine and oak forests, greater visual penetration was the best predictor of scenic beauty.[201]

An obvious factor related to differences in appraisals of beauty is culture. This was confirmed in a study that compared tourist and Balinese appraisals of the beauty of Balinese villages. Although the two groups did agree in most ways, there also were differences, which the researchers attributed to the tourists' misunderstanding of the meaning of certain landscape features.[202] Another study suggests that the beauty of water scenes can change with the growth of environmental awareness in the observer. The more observers realize that aquatic plant growth is one outcome of water pollution, rather than a natural phenomenon, the uglier the water scene appears.[203]

In general, appraisals of scenic beauty may be expected to vary with evolutionary, cultural, and individual experience factors.[204] To a certain extent, beauty is in the eye of the beholder. The real question is to what *degree* this is true, because those who favor the idea that beauty is mostly determined by features of the scene have strong evidence to present, too, and this will be discussed in the second half of this chapter.

Emotions: How Does It Make You Feel?

Is Affect the Same as Evaluation and Aesthetics? Presumably, environments that we evaluate as good and find beautiful will also make us feel pleasant. To some extent, then, appraisals of quality, beauty, and pleasant feelings overlap. However, there are good reasons *not* to conclude that the three kinds of appraisal are redundant.

1. Pleasantness is only one emotion we experience; other emotions may not neatly correspond to evaluation or beauty judgments.

2. Emotion (or the term many psychologists prefer, *affect*) is conceptually distinct from evaluation and beauty. The physiological, behavioral, and cognitive aspects of emotion are quite different from those involved in merely judging goodness or beauty. Emotion has been described as "a complex state of the human organism, involving not only feelings such as sadness, awe,

fear, rage, surprise, joy, but also bodily changes of various kinds, as well as impulses towards all forms of behavior."[205]

3. The built environment does not usually evoke in us strong, immediate emotions such as rage or ecstasy; it usually has a smaller but persistent and cumulative influence. The environment, therefore, may have an important impact on us in the long run without receiving much notice on a day-to-day basis. Thus, for several reasons, the emotional impact of settings deserves separate attention from evaluative and aesthetic appraisals of environments.

A Model of Emotional Response to Settings. Before directly discussing emotional appraisals, the work of two leading investigators of emotion in environmental psychology—James Russell and Albert Mehrabian—should be introduced. They view emotion as a mediator between the environment and personality (as preexisting influences), and behavior (as the outcome).[206,207] Originally, their research identified three primary emotional responses: pleasure, arousal, and dominance. Later, Russell's research led him to conclude that dominance is a poor third as a primary emotion, and he has concentrated on a model that includes only pleasure and arousal as primary emotions.[208] The remaining emotions, pleasure and arousal, are viewed as being independent from one other; that is, humans may experience any combination of them (see Figure 3–3). The model is a **circumplex**—a circular pattern of emotions that forms an infinite number of combinations of pleasure and arousal, its two main dimensions. Any of these emotions may be elicited by a setting.

In the Russell and Mehrabian framework, environmental variables (e.g., light, temperature, or the incoming speed of information reaching you) as well as personality variables (e.g., sociability or arousal-seeking tendency) are believed to influence the level of emotion you feel in a given setting. These emotions, in turn, influence such key behaviors as the desire to approach or avoid a setting, an employee's work performance, or interpersonal interaction in the setting.

The framework was tested in a series of studies in which verbal descriptions of settings were presented to research participants whose personality tendencies were

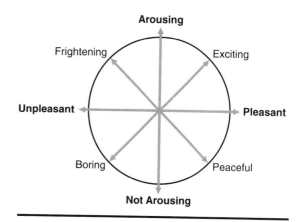

FIGURE 3–3 Two major dimensions of emotion and their hybrids form a **circumplex**, or circular ordering. Consider the emotions evoked by the setting you are in right now. Where would they fit on the circumplex?

known and who were asked to report how they would act in the setting.[209] The results can be complex, but one relatively simple example is representative. The curves in Figure 3–4 show Mehrabian and Russell's **pleasure-arousal hypothesis**: Individuals will want to approach physical settings that are, apart from their other characteristics, *moderately* arousing and *maximally* pleasurable. Note also that as the pleasantness of a setting increases, the maximum desire to approach it is predicted to occur at higher levels of arousal.

The solid lines in Figure 3–4 depict the actual experimental findings. As predicted, more pleasant settings were viewed as more approachable settings. For settings that were not particularly pleasant or unpleasant, the pleasure-arousal hypothesis was supported. Moderately arousing settings were more desirable than were low- or high-arousal settings.

However, for pleasant settings, approachability did not decline for highly arousing settings, as the researchers predicted; instead, it increased. For unpleasant settings, moderately arousing settings were the *least* desirable to approach, rather than the most desirable. The results of this and other studies appear to show that the emotional impact of the physical environment is indeed systematically related to behavior in them, even if the theory may require some fine-tuning to account for occasional deviations from its predictions.

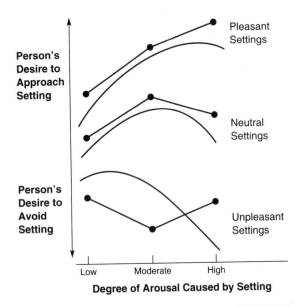

Low   Moderate   High
Degree of Arousal Caused by Setting

FIGURE 3-4 The pleasure-arousal hypothesis. The desire to approach a setting varies with the setting's pleasure- and arousal-eliciting qualities. According to the hypothesis, we most want to be in places that are very pleasurable and moderately arousing.

This research program often uses verbal descriptions of all the variables—personality, environment, emotions, and behaviors. This reliance on the self-report method has stimulated some critics to charge that the theory merely captures semantic associations among the variables, rather than the emotional impact of real behavior in real settings.[210] However, Russell and associates have defended their finding of a general structure for emotional qualities of settings by showing that the same dimensions emerge from a variety of rating methods.[211]

Meanings: What Is Its Significance?

Beyond the appraisals discussed so far is the question of meaning. Sometimes the word *meaning* is used broadly to characterize research on environmental perception, description, evaluation, or emotion, but in this chapter, the word will refer to four quite different processes:

1. *Place attachment:* the profound experience of being part of a place

2. *Ideological communication:* the way a building or place signifies some philosophical, architectural, political concept to those who view it
3. *Personal communication:* what the building "says" to observers about the occupants
4. *Architectural purpose:* appraisals of the building's function in relation to its form or appearance

Place Attachment. After we have long or intense experience with them, places can acquire great personal meaning. In contrast, most of the appraisals already discussed may be made after brief exposure to a place, although one's appraisal of quality, beauty, or preference might change after one has the benefit of longer experience with it.

Place attachment refers to the richness of meaning that develops with great familiarity.[212] It can develop for our homes, communities, or local nature settings. When place attachment grows, the meaning of place and the meaning of self begin to merge.[213] Thus, one meaning of place is that sometimes one's personal identity becomes inextricably bound up with it. We give ourselves names that reflect our place attachments: Britain has its Fenmen, the United States its New Yorkers, and Canada its Maritimers. University students identify with their schools, and residents of counties, states, districts, provinces, and territories identify with these jurisdictions. On a smaller scale, many people identify with their neighborhoods, boroughs, farms, houses, or even rooms.

One study explored what *home* means by asking people to list the meanings, experiences, knowledge, and emotions they associate with home.[214] Some of the most frequently mentioned meanings of home related to happiness, a sense of belonging, and self-expression. More broadly, the meanings of home could be grouped into three categories—those pertaining to self, social relations, and physical features.

Place attachment has some serious implications. Its first cousin, place identity, is an important dimension of an individual's personality, as we shall see in the next chapter. Place attachment can even kill. In a later chapter, we shall see that a major reason people do not abandon locations that are prone to natural hazards—such as floods, earthquakes, and hurricanes—is their deeply felt connection to a place.

Ideological Communication. The second dimension of meaning refers to the abstract concepts that a setting signifies or, despite its designer's intentions, fails to signify.[215] For example, one study found that buildings constructed by Hitler's government still communicate the Nazi image intended by their architects.[216] Buildings can reflect the ideals and aspirations of those who construct them; indeed, this is often a goal of the architect.

For example, **modernism** was an important architectural movement whose proponents believed in purity of form. They thought the rest of us would also appreciate the simple, clear, rectangular lines of their building facades. Modernists were weary of the excessive ornamentation and detail that characterized older styles; to them, *modern* meant clean lines. Skyscrapers with absolutely regular lines and symmetric strips of windows are typical modernist structures. Modernist architects often achieved this clarity of form and were widely admired (for a time) within their own circles. The public, however, has never much liked the modernists' "glass and steel boxes."

Charles Jencks, who was influential in developing a reformist architectural movement, thought he had a solution.[217] This movement, **postmodernism,** is based in part on the notion that two codes or sensibilities exist: one used by professional architects and one used by the rest of the population. A *code,* in this sense of the word, is an understanding or implicit agreement that certain stylistic elements signify or imply (i.e., mean) certain philosophies or values. Jencks believed that modernist buildings were designed by and to a professional code that was accepted and appreciated among architects. Modernist buildings meant *modern* (new, clean, clear) to architects. But the public interpreted the same buildings according to a different code; the same buildings meant *alienation* (cold, hard, forbidding) to them (see Figure 3–5).

Postmodernism attempts to incorporate both the architect's code and the public's code, so that they have positive connotations in both codes. Postmodern buildings do not all look the same or mean the same, but some common stylistic threads among postmodern buildings include hints of traditional architectural forms, more curves, and building portions that appear almost out of place or jumbled.

Postmodernist architects hope their buildings mean something positive in both the professional code

FIGURE 3–5   These are examples of a modernist building *(top)* and a postmodernist building *(bottom).*

(e.g., witty juxtaposition of historical styles and wise comments—through the design—on aesthetic principles) and in the public code (e.g., "Gee, that reminds me of my grandparents' farmhouse"). Because these intended meanings are positive, this should lead to greater popular as well as professional liking of postmodern buildings.

These ideas were tested by showing examples of modern, transitional, and postmodern buildings to architects and nonarchitects.[218] The results supported Jencks's dual coding notion—the idea that architects and nonarchitects employ different processes to pick up the meaning of buildings. Unfortunately, the nonarchitects were nevertheless unable to distinguish modern from postmodern buildings. Most architects are now aware of the existence of separate codes for themselves and nonarchitects, but often they have been unable to use that sensitivity to successfully convey their intended meanings to nonarchitects through their postmodern buildings.

Personal Communication. Like it or not, the buildings we live or work in "say" something to observers about us. Obvious conclusions are drawn about the wealth of persons who live in shacks versus mansions, for example. However, observers draw more subtle conclusions, too. Residents of higher-status neighborhoods are not only seen as wealthier but they are also viewed as having more favorable traits.[219,220]

Building materials influence judgments about the occupants, too. In one study, observers were shown houses made of brick, concrete block, weathered wood, stucco, flagstone, and wooden shingles.[221] Residents of concrete block houses were seen as cold and nonartistic and residents of wooden shingle houses were seen as warm and creative.

Architectural style also affects perceptions. In a study that compared perceptions of people who lived in six house styles (Tudor, Farm, Saltbox, Colonial, Mediterranean, and Spanish), researchers found that residents of Farm-style houses as most friendly and Colonial-style houses as least friendly.[222] Those who live in Tudor and Colonial houses were seen as being leaders; residents of Saltbox and Mediterranean styles were not. The identical building, given different labels, will elicit different meanings. For example, an apartment that is said to be public housing provokes less favorable reactions than the same apartment that is said to be a private condominium.[223]

Purpose. The fourth kind of meaning involves the way building form and function are understood by everyday observers. Much modern architecture is ambiguous; if viewers are not given clues (such as a sign over the entrance), they may not be able to decide what the purpose or function of the building is. One of the primary concerns of nonarchitects when looking at buildings is to discover the *purpose* of buildings they take the time to look at.[224] The reason for this concern, presumably, is that a crucial aspect of a building's meaning is bound up with the appropriateness of its form for its function. We might like the looks of a certain restaurant, as a restaurant, but we wouldn't like to *live* in the building. For example, a study in the Netherlands found that observers judged a building differently if it was said to be, for example, a city hall, a train station, or was presented with no functional label.[225]

Behavior that people believe occurs in a place is also an important influence on the place's meaning. Researchers showed 20 places to observers and asked them:

- Why might one go here?
- What might be done here?
- What activities probably occur here?[226]

The results suggest that place meaning is intricately connected to an individual's planned activities. Some places are quite behavior specific; that is, only a few activities are feasible in them (such as a phone booth). Others are much less behavior specific; many activities might occur in them (such as a beach). Places that are less behavior specific probably have broader meaning. Thus, if your plans are vague or include many possible variations, a behavior-specific place may have little value at the moment. But if you need to make a phone call, even a beach, with its many possible pleasant associations, might not be appreciated—at least until you can get back from making that phone call!

Risk: Is It Safe?

Virtually every day, we appraise the likelihood of danger in the places where we live, work, or visit. Perhaps some people are fortunate enough to proceed through their days without giving their own safety (or that of their children or loved ones) much thought. Unfortunately, most of us often feel compelled to judge how safe an environment is when we consider entering it.

Risk appraisals include perceived danger from crime, from accidents (such as traffic accidents), and from larger technological hazards (such as nuclear power or air pollution). Perceived risk and danger from natural hazards such as earthquakes or floods will be covered in a later chapter. Risk appraisals vary with the person (e.g., the elderly are more fearful than younger people), the neighborhood (e.g., some areas are more dangerous than others, or at least have that reputation), and the building (e.g., some houses appear more vulnerable to crime).

Accidents and Crime. A study of Scottish children examined which cues children use to appraise the risk of crossing roads.[227] These appraisals are obviously crucial for the safety of children: An incorrect appraisal can be fatal. The study found that younger children (5 to 7 years old) tend to use the presence or absence of cars *in their view* as their criterion for road-crossing safety. That is, they often do not consider oncoming cars that might be obscured from their view by parked cars or shrubs. By age 11 or so, most children factor the possibility of hidden cars into their appraisals of road-crossing safety (see Figure 3–6).

What influences appraisals of safety in parking lots, such as those at shopping centers?[228] Observers rated the attractiveness and security of 180 parking lot scenes in Georgia. Attractiveness increased as the amount of vegetation increased, but the rated security of the parking lots was high only when the vegetation was well maintained and appeared to part of a landscape design. Perhaps uncontrolled vegetation suggests to observers a uncared-for junglelike zone that would permit violence.

Another study proposed that prospect-refuge theory (discussed earlier), as a basis for environmental preference, would also predict which settings people appraise as safe.[229] When shown slides that varied in prospect and refuge, college students rated those that were high in prospect and refuge as safer; they also judged scenes that had more light as safer. Thus, one reason we prefer scenes with prospect and refuge is that we feel safer in them. Light helps us discern whether the scene has prospect and refuge qualities.

Which houses are appraised as vulnerable to burglary?[230,231] Convicted burglars say houses that provide fewer opportunities for surveillance (from the road and from inside the house), are more expensive, and have more exterior decorations and landscaping are more vulnerable to burglary. However, residents primarily believe that surveillability is the key, with actual barriers such as fences and locks playing a small role. These results suggest that when residents make physical changes to their houses to guard against burglary, they may focus on the wrong features.

Technological Hazards: Lay versus Expert Appraisals.
At the broader level, most of us are concerned about one or more technological hazards, such as nuclear power plants, toxic dump sites, and pollution outlets. Much of the research in this area focuses on the real problem of differences between experts and laypersons.[232] Many sociopolitical clashes occur because appraisals of safety and security by experts and nonexperts differ.

Before concentrating on the expert/layperson differences, consider that risk appraisals also vary *among* experts and *among* residents. For example, the risk from nuclear waste and nuclear energy is appraised as greater by life scientists than by physicists, chemists, and engineers, and experts' risk appraisals depend on which kind of institution they work in.[233] Among residents, risk appraisal differs with ethnic background,[234,235] sex and educational level,[236] perceived control,[237] dispositional anxiety,[238,239] the distance one lives from the hazardous site,[240] and the degree of environmental activism.[241]

FIGURE 3–6 When 5-year-olds cross the street, they often pay attention to cues that fail to protect them from oncoming traffic.

Among nuclear power plant employees, those who know less appraise the risks as greater.[242]

Appraisals of safety are multidimensional. One might consider the likelihood of the risk, how acceptable the risk is, how likely it is that exposure will lead to negative outcomes, the severity of the negative outcomes, how personally relevant the causes and consequences of the substance in question are, how much control one has over exposure to it, or how vividly the risk is presented.[243] This multidimensionality almost guarantees that relations among risk concepts will be complex.

Both residents and experts dread threatening facilities.[244] Residents' dread is expressed by the well-known Not in My Backyard (NIMBY) syndrome. Less well known is the experts' form of dread, the Locally Unwanted Land Use (LULU) syndrome, which is the expert's fear that NIMBYism *might* arise if facilities are proposed.

Resident or nonexpert opinions are often dismissed by experts. According to one viewpoint, resident reasoning comes in three flavors: ignorance or irrationality, selfishness, and prudence.[245] Put more positively, nonexperts think in more social and personal terms about the threat of hazardous facilities. After all, they, rather the experts, have to live near the threat. Resident appraisals may be amplified through social networks, although studies show that these appraisals are often quite rational.[246]

Expert views, in contrast, are formed through strong reliance on an objectivist, number-heavy, physical-characteristics approach to safety appraisal.[247] Experts and laypersons have different needs, goals, and methods of gathering information.[248] Laypersons' trust of public officials is low.[249] It is not hard to see why lay and expert safety appraisals clash. Now that these disagreements are well established through many public clashes, each side has begun to anticipate the others' position—LULU is one example, and nearly automatic mistrust of experts by many residents is another. Government agencies often claim they are committed to communicate information about risks to the public, but they do not live up to this commitment in practice.[250] The mistrust is mutual.

In order to get beyond these problems, we need more knowledge about how experts and nonexperts think about these issues. The goal is to create a decision-making framework that somehow integrates the experts' obsession with technical detail and the layperson's emphasis on personal and social concerns. Experts must cease dismissing laypersons' appraisals as irrational and begin understanding what is behind their fears.[251]

One research team has tackled this problem by comparing lay and expert views on the use of nuclear power in space, although their findings might apply to more down-to-earth problems.[252] An expertlike decision-making model was explicitly compared to a layperson's decision model in terms of the types of background knowledge and beliefs espoused, general beliefs, beliefs that are peripheral to the main issue, incorrect beliefs, and beliefs that are not part of the other side's model.

One suggestion that follows from these ideas is that of a **science court,** a democratic institution before which both sides would debate an issue.[253] The final decision would be made by educated citizens who were informed by expert opinion. However, a better approach may be to build more trust.[254] Trust may be increased by imposing strict government standards and by giving control over the operation of a facility to local residents.[255] Accurate information that is framed to take into account the personal and social concerns of residents probably helps.

◆ ***IN SUM,*** *environments may be described along many dimensions; a good poet or novelist probably is best able to select and employ the best dimensions for describing any particular setting. Researchers, nevertheless, have tried to develop standard sets of descriptors to obtain the average person's description of places. These standard sets have improved, but given the variety of settings and purposes for which settings are described, it may be both impossible and undesirable to develop a universal set of descriptors. One outcome of the many efforts to find such a set has been the finding that certain dimensions emerge repeatedly. Evaluative appraisals may take the form of stated preferences, ratings of quality, or rankings of goodness. Early research showed that such personal factors as age, sex, and familiarity with the place, and objective features such as room design, congruity, contrast, and complexity play a role. Newer approaches integrate person and place factors using concepts that involve person and environment.*

Preference is viewed as a complex outcome of these influences. Appraisals of landscape beauty depend on how observers weight different landscape elements in a scene, cultural meaning assigned to elements of the scene, the observer's level of environmental knowledge, and person-scene constructs such as visual penetration. Emotional response to environments usually is persistent and cumulative rather than sharp and brief. Nevertheless, it is a complex mix of behavioral, cognitive, and physiological responses. Settings evoke combinations of pleasure, arousal, and perhaps feelings of dominance in us. These emotions are linked to behavior in the pleasure-arousal hypothesis, which states that we approach or like places that are more arousing when they are also pleasant.

Environmental meaning includes four aspects: personal attachment or belonging, the building's communication of some architectural or philosophical concept, what a setting says about its occupants, and the communication of its purpose or function. Place attachment is an important process that involves some of the closest person-environment bonds we ever experience. Part of the art of architecture lies in finding a nonverbal, stylistic way to get a message from the creator of a building to its users. The latest general solution, postmodernism, still works only for some buildings. Buildings also communicate images about the people who live or work in them. Finally, meaning, in the sense of a building's perceived working function, has strong effects on its appreciation. We do not like buildings that have vague or inappropriate functional meanings.

Appraisals of security may be made in relation to crime, accidents, and environmental hazards about residences, neighborhoods, dump sites, power plants, or even the world as a whole. As with other appraisals, they vary from person to person and in relation to such physical variables as distance to the problem site and features of the site itself. An important difference is that between experts and everyday people, experts rely more on quantitative criteria in their appraisals of danger, whereas laypersons rely more on personal and social criteria. Efforts are underway to build bridges between these two groups.

♦ ENVIRONMENTAL ASSESSMENTS: ♦ COLLECTIVE JUDGMENTS OF PLACES

There can be many different impressions of a place. But it is also true, to a large extent, that perceptions of a place are similar. In this portion of the chapter, the vari-

eties of assessments and the differences between appraisal and assessments will be described.

Contrasting paradigms for assessing environmental quality from the human point of view (in contrast to mechanical means of monitoring environmental quality) will be discussed. The purposes and paradigms of observer-based environmental assessments will also be described. Finally, several typical investigations will be outlined, to give some flavor of current efforts to assess the quality of natural and built environments.

Distinctions and Definitions

Assessments versus Appraisals. Appraisals and assessments differ in four ways.

1. Appraisals are *person* centered; they focus on the way individuals think and feel about the places around them. Assessments are *place* centered; they focus on the quality of a setting from a broader human perspective. To understand how individuals appraise environments, their judgements of several places from their own world of experience usually are studied. To understand a place, judgments by several observers about one place usually are obtained.

2. Appraisals more often embody psychological constructs (e.g., emotion, meaning, concern, preference). Assessments more often are attempts to measure physical properties (e.g., environmental quality), using human perceptual skills. Even similar-sounding appraisals and assessments are conceptually different. For example, a judgment of preference (an appraisal) and a judgment of quality (an assessment) are distinct. Observers may assess the architecture of one city as being high quality but nevertheless *prefer* the architecture of another city.[256]

3. Assessments are more likely than appraisals to be undertaken in order to adopt or alter public policy. For example, the motive for much landscape assessment research is to help decide which vistas in parks ought to be preserved or developed.

4. Because assessments are place centered, observers with specific functional relationships to the place usually are selected. These assessors are often experts, either in the sense that they have professional training relevant to the setting (e.g., landscape architects assessing the quality of a university's botanical gardens) or in that they have a special interest in the setting (e.g., residents assessing the quality of a proposed housing development).

Varieties of Place Assessment. Long ago (within the short history of environmental psychology), Kenneth Craik described how social scientists were beginning to use psychological assessment techniques, long used primarily to assess persons, in the assessment of places.[257] The personality, intelligence, and other characteristics of individuals can be measured by careful human observation, and the same general set of skills may be applied to the assessment of physical settings. Craik described five kinds of place assessment that might be undertaken.

1. Physical and spatial properties of a setting may be measured. The slope of a valley, the height of a ceiling, the number of days of sunshine, and the number of rooms in a house are a few of the huge number of possible physical or spatial properties that might be assessed.

2. The number and variety of artifacts in a place may be assessed. What kind of furniture is in a living room? Which facilities does a campground have? What machines are in a manufacturing plant?

3. The traits of places may be assessed. Is that landscape *inviting*? Is that office *lush*? Is that home *majestic*? Environmental trait assessment must be distinguished from environmental appraisals, which represent the viewpoint of one individual. When a group of carefully selected and trained assessors agree that a certain trait applies to a certain place, we can be more confident that the trait is truly characteristic of the place, rather than a reflection of the needs and experiences of any one individual making the judgment. The term *personality* is used to describe the overall pattern of a person's traits, so the term **environmentality** may be used to describe the overall pattern of an environment's traits.

4. The behaviors that typically occur in a place may be assessed. As noted earlier, some places support many different human activities (e.g., a park), whereas others support relatively few (e.g., a field of wheat). Two similar places may enclose quite different sets of behaviors (your living room compared to your neighbor's living room).

5. The institutional attributes or social climate of places may be assessed.[258] Is a school organized or chaotic, warm or cold, supportive or not? Is a hospital comfortable, private, sterile?

In the years since Craik offered this typology, research has been unequally divided among the five kinds of assessments. The urgency of problems such as air pollution and the steady destruction of parklands and wilderness areas has led to legislation aimed at protection of the natural environment. The first step in environmental protection is to determine the location, extent, and severity of the present or potential damage.[259]

Thus, most efforts in the area of environmental assessment have consequently focused on one place trait—quality—and on one type of environment—the natural environment. Concern over the deterioration of ecosystems all over the globe has probably been the reason this topic has received so much attention at the expense of assessment research on other topics. The dramatic tone taken by some who express these concerns is exemplified by the words of a representative of an environmental defense organization who was speaking about only one aspect of environmental degradation—visible air pollution: "When we lose visibility . . . an important part of our vision as a people will be lost."[260]

We should not forget, however, that many other kinds of environmental assessment—such as those involving the great indoors, where we spend most of our time—are also important, and some indoor assessment work is now being done.[261] Much more environmental

KENNETH CRAIK
has provided an essential foundation for the study of environmental personality and environmental assessment.

assessment research, apart from that on the environmental quality of natural areas, remains to be done.

Technical Environmental Assessments versus Observer-Based Environmental Assessments. As noted earlier, most environmental assessments are done on environmental quality. In general, these assessments may be made by technical or observer-based means. **Technical environmental assessments (TEAs)** employ mechanical monitoring equipment or other physical means to produce a reading of environment quality. **Observer-based environmental assessments (OBEAs)** employ the perceptual abilities of humans to judge the quality (or other characteristics) of settings. The OBEA is a measure of the quality of the environment as it is *experienced.*[262]

Both TEAs and OBEAs are useful, depending on the goal of the assessment. TEAs are valuable, for example, for assessing levels of hazardous materials in air, water, and soil that humans cannot perceive. OBEAs are more useful when the goal of the study involves assessing quality in terms of the social, aesthetic, preferential, and satisfaction aspects of environmental change. For some purposes, such as measuring the visual impact of air pollution or the aural impact of noise, TEAs and OBEAs can play complementary roles. For example, TEA measures (e.g., the presence or absence of a view or the size of a living room) may significantly predict an OBEA measure (e.g., satisfaction with a nursing home).[263]

It is tempting to think of TEAs as objective measures and OBEAs as subjective measures, but this is inappropriate.[264] TEAs can be subjective in that assessors choose the times and places to sample the environment and must sometimes interpret the data according to their training and experience. More importantly, choosing which dimension of the environment to examine is subjective. OBEAs may be considered subjective because human observers are assumed to produce widely differing assessments; that is, they are not reliable. This *may* happen, but not necessarily. In many OBEAs, the level of agreement among observers is strikingly high.[265]

Nevertheless, no standardized OBEA yet exists. The variety in the names given them by different research groups (Perceived Environmental Quality Indices, Visual Impact Assessment, Multiphasic Environmental Assessment Procedure, etc.) is evidence that they are still in the developmental stage. This lack of standardization does not mean today's OBEAs are valueless. They may, in fact, be both impossible and undesirable to standardize, owing to the vast variety in both settings and assessment purposes. The optimal strategy may be to develop the best possible OBEA for each type of setting, just as TEAs employ many different specialized machines. Rudolf Moos and associates, for example, have spent years developing a standard instrument for the assessment of sheltered-care environments,[266] and Craik has spent years developing procedures for assessing landscapes.[267]

Uses of Observer-Based Environmental Assessments

Environmental appraisals are primarily of interest to those who wish to understand how individuals think and feel about environments. Environmental assessments have a different set of uses.[268] Several of these uses originate with public policy issues because concern for the deteriorating quality of the environment in the late 1960s and early 1970s culminated with laws requiring that environments be monitored. Both TEAs and OBEAs have been undertaken as part of the public push to find out just how economic development affects parklands, air, water, and urban areas. OBEAs have at least five purposes or uses.

1. OBEAs allow comparisons between human and mechanical measures of environmental quality. Large gaps between TEAs and OBEAs might indicate credibility problems for TEAs. Depending on whether the TEA or the OBEA is eventually found to be more accurate, more public education or improved TEA technology might be warranted. However, TEAs and OBEAs do not always differ; they may complement and confirm the other.

2. OBEAs assist in the development of TEAs. Through an OBEA, sites that are high or low in environmental quality can be identified. Next, physical characteristics that differentiate high from low environmental quality sites can be identified so that eventually, the environmental quality of sites can be assessed directly from their physical characteristics using TEAs. For example, consider a park manager who has many potential campsites to choose from but must select only a few for development. A panel of campers could be taken on a tour of potential sites and asked to rank the quality of each as a campsite. Then the physical elements common to sites assessed as high quality may be determined. Future campsite selection then could be based on knowledge of those key physical elements; another touring panel of campers would not have to be organized.

3. OBEAs provide knowledge of trends in environmental impact from the human point of view. OBEAs performed at regular intervals during the course of development in urban or park settings could inform policymakers of the seriousness of the impact at any given stage in a project. Similarly, the progress of environmental protection or enhancement programs could be monitored through OBEAs. For example, in England, the Thames River has been subjected to an intensive cleanup program. TEAs that indicate declines in pollution levels are valuable, but OBEAs can demonstrate that London's residents and visitors *notice* changes in the river's color, smell, and ability to produce fish. Indeed, such a study was conducted on a river in France: Technical indicators of water pollution were compared to the perceptions of riverside campers.[269]

4. OBEAs are useful for assessments of environmental quality that particularly relate to human interaction with the environment. For example, many physical characteristics of sound can be measured mechanically, but sound is not the same as noise. Sound only becomes noise pollution under certain conditions, which include the preferences, goals, and activities of the listeners in the setting. One person's intolerable screeching is another person's jazz festival!

5. OBEAs educate staff in the setting.[270] Park managers, nursing home operators, and planners often feel certain they know all the important issues in their facilities, but they do not. I once attended a meeting of a library board that had constructed a new branch library. It had been open for only a few months. The person who had spent over a year shepherding the project from start to finish questioned the need for an assessment of the library. "We have the best of everything there," he said. The chief librarian turned to him and said, "Bill, I hate to say this, but lighting has already been identified as a problem." Bill confused the goal of getting the library constructed in

time and on budget with the goal of ensuring that the building suited the needs of its users. Very often, "on time" and "within budget" are not good enough.

OBEAs may also be used to evaluate buildings, as illustrated in this anecdote. Environmental assessment is essential for architecture that is well tailored to the needs of building users. No one person knows all the strengths and weaknesses of a large setting such as a library or wilderness area. OBEAs utilize the observations of many individuals to educate those who manage settings. Because this architectural use of OBEAs is a large topic, it will be discussed in detail in Chapter 13 as part of the architectural design process, where the term for essentially the same activity is *postoccupancy evaluation (POE)*.

Paradigms and Methodological Considerations

Observer-based environmental assessment may be approached from at least four different paradigms.[271,272]

The Expert Paradigm. The expert paradigm involves the evaluation of environmental quality by trained observers. The training may be in any of several relevant fields, such as forestry, real estate, landscape architecture, resource management, construction, or engineering. The experts usually rate a setting using principles from their own field, which may include artistic concepts such as form, balance, and contrast, or forestry concepts such as timber age, density, and health. The expert OBEA, then, is an assessment of a specific dimension of environmental quality made by persons who are skilled in a particular field.

The Psychophysical Paradigm. The psychophysical paradigm uses classic psychological measurement procedures such as categorical ratings, the paired-comparison method, and rank ordering by observers to produce precise and reliable indexes called **scenic beauty estimations (SBEs)**.[273] The SBE method assumes that most of the power to predict judgments of environments resides in the scene rather than in the observer. Thus, in a logical extension of this belief, the psychophysical paradigm has been used to identify properties of settings that reliably lead to judgments of environmental quality.

The psychophysical paradigm, then, is observer based only in its initial stages, when human observers are used to discover which properties of scenes do result in assessments of beauty or quality. Later, if the paradigm is successful, environmental assessment does not require observers, because each and every observer is presumed to respond to a given scene in more or less the same way. Knowing that a setting has certain characteristics (and does *not* have others) should allow for the computation of its level of quality or beauty from a prediction equation.

Most research within the psychophysical paradigm concerns the aesthetics of landscapes, especially natural landscapes. Most people find the typical natural landscape more beautiful than the typical urban or suburban scene,[274] and that landscapes seem to produce more positive physiological effects than scenes of built environments.[275] The practical goal of this work has been to discover objective ways of deciding which vistas are beautiful to users of national parks. Is a wilderness scene more beautiful when it includes water? Is a forest view more beautiful when clearings are visible, or when dense tall trees fill the scene?

Research that systematically varies landscape elements in the scene—such as the amount, type, and location (center versus periphery, near versus far) of vegetation, water, and sky—supports the psychophysical approach by showing that physical elements can explain much of the variability in judgments of aesthetics, with no allowance for individual differences among observers.[276] The power of physical cues to predict judgments of beauty varies from study to study, depending on the selection of scenes and observers, but they are clearly a dominant force. In other words, this research suggests that most people will agree on the beauty of any given natural landscape. The challenge is to discover just which elements of the landscape are the most influential in defining beauty (see Figure 3–7).

Two recent studies explore this challenge. One study judged beauty as a function of the distance to a feature in a scene.[277] Six similar scenes were examined; each scene showed a grassy field in the foreground, a small ridge in the middle ground, and a large ridge in the background. Photographs were taken at various distances from the large back ridge in each scene. Scenic beauty varied with the distance to the back ridge but not in a straight-line fashion. The scene was judged more beautiful when the back ridge was either relatively near or relatively far, and less beautiful at intermediate distances.

In another study, the *placement* of vegetation in the scene was a significant predictor of beauty.[278] Scenes in which vegetation was seen in the center middle ground and in the center background were judged more beautiful.

The Cognitive Paradigm. The cognitive paradigm emphasizes human processing of information received from the environment. Observers are presumed to combine many features of the setting into broad assessments such as satisfaction or preference. The psychophysical

FIGURE 3–7 The scenic beauty estimate (SBE) method can offer a reliable quantitative estimate of this scene's beauty. Based on the method, this is a very beautiful scene.

and cognitive paradigms may be joined into a single entity called the *behavioral paradigm.*[279]

The Humanistic Paradigm. The humanistic or experiential paradigm focuses on the assessment of an active, sensitive observer who often adopts a phenomenological approach. The social and aesthetic concerns of an involved, sympathetic observer are reflected in humanistic OBEAs.

◆ ***IN SUM,*** *place assessments, in contrast to place appraisals, are place centered (instead of person centered), aim to measure physical properties (instead of psychological properties), are more often policy oriented (rather than oriented to the understanding of individuals), and more often employ observers with an expert or frequent-user relationship to the place being assessed. Place assessments may take the form of determining a setting's physical and spatial properties, artifacts and objects, traits, behavioral occurrences, or social climate. However, researchers have, so far, concentrated on one family of traits (environmental quality) in one kind of setting (wilderness parks). Place assessments may use technical or human means of observations. Each has its place; neither is necessarily more reliable or valid. Each also employs a variety of instruments (e.g., different machines for technical assessments, different questionnaires or rating forms for human observers).*

OBEAs have at least five purposes. They can allow for comparisons between TEAs and OBEAs, assist in the development of physical measures of environmental quality, provide data on environmental quality trends from the human perspective, provide assessments of quality along dimensions with particular human relevance, and educate the staff of the assessed setting as to its strengths and weaknesses. Four OBEA paradigms may be identified: expert, psychophysical, cognitive, and humanistic. Each has its own values and purposes, which result in different kinds of assessments.

◆ **TWO OBSERVER-BASED** ◆
ENVIRONMENTAL ASSESSMENTS

Over the last two decades, much theoretical and methodological progress has been made on OBEAs. Nevertheless, some policymakers remain suspicious of a process they see as an intangible.[280] OBEAs *are* needed, they *can* be useful, but they are not always *seen* to be useful by the policymakers who are in a position to fund them. Yet, be-

cause OBEAs have great potential value and because they are needed, researchers have worked hard to develop them. Here are the stories of two representative OBEAs.

The Scenic Quality of a Valley

The natural landscapes of many countries are being eroded quickly. Unspoiled landscape is an important nonrenewable resource.[281] Economic development has its benefits, but one of its primary costs is destruction of the land as a setting suitable for native animals and plants and as a place of beauty and quiet recreation for people. Recognizing that economic development will not cease, policymakers have enacted legislation that attempts to identify the best landscapes for preservation.

A series of studies reported by Erwin Zube and colleagues examined common assumptions about what constitutes scenic quality.[282] Many observers were shown slides of countryside in the northeast United States; others were taken into the field to see the vistas in person. Observers assessed the scenes using various rating methods. Some of the specific issues in question were (1) which features of the landscape lead observers to assess it as scenic, (2) whether assessors from different walks of life agree on what is scenic, and (3) whether slide-simulated scenes produce the same judgments of scenic quality as field viewing of scenes.

On the first issue, Zube and associates concluded that natural landscapes are more scenic than built ones. Humans "have yet to build a landscape equal in quality to the best in nature."[283] As for specific landscape characteristics, the authors reported that scenic quality generally increases with ruggedness (e.g., when much variation in vertical elevation appears in the scene), with the amount of shoreline visible in the scene, and with steepness, among other features. The image that comes to mind, then, is the classic postcard photograph of a sparkling lake set in tall mountains.

The second issue is agreement among different kinds of assessors. One cannot expect perfect agreement, but Zube and colleagues found quite strong tendencies for diverse groups to agree on the scenic quality of any given scene. The average correlation among groups, ranging from secretaries and students to professional environmental designers, was .77, which is very strong. This does not mean that assessors with different roles may not have somewhat different views or should not be asked to participate in OBEAs.[284] In fact, despite strong agreement among assessor groups, there are also significant differences. Zube himself has found age and cultural variations.[285,286] In the scenic valley study, these differences did not appear because only one culture was studied and because the age groups that appear to have different standards for scenic quality (children and the elderly) did not participate.

The third issue is whether simulations are effective in yielding the same assessments of scenic quality produced by field visits. Of course, the outcome is dependent on the quality of simulation employed. Zube and colleagues used color photographs and found very high correlations between assessments made after viewing the photos and after seeing the actual scenes.

Thus, this OBEA provided local authorities with a list of scenes in their district that have high scenic quality. The observer-based environmental assessment tentatively concluded that scenic quality is highest for unspoiled, rugged terrain with shorelines visible; that scenic quality is quite similar for young to middle-aged adults of different backgrounds but from the same culture; and that color photographs effectively simulate field-observed scenic quality.

The Environmental Quality of a Neighborhood

Fewer OBEAs of the built environment have been completed, but concern about the quality of housing, streets, urban parks, neighborhoods, and cities is at least as high as concern for natural settings. Most of us, after all, spend most of our time inside one building or another. Assessment of the quality of the built environment is obviously central to the slow process of creating more livable urban and suburban places.

Frances and Abraham Carp undertook a large-scale OBEA involving over 2,500 residents of the San Francisco area.[287] An extensive questionnaire yielded 15 factors, or groups of items, each pertaining to one aspect of neighborhood physical quality, such as air quality, outdoor noise, street maintenance, and aesthetic quality (see Figure 3–8).

An OBEA could stop here; it would yield an assessment of the physical strengths and weaknesses of each neighborhood studied on the 15 factors. The Carps, however, decided to go beyond this: They sought to discover relations between these assessments and objective features of the city, such as the distance to the nearest freeway, the number of different land uses within a quarter mile, and whether the block contains single-family or multiple-unit dwellings.[288] Eventually, as noted earlier in the discussion of OBEA uses, features of the environment that are known to correlate highly with OBEAs could be used as markers. Future assessments would need only measure the objective features to know if neighborhood quality is in trouble; the time-consuming process of recruiting many assessors for an OBEA would become unnecessary.

The Carps' research is one of the first steps in that direction. At this point, you might be thinking: Don't we

FIGURE 3–8 What are the consequences of living in urban neighborhoods that vary in commercial content, green space, and traffic?

already *know* when neighborhood quality is in trouble? Do we need fancy studies to find that out? In dramatically bad neighborhoods, OBEAs *are* probably unnecessary. But many mistakes have been made, even by professionals in the field. Some years ago, for example, a somewhat disreputable-looking neighborhood was redeveloped in Boston; residents were rehoused in shiny new buildings. Gradually, the planners discovered that the superficial seediness of the destroyed neighborhood was not important to the residents. Rather, the network of physical and social ties in the neighborhood had been destroyed by the redevelopment, and many residents literally grieved for their lost homes.[289] Neighborhood quality, as assessed by the individuals who matter most—the residents, was not nearly as bad as the redevelopers had thought. The planners' mistake was to assume that the physical traces *they* interpreted as indicators of poor neighborhood quality would also lead residents to think the neighborhood was in trouble.

Returning to the discussion on the Carps' study, the long list of potential physical markers was found to contain nine factors (clusters of items) like those listed earlier. The nine marker clusters were used to predict the 15 dimensions of quality. The more accurate these predictions, the more able planners would be to *accurately* gauge resident assessments of their own neighborhoods from physical features of the neighborhood.

Clearly, neighborhood OBEAs themselves can provide planners with valuable information about neighborhood quality from the residents' perspective. Connections between OBEA and physical markers of quality in neighborhoods are not yet as well established as the markers of scenic quality, for example. But the principles are the same and further research will improve knowledge of the relations between OBEAs and their physical indicators.

◆ SUMMARY ◆

Environmental concern is important for the survival of many plants, animals, and perhaps humans. Although

it appears strong, commitment may be not as strong as we think; certainly, its strength varies. Pro-environmental behavior does not always follow from environmental concern. Individuals appraise settings. In doing so, they may describe settings and make personal judgments of the setting's value, aesthetics, emotional impact, meaning, and security. Selected groups of observers can reliably assess places. Although many kinds of place assessments are possible, most so far have focused on the scenic quality of natural settings. Observer-based assessments (OBEASs) are more place and policy oriented than appraisals. They complement technical assessments (TEAs) and are particularly valuable for assessing dimensions of quality that are especially relevant to humans and can serve as educational tools. OBEAs that use expert, psychophysical, cognitive, and humanistic paradigms have been developed. The versatility of OBEAs is demonstrated in assessments of a scenic river valley and a neighborhood.

Suggested Supplementary Readings

Craik, K. H., & Zube, E. (Eds.). (1976). *Perceiving environmental quality: Research and applications.* New York: Plenum.

Daniel, T. C. (1990). Measuring the quality of the natural environment: A psychophysical approach. *American Psychologist, 45,* 633–637.

de Young, R. (1993). Changing behavior and making it stick: The conceptualization and management of conservation behavior. *Environment and Behavior, 25,* 485–505.

Dwyer, W. O., Leeming, F. C., Cobern, M. K., Porter, B. E., & Jackson, J. J. (1993). Critical review of behavioral interventions to preserve the environment. *Environment and Behavior, 25,* 275–321.

Kaplan, S., & Kaplan, R. (1982). *Cognition and environment: Functioning in an uncertain world.* New York: Praeger.

Nasar, J. L. (Ed.). (1988). *Environmental aesthetics: Theory, research, and applications.* New York: Cambridge University Press.

Wandersman, A. H., & Hallman, W. K. (1993). Are people acting irrationally? Understanding public concerns about environmental threats. *American Psychologist, 48,* 681–686.

4

PERSONALITY AND ENVIRONMENT

> The earliest mark of extraversion in a child is his quick adaptation to the
> environment, and the extraordinary attention he gives to objects, especially to his
> effect upon them.
>
> —Carl Jung[1]

"*You can't just sign up for those environmental review panels,*" *said Tom's friend.* "*Usually only experts or people who visit the place all the time are invited to participate.*" *Tom half-heartedly remarked that he went camping in the park several times a year, then he announced that he was off to the carrels to study again. This annoyed Jane slightly.*

    "*Why don't you come with the rest of us to study at Pat's place?*" *she asked.* "*Why are you always hiding out alone in that sensory-deprivation chamber?*" *Tom reflected.* "*I guess I've always needed to study in quiet,*" *he said.* "*Even in high school, when most kids played music in their rooms after being locked in by their parents to do their homework, I liked quiet for studying.*"

Jane accepted this at face value but remained skeptical. She had always benefited from studying with a group of people. She could sweeten the work with conversational breaks, ask questions about difficult concepts, and generally feel less lonely. "Well," she said, trying to change the subject to something less contentious, "what are you going to work on?"

"Becoming enlightened."

"What kind of an answer is that?"

"That is one of my major projects, you know," Tom said. "But I guess you're asking which school project I'm working on. It's an essay on the meaning of place. *I'm trying to describe, from my own point of view, why that carrel has become such an important place to me. It's almost like home."*

Jane counted to 10, trying not to blow up. "You and that carrel," she finally said. "What kind of person falls in love with a prison cell?"

Tom tried to be conciliatory, but he knew his own longstanding ways. "Sorry," he said, "I guess it takes all kinds."

◆   ◆   ◆

Personality may seem to be a strange topic in a book about environmental psychology. Often, personality is considered to be something *inside* us; the environment is *outside* us. One might, therefore, wonder what connections exist, if any, between personality and the physical environment.

This view is reinforced by a glance at the definitions of *personality* offered by some influential personality theorists. One says that personality is "a person's unique pattern of traits."[2] Another defines it as "the dynamic organization within the individual of those psychophysical systems that determine his [or her] characteristic behavior and thought."[3] If personality is inside us and the environment is outside us, perhaps they have no connections worthy of study.

Some reasons why this conclusion is wrong lead off the next section. After that, the ways that traditional personality variables help us understand person-environment relations are surveyed. Several systems for assessing **environmental personality**, the individual's behavioral tendencies that relate to or have consequences for the physical environment, are discussed. Finally, the chapter closes with a discussion of the uses to which personality may be put in designing environments.

◆ APOLOGIA, BACKGROUND, AND ◆ CURRENT SITUATION

Five Connections between Personality and Environment

There are five reasons why personality is an integral part of environmental psychology:

1. Some personality theorists—from the earliest times—have seen personality as intimately related to the physical environment. Even the trait theories, which seem to ignore the environment, intrinsically allow for situational factors when closely examined. For example, the original definition of *extraversion/introversion*, a trait we normally consider to be located inside the person, is based on the person's relationship to the environment. Carl Jung, who devised the concept, said the difference between the extravert and the introvert is based on the person's degree of preference for stimulation from outside.

Of course, merely asserting the existence of a connection between personality and environment does not make it exist. The second reason, however, confirms the first.

2. Knowledge of an individual's traits helps us to understand and predict environmentally relevant behavior. For example, knowledge of whether a person is dispositionally sociable and energetic significantly predicts the kind of behavior setting that person is likely to select when given a choice.[4]

3. Apart from traits or dispositions described by traditional personality theorists, such as extraversion or sociability, environmental psychologists have demonstrated that individuals have dispositions that are specifically relevant to person-environment transactions. For example, George McKechnie identified several environmental dispositions, one of which is environmental trust—a measure of an individual's tendency to feel secure in potentially threatening environments.[5]

4. Personal dispositions are central to one of environmental psychology's most important concepts: person-environment compatibility. One of the fundamental goals of designers and architects is to create a good fit between persons and their settings. To accomplish this, one must first be able to accurately assess both persons and environments. If these cannot be accurately assessed, one cannot be sure if a good match between them has been achieved. The assessment of persons yields a pattern of personal dispositions that is an important part of the person in the person-environment congruence concept.

5. Although the concept has not yet been developed much, we can turn around the notion of personality and apply it to places instead of people.[6] Plazas, neighborhoods, dwellings, and beaches have enduring characteristics, just like people. The term *environmentality*, which was introduced in Chapter 3, is appropriate here. Many of the methods and approaches developed over many years by personality psychologists for understanding persons may be used—with minor adaptations—to understand settings, too.

Roots of the Connection: Murray and Lewin

Henry Murray's Personology. Actually, the notion that personality and environment influence one another is ancient. Within the modern era, the idea was elaborated most clearly and forcefully by Henry Murray in the 1930s and 1940s, although others also discussed it.[7] In addition to his psychological interests, Murray was a brilliant all-around scholar who, besides having psychological interests, was a physician who graduated first in his class. He also wrote important literary works, including a classic interpretation of Herman Melville's *Moby Dick*. Not surprisingly, given this breadth of interests, Murray's vision of personality, which he called **personology**, recognizes and explicitly includes environmental factors.[8]

For Murray, the basic event for personologists to study is the **proceeding,** the initiation and completion of an important behavior sequence. He distinguished between *internal proceedings,* in which we try to represent, explain, and predict the world to ourselves (e.g., planning, daydreaming, solving problems) and *external pro-*

HENRY MURRAY
invented the concept of press, which included the physical environment.

ceedings, in which we interact with other individuals or the physical environment (e.g., conversing, sailing, working). External proceedings have two sides to them: one corresponds to our *experience* of the external proceeding and the other corresponds to an *objective* account of the behavior sequence. For example, when we sail, we think about and feel the weather, the water, and the boat. Yet, our sailing behavior, such as how long and how often we tack, could be measured objectively.

Murray viewed the environment itself as exerting **press,** "the power . . . to affect the well-being of the subject in one way or another"[9] (see Figure 4–1). Press may have a positive or negative influence on us. While sailing, for example, the weather may be warm and sunny with moderate winds or we may be capsized by a sudden squall. Press may be social or physical in nature. Most

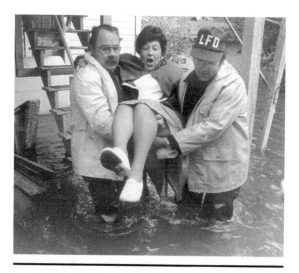

FIGURE 4–1 Here is one threatening form of environmental press!

important, press has an experiential side and an objective side, like the external proceeding. *Alpha press* is the environment considered from an objective, third-party point of view. *Beta press* is the environment considered from an individual's own perspective.

Alpha and beta press often closely correspond to one another, but on some occasions, they may differ strikingly. Discrepancies between alpha and beta press may indicate a person has a problem. Consider a situation in which a room is at 20 degrees Celsius (71 degrees Fahrenheit) and someone complains, "It's really cold in here." If we notice this gap between alpha and beta press, we may begin to divine some reason for it. Guessing the person may be coming down with a cold, we might ask, "How are you feeling?"

Murray offered several lists of press. These include aspects of both the physical and the social environment. In one list, designed to represent children's press, he included water, weather, and possessions, as well as parents, praise, and friendship.[10]

Kurt Lewin's Field Theory. Another theorist whose ideas brought the environment into greater prominence within psychology was Kurt Lewin, whose work was introduced in Chapter 1. His **field theory** was an attempt to represent the person and the environment in the graphic terms of topology, a branch of mathematics. The *person (P)* is viewed as existing in the *psychological environment (E)*, the person's representation of the physical and social influences in the surroundings. *P* and *E* together comprise the **life space,** the totality of facts inside and outside the person. From these assertions comes Lewin's famous formula, $B = f(P, E)$ (see Figure 4–2).

Outside the life space, the **foreign hull** consists of alien facts—that is, real aspects of the world that have no place in the life space of a particular individual. For example, there are many corners of the planet that we have never seen or heard of, but they do exist. Of crucial importance, however, is Lewin's contention that the boundary between the life space and the foreign hull is *permeable*. Alien facts may become psychologically important facts, perhaps when we visit one of those corners of the planet. That is why Lewin came to believe that the study of alien facts themselves—an enterprise he termed **psychological ecology**—is worthwhile.[11]

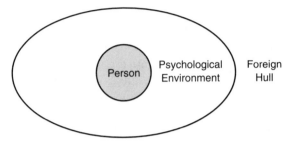

Person + Psychological Environment = Life Space

FIGURE 4-2 A simplified depiction of Kurt Lewin's view of persons-in-environments. Each person *(P)* exists in a psychological environment *(E)*, which, together, comprise the life space *(L)*. Outside *L* is the foreign hull *(F)*, that part of the objective world that this person has not incorporated into *L* through perception or awareness.

One implication of this permeability, then, is that aspects of the physical environment that never before affected an individual in any psychologically important way may begin to do so. Madame Curie was not particularly concerned about the consequences to her health of experimenting with radium. By now, however, we know all too much about the carcinogenic properties of radioactive materials. Concern about them *now* is an important part of living near a nuclear power plant.

A second, and perhaps even more important, implication of permeability is that permeability is bidirectional. That is, psychological facts also may influence alien facts. This feature of Lewin's theory was early formal recognition of an important current perspective of environmental psychologists: Persons should be viewed as active agents of environmental change. Often, we are able to choose which setting we wish to use for a given purpose, to alter that setting if need be, and, on a larger scale, to influence decisions made on environmental issues by governments, business firms, and other organizations.

As we become aware of more and more elements of the physical environment that affect us, we incorporate more of the foreign hull into our life spaces. This increased awareness does not mean that all of us become environmentally active. Rather, most of us become more active at least in our own territories, many of us become more active on a larger scale, and nearly all of us could be more active agents of environmental improvement.

Another implication of permeability is that we sometimes affect the foreign hull unintentionally, without realizing either that we have had an effect or the magnitude of that effect. On the societal level, that is what happened with the widespread use of DDT. For years, we did not realize that it was working its way up the food chain and endangering predatory birds by weakening the walls of their eggs. On a personal level, one's decision to reduce, reuse, and recycle affects individuals, organizations, and the physical environment far beyond one's own life space.

Lewin's theory seems very simple, but it is conceptually powerful and has had enormous impact in psychology. In environmental psychology, it is the direct basis of several current theories, including ecological psychology and social ecology. The theory has been criticized, however, as unclear about the difference between *E,* the psychological environment, and *P,* the physical environment.[12,13] Critics maintain that Lewin confuses the objective environment and the person's psychological representation of the environment. This confusion has probably made the theory *more* influential rather than less so. Social psychologists have fruitfully taken *E* as the person's cognitive representation of the social and physical world. Some environmental psychologists have fruitfully used *E* as the objective physical world. *Both* groups have found the theory a useful guiding framework for research.

Much applied and nonapplied research has been based—sometimes directly, sometimes loosely—on Lewin's ideas. The applied work often employs Lewin's own concept, **action research,**[14] a specific procedure that aims to change and improve social and physical conditions.

◆ *IN SUM, personality is a part of environmental psychology because traits or dispositions do not merely refer to persons but include consideration of how persons interact with their environments, help predict the behavior of individuals in the environment, specifically characterize our environmental tendencies, and form an important part of the person half of person-environment compatibility. The important early formulations of Henry Murray and Kurt Lewin are reviewed because their ideas are still influential. Henry Murray's personology introduced the concepts of alpha and beta press (the actual and perceived power of the*

environment to affect our welfare), and internal and external proceedings (subjective and objective accounts of the initiation and completion of a behavior sequence). Lewin's field theory, which conceptualized persons as actively interacting with their environments in their life spaces, produced the famous formula B = f(P, E). Our representation of the physical environment and some elements of the unrepresented physical environment (the foreign hull) affect our behavior and experience. Lewin's action research concept, in which theory and application are fused, guides many environmental psychologists today.

◆ TRADITIONAL PERSONALITY ◆ DIMENSIONS

When environmental psychology was new, no one had yet developed measures of personality specifically concerned with person-environment transactions. Those who believed that the study of personal dispositions might help us understand behavior in the environment were forced to employ existing measures of personality. Although traditional personality measures were not designed to predict environmentally relevant behaviors, some appeared to be useful. Environmental psychologists therefore attempted to use them, in the absence of custom-designed constructs, to help elucidate environment-behavior relations.

For example, the frequency of engaging in six outdoor recreation activities was correlated in one study with scores on a general purpose personality test.[15] The results demonstrated that personality is modestly related to one's choice of outdoor activities. Of course, these traditional measures were not great predictors of environmental activities, but they performed fairly well.

This section surveys the outcomes of traditional personality measures in relation to environmental behavior. Two traditional constructs, sociability and locus of control, form the bulk of this survey, but a few other traditional constructs also have been studied.

Outgoing versus Reserved Personality

One fundamental dimension in traditional personality theory is tapped by constructs such as extraversion/introversion, sociable/unsociable, and warm/cold. These constructs are not identical, but generally they all differentiate individuals who enjoy being with others from those who do not.

Social Space. Sociability is predictive of many environmentally relevant behaviors, particularly an individual's use of space. Specifically, this includes preferred interpersonal distance, reactions to high-density situations, and furniture arrangement preferences.

Most studies show that outgoing individuals prefer to be physically closer to others than do reserved individuals[16] (see Figure 4–3). For example, extraverted individuals spend more time in hotel lobbies and in bars, where more social interaction occurs.[17] Another study showed that more reserved professors arrange their office furniture differently from more outgoing professors.[18] Faculty offices may be characterized as open (when the desk is placed against a far wall, so it does not constitute a barrier between professor and visitor) or closed (when the desk intervenes between professor and visitor). Outgoing professors more often used the open furniture arrangement.

If sociability were the only influence on social space choices, similar results probably would always be found. However, at least four other kinds of factors also affect our preferences.

1. Social factors (such as the number of visitors to the professors' offices in the study just described) might influence a person's furniture arrangements.[19] Similarly, one might predict that sociable persons would enjoy

crowding more than less sociable persons, and that less sociable persons would enjoy being alone more than social persons. In a study of dormitory residents, outgoing students who lived in high-density dorms reported less stress than reserved students who lived in high-density dorms (as predicted); however, the two groups experienced about the same amount of stress in low-density dorms (where one might expect outgoing students to experience more stress).[20]

2. Demographic factors can moderate relations between personality and environmental behavior. For example, one study found that more sociable people tend to have more seats per square foot in the entertainment area of their homes than less sociable people do. They also have more couches and benches (closer seating) than chairs (more isolated seating).[21] However, these findings are much more true for women than men.

3. Behavior often is a function of multiple dispositions, not merely one. In a study that examined this idea, participants were asked to draw chairs in a diagram of a room, placing the chairs where they would feel comfortable talking to another person in 18 different social situations.[22] In general, warm individuals placed their chairs closer to the other person than did cold individuals; this is a straightforward relation of the type already discussed. But a more complex pattern was also evident. Those who were colder and *more* ambitious chose significantly larger distances than those who were colder but *less* ambitious; among warmer individuals, ambitious and nonambitious individuals did not choose different distances.

Thus, if we combine knowledge of at least two dispositions of a person, we can make better predictions about that person's preferred interpersonal distance than if we considered only one disposition.

Landscapes, Sense of Direction, and Noise. Some evidence suggests that outgoing individuals evaluate landscapes differently than do reserved individuals.[23,24] In one study, individuals who reported needing the support of others found landscapes near San Francisco more serene, beautiful, and cultivated than those who reported needing less support from others. In another study, outgoing individuals perceived landscapes in the

FIGURE 4–3 Some like to be close.

same area as more active and busy than did reserved individuals. These studies demonstrate that personality is connected to environmentally relevant behavior in some nonobvious ways.

Another nonobvious personality-environment relation is the finding that the outgoing/reserved dimension is related to one's sense of direction.[25] More sociable individuals, it seems, are better able to point out correct geographical directions than less sociable individuals. As further evidence that such relations are really not obvious, when the researcher asked participants how good their sense of direction was, no differences were found between outgoing and reserved individuals. Thus, even those who use their sense of direction more effectively seem to be unaware that they are more skilled than others!

Finally, as predicted by Jung when he first described the concept, extraverts and introverts respond to incoming stimulation, such as noise, differently. In worklike tasks, the performance of neurotic introverts was more adversely affected by noise than was the performance of nonneurotic extraverts.[26] Of course, it is hard to know from this study whether the participants' neuroticism or their extraversion was the more important factor. In another study in which neuroticism was not a factor, extraverts were more annoyed by noise from jet aircraft when the ambient lighting is bright, whereas introverts were more annoyed by it when the lighting is dim.[27]

Locus of Control

Some of us feel that we can exert a reasonable amount of control over our destinies; others believe that their lives are strongly influenced by powerful others or by fate. This belief that control is primarily inside or outside oneself (internal versus external locus of control) has been examined in relation to environmentally relevant behaviors because of its seemingly obvious connection to person-environment relations.

In fact, however, most locus of control measures refer to a belief that our lives are controlled by fate, luck, chance, or powerful other people rather than the physical environment. Thus, traditional locus of control measures are not conceptually related to the physical environment. Nevertheless, traditional locus of control has been a significant predictor of environmental behaviors.

Among these are use of social space, response to environmental hazards, pro-environment activities, and preferences for architectural style.

Social Space. Internal versus external locus of control is related to preferences for interpersonal distance and reactions to high population density. Those who believe their lives are controlled by external forces seem to prefer larger interpersonal distances.[28,29] Perhaps those who believe that other people exert considerable influence over them feel more secure if they are literally out of reach.

Internals apparently tolerate high densities better than externals.[30,31] In high-density living conditions, a lack of perceived control causes increased psychological distress.[32,33] Possibly internals have learned more and better coping strategies: Those who believe life is reasonably controllable naturally fulfill that belief by developing more and better methods of handling difficult situations, such as high density.

Environmental Hazards. Internals and externals respond differently to some environmental threats.[34] Internals believed that luck had less to do with the damage resulting from tornados than did externals, for example. More significantly, internals actually took more recommended precautions than externals did.

However, as usual, life can be a little more complicated, as seen by researchers who investigated how Los Angeles residents respond to another hazard, air pollution.[35] From the research just described, we might expect that internals would cope with smog by engaging in more preventive behaviors than externals would. This was the case for internals who *recently arrived* in Los Angeles; they did take more anti-pollution steps. Unfortunately, however, *long-term* residents who were internals took as few preventive measures as external long-term residents. Adaptation, sadly, seemed to dampen the anti-pollution behavior of internals (see Figure 4–4).

Pro-Environment Actions. Locus of control is related to responsible environmentalism; generally, those who are more internal engage in more environmentally responsible behaviors and are more likely to be political activists.[36,37,38,39] Regular recyclers were compared with nonrecyclers in one study; recyclers were significantly

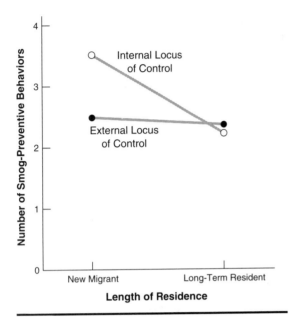

FIGURE 4–4 Whether one copes with smog by engaging in behaviors that reduce its impact is a function of both personality and length of residence. *Internals* who move to Los Angeles initially cope more than newly arrived *externals*, but as time passes, their coping behavior sags to the level of externals.

more internal.[40] Internals recycled more, even though they also had higher scores on a scale measuring environmental cynicism—that is, they were less optimistic than nonrecyclers that their efforts would solve environmental problems. Perhaps the internals recycled more because, as measured on another scale, they more strongly believed that environmental problems were their personal responsibility.

Some interactions between locus of control and other factors need more research. For example, in another study of locus of control and anti-pollution behavior, internals engaged in five pro-ecology activities (e.g., joining an environmental group or writing to the government on ecological issues) more than externals.[41] This is what one would expect. But the researchers also measured the optimism of their participants and found that optimistic internals engaged in more activities than did pessimistic internals.

This interaction between locus of control and optimism contrasts with the results in the previous study of

recyclers, in which pessimists recycled more. More research is necessary to resolve this discrepancy. However, it is safe to conclude that, in general, those who believe they have some control over their lives do engage in more responsible environmental activities.

When individuals do not feel that they control their lives, both the environment and the self may suffer. Researchers have speculated that a lack of perceived control might lead to frustration, which might mainfest itself as vandalism or other environmentally destructive behavior.[42,43] As for the self, among the exotic few who have spent the winter in Antarctica, those who feel powerless have the most difficulty adjusting to the harsh environment.[44]

Preferences for Architectural Styles. Locus of control may also be related to preferences for architectural style. Researchers showed slides depicting classical building styles (Renaissance and 1950s international) versus romantic building styles (baroque and 1950s naturalism).[45] Individuals with a tendency toward external locus of control preferred romantic-style buildings; those tending to internality preferred buildings in the classical tradition. To explain this, the researchers speculated that perhaps internality implies the exercise of control, and this preference for control carries over into a preference for more controlled styles and environments. Classical building styles, most architects would agree, include more straight lines and are more severe than the more flowing, rolling lines characteristic of romantic styles.

Other Traditional Dimensions

The outgoing/reserved and internal/external locus of control dimensions have received the most research attention, but a variety of others also have been examined. One of these might be termed **psychological health,** measured as ego strength, adjustment, self-confidence, or lack of neuroticism. Individuals in good psychological health seem to withstand better the stresses of poor housing,[46] choose more beneficial settings,[47] and even have a better sense of direction.[48]

Conventionality and traditionalism have also been examined. Professors with traditional orientations to education reflected this through closed office arrangements, although this was moderated by the number of students the professor advised.[49] As one would expect, more unconventional individuals choose more unconventional places to be,[50] and less conservative individuals recycle more.[51]

Finally, the relevance of a person's cognitive style to environmental issues has been examined.[52] One system for describing the way we think holds that a pair of dimensions characterizes much of our cognitive activity.[53] The objective/subjective dimension refers to preferences for "the hard, cold facts" versus preferences for one's own feelings and values. The analytic/holistic dimension refers to a preference for breaking down problems into their parts versus considering the problem as a whole in its context (see Figure 4–5).

These dimensions can be combined to form quadrants that represent four cognitive styles. The person who tends to be both analytical and objective is the **analytical scientist,** who focuses on objective facts in a reductionist manner. Perhaps the usual chemist typifies this style. The **systems theorist** prefers an objective approach but is not so reductionist; the whole interacting system is the focus. Perhaps most biologists adopt this cognitive style. The **humanist** tends to think in subjective and holistic terms. This person often is the dissident scientist who argues that facts have their place, but in the larger context, our feelings and values must be taken into account. The **mystic** prefers a subjective but analytic thinking style. The main concern is to explore the elements of one's own reaction to the external problems the others are working on. The mystic is unlikely to be a scientist, but perhaps a poet or spiritual seeker. Can you see how persons with these different cognitive styles might think about nuclear power or pesticide spraying?

A related construct, cognitive complexity, influences how we think about environmental issues. **Cognitive complexity** is the degree to which a person's thoughts about a problem range from simple, concrete, and dichotomous (good/bad, right/wrong) to complex. It is also the degree to which a person considers self and others, weighs many alternatives, thinks about consequences, and is open to compromise. As one might expect, individuals with greater cognitive complexity think about environmental issues in a more complex way.[54] They see both sides, have doubts, and are more likely to integrate all the concerns into a compromise proposal.

Personality *and* Environment

As discussed earlier, personality and the physical setting often act together to influence behavior. To illustrate this in some detail, consider a study of participation in conversations.[55] Neither personality (defensive versus trusting) nor seating arrangement (row versus half-circle) *independently* predicted participation. However, participation was significantly higher for defensive individuals when the chairs were arranged in a row and for trusting individuals when the chairs were arranged in a half-circle.

Apparently, when half-circle seating arrangements face participants toward one another, which allows for more visual surveillance than a straight row, the wariness of defensive individuals is increased and they "clam up." Trusting individuals, in contrast, apparently feel uncomfortable holding a conversation in a row arrangement and participate less than they would in a half-circle. To predict conversational participation, one needs to know not only an individual's personality but also the seating arrangement.

◆ *IN SUM, some traditional personality measures assist in the understanding of environment-related behavior even though they were not designed for that purpose. Outgoing individuals generally prefer smaller interpersonal distances and may experience less stress in higher-density*

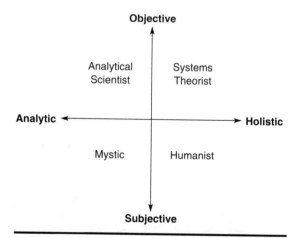

FIGURE 4–5 Two dimensions of cognitive style (analytic/holistic and objective/subjective) describe four general ways of thinking about the environment.

situations. They arrange furniture in a more open manner, perceive landscapes differently, and have a better sense of direction than reserved individuals. Persons with an internal locus of control also prefer smaller interpersonal distances and tolerate high density better than those with an external locus of control. Internals often engage in more pro-environment activities, such as recycling, although other factors can alter this. They also may prefer more "controlled" architecture. Psychological health and conventionality have also been linked to environmentally relevant behavior. Some behavior has been shown to be influenced by the joint effects of personality and the physical setting.

◆ ENVIRONMENTAL PERSONALITY ◆ DIMENSIONS

A basic premise of personality theory is that researchers should use only dispositions that have been designed for the domain of behavior to be studied. According to this premise, all the foregoing research was ill advised. But, as noted earlier, pioneer environmental psychologists had no purpose-built measures to use in studies of personality and the environment. Such measures have had to be constructed, and this takes time.

Because purpose-built measures are newer than the traditional ones, research on the measures designed specially for environmental psychology is not plentiful. Some research is aimed at assessing the reliability and validity of the new measures. Nevertheless, enough research is available to give some flavor of the potential uses of the new measures. A survey of each construct and some research using it follows.

Person-Thing Orientation

The Construct. One of the earliest environmental personality concepts posits that some individuals are primarily attuned to objects and environments and others are more attuned to people.[56,57] (Are you tuned into the environment or something else?) This simple distinction seems appropriate as the first environmental personality dimension. However, person-thing orientation is a trifle more complicated than that.

The developer of this concept, Brian Little,[58,59,60] proposes that we can be high or low on each of the two

orientations, which creates four possible orientations. Two of these are obvious: **Person specialists** and **thing specialists** are high on one dimension but low on the other. However, others are **generalists,** who show marked interest in both people *and* things, and **nonspecialists,** who are not very interested in either people *or* things. Knowing which of these types best characterizes an individual should enable us to predict some of that person's behavior, including environment-related behavior. Which type would most likely take a computer course? Which would prefer a social psychology course? Which type is best suited to a course in environmental psychology?

The person specialist, according to Little, is likely to have a smaller personal space zone, to use first names in conversations more, and to send more letters. The thing specialist, when not working on a computer or a collection, probably prefers solitary nature walks or gardening and reads magazines that focus on hobbies, electronics, or other *things* (see Figure 4–6).

The generalist cares about both people and things, but may have a problem with information overload. This type person, for instance, may be frustrated when attempts to involve an acquaintance who is a computer addict (thing specialist) in, say, a computer club prove futile, and when it is nearly impossible to involve a friend who is majoring in social work (person specialist) to even look at a computer.

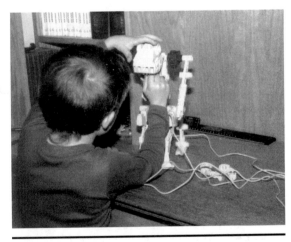

FIGURE 4–6   Most thing specialists like to tinker with complex objects.

Individuals in the nonspecialist category care most about themselves. Little suggests that a better name for this type might be *self-specialist*. These individuals spend much time attempting to understand and predict their own behavior, and perhaps telling you and everyone else about their progress or lack of progress, which severely limits the amount of time they have to devote to others *or* the environment.

Little's measures of these constructs, called the *Person-Thing Orientation scales,* are in questionnaire format. A different measure of the same basic concept is called **thing-cognitive complexity**.[61] Adapting a technique from the personality theorist George Kelly, the repertory grid,[62] Friedman attempted to assess the complexity of an individual's conceptualization of things. Individuals who are very thing-cognitively complex have many different ways of distinguishing or grouping things or environments. Do you know people who can tell you a million things about different models of computers and others who do not know a Mac from an IBM?

Research Findings. How might our disposition to specialize in persons or things (or both, or neither) relate to our transactions with the environment? Little has reported that person specialists do indeed have more constructs with which to differentiate other individuals; they are more knowledgeable about the myriad types of individuals that exist.[63] Thing specialists use more physicalistic constructs when assessing places, compared to those with low thing scores.

In another study, Little asked Berkeley (CA) residents to generate constructs that would distinguish among three local shopping areas. Generalists produced the largest number, but person specialists again produced more people-oriented constructs and thing specialists produced more physical constructs. These results show that the person-thing orientation scale has some validity; individuals behave as their score leads us to expect they would.

Another study reports a less obvious finding.[64] Residents of Vancouver, British Columbia, were asked to estimate urban distances (on the order of 6 kilometers). Everyone tended to overestimate actual distances, but there were large differences in the amount of error. Generalists only overestimated by 8 percent, followed by thing

specialists at 15 percent, person specialists at 33 percent, and nonspecialists at 45 percent. Can you explain these results, based on the person-thing orientation construct?

Environmental Personality Inventory

The Constructs. A second early environmental personality typology was constructed by Joseph Sonnenfeld.[65] It includes four concepts.

1. Environmental sensitivity. This dimension measures the amount and complexity of the environment's perceived impact on oneself. When asked whether their home environments have positive, negative, or neutral connotations to them, environmentally sensitive individuals report that many features do have connotations of one sort or another.

2. Environmental mobility. By asking individuals to rank how much they would like to visit certain places around the world and how risky and exotic they believe each place to be, Sonnenfeld derives a measure of the individual's mobility. In general, highly mobile individuals are those who would very much like to visit or even migrate to the places they believe are risky and exotic.

3. Environmental control. This dimension measures how much individuals believe the environment controls them, or vice versa, in the case of natural hazards. In the case of flooding, individuals differing on this dimension might prefer to avoid flood plains, work to control flooding, learn to live with floods, or even appreciate the excitement and challenge that floods provide.

4. Environmental risk taking. This is the measure of one's propensity to take risks and to evaluate various activities as being risky or not. Some people climb rock faces, raft down whitewater rivers, or race cars, but others would never engage in these activities. Sonnenfeld's construct, however, also includes the individual's beliefs about whether these and other more activities are or are not risky. Thus, Chris may believe mountain climbing is very risky, yet climb rock cliffs every weekend, whereas Pat climbs frequently but does not believe climbing is very risky. Lindsay believes climbing is risky and avoids it, and Jamie believes that it is not risky but never cares to go. Environmental risk taking is a combination of whether one takes risks and whether one is aware that one is taking risks.

Research Findings. Sonnenfeld reports a variety of demographic differences on his scales.[66] For example, older people and women had lower environmental risk-taking scores; risky and exotic places were more preferred by younger males, but not in the same way: People in business, industrial, and engineering occupations, for example, preferred exotic but *not* risky destinations. Those in creative occupations preferred more exotic locales; those in medicine-related fields—perhaps oddly—preferred the more risky locations. Individuals who lived or would like to live in urban areas scored highest on environmental sensitivity, but those who were *raised* in large cities scored the lowest. Researchers who used a different measure of environmental sensitivity found that it is strongly related to self-reported pro-environmental behavior.[67,68]

The Environmental Response Inventory

The Constructs. The most ambitious effort to measure environmentally related personality to date is George McKechnie's Environmental Response Inventory (ERI), which contains scales to measure eight concepts.[69] McKechnie calls the ERI a broad-band assessment instrument, meaning that, for the first time, an attempt is made to measure most or all personal dispositions relevant to our everyday interaction with the physical environment.

This raises a question: How many such dispositions are there? So far, personality researchers who specialize in environmentally relevant behavior have no overall guiding theory to supply an answer to this question,[70] although to develop such a theory would be a very worthy goal. Thus, although the ERI includes more concepts than any other assessment method to date, it cannot be regarded as comprehensive. Nevertheless, the ERI definitely is the single-most complete environmental personality assessment system we have.

The ERI was developed in a complex, multistage test construction sequence. After much creation, exploration, evaluation, shortening, and testing of the scales, the following eight concepts were considered to be adequately measured by scales that are each about 20 questions long.

1. **Pastoralism**. The tendency to oppose land development, preserve open space, accept natural forces as influences, and prefer self-sufficiency
2. **Urbanism**. The tendency to enjoy high-density living and appreciate the varied interpersonal and cultural stimulation found in city life
3. **Environmental adaptation**. The tendency to favor the alteration of the environment to suit human needs and desires, oppose development controls, and prefer highly refined settings and objects
4. **Stimulus seeking**. The tendency to be interested in travel and exploration, enjoy complex or intense physical sensations, and have very broad interests
5. **Environmental trust**. The tendency to be secure in the environment, be competent in finding one's way around, and be unafraid of new places or of being alone
6. **Antiquarianism**. The tendency to enjoy historical places and things, prefer traditional designs, collect more treasured possessions than most other individuals, and appreciate the products of earlier eras
7. **Need for privacy**. The tendency to need isolation, not appreciate neighbors, avoid distraction, and seek solitude
8. **Mechanical orientation**. The tendency to enjoy technological and mechanical processes, enjoy working with one's hands, and care about how things work

We see in these dimensions certain similarities to the earlier systems. Stimulus seeking is not unlike Sonnenfeld's environmental mobility. Mechanical orientation is similar to Little's thing orientation. Nevertheless, McKechnie's system includes some new dimensions and provides us with a set of concepts that can all be measured at the same time with the same basic instructions and materials. More important, it allows for the beginning of research into the question of how many dimensions of interest to environmental psychologists exist and how they are interrelated. For example, from McKechnie's own work, we know that antiquarianism and pastoralism are strongly correlated (but not so alike that they are redundant), whereas environmental trust and environmental adaptation are completely uncorrelated. Ultimately, one goal is to know all the important dimensions and how they fit together.

Thus far, we have focused on the dimensions of environmental personality one at a time. McKechnie's broadband approach opens another possibility: to assess an individual's *pattern* of personal dispositions. For idiographic applications such as designing a home or workspace for one individual, knowing that person's configuration of environmental tendencies could be of considerable value. For example, McKechnie described how the ERI may be used to graphically illustrate the differences between conservation group members, government officials, and members of a fishing and hunting club, or the differences within a profession, such as student planners versus practicing planners.[71] With eight or more tendencies to consider, this could be a complex decision, but let's consider a relatively simple hypothetical case.

Morgan scores very high on stimulus seeking and antiquarianism, and Leslie scores very high on antiquarianism and very low on stimulus seeking. To keep matters simple, assume both have average scores on the other scales. I see Morgan in an office covered with photos of safaris and mountaintops. On the desk are some pieces-of-eight found while diving in the Caribbean. There is a set of genuine armor in the corner. An antique map collection fills an entire wall. I see Leslie in an office that also reveals the collector tendency. However, Leslie is into stamps and coins; display cases figure prominently in one corner of the office. In contrast to the electric blue carpet and orange walls of Morgan's office, Leslie has brown carpet and weathered barn-board on one wall. Subdued lighting, Victorian leather furnishings, and bookshelves full of first editions complete the scene in Leslie's office.

The ERI's value has been increased by an adaptation of it for use with children.[72] Many ERI items were adapted to reflect the activities and interests of children as young as age 9, which resulted in the Children's Environmental Response Inventory (CERI). It should allow researchers to discover the tendencies of individual children, understand why they like and dislike certain settings, and assist in planning children's settings.

Another elaboration of an ERI theme develops more differentiated measures of the individual's disposition toward the past, or *antiquarianism*[73] (see Figure 4–7). In a study of historic and prehistoric sites in Toronto, four subspecies of the antiquarian personality were uncovered.

FIGURE 4–7 Some like them antique.

Conservation is the tendency to support (or not) the preservation of historic buildings and archaeological sites. **Heritage** is the tendency to appreciate (or not) the past as a cultural entity that has value in the present as a source of national identity or of lessons that could usefully guide today's decisions. **Experience** is the tendency to desire (or not) direct experience with historic or prehistoric places, such as wanting to visit reconstructed pioneer villages or living in a nice old house. **Interest** is the tendency to think often (or not) about or reflect on past events and places. All four scales are highly correlated with antiquarianism, but the developers of these subspecies offer them as tools for use when the researcher is specifically interested in the different aspects of dispositions toward the past and its artifacts.

Research Findings. McKechnie proposed the ERI as a broad-band assessment tool useful in any research setting where it is desirable to obtain information about how individuals think about and relate to the everyday physical environment.[74] To this end, the ERI was used to predict how students and residents of towns would judge 10 everyday buildings on a university campus and in the small town surrounding it.[75] Participants were shown color slide sequences of the buildings and asked to rate them on several dimensions.

The buildings were divided into several objective categories: newer versus older, larger versus smaller, brightly lit versus dimly lit, and buildings with people versus buildings without people. Pastoralists, antiquarians, and mechanically oriented participants preferred pictures of buildings in which people were not visible over those in which people were present. Recall that these three personality types share strong interests in activities that do not emphasize people.

Raters high on environmental adaptation liked larger and newer buildings more than older and smaller ones, but antiquarians, as you might expect, preferred older buildings to newer ones. At a more general level, participants rated the buildings as a whole—that is, an approximation of what they thought of everyday architecture in general. Those high on environmental adaptation liked the buildings; pastoralists and antiquarians disliked them. The study concluded that the ERI is indeed a promising tool for understanding which sorts of individuals are likely to prefer which sorts of buildings.

A current problem in medical training is that graduates gravitate more often to urban than to rural areas, resulting in unequal medical services to the population. The ERI was used to identify differences among optometrists who chose to practice in inner city, urban, suburban, and rural locations.[76] Those who located in more urban areas scored higher on the urbanism scale. This finding has two implications. First, it shows that the ERI has some degree of validity (those who score high on an ERI urbanism scale generally do elect to live in cities). Second, it suggests that the ERI might be used to identify or screen applicants for medical school who are likely to prefer practicing in rural areas, should a medical school be prepared to rectify the imbalance in medical services to rural areas.

Nature Orientation

The Constructs. Another set of measures to assess environmental personality includes two items concerned with items toward the great outdoors.[77] The **nature** scale taps the tendency to enjoy wilderness, woodlands, campfires, and other outdoor activities in relatively undeveloped places. The **romantic escape** scale also measures one's tendency to get out into natural settings, but there is a difference in motivation. The person high on the nature scale wants to head *to* the woods, whereas the

romantic escapist wants to flee *from* the urban-suburban life.

Quick, what is the very first word that comes to mind when you read the next word? *Den.* Hold on to the word that came to mind for a moment while I explain. So many people are interested in nature these days that some responses to nature scales may represent fashionable answers rather than real interest. For this reason, a measure called the **natural environment awareness word association test** (NEAT) was developed.[78]

The NEAT uses a nonreactive, word-association approach to overcome the so-called fashionable problem; it assumes that word associations tap a person's true beliefs better than questionnaire items.[79] Thus, if the first word that came to your mind was *cave, bear,* or *wolf* (or another nature word), score one for your nature sensitivity; if it was *room, study,* or *fireplace* (or other building or building-relevant word), then score one for your architectural (nonnature) sensitivity. Repeated over 75 words that can have either nature or nonnature associations, the NEAT measures how nature oriented or nature sensitive a person is.

Research Findings. Individuals with different scores on the Kaplan nature scales do not merely engage in different activities; they do so for different reasons. For example, those who score high on the nature scale engage in their favorite activities in order to gain peace and quiet, to be involved in the process that characterizes the activity, and to be outdoors in natural settings.[80]

Environmental Stimulus Sensitivity

The Constructs. Are some people more tuned-in to the environment—not only to nature, but to their surroundings in general? Are some people more able or less able to screen out environmental stimuli than others? Are there individual differences in environmental vulnerability?[81] One family of environmental personality tests is geared to measuring such differences.

Two measures, developed separately, both deal with how the individual processes incoming stimulation from the environment. The **stimulus screening** concept developed by Albert Mehrabian examines an individual's responses ("slow to be aroused" or "quick to adapt") to different kinds of stimuli (sound, texture, odor, and heat) that arrive in different patterns (novel, complex, or sudden).[82] The goal is to assess an individual's *automatic* screening of irrelevant stimuli. Screeners are those who are able to overcome the distraction that irrelevant stimuli cause nonscreeners (see Figure 4–8). In general, screeners are believed to be less "arousable" than nonscreeners.

The **Noise Sensitivity Scale**, developed by Neil Weinstein, focuses on one's emotional response to noise in the immediate area.[83] Weinstein constructed it under the assumptions that people differ in their initial response to noise and in their abilities to adjust to noise that continues. Noise sensitivity appears to be related to a more general tendency of individuals to be critical or uncritical of their physical surroundings.[84]

Research Findings. These stimulus-sensitivity scales have been shown to predict several environment-related behaviors. For example, we all have our favored and less-favored places, but screeners and nonscreeners differ in how they respond to these settings. Nonscreeners seem to resist entering disliked settings more than screeners do; once there, they may socialize with others less and work less than screeners do.[85] These findings appear to have important implications for both environmental designers and personnel managers.

NEIL WEINSTEIN
devised the Noise Sensitivity Scale and has investigated the effects of noise and responses to radon gas.

Another study of screeners' behavior examined the responses of residents to dormitories of different designs.[86] In general, long corridor designs are seen as more crowded and are associated with more behavioral helplessness. However, screeners who lived in long-corridor dormitories adapted to the situation more successfully than did nonscreeners.

Research on noise sensitivity shows that the scale can predict responses one would expect it to predict. For example, more noise-sensitive individuals usually perform worse in noisy conditions,[87,88,89] choose lower levels of noise,[90] listen to music less while working or reading, are more annoyed by noise from nearby roads, report more interference from noise with their daily activi-

FIGURE 4–8 Screeners are better able to study in high-stimulus surroundings such as this than nonscreeners.

ties,[91,92] and are more sensitive to other kinds of stimuli.[93] Noise-sensitive college students were more bothered by dormitory noise at the beginning of the school year, and became more disturbed by it by the end of the year.[94] Noise-sensitive students also have a history of lower academic performance, perhaps because of their sensitivity.

These findings are not surprising, but they do demonstrate that individuals who are likely to have negative experiences with noise sources can be identified. Planning for the needs of noise-sensitive individuals is important, because they apparently cannot adapt to noise over time.[95,96] Noise sensitivity is not strongly related to objective noise level.[97] Some people are more sensitive to the same level of objectively measured noise than others. Also, objective noise level can be unrelated to health or sleep complaints, whereas noise sensitivity in the same space *is* significantly related to health and sleep problems.[98] Thus, planning should not be based simply on objective noise levels; we must determine who in the noisy setting is noise sensitive and plan for them in particular.

Control-Related Environmental Dispositions

The Constructs. As noted earlier, the external dimension of traditional locus of control measures does not refer to the physical environment, but to fate, luck, chance, or powerful other people. But control over certain parts of the physical environment *is* important to people, so environmental psychologists have created special scales to measure perceived control in physical settings. Perceived, actual, and desired[99] control over features of the physical environment are all important.

Some of these new control scales are designed for specific environments or purposes. For example, one assesses apartment tenants' degree of perceived control.[100] Another, the **Environmental Appraisal Inventory (EAI)**, concentrates on perceived control over environmental hazards.[101] Across 24 human- and nature-made hazards, some people feel they have more control; others feel more powerless. The EAI also measures how threatening these 24 hazards are to the person, and a recent extension of it assesses how responsible persons feel for each hazard.[102]

A concept closely related to control is the belief that things can be improved, or optimism that, *collectively*, people can control the problem even if you cannot personally do so. Such a test, called the **Environmental Modifiability Test**, was developed for the specific case of air pollution.[103]

A third specialized tool, the **Environmental Action Internal Control Index**, assesses locus of control within the context of pro-environment behavior.[104] It predicts (and initial studies confirm) that internals on the scale will engage in more environmentally responsible actions than externals.

These three scales measure control in rather special environmental conditions—for renting, hazards, and ecologically oriented behavior. A more general tool for measuring perceived control in everyday settings is needed. Such an instrument is presently under development.[105] The **Survey of Personal Influence in Common Environments (SPICE)** assesses perceived control (and the *importance* of having control) over many elements of three everyday physical settings—home, work, and school—and in public places (e.g., streets or retail stores) in which most of us spend most of our time.

Research Findings. Most of the environmental control scales are quite new and have many potential purposes, although very little research has been done with them. However, one finding is that persons with a greater perceived control over environmental hazards are also more committed to safeguarding the environment.[106]

Studies show there may be a big psychological difference between *perceived* and *actual* control. In an office work setting, employees who perceived that they had control over the room temperature were more satisfied, but when they were given actual control over the temperature, they were less happy.[107] Apparently, the employees (and maybe the rest of us) like to feel we have control, but exercising that control takes effort and the cost of this effort cuts into our satisfaction.

◆ *IN SUM, personality dimensions constructed especially for person-environment relations are relatively recent. Five groups or kinds of dimensions have been developed: orientation toward persons and orientation for things (or both or neither), those concerned with perceived or desired control over the physical environment, sensitivity to environmental stimuli, and affinity for nature. Two attempts to assemble a spectrum of environmental personality dimensions are the Environmental Response Inventory and the Environmental Personality Inventory. Personality theory predicts that such measures will be more useful than traditional personality measures for helping us understand person-environment relations because they are tools made specifically for the job.*

◆ SOME USES OF PERSONALITY ◆ IN ENVIRONMENTAL DESIGN

I have described in some detail the different approaches to assessing those aspects of personality most relevant to environmental psychology and some of the research linking those instruments to environmentally relevant cognitions and behaviors. Perhaps you are still wondering just how such knowledge might be used. Kenneth Craik has described three categories of uses to which personality assessments may be put: description, comparison, and prediction.[108]

Description

Description may be accomplished by the judicious use of any or all of the environmental personality measures described earlier. Whether they are used to describe a single person or the typical member of a certain group, environmental designers cannot take the person into account until the person's qualities are known. Description answers the question: Who is the individual for whom this space will be designed? In addition, the question might be turned around: Who are the architects, the designers, the managers of water resources, the facility managers who allocate and maintain space in organizations? Knowing *their* personalities helps us understand how they will tend to design and manage the environment.

Comparison

Comparison allows planners, architects, designers, and others to know the *differences* between individuals or groups. For example, knowledge of the differences in personality of typical snowmobilers and cross-country skiers should help park planners to design better new recreation areas and to develop effective policies for ex-

isting ones. Many other possible group comparisons might be made as part of the design process. Is the typical student different from the typical professor in terms of environmental tendencies? Are nurses different from physicians? Patients from both? In every behavior setting, there are several user groups. If their typical personalities are different, how so? Clarifying these specific differences should help designers create settings that better fit the needs of each group.

Prediction

The third use of personality knowledge is prediction. The assessment of individual differences frequently allows a forecast of the satisfaction, productivity, or some relevant behavior of an individual in a given environment. For example, recall that the ERI was used to predict which medical students will migrate. The other uses of prediction from environmental personality measures parallel the chapters of this book. They may be used to understand how individuals think about their surroundings, use the space around them, and manage their resources.

◆ SUMMARY ◆

This chapter describes the seemingly unlikely connections between personality and environment. Reasons why environmental psychologists should consider personality are offered. The classic theories of Henry Murray and Kurt Lewin are described. The ways that traditional personality variables (such as outgoing/reserved and internal/external locus of control) help explain behavior of interest to environmental psychology are noted. Six systems for assessing environmental personality, and some research using them, are described. The uses of personality assessment in environmental design include description, comparison, and prediction. Knowing the behavioral tendencies of those who are to use or control a setting may help designers produce a more compatible fit between occupant and habitat. Knowing how individuals and groups *differ* on key personality dimensions can help the designer become more aware of how settings for different people should reflect their distinct psychological makeups. Knowing the environmental personality of individuals allows better prediction of their satisfaction with and performance in different physical settings.

Suggested Supplementary Readings

Craik, K. H. (1976). The personality research paradigm in environmental psychology. In S. Wapner, S. B. Cohen, & B. Kaplan (Eds.), *Experiencing the environment*. New York: Plenum.

Fridgen, C. (1994). Human disposition toward hazards: Testing the Environmental Appraisal Inventory. *Journal of Environmental Psychology, 14*, 101–111.

Little, B. R. (1987). Personality and environment. In D. Stokols & I. Altman (Eds.), *Handbook of environmental psychology*. New York: Wiley.

McKechnie, G. E. (1977). The environmental response inventory in application. *Environment and Behavior, 9*, 255–276.

CHAPTER **5**

PERSONAL SPACE

The best way to learn the location of invisible boundaries is to keep walking until somebody complains.

—Robert Sommer[1]

*A*fter studying for hours in his carrel, Tom felt like taking a break and decided to go to a movie. At the theater, he found himself in a long line. Someone behind him stood so close that Tom felt uncomfortable and tense.

Across town, Jane was introduced by a friend to an international student. He seemed pleasant enough, but for some reason, he stood so close to her that she felt overwhelmed and wanted to get away from him. Jane backed away, but he seemed pushy, and she spent half an hour feeling cornered in a conversation.

After the movie, Tom happened to meet an acquaintance of Jane's while walking home, Marta. She insisted that he come to a postgame celebration. He wasn't romantically interested in her, but he thought the party might be interesting. As they walked, Marta suddenly took Tom's arm and the two of them were shoulder to shoulder. Tom hoped none of his friends would see him and Marta this way.

◆   ◆   ◆

The best way to explain personal space may be to ask you to place yourself in these situations faced by Jane and Tom—scenarios in which you are too close to someone. Most of the time, when you are comfortable about your distance to others, you are not even aware of personal space.

This chapter will concentrate on one of the most widely studied areas of environmental psychology. Over 1,300 studies on personal space have been reported. It has been described as hidden, silent, and invisible, yet everyone possesses and uses personal space every day. If you never have considered personal space before, this chapter may change the way you think about yourself and others. After defining personal space and describing the major ways of measuring it, the factors that affect its size will be surveyed. Next, the ways personal space is connected to a variety of other behaviors is described. Then its functional value is discussed and some integrative theories are presented. Finally, the role of personal space in environmental design is illustrated with several examples.

◆ WHAT IS PERSONAL SPACE? ◆

A Basic Definition

A simple definition of *personal space* was offered by Robert Sommer years ago: "Personal space refers to an area with invisible boundaries surrounding a person's body into which intruders may not come."[2]

But almost nothing in environmental psychology is simple. This bubblelike image of personal space has been challenged.[3] First, it implies that personal space is stable, when, in fact, it stretches and shrinks with circumstances. Second, it is not really personal but interpersonal. Personal space exists only when we interact with others. Third, it emphasizes distance to the exclusion of strongly related aspects of social interaction such as angle of orientation and eye contact. Fourth, it suggests personal space is an either-or phenomenon (either we are intruded upon or not), when intrusion is more like a gradient than a boundary.[4]

Therefore, I will define **personal space** as the geographic component of interpersonal relations. That is, it is the distance and angle of orientation (such as side by side or face to face) between individuals as they interact.

Three Elaborations

The concise definition just offered contains within it numerous important implications that are developed in this chapter. Three aspects of personal space are described to illustrate some of these implications.

A Personal, Portable Territory. Territories are places where entry is controlled. Some outsiders are allowed in; others are not. Personal space differs from most other territories in that it is portable. Wherever you stand or sit, you are surrounded on all sides by personal space. Yet, unlike the sharp borders of property lines, the borders of this personal space are gradual (see Figure 5–1). Unauthorized intrusion into this personal territory is either an accident (someone not watching where he or she is walking bumps into you) or intentional (you get mugged). Authorized intrusion is possible, too (your mother gives you a hug).

ROBERT SOMMER
has pioneered the study of personal space, social design (see Chapter 15), and many other specific behavior settings.

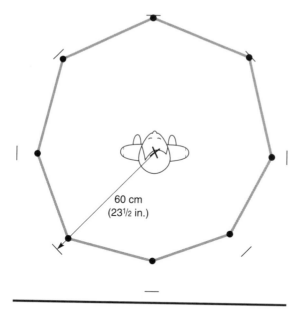

60 cm
(23½ in.)

FIGURE 5–1 The shape of personal space. The lines represent average distances around the bodies of students when approached by a young male researcher until they told him they felt uncomfortable about his closeness.

A Spacing Mechanism. Observers of birds[5] and animals[6] have long known that certain species maintain characteristic distances between individuals of that species (see Figure 5–2). These distances have biological value; they regulate fundamental processes such as food gathering and mating. At certain times, some species,

such as sea lions during breeding, have almost zero personal space; other species, such as wolves living in the tundra, have very large ones.

A Communication Channel. Personal space is a way of sending messages. According to Edward Hall,[7] a pioneer personal space researcher, interpersonal distance informs both participants and outside observers about the very nature of the participants' relationship. For example, you have probably seen couples strolling along, arm in arm. In our culture, the inevitable message is that this couple is in love.

Hall described eight gradations of interpersonal distance (see Figure 5–3).[8] Each one provides participants with a slightly different set of sensory information, and each indicates a slightly different relationship between the participants. The eight distances are composed of the near and far phases of four main distances.

1. *Intimate distance.* The near phase of intimate distance (0–6 inches or 0–15 centimeters) is for comforting, protecting, lovemaking, wrestling, and other full-contact activities. People who interact at this distance are on intimate terms, or they are behaving within a strict set of rules (e.g., wrestling), or they are expressing strong negative emotions (e.g., an angry baseball manager heatedly disputing an umpire's decision).

The far phase of intimate distance (6–18 inches or 15–45 centimeters) is used by individuals who are on very close terms. (Note, incidentally, how the English

FIGURE 5–2 The study of personal space originated with the observation that both animals and humans use consistent interorganism spacing.

Interpersonal Distance Zones

Intimate:
Near Phase: 0–15 cm (0–6 inches)
Far Phase: 15–45 cm (6–18 inches)

Personal:
Near Phase: 45–75 cm (18–30 inches)
Far Phase: 75–120 cm (2½–4 feet)

Social:
Near Phase: 120–200 cm (4–7 feet)
Far Phase: 200–350 cm (7–12 feet)

Public:
Near Phase: 350–700 cm (12–25 feet)
Far Phase: over 700 cm (25 feet)

FIGURE 5–3 Edward Hall first described four major interpersonal distance zones based on the social relation between the two persons.

language contains many words that describe the state of relationships in terms of interpersonal distance, such as *close, in touch, distant,* etc.). A typical behavior at this distance is whispering. Generally, the participants in an interaction at this distance are very good friends.

2. *Personal distance.* The near phase (18–30 inches or 45–75 centimeters) is the zone for those who are familiar with one another and on good terms. Good friends or a happy couple will use this distance to talk. Hall says that if your spouse enters this zone, acquaintances will hardly notice, but if someone else of your spouse's sex comes this close to you, that is "an entirely different story."[9]

The far phase of personal distance (2.5–4 feet or 75–120 centimeters) is used for social interactions between friends and acquaintances. If you observe two classmates who are acquainted but not special friends talking in a hallway, chances are they will be standing in the far phase of personal distance.

3. *Social distance.* Despite the name, this zone is used more for interaction between unacquainted individuals

or those transacting business. The near phase (4–7 feet or 1.2–2 meters) is the distance someone might select while being introduced to a roommate's mother or while buying a stereo.

The far phase of social distance (7–12 feet or 2–3.5 meters) is typical of more formal business transactions. Perhaps Hall should have called it *business distance.* Here, there is little sense of friendship or even of trying to be friendly. The interaction is best described as the meeting of two organizations' representatives. For example, if the company owned by your roommate's mother is about to buy out the stereo store, she and the stereo salesperson's boss might interact at this distance.

4. *Public distance.* This zone is used less often by two interacting individuals than by speakers and their audiences. The near phase of public distance (12–25 feet or 3.5–7 meters) would be used by a lecturer whose class has grown just large enough that speaking from a seated position no longer feels comfortable. When someone is speaking to a group of 30 or 40 people, the average distance between speaker and listener is likely to be in this range.

The far phase of public distance (over 25 feet or 7 meters) is used when ordinary mortals meet important public figures. If you were formally introduced to a head of state, you would probably halt your approach at about this distance. Because it is not easy to hold a normal conversation at this distance, the important public figure must beckon you closer if communication between the two of you is to occur.

The three conceptions of personal space (territory, spacing mechanism, and communication channel) are complementary. Later in this chapter, when we examine theories of personal space, we will see that most of them are based on these three fundamental elements.

Awareness and Choice

Did you already know about personal space before you read about it here? Certainly, you approximate Hall's distances; your spacing from other individuals is not random. In fact, you choose distances much more finely than suggested in Hall's categories because you take other factors into account. But were you aware, until you read the first part of this chapter, of these behavioral choices you have been making? As an old sage once said, you don't have to know the laws of physics to shoot a basketball accurately. Similarly, most of us use personal space every day according to certain rules, yet we have a low level of awareness of these rules and the distancing process.

The rules governing personal space are acquired. Children gradually learn them; eventually, they learn the rules so well that they no longer need to clog their moment-to-moment cognitive processing with them. When personal space rules are broken, however, there can be negative consequences. First, of course, when someone else is too close or too far away, you feel uncomfortable. Anecdotal[10] and experimental evidence[11] suggest that a second negative consequence occurs when others approach us too closely: We attribute unfavorable traits to them. We conclude that the other person is pushy, rude, cold, or aggressive. Of course, for some people, these attributions are correct! In other situations, however, too-close interpersonal distances are in-

appropriately interpreted and people develop inaccurately unfavorable impressions of others.

Awareness of personal space has another dimension to it. Notice that all the foregoing descriptions of it refer to objective distances. Environmental psychologists measure these distances from a third-party vantage point. But when personal space is actually used on the street, in hallways, or in the office, one operates on the base of *perceived,* not objective, interpersonal distance. Personal space also is a subjective experience. For years, influential reviews of the personal space literature[12,13] have called for research into the cognitive aspects of personal space. Yet, of the hundreds of experiments on personal space, only a handful have investigated the experience of personal space.

One perspective is that there are two kinds of personal space.[14] **Alpha personal space** is the objective, externally measurable distance and angle between interacting individuals. **Beta personal space** is the subjective experience of the distancing process. Like all experiences, it must be measured indirectly. Beta personal space is the individual's sense of distance and angular orientation in social encounters.

One way to investigate beta personal space is to ask individuals at normal interpersonal distances to estimate the distance from themselves to the other person. In one study, beta personal space, measured as the perceived distance between self and other, was 24 percent larger than alpha personal space, the actual interpersonal distance.[15] In normal social interaction, we seem to believe that we are farther away from the other person than we really are.

Also, an **asymmetry effect** in beta personal space has been demonstrated: We generally perceive another person to be closer to us than he or she actually is (i.e., when asked "How far is Tom from you?"), yet we perceive ourselves to be farther from the other person than we actually are (i.e., when asked "How far are you from Tom?").[16] Apparently, we typically think others occupy more of *our* space than we occupy of *their* space. The asymmetry is opposite to this (we think we occupy more of *their* space than they do of ours) only when few others are around and we are not very self-aware at the moment.[17]

◆ **IN SUM,** *personal space refers to the interpersonal distance and orientation chosen during social interaction.*

It involves elements of territoriality, spacing, and communication. Alpha personal space is the objective distance between interacting individuals, and beta personal space refers to our experience of that distance.

◆ **MEASURING PERSONAL SPACE** ◆

There are three general ways to measure personal space, although each has variations. Each method has its advantages and disadvantages in ease of performing the measurement, effectiveness in tapping the key dimensions of personal space as viewed by the different theories, and reliability and validity of the measurement. These are the simulation, the stop-distance, and the naturalistic observation methods.

Simulation Methods

Simulation methods involve placing small felt figures on felt boards or making marks on paper. Although simulation techniques were widely used in the early days of personal space research, their limitations have caused a great decline in their use. Four of these limitations are that individuals (1) are not in real person-to-person interactions when their personal space is being measured, (2) must remember distances from previous (actual) encounters, (3) must adjust for scale (and may not do so very accurately), and (4) are quite conscious of the distancing process (and usually are not in real interactions). To the extent these methods measure the cognitive aspects of personal space, they may be useful measures of beta personal space, but not alpha personal space. The following methods overcome most of these limitations and are better for measuring alpha personal space.

The Stop-Distance Method

Researchers who desire a more realistic measure of alpha personal space have often used the stop-distance technique. In this method, participants are usually studied in a laboratory situation, but in a live encounter. The participant usually is asked to stand some distance away and then to walk slowly toward the experimenter and to stop at the point of discomfort. Sometimes the experimenter approaches the participant, who asks the experimenter to stop when the participant feels uncomfortable. The resulting interpersonal distance is taken as a measure of alpha personal space. Occasionally, this procedure is repeated for different angles of approach, but most often the two participants face one another during the measurement.

The stop-distance method is very reliable; it tends to yield similar distances each time personal space is measured.[18] What about its validity? Two of the disadvantages of the simulation methods (as measures of alpha personal space) are overcome in the stop-distance method. The subject need not rely on memory and is not asked to scale down personal space distances. However, one apparent disadvantage remains; the participant is very aware of the distancing process.

Whether awareness is a problem is a matter of some debate. Even though measures in which subjects are aware of the distancing process correlate poorly with measures in which they are not, the *effects* on both (e.g., gender differences or levels of acquaintance) are about the same.[19] However, this may not hold for other variables that affect personal space.[20]

The issue would not matter if we could devise stop-distance techniques that avoid participant awareness. Recently, this was done; the researcher simply asked participants who entered a room at a door some distance away (and did not know the study was about personal space) to "come over here and we'll get started."[21] When the participants approached and stopped where they liked, a measurement was made that overcame all three problems with the simulation methods. Objective distances may be measured with special pressure-sensitive floor mats.[22]

Naturalistic Observation

I can almost hear you asking: Why not simply study personal space by measuring the unplanned interpersonal distances of individuals in natural settings? This would dispose of all three disadvantages. It may, but there are three other reasons why naturalistic observation is not often used. First, some environmental psychologists believe it is unethical to measure the behavior of people without their prior informed consent. This can be overcome by asking for consent to use the data afterwards, but there are other problems.

Another crucial problem is that measurements made under natural conditions are subject to many uncontrolled variables. For example, if you went to a park and measured personal space between pairs there, the pairs probably would include many levels of friendship, topics being discussed, roles, and combinations of personality. Without knowing the status of each person on these variables, it would be hard to explain why some pairs stood at large interpersonal distances but others stood at small ones. The problem with naturalistic measurement of personal space is not so much in determining the size of personal space, but in determining the *reasons* for differences in personal space—and that is usually the purpose of the study.

Third, the measurement itself can be tricky. Would you simply estimate the interpersonal distance of each pair from a distance? That would not be very accurate. Would you casually stroll up to them and ask the pair to freeze so you could stretch a tape between their chests? Even if you are bold enough to do this, your quarries probably would shift their positions by turning to look at you. They may even move back a step or two or run away from this obviously deranged intruder! You could try to photograph the pairs so you could get the distances from the pictures, but there are considerable technical difficulties in translating photographic distances to life-size distances, particularly if the angle of the camera shot is not exactly perpendicular to the conversing couple. These difficulties can and have been overcome, but not often and not easily. That is why simulation and stop-distance techniques are used more often than naturalistic methods.

◆ *IN SUM, personal space has been measured using simulation, stop-distance, and naturalistic observation methods. The simulation techniques have flaws, but may be better suited to studying beta than alpha personal space. The stop-distance technique can, in some variations, overcome these flaws. Naturalistic observation can be technically difficult and often does not allow the investigator to distinguish among different possible reasons for variations in personal space. The researcher must be aware of both the advantages and disadvantages of each method, the theoretical implications of selecting a method, and the pitfalls involved in actually making the measurement. Let us turn now to a survey of the major influences on the size of personal space.*

◆ INFLUENCES ON PERSONAL SPACE ◆

What size is personal space? This simple question has been the focus of many investigations since 1959, when the first study of human personal space was published by Robert Sommer. As you might expect, the simple overall conclusion about the size of personal space is this: It depends. What it depends on are influences that fall into four broad categories: personal, social, physical, and cultural factors.

Personal Influences

Personal space is a function, in part, of the characteristics each individual carries from situation to situation, such as gender, personality, mental health, and age. Each of these characteristics has an important role in personal space, although we must remember that in any real-life distancing process, many influences—including those from the social, physical, and cultural categories—are simultaneously at work.

Gender. Generally, male/male pairs keep the largest distances,[23,24,25,26,27] followed by female/female pairs and male/female pairs.[28,29] However, varying results can be found.[30,31] One possible reason is that sex differences in personal space reflect differences in the socialization of males and females rather than biological differences. Depending on their upbringing and other social and cultural influences, men may interact more closely than women. For example, in a study that focused on gender, race, and age simultaneously, gender influenced personal space only in interaction with race, age, and the other person's gender, not by itself.[32]

A study of children at play showed that girls stay closer to adults when boys and girls play together than when all the children in the play group are girls.[33] Male/female pairs may use much more space when the two are strangers than when they are lovers. Thus, gender simply is not as powerful a determinant of personal space, on its own, as are other variables.

Age. Personal space increases with age.[34] Infant personal space is hard to measure because infants have little independent mobility. Developmental psychologists do, however, know that some infants like to be hugged and others resist contact. Perhaps these young resisters would have larger personal space zones than the huggers if someone could find a way to measure them. By the age of 18 months, however, children do choose different interpersonal distances depending on the person and the situation.[35] By about age 12, children use personal space approximately the way adults do.[36]

Again, other factors play a role, although not to the extent they do with gender. In fact, gender is one such factor. In one study, the personal space of males and females from ages 5 to 18 was measured[37] (see Figure 5–4). As usual, older children displayed larger interpersonal distances than younger children. But an age-by-gender interaction was also significant. Rather than boys or girls having larger personal space in general, older boys chose larger distances than older girls, but there was no difference in the size of personal space among the younger boys and girls.

Culture is another factor that can modify the age trend in personal space. For example, children in Puerto Rico increase their interpersonal distance at a later age than Puerto Rican children living in New York.[38]

Incidentally, surprisingly little is known about personal space after early childhood. As we become more aware of important developmental changes in middle and late adulthood, we realize that personal space may

change during these phases of life, too. But so far, no one has investigated this possibility.

Personality. Some reviewers have concluded there is no consistent relation between personality and personal space.[39] This may be because the relevant research has not always been well planned.[40] Some failures to find connections probably occurred because personal space was investigated in relation to dimensions of personality for which there was no good reason to expect a relation.

But in which domain of personality *might* significant relations with personal space be expected? Probably the domain that is theoretically most relevant to personal space is interpersonal behavior, including such dispositions as dominance/submissiveness, warmth/coldness, and extraversion/introversion.

Indeed, when the personal space-personality connection within the interpersonal domain is examined, clear trends appear. People who are more extraverted, affiliative, or interpersonally warm have smaller personal space zones.[41,42,43] Those who are field dependent (rely on external cues to make judgments) tend to be warmer and friendly and tend to choose smaller interpersonal distances.[44] One study investigated the whole interpersonal behavior domain.[45] The strongest correlations involved extraversion and gregariousness (smaller personal space) and coldness and quarrelsomeness (larger personal space). Individuals who are typically worried about how their views will be received by others keep larger distances.[46]

Another personality domain where personal space appears relevant is temperament. One temperament variable, trait anxiety (as opposed to short-term or state anxiety) has consistently been linked to larger personal space zones.[47,48,49,50] Type A personalities, persons who are characteristically rushed and competitive, also tend to claim greater personal space.[51]

Psychological Disturbance and Violence. Individuals who have some form of emotional problem often have unusual personal space zones. Because most psychological disturbances involve anxiety and difficulties in communication, interpersonal relationships, and perceptual processes, this is not surprising.

The very first empirical study of human personal space[52] examined the interpersonal distances chosen by

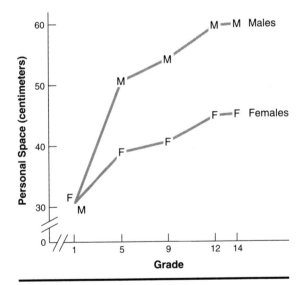

FIGURE 5–4 Personal space increases with age, and males show larger increases than females.

schizophrenics. Compared to hospital employees and nonschizophrenic patients, schizophrenics sometimes chose much greater seating distances and sometimes chose much smaller ones.[53] A later study reported that schizophrenics choose larger distances.[54]

One interesting study illustrates the relation between *degree* of disturbance and *size* of personal space.[55] The personal space of newly admitted schizophrenics, who were presumably quite disturbed, was found to be very large. The personal space of the schizophrenics was measured every three weeks during their hospital stay. As the schizophrenics improved (by independent judgment), their personal space moved much closer to that of nonpatients.

In an early study of prisoners, the interpersonal distance of those with a history of violence was found to be larger than that of nonviolent persons.[56] It seemed that those who have clashed with others need to keep a larger "body buffer zone" for security reasons. More recent research indicates that only violent prisoners who understand nonverbal behavior less and tend toward psychoticism more have larger interpersonal distances.[57] Also, when violent persons are allowed to control the distance-choosing process, they choose much smaller distances.[58]

Disabilities. Few studies have examined the interpersonal choices made by people who are disabled. However, one study showed that pairs of children with hearing impairments use greater distances than pairs of children with no hearing disability.[59] Another found that children with full-syndrome autism keep closer to adults than children with inactive autism, hyperactivity, or mental retardation.[60]

Social Influences

Collectively, the individual characteristics just reviewed add up to a generalized personal space tendency that an individual carries from situation to situation. But once the individual enters any social situation, personal space is influenced by a new range of factors. The social qualities of a situation may be broadly grouped under the headings of attraction, fear/security, cooperation/competition, and power and status. We will consider the effects on personal space that each of these qualities exerts.

Attraction. Attraction, acquaintance, and friendship all refer to the degree of positive or negative feelings and thoughts one person holds toward another. One of the strongest generalizations in personal space research is that attraction draws us physically closer. In a classic study, drawings of individuals described as good friends were placed closer together than were drawings of strangers.[61] These results have been confirmed in naturalistic observations,[62] other cultures,[63] and for children.[64] A study of married couples showed that husbands and wives sat closer than pairs of wives, who sat closer than pairs of husbands, and the greatest distance was between men and women who were not married.[65] These results suggest that attraction is a stronger influence on personal space than sex.

Some researchers have examined similarity between individuals and pleasantness of manner, two influences that presumably operate like attraction. The same results are found: As similarity and pleasantness of manner increase, personal space decreases.[66,67,68]

Emotional displays also affect personal space. Women who see either happiness or sadness in someone's face move relatively close. However, men move closer to happiness than to sadness. Both sexes keep a distance when they see fear.[69] When two people are engaged in an emotionally intense discussion, others are less likely to walk between them than if no strong emotion is apparent.[70]

A few studies have investigated the negative side of interpersonal relations. In one study, college men were scolded for being late for the experiment.[71] The experimenter told the participants, none of whom was actually late, "It said on the sign-up sheet to be on time—what's the matter, can't you read?" After a few similar insults, personal space was measured with the stop-distance technique. Not surprisingly, participants who were insulted chose larger personal space zones than did participants who were not insulted. The larger zone was specific to the insulter; participants did not show larger zones when another person measured their personal space. Criticism and insults lead to dislike, which leads to increased distance.[72]

Fear/Security. People choose closer distances when they feel secure and larger distances when they feel unsafe or fearful. For example, when told that a stranger was a nonoffender, a nonviolent offender, or a violent offender, people chose increasingly larger distances.[73] In another study, subjects chose closer distances to an older, well-groomed female than to a scruffy, younger male.[74] Presumably, the female inspired less fear than the male.

Disabilities or other visible stigmata often unfairly lead to greater distancing by others. Participants choose greater distances when the other is a mental patient, an amputee,[75] a drug user, disabled (wheelchair-bound),[76] a user of a white cane,[77] a homosexual, or a fat person.[78] The larger distances may, in part, be based on fear of the unfamiliar and on the difference between the person and society's desirable stereotypes. Stigmatized persons are sensitive to the increase in distance. They realize that although other persons may still be helpful, such as in giving directions when asked,[79] their choice of greater interpersonal distance is a telltale sign of their true, unfavorable attitude.

Cooperation/Competition. A third quality of the social situation concerns the competitive or cooperative nature of the interaction. In a series of simulation studies on this topic, individuals indicated they would select closer seats when they were cooperating, as you might expect.[80] Moreover, these studies suggested that angle of orientation is important. In competitive situations, subjects said they would choose more direct orientations (face to face), but in more cooperative situations, they would choose less direct orientations (side by side).

In naturalistic settings, the customs and physical layouts of particular places will alter these tendencies[81] (see Figure 5–5). For example, if you went to a fancy, dimly lit restaurant with your dearly beloved—presumably a situation that is more cooperative than competitive—you would probably select seats facing one another. Two men sitting in a singles bar waiting for the right woman to appear—presumably a more competitive than cooperative enterprise—are more likely to sit side by side against the wall.

The competitive or cooperative quality of a social situation may even affect personal space in *subsequent* situations. In one study, subjects played a game with a confederate of the experimenter.[82] The confederates were instructed to use either a very cooperative or very competitive strategy in the game. The interpersonal dis-

Seating Arrangements

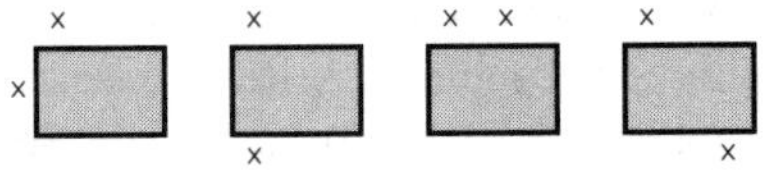

Bars				
Two Men	14%	34%	52%	
Man and Woman	15%	15%	70%	
Restaurants				
Two Men		100%		
Man and Woman		82%	16%	2%
Two Women		86%		14%

FIGURE 5–5 These seating choices were observed in three bars and a restaurant. Both the type of setting (bar versus restaurant) and the sexes of the pair (MM, FF, MF) affect seating choices.

tance of the subjects was observed in another room during a second phase of the experiment. Those who had played with a cooperative confederate selected smaller distances than those who had played with a competitive confederate.

Power and Status. A fourth quality of a social situation pertains to the status, power, or dominance of participants. Generally, others whom we perceive to be of higher *or* lower status are granted (or banished) to a greater distance. For example, when a high-status person stood near a campus water fountain, fewer passersby used the fountain than when no one stood near it.[83] Another study found that students sat closer to fellow students and farther from both higher-status others (professors) and lower-status others (a student said to be failing).[84] Thus, personal space is related more to *differences* in status than to the amount of status;[85] the greater the difference, the greater the interpersonal distance.[86]

Physical Influences

Personal space is also influenced by the physical setting context of the interaction. Close distances are more uncomfortable when lighting is dimmer.[87] Smaller distances seem to be preferred in wide or narrow rooms.[88] Individuals appear to use more space in corners of rooms than in the center.[89] Subjects who were told to pretend they were theater directors placed actresses farther apart in office waiting rooms than in lobbies or on street corners.[90] Males seem to need more space when the ceiling is lower.[91] Individuals choose larger distances indoors than outdoors.[92] The general conclusion appears to be that we prefer more space between us when the overall supply of physical space is low. However, there are circumstances under which people use more space outdoors than indoors: Children spread out when they go outside to play compared to their interpersonal distances while playing indoors.[93]

Another dimension of the physical setting is the number of other people around and what they are doing. A laboratory study found that persons who had been isolated for 90 to 150 minutes selected larger distances than those isolated for shorter periods, and larger distances if they thought others would be watching them.[94] Is this true in everyday life? If so, office workers who toil in relative isolation should need more space than those who work with others more. The personal space of women who spent their working day entering data on video display terminals was compared with that of women in the same building whose jobs offered much more social interaction.[95] The isolates did prefer significantly *more* personal space. Apparently, working in isolation either attracts individuals who already prefer more space or, perhaps, isolates adapt to the isolation and feel less comfortable with other people.

An unusual study examined the effect of weightlessness on interpersonal distances, in an effort to help understand social interaction in outer space.[96] Weightlessness produces some very odd person-to-person orientations, such as floating prone positions or head-to-toe arrangements. Generally, the largest interpersonal distances result for the most unusual orientations.

Cultural, Ethnic, Religious, and Legal Variations

Nearly all the research discussed so far was performed in North America. Yet Hall's original point was that space utilization varies across cultures: Based on his own observations of Arabs, French, South Americans, Japanese, and English, Hall believed that his four zones retained their order but not their size. Let Hall tell his own story.

I had the good fortune to be visited by a very distinguished and learned man who had been for many years a top-ranking diplomat representing a foreign country. . . . Dr. X was interested in some of the work several of us were doing at the time and asked permission to attend one of my lectures. He came to the front of the class at the end of the lecture to talk over a number of points made in the preceding hour. While talking he became quite involved in the implications of the lecture as well as what he was saying. We started out facing each other and as he talked I became dimly aware that he was standing a little too close and that I was beginning to back up. Fortunately I was able to suppress my first impulse and remain stationary because there was nothing to communicate aggression in his behavior except the conversational distance. . . . Someone who had been so successful in the old school of diplomacy could not possibly let himself communicate something offensive to the other person except outside of his highly trained awareness.

By experimenting I was able to observe that as I moved away slightly, there was an associated pattern of interaction. He had more trouble expressing himself. If I shifted to where I felt comfortable (about twenty-one inches), he looked somewhat puzzled and hurt, almost as though he were saying: "Why is he acting that way? Here I am doing everything I can to talk to him in a friendly manner and he suddenly withdraws. Have I done anything wrong?"[97]

Such an interaction with a less-sensitive observer than Hall (who eventually rooted himself at the close distance to facilitate the discussion) could have had undesirable repercussions. Remember, we begin to attribute negative characteristics to those who interact with us at inappropriate distances. This can, and indeed *has*, contributed negative cultural stereotypes.

An early experiment examined cultural differences in some detail.[98] Groups of four male students came to the laboratory and were told they would be observed but were given no other instructions. Half the groups were composed of Arabs, half of Americans. The average interpersonal distance chosen by Arabs was about the length of an extended arm, but the average interpersonal distance of the Americans was noticeably further. The Arabs touched one another much more often and their orientation was much more direct. Generally, the Arabs were much more "immediate"[99] than the Americans. Such findings have led to some overly simplistic generalizations of stereotypes.

For example, one researcher asserted that cultures may be described as either *contact* or *noncontact*.[100] Yet, two studies[101,102] found that students from allegedly contact cultures (Latin America, Spain, and Morocco) sit farther apart from one another than do students from a noncontact culture (American). Further, not all Latin Americans use the same amount of space.[103] Costa Ricans, for example, choose smaller interpersonal distances than do Panamanians or Colombians. There are differences among Europeans, too: Dutch pairs use more space than French pairs, who use more space than English pairs.[104]

Inconsistent subcultural differences have been reported, too. Several studies have shown that African Americans use more space than whites, but others have shown the reverse or no differences. Like some other black/white differences, the reason may be socioeconomic rather than cultural.[105] Another study supports this conclusion; it showed that black/white differences in personal space decreased as the amount of school experience increased.[106]

Despite a few overgeneralizations, personal space does vary with culture. For example, Arab and American males have similar personal space (another contradiction of earlier results!), but Arab and American females do not.[107] Arab females keep larger distances from their male friends than Arab males do; they place them about as far away as they place male strangers.

Thus, distancing is a complex process. As another example, Japanese use more distance in conversations than Americans, who use more than Venezuelans. But when Japanese and Venezuelans speak English instead of their native tongue, their conversational distance moves toward that of the Americans.[108] Language, an important part of culture, can modify one's cultural tendencies to use more or less interpersonal distance (see Figure 5–6).

Another important part of culture is religion, and even it is related to personal space choices. A Nigerian study found that personal space between members of different religions was larger than that between members of the same religion.[109] Pairs of Muslims used smaller interpersonal distances than pairs of Christians.

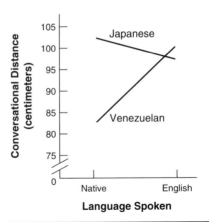

FIGURE 5–6 Interpersonal distancing is affected by the language spoken by conversation partners.

Edward Hall's original goal was to find some reasons for antagonism between cultures; he suggested that the differential use of space was one key factor. One researcher tested this idea by teaching English students how to act more like Arabs in their nonverbal behavior.[110] Arabs who interacted with the trained students liked them more than students who had not received training. Consider the implications for diplomats and for ordinary tourists!

Finally, personal space sometimes is influenced by legal means. For example, spouses sometimes are ordered by courts to keep a certain distance from their partners after they have pestered, harassed, or abused them. In Boulder, Colorado, the city council passed an ordinance that required pro-life demonstrators to keep their distance from women entering an abortion clinic.[111] Pro-life groups challenged this legal enforcement of personal space in court, but, based partly on the testimony of Edward Hall and others, the court upheld the ordinance.

◆ **IN SUM,** *personal space may be predicted, in part, from knowing an individual's characteristics. Males typically use larger distances than females. Young adults typically use more personal space than children. Interpersonally warm and nonanxious individuals have smaller personal space than others. Psychological disturbance often leads to more variable or inappropriate personal space. Persons with a history of violence often choose larger interpersonal distances. However, combinations of these and* *other factors may change these trends in everyday situations. Social and physical features of the situation also alter interpersonal distance. Attraction, cooperation, and equal status are associated with smaller personal space; stigma and unequal status lead to larger personal space. Orientation, as opposed to distance, is less well understood. We seem to prefer more space when the physical environment offers less room.*

Culture is a major modifier of interpersonal distance. There is some evidence for a continuum that ranges from the closeness of Arabs and Latin Americans to the distance of English and Germans. But differences within these groups, occasional results that do not fit this neat pattern, and other factors such as the language spoken during a particular interaction all may affect personal space. All these factors combine in everyday settings to produce interpersonal distances that are different from what would be expected from consideration of each influence by itself.

♦ PERSONAL SPACE AND ♦ HUMAN BEHAVIOR

In this section, we will survey what happens when individuals deliberately invade others' space or innocently choose inappropriate interpersonal distances. The notion of *appropriate* distance is central to personal space. In each situation, only a small range of distances is acceptable. In his story, for example, Edward Hall first considers the possibility that the diplomat is aggressive. On the too-close side, inappropriate distance will be perceived as invasion of personal space; on the too-far side, it will be perceived as aloofness or coldness. Furthermore, recall that Hall's diplomatic admirer actually began to have communication difficulties when Hall moved too far away from him.

Flight and Affect

If you have ever had your personal space invaded, you probably felt at least a short burst of emotion.[112] Even when the invasion is excusable—as, for example, in a crowded elevator—some negative emotion usually surfaces. We might then hypothesize that appropriate distance in a given situation is associated with positive or neutral affect, but too-close and too-far distances lead to a bad feeling.

Surprisingly few studies have directly tested this idea. However, if avoidance behaviors such as leaving the scene are the result of negative emotions, there is abundant evidence in favor of this simple hypothesis. The classic evidence comes again from the work of Robert Sommer.[113] He began by simply sitting down quite close to (6 inches or 20 centimeters) other men who were sitting alone. The men happened to be mental patients at the hospital where Sommer worked, but, as we shall see, the results are similar for other groups of people.

After 1 minute, 30 percent of Sommer's participants had moved from their place. After 10 minutes, 55 percent had moved away. Each man whose space was invaded was matched with another seated man whose space was not invaded. After 1 and 10 minutes, 0 percent and 25 percent, respectively, of these controls had moved. We might infer, then, that when someone sits down within your personal space, there is a good chance you will find a reason to leave sooner than you would have otherwise. Later, one of Sommer's female students invaded the personal space of women studying alone in a university library. The closer she sat, the faster they left. Incidentally, less than 2 percent of all the individuals in these studies responded verbally by asking the invader to move or leave.

Next, the status of the invader was examined.[114] When the invader was dressed as a faculty member, students fled more quickly than when the invader was dressed as a student. In a shopping mall, women left their seats early when a low-status person sat close to them, but men did not.[115]

A person's sex-role orientation also plays a role. Men with traditional masculine orientations and women with androgynous (balanced masculine-feminine) orientations dislike frontal invasion of their space more than androgynous men and traditional feminine women.[116]

In these studies, negative affect is implied but not directly studied. Another study examined the feelings of individuals who were asked to stand too close, about normal, or too far from another individual.[117] Participants reported feeling most negative about the far distance. They said that they felt no worse about the close distance (12 inches or 30 centimeters) than about the normal distance (24 inches or 60 centimeters). This was true for pairs who were strangers as well as for pairs who were friends. The finding that very close distances do not lead to negative emotions is surprising. Emotion was measured by self-report in their study; it is possible that the subjects simply did not report their true feelings.

Other studies indicate that when friends come very close, positive rather than negative feelings often result,[118] but when the invader is a stranger, particularly a male stranger, negative feelings are aroused.[119]

Attraction

Intuitively, we might hypothesize that appropriate use of space leads to attraction—or at least does not harm personal relations—whereas inappropriate use of space leads to dislike. Research does support this conclusion, but a problematic word in this simple statement is *appropriate*. The very same distance may be appropriate for one person but not for another. For example, men tolerate invasions by women more than women tolerate invasions by men.[120] What about the *angle* of the approach? In an early study, a researcher went to the campus library and looked for a student sitting alone.[121] The researcher then selected a seat next to, one seat away from, or directly across from the student, pretended to read for a short while, and then left.

Then, a confederate immediately came upon the scene and asked a few questions about the subject's opinion of the researcher. Both male and female students liked the female researcher who sat very close to them more than they liked the male researcher who sat very close to them. Thus, appropriateness of distance partly depends on the gender of the person who invades your personal space. Female students expressed greater attraction for confederates who sat *across* from them, but male students preferred confederates who sat *next* to them.

In a study of nurses and patients, male patients liked being touched by female nurses more than female patients did.[122] Ironically, the *nurses* believed that women were more receptive to their touch. Also, the nurses themselves were more comfortable touching their female patients.

Where do men and women sit in everyday settings? In an observational study, 82 percent of male/female pairs sat across from one another in restaurants, but in

bars, 70 percent of male/female pairs sat next to one another.[123] This may be due both to different seating arrangements in bars and restaurants and to the preferences of couples. Either way, it seems that at a restaurant, early in the evening, couples usually choose to sit in a pattern which, based on the library study just discussed, facilitates *her* attraction. But later in the evening, at the bar, they choose to sit in a pattern that facilitates *his* attraction (see Figure 5–7).

Our reactions also depend on the invader's apparent motives. We distinguish between intentional invasions and invasions others are forced into, such as in a crowded elevator. When the invasion is seen as intentional, we evaluate the invader negatively, but when we think the person could not avoid the invasion, the opposite is true.[124]

One consequence of attraction is the formation of shared or group personal space. Pairs or larger groups walking along a hallway, for example, seem to form a cohesive whole that becomes an invasion-resistant group space.[125,126,127]

Arousal

Inappropriately close interpersonal distance is often viewed as an invasion. We feel uncomfortable; on the physiological level, arousal occurs. This arousal was demonstrated in an unusual and widely discussed

FIGURE 5–7 Male/female seating reflects mutual attraction.

study.[128] The researchers hypothesized that arousal due to spatial invasion would manifest itself in altered patterns of urination. In a lavatory, a hidden camera measured how long it took men to begin urinating and how long they urinated when they were alone, when another man stood one urinal away, and when another man stood at the adjacent urinal. As predicted, urination took longer to begin and lasted less time when someone stood closer. Arousal due to closeness seems to have literally tensed up the subjects.

Social Influence

Can an individual influence someone merely by adjusting the interpersonal distance? Research participants were shown films of discussions. Actors who used smaller interpersonal distances and less direct orientations in the film (more side by side than face to face) were judged by the film observers to be more persuasive.[129] Notice that this study does not show that individuals who stand close are actually more persuasive—but merely that outside observers *perceive* that they were more persuasive.

Another study assessed the actual change in listeners' attitudes when a speaker voiced an opinion at close, medium, and far distances.[130] The far speaker had the most influence, contrary to the earlier conclusion. Possibly, far speakers are be more persuasive because listeners are less guarded when the persuader is beyond normal interpersonal distance for persuasion. The two studies illustrate, however, that perceptions do not always match behavior.

Attribution and Impression Formation

Consider the following film scene. You see a man sitting at his desk in an office, sorting through papers. Another man knocks at the door and enters. In one version of the film, the second man begins to speak to the first man from just inside the door. In the second version, he walks over to the desk, produces some papers, and then begins to speak. Observers of this film judge the visiting man to be a subordinate if he stays just inside the door, but more equal in status to the other man if he walks over to the desk.[131]

In a later study, subjects engaged in a discussion with someone who happened to be a confederate.[132] The confederate sat at four different distances but gave the same answers in response to the subject's questions. When asked to judge the personality of the confederate, subjects evaluated the confederate more negatively at larger distances. When a confederate in another study selected a larger-than-normal distance, participants evaluated the confederate as more rejecting and aggressive.[133] A study of police in the Netherlands reports that when suspects engaged in defensive nonverbal behavior in response to a police invasion of their personal space, the police officer interpreted this (often incorrectly) as a sign that the suspect was guilty.[134]

What if the impression comes first—that is, you enter a social situation in which you expect to meet someone with a given set of characteristics? Participants in one study were told they were about to meet someone who was warm and friendly (or who was unfriendly).[135] The participants chose smaller interpersonal distances for the warm and friendly confederate. Similarly, observers will attribute intimacy to pairs of individuals they note are physically close together.[136,137]

An important point about these attributions is that they may or may not match individuals' behavior, as we saw earlier in the case of persuasive attempts. The man who stops just inside the office door to talk may simply be a very polite boss rather than a subordinate; individuals who choose large interpersonal distances may not have unpleasant personalities; and couples who walk very close to each other may not be lovers. But these studies indicate that observers will form such impressions, accurate or not. What impressions are *your* interpersonal distance choices creating in the minds of others?

Helping Others

Interpersonal distance seems to affect the desire to help others, but again the relations are not simple. In one study, the personal space of pedestrians was invaded, then the invader dropped something. Even when the dropped object was an important one, moving pedestrians whose space was invaded helped (by picking up the object) less often than did moving pedestrians whose space was not invaded.[138]

Even when the invader is not to blame—when circumstances clearly caused the invasion—helping is diminished.[139] This makes sense. We would not expect a person who has just been invaded—for whatever reason—to be overly generous. Yet, in a subsequent study, requests for help were *more* successful after an invasion.[140] Its authors suggest that conflicting results may be due to different attributions by the invaded individuals in the two studies. In the first study, the invader may have been seen as personally unpleasant, but in the second study, the importance of the request was salient; the invasion was not perceived as intentional.

A new study was devised to clear up the confusion by explicitly examining the need of the invader. When the invader pleaded a great need for help and stood near, pedestrians offered the most help. When the invader stood near but did not stress that the course project was essential, pedestrians offered the least assistance. At a relatively far distance, this situation was reversed: Invaders who pled low need received more offers of assistance than those who pled high need.[141]

Not only is this study valuable for the way it reveals how personal space and helping behavior are linked but also for once again showing how variables interact to produce results that are not clearly predictable from either variable alone. The earlier studies reached conflicting results because they each emphasized one variable but did not adopt a multivariate approach.

But does increased arousal lead to more helping or less helping? One study found that those who were invaded did help more;[142] the authors speculated that giving assistance served to reduce the arousal of the person who was invaded. In another, the invader's appearance was discovered to be important: Invaders who look like punk rockers were given less help than more typical-looking invaders.[143] Interestingly, the two received the same amount of help when they asked for help while standing relatively far away. Invasion by needy or average-looking persons seems to elicit a positive or helpful form of arousal, but invasion by atypical persons seem to cause anxiety (a negative form of arousal) and rejection of their requests.

Working in Small Groups

Imagine working on a project with a small group of others. Will the pattern of distances and orientations among you influence productivity or the way the mem-

bers interact? Early research showed that individuals very often say (on questionnaires) that they would select face-to-face arrangements for competition.[144] However, another study indicates that face-to-face seating seems to lead to cooperation, not competition.[145] Male subjects were asked to play a game in which either a cooperative strategy or a competitive strategy could be used to win. The subjects were asked to sit next to each other or across from each other; in both arrangements, the subjects either could see one another or not (a visual barrier was used to accomplish this). Cooperation was greatest in the face-to-face, visual-access condition. So, although such an arrangement is often viewed as competitive, it actually seems to elicit cooperation.

This may happen because the face-to-face arrangement makes the other person very salient. When the other person has so much visual presence, we may be loath to compete, fearing that competition will produce conflict and negative emotions. Perhaps individuals responding to a questionnaire underestimate the emotional power of a face-to-face arrangement; that is why they report that they would sit face to face for competitive activities (the stereotypical arrangement), but actually cooperate more when placed in a real face-to-face situation.

In another study, groups of four men and women asked to cooperate with each other or to compete as individuals while at small or large distances.[146] Their task was to solve a complex maze. When the instructions called for subjects to compete with each other, performance was better at the larger distance (5 feet or 150 centimeters) than at the smaller one (2 feet or 60 centimeters). When the subjects were asked to cooperate, however, the smaller distance led to better performance.

In the previous study, then, placing a group member in a more visually immediate position, even though it was farther away, led to more cooperation. In this study, bringing individuals closer (without a change in orientation) led to better performance when they were asked to cooperate, but the more distant arrangement facilitated performance when the subjects were instructed to compete.

Cooperation, it seems, occurs more and leads to better performance when group members are made very aware of each other either because they are face to face or because they are very close. Competition occurs more and is associated with higher productivity when the competitors are less directly oriented or are simply farther apart. These conclusions must be tentative and limited, but the questions they deal with are very important. Millions of employees work in settings where the seating arrangements are based on custom, fashions in office decor, or no rationale at all. These studies suggest that cooperation and productivity may be enhanced by moving the furniture.

◆ *IN SUM, personal space is intimately intertwined with numerous facets of human behavior. Changing the interpersonal distance may allow one individual to exert social control over another.*[147] *Moving close in a positive relationship may lead to greater attraction, but doing so when the other person is a stranger leads to flight. Impressions are often formed on the basis of interpersonal distances we observe in others, but these attributions are not always valid. Help may be forthcoming when individuals are relatively near others* and *impress their need on the other. Cooperation occurs more and leads to better performance when individuals are* immediate *(closer and facing one another). When they are less immediate, performance is better in competitive conditions. Some of these behaviors change if the other person is of the opposite sex, different in status, or creates certain impressions through appearance or apparent motives. Our behavior is complex! Let's examine some ideas that offer clarifying principles.*

◆ THEORIES OF PERSONAL SPACE ◆

So far, we have defined personal space, described how it may be measured, discussed many influences on it, and surveyed some of its effects on other human behaviors. It is time to attempt to draw together these strands of a complex process. Just how does personal space work?

Learning Personal Space: Social Learning Theory

Most environmental psychologists believe personal space is culturally acquired. However, we should not forget that although many differences exist between cultures and even subcultures,[148] all humans seem to require some amount of personal space. In that sense, personal space is not culturally acquired but is part of our genetic inheritance as human beings. Not every species is as socially inclined as ours. Therefore, in phytogenetic terms, personal space is genetically acquired, but once we restrict our study to humans, the differences in personal space are the result of personal, social, physical setting, and cultural influences.

The only theory concerning the acquisition of personal space borrows from an approach prominent in other areas of psychology. **Social learning theory** asserts that personal space is a gradually learned behavior resulting from an individual's history of reinforcement.[149] Parents and others often deliver verbal reinforcements to children about the appropriateness of their interpersonal distance: "Don't go near strangers." "Give your Auntie Maud a big kiss, now." "Stay close to your brother on the way to school."

Children apparently do learn the rules early. Before they are 2 years old, children stay closer to their mothers in more stressful and more structured situations, and roam farther away in free-play situations.[150] By the age of 3, children have already learned to stay further from boys than girls, a pattern that generally holds throughout life.[151] By the age of 4, children already follow at least four personal space rules.[152]

1. Boys keep greater distances from boys than girls do from girls.
2. Children stay closer to acquaintances than to strangers.
3. Children stay closer together in a formal setting (such as the teacher's office) than in an informal setting (such as their own playroom).
4. If another child is a stranger and the setting is formal, children keep a larger distance than they would from the same stranger in an informal setting. But if the other child is a friend and the setting is formal, they keep a smaller distance than they would even in an informal setting (see Figure 5–8).

We also apparently learn some unfortunate prejudices, such as ageism, by the time we go to school. For instance 6-year-olds (but not 4-year-olds) choose large distances from elderly persons (particularly elderly women) than from adults who are not elderly.[153] If we learn this much so young, consider the number of personal space rules we must know by adulthood.

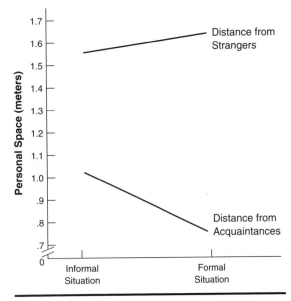

FIGURE 5–8 Even by age 4, children choose different interpersonal distances depending on the situation (formal versus informal) and their relationship with another child (an acquaintance versus a stranger).

Affiliative-Conflict Theory

Without a doubt, the most fertile theory about the function of personal space was originally formulated by Michael Argyle and Janet Dean.[154] Like optimal stimulation theory, the central idea is that we have a balance point; the difference is that instead of balancing immediate sensations such as brightness or odor, we balance our social needs.

Affiliative-conflict theory maintains that, like cold porcupines, we have conflicting social motives—a desire to draw closer to others and, at the same time, a desire to move away from others. These conflicting tendencies arise because we are simultaneously attracted to others or want information from them but also wish to retain our individuality and freedom or may not want to reveal information about ourselves to others.

In several nonverbal channels—not only interpersonal distance but others such as amount of eye contact, smiling, and intimacy of the discussion topic—individuals are presumed to seek an equilibrium between their approach and avoidance tendencies. In stable interpersonal

relationships, the various channels add up to a certain level of intimacy, the equilibrium point. If, for some reason, one of the individuals in the relationship alters the equilibrium, then the other individual will, according to the theory, compensate by adjusting one channel or another so as to reestablish the previous level of intimacy. As an illustration, imagine that you and an acquaintance are strolling along to the cafeteria together, chatting about one of your classes. When you arrive at the cafeteria, you discover that the lines are long. You squeeze into a line anyway because you are both quite hungry.

Now you are inappropriately close to your acquaintance; neither of you can avoid the closeness, under the circumstances. Affiliative-conflict theory predicts that the resulting disequilibrium in the interpersonal distance channel will be compensated for in other channels. You might reduce eye contact or shift the conversation to less intimate topics. Affiliative-conflict theory has been tested many times; most studies support its basic tenets.[155,156]

This equilibrium varies with circumstances. For example, when interpersonal distance shrinks, eye contact often is reduced too, but the amount of this reduction depends on (1) whether one of the persons actively moves closer (as opposed to already being close), (2) who is speaking and who is listening at the time, (3) whether the pair are friends or strangers, and (4) whether the pair are of the same or opposite sexes.[157] Eye contact is likely to be avoided when a same-sex stranger moves closer. The degree to which compensation occurs also depends on personality. Individuals who are more arousable compensate less than those who are less arousable.[158]

Affiliative-conflict theory is still evolving.[159] Four recent models represent refinements and extensions of it.

Social Penetration. A major shortcoming of affiliative-conflict theory is its failure to account for certain changes in relationships. When you fall in love, an increase in the nonverbal intimacy of one partner often will be *reciprocated* by the other, rather than compensated for. Instead of moving away when you move close, the other person maintains the shorter distance or even moves closer to you. In general, when relationships are growing, changing, or dying, affiliative-conflict theory may fail to predict individual responses to disequilibrium.[160]

Irwin Altman and colleagues proposed a form of affiliative-conflict theory that deals with these changes. Their dialectical approach posits that compensatory *and* reciprocal behaviors will occur as individuals gradually adjust to changes in their desired level of interaction with others.[161,162]

Limits of Compensation. Does the basic notion that people will compensate for inappropriate distances work at *any* distance? John Aiello and colleagues have shown that compensation processes do not work well outside a certain range of distances[163,164] (see Figure 5–9). This is partly due to growing discomfort as interpersonal distance becomes more and more inappropriate.

In one study, observers were shown videotapes of pairs interacting at different distances. The observers judged the degree of comfort that individuals in the film would feel at the different distances. Maximum comfort was perceived at a moderate distance; at shorter and longer distances, the comfort ratings declined.[165] Outside a **critical discomfort region,** the usual channels cannot easily be used to restore equilibrium.

In several studies, Aiello and colleagues have also found sex differences in the distances at which the critical discomfort region is reached.[166,167,168] Males show more discomfort as the distance grows inappropriately *close,* but females show more discomfort as

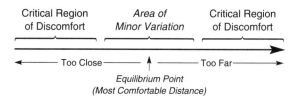

The Interpersonal Distance Continuum

FIGURE 5–9 Interpersonal distance is better viewed as a comfort continuum than as a fixed distance. As distance from an optimal equilibrium point increases or decreases, discomfort grows. Compensatory behaviors (such as averting one's eyes or changing the topic of conversation) can ameliorate mild discomfort from distances that are somewhat too small or large, but not the greater discomfort caused by very large or very small interpersonal distances.

the distance grows inappropriately *far.* Women who were too far away from the other person had greater difficulty using any of the other channels to reestablish equilibrium.

Arousal Cognition. In most versions of affiliative-conflict theory, compensation and reciprocation are believed to occur at a very low level of cognitive awareness. However, not all theories discount the role of cognitive processes. If you move too close to someone, you become aroused. There is nothing surprising about this arousal; the only mystery might be whether the arousal is negatively toned (annoyance-anger) or positively toned (pleasure-sexual).

Miles Patterson, the chief spokesperson for the arousal approach, believes that changes in arousal have a cognitive component. He asserts that we are aware of changes in our arousal and we tend to label that change positively or negatively. Patterson predicts that arousal shifts accompanied by positive affect will lead to reciprocation. Only negatively labeled arousal-shifts, according to Patterson, lead to the compensatory behaviors described by Argyle and Dean in their affiliative-conflict theory.

Approach Avoidance. Argyle and Dean's original formulation of affiliative-conflict theory suggested that we use interpersonal distance (and other nonverbal behaviors) to balance conflicting desires to approach and to avoid the other person. Eric Knowles examined this assumption more closely and postulated three clarifications of the approach-avoidance assumption.[169,170] These clarifications, by the way, also represent a more articulate definition of the comfort concept used by early theorists.

1. Nearly every interpersonal situation involves avoidance tendencies. Even in rewarding relationships, we wish to avoid getting *too* close, involved, or committed.
2. Some interpersonal situations result in approach tendencies; we do want to become involved with some individuals.
3. Discomfort in interpersonal situations results from a discrepancy between approach and avoidance tendencies.

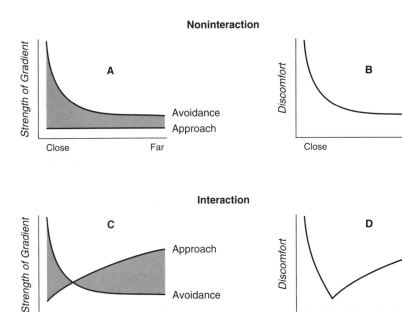

Noninteraction

A — Strength of Gradient / Close — Far — Avoidance / Approach

B — Discomfort / Close — Far

Interaction

C — Strength of Gradient / Close — Far — Approach / Avoidance

D — Discomfort / Close — Far

FIGURE 5–10 A more complex view of personal space holds that discomfort depends on whether we are involved in an interaction with the other person and on the strength of our approach and avoidance tendencies toward the other person. When we are *not* interacting with the other person (*diagrams A and B*), discomfort does not increase as distance increases. However, when we *are* interacting with the other (*diagrams C and D*), discomfort is lowest at an optimal middle distance; we become *more* uncomfortable when the distance grows too large.

These clarifications are shown in Figure 5–10. In interpersonal situations, individuals who are near one another may be interacting or not (external forces may have put them in proximity, such as in a crowded elevator, bus, or room). The shaded areas in diagrams A and C represent the discrepancy between approach and avoidance tendencies at close and far distances. Diagrams B and D depict the resultant discomfort experienced by a person at these distances.

◆ **IN SUM,** *an individual's acquisition of the rules concerning interpersonal distance are probably well characterized by social learning theory and affiliative-conflict theory. More encompassing theoretical integrations have begun to appear. The social penetration model emphasizes the role of personal space in the rise and fall of relationships. The limits-of-compensation model highlights the outer limits of interpersonal distance, showing that as discomfort grows, interaction becomes more difficult. The approach-avoidance model hypothesizes differences between the desire to get close to someone and the desire to keep one's distance. Discomfort is seen as the discrepancy between the two desires.*

◆ **PERSONAL SPACE AND** ◆
ENVIRONMENTAL DESIGN

In the early days of personal space research, some researchers dreamt that personal space would be the central part of architectural planning. Robert Sommer subtitled his classic book on personal space *The Behavioral Basis of Design.* Only five years later, however, Sommer realized that personal space will never be *the* cornerstone of architecture.[171] There are simply too many other considerations: Local regulations, sites, other social factors, budgets, materials, and aesthetics are also important.

Personal space may not be the essence of environmental design, but it is one important consideration among others. Edward Hall remarked that research on interpersonal distance cannot tell an architect how to design a building, but it certainly can provide the architect with information that can be worked into a design. Designers have become very much more sensitive to the spatial needs of their clients since Sommer's and Hall's books were published.

A number of researchers have specifically examined the role of personal space in the built environment. Most of these studies have concentrated on personal space as reflected in seating arrangements in such public spaces as libraries, airports, schools, offices, and restaurants. Most research has centered on the effect of furniture arrangements on social interaction. Some arrangements seem to foster social interaction and others seem to hinder it. Here are some case studies of personal space in architectural design.

Sociopetal and Sociofugal Arrangements

An insightful psychiatrist, Humphrey Osmond, coined the terms **sociopetal setting** to describe settings that facilitate social interaction and **sociofugal setting** to describe settings that discourage social interaction.[172] Osmond himself did not restrict the terms to seating arrangements. He describes, for example, hallways as sociofugal and circular rooms as sociopetal. Most subsequent research, however, has emphasized the sociopetal or sociofugal qualities of seating arrangements.

A typical sociopetal arrangement is the dining table in most homes, where family members sit around the table facing one another. A typical sociofugal arrangement is a set of chairs bolted so that chair occupants face outward, away from one another, in different directions. Most seating arrangements fall along a continuum from one extreme to another (see Figure 5–11).

Initially, we may conclude that sociopetal arrangements are good and sociofugal arrangements are bad. After all, don't we wish to foster social interaction everywhere possible? Not necessarily. There are situations in which a minimum of social interaction is the best pattern. For example, in the reading room of a university library, most of us expect others to work quietly. In some community libraries, however, librarians may wish to encourage users to discuss issues and ask questions. This, in fact, is the very heart of the matter. Neither sociopetal nor sociofugal designs are inherently good or bad. The questions are: Which behaviors are *valued* in this particular setting and Which arrangement will encourage these behaviors?

However, designers cannot expect to cause valued behaviors to occur merely by creating one seating arrangement or another. Research shows that seating arrangements that orient individuals toward one another do not always facilitate conversation.[173] This may

FIGURE 5–11 Sociofugal *(top)* and sociopetal *(bottom)* seating affects social interaction.

be because other factors, such as personality, also affect sociability.[174] However, sociopetal and sociofugal seating arrangements probably encourage or facilitate more or less social interaction.

Libraries

Researchers began one study by simply noting how the patrons of a university library reading room used the space.[175] The goal, however, was to develop an approach that might predict how patrons in any roughly similar setting would use the available spatial arrangements. The researchers recorded which seats were taken, in what order, for how long, and by what sort of user. An old rule of thumb says that after about two-thirds of the seats in a room are taken, some new arrivals will leave rather than take a seat. The initial model assumed that within the near phase of Hall's social distance (a radius of 6 feet or about 2 meters), once a seat was taken, other seats in the zone would be avoided. This was confirmed, but there was also a strong tendency for users to select unoccupied tables if they were available. Individuals avoided choosing side-by-side arrangements, but when they did sit side by side, conversation almost always ensued.

Such data could be utilized by a mathematical model to assist in designing or renovating library reading rooms. If the model is provided with basic facts such as the number of seats available and the physical arrangements of the seats, then information on user preferences or informal rules may be used to build up a predicted pattern of usage for alternate designs for a reading room. Some of the usage rules that emerged from this study are:

- The most desirable seats are those at vacant tables.
- If a table is occupied, the next most desirable seat is the one furthest from the other person.
- Seats that allow a back-to-back arrangement are preferred over side-by-side arrangements.
- When the room is over 60 percent full, users will go elsewhere.

Some universities already use models like these to predict the flow of students from dormitory to cafeteria to classroom to study spaces.

Restaurants and Bars

Establishments that sell food and drink for on-site consumption can vary tremendously in design. Certain aspects of design are controlled by local laws; every jurisdiction seems to have its own bizarre rules about the serving of liquor. But many others are controlled by the proprietor's own version of the clientele's tastes or whether the proprietor's goal is to turn over the clientele quickly or slowly.

Mark Cook studied seating in bars and restaurants.[176] Several of his findings are relevant here. First, questionnaires about seating preferences do not match actual behavioral choices very well. Second, actual seating choices vary considerably, depending on whether the diners are of the same sex. Third, actual seating patterns in restaurants differ from those in bars. Observations such as these provide valuable information for architects who are commissioned to build or renovate a restaurant or bar.

Sherri Cavan obtained her Ph.D. by hanging around bars in San Francisco. Of course, she was not merely hanging around; she was engaged in participant observation of the behavior patterns of the customers.[177] She observed the social isolation and interaction patterns at the bar itself and at the tables. There is a definite pattern to the interplay between an individual's goals and the layout of the space.

A person who wishes to drink alone, Cavan found, should select a distant bar stool or table, hunch over, and stare into his or her drink. Even this behavior may not keep others away; bars are widely perceived as settings that are expressly created for social interaction. However, the bar itself usually has a more sociofugal arrangement than the tables, so the lone drinker has a greater chance of avoiding social contact.

Cavan found that patrons rarely initiated a conversation over a span greater than two bar stools. If two men begin to talk over a single empty stool, they are unlikely to move to the empty stool. But if a man and woman begin talking over any number of empty stools, the gap will rather quickly be erased.

A basic principle of design is illustrated by the bars studied by Cavan. Proprietors of such establishments discovered long ago that some customers like sociopetal arrangements and others prefer more sociofugal ones. The solution is to give the customers their choice. Studies like Cavan's can assist in the design process by suggesting the proper mix of seating for a given clientele, location, and size.

Counseling Settings

A basic component of many counseling clients' problems is difficulty in communication. Schizophrenics typically do not communicate much or well. Neurotics may communicate too much but not pleasantly. Even family problems are often based in communication difficulties. Seating arrangements during psychotherapy may be an important part of success or failure in this delicate situation.

Chairs themselves can be psychologically significant.[178] For example, if a person feels ready to crumble emotionally, the therapist could do much better than to offer a folding chair. The chair arrangements recommended by the leaders of four prominent schools of psychotherapy are enlightening.[179] Freud's approach is very sociofugal; the patient lies on a couch with the analyst sitting at the head of the couch, entirely out of sight. This psychologically distant arrangement is congruent with Freud's belief that such an arrangement facilitates the free expression of repressed ideas.

Harry Stack Sullivan, the father of a more interpersonally oriented school of psychotherapy, recommended an arrangement in which the client and therapist face one another directly, across a desk. Sullivan, who specialized in helping schizophrenics, believed this direct orientation promoted communication with the small part of the schizophrenic's personality that still wants to communicate. However, such a direct orientation may overload the therapist; Sullivan ended his own life.

William Reich, representing a body-oriented form of psychotherapy, asked his patients to lie on a couch with the therapist sitting beside the couch, facing the patient. This arrangement was rooted in Reich's belief that character defenses in individuals with psychological problems are reflected in rigid muscles and other bodily manifestations. Reich's furniture arrangement was designed to allow the therapist to touch and massage the patient frequently during therapy.

Another school of thought is Fritz Perls's gestalt therapy. Perls believed there should be *no* fixed arrangement of chairs. In fact, he would often direct clients in group therapy to move themselves or the furniture around for different activities, such as role-playing or recounting dreams. Perls sometimes ordered clients to abandon the furniture entirely in favor of the floor.

◆ SUMMARY ◆

Personal space is the distance and orientation component of interpersonal relations. It has objective (alpha) and experiential (beta) aspects. The best way to measure alpha personal space is probably the disguised stop-distance technique. Simulation methods may be useful for measuring beta personal space. Interpersonal space generally grows with age and interpersonal coldness. Males have larger personal spaces and psychologically disturbed individuals have more variable personal space. Personal and situational influences interact, so caution

must be exercised in predicting interpersonal distance in everyday social transactions. Attraction and cooperation generally lead to smaller interpersonal distance, but stigma and unequal status lead to larger interpersonal distances.

When the physical setting is less spacious, people select larger interpersonal distance. Cultural differences in interpersonal distance exist, but other factors often operate to alter the simple stereotype of contact versus noncontact cultures. Interpersonal distance may be used to influence others. Inferences about others are often drawn on the basis of the interpersonal distance they choose. Close distances may lead to reciprocation or to flight, depending on the quality of the relationship. They may also evoke helping in others, if a person's need is clearly expressed. Closeness in cooperative circumstances and distance in competitive circumstances lead to better performance.

Integrative models of personal space incorporate its functions as a communication medium that protects us from stress by allowing control of stimulation from others in interpersonal encounters. They emphasize the dynamic nature of relationships, the role of cognitive appraisal, and the management of approach-avoidance conflicts. Personal space is one important behavioral basis for the humane design of buildings. As the costs of construction rise and more of us are crammed closer and closer together, increasing attention must be paid to the arrangement of space. Personal space transactions are omnipresent and crucial to social interaction, yet they are often unplanned for and go unnoticed. At the very least, we can conclude that designers should offer either a variety of seating arrangements or flexible arrangements so that individuals can find comfortable spaces for interaction.

Suggested Supplementary Readings

Aiello, J. R. (1987). Human spatial behavior. In D. Stokols & I. Altman (Eds.), *Handbook of environmental psychology.* New York: Wiley.

Hayduk, I. A. (1983). Personal space: Where we now stand. *Psychological Bulletin, 94,* 293–335.

Knowles, E. S. (1989). Spatial behavior of individuals and groups. In P. B. Paulus (Ed.), *Psychology of group influence* (2nd ed.). Hillsdale, NJ: Erlbaum.

Sommer, R. (1969). *Personal space: The behavioral basis of design.* Englewood Cliffs, NJ: Prentice-Hall.

CHAPTER 6

TERRITORIALITY

WHAT IS TERRITORIALITY?
Types: Primary, Secondary, Public, and More
Types of Infringement
Types of Defense

MEASURING TERRITORIALITY
Field Studies and Field Experiments
Surveys and Interviews
Naturalistic Observation and Unobtrusive Measures

INFLUENCES ON TERRITORIALITY
Personal Factors
The Social Context
The Physical Context
Culture and Ethnic Factors

TERRITORIALITY AND HUMAN BEHAVIOR
Personalization and Marking
Aggression and Territorial Defense
Dominance and Control

THEORIES OF TERRITORIALITY
The Role of Genes and Evolution
An Interaction Organizer
Behavior-Setting Theory

TERRITORIALITY AND ENVIRONMENTAL DESIGN
Neighborhoods
Hospitals

Territory . . . is valued for the way it facilitates making sense, for the opportunity for choice and control it provides, as well as for the many positive associations it comes to have.

—Stephen and Rachel Kaplan[1]

Jane wanted a raise. To improve her chances of talking the boss into it, she prepared a mental list of her accomplishments since her last raise, thought about the order in which to present them, and even planned how she would enter the office, where to sit, and how much eye contact to make with the boss. Precisely at the appointed hour, she knocked on Mrs. Black's door. As she did so, she felt but then suppressed the notion that Mrs. Black's office would be very nice to have someday. It had that solid door, that brass nameplate, those leather chairs, and those little conference tables scattered around.

Summoned inside, Jane realized that somehow she hadn't entered the room with all the panache and presence she had hoped for. Mrs. Black leaned back in her chair with her back to a huge sunny window. Jane could hardly make out the expression on Mrs. Black's face because of the light stream-

118

ing from behind. At the same time, Jane suddenly thought, her own face was so exposed to the bright light that she was squinting.

Jane tried to express her reasons for seeking a raise, but somehow the whole idea now seemed rather lifeless. She stammered out her list, confusing her order and even forgetting some reasons. Finally, although Mrs. Black was pleasant enough, Jane ceased the painful recital knowing that it had not been very convincing.

Mrs. Black said she would "think the matter over." Jane returned to her small work space partitioned off in the middle of many other small spaces. She felt comfortable there, at least, but she did not at all feel optimistic about her raise.

◆ ◆ ◆

Territoriality is an extremely widespread phenomenon. Once you recognize them, indicators of human territoriality are everywhere: books spread out on a library table to save a place, nameplates, fences, locks, barriers (see Figure 6–1), No Trespassing signs, even copyright notices. Despite its pervasiveness, territoriality has not received the amount of study it deserves. There are difficulties in precisely defining it, in actually doing research on it, and even in reaching agreement that humans truly exhibit territoriality.

This chapter explores the meaning of territoriality, describes how it has been measured, surveys the factors that influence and are influenced by it, discusses several theories of territoriality, and shows how it may be used to design better human environments.

◆ WHAT IS TERRITORIALITY? ◆

Perhaps it is best to preface a formal definition of territoriality with an impressionistic one, so you get a feel for the kinds of concepts involved. Julian Edney observes that territoriality involves physical space, possession, defense, exclusiveness of use, markers, personalization, and identity.[2] To this list, one could add dominance, control, conflict, security, claim staking, arousal, and vigilance.

Many definitions of *territoriality* have been proposed, each including one or more of these elements. Most psychological definitions stress that territoriality involves behavior and cognition related to a place. The lack of agreement on definitions is a matter of emphasis—that is, which elements from the preceding list are emphasized. One difficulty is that some elements never are actually manifested by the territory holder, although the potential for them to be manifested is clear. For example, a key element in many definitions is defense of a territory. Yet, some territories are never challenged, so that the individual in control of the territory is never actually forced to defend it.

FIGURE 6–1 Territoriality in the form of steel.

JULIAN EDNEY
has written some of the most insightful articles on the nature of territoriality.

Territories may be controlled by individuals or by groups; they are usually physical (but some theorists have considered ideas as territories, as in the notion of copyrights or patents); and they consist of space (but some theorists consider objects that individuals possess and defend to be territories). We ordinarily think of large areas (e.g., cities or nations) as territories, but individuals and small groups of people may respond in a territorial manner only to small-scale settings (e.g., a room or a residential block).[3]

A simple formal definition, therefore, is not easy to offer, but the following will serve as our operating definition: **Territoriality** is a pattern of behavior and attitudes held by an individual or group that is based on perceived, attempted, or actual control of a definable physical space, object, or idea that may involve habitual occupation, defense, personalization, and marking of it. **Marking** means placing an object or substance in a space to indicate one's territorial intentions. Male dogs mark fire hydrants. Cafeteria diners leave coats or books on a chair or table. Prospectors stake claims. **Personalization** means marking in a manner that indicates one's identity. Employees decorate their work spaces with pictures and mementos. Some car owners purchase vanity licence plates. Gang graffiti is a way of saying "We control this area."

Types: Primary, Secondary, Public, and More

There are millions of territories in the world; some are large, others are small, some are nested within others, and some are shared. To understand how territoriality works, it is useful to find a system for classifying territories. If a good system is discovered, we can then study selected territories of a given type and reasonably assume that our findings apply to other territories of the same type. The two main systems that have been proposed overlap and can both be described as varying in centrality,[4] the degree to which the territory is psychologically important to us.

The Altman System. One system of classifying territories was developed by Irwin Altman.[5] A key element in Altman's typology is the degree of privacy, affiliation, or accessibility allowed by each type. **Primary territories** are spaces owned by individuals or primary groups, controlled on a relatively permanent basis by them, and central to their daily lives (see Figure 6–2). Examples include your bedroom or a family's dwelling. The psychological importance of a primary territory to its occupant(s) is always high.

Secondary territories are less important to us than primary territories, but they do possess moderate significance to their occupants. A person's desk at work, favorite restaurant, locker in the gym, and home playing field are examples. Control of these territories is less essential to the current occupant and is more likely to change, rotate, or be shared with strangers.

Public territories are areas open to anyone in good standing with the community. Beaches, sidewalks, hotel lobbies, trains, stores, and ski slopes are public territories. Occasionally, because of discrimination or unacceptable behavior, public territories are closed to certain individuals. Bars and taverns, for example, are public territories to anyone of drinking age. However, someone who causes trouble may be banned from a bar. Bouncers are agents of territoriality. In contrast to primary territories, which generally are closed to outsiders, public territories are open to all outsiders who are not specifically excluded.

Altman describes two other types of territories, although they are not universally considered territories.[6] **Objects** meet some of the criteria for territories—we mark, personalize, defend, and control our books, coats, bicycles, and calculators. **Ideas** are also, in some ways, territories. We defend them through patents and copyrights. We have rules against plagiarism. Software authors try to protect ownership of their programs.

Must territories be places? This is certainly implied in the everyday meaning of the word. However, the no-

FIGURE 6–2 These are samples of one person's primary, secondary, and public territories.

tion of territoriality came to environmental psychology from those who study animal territoriality. Animals exhibit little territoriality toward objects or ideas. Perhaps our reluctance to consider objects and ideas as territories stems from our familiarity with the word *territoriality* as it is used in animal research, where it refers to space. Perhaps objects and ideas are the most human of all territories, in the sense that they are based in cognitive processes that are more developed in humans than in any other species.[7] Nevertheless, it must be said that very little research has yet examined objects or ideas as territories.

The Lyman and Scott System. A typology by Lyman and Scott overlaps, to some extent, with Altman's, but the former proposes two types of territory that are not directly comparable to the latter.[8] The first of these is **interactional territories,** which are areas temporarily controlled by a group of interacting individuals. Examples include a classroom, a family's picnic area, and a football game in the park. Little overt marking of these territories may occur, yet entry into them is perceived as interference, rudeness, or "crashing."

Lyman and Scott also regard the physical self as a **body territory**. This is not the same as personal space, because the boundary is at one's skin rather than some distance away from it. Bodies may be entered with permission (as in surgery) or without permission (as in a knife attack), but individuals mark and personalize their bodies with makeup, jewelry, tattoos, and clothing, and they certainly defend and try to control access to their bodies.

Types of Infringement

Research and experience indicates there are several ways that a territory may be infringed upon.[9] The most obvious form is **invasion,** in which an outsider physically enters the territory, usually with the intention of taking control of it from its current owner. One example would be a spouse taking over a sewing room to install the family's new computer.

The second form of infringement is **violation,** a more temporary incursion into someone's territory. Usually, the goal is not ownership but annoyance or harm. Vandalism, hit-and-run attacks, and burglary fall into this category. Sometimes, a violation occurs out of ignorance, as when a boy who cannot yet read stumbles into a women's washroom. Other times, the violation is deliberate, such as computer pranksters worming their way into others' machines. Violation may occur without the infringer personally entering the territory. Jamming radio waves, playing loud music, and computer viruses are examples of territorial violation.

Infringement sometimes depends on one's perspective. For example, court orders for searches and seizures are based on assumptions about privacy that are not always shared by residents of the dwelling to be entered; the court may not view such entrances as invasions, but residents often do.[10]

The third form of infringement is **contamination,** in which the infringer fouls someone else's territory by putting something awful in the territory. Examples would be a large chemical company leaving poisonous waste in the ground for later residents to deal with, a houseguest leaving the kitchen filthy, and a pesticide spray drifting into your yard.

Types of Defense

Just as there are a variety of ways to infringe on territories, there are different ways to defend them. However, we should remember that territories are not always infringed and that when they are infringed, they are not always defended. According to Mark Knapp, six factors affect whether, and how much, territory holders respond to infringement.[11]

1. *Who* is the infringer? Friends and peers, for example, are more often welcome (we may not even think of their entrance as an infringement) than strangers and individuals who are different from ourselves in some important way. One study even shows that infringement by the right person can have positive consequences. Women on beaches were asked how often their territory was invaded by men.[12] On average, the women reported about one invasion per visit. Many intrusions were unwanted (over half the women said they wanted to dissuade men from approaching), yet quite a number of intrusions resulted in dates and 10 percent of the women were currently going out with someone who had encroached on their beach territory!

2. *Why* did the intruder infringe? Some infringements are accidental and some are made by individuals who honestly did not know their mistake, but others are perceived as intentional. Obviously, we will react more strongly in the later instance.

3. *Which type* of territory was invaded? Primary territories and body territories, for example, are likely to elicit stronger defensive reactions to intrusion than are secondary and public territories.

4. *How* was the infringement accomplished? A touch applied to a body territory will be defended against more strenuously than a stroll across someone's grass. Of course, as noted earlier, whose touch it is and the apparent reason for the touch are also relevant.

5. *How long* was the infringement? Presumably, defensive reactions to seemingly short infringements are weaker than those to seemingly long infringements.

6. *Where* did the infringement occur? Did it occur in a place where alternative territories may be found? In general, infringements of territories where there is plenty of space (so that the territory holder may simply move to another spot) will not result in defensive actions as vigorous as those in response to infringements of irreplaceable territories. Consider the difference, for example, in your reaction to someone taking your seat in a theater when the house is sold out compared to when the theater is half empty.

Knapp divides defenses into two general types: prevention defenses and reaction defenses. Such markers as coats, towels, signs, and fences are **preventive defenses.** One anticipates infringement and acts to stop it before it occurs. Reactions, on the other hand, are responses to an infringement after it actually happens. Examples of **reaction defenses** range from slamming doors and physically striking out at the infringer to court actions for patent or copyright violations, or simply occupying a place (such as a pay phone) longer than you otherwise would have.[13]

A third type of defense is the **social boundary defense.**[14] Used at the edge of interactional territories, the social boundary defense consists of a ritual engaged in by hosts and visitors (see Figure 6–3). For example, you needed a password to get into the speakeasies of the

FIGURE 6–3   A social boundary is a type of defense.

1920s. Bushmen groups in Africa who meet at a border exchange certain greetings before they allow outsiders into their territories. The equivalent in the developed world is the customs office at the border. Social boundary defenses serve to separate wanted visitors from unwanted ones through social interaction.

◆ *IN SUM, seven types of territory may be distinguished: primary, secondary, public, interactional, body, object, and idea. These different types probably overlap to some extent. No one as yet has refined a category system that has a place for every type and every type in its place. The seven types of territory may be infringed upon in three general ways: invasion, violation, and contamination. In turn, territory holders may utilize preventive, reaction, or social boundary defenses.*

◆ **MEASURING TERRITORIALITY** ◆

Territoriality, by its very nature, is nearly impossible to study in a laboratory. Territoriality takes time to develop, and subjects in laboratory studies usually spend an hour or less in the lab. Ownership and control are central to territoriality, and subjects have very little opportunity to experience these in the experimenter's laboratory. This inability to study territoriality in the lab has two unfortunate consequences. First, laboratories offer considerable experimental control; without it, conclusions about the causes and effects of territoriality are

difficult to make. Second, because of the many difficulties of field research, relatively few studies of human territoriality are available.

The primary methods for studying human territoriality are field studies and field experiments, surveys and interviews, and naturalistic observation of territorial behavior. Let us consider some examples of each approach.

Field Studies and Field Experiments

You may recall from Chapter 1 that field experiments are attempts to exercise experimental control and random assignment of subjects in real-world settings. However, field studies, also performed in real-world settings, focus on naturally occurring correlations or differences between variables because the researcher cannot randomly assign subjects or exercise control over the variables. Studies of territoriality provide a good opportunity to illustrate the difference between the two.

Field experiments require unusual creativity and perseverance to design and carry out. A rare example is a study of territoriality and decision making.[15] The purpose of this study was to discover whether being in one's own territory gives a person greater influence than a visitor on the outcome of a mutual decision. In addition, the researchers wanted to find out whether dominance (as a personality trait) influenced the process. They asked groups of three students to meet in a room in which one student was the resident and the other two were visitors. The group was asked to discuss a budget problem and reach a consensus.

Both random assignment and control over the variables were used, so the conclusions could, with some justification, be said to represent causal links (rather than mere associations) among territoriality, dominance, and decision making. The random assignment involved choosing on a chance basis which subjects participated in their own territory and which of them were asked to be visitors. Control of the dominance variable was achieved by assigning one low-, one medium-, and one high-dominance participant to each group of three decision makers.

Dominance did not affect decision making much. Instead, the final consensus reflected the territory owner's point of view in the debate much more than it reflected the visitors' point of view. The results suggest that if you want decisions to go your way, you should try to get others to discuss the decision at your place. This strategy, it appears, works whether or not you have a dominating personality.

In a typical field study, several variables are measured but not controlled by the researcher, and there is no random assignment to the experimental conditions or settings. For example, one study investigated territoriality on beaches.[16] Sunbathers tend to mark off territories using radios, towels, and umbrellas. The results showed that females claim smaller territories than males, and that mixed-sex groups and larger groups claim less space (per person) than do same-sex groups and smaller groups. However, because participants were not assigned randomly to the different types of groups, we cannot be sure that group size, for example, *causes* differences in the size of territories. Some third factor may cause certain individuals to go to the beach in larger groups *and* cause these individuals to space themselves rather closely, so that the group as a whole claims a relatively small space on the beach.

Surveys and Interviews

Another way to study territoriality is to ask individuals about their behavior and experiences. Self-report methods such as surveys and interviews have the disadvantage that respondents may not be able or willing to report their behavior accurately. However, these methods usually have two advantages: The researcher's resources can be stretched to include a much larger number of individuals in the study, and the opinions, beliefs, feelings, and other cognitions of respondents can be studied.

A good example of the interview approach is a study of 185 residents of high-rise buildings in Israel.[17] Every member of 45 families, including children over age 5, were asked about their actual territory-relevant behaviors and cognitions. For example, residents were asked where in the apartment they chose to engage in specific activities (a behavior question), and who, in their opinion, owned various places within the apartment (a cognition question).

Not every self-report technique involves the traditional question-and-answer format. In a study that examined how different arrangements of fences, planting, curbs, and ornaments affected resident perceptions of the property's security, participants were shown line drawings.[18] In the drawings, the different arrangements were systematically varied to find out how each of them affected the resident's estimate of the likelihood that passersby might cut across the property, steal a bike parked on the property, and so on.

Naturalistic Observation and Unobtrusive Measures

A third strategy for studying human territoriality is to observe ongoing territoriality behavior in a careful, structured way. The researcher may watch how children occupy and defend certain areas of a school playground, for example. When unobtrusive measures are employed, the researcher may count the number and location of items that individuals deploy to control a space. For instance, my university's cafeteria is so heavily used that experienced students going to lunch first locate a vacant seat, where they deposit their books on the table and their coat on the back of the chair, *then* go to the food lines.

Two typical unobtrusive measures of territoriality are marking and personalization (discussed earlier in this chapter). If you wished to discover whether some ethnic groups express territoriality differently, you could unobtrusively compare the amount they personalize their front yards. One study did this and found that inner-city Slavic Americans personalized their yards more than their non-Slavic neighbors. The Slavs landscaped their yards more, maintained their houses better, and placed more potted plants in view.[19]

◆ *IN SUM, territoriality is nearly always investigated in the field. Researchers occasionally perform true experiments, but more often, they examine correlations between territoriality and other behaviors and attitudes, ask for self-reports of territoriality activities, or observe how individuals mark or personalize territories. Because each method has both strengths and weaknesses, researchers should, if possible, employ several methods to answer the research question. If only one method can be used, care must be taken to select the method best suited to the particular research question. For example, if the hypothesis concerns territorial behaviors, naturalistic observation of the behavior is preferable to a questionnaire about the behavior. However, if the question concerns territorial cognitions, a questionnaire or survey is preferable.*

◆ **INFLUENCES ON TERRITORIALITY** ◆

Who is territorial? Under what social and physical conditions does territoriality emerge out of the complexities of human behavior as a distinct pattern? Territoriality is a function of personal, social, physical, and cultural factors.

Personal Factors

Sex. Territoriality varies with such personal characteristics as sex, age, and personality. Perhaps the most consistent finding is that males claim larger territories than females. This was true in the beach study discussed earlier,[20] in a study of territoriality in dormitories,[21] and in some earlier studies. In the dormitory study, residents were asked to draw on a map of their double-occupancy room which areas the participants considered their own, which parts belonged to their roommate, and which were shared territories. Males drew larger "own" territories than females.

Men still hold high-status occupations more often than women, and thereby claim larger spaces at work more often. The dormitory study suggests that men are more territorial, even before they acquire higher status—that is, when both men and women are still in the student phase of their lives.

What of territories in the home? Is a man's home his castle, or does the woman make up for her lack of territory in a work setting by claiming more space at home? A study of Israeli families provides some intriguing answers.[22] First, both parents agreed that the kitchen belongs to the woman. In apparent contradiction, however, over 30 percent of the fathers said the *entire* home was theirs. On the other hand, more fathers (48 percent) than mothers (27 percent) said they had *no* place of their own at home. Generally, then, mothers were quite consistent in believing that the home, as a whole, was a shared territory, but that their own territory was the kitchen.

Men delivered a more confused image, more often saying the entire home was theirs, yet granting the kitchen to their wife and also frequently reporting that they actually had no territory at home. Depending on the beliefs in any given home, such a mix of territoriality beliefs could lead to considerable disagreement about who is allowed to do what in which areas of the home.

Territoriality at work seems to vary with employees' need for control.[23] Those who most minded a potential invasion of their work space were employees who most minded taking directions from others who were not their supervisors and those who minded personal space invasions the most—that is, people who resent others trying to control their social space.

Personality and Intelligence. What about other individual differences in territoriality? Are some personality types more likely to claim and defend territories than others? In the investigation of territoriality in shared dormitory rooms, more intelligent residents of both sexes marked off larger areas for themselves, residents of both sexes who came from larger homes marked off more space for themselves, and males who were more apprehensive marked off larger territories.[24] Females who were more self-assured but *less* dominant marked off larger territories. These results suggest that gender and personality play an intertwined role in territoriality.

Competence. A study of territoriality among elderly residents of a care facility indicates that one's level of competence affects territorial functioning.[25] Residents who require less help to get around reported being more territorial not only in public territories but also in their primary territories. Residents who were more mentally alert were more territorial in their primary territories, but those who were less mentally alert were more territorial in public territories.

The Social Context

Territorial functioning has been linked to at least five social factors: neighborhood social climate, social class, competition for resources, legal ownership, and task.

Social Climate. The social climate of a neighborhood appears to influence territoriality. A study of 12 Baltimore districts found that congenial social climates were associated with improved territorial functioning.[26] In more congenial neighborhoods, residents were better able to distinguish neighbors from intruders, experienced fewer problems of territorial control, and felt more responsibility for neighborhood space.

Social Class. Territoriality varies with the socioeconomic level of a neighborhood and its residents. At the lowest level are the homeless, who try to create primary territories out of space that is viewed as public territory by most people, such as doorways, lobbies, stations, and parks.

Next are young adults, who may officially have some space in their parents' residence but cannot engage in some activities they value at home. They often use cars as primary territories for social interaction, disapproved activities, and sometimes as a means of expressing anger and frustration.[27]

In lower-class neighborhoods, a person's house serves as a primary territory, but ownership and control often ends at the front door. Just beyond that door, outside the house, unwanted activities may occur, but the resident often feels control over the space outside is impossible and ceases attempts to control it.[28] In middle-class neighborhoods, a sense of territory more often extends to the yard outside and, to some extent, up and down the neighborhood street.

In upper-class neighborhoods, territorial functioning sometimes extends to the whole neighborhood. I once took my dog for a walk in a suburban California neighborhood and was actively watched by residents and even asked as I walked down the street what I was doing there. Although I had no evil intentions, I soon left and I left feeling as if I *were* guilty of plotting a burglary. The most territorial neighborhoods are wealthy enclaves that are literally walled in and have 24-hour security guards (see Figure 6–4). One such "gated city" in California has over 600 houses.[29]

Competition for Resources. A third social factor in territoriality is competition for resources. You might expect more territorial behavior when individuals must struggle with others for resources. Everyday experience suggests that when cafeteria chairs, space in the library, or any other resource is in short supply, individuals will begin to mark, personalize, claim, and defend territories to preserve their share of the resource.

On the other hand, some **cost-benefit theories** of animal territoriality predict that territoriality is greatest when resources are abundant, because that is when the benefits of territoriality are worth the effort of defending them.[30] When resources are scattered and scarce, these theories say, territories must be larger to provide enough food. The effort of defending such a large space outweighs the meager living the animal can obtain from it. Thus, animals living in conditions where resources are difficult to find abandon territoriality in favor of a catch-as-catch-can approach.

Considerable evidence from animal field studies supports this cost-benefit model, but does it apply to humans? Among a variety of so-called primitive peoples, the model seems to apply in some cases and not in

FIGURE 6–4 This is a residential show of territoriality.

others. Elizabeth Cashdan has supplied some reasoning and evidence, from her study of African Bushmen, that help explain this.[31] In her view, territoriality occurs when there is competition for resources. However, different forms of defense are used when the resources are abundant than when they are scarce. When resources are abundant, territories tend to be small (because groups need not search far to obtain all they need) and defense takes the form of perimeter displays and skirmishes. That is, the boundary itself is the focus of territoriality actively. When resources are scarce, perimeter defense is no longer practicable, and animals might give up territoriality entirely.

But humans, Cashdan says, control their territories through social boundary defense mechanisms in which owner-groups focus on reciprocal access to territories by members of competing owner-groups. The boundary itself is no longer so important; instead, visitors to a territory must go through various permission rituals to enter an owner's territory. Once they "pay their dues," they are welcome to share in the resources of the territory.

Cashdan found that the Bushmen, contrary to cost-benefit theory, are more territorial when resources are scarce than when they are plentiful. That is, Bushmen more often deny outsiders access to the resources they control when resources are limited. If this holds for our culture, too, it would confirm that territoriality operates differently in humans and animals.

Legal Ownership. Another social factor in territoriality is legal ownership. Both renters and homeowners control residential territory in the sense we have defined territoriality, but legal ownership appears to increase the homeowner's territorial behavior.[32] Specifically, homeowners engage in more personalization than renters, although this is not surprising, given the greater commitment of resources made by homeowners.

Task. One more social situational factor may affect territoriality. When we are in a public territory but engaged in a specific task, we may defend that territory more than if we are not doing anything particular. A study of callers at public telephones found that people continued their calls longer when someone was waiting for the phone than when no one was waiting for it[33]—just what you always suspected!

The Physical Context

How might the physical setting influence someone to be more or less territorial? Most evidence bearing on this question has emerged from the observations and ideas of Jane Jacobs[34] and Oscar Newman[35] that led to **defensible space theory**. The theory deals with residential crime and fear of crime—two phenomena related to territorial invasion. It proposes that certain design features—such as real or symbolic barriers to separate public territory from private territory and opportunities for territory owners to observe suspicious activity in their spaces (surveillance)—will increase residents' sense of security and decrease crime in the territory.

Quite a number of field studies have tested defensible space theory, and most of them provide at least mild support for it.[36,37] For example, one would suspect more crime in areas that offer fewer opportunities for surveillance and do not appear to be controlled by anyone. A study of the locations of stripped-down cars supported these ideas.[38] A study of crime in university residence halls showed that halls with defensible space features (e.g., more areas that residents could control and more surveillability) suffered less crime than halls on the same campus without such features.[39]

Convenience Stores. Convenience stores are frequent robbery targets. Those with smaller parking lots and those that do not sell gas, both of which decrease the surveillability of the store's interior, are held up more, as are stores in more socially disorganized neighborhoods.[40] A fascinating study of bank robbery found that several design features are related to increased chances of a holdup.[41] Among these, more robberies occur when the bank has a smaller lobby, a compact square lobby (as opposed to a wide rectangular lobby), and larger distances between its teller stations. These features may also be influential because they affect surveillability in the bank lobby. But a key question, of course, is whether criminals themselves respect properties with defensible space features more than those without these features.

Here, the theory may require some adjustments. These adjustments concern the underlying reasons for the effectiveness of defensible space features. The features are architectural, and we learned much earlier that it is simplistic to believe that the physical environment determines behavior in a direct way. People often interpret the same environment differently, and some difficulties with defensible space theory occur because criminals do not interpret defensible space features as the theory predicts.

Homes. In one study, convicted burglars examined photos of 50 single-family dwellings and rated each one's likelihood of being burglarized.[42] The defensible space features of the houses were then assessed. As the theory predicts, easily surveillable houses were judged unlikely targets. However, actual barriers (e.g., fences and visible locks) had no effect on the vulnerability of the houses; the theory predicts they should. Symbolic barriers, such as extra decorations or fancy gardens, are supposed to communicate to criminals that the residents are especially concerned about their property and are therefore more likely to defend it; symbolic barriers should make burglars shy away. However, the burglars saw houses with symbolic barriers as *more* vulnerable to burglary (see Figure 6–5).

Why? Interviews after the study revealed that burglars viewed actual barriers as challenges that they could overcome; most fences and locks were not actual barriers to them. The symbolic barriers were interpreted not as signs that the residents were especially vigilant, but as signs that the house probably contained more than the usual amount of valuables. If a resident has the time and money to decorate the house and garden, the burglars reasoned, the resident probably has a house full of goodies.

Burglars cannot accurately pick out houses that have been burglarized from those that have not, but they do use social and physical cues in their guesses.[43] As in the previous study, burglars do not see locks and bars as serious impediments, but they worry about neighbors seeing them and the residents' territorial concerns.

Residential Streets. Let's consider the resident again; defensible space theory asserts that both the resident and the criminal are affected by defensible space features. Certain streets in St. Louis have defensible space features, including gatewaylike entrances, alterations that restrict traffic flow, and signs that discourage traffic.[44] Residents who live on such streets are more often seen outside their homes, walking and working in their

FIGURE 6–5 Based on the text, which house is more likely to be burglarized. Why?

yards. Such behaviors may not be overtly territorial; residents may not think of themselves as guarding the neighborhood, yet they seem to have the effect of discouraging antisocial activity. Presumably, intruders are discouraged by this naturally occurring surveillance.

These conclusions are based on naturalistic observations, so they cannot be considered causal statements. However, it does appear that restricting traffic flow may direct some potential trouble away from the neighborhood and make outdoor activities more pleasant for residents. This, in turn, discourages those few potential intruders who pass through the neighborhood from criminal activity.

Different street forms may facilitate behaviors that are more positive than merely driving burglars away. In comparison to through streets, culs-de-sac seem to promote greater neighborhood attachment among residents.[45] Closer neighborhood ties were reflected in greater concentrations of holiday decorations on culs-de-sac.

Urban neighborhood crime can be predicted from selected physical cues, including signs of disorder. In a study of a 48-block area that contains over 500 residences, these physical cues could predict crime better than the estimations of residents who lived in the neighborhood.[46]

Culture and Ethnic Factors

Are some cultural and ethnic groups more territorial than others? Do different cultures express their territoriality differently? The first question has not yet been clearly answered. A reasonable speculation would be that all human cultures are equally territorial, at least after differences in living conditions are taken into account. A related proposition would be that territoriality is merely expressed differently in different cultures.

One investigation of territoriality on French and German beaches[47] was closely patterned on an earlier U.S. study,[48] so that the beach territoriality of Germans, French, and Americans could be contrasted. The three cultures were similar in *some* respects. For example, in all three cultures, larger groups claim smaller per-person spaces, groups composed of males and females claim smaller per-person spaces, and females claim less space than males.

In other respects, however, the cultures differ. The French seem less territorial. They had some difficulty with the very concept of territoriality, often saying that "the beach is for everyone." The Germans engaged in much more marking. They frequently erected sand-castle barriers, signs declaring that "their" area of the beach was "reserved" between two particular dates, and signs indicating that certain areas were reserved for certain groups (families with children here, nudists there, etc.). Finally, territorial *sizes* were quite different among the three cultures, but the *shapes* of the territories were quite similar. The Germans more often claimed very large territories, but in all three cultures, individuals marked out more elliptical territories and groups marked out more circular territories.

A study of how two cultures (Greek and American) respond to litter demonstrates again how territoriality is similar yet different across cultures.[49] The experimenters deposited a bag of litter in one of three places: in the front yard, on the sidewalk in front of the house, or on the street curb in front of the house. Bags of litter in the front yards were removed equally quickly in both cultures, but the Americans removed litter placed on the sidewalk or curb faster than Greeks did.

Are Americans therefore more territorial than Greeks? The researchers say no; the difference lies in the way the two cultures think of territory around their homes. Americans think of the sidewalk and curb as semipublic—or one might say semiprivate—so they clean up the litter in "their" territory faster than Greeks. Greeks, the authors suggest, think of the sidewalk and curb as public territory; therefore, litter on it is not of great concern to them.

Even the study of home personalization comparing Slavic-Americans to their non-Slavic neighbors, which found certain differences (discussed earlier), found *no* differences in other comparisons. For example, Slavic and non-Slavic neighbors[50] personalized their front door with initials at the same rate. Thus, territoriality varies across cultures in some ways but is similar in other ways.

Territoriality is often quite evident in a culture's youth gangs, who must face other gangs on what is nominally public territory. A study that compared British and American gangs found the American gangs express much more territoriality.[51] Does this mean that U.S. youths are more territorial than British youths? Once again, not necessarily. Youths in Great Britain and the United States have quite different living conditions. British gangs tend to be a working-class reaction to middle-class values. Because working- and middle-class Britons do not live in the same areas, the gangs need not establish competing territories in their own neighborhoods. They are not fighting one another so much as they are fighting the middle class. American gangs, however, tend to be composed of different racial and ethnic groups who do share the same general neighborhood. Territories are carved out and defended because the gangs *are* competing against one another.

Finally, one study reports racial differences in territoriality at drinking fountains.[52] Both blacks and whites were reluctant to intrude on drinkers of the other race, but whites were more reluctant than blacks to intrude. Members of both races tended to drink longer when they were intruded upon than when they were not intruded upon, as if to assert control over their drinking territory.

◆ *IN SUM, personal, social, physical, and cultural factors can lead to differences in territoriality. Males appear, in general, to manifest more territoriality than females. Territoriality appears to vary with five social factors: ownership, positive social climate, competition for resources, social class, and task. As for physical setting sources of territoriality, defensible space theory argues that physical arrangements increase territoriality feelings and behavior, and that this increase leads to a decline in territorial invasions. The physical arrangements may be at the block or neighborhood level (altering traffic flow) or at the house level (fences and plantings). Research generally favors the theory, but the evidence is not conclusive. In fact, some defensible space features may work in the opposite-from-expected direction; more research is necessary. Cultures differ in their* expression *of territoriality, although the question of whether some cultures are more* territorial *than others has not been clearly answered.*

FIGURE 6–6   Here is a sample of personalization in a work space.

◆ TERRITORIALITY AND ◆
HUMAN BEHAVIOR

Territoriality functions as a central process in at least eight types of human behavior: personalization, marking, aggression, dominance, control, winning, helping, and inaction.

Personalization and Marking

Personalization and marking occur in a wide variety of settings, including some you might not expect (see Figure 6–6). For example, restaurant diners were found in one study to mark their plates by touching them about three times more often when the plate was served by another person than when they served themselves.[53] Because diners probably do not consciously mark the plate as their own in this manner, it appears that some of our marking behavior occurs out of our awareness.

A similar pattern was found in a video-game arcade.[54] Naturalistic observation of players suggested that players touch the machines to establish territory and touch them longer when others intrude on them. When a confederate of the investigators touched the machines, other players were discouraged from using them.

Of course, personalization and marking are also quite deliberate at times. When we erect signs reading "No Hunting" or "No Trespassing" or "No Agents, Vendors, Solicitors, or Sales Agents," we do so with a clear and conscious purpose. Urban gangs mark their turf boundaries with spray-painted signs on the walls of buildings.[55] We must be careful, however, not to assume that every sign or piece of graffiti is a territorial marker. Graffiti may be mere vandalism, and someone may put a coat on the back of a chair because there is nowhere else to hang it.

Personalization and marking serve notice of our claim, but if they are ignored, we often do not follow through with stronger defenses of the territory. Especially when the territory is a public one, such as space at a library table, when an intruder disregards an occupant's territorial markers, the occupant often abandons the space rather than actively defend it.[56]

Personalization has positive side effects. When residents of a psychiatric ward were allowed to personalize their territories, the social atmosphere of the ward improved.[57] Unfortunately, many organizations discourage personalization. One university, however, encourages it by holding an annual door-painting contest in its dormitories. Personalization of dormitory rooms has also been linked to staying in school (as opposed to dropping out), although many other factors influence such a decision.[58]

Aggression and Territorial Defense

In the popular mind, perhaps spurred by accounts of violent disputes over territory in some animal species or by media accounts of human territorial conflict, territoriality and aggression go hand in hand. At the national level, too, the tragedy of war is all too common. However, aggression receives more attention than peaceful coexistence. Research in environmental psychology suggests that aggression over individual and small group territories is actually not very common.[59] This, in part, is because humans have developed so many nonviolent ways of settling disputes—language to negotiate with, customs to guide behavior, and a legal system to settle most disputes.

This is not to say individuals do not defend their territories. All the nonviolent means just listed, and more (e.g., yelling and dirty looks) *may* be used as territorial defenses. Defense of territory through marking, personalization, and other means is common, but violent defenses are uncommon. One such nonviolent defense is vigilance. In an early field study, residents of houses with defense displays (e.g., signs reading "Private Property, Keep Out") responded to a knock at the door significantly faster than residents without defense displays.[60] As noted earlier, territory holders may simply occupy a public space longer.[61]

Unfortunately, aggression does occur under some circumstances. The more the territory is valued, for example, the more likely it will be actively defended.[62] Many societies even condone violence in the defense of a primary territory. For example, homeowners have been acquitted when they shot burglars in their own homes. Aggression may also occur when territorial boundaries are vague. When the boundaries between the turf belonging to urban gangs is not clearly agreed upon, more violence occurs than when boundaries are clearly agreed upon.[63]

We may speculate that violence is used as a territoriality defense when all other means have been ex-

hausted, when an individual is unaware of alternatives, or when an individual is denied other means—such as when some groups, through poverty or discrimination, are denied equal access to the justice system. Sometimes, defense is impossible—such as when we are too weak to resist an invasion, when it happened despite our efforts, or when it happened while we were away. Invasion leads to victimization or emotional loss that transcends the material loss. Burglary victims are naturally more upset when the burglary includes more destruction of the house and the loss of personally meaningful items.[64]

Dominance and Control

These two terms do not quite mean the same thing.[65] Territoriality has most often been associated with dominance, a social behavior that implies winning. Sometimes, dominance or rank in a hierarchy is closely associated with the amount and quality of territory an individual holds, but sometimes it is not.

Human territoriality may be more closely tied to control, a broader concept than dominance. **Control** refers not only to influence over other individuals but to influence over space, ideas, and other resources in the territory. Control may be *active*, as when control is exercised offensively and is initiated by the territory holder, or *passive*, when the territory holder acts defensively, responding to or resisting a challenge by outsiders. We should think more in terms of control, particularly passive control, when considering human territoriality. Individuals rarely engage in direct attempts to assert dominance, but they often may be seen engaging in nonviolent behavior that promotes their control over territories. For example, in a dispute concerning a boundary between two properties, individuals are much more likely to engage in a courtroom battle of words than in fisticuffs.

Dominance and Territoriality. In an early study of territoriality and dominance in mental hospital patients, the middle and bottom thirds of the dominance hierarchy among both adults and child patients possessed territories on the ward in keeping with their position in the hierarchy. The middle third of the patients had large central territories and the bottom third had small remote territories.[66,67] The top third of the hierarchy, though, had no particular territory—they wandered freely throughout the setting. In one sense, they had *no* territory; in another sense, the entire setting was their territory.

Another study linking personal dominance with territoriality was conducted in a residence for women who are profoundly retarded.[68] The researchers first constructed a dominance hierarchy, based on the women's actual behavior (how often they initiated and participated in social interaction). The more dominant women had larger territories. Women who were adjacent in the dominance hierarchy (e.g., numbers 3 and 4) tended to have territories that were far apart. This practice may serve to minimize aggression; if women adjacent in dominance also had adjacent territories, they might engage in more active competition for territory.

In a study of dominance and territoriality in a school for young male offenders, territoriality was correlated with dominance as long as membership in the group remained unchanged.[69] However, when two very dominant individuals left the group, conflict increased and the correlation between dominance and territorial behavior decreased. Later, as group membership grew stable again, the links between territoriality and dominance strengthened among the middle and bottom thirds of the hierarchy. The most dominant individuals, however, were still struggling and had not yet established clear territories. The researchers concluded that, with more time, the group's original strong ties between territorial behavior and dominance might reemerge.

However, there is another possible outcome. The most dominant residents might have established territories that allowed them to move freely throughout the setting. The important point, however, is that the strength of dominance-territoriality relations varies with the situation; shake-ups in the composition of a group as well as other social factors can strengthen or weaken them.

Dominance and territoriality are not always related neatly in humans.[70] The relation also depends on who the individuals are (e.g., mental patients versus corporate executives), how dominance is measured (e.g., as a personality variable, as popularity, or as the number of interactions one initiates), social dynamics (e.g., how the organization is run), and the value of the territories involved (e.g., sometimes space, as in a mental hospital ward, may not be worth fighting for).

Control and the Home Field Advantage. Does the *possession* of a territory help humans dominate activities in it, to win? We have already seen that decisions made on our own turf reflect our own positions on the issue more than they reflect others' positions.[71] The courtroom is one place where victories and defeats occur. In an intriguing assessment of a North Carolina courtroom, objectivity and equality between the prosecution and defense were not always reflected in the physical arrangements of the courtroom.[72] After observing the locations of the judge, jury, prosecution, and defense of the courtroom, the researchers concluded that the prosecution had a significant advantage over the defense. For example, the prosecution was located nearer the jury, allowing prosecutors to subtly convince jurors that they were literally on the same side in the case.

Further evidence of the value of a primary territory came in a study of asking favors.[73] The favor was a request to sign a petition that advocated a viewpoint contrary to the beliefs of subjects. Subjects—particularly men—were most willing to sign such a petition when they were in a "nonterritory" than when they were in a primary territory. Apparently, a good way to avoid being talked into something you do not agree with is to hold the discussion in your personal territory.

Territorial control also appears to affect the outcome of sports events—a phenomenon known as the **home field advantage**. In every league, teams bemoan road trips. Road trips mean travel, which becomes wearisome, which means the odds of winning are lower. Or are they? Is the home field advantage myth or reality?

Several studies have examined the home and away records of teams in hockey, basketball, baseball, and football.[74,75] The researchers found that the home advantage exists but is greater in some sports than others. In the baseball season they examined, home teams won 53 percent of their games. This advantage is small, considering the legends in the game about grounds keepers "doctoring" the playing field to suit the home team or to foil visiting base stealers and bunters.

Football teams win about 57 percent of home games. Professional hockey teams win about 60 percent (wins plus ties are about 70 percent), basketball teams win about 62 percent, and soccer teams win about 67 percent at home. The researchers considered numerous reasons for their findings but concluded that the main reason was fan support, magnified by the form of the physical environment (see Figure 6–7).

Hockey and basketball fans cheer their teams in closed buildings; this intensifies their vocal support for the team, compared to the effect fans can have in baseball and football, where cheers partially dissipate into open skies. Indoor venues also decrease the distance from fan to player, which increases fan input even more. A study of booing at basketball games[76] revealed that home team performance increased slightly just after booing by its fans and that visiting teams committed more fouls and generally performed worse just after the booing. A different study found that found that pro basketball stars (but not nonstars) have fewer fouls called on them during home games.[77] Both studies suggest that referees are influenced by crowds. The home advantage is stronger, then, for indoor sports than for outdoor sports. A study of hockey games showed that the home advantage grew when the *density* of the crowd increased.[78]

The home field advantage can backfire when the pressure to succeed becomes extreme. In baseball's World Series, home teams win over 60 percent of first and second games but less than 40 percent of seventh games, when the whole series is decided in one game.[79] Yet, during the regular season, the home advantage generally is stronger for better teams—those who end up in the World Series. A baseball researcher sorted baseball teams by overall winning percentages and found that those winning 55 to 65 percent of their games averaged 12 percent more wins at home than on the road, but teams winning 33 to 43 percent averaged only 7 percent more wins at home.[80] This finding underscores the connections between dominance, control, and territoriality. Even mediocre teams benefit from the home field advantage, but the strength of generally strong teams is magnified at home (see Figure 6–8).

In everyday life, we notice that visitors and hosts enact rituals; the visitor is usually expected to act in a restrained, cautious manner, and the host usually encourages the visitor to feel at home. The implicit assumption on both sides is that the host is in control. The guest's

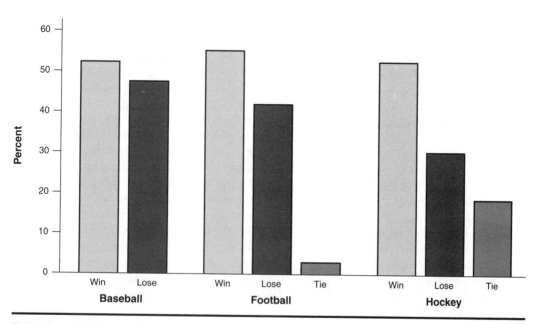

FIGURE 6–7 Outcomes of home games in three professional sports. Differences in winning percentages are not large, but with ties as possible outcomes to their games, hockey teams lose much less often at home than do baseball teams.

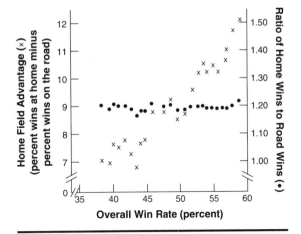

FIGURE 6-8 A puzzle based on the home team effect. Baseball teams with better records win more often at home (see xs). However, this is not simply because they have a better overall win record: Winning teams win a greater percentage of games at home than their overall record would predict, and losing teams win less at home than their overall record would predict (data from James, 1984; see note 80). Even more striking (see dots on graph), the home field advantage appears to be a constant. Regardless of their overall record, baseball teams win, on average, about 21 percent more home than away games.

role is to acknowledge this; the host's role is to graciously surrender it.

Nevertheless, the visitor's maxim is "When in Rome, do as the Romans do." Sometimes we are *too* ready to yield to arrangements in places we do not control. In a study of environmental awareness, I found that students working on a lab assignment for a psychology class went to great lengths not to disturb a furniture arrangement that caused them considerable difficulty in moving around the lab.[81] The students' lack of action was partly due to their lack of awareness of the physical environment, but some of them later pointed out that "one does not move furniture around except in one's own home." In the lab, there were no prohibitions against moving furniture around, especially if it was interfering with progress in the lab. Yet, the students felt that "they" (the lab instructor? the janitor? the university President?) must have wanted the furniture that way. The students felt such a lack of control that they did

not even raise the issue of restructuring the furniture arrangements, let alone actively lobby for a change or change things around themselves.

An important consideration in the relation between territory and control, therefore, is whether the territory is primary, secondary, or public. The students in the lab, for example, clearly viewed the lab as a secondary or, more likely, as a public territory rather than a primary one.

We should have most control in primary territories. Do individuals at least believe they exert more control in primary territories than in the other kinds? Subjects in one study did report feeling more in control when they occupied primary territories (e.g., bedrooms with the doors closed and bathrooms) than they did in secondary territories (e.g., their backyards and the sidewalks in front of their houses) or in public territories (e.g., streets, supermarkets, and recreation areas).[82]

One study investigated when pedestrians are more likely to invade the little interactional territory formed by two people talking. Pedestrians were more likely to walk between the two conversing people when they were in a secondary territory (their own dormitory corridor) than when they were in a public territory (a classroom building corridor).[83]

◆ *IN SUM, we have seen that territoriality is associated with a variety of behaviors: personalization, marking, aggression, dominance, control, winning, helping, and inaction. Personalization and marking are very common (but territoriality is not the basis of every public display). It may occur with or without awareness, it may signal ownership but does not always lead to active defense, and it seems to offer psychological benefits to the territory holder beyond merely informing the world of a territorial claim.*

Popular writers have exaggerated the relation between overt aggression and territoriality in humans; some are too willing to generalize from animal behavior. This does not mean humans never defend territory violently (witness the hundreds of wars and assaults that occur at the national and individual levels), but many more everyday disputes are settled nonviolently.

Territoriality does seem to help us control and dominate our territories, but this end is usually accomplished through passive means that do not involve direct bullying of others. In the home field advantage in sports, for exam-

ple, fan support or perhaps "doctoring" the field is used in attempts to control the outcome of the game. Also, we are unlikely to alter furniture or other arrangements in public territories because we do not see them as our own, even when no one else claims the space as a primary territory.

◆ THEORIES OF TERRITORIALITY ◆

What governs territoriality? The ancient debate in psychology between inheritance and learning as determinants of behavior may be more relevant to territoriality than to any other topic in this book. Are our territorial tendencies part of our genetic heritage?

The Role of Genes and Evolution

Many animal species are clearly territorial with a heavy genetic influence, leading some theorists to treat human territoriality as a direct extension of animal territoriality. In the forefront of this approach are many European ethologists and some North American writers who have been quick to suggest an instinctual basis for human territoriality.[84] The ethological approach, whether applied to animals or humans, emphasizes the aggression and defense elements of territoriality.

There is no proof that human territoriality is inherited, despite the parallels that can be drawn between some human behaviors and some animal behaviors. Indeed, some writers appear to overlook the fact that not all animals are territorial; we could, with equal justification, point to our mammalian heritage in support of the position that humans are *not* instinctually territorial. For example, some of the great apes, our closest relatives, exhibit very little territoriality.

Ralph Taylor has carefully considered the possible evolutionary and genetic bases for human territoriality.[85] His view is that territorial functioning is a product of our evolutionary heritage. Our ancient history as bands of hunters roaming the African savannah shaped the general nature of our present territoriality. According to Taylor, because territoriality developed in a small group context, even today it applies only to individuals and small groups, not to large aggregates such as nations.

Taylor maintains that the behavior processes involved in our present territorial functioning are similar in form to those evolved long ago, even if they no longer

RALPH TAYLOR
is a leading researcher of territoriality and urban neighborhoods.

serve quite the same purpose or have the same consequences. Finally, Taylor asserts that the evolutionary basis of territoriality does *not* mean that it is "hard-wired" into our genes. Instead of concentrating on aggression and defense, environmental psychologists tend to focus on habitual occupation of space and how it affects the social behavior and cognition of occupants and visitors.

An Interaction Organizer

Recall that human territoriality is not often characterized by attempts to dominate visitors.[86] Rather, according to Julian Edney and others, human territoriality serves to *organize* human behavior so that violence, aggression, and overt domination are unnecessary. When an individual or group controls a setting, many aspects of behavior become ordered, including choice of activities, access to resources, and behavioral customs. Many individuals who have been employed by others dream of owning a business themselves, partly for financial reasons, but also so they can organize and control the policies and physical aspects of their workplace. For example, children want their own rooms so that their activities and decorations do not have to be negotiated with a sibling. Thus, one motivation for seeking territory is to have the opportunity to obtain these organizing prerogatives.

Organization and order are provided by territories to communities, small groups, and individuals. First, communities benefit mainly because territories geographically fix individuals—that is, because each of us spends considerable time in specific territories. If community members spent time in many different places, we would have a difficult time locating those with whom we want to interact. Thus, territories provide individuals with reliable access to the contacts they need. The community, as a whole, is better off because time and effort spent in communicating with others is much less than if we had to look everywhere each time we wanted to speak with someone.

Small groups benefit because territorial ownership seems to generate expectations about how visitors and hosts will behave. Clubs and drinking establishments, for example, often have written or unwritten rules of conduct. I once saw a sign erected by the proud owner of a new backyard swimming pool: "We don't swim in your toilet, please don't pee in our pool!" These conventions (particularly those more serious than the pool owner's sign) increase order and security by providing a mutually acceptable set of ground rules on which social behavior can be transacted. As noted earlier, these conventions generally assign control to the host, but the host uses this control to be considerate of the visitor's needs. For example, the host offers the visitor a choice of drinks, serves the visitor first, and suggests where the visitor should sit.

And last, individuals benefit from the organizing function of territories. Because they control social and resource management aspects of the territory's operation, territory holders are better able to plan and anticipate future events. Familiarity with the territory also gives individuals a sense of competence that would be impossible if they moved randomly from place to place. Individuals gain a sense of identity by simply being spatially separate from others. Also, individuals typically enact long chains of related behaviors. When these occur in a single place, they are better organized and ordered because of the individual's familiarity with the territory. An everyday example is cooking a meal. The process is much easier in our own kitchen than in someone else's because we know where the ingredients and implements are stored.

Behavior-Setting Theory

Ecological psychologists view territorial behavior from a behavior-setting perspective. The organizing function of territoriality is quite similar to concepts from the work of Roger Barker, the father of ecological psychology.[87,88] For example, recall from Chapter 1 that in ecological psychology a program is "a prescribed sequence of interactions between people and objects in the setting."[89] Other concepts from ecological psychology explicitly incorporate the notion of control. For example, **sensing mechanisms** and **executive mechanisms** (usually a person in control, but sometimes a servomechanism such as a thermostat) examine the setting for incorrect conditions and correct them. In general, the ecological-psychology approach of the behavior setting[90] overlaps considerably with Edney's ideas about organization and control.

◆ **IN SUM,** *theories of territoriality remain diverse and speculative. Ethology, evolution, organization, control, and behavior settings are quite disparate concepts around which to construct a theory of territoriality. If we assume that each of them is partially correct, a future theory that synthesizes them coherently will surely picture human territoriality as an extremely complex process. Despite the diversity in theory, environmental psychologists know enough about territoriality to use it in their contributions to better environmental design. We turn now to that enterprise.*

◆ **TERRITORIALITY AND** ◆
ENVIRONMENTAL DESIGN

When applied to particular design situations, territoriality should be facilitated in the plans wherever it appears to serve the needs of clients. That is, based on our list of human behavior patterns that are linked to territoriality, designs for territoriality should attempt to reduce aggression, increase control, and promote a sense of order and security. A rather bold conclusion, supported by some research and refuted by none so far reported, is this: The more a design can provide primary territories for every person at home, school, and work, the better.

Of course, one important restriction on the supply of primary territories is money; space costs can be high. A second restriction is the policies of some organizations, which require that employees be under the direct surveillance of a supervisor. A third restriction is that some jobs, by their very nature, require that other employees or the general public have access to the individual holding the job. The only refuges of frontline employees are the staff room and the coffee break.

On many jobs, groups must work together in close communication most of the day. Individuals in such jobs may not perform best if each one is located in a separate primary territory. However, territories may be occupied by groups. Such work groups should have their own collective primary territory. In many home, work, and institutional settings, more could be done to provide primary or secondary territories for individuals and groups. Very often, no one has seriously considered how the lives of affected individuals would be improved by access to an owned space.

This section will examine some suggestions for territorializing neighborhoods and hospitals. The design recommendations were developed for these specific settings, but with a little imagination, we can conceive of designs for other settings using the same principles. Changes in the design of larger settings (such as neighborhoods) are more difficult to implement than changes in small settings (such as our own homes). Nevertheless, whole neighborhoods *have* been territorialized to varying degrees.

Neighborhoods

Cities are often asked to block off streets in order to restrict traffic flow through the neighborhood when residents believe too much traffic flows through their streets. Commuters, of course, believe the streets are there to help them get to and from work efficiently. Concerns about children's safety and traffic noise are the neighborhood residents' explicit reasons for the barriers, but the move to territorialize the neighborhood may have less obvious benefits.

Blocking off streets serves to give residents a sense of control and identity. The cars that now move through the streets are neither so numerous nor so foreign; they are owned by neighbors. Because there are fewer cars, residents have a better chance of recognizing strange ones. This may serve to reduce crime because "different" cars are noticed by residents. Burglars who have several neighborhoods to choose from would be better off selecting a more anonymous neighborhood. Defensible space theory would support neighborhood design changes that increase the residents' sense of ownership, eliminate space about which no one in particular feels vigilant, and increase space that is easily watched by residents.

Changing whole neighborhoods, unfortunately, is politically difficult. Traffic barriers, for example, are opposed not only by commuters who are inconvenienced but also by residents of neighborhoods that will experience increased traffic as a result of the new barriers. Smaller-scale changes—to individual houses, for example—are much easier politically, but some of them cost that individual homeowner more.

Of course, the problem sometimes can be solved by creating a different street pattern either when the neighborhood is originally designed or by rearranging the street pattern in a block. One study demonstrated that residents of culs-de-sac believe that they have exclusive use of their street, can better distinguish neighbors from strangers, and have safer and better-maintained streets than residents of through streets.[91]

Hospitals

No one likes to be hospitalized. Besides the obvious reason (that being in a hospital means illness or injury), another reason we may not enjoy our stay is the way space is managed in hospitals. Unavoidably, we go to a setting where we have no preestablished territory. Immediately, this affects our sense of control and security. Even if we are given a private room or our own bed, we are compelled to perform behaviors (such as sleeping, grooming, and discussing private matters) in a secondary territory that we are used to performing in our own primary territories.[92] If we have no lockable cupboard, for example, our usual sense that we can control our possessions is compromised.

The answer is to allow patients personalization and control wherever possible. Lockable cupboards, viewable bulletin boards, and more table space to display photographs, books, and other meaningful possessions are some suggested design changes. An even simpler rule may be to ask staff to respect the way patients arrange small objects within their reach. Some evidence that the creation of primary territories does have a beneficial effect comes from a study in a nursing home.[93] In double-occupancy rooms, visible markers that divided the room into two separate spaces increased residents' self-esteem and sense of adequacy.

As in most situations, however, there are strong pressures against some of these design changes. Some staff members complain that tables are cumbersome, cupboards take up valuable space, and bulletin boards are expensive. Some staff object to the inefficiency caused by idiosyncratic arrangements of furniture and personal possessions. The issue is whether institutions primarily exist for the welfare of the patients or the staff.[94] Surprisingly often, judging by the arrangements of hospitals and other institutions, the answer is that staff needs come first.

Staff needs, of course, are legitimate. However, too often, patient needs are underserved because their illness, injury, and temporary status reduce their ability to voice their needs in an effective way. Yet, although each patient is temporary, a permanent stream of similar patients with similar needs flows through the hospital; eventually, each of us will be there.

The best solutions to the staff versus patient design dilemma will be reached when designers carefully examine both groups' needs and base architectural changes on the costs and benefits to both groups. More changes favoring patient privacy and territoriality over staff efficiency are needed because, to this point, staff needs usually have prevailed.[95]

In the end, the premise of this section is that many spatial arrangements, despite some existing barriers, could be improved considerably so that everyone in a building is better off. Environmental designs that creatively include territoriality can significantly improve quality of life.

◆ **SUMMARY** ◆

Territoriality in humans is a pattern of behavior and experience related to the control (usually by nonviolent means such as occupation, law, custom, and personalization) of physical space, objects, and ideas. Seven forms of territory are identified; several infringement and defense strategies are employed in jostling for territory. Field experiments and studies are best for studying territorial behavior, but territorial cognitions are best studied by interviews and questionnaires. Males are often more ter-

ritorial than females. Certain arrangements of dwelling exteriors and street plans may enhance residents' territoriality and reduce crime. Ownership, positive social climate, resource competition, social class, and task are social factors that seem to increase territoriality.

Behavior related to territoriality is usually passive but oriented toward controlling space. Personalization, marking, and status are used more often than physical aggression. Theories of territoriality focus on its organizing function, behavior-setting theory, and evolution. Designers should incorporate knowledge about territoriality to build better homes, offices, and institutions. The overall goal is to provide individuals with territories that allow them as much control as they are capable of responsibly exercising and as the organizational context allows. When this can be accomplished in a design, territory holders will benefit from a greater sense of self-determination, identity, and perhaps even safety.

Suggested Supplementary Readings

Brown, B. B. (1987). Territoriality. In D. Stokols & I. Altman (Eds.), *Handbook of environmental psychology*. New York: Wiley.

Cornuneya, K. S., & Carron, A. V. (1992). The home advantage in sport competition: A literature review. *Journal of Sport and Exercise Psychology, 14*(1), 13–27.

Edney, J. J. (1974). Human territoriality. *Psychological Bulletin, 81,* 959–975.

Edney, J. J. (1976). The psychological role of property rights in human behavior. *Environment and Planning: A, 8,* 811–822.

Newman, O. (1972). *Defensible space.* New York: Macmillan.

Perkins, D. D., Wandersman, A. H., Rich, R. C., & Taylor, R. B. (1993). The physical environment of street crime: Defensible space, territoriality, and incivilities. *Journal of Environmental Psychology, 13,* 29–49.

Taylor, R. B. (1988). *Human territorial functioning: An empirical, evolutionary perspective on individual and small group territorial cognitions, behaviors, and consequences.* New York: Cambridge University Press.

Wollman, N., Kelly, B. M., & Bordens, K. S. (1994). Environmental and intrapersonal predictors of reactions to potential territorial intrusions in the workplace. *Environment and Behavior, 26,* 179–194.

CHAPTER 7

CROWDING

Rather than attempting to provide spacious gardens or solitude in search of some impossible pastoral existence, building design should encourage healthy, lively contact among neighbors.

—Jonathan Freedman[1]

The best band to hit town in months was playing at The Zanzibar Club. The recent slump in the supply of good music guaranteed that lots of people would be there Saturday night, but Tom couldn't believe the scene when he arrived. Lines stretched around the block. He and Jane just got in as the manager started mumbling something about fire regulations.

Tom was already a little grumpy after a long search for a parking spot, the "special" cover charge, and the seats behind a column that partially blocked their view of the bandstand. Somehow Jane had managed to stay cheerful through all this—a bit too *cheerful for Tom. She asked him again if he wanted to dance.*

"Are you kidding? Not one more person could fit on that dance floor."

Jane tried to improve Tom's mood, pointing out friends in the crowd, telling him about the good grade she got on her chemistry exam, and remarking that the band was playing Tom's favorite tune. She seemed not to notice the noise, heat, sweat, and smoke. Tom couldn't seem to rise above the sea of awful sensations to appreciate Jane, the music, or the boisterous atmosphere.

To Tom, the place seemed unbearably full of generally unspeakable folks. To make matters worse, an old friend of Jane's sat down at their table and the two of them engaged in a marvelous series of recollections of the old days. Tom struggled to overcome his hostile mood, realizing it was endangering the whole evening, but he couldn't escape a sense that it was all too much to take and that he couldn't do much about the situation. He decided to leave before things got worse. Interrupting Jane and her friend, Tom announced that he was going home. Jane looked up at him and . . . .

◆ ◆ ◆

◆ CROWDING, DENSITY, ◆ AND POPULATION

The world is increasingly crowded. Most of us have experienced the frustration of crowded roads, living space, working space, or leisure space. Traffic jams, tripled dormitory rooms, squeezed employees and prisons, and campgrounds with waiting lists are some of the many situations that produce crowding stress.

The World Population Context

Crowding at the personal level, as in the preceding examples, has an immediate impact on us, but it occurs against the backdrop of an absolutely staggering population increase at the global level. Despite many efforts at population control, the world's population curve is nearly vertical; it currently requires only three or four decades to double (see Figure 7–1).

China passed the 1.2 billion population mark on February 15, 1994.[2] Despite its famous one-child-per-family policy, there are so many women of child-bearing age that its population still is rising rapidly—about 21 million people per year. It is true that much of this increase seems far removed to those who live in developed countries where zero or near-zero population growth has been achieved. Despite knowing the numbers, we have a tendency to deny that a threat exists or we deceive ourselves about the eventual outcomes.[3]

Nevertheless, in one way or another, the population explosion is bound to touch our lives. At the very least, scenes of famine on television will upset us and motivate

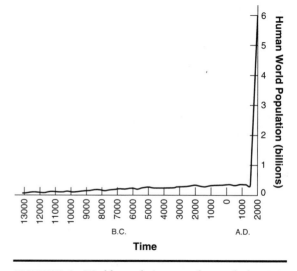

FIGURE 7–1 World population growth over the last 140 centuries.

some to offer food or financial aid. At the most, economic and political upheaval in countries where the populace has become desperate will serve to disrupt lines of supply to, and the quality of life in, countries that have no population problem themselves (see Table 7–1).

So, are we about to run out of room or resources? You might think so, but conservative economists such as Julian Simon argue that all the people in the world could fit into Texas and have 1,352 square feet for each person.[4] Texas covers less than half of 1 percent of the world's land surface, the argument runs, so there must be plenty of space for more people. Also, world popula-

TABLE 7–1 **Populations and Densities of Some Cities and Countries**

Country City	1990 Population (Millions)	Density (People per Square Mile)
Australia	16.9	6
Sydney	3.5	10328
Brazil	152.5	46
Sao Paulo	18.0	38528
Canada	26.5	7
Toronto	3.1	20001
Hong Kong	5.7	280350
France	56.4	267
Paris	8.7	20123
Japan	123.6	860
Tokyo-Yokohama	27.0	24463
Mexico	87.9	115
Mexico City	20.2	37314
Nigeria	118.8	333
Lagos	7.6	129705
Philippines	66.1	570
Manila	9.9	50978
United Kingdom	57.4	609
London	9.2	10551
United States	250.4	69
Los Angeles	10.0	8985
New York	14.6	11473
World (Land Area)	5318.0	101

Note: Some cities have large low-population areas as part of their official boundaries (e.g., Los Angeles and Hong Kong) and other cities border high-population areas that are legally separate cities (e.g., Toronto and New York). To provide realistic density figures, the computations are for each city's actual built-up area rather than its legal boundaries, which can yield misleading density figures. The city densities in the table are computed for the city's "continuous population cluster" with a density of at least 5,000 persons per square mile (about 8 persons per acre), which is equivalent to light suburban development.

tion is only increasing at about 1.6 percent per year. Finally, if we are running out of resources, the price of resources should be rising, in inflation-adjusted terms, but they are not. Presumably, this is because we continue to discover new sources of resources and more efficient ways of extracting those resources.

Is there a world population problem? This is an issue about which economists and demographers will continue to argue. Our task is to understand the causes of crowding and the effects of high density at the human scale—in rooms, residences, workplaces, and communities. At this level, we know that many individuals feel crowded, like Tom, and that high density has some negative effects. But no matter what Tom thinks, you should know that not all the news is gloomy; sometimes, high density can be quite pleasant—just ask Jane. The concluding section of this chapter describes some of the architectural innovations that have succeeded in alleviating crowding stress.

Crowding versus Density

Crowding has an everyday meaning as well as several technical meanings. In some ways, these meanings overlap; in other ways, they do not. In everyday conversation, it does not much matter exactly how we use the word, but environmental psychologists have learned the hard way that it is important to make certain distinctions clear if we hope to achieve a clear understanding of crowding. One reason for this is that we behave quite differently when we are subjected to the different forms of density. Early studies reached contradictory findings because researchers had not yet learned the importance of distinguishing among the varieties of crowding. Let's tour some key distinctions.

Crowds versus Crowding. To early social scientists, crowding meant the formation of large, temporary groups of emotional individuals. These could include swarms of peaceful concert-goers or fair patrons, but more often, they meant lynch mobs, rioters, or panic-stricken disaster victims. The formation of crowds was generally traced to irrational motives or a desire to be immersed in a feeling of universality.[5,6] Although it might seem that joining such a crowd would *increase* arousal, some theorists see crowd joining as a form of tension *release*[7] and others see rioters as people who seek power, complete with safety, anonymity and decreased responsibility[8] (see Figure 7–2). Many descriptive studies of evangelical meetings, mutinies, theater fires, bar fights, and mass desertions during battle were conducted in the first four decades of the twentieth century.

Crowds and *crowding* differ and research reflects their differences. Modern crowding research focuses on an individual's experience, although recent theorists have tried to emphasize that crowding is, after all, a group phenomenon.[9] Crowd researchers, in contrast, naturally focus on the formation of crowds,[10] their shape and structure,[11] their movement,[12] and their control.

One analysis concludes that the key characteristics of crowds, insofar as their potential destructiveness is concerned, are the anonymity and suggestibility of the crowd members and the unpredictability of the crowd's behavior.[13] If the crowd does turn to anti-social activities, the analysis suggests that the best ways to disperse it (if possible) are to:

- Create new stimuli that are stronger than whatever formed the crowd.
- Shift the crowd's attention.
- Make participants realize their personal identities and values.
- Divide the opinions of participants.
- Isolate the leaders.

The older research on crowds usually considered broader social, political, and economic influences. This approach was strengthened by reports of strong connec-

FIGURE 7–2 Most research on *crowds* was conducted before World War II; most *crowding* research was conducted later, especially in the 1970s.

tions between indicators of economic activity and mob violence. For example, cotton price decreases in the southern United States between 1882 and 1930 were strongly correlated with increases in mob lynchings in those years.[14]

Crowd research declined after the 1940s and crowding research increased dramatically. It is tempting to explain this by saying that the subject of crowd research (the highly charged, temporary aggregation of people) is less common now; we do not have many lynchings today. True, but crowds still exist. Remember the 1992 Los Angeles riots? Violence in sports crowds?[15] Street gang clashes? Schoolyard brawls with rings of onlookers? After-Christmas clearance sales? Swarming by youths? Perhaps crowd research needs a revival.

Crowding versus Density. The terms *crowding* and *density* were used more or less interchangeably until Daniel Stokols made a distinction that is now generally accepted.[16] **Density** is a measure of the number of individuals per unit area. It may be calculated for any area from the whole earth (by the way, there are about 100 inhabitants per square mile of land in the world), to nations, cities, neighborhoods, buildings and homes, and even rooms. However, whether it is measured in people per square meter or people per square kilometer, the same principle holds: Density is an objective measure of individuals per unit of area.

Density is an objective measure, but it can be measured at different physical scales. The distribution of population is such that one may live in a densely populated city that is situated in a large, nearly uninhabited area (this is how most Canadians live, for example) or in a dense, evenly populated rural region. For example, in Java, the population density is about 1,000 people per square kilometer (almost two-thirds of a mile), even though Java is largely rural. The room, building, neighborhood, city, region, and nation in which an individual is located probably all have different densities. One key issue in research has concerned the differences that each of these densities have on human behavior. Later, we will discuss some of the research bearing on this question.

Crowding, on the other hand, refers to a person's *experience* of the number of other people around. Rather than a physical ratio, crowding is a personally defined, subjective feeling that too many others are

DANIEL STOKOLS *made an important distinction between crowding and density and has played a leading role in the social ecological approach to environmental psychology.*

around. Crowding *may* correspond to high density,[17] but often the connection is not as strong as you might think. I have felt crowded by one other person in a large room and not crowded when I was with thousands of other people at a concert. Crowding is a function of many personal, situational, and cultural factors.

The relatively small relation between crowding and density has been demonstrated many times. For example, in a large study of households in Chicago, room-level density was correlated with two measures of crowding: the residents' perception that too many demands were placed on them and their perceptions of privacy loss.[18] Both correlations were about .30, meaning that less than 10 percent of the variation in the experience of crowding was explained by density. In a study of Australian workers, crowding and density were significantly correlated with entirely different aspects of job satisfaction.[19] In a study of prisons, crowding was related to physiological stress, but density was not.[20]

Perceived density is a related but distinct concept. It refers to an individual's *estimate* of the density in a place, accurate or not, rather than the actual ratio of individuals per unit area.[21] This distinction is based on the hypothesis that behavior sometimes is influenced more by one's perception of density than it is by density itself. For example, one researcher interviewed campers in a national forest about crowding and density in their vicinity.[22] Campers had relatively inaccurate estimates of the actual density of others in the nearby forest, and the correlation between actual density and perceived density was very low. The campers' behavior was more related to perceived density than to actual density.

Once we perceive that density is high, we experience **affective density,** the emotional response to the realization that "lots of people are here." When affective density is negative, as in "I never dreamed the place would be so jammed," we experience crowding. When affective density is positive, as in "What a great party—*everyone's* here!" **functional density** occurs.[23] Perceived density is transformed into negative affective density (i.e., crowding) when we have a specific task to complete and realize that the density will make our job difficult.[24]

Social Density versus Spatial Density. Although density is the ratio of individuals to area, it may vary in two ways. Consider a classroom with 30 students. The density could be doubled either by adding another 30 students to the room or by slicing the classroom in half and putting all 30 students in half of the former space. Mathematically, these two procedures lead to the same density, which is twice the previous density. Psychologically, however, the two procedures lead to different outcomes.[25] When the number of individuals in a fixed space is varied, we are investigating **social density**. When the amount of space available to a fixed number of individuals is varied, we are investigating **spatial density**.

Inside Density versus Outside Density. Some researchers study crowding at the room or building level of analysis, whereas others focus on crowding at the block, neighborhood, community, or even national scale. Densities inside and outside a single building can vary dramatically. In Hong Kong or Manhattan, density measured as the number of people per block is very high. Yet, one person may live in a four-bedroom apartment, while, in the same city, a one-room apartment is shared by a whole family. **Indoor density** is the ratio of individuals to space inside buildings, whereas **outdoor density** is the ratio of individuals to space outside buildings. The contrast in density from indoors to outdoors in these two cases may be related to quite different experiences and outcomes[26,27] (see Figure 7–3).

Density versus Proximity. The distinction between inside and outside density is viewed by some environmental psychologists as a preliminary, incomplete measure of more important factors: how many others are present and how close they are. The indoor versus outdoor density distinction may be seen as a mere approximation of the key measure—the actual proximity of others.[28] This

FIGURE 7–3 This high-rise apartment building has been called an eyesore and many behavior problems are associated with it.

is because most measures of density implicitly assume that individuals are evenly distributed across the area. But, of course, in most settings, individuals are clustered in groups. Crowding may be more related to the number and nearness of others in such clusters than to area-based measures.

A mathematical formula for density measured as proximity has been developed[29] and refined.[30,31,32,33] The **Population Density Index** essentially is the average distance between all pairs of individuals in a setting, adjusted for the area of space they collectively occupy. Some researchers believe that proximity-based measures of crowding will clear up certain confusions in previous research and provide better predictions of behavior.

A study by Eric Knowles tested this idea.[34] His proximity concept is modeled on the law of gravitation and is part of a larger approach to the psychology of social influence called *social gravity theory* or *social physics theory*. In a manner analogous to the gravitational effects of planets and stars in space, effects on an individual are posited to be a function of mass (number of others present) and their distance.

As Knowles predicted, judgments of crowding closely paralleled a proximity index composed of these variables. From the results, Knowles proposed a more general law of social interaction: The effects of others on an individual will *increase* with the square root of their number and *decrease* with the square root of their distance. Further research will establish whether this social physics vision of density and crowding is correct.

Three Components of Crowding. Many studies have shown that crowding has at least three aspects.[35,36]

1. Crowding is based on some situational antecedent—for instance, too many people (or even one person) approach too close, your goal is blocked by a glut of people ahead, space is reduced by the arrival of a visitor or a new roommate, or needed resources are swamped by congestion.[37]

2. Crowding implies emotion or affect, usually negative.

3. Crowding will produce some kind of behavioral response, ranging from overt aggression (rarely) to less dramatic actions such as leaving the scene, avoiding eye contact, or withdrawing from social interaction.

Each of these three dimensions might be represented by many specific examples. A key study by Montano and Adamopoulos described the main situational, affective, and behavioral aspects of crowding.[38] The researchers used a complex series of steps involving the selection of a variety of different crowding situations, ratings by individuals as to how they would act and feel in each situation, and analyses by a sophisticated statistical technique. This enabled Montano and Adamopoulos to conclude that there are four major situation modes, three major affective modes, and five major behavior modes in the crowding experience.

1. The **situation modes** include experiences in which we feel that our behavior is constrained, we are being in-terfered with physically, the mere presence of others causes us discomfort, or our expectations have not been met.

2. The **affective modes** include negative reactions to others, negative reactions to the situation, or positive feelings. The latter may seem surprising. However, Montano and Adamopoulos discovered that positive emotion is associated with crowding when individuals feel they have successfully coped with it. Positive emotion apparently is part of the crowding experience only when we believe we have overcome it.

3. The primary **behavior modes** in response to crowding include assertiveness (protesting, expressing an opinion, changing the environment), activity completion ("Let's finish this up and get out of here!"), psychological withdrawal (staying, but trying to tune out the crowding), immediate physical withdrawal ("Let's *not* finish this up, I'm leaving *now!*"), and adaptation (making the best of the situation by interacting with others, watching the fun, or making the physical setting more comfortable).

Montano and Adamopoulos's three-mode definition portrays crowding as a multidimensional phenomenon. By multiplying out the factors ($3 \times 4 \times 5$), we see that 60 kinds of crowding experience are described by their model. Although further research may refine the model, it is the kind of specific, multidimensional approach needed to adequately characterize the complexity of crowding.

How Crowding and Density Are Studied

If you wanted to do a study of crowding, what methods or approaches could you take? Three major methods are used, although many variations are employed in the hundreds of studies so far reported. These are the aggregate, field, and laboratory methods.

The **aggregate approach** usually examines the relation between some measure of density and some pathological consequence. Typical aggregate measures include the density of a city, census tract, block, or building. In general, research following this approach has shifted toward smaller and smaller scales. Large-scale aggregate studies now often focus on persons per room,[39] because research at the smaller scales has generally been more productive.

Aggregate studies usually search for connections between density and such outcomes as social breakdown and disease. Any links found must be treated cautiously, because the studies do not use experimental techniques that allow the researcher to draw causal conclusions. Aggregate studies also usually ignore the immediate interpersonal and experiential aspects of crowding. They are better considered as investigations of the broad, cumulative effects of living in high density.

Field studies take place in natural settings, but they usually attempt to satisfy some of the demands of experimental rigor by studying natural density variations in otherwise comparable settings. The university dormitory often has been studied this way; financial problems sometimes require universities to put three or more students in rooms meant for two. Field studies combine some of the advantages of pure experimental designs with a degree of external validity (applicability to everyday settings).

The **laboratory experiment** offers the greatest opportunity for drawing causal conclusions because the experimenter has more control over the variables and can randomly assign subjects to conditions. Laboratory studies have focused on all aspects of crowding, including antecedents (such as high density), the subjective experience, and many different consequences or outcomes.

Laboratory studies may sound ideal, but, in practice, they typically have two drawbacks: brevity of exposure (usually an hour or even less) and lack of external validity. Yet, laboratory studies offer the best chance to carefully observe certain crowding-related processes, such as physiological changes, interpersonal transactions, nonverbal behavior, and other fleeting and difficult-to-measure behaviors. The strength of a pure experiment is that it allows for a proper scientific test of a theory—something that aggregate and field studies are not able to do.

The ideal method is the **field experiment**, which combines random assignment and experimenter control of variables with longer term exposure to high density. Unfortunately, field experiments are very difficult to carry out.

◆ **IN SUM,** *the phenomenon of crowds—although intriguing—has declined as a research topic. Crowding is the experience of the spatial restriction caused by other people, whereas density is a physical ratio of persons per unit area. Perceived density is an individual's estimate of this ratio. Crowding, density, and perceived density are not always correlated with one another. The notions of social versus spatial density, indoor versus outdoor density, and proximity have been advanced as ways to refine the density ratio into a variable with more predictive power. Crowding includes situational, emotional, and behavioral dimensions. Aggregate studies offer the best avenue for examining the gross effects of density on entire populations. Field studies offer the advantage of a real-life setting, but lack random assignment of subjects to conditions and experimenter control of variables. Laboratory experiments offer an opportunity to draw causal conclusions but may lack external validity. The field experiment is an ideal investigation that is capable of investigating effects on individuals and of claiming some relevance to everyday life.*

◆ INFLUENCES ON CROWDING ◆

Under what conditions do you feel crowded? You might laugh at such a seemingly naive question. Don't people simply feel crowded when too many other people are around? Not exactly; environmental psychologists find that many factors lead some individuals to feel crowded and others to feel uncrowded, even in the same objective setting. For example, certain personal characteristics are associated with a lower tolerance for proximity to others. In addition, for any given individual, certain physical and social situations lead to the experience of crowding but others do not.

A major task of researchers is to identify the personal and situational variables that lead individuals to label and experience *crowded*. Figure 7–4 is a basic model of crowding. What we know about this follows.

Personal Influences

Personality and Attitudes. What sort of individual is likely to feel crowded when, under similar circumstances, others do not? Personal control is an important component of crowding.[40] A key aspect of this is **locus of control**—the tendency of individuals to believe (or not) that they exercise considerable influence over their own lives. Individuals who believe this more (**internals**) generally

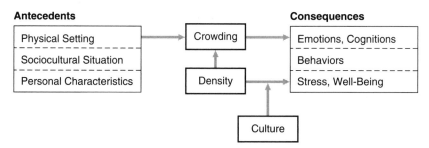

FIGURE 7–4 An overview of crowding and density. Crowding depends not only on density but also on a person's characteristics, the physical setting, and social and cultural factors. Once crowding occurs, it affects—mostly negatively—emotion, cognition, behavior, and well-being.

have been found able to handle the stress of crowding better than those who believe it less (**externals**),[41] although not every study supports this conclusion.[42]

One exception was a study of dormitories where some students had to live three to a room while others lived two to a room. Internals were found to experience *more* stress than externals.[43] This unexpected finding may occur when, under some levels or types of density, externals resign the struggle, while internals continue to fight the situation or search for a successful coping strategy, and thereby incur more stress.

Regardless of how much control individuals think they have, they may *desire* more or less control. In a study that asked participants to solve puzzles in a setting that almost required them to interfere with one another, those who had expressed a greater desire for control in a survey several weeks earlier reported being more crowded.[44]

Another personality variable relevant to the crowding experience is affiliative tendency or **sociability**. Individuals who generally like to be with others seem to have a higher tolerance for dense situations than individuals who are less affiliative. Two studies have shown that this tendency does moderate the crowding experience. In one, participants with higher affiliation scores placed more stick figures in a model room before they considered the room to be crowded.[45] In the other, residents in a dormitory who were more affiliative experienced more stress when they were assigned to a low-density dorm than when they were assigned to a high-density dorm[46] (see Figure 7–5). Apparently, high affiliators find it easier to deal with a social overload (higher density) than a situation requiring them to be independent (lower density).

In another study of high-density dormitories, the crowdedness of students who varied in **stimulus screening** was compared.[47] The researchers hypothesized and found that screeners could cope with the social overload inherent in high-density situations better than nonscreeners could.

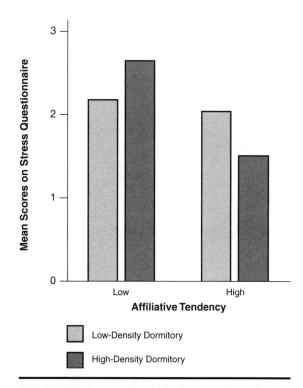

FIGURE 7–5 Stress varies with both personality and density. In low-density dormitories, stress levels are similar for affiliative and nonaffiliative residents, but at high density, stress is greater for nonaffiliators and less for affiliators.

Certain attitudes and cognitive processes also predispose individuals to crowding. For example, outdoor recreationists who hold more "purist" attitudes about wilderness are likely to experience crowding more than those who are not as purist.[48] When the others in the setting can be grouped into categories, crowding is reduced.[49] It is as if the number of others is psychologically reduced when they are cognitively lumped into groups.

Psychiatric Status. India is a country with very high densities in some areas. Does high density affect the crowdedness of people suffering from psychological disorders? In a city with a population density of 200–300 persons per acre, the crowdedness of people with and without disorders was compared.[50] Those with disorders (schizophrenia, affective disorders, and neuroses) all felt significantly more crowded than those without disorders, and the more severe the disorder, the more crowded the individual felt.

Preferences, Expectations, and Norms. Crowding partly depends on how many people one expects or considers normal in a given situation. A person expects throngs of people at a fair, and thus does not feel crowded among many people there. However, that same person outdoors enjoying nature may feel crowded after encountering only a few other people.

An investigation in an Alaskan park found that campers experienced crowding depending on their preferences and expectations about density.[51] Those who *preferred* higher densities felt less crowded; those who *expected* higher densities than they found felt less crowded. Incidentally, these preferences and expectations were better able to predict crowding than could an objective measure of density.

Similarly, a survey of over 3,000 persons engaged in outdoor recreation activities found that crowding was more closely related to one's *preferences* for encountering many or few others and one's *expectations* for encountering many or few others than to the actual number of others encountered.[52] A study of recreational river floaters found that crowding significantly increased as the difference between beliefs about the normal number of floaters and the number of other floaters encountered increased.[53]

These findings complement earlier laboratory findings.[54] When subjects expected 10 others to join them in

a room, they reported feeling more crowded than subjects who expected only 4 others to join them, even though the same number of others (only 2) arrived in both conditions. The results of the Alaskan park study just mentioned suggest that these subjects would have reported less crowding after they discovered that fewer others actually arrived than they had been led to expect.

Experience. Personal experience with high-density situations or familiarity with a behavior setting where crowding occurs may affect the degree of distress that is experienced. The trouble is, these effects are not always the same—sometimes experience helps and sometimes it does not.

Several studies support an adaptation effect; that is, persons with a history of exposure to high density tolerate it better in new settings.[55] For example, one study investigated the responses of bookstore patrons who either were or were not experienced with the store, at the beginning of the school term when the bookstore was very busy.[56] As might be expected, those who were experienced with the store were able to use the store to find information more effectively than those who were less familiar with the store. That is, experience with high density helped rather than harmed bookstore patrons.

This does not always hold, however. When downtown residents of a college town were interviewed, a researcher found that residents with more high-density living experience reported having more arguments with other residents than did residents whose past residential experience was with lower-density housing.[57] Because these are correlational findings, causal conclusions are not possible. But perhaps a history of high-density living does not give residents of higher-density housing the kind of interpersonal lessons that allow for more harmonious house sharing.

In outdoor settings, experience can also work differently. Those with more experience in a particular activity or setting, such as long-time canoeists on a certain river, tend to feel crowded more easily than newcomers.[58]

The resolution of these variations may lie in the kinds or lengths or locations of one's high-density experience. For example, a distinction between crowding in primary and secondary environments may be useful.[59] **Primary environments** are those in which one spends much time, usually with personally significant things.

The home and one's longtime favorite fishing spot are two examples. **Secondary environments** are those involving usually brief and relatively unimportant interactions with strangers. A bookstore and a pharmacy are examples.

Perhaps experience can help us cope with high density in secondary settings, but it cannot overcome the effects of high density in primary settings. Indeed, crowding has been shown to be more aversive in primary environments than in secondary environments in some studies. Also, whether one's high-density experience is in the same setting, the same type of setting, or a totally different setting may be important. Is your experience, for example, in *this* bookstore, other bookstores, or at home? The role of experience needs more research.

Experience in high-density settings may allow one to successfully adapt physiologically, if not interpersonally. In a large-scale Toronto study, men who grew up in high-density households were less likely than men who grew up in low-density households to have stress-related diseases when they lived in high-density residences as adults.[60]

Crowding is a complex experience, and it has complex causes. More recent research shows that crowding can be understood better if a person's prior experience in high-density situations, expectations about a future situation, and the future situation's actual density are all considered.[61]

Gender. Sex, probably through differential socialization, also predisposes men and women to react differently to high density. Research performed in laboratory settings usually finds that men respond to high density more negatively than women; their mood, attitudes toward others, and social behavior are more hostile. In these situations from which there is no easy escape, women seem to handle the stress better.[62]

Possibly this occurs because women more often define the situation as one that calls for sharing the distress; men are less able to share distress, perhaps because they are discouraged from showing emotion.[63] Alternatively, men may handle high density less well because they prefer greater interpersonal distances.[64] Whatever the reason, the sexes exhibit this difference as early as 9 years of age.[65]

In field studies, however, these sex differences often are reversed. Studies of dormitory residents living two

JOHN AIELLO
has contributed many valuable studies toward the understanding of crowding and personal space.

to a room versus those living three to a room usually,[66] but not always,[67] find that women report more crowding than men. A key reason for this reversal appears to be the amount of time men and women actually spend in their rooms. Men more often cope with the high density by leaving their rooms, something they are less free to do in laboratory studies. Women, perhaps more fearful of going out or more involved with their roommates, spend more time in their rooms, thereby incurring more stress and health problems.[68] Thus, the tendency of women to share crowding distress may benefit them in short-term, low-control situations but harm them in some longer-term, high-control situations.

Mood. Will you feel more crowded if you are in an enjoyable or unenjoyable situation? In this case, the answer is just what you would think: People feel more crowded when the situation is not very enjoyable.[69]

Culture. The interplay between high density and culture has received considerable attention and will be discussed in a later section. Far fewer studies that compare the crowding experiences of different cultures are available. Even in an international symposium that focused exclusively on crowding, not a single research paper compared the ways that members of different cultures experience crowding.[70]

One study did compare the crowding of Asians and Mediterraneans who resided in the same dormitory in North America.[71] Based on some anthropological observations,[72] the researchers expected that when space is in short supply, Asians would prefer social barriers and Mediterraneans would prefer physical barriers. Thus, the researchers predicted, Mediterraneans would report more crowding than Asians when placed in the relatively constricted physical space of a single dormitory room. This was confirmed.

Community Size. Do people who come from rural, suburban, and urban regions experience crowding differently? You might expect that people from low-density areas would experience more crowding than people from high-density areas if they move to a high-density area. Indeed, a large study of residential crowding in Chicago found that individuals raised in the country were more reactive to crowding than individuals raised in the city.[73] However, in a Florida study, dormitory residents from suburban homes reported more crowding than residents from urban or rural backgrounds.[74] In general, it may be that moving from a low-density residential area to a high-density area leads to more crowding, but the inconsistency in the Florida study suggests that other factors, such as amount of space in the childhood home (regardless of whether it was rural, suburban, or urban), are also important.

Social Influences

The preceding section surveyed the influences on crowding of characteristics that individuals acquire before they enter any particular situation. This section examines social influences on crowding. Individuals' personal characteristics predispose them to experience more or less crowding, but the influence of others in that setting can either worsen or ameliorate crowding stress. Some of these social factors include:

- The mere presence and behavior of nearby others
- Coalitions that tend to form in small groups
- The quality or type of relationship among the individuals
- The kind of information that crowded individuals receive

The Presence and Behavior of Others. High density means many others are around you, but crowding may or may not be intensified by it, depending on what those others are doing. For example, if the others are watching you do something, your performance is likely to improve or deteriorate, depending on if you are good at the task, what rewards you expect, and if your attention is on yourself or the audience (see Figure 7–6).

For example, in one study, the performance of simple learning and memory tasks declined as the number of onlookers rose from two to eight, even though their physical closeness (in the range of 1 to 7 yards away) did not affect performance.[75] However, if the others are not focused on you, but are merely present, then the *distance* between you and others may be more important than the *number* of others.[76] In a field setting, dormitory residents felt crowded in proportion to the number of visitors they had.[77] Residents who received more visits were also more dissatisfied with their rooms, roommates, and studying.

River rafters (in contrast to an earlier study of river rafters) felt more crowded as a function of how many other rafters they saw, *not* their expectations about how many others they would see.[78] However, more people does not always mean more crowding. A study of exercise classes found that crowding was worse in medium-sized classes than in either large or small classes.[79]

Being crowded can, in the future, lead to feeling crowded. A study of tourists who took a boat ride in order to visit a historic fort found that those who felt crowded on the boat felt more crowded at the fort—a phenomenon the investigators call **carry-over crowding**.[80] Crowding at the fort was not strongly related to density at the fort; it seems that being crowded enroute itself caused crowding at the destination.

FIGURE 7–6 Performance can depend on the number and distance of onlookers.

If others are touching you, crowding is worse than if they are not, even though density is unchanged. In a laboratory study, subjects' physiological responses, moods, performances, and tolerances for frustration were measured during a 30-minute exposure to extremely high density (four individuals in about 1 square yard) or low density (four individuals in about 15 square yards).[81] In the high-density condition, some individuals were separated by barriers (yard-high Plexiglas partitions between bodies) to prevent physical contact, which was unavoidable when others were not separated by barriers.

Physiological arousal increased significantly over the 30 minutes for all subjects, and men's arousal was higher than women's. The arousal of men who were forced to touch increased faster than that of men who did not touch, but this did not happen for women. Men reported being in worse moods than women after being in the situation where touching was unavoidable, but women reported worse moods when there were barriers. Subjects in the crowded-touch situation showed lower toleration for frustration on certain tasks than did subjects in the crowded-nontouch situation. The researchers concluded that touching while in high density is more stressful for men than nontouching in high density, but women seem less stressed by touching.

A field study sheds some light on how the behavior of nearby others affects crowding in natural settings.[82] In the Alaskan park crowding study described earlier, the researchers discovered that the number of others in the campground was not a major reason for campers to feel crowded. Instead, campers felt crowded when others engaged in activities they disliked: "My crowded feelings were directly related to the neighboring campers. If they were noisy, inconsiderate, or loud, I wanted to flee to the backcountry." Another camper felt crowded because he happened to pick a site that other campers frequently walked through. In contrast, others did not feel crowded, even when forced to share a campsite (after discovering that every empty site was taken) because they discovered they liked the people with whom they shared their site.

An important issue is whether the interference with our activities is intentional or not.[83] Interference that we believe is directed at us is **personal thwarting,** and interference we believe is not directed at us personally is **neu-**

tral thwarting. Personal thwarting produces more stressful crowding than neutral thwarting. Your assessment of *why* someone touches you or barges through your campsite is an important determinant of intensity.

Coalition Formation. In residential settings, many studies support the idea that increasing social density increases crowding.[84] Most of these studies have examined the consequences of adding a third roommate to a university dormitory room and have found them to be negative.[85,86,87,88] When social density increases, privacy is lowered, the same number of resources must be spread thinner, more physical interference is encountered, and one's sense of control is reduced.

One consequence of increased social density is that triads sometimes degenerate, interpersonally, into a pair (or coalition) plus one isolated roommate. Isolated residents experience the most stress, tension, bad feelings, loss of control, and even poorer grades,[89,90,91,92] whereas residents who form part of a coalition experience less stress; in fact, they may experience no more stress than residents of double rooms.[93] In further support of the notion that stress is primarily suffered by isolates, one study found that residents of four-person rooms reported no more stress than residents of three-person rooms.[94] Presumably, two pairs form and no one is isolated. Thus, the stress of crowding is moderated by the formation of pairs.

Interpersonal Similarity. A related social factor that also moderates crowding is the similarity of attitudes among those who must share space. A laboratory study of short-term crowding found that when participants were led to believe that another participant held very similar views to their own—that is, they could expect interpersonal compatibility—they reported less crowding than when they were led to believe the other participant held dissimilar views.[95] Crowding was most intense when the incompatible other person gazed at the participant more. These findings were the same in rooms that differed in size by a factor of three. Thus, crowding was significantly affected by how well participants expected to agree with another person and how much that person gazed at the participant, but not by changes in spatial density.

This effect can be asymmetric when the similarity or lack of it pertains to activities rather than attitudes—

for instance, when river paddlers feel crowded by motorboaters, but motorboaters do not feel crowded by paddlers.[96]

The Provision of Information. Crowding is also affected by the amount and type of information one is given before and during a high-density experience. Participants in a laboratory study were led to believe that they were the first of 10 subjects to arrive at a fairly small room.[97] The participants reported feeling more or less comfortable depending on the kind of information they were given about the imminent high-density situation. Those who received no information at all or received messages concerning their likely *emotional* reactions ("You may be uncomfortable because others will be close to you") reported feeling more discomfort than those who received *situational* messages ("Others will be close to you").

In a follow-up field study, researchers gave different kinds of advance warning to patrons of a busy (high-density) bookstore.[98] In addition to situational and emotional information, some patrons were given sensory information (the physiological sensations they were likely to experience) and others were given positive information (that the large numbers of other patrons might make them feel more comfortable and more productive). Situational messages produced the least discomfort of all, significantly less than giving patrons no information or positive information. Emotional and sensory information reduced discomfort for patrons who were familiar with the bookstore, but not for those who were unfamiliar with it.

One researcher even claimed to prove mathematically that waiting in line increases psychological stress[99] and suggested that this stress would be reduced by providing people in lines with realistic information about how long it would take to be served. Just such information is now widely available in banks and amusement parks.

If we wished to put this knowledge into practice, we probably would not be able to distinguish patrons who are familiar with the store from those who are not. If, however, we gave all patrons situational information, it should significantly reduce crowding in a busy store. Accurate, objective information about impending high density serves to validate one's experiences, thereby making it less aversive.

Recreation researchers also conclude that crowding could be reduced by providing realistic information to prospective visitors on how many people are already using various sites.[100] Information may be provided verbally, as it was in the preceding studies, but a more practical alternative may be to present the appropriate information on a sign. Researchers investigated whether signs offering simple directions and information (such as "Pick Up Visitor Forms Below") would alleviate crowding in the lobby of a prison administration building that is often densely populated.[101] Visitors felt significantly less crowded, confused, and angered after the signs were introduced, compared to visitors interviewed before the signs were introduced. The time required to complete the registration process was shorter and the visitors made fewer navigational errors in the lobby.

Physical Influences

The third major influence on how crowded we feel is the physical setting. High density itself is the most obvious such factor, but, as we have seen, it does not always lead to crowding. Other physical factors associated with crowding include:

- Which scale is under investigation (room, building, neighborhood, city)
- Architectural variations (ceiling height, furniture arrangement, window placement, partitions, barriers, etc.)
- Place variations (home, work, beach, etc.)
- Weather

Scale. How might scale affect crowding? Answer the following questions for yourself: Is your city or town too crowded for you? Is your neighborhood too crowded for you? Is your residence too crowded for you? If you are like respondents in one study, your answers to these three questions are not necessarily the same.[102]

If crowding is indeed a function of which scale we consider, what leads a person to feel crowded (or not) at each level? To answer this, researchers measured several physical indices (densities, distances to commercial-industrial areas, freeways, and parks) and several psychological indices (attitudes about urban development, privacy, this city compared to other cities, traffic, etc.).

They found that crowding at the smallest scale (one's residence) was equally well predicted by physical and psychological factors, but crowding at the larger scales was much better predicted by the psychological scales.

It is possible that these results were due in part to the researcher's particular selection of measures chosen to represent the physical and psychological domains. But the relation between crowding and objective measures at the smaller scales has been confirmed by other studies.[103] Therefore, crowding apparently depends on which scale is being considered and the fact that different factors at each scale lead individuals to conclude they are crowded.

Architectural Variations. Crowding is affected by the arrangement of space in rooms and buildings. This section considers studies of preexisting variations in architecture and changes made by building users. A later section surveys the results of active architectural interventions by environmental psychologists, designers, and other outsiders.

Studies of high-rise dormitories clearly show that when the design involves long corridors, as opposed to clusters of suites or short corridors, residents experience more crowding and stress[104,105,106] (see Figure 7–7).

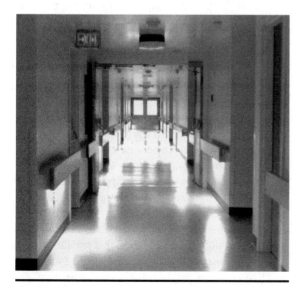

FIGURE 7–7 Long residential corridors increase crowding.

Living in a high-rise building (compared to a low-rise building) may lead to greater feelings of crowdedness and other negatively toned attitudes such as less perceived control, safety, privacy, building satisfaction, and lower quality of relationships with other residents.[107] This pattern of results may be modified, however, by how high one lives in the high rise. One study found that residents of higher floors felt less crowded than did residents of lower floors.[108] This may be because fewer strangers venture to the upper reaches of a building or because views out the windows of upper-level apartments provide more visual expanse[109] or visual escape[110] than do lower-level windows. Upper-level rooms are experienced as lighter and less crowded.[111] However, one study did find that crowding was not related to floor height or to view,[112] so more research on these architectural variables is needed.

Rooms that receive more sunlight are perceived as less crowded by women[113,114] and perhaps by men.[115] Sunlight cannot easily be made to enter north-facing windows, but crowding may be reduced by brightening a room with light colors or graphic designs.[116]

Another architectural feature, ceiling height, affects crowding; higher ceilings, as you might imagine, are associated with less crowding.[117] Could even the walls of a room affect crowding? A study of scale-model rooms of identical floor areas indicated that rooms with curved walls produced more crowding than rooms with straight walls.[118]

Furniture arrangement can make a difference, too. When seats were arranged sociofugally in one study, so that individuals tended to face away from one another, the room was rated as more crowded than when seats were arranged sociopetally with individuals facing one another.[119] When individuals face each other, the overload approach would predict more crowding, which did not occur. Perhaps sociopetal seating does not lead to more crowding when social relationships in the group are reasonably good.

Place Variations. Some places often have, or are expected to have, more visitors than others. Crowding, therefore, partly is a function of place. A popular (high-density) beach may not evoke as much crowding in its visitors as a secluded (low-density) beach that happens to have a few more visitors than usual.[120] *Within* a place, the potential for crowding also can vary. In a backcountry park, for example, a sense of crowding is more likely around the campsites than along nearby trails.[121]

Places that show strong evidence of other people, even if those people are gone, can elicit more crowding. When visitors to wilderness areas see litter and other evidence of past visitors, they report feeling more crowded than visitors who see no degradation of the setting.[122]

Weather. An unusual study conducted in India points toward a conclusion that is probably true everywhere.[123] Passengers in motorized rickshaws were asked how crowded they were on hot and very hot days. Even when the same number of passengers were riding in the rickshaw, more crowding was reported when the temperature was higher. High temperatures apparently can increase crowdedness.

◆ *IN SUM, this section reviews the influences that lead us to feel crowded. At the personal level, personality, attitudes, psychiatric status, expectations, norms, mood, and preferences influence whether an individual experiences a given situation as crowded or not. We may conclude that internal locus of control, high affiliative tendency, a tendency to screen unwanted stimuli, nonpurist attitudes about the setting, a preference for high density, and an expectation for low density predispose us to experience less crowding when density is high. Researchers have not yet clarified how different cultures respond to crowding (as an experience). Personal experience with high density may reduce crowding stress in secondary but not in primary environments. In confined settings, women usually manage high density better, but men seem to cope better when escape is possible.*

Social influences either can worsen crowding or ease it. Sheer numbers of others will sometimes, but not always, produce more crowding. If others are watching or touching us (particularly if we are male), or if we are engaged in activities we dislike, crowding may be worse even when density is equivalent. Being left out produces more crowding stress than sharing space with another person with whom one is compatible. Objective, accurate information about high-density settings reduces crowding. Crowding is likely to be worse depending on the place—when density is higher, the building is higher, the corridors are longer, the ceiling is lower, the walls are curved, sunlight rarely finds

its way in, and perhaps if one lives or works on the lower floors of a tall building and arranges the furniture in certain ways. Crowding definitely is not a mere matter of how many other people are around.

◆ **HIGH DENSITY, CROWDING,** ◆
AND HUMAN BEHAVIOR

We have seen that certain personal, social, and physical influences may cause a person to feel crowded. High density is just one such influence, and it does not always lead one to feel crowded. This section begins with the individual in a densely populated setting or already feeling crowded. We will discuss the effects that density and crowding have on individuals.

Animal Research

The effects of high density on animals have been extensively studied, sometimes with understanding of animal behavior as the terminal purpose,[124] and sometimes with animal responses viewed as generalizable to human behavior.[125,126] Although animal research may be valuable in its own right (e.g., as a basis for planning nature reserves, national parks, or zoos), we must be very cautious in generalizing findings from animal studies to humans.

Animal responses to high density are more stereotyped because they have less cognitive capacity; their behavior more directly results from biological programming. Some animals naturally live in much higher or lower densities than humans. Their preferred densities sometimes vary with the season. Humans often have more opportunity to leave a high-density situation or more ability to cope in a larger variety of ways.

Nevertheless, animal research has stimulated much human crowding research because its findings have provided challenging hypotheses for research with humans. The most influential work of this type was done by John Calhoun.[127,128,129] His studies of Norway rats enclosed in four adjacent pens with adequate supplies of food, drink, and other necessities of life are landmarks in the study of crowding. Calhoun found that female rats distributed themselves about equally in the four pens, which were connected, but that a few dominant males controlled each of two end pens. All other males had to live in middle pens; density in these pens was very high and all manner of horrible consequences occurred in these **behavioral sinks**: aggression, impaired maternal behavior (up to 96 percent of the young born in this area died before weaning), hyperactivity, cannibalism, and bizarre sexual activity.

However provocative Calhoun's research has been, its validity even for animals has been questioned. Norway rats are not usually penned in this manner. Rodents in natural settings faced with high density simply emigrate.[130] Calhoun's housing design was set up so that behavioral sinks almost had to develop. If one wishes to know just how awful life can be under a worst-case scenario, the research has value. As an attempt to discover how humans or even rats behave in natural settings, the research is less valuable. Depending on our moral views on animal research, we might even question the ethical wisdom of Calhoun's work.

In this book, high density and crowding are viewed as part of an integrated and complex process. A variety of factors, including high density, lead to crowding (as a subjective state). High density (sometimes without any sense of being crowded) has a variety of effects, even including some positive outcomes. One major task of environmental psychology is to discover the conditions under which high density will have negative effects and those under which it will have positive effects.[131] We next survey the effect of high density on physiological stress, mental health, alcohol use, child development, performance, social interaction, visiting public places, and culture as a moderator.

Physiological Stress and Health

Many investigations of human response to high density have shown that it leads, both in short-term laboratory studies and in long-term field studies, to physiological stress and arousal.[132] Specifically, high density affects blood pressure and other cardiac functions,[133,134,135] skin conductance and sweating,[136,137,138] and other physiological indicators of stress.[139]

Given that high density has these physiological effects, does it actually lead to health problems? Remember that arousal is not necessarily bad; some awfully good times are accompanied by high-arousal levels. Unfortunately, joyful high-density occasions have rarely been researched. On the negative side, high density can precipitate illness merely based on the ease with which disease organisms can move from person to person.[140] Moderate to high residential density, such as is found in prisons, is correlated with an increase in health complaints.[141,142] Health is affected by high inside density, but not by high outside density.[143,144]

A study of Thai households suggests that high density does not always lead to ill health.[145] Instead, ill health was associated with crowding in these households. Thus, *feeling* crowded may cause poor health independently of density levels.

Personal factors may worsen crowding, as we have seen; the same is true for the effects of crowding and high density. For example, individuals with preferences for larger interpersonal distances experience more physiological stress in high-density situations than do individuals who prefer smaller interpersonal distances[146] (see Figure 7–8).

Psychological Stress and Mental Health

Does population density or feeling crowded cause mental health problems? It may, but the answer is not as sim-

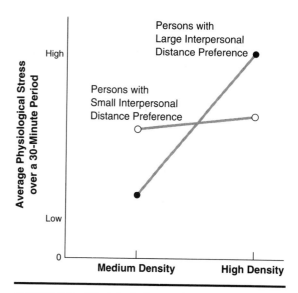

FIGURE 7–8 Physiological stress rises with increased density much faster for those with large interpersonal distance preferences than for those with small interpersonal distance preferences.

ple as the question. A Chinese study of over 100 districts did find that mental health declined as density increased,[147] but, of course, high-density districts differ from low-density districts in ways other than the concentration of people. High-density areas are more industrialized, for example, and sometimes are populated by different income or ethnic groups.

Studies at the aggregate level naturally overlook finer-grained influences. When mental health is examined in relation to household density, a somewhat different picture emerges. A Filipino study did show that higher residential densities were correlated with more symptoms of mental disorder,[148] but an English study found that both high *and* low indoor density was associated with poorer mental health.[149] Another examination of all admissions to 44 psychiatric facilities discovered that individuals who lived alone (low indoor density) were at greater risk, but only when outdoor density was also low.[150]

An even closer look at density and mental health showed that, both in India and the United States, after controlling for some other possible influences, psychological disturbance was more common in homes with both high density and "social hassles."[151] Psychological disturbance increases with both indoor density and less social support in the household,[152] but perceived control explained *when* social hassles and high density resulted in greater psychological distress. Psychological distress results from crowding when perceived control is lower.[153]

One way to integrate all these findings is to suggest that both low and high indoor density lead to low levels of social support, and that increases the risk of mental health problems. How can high indoor density be associated with *less* social support? Individuals who have too little room may squabble more, spend more time away from home, or hide away from others in some corner of the house to gain some privacy. All these activities may reduce social support, even though many people share the dwelling.[154]

Alcohol Use

The use and abuse of alcohol have many causes. There is evidence that high density is one factor. At the room level, numerous studies show that persons in groups drink more than persons alone,[155,156,157] not so much because they drink faster, but because they stay longer. At the household level, a Pennsylvania study showed that increased cirrhosis of the liver was associated with increased household density.[158] Similarly, a dormitory study found that drinking was greater when more students shared a room.[159]

At a broader scale, more people die of cirrhosis of the liver in U.S. states with higher population density;[160] also, Norwegian women who live in more densely populated areas drink more.[161] The next time someone offers you a drink when lots of people are around and you live in a high-density household in a high-density city, you may drink more than you otherwise would!

Child Development

High household density appears to endanger children. The ear and eye health of over 1,000 black children in Washington, DC, was related (in order) to lower family income, higher household density, and lower neighborhood income.[162] Among Haitian-American children, increased household density was related to slower psychomotor development.[163] In black South African children, higher household density means smaller physical growth and slower development.[164] In New York, children in preschool programs who came from higher-density homes were found to engage in more scattered behaviors, to persist in any given play activity for shorter periods, to resume interrupted activities less often, to play with other children less, and to receive higher behavior-disturbance scores than children from lower-density homes.[165] Thus, the growth, development, and behavior of children all appear to suffer when household density is high.

Performance

The relation between density and task performance depends on the nature of the task, which measure of performance is used, who is watching the performance, one's expectations about density in the situation, and one's personal space preferences.

Simple versus Complex Tasks. Early studies found that moderately high densities did not affect the performance of relatively simple tasks in which individuals sat in one place for an hour or so and worked without interacting with others. Later studies found that performance is affected if some of these conditions are different.

One study varied spatial density by a factor of six (about 1 versus 6 square yards per person) and asked individuals, participating in groups of 10, to perform several tasks requiring basic information processing and decision making.[166] Simple and complex versions of each task were presented. On most of the tasks, performance of the complex version was worse in the high-density condition, but performance of the simple task did not vary with density. High density may affect the performance of complex but not simple tasks.[167] This was confirmed and extended in a study that showed complex task performance was adversely affected in high density when workers had larger personal space preferences.[168]

Tasks That Require Physical Interaction. In many high-density settings, performance depends on the physical interaction of individuals, either through direct communication or because they must move around the setting to acquire, process, and deliver materials. Offices, retail stores, and laboratories are everyday places where this occurs. In a study of this possibility, researchers asked participants to perform a simple office task (collating paper) under two conditions: when pages of the manuscript were placed in an orderly sequence and when the pages were placed around the room in no particular sequence.[169] In the first condition, participants were not forced to interact physically as they performed, but in the second they were. Performance was not different in high- and low-density conditions when the task did not require physical interaction, but was significantly worse in high-density, high-interaction conditions compared to high-density, low-interaction conditions.

Who's Watching? One lab study investigated performance when density varied and everyone present watched one person learn to trace a maze.[170] Learning *rate* declined as audience size (and social density) increased. However, during rest periods, participants in the high-density conditions forgot less of what they had learned than did participants in low-density, low-audi-

ence conditions. Performance, therefore, was both worse (slower learning) and better (less forgetting) as density and audience size increased (see Figure 7–9).

Expectations and Norms. Expectations about the situation also affect performance. Individuals who are subjected to high density and believe they will not do well on the task perform poorly.[171] Expectancies about density itself also affect performance. Students who were led to expect a high- or low-density situation but then encountered the reverse situation performed more poorly than students who found what they expected.[172] This is reminiscent of work we discussed earlier in which accurate forewarning of high density to bookstore patrons helped them feel less crowded.

A person who grows up in high-density conditions may find ways to adapt to it, may consider high density normal, may prefer it, and may perform better in it. In a study of noise and complex task performance, those who had more experience living in high density performed better than those who had less high-density living experience.[173]

Social (and Anti-Social) Behavior

What are the effects of high density on social relations? The answer depends on several considerations, of which

FIGURE 7–9 Being watched can affect work performance, depending on how far away the observers are.

the two most important are scale (rooms to communities) and type of social relations. High density has now been shown to affect six aspects of social behavior:

- Social pathology
- Aggression
- Dislike and hostility
- Unhelpfulness
- Social withdrawal
- Humor

Social Pathology. Early aggregate studies reported positive correlations between population density and various forms of social pathology such as crime, divorce, suicide, and mental illnesses. This led to the widespread belief that cities, by their very nature as densely populated areas, were bad places to live.

More recent studies have tried to separate the effects of city size and population density, and to control for the effects of important poverty, education, and ethnic mix. A large city is not necessarily a densely populated city, as Table 7–1 showed (earlier in the chapter). One examination of the statistics for 175 U.S. cities found that some forms of pathology were related to city size but not density, or vice versa.[174] For example, murder rates increased with city size but were not related to density. Robbery and car theft rates strongly increased with city size and also increased with density. Burglary rates were *lower* in higher densities but were unrelated to city size. The ratio of divorce to marriage also was lower in bigger cities but it was not related to density. The incidence of poverty did not alter these results. Thus, whether cities are dangerous depends on which form of danger one means, and whether the city is large, densely populated, or both.

Aggression. High density, especially for males and especially over a long-term exposure, increases aggression. In short-term laboratory studies, high spatial density is likely to produce such mild forms of aggression as taking the central chair in a room[175] or, in a hypothetical court case, sentencing a convict to a longer sentence. In an investigation of a mild form of aggression in a field setting, the frequency with which passersby violated the personal space of a person standing near a fountain was observed.[176] Under high social density, but not high spa-

tial density, the researcher's personal space was invaded more often than under low-density conditions.

Men may feel more aggressive in short-term exposure to high density, but they are socialized not to express it directly. Men in longer-term, high-density situations, such as convicts, are more likely to act aggressively. Very high relations between density and violence in southern U.S. prisons have been reported.[177] One prison in Mississippi experienced a 30 percent reduction in population over a period of a few months; the rate in inmate assaults on other inmates dropped during that period by about 60 percent. Later, the prison experienced a 19 percent increase in population, and a 36 percent increase in assaults followed.

Of course, these are correlational data and other factors may have been at work. However, similar patterns of aggression have been reported in many prisons, despite researchers' efforts to take other possible factors into account.[178] Similar results have been reported in other kinds of institutions. A Swedish investigation of aggression in a psychiatric unit concluded that increases in social density were associated with increases in aggressive behavior.[179]

Children are less socialized than adults; do they behave more aggressively in high-density conditions? One study found that higher social density (about 1.5 square yards per child) did produce more aggression.[180] Higher spatial density, on the other hand, leads to a slight (nonsignificant) decrease in aggression.[181] Once again, a sex difference was found; boys were more likely to aggress than girls.

Exactly why does high density increase aggression? Perhaps it has to do with resources. Increased social density often means fewer resources per person; increased spatial density often means no decrease in resources (except space itself). If this is true, increased aggression in higher social density may be due to increased competition for desirable resources, whether they are toys among preschoolers or good seats in the lounge for adult prisoners. Indeed, when resources were made scarcer on a playground, aggression among preschool children did increase.[182]

Sadly, children may be victims of violence more often when they live in high density. A Baltimore study found that when residential density exceeded 1.5 persons per room, incidents of child abuse increased significantly.[183] Thus, high residential density means that children are more likely to receive very different but equally unpleasant experiences of neglect and abuse.

Overall, it seems that males have a more difficult time handling lack of space. They can manage to avoid aggression if the high-density situation does not last very long or if there is a way out (e.g., leaving one's crowded dorm room). But if thrown together with other men for long periods, they are more likely to act aggressively in proportion to increases in density and, perhaps, in proportion to decreases in resources.

Dislike and Hostility. Particularly when high density is undesirable (it was not our choice or it occurs in an unpleasant place or it occurs for an extended period), social outcomes are generally negative—others in the situation seem less attractive or people feel more hostility.[184] Consider for yourself the difference between spending an hour packed into a tiny room for a laboratory experiment, which you agreed to participate in to gain points in a class, and spending an hour packed into a tiny room that contains a rollicking party with good friends, good food, and good music. When negative feelings develop they can do so quickly. The mere *anticipation* of high density can lead to less liking of others.[185]

Unhelpfulness. If high density usually creates negative attitudes toward others, one must predict that antisocial or asocial behavior will follow. For the most part, that is exactly what happens. Children from ages 9 to 17 who were exposed to extremely high spatial density (about one-quarter square yard per person) for little more than half an hour displayed more competitive strategies in a game played afterwards than others who were not exposed to high density.[186] University students showed the same effect, even though they had about four times the amount of space per person, which still amounts to very high density.[187] Among South African children in a high-density day-care center, cooperation and social play were less common when the density was even higher than usual.[188]

There is even more evidence that high density usually leads to less helpfulness. In one study, stamped and addressed envelopes were "accidentally" dropped by experimenters in high-, medium-, and low-density dorms.[189] Residents of high-density dorms more often left the letters on the floor; residents of low-density dorms more often picked them up and mailed them. In another study, cafeteria patrons respected a sign requesting them to return their trays from their tables to the dishwashing area less often when the cafeteria was more densely populated[190] (see Figure 7–10). Finally, six kinds of helpfulness were counted in 36 small, medium, and large U.S. cities.[191] The strongest predictor of helpfulness was (low) density—stronger than city size. Low density predicts helpfulness better than smaller city size.

Social Withdrawal. Individuals subjected to high density often respond by withdrawing from social interaction. A classic example is the commuter who is engrossed in reading a newspaper on a busy train as much to avoid social contact as to learn what is in the news. Long-term exposure to high community density is associated with social withdrawal, at least among males.[192]

Social withdrawal is manifested in various ways: leaving the scene, choosing less personal topics to talk about,[193] making remarks about leaving, adopting a de-

FIGURE 7–10 High density in eating areas may reduce responsiveness to pleas like this one.

fensive posture,[194] turning away, avoiding eye contact, increasing interpersonal distance,[195] and so on. In the dense South African day-care center mentioned earlier, children were more often observed in "unoccupied" activities when the density was especially high.[196]

A corollary of this idea is that people who live in high density, who presumably are more socially withdrawn, will mind being ignored less than people who live in less-dense settings. One researcher investigated whether residents of corridor-design or suite-design dormitories react more negatively to being ignored.[197] Because corridor designs usually require residents to share bathrooms and lounges more than do suite designs, they have higher social densities in public areas. No one who was ignored during a discussion liked the experience, but corridor-design residents who were ignored reported the *least* discomfort and suite-design residents who were ignored reported the *most* discomfort, as predicted.

Indirect evidence of withdrawal comes from studies of social support, preferred personal space, and child neglect. Dorm residents who lived in higher densities report lower levels of social support.[198] Persons who live in higher-density homes were less likely to seek or offer social support in a stressful lab situation.[199] In India, individuals preferred larger interpersonal distances in high-density conditions.[200] Baltimore children who lived in high density (over 1.5 persons per room) were significantly more likely to be neglected.[201] As if to compensate for the excessive number of others around, people seem to reduce social interaction with others.

Humor. The effects of density on social interaction discussed so far are pretty grim. There does appear to be one bright spot—high density may enhance humor. In one study, groups were shown humorous films.[202] At the end, one person began clapping to indicate appreciation of the film. When this occurred in high density, more others joined the clapping than when it occurred in low density. In another study, participants listened to some comedy records.[203] Those in high spatial density conditions thought the comedians were funnier than did those in lower spatial density.

Humor appreciation may be enhanced in high density either by a contagion effect[204] or by tension release.[205] If one person defines a film as very funny by going to the trouble of applauding it, applause may spread contagiously in high-density situations. The other explanation assumes that high density creates more tension, and when an opportunity to dispel some of it arrives (a joke is heard), more laughter and appreciation of the joke follows.

Unfortunately, there is a somber note even in the humor research. Some studies show that high density may reduce appreciation of humor and diminish the power of humor to produce good feelings.[206,207] However, because this varies with age and sex, more research is necessary to clarify the effects of density on humor.

Visiting Public Places

An old rule of thumb claims that when a church is two-thirds full two-thirds of the time, some parishioners will leave. That is, the functional capacity of a public place is less than the actual number of seats or spaces in it. A similar idea was tested in a study of a nature visitors' center in West Virginia.[208] Visitors who arrived when 59 or fewer people were already there stayed 29 percent longer than visitors who arrived when 60 or more people were already present. Among first-time users of a library, the number of questions asked dropped as social density increased.[209] Presumably, high density in the visitors' center and the library limited the learning of their patrons.

Managers of public facilities need to know that the objective capacity of their setting probably is greater than its practical capacity. When the facility has a relatively high density, visitors will leave sooner or simply not come, although if there is a similar setting nearby, they often will adapt by going there instead.[210] This is particularly true for task-oriented visitors, as opposed to people who are just hanging out.[211]

Once again, however, perceived control can help. In a hypothetical bank situation, customers felt more pleasant under high-density conditions if they believed they had some control over the situation.[212] When shoppers were given some cognitive control by receiving information about the effects of crowding, they felt better and shopped more efficiently.[213]

Culture as a Moderator

The consequences of crowding and high density depend in part on our cultural background. Earlier we discussed cultural differences in the experience of crowding. Now we take up the issue of high density's effects in different cultures. We will see that culture acts as an intermediary for high density, sometimes providing its members with a kind of shield against the negative effects of high density and sometimes failing to equip them with effective means of coping with high density. In a typical study, high school students in Toronto from an Asian ethnic background were found to tolerate high density better than students with southern European roots, who tolerate it better than those with British backgrounds.[214]

Crime and Fear of Crime. Perhaps the most important conclusion we can draw from this worldwide research is that high density does not necessarily cause personal or social pathology. For example, the density of Hong Kong is about four times that of downtown Toronto, yet its crime rate is about one-fourth that of Toronto, and Toronto has a much lower crime rate than many other large cities in North America.[215] The same study did show, however, that the *fear* of crime appears to be more related to high density than to actual crime rate. Although high density at the community scale may be related to more social pathology in some North American places,[216] it is not in other places, such as the Netherlands,[217] parts of Africa,[218] and India.[219]

Cultures Gradually Learn. One relevant factor appears to be the age of the culture. Crowding is often associated with social breakdown in cultures that are relatively young. A clear possibility emerges that young cultures have not had time to evolve ways of coping with high density. More violence, mental and physical illness, and crime are often found in them. As centuries pass, customs that regulate high-density social interaction develop so that potential trouble is avoided.

Waves of immigration have benefited the United States in many ways, but have also produced continuing unrest in high-density areas as recent immigrants experience clashes between the values and customs of their old and new countries. African Americans, who have been most closely associated with social breakdown in some studies,[220] have gone through this process twice. First, over a two-century period, they were imported as slaves; second, over the last century, they were given nominal and, gradually, genuine freedom into a largely unwelcoming culture.

A large-scale study of Chicago[221] found important differences in the responses of blacks, Hispanics, and others (mostly whites) to high density. Even after controlling for education, poverty, sex, age, and other possibly influential variables, blacks were found to be most reactive to high density, particularly as it impinges on their privacy. Hispanics were least responsive to it, perhaps because of cultural norms favoring close interpersonal proximity. But because Hispanics live under relatively high densities, their cultural predisposition for closeness sometimes is inadequate to prevent negative outcomes of high density. Thus, although in terms of density, blacks are intermediate between whites and Hispanics, the cultural preference of Hispanics for closeness means that high density has the greatest impact on blacks.

A century or two seems a long time to North Americans, but when compared with the 30 or 40 centuries of experience that some cultures have, North America is still in its infancy.

Cultural Strategies for Handling High Density. What are some of the strategies used by experienced cultures to make high density bearable or enjoyable? The !Kung of Southwest Africa live in camps that place thin-walled dwelling places within an arm's length of each other, but they have few problems with density and even seem to prefer it. The !Kung have a valuable mechanism to peacefully regulate their social interaction.[222] Members may leave the group they live with and move to another, or even begin their own group, without incurring the opposition that such moves often evoke in other societies.

The Chinese have also dealt with high density so well that they often choose high density even when offered a low-density alternative.[223] In Hong Kong, low-cost apartments are designed to offer about 3.5 square yards per person. Thus, an apartment for a family of five would contain less than 200 square feet. A construction supervisor, when asked why designers did not consider providing more space per person, replied that if the apartments were designed to offer 6 square yards per person, many tenants would sublet part of their space.[224]

In many Chinese households, there are firm rules about access to one another's space, and children may be punished for even looking into another family's space.[225] Interaction between specific groups—such as men and women, high- and low-status individuals, and adults and children—is circumscribed by definite rules. Household sounds that might be labeled noise in other cultures are viewed instead as a sign of action and life. Adults may discipline the children of other adults without being perceived as interfering. Finally, a relatively low level of emotional involvement is expected. One reason many recent communal living experiments in North America failed may have been unrealistic expectations that high-density living can be successfully combined with high levels of emotional involvement.[226]

Because the Chinese have successfully adapted to high density, it is tempting to conclude that most Chinese like crowding, but this is a myth. In a survey of San Francisco's Chinatown, nearly all Chinese residents stated that crowding is undesirable and harmful[227] (see Figure 7–11). If it is incorrect to conclude that the Chinese like crowding, at what level of high density do they begin to feel crowding stress?

Some cultures may adapt to and even prefer higher densities than do others. At least two circumstances of the high-density situation must be considered: first, whether a person chooses high density or was forced into it, and second, with whom the person shares space. When Chinese people choose to sublet some household space as a way to supplement income, it often is seen as

an important way of helping the family. The knowledge that one is assisting helps householders to avoid experiencing the resultant high density as crowding. Also, many Chinese find high density acceptable or even preferable when the dwelling is filled with family, but not if it is filled with outsiders.

In East Africa, three cultures that live in densities varying by a 1:3:6 ratio were compared.[228] The culture that lives in the highest density (the Logali) have the strongest norms against close personal contact, both physical and emotional. In nearby cultures, friends may often be seen holding hands, but this is discouraged among the Logali. Once again, low emotional involvement emerges as a mechanism by which high density is managed.

Other high-density societies have developed architectural and behavioral preferences that are compatible with high-density living. For example, both the Japanese and Dutch have developed special affection for objects that take up very little space, such as jewel boxes, bonsai, and miniature paintings. In the Japanese home, the same room is used for more than one purpose; elaborate rules govern the use and transformation of space from one function to another.

In both Japan and the Netherlands, citizens create mini-communities within high-density areas.[229,230] In Tokyo, many such districts each provide easily accessible places for individuals to meet and interact, so that each person's small home need not absorb any further population pressure. However, the Japanese also view crowding as a negative experience, and recent dramatic increases in community density have undermined some of their traditional coping strategies.[231] Dutch towns tend to be very compact and separate, with accessible green space between them, allowing an uncrowded feeling in a very densely populated land.

◆ **IN SUM,** *high inside density usually leads to physiological and psychological stress, at least for those who prefer larger interpersonal distances or who are socially isolated. Both low density (living alone) and high density (when combined with social hassles and a lack of social support) may increase the risk of mental disorders. High density at all scales from room to region appears to increase alcohol consumption. It also seems to harm the physical and psychological development of children and expose them to more abuse and neglect. Performance may be harmed un-*

FIGURE 7–11 Are residents of Chinese districts really crowded?

der high density when the task is complex, when others are watching, and when performers must physically interact to accomplish the task. When a person's expectancies about density are unfulfilled, performance may suffer. Performance may even be worse in low density if the performer expected high density. Some aspects of performance may even improve when density or audience size are increased.

High density often has negative effects, but under some conditions—perhaps when we perform activities in which we are already competent—it may improve performance. Inescapable high inside density harms a wide range of social behaviors, particularly for men. Except in prison, those effects usually take more passive forms (lack of helpfulness) than active forms (violence). High density can enhance humor but it almost always creates negative emotion. Centuries of experience may be necessary before a culture can live successfully with high density. If newer cultures wanted to learn from older cultures, they might:

- Encourage more psychological distance between individuals.
- Allow more times and places for escape.
- Develop stricter norms about what may be said to whom.
- Restrict who may go where within the home and how each space within the home is to be used.
- Discourage social interaction with acquaintances inside the home but encourage it in public places
- Learn to appreciate higher levels of social stimulation.

◆ THEORIES OF CROWDING ◆

Now that we have reviewed a considerable body of knowledge about what leads an individual to feel crowded and the effects of high density, the time has come to attempt an integration of the research findings. Fortunately, a rich panorama of integrative formulations has already been proposed. Half a dozen major theories of crowding have been advanced, as well as many smaller proposals, distinctions, and refinements.

The theories differ mainly in the explanatory mechanisms they propose and on which part of the process they focus. Some emphasize factors that lead an individual to label a situation as crowded. Others center on the psychological process that takes place during the crowding experience. Finally, some primarily focus on

the outcomes of crowding. Theories of crowding also differ in complexity, level of analysis, underlying assumptions, and testability.[232]

Building on various attempts to organize thinking about crowding, this section presents an overall framework that has a place for each of the major theories (see Figure 7–12). The framework is a temporal-sequential description of the antecedents, processes, and consequences involved in crowding.[233] It begins with the assumption that a variety of influences (personal, social, and physical) leads, via perceptual-cognitive and physiological mechanisms, to a stressful state labeled *crowding*.

This crowding stress is more specifically defined by psychological processes such as perceived lack of control, stimulus overload, and behavioral constraint. These crowding processes, in turn, lead to a variety of consequences—coping, helplessness, behavioral deficits (and occasional benefits), and physiological aftereffects.

The framework also recognizes that high density may lead directly to some kinds of outcomes, without the individual's awareness of being crowded. That is, the processes characteristic of the crowding state may not always be evoked; high density may directly lead to some outcomes without the individual labeling the experience as crowded.[234] Let's take a closer look at the components of this model. Each of the major theories will be covered as part of the component in which it best fits.

Antecedents

Personal. Most crowding theories acknowledge that individual differences play a role in crowding, but none is *primarily* concerned with personal factors. Researchers seem content at present to amass lists of personal factors that lead to crowding. This is an area of crowding that requires more theoretical integration. However, a tentative list of such factors might include being male, coming from a relatively new culture, being either unfamiliar or very familiar with the setting in question, being a nonscreener, tending to external locus of control, preferring low density in general (or having a large personal space zone), anticipating a different level of density than is actually experienced, and being a specialist or "purist" in the setting.

Social. To put it mildly, a leading cause of crowding is too many others around. Two theories focus on the

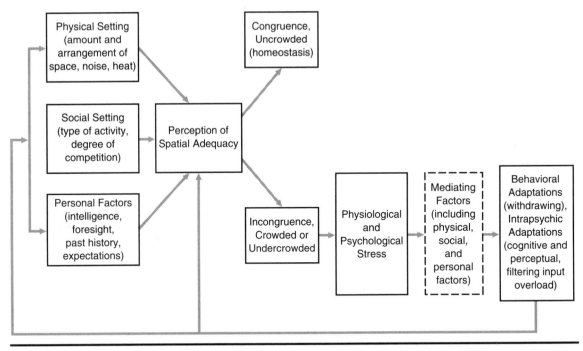

FIGURE 7–12 An integrative model of crowding.

number of people in the immediate vicinity as a central concept in crowding. The first is Jonathan Freedman's **density-intensity theory.**[235] In this approach, density is paramount; crowding is almost incidental. Bear in mind that Freedman's second and third uses of the word *crowding* in the following passage refer to what this chapter calls *density*—the physical measure:

> Some authors have assumed that crowding means stress and have defined it accordingly. . . . This obviously takes as conclusion what is at issue—how crowding [density] affects people. We are not asking whether crowding [density] is stressful, helpful, or anything else, so we must not assume that it is any of these. Stokols did make the important distinction between physical and psychological crowding, the former referring to the amount of space and the latter to the internal feeling. But he then seems to emphasize the latter, whereas it is mainly the former that must be studied.[236]

Freedman proposes that density itself is not harmful, but that it merely *magnifies* whatever else is going

on. If that is negative, then density will worsen the situation. High density in prisons has adverse effects not because of the high density itself, but because prison is basically an awful setting. Inmates are there involuntarily, the prison population includes some fundamentally unpleasant people, and the architecture and decor are not exactly uplifting.

If, on the other hand, the atmosphere is positive, then density will intensify it. Freedman, a champion of urban life, has implied that, for the average urban person, density more often magnifies pleasant reactions than unpleasant ones. He even claims that animals are not adversely affected by high density.[237] But, in the end, his position is that density is *neutral* and the task of social scientists is to specify the conditions under which high density leads to happy or unhappy outcomes (see Figure 7–13).

A second number-of-people approach is that of Eric Knowles, who observes that all density measures ignore the fact that individuals are rarely distributed evenly across a room, neighborhood, or city.[238] The key elements in his **social-physics model** are the distances

FIGURE 7-13 City life certainly is not all crowding and stress.

from others to an individual and whether the others form an audience, are merely present, or happen to be a few yards away but on the other side of a wall.

Knowles and others have presented evidence that a social-physics approach predicts observers' ratings of settings as crowded or uncrowded.[239,240] Perceived crowding in these studies is more closely approximated by a logarithmic or other exponential function of density than by density itself. These functions, resembling laws developed in another area of psychology called *psychophysics,* reflect the basic idea that social influence depends on the number and distance of others from the individual.[241]

A third social theory of crowding asserts that who one encounters and what they are doing is crucial.[242] Considerable evidence from outdoor recreation studies shows that crowding increases when one encounters others who are different. For instance, they are mountain bikers and you are a hiker, or they are in a large group and you are in a small group, or they come from a different place. Similarly, what the others are doing increases crowding. For example, they are noisy and your group is quiet or they are canoeing where you are fishing. Obviously, these factors would also apply in urban settings, where "different" people clash in a park or someone is listening to the radio where you are trying to study.

Physical. Although research exists that documents links between architectural variables and crowding, no theory primarily concerns itself with them. Crowding may be reduced by the judicious use of partitions in large open residential or work spaces and perhaps by such factors as which floor one lives on, what color and temperature the room is, the height of the ceiling, and whether the room receives much sunlight. Geographically, crowding perceptions depend on which scale is considered—room, neighborhood, or community.

One theory does include physical objects, although it is not usually considered a theory of crowding. This is the ecological approach of Roger Barker and Allan Wicker, which relies on different terminology than most theories of crowding (*overstaffing* is the nearest equivalent term).[243,244] Ecological theorists emphasize resource shortages as a key element of crowding. Physical resources can mean crayons in a preschool, tools in a shop, computers in an office, or books in a classroom.

To control crowding, access to the few available resources must be restricted, which leads to lines, priority rankings, waiting lists, and restriction of entry to the setting. Space itself might be in short supply, in which case overstaffing is similar to high density. The point is: Shortages of space are just one kind of resource shortage that may cause crowding.[245]

The flip side of a resource shortage is, of course, an excess of people. Whether resource shortages or an excess of people is the focus of attention depends on which of the two is more easily altered. If public schools are overcrowded, we do not look for ways to eliminate children! If a national park is overcrowded, we consider ways of restricting access to it through booking or quota systems.

Psychological Processes

Certain personal, social, and physical antecedents give rise to crowding stress. At least six stress processes have been described, although considerable similarity among them is apparent. We will organize most of these within two broad processes: personal control and overload.

Personal Control. Perhaps the most inclusive of the two processes is personal control. When individuals are crowded, an essential feature of the experience is that they have lost much of their ability to control what happens to them. The world either becomes unpredictable or predictably undesirable. Traffic jams are a perfect example. You want to get home or to work, but the traffic takes away your ability to control the rate at which you drive. You do not know how long it will take, but you are quite sure it will take longer than you wish (see Figure 7–14).

In their integration of crowding and personal control, Donald Schmidt and John Keating distinguish between three forms of personal control: cognitive, behavioral, and decisional.[246] They believe that even under high-density conditions, if we are able to attain one or more of these forms of control, crowding stress will be reduced. For example, earlier this chapter discussed how accurate signs and information reduce crowding; this strategy may be successful because the information imparts a sense of **cognitive control** to individuals in densely populated areas.

Behavioral control refers to the ability (or lack of it) to act toward a goal. The studies showing that crowding is worse when physical interaction hampers efforts to accomplish a task are examples of crowding caused by a lack of behavioral control. When you are enjoying a great game in a packed stadium, you are not especially crowded. But when the game is over and you move toward your car, the crush of fellow fans greatly reduces your behavioral control.

Decisional control refers to the amount of choice available in a setting. When individuals perceive strong limitations in their options, they are apt to feel crowded. If you enter a nearly full theater and discover that the only remaining seats are behind people wearing large hats, your decisional control is reduced to nil.

Control-based theory may be seen as including or superseding some of the other theories. The behavioral-constraint[247] and behavior-interference[248] theories developed out of research that demonstrated that crowding results when actions are restricted or goals are blocked. However, both formulations are very similar to the idea of behavioral control. Another early theory within the control perspective was that crowding represented a loss of freedom of choice[249] and an increase in frustration. Control theory would view this as an example of reduction in decisional control.

Overload. A second major theory of crowding as a psychological process involves the notions of social and informational overload.[250,251] The idea that densely populated cities are likely to stimulate residents beyond their capacities to process the information they receive has a long history.[252,253]

It is possible to view the overload approach as a branch of the control approach; a person's overloaded behavioral, cognitive, and decisional control are probably impaired.[254] However, the overload approach is sufficiently different that it deserves separate treatment. It focuses on the relation between the amount of incoming information as compared to the individual's preferred level of stimulation and current ability to absorb it.

Current ability and *preferred level* refer to the adaptation-level theory idea that individuals, at different times, adapt to different levels of incoming social and informational stimulation.[255] When that level is exceeded, crowding due to overload is experienced. In general, by concentrating on the match (or mismatch) between actual incoming stimulation and preferred level of stimulation, overload approaches emphasize the cognitive aspects of the crowding process.

FIGURE 7–14 Sometimes getting to or from the city can be stressful.

Consequences

Once individuals are crowded and perceive a loss of personal control or experience a serious overload of information, they respond physiologically, behaviorally, and cognitively. Some of these responses may help to reduce stress; others are manifestations of the stress. Some responses are more or less immediate; others are delayed. If we can find a successful way to cope with crowding stress, then some of its negative consequences can be avoided.

Physiological Consequences. Inescapable high density, such as that experienced in an overpopulated prison, can lead to heightened blood pressure, illness, and other biochemical changes.[256] Even the ultimate physiological consequence—death—is strongly correlated with population density in a psychiatric facility. If high density has any positive physiological effects, as Freedman's density-intensity theory predicts, they have not yet been demonstrated.

Behavioral Consequences. A wide spectrum of behavioral consequences have been reported. Heightened physiological activity means that even in everyday settings, people walk faster when density is higher.[257] Overload theory predicts that individuals will try to cope by escaping the setting. Indeed, this chapter has discussed studies showing that residents of densely populated dormitories, especially male residents, simply spend little time in their dormitory.

Another response, less desirable, is the development of **learned helplessness**. The personal control approach in particular predicts that a persistent lack of control teaches individuals that attempting to cope is fruitless. Children who spend much time in overpopulated classrooms may eventually give up attempting to learn.[258]

Anti-social behavior, ranging from withdrawal to overt aggression, is another possible consequence of crowding. These responses may be primarily associated with deficits in perceived personal control. When our goals are frustrated, constrained, blocked, or interfered with, reactance is likely to develop. **Reactance** is the tendency to maintain or restore freedom of choice when it is threatened.[259] How reactance is expressed probably depends on our personal history. Prisoners too often find violence a convenient vehicle. Some who are chronically faced with high density merely become stonelike, shutting others out. Others develop devious ways to strike back at whoever or whatever they perceive to be the source of their stress.

Cognitive Consequences. Crowding can be dealt with by changing the ways you think about or perceive the world. The overload approach postulates that crowded individuals simply filter out some aspects of life around them. Stanley Milgram suggested that the reason city dwellers sometimes walk past persons who are collapsed on the street is not because they are less kind, but because they are forced to rank-order their social priorities to manage the extremely heavy amount of stimulation they face each day.[260] Unfortunately, there are many needy individuals on the streets of large cities; most individuals could not manage a normal life if they attended to the needs of every needy person they encountered.

◆ **IN SUM,** *certain personal, social, and physical antecedents lead to the experience of crowding. Among these are a variety of individual differences, resource shortages (behavior-setting theory), the number of other people nearby (density-intensity and social-physics theories), who those others are, and what they are doing. Sensory overload and a lack of personal control are psychological processes central to the experience of crowding. The consequences of crowding include physiological, behavioral, and cognitive effects, including health problems, learned helplessness, and reactance.*

◆ CROWDING AND ◆ ENVIRONMENTAL DESIGN

When crowding is the problem, the obvious design solution is to provide more space. But there are two problems with this commonsense solution. First, economic considerations do not always favor creating more space. Second, as we have seen, crowding is not always the result of high density. We shall see that certain *arrangements* of space can also be effective antidotes to crowding. In some cases, optimal arrangements may even be better solutions to crowding than simply providing more space.

Residences

High density in any primary environment is likely to be a problem. We spend much time in primary environments, engage in some of our most important activities in them, and interact in them with those who are most important to us. Home is our most important primary environment. I am aware of no study that reports positive effects of high density on the home. Can anything be done when in-home density is unavoidably high?

Most studies of residential crowding as an experience or as an interpersonal process have been conducted in dormitories. Some of these examine the effect of actually changing some aspect of the dormitory to see if crowding is ameliorated. In one such attempt, Andrew Baum and Glenn Davis followed up on a suggestion[261] that where corridors are long, crowding might be reduced by shortening them.[262]

Baum and Davis's architectural intervention was quite simple. They arranged for a wall and double doors to be installed in the middle of a long dormitory corridor. After several weeks, residents on the divided-corridor floor felt significantly less crowded than did residents of a similar floor that remained undivided. Even though the double doors were not locked, the division of the floor into two halves seemed to have reduced overload, encouraged separate use of public facilities (such as bathrooms) by the two groups of residents, and assisted in friendship formation.

Others have offered a variety of possible interventions. Crowding could be lessened, even in a four-barewalls setting, if residents were given the means to divide up the space.[263] Even partitions or light movable walls, though not soundproof, at least restrict visual surveillance among individuals who are forced to share a room. They may, therefore, reduce sensory overload and improve the residents' sense of control. Sometimes, full control over a small space is preferable to shared control over a larger space. Also, the freedom to personalize primary space can impart a sense of control that, in turn, can reduce the amount of crowding individuals experience.

Recall the notion of perceived density. Some designs (such as stark high-rise apartment blocks) look as if they are chock-full of people, when alternative designs could give the appearance of lower density. Lowrise buildings of equal density (measured at ground level) would cover more ground, but if they were intermixed with such nonresidential settings as shops, libraries, or neighborhood pubs, they would *seem* to have lower density.[264]

Wilderness Parks

Many wilderness areas have become popular spots for camping and other outdoor activities. This has become so prevalent in parks that combine great beauty with proximity to large cities that parts of them have essentially been converted into full-scale towns. Crowding may occur in the urbanized entry areas of parks and in the areas reserved for camping and related activities.

For example, attempts have been made to deal with crowding and other problems at bus stops in the urbanized part of Yosemite National Park in California.[265] The bus was introduced by park managers to reduce traffic in the rest of the park. It transports passengers to campgrounds, trail heads, stores, motels, and other places in the park. Unfortunately, youthful zest seemed to encourage not only frequent use of the free service but also some undesirable ways of using the bus, such as running on board and pushing (the patrons also entered through windows, shouted, drank, and hung out the windows).

To curb some of the disorderly activity, a post-and-chain queuing device was installed at the bus stop. It was not pretty, but behavioral observations demonstrated that it did reduce running and pushing and increase the orderliness of boarding. Unfortunately, this change was not perceived by bus drivers; in fact, they believed no change had occurred. Passengers, at least initially, did not like it either. Before the results of the behavioral observations could even be tabulated, park authorities decided the queuing device was inappropriate for a national park, and they tore it out.

In the back areas of parks, there are also problems with too many campers. The standard approach of park managers to high density in campgrounds is to restrict entry. However, as we have seen, the *number* of campers may not be as important as their *activities*.[266] Campers have a variety of different purposes: Some desire a pure wilderness experience, some hope for a chance to be with their children in an outdoor setting, and others see an opportunity for a great party.

Crowding in campgrounds may be due more to the unfortunate proximity of campers who have incompatible goals than an overall shortage of space. **Behavioral**

zoning might work in parks so that campers with similar values and activities will find themselves in compatible company. The national park equivalent of smoking and nonsmoking zones might include party zones, family zones, and wilderness-isolation zones. Overall park density would be about the same, but crowding might well be less.

Prisons

Prisons are unpleasant; densely populated prisons are worse for every negative outcome studied, including more suicide, aggression, death, illness, and rule violation.[267,268,269] However, these findings may be moderated by other factors, such as inmate age, turnover, and other prison characteristics.[270,271] The view that high density directly causes any behavior is naive determinism, but high density does influence various inmates and prison officials differently, and some of those influences result in negative outcomes.

Although authorities have constructed much new prison space, it can be extremely expensive. When more individuals are convicted and sentencing is tougher, prison populations increase at the same time that public interest in providing more space is at a low ebb. Nevertheless, a few environmental psychologists have examined the effects of spatial arrangements in prisons, trying to find those with the least negative impact. Verne Cox, Paul Paulus, and Garvin McCain compared the responses of inmates to quite a range of spatial densities and found few ill effects. Whether an inmate has 5 or 10 square yards to himself or herself seems to matter little.

On the other hand, varying social density is quite different. When the number of inmates per cell rises, so does crowding and the incidence of illness complaints. Double-inmate cells are associated with more rule violations than single-inmate cells. Larger, open dormitories seem to produce psychological disturbances more often than do single-inmate cells.

Cox, Paulus, and McCain concluded that the best alternative for high-density prisons is to provide single-inmate cells (even if they contain only 5 square yards) rather than house prisoners together in groups. They reported studies indicating that simple cubicles placed in otherwise open dormitory space are beneficial to prisoners. Mere cubicles may not be as desirable as completely separate cells, but they seem to provide enough personal control among inmates to be superior to open dormitories.

PAUL PAULUS,
who produced much valuable research on the effects of prison crowding, now examines housing issues.

Crowding, like personal space and territoriality, has become a legal matter. U.S. federal courts have issued rulings about the availability of space in prisons, which is a start. However, the rulings are based on the total number of inmates and the total amount of space in the prison. Such institutionwide guidelines still ignore differences among prisoners, such violent versus nonviolent background.[272]

◆ SUMMARY ◆

Crowding is a subjective experience that is only mildly related to high density, a physical index. Aggregate and laboratory approaches to its investigation have their places as research methods, but field studies or field experiments may be the best overall methods. The experience of crowding is accentuated by personal factors (personality, expectations, attitudes, sex), social factors (the number, type, and actions of others, and the degree of attitude similarity), and physical factors (architectural features and spatial arrangements). Prolonged high indoor density often impairs mental and physical health, task performance, child development, and social interaction. Individuals and cultures attempt to cope with it, but sensory overload and lack of personal control lead to many negative outcomes.

Short-term high density may have positive outcomes when social and physical conditions are positive; high outdoor density, as in large cities, certainly can provide an enjoyable variety of social and cultural experiences. To reduce the negative effects of high density through environmental design, providing more space is not necessarily the answer (although that can help). Rather, careful environmental design (such as partitions and behavioral zoning) can ease crowding within the limited space that is characteristic of many settings.

Suggested Supplementary Readings

Aiello, J. R., & Baum, A. (Eds.). (1979). *Residential crowding and design*. New York: Plenum.

Baum, A., & Paulus, P. (1987). Crowding. In D. Stokols & I. Altman (Eds.), *Handbook of Environmental Psychology*. New York: Wiley.

Epstein, Y. M. (1982). Crowding stress and human behavior. In G. W. Evans (Ed.), *Environmental stress*. New York: Cambridge University Press.

Evans, G. W., & Lepore, S. J. (1993). Household crowding and social support: A quasi-experimental analysis. *Journal of Personality and Social Psychology, 65,* 308–316.

Gove, W. R., & Hughes, M. (1983). *Overcrowding in the household*. New York: Academic Press.

Gurkaynak, M. R., & LeCompte, W. A. (1979). *Human consequences of crowding*. New York: Plenum.

Hui, M. K., & Bateson, J. E. (1991). Perceived control and the effects of crowding and consumer choice on the service experience. *Journal of Consumer Research, 18,* 174–184.

Kuentzel, W. F., & Heberlein, T. A. (1992). Cognitive and behavioral adaptations to perceived crowding: A panel study of coping and displacement. *Journal of Leisure Research, 24,* 377–393.

Levine, R. V., Martinez, T. S., Brase, G., & Sorenson, K. (1994). Helping in 36 U.S. cities. *Journal of Personality and Social Psychology, 67,* 69–82.

Montano, D., & Adamopoulos, J. (1984). The perception of crowding in interpersonal situations: Affective and behavioral responses. *Environment and Behavior, 16,* 643–666.

Paulus, P. B. (1988). *Prison crowding: A psychological perspective*. New York: Springer-Verlag.

CHAPTER 8

PRIVACY

Each individual must . . . make a continuous adjustment between his or her needs
for solitude and companionship.

—Alan F. Westin[1]

There was a knock at the door. After scrutinizing her visitor through the peephole and deciding that the plump, matronly woman was not threatening, Jane answered the door. She found that her friendly neighborhood census taker wanted to ask her a few questions. "Well, I guess that would be OK," Jane said hesitantly.

After a few standard questions, the census taker started asking strange things, such as how many bathrooms were in the house and what Jane's income was. The questions became increasingly personal, Jane thought, and finally she refused to answer. The census taker smiled, said that answering the questions was mandatory, and left, saying that her supervisor would return later to obtain the answers.

Just as Jane closed the door, the phone rang. It was that wuss from her biology class, bugging her again about going out. He didn't seem to get the message when she politely refused, so she bluntly told him never to call again. The phone rang again immediately. "Phones!" Jane fumed to herself. "I gotta get that caller's number display on this phone." Gingerly picking up the receiver, certain it was the wuss again, she said, "Hello?"

When she heard Tom's familiar voice asking her if she'd like to try the new Japanese restaurant, she was relieved. "I'm really sorry about The Zanzibar Club, Jane," he said. "Sometimes I just can't take all that noise. Over dinner, I'd like to talk about some of the apartments I've been looking at for us," he said. "Seems like we have to choose between enough space to stretch out in and going to school next year. I don't see how we can afford both."

Jane felt apprehensive again. "I guess we've never really taken a look at how much space we need or, in this case, how little space our relationship can survive," she said.

Seated on the mats in a little room in the Japanese restaurant, Tom and Jane tried to talk about it, but there were two problems. For one thing, there seemed to be many more interesting and easy things to talk about. For another, the biology wuss somehow had landed not only in the same restaurant but in the next room. Jane was able to prevent his leering looks by closing the curtains, but the creep was laughing and talking so loudly with his friends that Tom and Jane could hardly carry on a conversation.

◆ ◆ ◆

Privacy, like personal space and territoriality, is a process that is an extremely important dimension of our daily lives, but one we often manage at a low level of awareness. To accomplish our privacy goals, we must be skilled at balancing our own desires, those of others, and the physical environment.

To many people, privacy means two things. One is being apart from other people; the other is being sure that other individuals or organizations do not have access to one's personal information. However, these two everyday meanings represent only part of the meaning of privacy. For example, one prominent view of privacy in environmental psychology is that privacy processes sometimes lead individuals to seek *more* social interaction.

Privacy is addressed not only by psychologists but also by political scientists, sociologists, anthropologists, and lawyers, reflecting its social, cultural, and legal aspects. Privacy is manifested in our behavior, preferences, values, needs, and expectations. It is facilitated or eroded by the physical design of our homes, workplaces, schools, public places, and institutions. Invasions of privacy occur when someone physically intrudes on us or when someone collects information about us that we do not want them to have.

Some of us need more privacy than others; some of us need different *kinds* of privacy; all of us need more solitude at certain times and less at others. Privacy is closely related to territoriality, crowding, and personal space. It is part of the way we speak, our nonverbal behavior, and our psychological development. It is intimately involved with other important psychological processes, including emotion, identity, and our sense of control.

All of these facets of privacy are interesting in their own right, but understanding privacy serves a larger purpose: assisting in the design of better built environments. We cannot accomplish this goal without knowing how to measure privacy, what personal and situational factors influence it, and how privacy is related to other behavior processes. We must also have useful models of privacy's workings. After surveying what is known about all these facets of privacy, this chapter concludes with a section on the most important privacy issue: how to optimize it through environmental design.

◆ WHAT IS PRIVACY? ◆

We have seen that privacy means many things to many people. Any attempt to define it precisely risks excluding some important aspects of privacy; overly broad definitions risk meaninglessness. Probably the best definition of privacy yet developed is one by Irwin Altman. Privacy, he wrote, is "selective control of access to the self

IRWIN ALTMAN'S
theory of privacy and related social-environmental processes has been very influential.

or to one's group."[2] Altman's definition captures the essence of privacy—the twin themes of management of information about oneself and the management of social interaction. That is, "access to self" may refer either to information about oneself or to social interaction with oneself.

Altman's definition also has room for other dimensions about privacy. One involves the number of individuals encompassed, despite the "self" part. Normally, one thinks of individuals seeking privacy, but sometimes people seek to be alone with one or more selected others.[3] Everyone dreams of being alone in a favorite spot with a special someone—that is, *two* people seeking privacy together. At other times, classmates, businesspeople, or football players huddle together in groups, excluding others. That is why Altman's definition includes groups (see Figure 8–1).

The words *access to the self* in Altman's definition also refer to a range of sensory avenues. For example, heads of state may stand on a prominent balcony so that citizens have visual access to them, yet no individual citizen may be granted a private audience. You may seek privacy by going into your room to study but be bothered by music or conversation produced by others. Many others grant us both visual and acoustic access to them (e.g., in a conversation) yet not allow us to touch them. Office employees in open-plan offices often have visual privacy but complain that their acoustic privacy is poor.

On the other hand, even strippers past their last shred of clothing on stage may still have considerable privacy.[4] Visual access to their bodies is complete, to be sure. But when strippers successfully adopt a blank, closed expression, they manage to control access to a more important part of themselves. They are denying the customers access to their thoughts, interests, and any shred of social involvement. This is an extreme example, but it illustrates one complexity of privacy: Some channels of communication may be open while others are not.

The notion of open and closed channels leads us to a final but crucial observation on Altman's definition. *Selective control* implies that access may be granted as well as denied; privacy is not merely shutting out others. It often includes enjoying social interaction and gladly sharing information about yourself with others. The key

FIGURE 8–1 Being alone is just one form of privacy.

word is *control*. A person who has optimal privacy is *not* a recluse but someone who is able to find either companionship *or* solitude easily (social interaction management) and who is able to share or halt the flow of self-related information (information management).

◆ MEASURING PRIVACY ◆

Those who would measure privacy well must carefully consider its complex definition. Although it is acceptable to measure one or two aspects of privacy if the research goal includes only those aspects, a comprehensive measure should (1) include privacy's social as well as informational themes, (2) acknowledge that pairs and larger groups as well as individuals may seek privacy, (3) note that privacy may vary across the various communication channels as well as over time, and (4) recognize that seeking privacy may actually lead an individual to search for a party to attend (see Figure 8–2).

Privacy may be measured as a behavior, a value, a preference, a need, and an expectation. For example, one researcher erected some "privacy booths" in an elementary school classroom and observed the children's actual use of and *behavior* in the booths.[5] Others have examined individuals' privacy *preferences*. In one study, the privacy preferences of dormitory residents were affected by crowded living conditions.[6] The privacy *values* in question are often those of others toward our privacy.

FIGURE 8–2 Companionship is part of the privacy process, too.

One authority claims that many adults do not believe adolescents are sufficiently developed as persons to warrant privacy; that is, adults often do not value adolescents' privacy.[7] Finally, people may have high or low *expectations* for privacy. Prisoners, for example, have very little privacy and do not expect much. When they move to new facilities, though, even prisoners may expect an increase in privacy.[8] Their low expectations for privacy do not mean that prisoners do not *need* privacy, though—perhaps many problems in prisons originate with prisoners' unmet privacy needs.

No comprehensive measure of privacy has yet been developed. Most privacy investigations have studied privacy with surveys, questionnaires, or interviews. After all, in order to study privacy behavior by field observation, the investigator is almost forced to violate the subject's privacy! The few naturalistic observations of privacy have been done in schools, offices, institutions, or other secondary territories in which the subjects' more sensitive areas of behavior will not be under surveillance.

Questionnaire measures of privacy are often based on the pioneering typology of Alan Westin, who reasoned that privacy has four faces: solitude, intimacy, anonymity, and reserve.[9] **Solitude** is the popular but limited notion of privacy: being alone. **Intimacy** refers to group privacy, as when a pair of lovers wish to be alone together. **Anonymity** is the form of privacy desired when a person wishes to be among others but does not want to be personally identified or to interact on a personal basis. For example, monarchs, presidents, and rock stars occasionally desire to walk among their people, as just another person, to see what normal life is like. Ordinary individuals, too, sometimes desire anonymity. Do you ever go to the mall simply to absorb the bustling atmosphere without wanting to interact with anyone as yourself? The last form of privacy in Westin's typology is **reserve**, the creation of a psychological barrier against intrusion. In public or in private, reserve means that a person wishes to limit communication about himself or herself to others.

Three researchers have developed measures of privacy based on Westin's ideas. The first focused on privacy in neighborhoods.[10] From an original set of 86 questionnaire items, 6 privacy factors were identified; 4 of these were very similar to Westin's privacy types. The additional two were variants on the theme of solitude.

Seclusion refers to living away from the sights and sounds of traffic and other people. **Not neighboring** refers to a dislike of casual visiting and general contact with neighbors.

The second researcher also confirmed Westin's four basic factors, but suggested two refinements.[11,12] One refinement is to separate intimacy into two forms: **intimacy with friends** and **intimacy with family**. The suggestion is that these two forms of intimacy are psychologically distinct. The other refinement is to distinguish isolation from solitude: **Isolation means being alone with no one else nearby**, whereas **solitude** means being alone in the midst of others. You seek isolation when you want to live alone on a desert island; you seek solitude when you want to be alone in your room, but have other people nearby, such as in other rooms of the house.

The third researcher focused on wilderness privacy.[13] Once again, a set of items based on Westin's and others' ideas was constructed. Two factors that emerged from the analysis of responses by students and backpackers were similar to Westin's intimacy and anonymity factors. A third factor resembles isolation or seclusion, as already defined. Two other factors are quite different from all those previously discussed. Both involve privacy as a sense of freedom. **Individual cognitive freedom** means the opportunity to do more or less as you please and to pay attention to whatever you like. **Social cognitive freedom** emphasizes freedom from the expectations of others, such as your family, boss, or friends. Both might be described as privacy in the sense of being "free to be the real me." Note the similarity of these two concepts to the idea of a free territory, discussed in Chapter 6.

◆ **IN SUM,** *privacy means selective control of access to self, either in person or in terms of information about oneself. It may be considered as a preference, expectation, value, need, and behavior. Privacy means going toward others as well as going away from them; privacy is optimizing social interaction and information transfer, not merely restricting them. Westin proposed solitude, intimacy, anonymity, and reserve as the basic forms of privacy. Empirically derived questionnaire measures support Westin's speculations and add several others. The five basic factors of privacy appear to be solitude (or isolation, seclusion, or not neighboring), intimacy (with friends or with family), reserve, anonymity, and freedom (from constraints and expectations).*

◆ INFLUENCES ON PRIVACY ◆

Differences in privacy behavior, values, preferences, needs, and expectations originate with differences in personal characteristics, social situations, physical settings, and culture. Some people, because of their culture, personality, or other characteristics, require more privacy or express privacy needs differently from others. Certain social situations or physical settings, regardless of who is in them, engender different privacy needs. Let's examine the personal factors first.

Personal Influences

Residential History. Differences in a person's background are related to privacy preferences. Individuals who grow up in homes they felt were crowded prefer more anonymity and reserve as adults.[14] Those who spend more time in cities prefer more anonymity and intimacy. Wanderers (persons who live someplace other than where they grew up) prefer less intimacy, as you might predict of individuals who found a reason to leave their families and friends behind.

Sex. There are also sex differences in privacy. In a study of dormitory residents, men and women responded differently to two-person and three-person room arrangements.[15] Men assigned to two-person rooms increased their preferences for all forms of privacy (compared to their preferences before they moved into the dorms), but men assigned to three-person rooms actually decreased their preference for solitude (their preference for other forms of privacy were unchanged).

Why would men assigned to two-person rooms begin to prefer *more* solitude and those assigned to three-person rooms prefer *less* of it? The researchers discovered that men in three-person rooms stayed away from their residences more. Perhaps those in two-person rooms were not crowded enough to take concrete steps (stay away from their room), but they were crowded enough to wish for more solitude. (Many of these young men had their own rooms at home.) Apparently, men in three-person rooms really were crowded; they coped with the higher density by deciding they really did not want to be alone so much after all (thus bringing their preferences into closer agreement with reality) and by avoiding their rooms more (see Figure 8–3).

Women, on the other hand, did not show changes in preference for privacy when they were assigned to two-person versus three-person rooms. They spent as much or more time in the three-person rooms as in the two-person rooms. We should not conclude that women *value* privacy less than men, however. Women may enjoy the company of others more and, when asked to live in higher-density situations, may have learned a greater repertoire of privacy-regulating mechanisms *within* the social context. In contrast, men seem to cope by adjusting the value they place on privacy and by escaping the social context if they can.

Another study of dormitory living supports this idea.[16] This study focused on informational privacy. Women told roommates more about interpersonal matters than men did, and friendship among women was more closely tied to intimate disclosure than friendship among men. The researchers suggest their results are consistent with the image of women as social-emotional specialists, or person specialists. Among nursing home residents, women prefer environments that allowed for controlled disclosure, places to speak confidentially, more than men.[17] This can be interpreted as further support for the greater socioemotional interests of women. These studies give a flavor of the differences between the sexes in privacy preferences and behaviors.

Personality. Some psychologists have investigated the relations between privacy and personality dispositions. Persons with higher needs for privacy felt less confident and more anxious, in one study.[18] Another indicates that individuals who feel they do not have enough privacy are more distractible.[19] A third study confirms this general picture. People who are more reserved and those who seek more solitude and anonymity tend to have lower self-esteem.[20] Introspective individuals are more likely to be reserved and less likely to seek intimacy with their families.

Social Influences

Personal characteristics influence privacy, but so does each social situation we find ourselves in. If you have just returned home from a night on the town with your beloved, you will probably want more solitude than if you would like to discuss this weekend's big game with some friends. If you are discussing your finances with a bank manager, you probably want more intimacy than if you were responding to a questionnaire on your attitudes toward campus architecture. In general, our desire for privacy varies with the social situation.

Let's consider how the management of information relevant to self is affected by the social situation. Who wants private information about you? What will be done with it? What kind of personal information is wanted? What social consequences will follow should the information become widely known? Employees in one study were interviewed about their experiences, intentions, beliefs, and values concerning informational privacy.[21] For example, which organizations (an employer, a lending institution, a law enforcement agency, a credit grantor, an insurance company, or a taxation agency), if any, *should* be allowed to collect, store, use, and disseminate information about you?

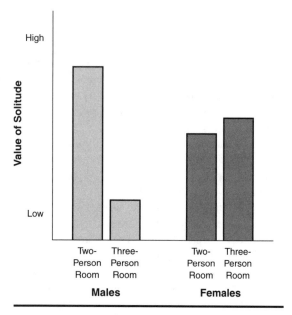

FIGURE 8–3 In higher-social-density dormitory rooms, male students place less value on solitude. Why?

The employees said lenders should be allowed more information than law enforcement agencies. Which organizations actually *do* collect, store, use, and disseminate information about you? The employees in the study believed that their employers do so much more than credit-granting agencies (see Figure 8–4).

Under which circumstances do people believe their informational privacy has been invaded? Over 2,000 employees in several corporations were pre-sented with a hypothetical situation in which an employee was applying for a promotion and queried more broadly about informational privacy at work.[22,23] The employees felt their privacy was compromised more if the information:

- Concerned their personality rather than their performance
- Was obtained without their permission rather than with their permission
- Was disclosed to outsiders instead of insiders
- Had negative rather than positive consequences for them
- Seemed irrelevant for the purpose it was requested

A consistent undercurrent in these studies is the individual's concern with *control* of information about self. Consider, for example, the finding that privacy is believed to be compromised more when (1) information is obtained about personality (over which we have little control) than when it is obtained about performance (over which we have more control); (2) we do not give permission for it to be collected; and (3) it is given to outsiders (who may speed the spread of the information beyond our control). This concern with control was confirmed by another study, in which subjects also read an employment application scenario.[24] Again, subjects believed their privacy was invaded if they had not granted permission for the information to be collected.

What about social influences on the interpersonal interaction side of privacy? Among single-family dwelling residents, sharing a residence with more people was correlated with a smaller preference for being alone.[25] This study was conducted in a middle-class neighborhood, however. The same results may not be found when residents have fewer resources or fewer options for moving.

In terms of acquaintances and friends, we can expect that individuals who have recently experienced considerable social interaction will want less and that those who have experienced relatively little will want more. Altman's theory predicts that people naturally oscillate—in terms of what they would *like* to experience—from the hermit end of the privacy spectrum to its social end and back again, endlessly.[26]

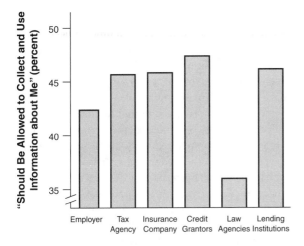

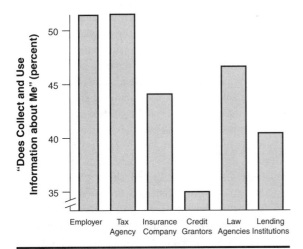

FIGURE 8–4 Values ("Who should") and beliefs ("Who does") about informational privacy vary. Note the discrepancies between values and beliefs for different kinds of organizations.

Physical Influences

What about the environment itself might be associated with greater privacy preferences or dissatisfaction with privacy? Numerous studies report that satisfaction with privacy at work is related to the degree of physical enclosure one is allowed. A study of office workers who changed offices found that employees who left offices with walls for open-plan offices said they felt a significant decline in privacy[27] (see Figure 8–5). In another study of office workers, the best predictor of satisfaction with privacy was simply the number of partitions around the employee's workstation.[28]

These studies suggest that satisfaction with privacy is, as might be expected, a function of how much the

ERIC SUNDSTROM
has performed key research on privacy and crowding at work.

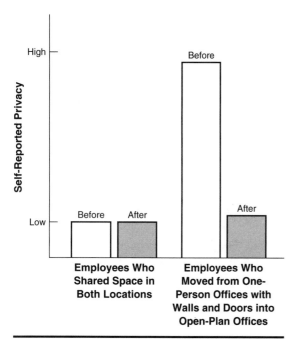

FIGURE 8–5 This shows privacy in traditional (walled) and open-plan (partitioned) offices. Employees of a large corporation who were moved to new offices rated their privacy before and after relocation. Level 1 employees shared space at both locations. Level 2 employees moved from a traditional office shared with one other person to an individual enclosure with 60-inch-high partitions. Level 3 and Level 4 employees moved from traditional offices with doors to doorless individual enclosures with 60-inch and 78-inch partitions, respectively.

physical environment allows us to regulate access to self. Walled offices and partitions allow solitude, but one can always step out into the social stream of the hallway. Open-plan offices force us toward the social stream and make solitude virtually impossible.

What about privacy at home? Residents of houses with open plans (where more rooms are visually open to one another) also preferred less solitude. At work, then, open spaces are associated with dissatisfaction with privacy, but at home, open spaces are associated with preferences for less privacy. At work, we may prefer closed spaces because coworkers are not always our favorite companions, whereas at home, open spaces shared with family or friends are more welcome.

Other environmental factors are also related to privacy in the home setting. For example, as you might expect, persons whose homes insulate quiet activities from noisy ones are more likely to be satisfied with their privacy than those whose homes fail to separate noisy activities from quiet ones. In addition, individuals who are far from neighbors and cannot see very many other houses from the windows are more likely to be satisfied with privacy.[29]

Some research focuses on the different dimensions of privacy (intimacy, solitude, etc.) rather than treating privacy as a global, unified process. For example, in the housing research just described, those who live in less spacious surroundings generally preferred less privacy, but this finding did not always hold. When many houses were visible from their windows (suggesting a high-density neighborhood), residents tended to prefer less seclusion. However, they also tended to prefer *more* reserve.[30] Clearly, privacy is not a unitary phenomenon. Each kind of privacy can be differently influenced by the physical environment.

Prisoners are often subjected to low levels of privacy. One study examined both the privacy preferences and the privacy expectations of prisoners who were moved from an old facility to a new one.[31] The old jail housed four inmates in each 6-square-meter (64-square-foot) cell. The new jail offered a 6-square-meter cell to each inmate. Privacy preferences changed little after the move, but expectancies for some types of privacy (solitude and intimacy) rose significantly.

Because the prisoners had preferred more solitude and intimacy than they expected in the old jail, but expected about as much as they preferred in the new jail, we can guess that they were more satisfied with their new jail. It is hardly astonishing, of course, that people are happier when space quadruples from 1.5 square meters per person to 6 square meters per person, but the study demonstrates that expectancy is an important component of the privacy process.

What about the influences physical setting has on informational privacy (as opposed to interpersonal privacy)? Only a few studies have investigated this. The emphasis in these information-oriented studies is on self-disclosure—how much self-related information one person chooses to tell another. For example, "soft" rooms—furnished with cushioned chairs, rugs, wall decorations, and incandescent lighting—have been found to elicit more intimate self-disclosure than "hard" rooms—with bare floors and walls, hard chairs, and fluorescent lighting.[32]

A subsequent study attempted to determine whether the increase in the communication of intimate information was more a function of lighting, the decor, or both (this could not be determined in the earlier study).[33] Softer decor did result in slightly more intimate communication. Across two occasions about an hour apart, intimacy was actually greater in brighter-light conditions. However, all forms of communication (not only intimate communication) decreased over time. Participants may have simply gotten sleepy after an hour or so in the dim light! Nevertheless, these studies show how the physical setting can affect informational privacy.

The interpersonal and informational sides of privacy are linked. This link is demonstrated in a study of dormitory roommates.[34] Students who had lived together in a residence hall for 4 months were asked how much they had disclosed to others who lived on their

floor. Roommates disclosed more about themselves to each other than did students who merely lived on the same floor. Assuming that roommates share space more than hallmates, the study indicates that less privacy in the shared-space sense is associated with less privacy in the sense of information sharing.

Cultural Influences

Do individuals from different cultures require the same amount of privacy, or do some cultures desire more than others? First, there is no doubt that different societies *appear* to vary widely in the amount of privacy that members actually have. In some Arab societies, the ideal home has high solid walls around it. Elsewhere, housing patterns can be quite different. I briefly lived in a tiny fishing village in southern India where all the families had grass huts very close to each other, so that very little regulation of privacy was possible, yet the villagers did not seem to desire more separation from their neighbors.

However, appearances can be deceiving. Desired and achieved privacy may be as high in the Indian society as in the Arab society. This is illustrated by the Iban society of Sarawak, in Borneo. The Iban live in longhouses with very little privacy in the First World sense of the term—the opportunity for solitude or intimacy behind closed doors. Are the Iban desperate for privacy, or do they not desire as much privacy as individuals in developed countries?

The Iban seem to need about as much privacy as North Americans do, but they achieve it through different mechanisms.[35] These mechanisms are largely social conventions instead of the physical means on which North Americans rely. For example, the Iban have special maneuvers for changing clothes in public that preserve their modesty. They have rules against criticizing others' children, which helps to keep disputes among adults to a minimum. The longhouse is closed to outsiders on many occasions. Beginning at puberty, the sexes use separate sleeping areas. Together, these conventions help the Iban achieve privacy without walls.

The Gypsies, who often live in mobile wagons, also lack physical settings for privacy. They have developed the following rule, among others, to allow members privacy.[36] On rising each morning from sleeping around the campsite, Gypsies decide when to wash their faces. If they feel grumpy, need some time to think, or just want to be alone, they simply do not wash their faces. Others would not be so rude as to interrupt this self-imposed social isolation until those seeking solitude have washed their faces.

A man who lived with Gypsies for 10 years says they have a different view of privacy from the Gaje (the non-Gypsy). Gypsies view privacy as a two-way concept. One does not pry by watching others change their clothes or perform the so-called functions of nature. Also, however, the person who seeks solitude has the responsibility to avoid places and times where others could easily observe these private activities.

A wise old Gypsy woman declared that privacy is a state of mind. To the Rom (the name Gypsies have for themselves), the Gaje's practice of building walls and doors is an insult to others: It suggests that others would not respect your privacy by looking away. At the same time, the doors and windows are an enticement or challenge to pry, spy, or peep on someone so distrusting that he or she hides behind closed doors. Privacy, therefore, is a state of mind because it involves—even requires—courtesy, tactfulness, restraint, and respect to manage an unwalled life.

Thus, it appears that cultures are not different in the amount of privacy they desire. However, they do vary considerably in how they achieve that privacy.[37]

◆ *IN SUM, privacy preferences, expectations, needs, and satisfaction are influenced by personal characteristics, the social situation, the physical setting, and the culture. City-raised individuals prefer more anonymity and intimacy. Women seem to manage privacy in close groups by discussing more interpersonal and intimate matters; men often achieve privacy by removing themselves from the setting and talking less about delicate matters. Personality studies suggest that individuals who have greater-than-average privacy needs are less sure of themselves and more anxious.*

Informational privacy primarily is affected by who wants information from us, what information they want, and how they attempt to obtain it. Some privacy fears could be reduced if employees gave informed consent to the gathering of information about them. The physical setting has important effects on privacy preferences, expectations, and satisfaction. For example, open space at work often breeds dissatisfaction, whereas at home, it is preferred.

These influences are indoors, such as the doors and partitions surrounding us, and outdoors, such as the distance between houses and the number of neighbors visible from one's house (see Figure 8–6).

Room lighting and decor can influence the type and amount of information we communicate to one another. Members of different cultures probably have similar privacy needs but, depending on how the environment supports those needs, may use different means of achieving privacy. Next, we explore how privacy is connected to other important psychological processes.

◆ PRIVACY AND HUMAN BEHAVIOR ◆

We have seen that privacy is influenced by personal and situational factors. It is also inextricably linked with other important behavior processes. Once again, we are indebted to Alan Westin for describing most of these essential functions.[38]

1. Privacy is clearly related to **communication**. Both the informational and interpersonal themes of privacy are deeply involved with communication.
2. Privacy is intimately connected to our sense of **control**, or autonomy. The ability to choose solitude or the company of others endows us with a sense of self-determination; not having that choice makes us feel helpless.

FIGURE 8–6 This house is next to a public park—not a great site for privacy.

3. Privacy is important to our sense of **identity**. Solitude and intimacy, in particular, can be used to evaluate our progress in life, who we really are, what our relationship to others is, and what it ought to be.
4. Privacy allows for **emotional release**. In private, we can weep, make faces at ourselves in the mirror, sing loud crazy songs, and talk to ourselves.

Westin's four functions of privacy provide a good framework for research on the relation between privacy and other human behaviors. Privacy is connected to more than these four functions, however. It is also related to child development and how we adapt to space. We will first survey the research substantiating Westin's four functions of privacy, then discuss the links between privacy and other behavior processes, and conclude with a section on the links among privacy, personal space, territoriality, and crowding.

Communication

One reason we seek privacy is for protected communication.[39] When we wish to talk to a friend, lawyer, teacher, counselor, or coworker about something personal or important, we try to find a private place. Many important private exchanges would never occur if we could not take a drive or find a private place to talk with that special person.

Privacy and communication at work have been the subject of several investigations. As noted earlier, employees who moved from walled offices to open-plan offices were dissatisfied with privacy.[40] A key reason for the dissatisfaction of these employees was the loss of protected communication; they felt that the confidentiality of their conversations had suffered. As another example, I recently received a call from an acquaintance in another city. It was basically a business call, but the caller waited until after 5 P.M. local time so the call would come in after hours, when other employees were away. These are merely two of many instances in which people seek privacy for the purpose of protected communication.

Control

Westin describes how privacy can facilitate an individual's sense of control or autonomy. Beginning on the bleak side, those who have little solitude of their own choosing and yet cannot see others they would love to be with (e.g., institutionalized individuals) have little control over their physical or social environment. Having little control leads an individual to feel deprived of autonomy or independence.

On the more fortunate side of life, wealthy individuals are able to control their access to others and others' access to them nearly all the time. They can exclude others with an endless succession of private rooms, private offices, private clubs, private transportation, and private elevators, and they can entice others with luxurious surroundings and other goodies.

There are more studies of individuals who greatly lack privacy than of individuals who have it in abundance. This in itself is a comment on privacy and research. Those with privacy often also have more power; they can more easily refuse to be studied or find an excuse not to be part of a study. One study of prisoners, for example, looked into prisoners' sense of control in relation to their privacy.[41] In their former (cramped) quarters, the more prisoners preferred solitude and reserve, the less control over their lives they felt. One outcome of moving to their new, more spacious quarters was a significant change in this relation between privacy and control. In their new quarters, the more prisoners valued solitude and reserve, the greater their sense of control. The physical setting changed the relation between privacy and control. In this case, the prisoners' actual preferences for solitude and reserve did not change with the move to new quarters, but presumably their sense of control increased significantly. Those who particularly valued solitude and reserve were able, in their new more private surroundings, to feel they had greater control over their lives.

A study of wilderness solitude found that one of its desirable features is that, compared to the pressing demands of everyday urban life, wilderness allows us to control what we pay attention to and which activities we engage in.[42] The author suggested that people do not go to the wilderness primarily to be isolated but to be able to experience the "cognitive freedom" involved in controlling their experiences. "Getting away from it all" to the wilderness means escaping from a place where a person is subjected to many controls to a setting where *the person* can decide what to do.

Control over information may even be related to physical health. When hospital patients have better control over information pertinent to their health (such as diagnostic and treatment information), they cooperate more and experience less stress.[43]

In a series of studies, Carol Werner and colleagues studied privacy and control.[44] One appealing feature of these studies is that they investigated realistic situations, such as a typical person being interrupted while working on an important task. One study showed that signs and chairs can strongly support the feeling that people control the space where they are working. When working in a room that had a sign saying "Come in" and a chair inside the room (and none outside it), very few individuals asked a person who entered the room to leave. When the sign said "Do not disturb" and there was a chair outside the door (and none in the room), nearly everyone asked the person who entered the room to leave.

A second study showed that this occurred at least partly because the sign made the occupant of the room feel that he or she "had a right" to ask the intruder to leave. In these studies, the occupant's assertiveness made a difference. Less assertive occupants felt they were not so much throwing out an intruder who was harming their work performance as helping a lost person find his or her correct place. More assertive occupants conceived of the entrance as an intrusion that threatened their control and therefore their work performance.

Another study suggested that when occupants have a legitimate place to which they can direct intruders, they are more likely to do so. Especially for less assertive persons, being able to say (for example), "The smoking area is over there" is easier than saying, "Please don't smoke. This is a nonsmoking area."

CAROL WERNER
is a leading researcher in privacy and related topics.

In a fourth study, office workers' methods of establishing control over their work space was examined.[45] On typical days, employees might use no mechanisms, or use two that conflict, such as posting a "Do not disturb" sign but leaving the door open. But when they really want privacy, they employ multiple, redundant methods. They might, for example, close the door, put up a sign, stay late, and use a secretary to screen calls. In general, control over information and control over access to others are central to the concept of privacy and are closely related to one's general sense of self-determination in life.

Identity

Privacy is an important part of our sense of self, or identity. This may seem a strange declaration; what does either informational or interpersonal privacy have to do with self-definition? Westin demonstrates how privacy is essential to enable us to integrate all the information from daily exchanges with others.[46] Sometimes, it is not easy to make sense of all the things that happen to us while we are still on the public stage. Privacy allows us the time and space to reflect on the meaning of events, to fit them into our understanding of the world, and to formulate a response to them that is consistent with our self-images.

For example, if you have ever felt swept away by love in a new relationship, you can understand this function of privacy. Certainly, the first rush of love is a pleasant experience, but a common associated feeling is that you are losing your self while gaining a relationship. Even when, in the first stages of such a relationship, part of you very much desires intimacy, another part often wants solitude or reserve. Generally, you need to take a step back even from a very pleasant experience to evaluate whether this is "the real me" or whether entering the wonderful relationship might not alter your very identity in ways you do not want it to.

This notion of privacy as a facilitator of identification is taken seriously enough by some theorists to be considered the central idea in their privacy framework.[47] Unfortunately, identity is not an easy concept to empirically investigate. Support for the centrality of identity comes largely from sociological analyses of novels and plays. This does not detract from the value of identity for privacy; it merely means that empirical support for the idea is difficult to obtain.

Emotion

The fourth function of privacy, in Westin's approach, is to allow for emotional release.[48] Society discourages public emotional displays except under exceptional circumstances such as weddings and funerals. People often feel more emotion than they are able to display, so privacy serves as a vehicle for emotional release. A person may feel very bad, for example, and head for the nearest secluded place to cry.

But more positive emotional release problems arise, too. Have you ever been to a concert so good that on the way home in the car you sang and yelled, riding the excitement? If you stopped to eat on the way home, you may have walked into a restaurant full of people who did not share your exhilaration. Perhaps you contained your excitement so that the others did not think you were crazy and, if so, you likely felt frustrated at the restraint you imposed on yourself.

Another example of emotional release, closer to the informational theme of privacy, is the tradition of "off the record" comments made by politicians to reporters. Politicians must present only part of themselves to the public if they wish to survive; they know and feel much more than they can afford to tell the public. The pressure of this knowledge inevitably builds up—especially on a long road trip where a spouse or trusted aide may not be available.

This inevitably leads to candid conversations between politicians and reporters on the same trip who can be trusted to honor the off-the-record tradition. In these private conversations, politicians may criticize their own party's policies or admit to fear that a recent public statement was ill advised. The reporter must honor the unwritten code against publishing remarks such as these in order to maintain a trustworthy status not only with that politician but with all others. If the confidential information is publicized, word will quickly spread that the reporter cannot be trusted to keep off-the-record comments off the record, and a valuable asset—trust—will be lost.

Child Development

The privacy needs of infants are unknown, but it is probably safe to assume that infants have little need for solitude, reserve, or anonymity, although they do need physical intimacy. But as the child develops, so does the need for the other forms of privacy.

Informational privacy becomes an issue when the preadolescent is first given a diary (and the parent wrestles with the temptation to read it). "Keep Out" signs begin to appear on the adolescent's door. Too few studies have examined the process by which infants with no privacy needs develop into adults with important and diverse privacy needs. This may be because adults often forget that children value and deserve some solitude.[49] Nevertheless, a few key pieces of research have begun to explore the development of privacy.

Maxine Wolfe has extensively studied how the meaning of privacy develops in children[50] (see Figure 8–7). She began by simply asking children what the word *privacy* meant. Their answers were coded according to whether they contained certain themes—such as being alone, managing information, controlling access to specific places, autonomy, quiet, being undisturbed, and so on. Being alone was the theme most mentioned by children of all ages, followed by informa-

FIGURE 8-7 Privacy needs increase during childhood and adolescence.

tion management. The youngest children (ages 4 to 7) mentioned aloneness less often than the older children (ages 8 to 17) in their definitions of privacy. Information management themes were expressed more by the older children (ages 13 to 17) than by the younger ones (ages 4 to 12). Interestingly, control of access to a place peaked as a definitional theme in the middle age group (ages 8 to 12).

If we think of the definitions of the meaning of privacy, but also of a child's present need for privacy, this peak at 8 to 12 years of age may represent a dilemma of preadolescence. At that age, the need for solitude is growing but the child still has a restricted range of places to go outside the home. The only way for the child to obtain solitude is to go into his or her bedroom and close the door. Many struggles between parents and children in this age group develop over access to the child's bedroom. The parents have not yet fully recognized the child's growing privacy needs and still feel they have the right to enter at will; the child wants the opportunity to be alone.

However, the battle over access to a place is often over by adolescence because the parents have finally adjusted to the child's need for solitude and intimacy *with friends*. The adolescent now has a larger range of destinations outside the home and can find solitude and intimacy in many more places than his or her bedroom. At that point, the theme of "a place of my own" fades from the child's definition of privacy because the place issue has subsided.

The autonomy theme—being able to do what you choose—was the least common one in Wolfe's study. However, it is the only theme that significantly increased from early to middle to late childhood. It appeared in about 6 percent of the 4- to 7-year-olds' definitions and in about 23 percent of the 13- to 17-year-olds' definitions.

Other researchers have investigated the privacy behavior of children.[51] One common behavioral expression of a person's need for privacy is closing bedroom and bathroom doors. Children of different ages were asked when and how often they closed their doors. Children who live in houses with more bedrooms and bathrooms close the doors more often. By the adolescent stage, however, the number of bathrooms does not matter—even when there was only one

bathroom, 100 percent of the 10- to 17-year-olds said they closed the door.

Adaptation and Regulation

Another area of privacy and behavior includes the mechanisms by which we regulate privacy. When we have less privacy than we desire, we may adapt so that we no longer believe we need as much as before. In the short term, we may avoid others or seek them out to obtain the amount of social contact we desire. In the long term, some evidence suggests that if we continue to have less privacy than we desire, we adapt by changing our social goals to fit reality. Let's take a look at the evidence.

First-year university students who live in dormitories are especially sensitive to the privacy process. Uprooted from their family homes, they usually need social contact. Thrown together with many others in a residential building, they also sometimes need to get away from others. As everyone who has experienced dormitory life knows, the first year is full of ups and downs related to overexposure and underexposure to other people. Which mechanisms do dormitory residents use to open and close themselves to others? What are the long-term effects of employing these mechanisms?

Researchers asked students how they handled contact with others.[52] The most popular means of seeking others out were, as you might expect, phoning others, visiting others' rooms, leaving one's own door open, and inviting others to one's room. To avoid contact, students closed their doors, sought quiet places, tuned out noise, and went for walks alone. Not all students, however, use the same number or kinds of mechanisms. Hypothesizing a connection between the use of privacy mechanisms and success in school, the researchers compared the number of privacy mechanisms used by students who were still in school about one year later versus those who had dropped out of school. Those still in school were found to have reported using both more contact-seeking mechanisms *and* more contact-avoidance mechanisms than the dropouts.

Although other factors must have played a role too, the implication is that students who know how to regulate their privacy better will do better in school. This does not mean that better students always avoid others; notice that they also used more contact-seeking mechanisms. The mechanisms that were used more by the dropouts are revealing: They went to the dorm lounge more (to seek contact) and they turned up their stereos loud (to avoid contact). The latter mechanism, in particular, may be seen as maladaptive; if someone plays loud music to drive others away, he or she probably cannot study very well either.

Do people adapt to the level of privacy offered by physical settings they use, or do their privacy needs contrast with what is offered? This issue is illustrated by a study of privacy in a nursing home in which the preferences of elderly residents who lived in open wards was compared with those of residents who lived in private rooms.[53] Private room residents—who presumably could regulate their privacy more easily—desired *more* privacy than ward residents. It seems that those who have more privacy desire more, and those who have less desire less. The results support the idea that individuals adapt to the level of privacy their surroundings offer.

Assuming individuals *can* adapt to settings with apparently low levels of privacy, such as wards, is this a healthy adaptation or an unhealthy one? The authors suggest that the residents accept their living conditions as unchangeable. This acceptance grew with the length of time the resident had been institutionalized.

If this adaptation is healthy, or at least not particularly harmful, designers could save space by designing *fewer* private areas. But if residents in the nursing home study expressed satisfaction with open wards out of fatalism, and if privacy is important for resident welfare, then *more* private spaces should be built.

Relation to Crowding, Personal Space, and Territoriality

What are the relations among the space management processes to which the last four chapters have been devoted? Some environmental psychologists believe one or another of them to be primary, with the other processes serving the individual's interests in the primary process. For example, Altman views privacy as the central concept among the processes. Personal space and territoriality are, in his model, mechanisms by which a person regulates privacy. Crowding is the failure to obtain privacy, and too much privacy is loneliness (see Figure 8–8).

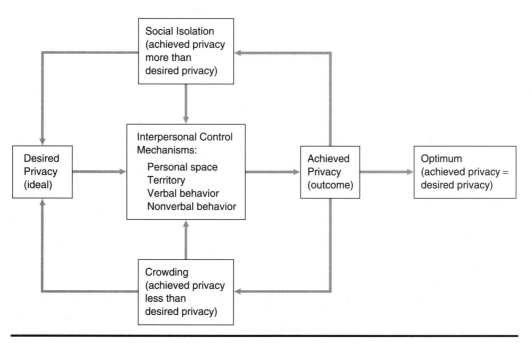

FIGURE 8–8 Altman's perspective on privacy as the central process among our space-regulation behavior processes.

Others have adopted different views—for example, that privacy is a process meant to serve one's territorial interests.[54] Or, as we have noted, certain concepts from one process (e.g., the idea of a free territory) strongly remind people of concepts from another process (e.g., social and individual cognitive freedom, described earlier as a type of privacy). How much do personal space, territoriality, crowding, and privacy overlap?

Theoretical advancement in this area obviously depends on straightening out the relations among these concepts. To that end, students were asked in one study to describe places they choose for solitude and for intimacy.[55] Different kinds of territories were selected for the two kinds of privacy. For example, individuals seeking solitude more often chose public territories, but individuals seeking intimacy more often chose primary territories.

The researchers concluded that neither privacy nor territoriality is more fundamental, but that they are linked on an equal basis, as follows. An individual who desires privacy seeks a particular kind of territory. Once established in that territory, however, both privacy and other needs are served by the individual's possession of the territory. That is, privacy is foremost at some stages in the sequences of social behavior, but territoriality is foremost at others.

Other investigators chose to study the differences between privacy and territoriality by asking individuals where they preferred to engage in a variety of everyday activities.[56] They offered four alternative types of space: (1) home territory with solitude, (2) home territory without solitude, (3) solitude in someone else's territory, and (4) no solitude in someone else's territory. The participants made strong distinctions among the four combinations about where they would like to do various things, which indicates that privacy and territoriality were clearly distinct concepts to the participants.

A second study found further differences between privacy and territory. Participants who were given no solitude tended to attribute their behavior to the influence of others; those who were given a place to territorialize tended to attribute their behavior to their own personality. The authors concluded that privacy and territoriality must be distinct if they produce these different influences on cognitive activity.

A Japanese study helps to distinguish privacy and territoriality as they relate to another of the processes—crowding.[57] Participants were asked how they would feel in a variety of social situations. Across situations, when participants' needs for privacy and needs for territoriality rose, the tendency to experience crowding also rose. Because privacy and territoriality are both associated with a tendency to feel crowded, we might conclude they really are the same construct. However, privacy orientation and territoriality orientation were *not* correlated. This suggests that although they both lead a person to feel more crowded, they do so for different reasons.

The Japanese study did not determine what those different reasons are. One possibility, however, is that privacy primarily refers to social and informational access and territoriality primarily refers to spatial access. The two kinds of access may be sometimes desired at the same time, or one kind of access may facilitate the other kind of access, but there are many occasions when the two kinds of access have nothing to do with each other. For example, someone may want a territory for its economic value or for its personal significance; social-informational access (privacy) is irrelevant. Or, a politician on a campaign visit may wish to maximize social access to voters; while the politician concentrates on that activity, territoriality is minimally at issue.

◆ *IN SUM, a major goal of social behavior is to regulate the amount of contact we have with others. Those who know how to use the environment to accomplish this may be more successful in the social realm and in other areas of life. Some individuals adapt to or accept situations that would seem to offer too much or too little social contact. Others, faced with a shortage of physical mechanisms for regulating social interaction (recall the Gypsies), develop creative solutions to the problem. As a key process in our dealings with others, privacy is inextricably linked to communication, autonomy, identity, emotional release, and growing up. The use of many privacy regulation mechanisms may be one hallmark of success; satisfaction with little privacy is a sign of growing institutionalization.*

The four space management processes (personal space, territoriality, crowding, and privacy) overlap in some ways. For example, in one way or another, they all pertain to an individual's control of access to self. At the same time, they each have unique functional value to the individual and are useful in understanding separate areas of person-environment transactions. Thus, they should not be crammed into a single super-process, nor should their commonalities be ignored. Researchers have correctly begun the task of specifying just when and how the processes are similar as well as when and how they are distinct.

◆ THEORIES OF PRIVACY ◆

We shall see that one theory dominates thinking about privacy, although there are alternatives. Some of these models interpret privacy primarily as a reflection or mechanism supporting some other process. Others view privacy as a vehicle by which individuals define and maintain their identity.[58] Still others emphasize how privacy is interwoven with many aspects of our lives. We will survey some of the narrower and some of the broader approaches to privacy. The dominant theory, proposed by Irwin Altman, is described first, and then some attention is given to the alternative ideas.

Selective Control of Access to Self

Altman conceptualizes privacy as a three-dimensional process.[59,60] First, privacy is a **boundary-control process.** Individuals do not merely attempt to exclude others; they also find themselves seeking out others. The gate to the self swings both ways.

Second, privacy is a **dialectical interplay** between one's desires to be alone and to be with others. Both desires are present, but sometimes one is uppermost and sometimes the other is uppermost.[61] The individual does not seek more and more solitude, reserve, or anonymity; often, intimacy or being together is the goal of social activity. People swing back and forth, the theory says, from wanting to be with others to wanting to be alone.

Privacy is an optimizing process. We always try to match reality with our current desired level of social interaction. According to Altman, the ultimate in privacy is being alone when we want to *and* being with others when we want to. However, that does not mean that all of us desire the same amount of social interaction over a given time period.

Some individuals want to be alone more than others. Therefore, some individuals might rarely see others, yet still be dissatisfied with their privacy because they never want to see anyone. Others might be with friends most of the time and still be dissatisfied; their optimum level of socializing is very high. Privacy is having the *right* amount of social contact, whether that is a large or small amount.

In the third dimension of Altman's model, individuals and cultures employ a variety of means to optimize their privacy; that is, privacy is a **multimechanism process.** As we saw earlier, there is some empirical support for the idea that privacy is a cultural universal. Even societies without walls find ways to allow members ways to achieve privacy. Most people tend to think of privacy in terms of doors and walls, but privacy may be regulated by other mechanisms.

Nonverbal behavior is one mechanism (see Figure 8–9). A person who desires solitude may convey that desire to another person who comes near with a look that clearly says, "Leave me alone." Verbal behavior is another mechanism. Have you ever delivered an invitation to "drop by sometime" knowing that you would probably never specify exactly *what* time, mainly because you do not really want that particular person close to you? The situation can arise when you feel compelled by social pressure to make the invitation, but you do not really want to. Your parents keep asking you to invite their friends' son over for dinner. You think he is a jerk; the feeling may be mutual. Now, having made the invitation as above, you can claim that you invited him over but he "just doesn't seem too enthusiastic."

FIGURE 8–9 Privacy in public spaces chiefly means avoiding unwanted interactions; we use nonverbal behavior such as turning our backs to outsiders to accomplish this.

Clothing can be another privacy mechanism. Consider the use of the veil in traditional Moslem society and the use of sunglasses, even on cloudy days, by some members of North American society.

Altman's descriptive framework of privacy is the most comprehensive in environmental psychology. However, it is not a theory in the classical sense; rather, it is a proposal that environmental psychologists shift from atomistic, homeostatic models to more holistic, process-oriented models of privacy.[62] In reviewing it and others, critics conclude that Altman's model of privacy is the best in many ways but that it does have some shortcomings.[63,64] For example, Altman employed concepts that have multiple definitions, such as self, boundaries, and optimum level of privacy, and the critics fear that confusion may result when the framework is used in research. Altman himself views the theory's value as heuristic—that is, as ideas that should provoke new questions and further research.[65] In the following sections, other points of view are described in the search for a better theory of privacy.

The Life Cycle

Maxine Wolfe expanded our conception of privacy to include a clear role for developmental factors. Wolfe and colleagues show how the management of social interaction and the management of information take on fresh meaning when the individual's life cycle is considered. As we have seen, young children have little sense of privacy. By adulthood, most individuals have strong privacy preferences. What more can be said about privacy across the life span?[66]

The development of the self is based on a gradual realization that self and nonself are distinct; this distinction is closely related to the individual's understanding of privacy and the availability of privacy. Small children like lots of physical intimacy, but as their selves develop through adolescence, their desires for parental intimacy drops (below zero sometimes!).

Then, in love for the first time, the young adult's desire for intimacy is practically insatiable. Next, consider the parent of several young children, who often has too much intimacy and too little solitude. The same parent 15 years later may suffer from an *over*supply of solitude (the empty-nest syndrome) when the children have

all left home. Finally, and unfortunately, many old people also experience an oversupply of solitude: They are lonely.

Finally, Wolfe and colleagues remind us that privacy always has a time dimension to it. This is obvious in that the life cycle is a temporal dimension. But another interesting aspect of privacy and time is that individuals at one life stage may not be able to understand and appreciate the privacy needs of individuals at another life stage. Children may not understand the needs of their parents because they have not yet experienced adult situations. Also, adults seem to forget their own adolescence when they underestimate the desire for privacy as well as the competency for privacy of their own adolescents.[67]

A Hierarchy of Needs

In the course of studying privacy in offices, Eric Sundstrom and associates have raised the possibility that privacy needs are organized in a hierarchical fashion.[68] That is, certain aspects of privacy are more salient at lower job levels, whereas other aspects are more salient at higher job levels, The general outlines of the theory are reminiscent of Abraham Maslow's theory of motivation, in which individuals are said to have needs that must be satisfied in a specific hierarchical order.

Employees at the lowest level in many organizations are also the most visually conspicuous. Working in the view of many others, their greatest privacy need, according to Sundstrom, is for social control—in particular, regulating the amount of person-to-person contact so it is not overwhelming.

At the middle level in many organizations, employees have walled offices; keeping others away is no longer as big a problem. The need is still there, but it often has been met. However, because their work often requires more concentration than that of lower-level employees, their main privacy need is for a setting that allows freedom from distractions, such as noise floating down a hallway.

Nearer the top of the organization, neither social control nor distractions are the main problem. Again, the need is still there, but it has been taken care of. Walls and secretaries protect the executive from unwanted intrusions. Yet, the executive still has a need for privacy, but of a different sort. Executives desire privacy in the sense of protected communication and conversational confidentiality.

Thus, as an employee rises up the privacy hierarchy, his or her privacy needs change. In one sense, the executive has more privacy than the secretary, reflecting the difference in their power. Yet, it may be that their different privacy needs are experienced equally strongly. Executives *may* be less satisfied with their privacy than secretaries.

At first glance, Sundstrom's theory appears to apply only to the work setting. Yet, its basic premises may well apply much more widely, wherever there are power or status differences that are reflected in the privacy-facilitating qualities of individual territories. Although it has not been tested outside the workplace, Sundstrom's theory may also apply in schools, homes, and institutions equally well.

Don't Forget the Physical Environment

Our review of research earlier showed that the physical setting affects privacy. Although the environment often supports or denies privacy, it has not been clearly included in the privacy theories described so far. John Archea believed this is odd, especially for environmental psychologists.[69] Archea argued that privacy theories must include the environment as a full partner in the model, not as a fuzzy backdrop.

Archea reminded us that we vary privacy largely by changing and selecting sites for our behaviors. Because he viewed privacy primarily as an **information distribution process,** Archea believed that the physical environment regulates the flow of privacy. Depending on how it is arranged or designed, it can concentrate, diffuse, segregate, or localize information. Think of visual or auditory information as light or water, and then consider how walls, doors, and windows affect the flow of this light or water. Archea asked designers to analyze physical settings to determine how each one affects the flow of information in these four ways. He also noted that such analyses are not often done.

As a simple example, consider the difference between solid walls and partitions in a psychotherapy clinic. The difference between these two kinds of room dividers will probably have a large effect on the flow of spoken information between client and counselor, as

well as between that client-counselor pair and another client-counselor pair in the next room (see Figure 8–10).

Archea also pointed out that in different physical settings, individuals may be visually conspicuous to others or not. Think, for example, of the surroundings you would select for solitude versus those you would select for intimacy versus those you would select for anonymity. Compare the differences in the three settings that would hinder or promote your visibility in each one. Windows, walls, doors, and line of sight to others are some features that crucially alter visibility. In general, Archea argued that we could understand privacy much better if we specifically considered the properties of physical settings in studies of privacy more often.

◆ ***IN SUM,*** *as we reflect on these theories of privacy, an overriding impression is that we do not yet have a theory with a claim to completeness. Altman's model dominates the area, but other theorists remind us that one aspect or another of privacy has not received due consideration. Privacy may be an optimizing boundary-control process, but there are some problems with the definition of (and therefore with the measurement of) key terms in this approach. Central to the issue is whether privacy is fundamentally a self-defined concept or an objectively definable one. When privacy is considered a subjective and dynamic phenomenon, it can be difficult to measure, and scientific tests of theories holding this position may be difficult. Archea, for example, observed that privacy has a strong environmental component, although he recognized the psychological aspects of privacy (e.g., that we select our settings whenever*

FIGURE 8–10 Meetings at the table in this room will not be very private, either visually or acoustically.

possible). Wolfe notes that privacy preferences, expectations, and satisfaction vary over the life cycle. Sundstrom observes that at any one point in the life cycle, our privacy needs vary as a function of our status.

◆ **PRIVACY AND** ◆
ENVIRONMENTAL DESIGN

The goal of the designer must be to give everyone as much privacy as possible. This does *not* mean constructing houses, offices, schools, institutions, and outdoor spaces so that each person has a separate walled compartment! All the theorists agree that privacy can mean openness to others as much as it means being closed to others. The important thing is to live and work in settings that allow an individual to *regulate* access to others. We turn now to specific design examples in housing and offices.

Privacy in Housing

A residence is already a relatively private space. In the developed world, the walls and doors provided by our houses probably are the most common mechanisms we use to manage privacy, even though some surveys report that many individuals associate residential privacy with exterior factors such as lot size and distance from neighbors.[70,71] If a house is large enough, privacy is not a problem unless it is so large that family members become isolated and alienated from one another. More often, unfortunately, the problem is insufficient space or poor arrangement of the available space.[72]

Privacy may vary as a function of design in the semiprivate spaces of multiunit housing projects. In New York, researchers studied privacy in the lobbies, elevators, and other public areas within low-rise and high-rise buildings.[73] Naturally, such areas offer less solitude or intimacy than a person's own apartment, but the study found that the semipublic areas in the low-rise design were judged by residents to offer more privacy than the semipublic areas in the high-rise design. In support of the notion that satisfaction with privacy does not mean being isolated, the low-rise tenants were more socially active and belonged to more voluntary organizations than the high-rise tenants. In a study that compared privacy in dormitories with long-corridor designs with that in short-corridor designs, residents of long-corridor dormitories reported more difficulty in maintaining adequate privacy than did residents of short-corridor dormitories.[74] In both studies, lack of privacy may result when residents must pass more strangers in the public areas of their building.

Christopher Alexander is an architect who has thought about privacy in housing for many years. One solution devised by Alexander when indoor space is limited is the **privacy gradient**.[75] Based on careful consideration of cultural practices and interviews, Alexander arranged space in low-cost Peruvian homes from the most public, near the entrance, to the most private, located farthest from the entrance (see Figure 8–11).

The balance between privacy (in the sense of solitude or intimacy) and community (relations with neighbors) can be difficult to balance in a housing design. Even projects that attempt to follow Alexander's principles do not always succeed in usefully balancing privacy and community.[76] Clearly, there is no single universal design that guarantees residential privacy. Each

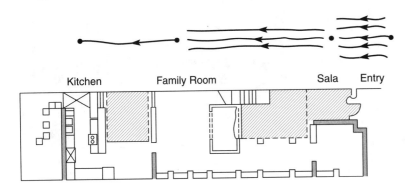

Kitchen   Family Room   Sala   Entry

FIGURE 8–11 Here is an example of the privacy gradient incorporated into Christopher Alexander's plan for low-income housing in Peru.

family or client's needs must be carefully considered if the designer is to provide a cost-efficient yet private dwelling. However, certain groups of residents are sufficiently similar that some design considerations may apply to most buildings serving them.

Privacy in Offices

Privacy at work is a growing issue. Recent studies of the visual, acoustical, social, and informational privacy in offices suggest that many arrangements are far from satisfactory.[77,78] Another expert observes that arrangements are all too often made on such crude considerations as the number of employees per square foot, when they should be made on the basis of work efficiency.[79] Yet, employees consider privacy very important. One study of faculty offices found that privacy was considered more important than amount of space, temperature and ventilation, furniture, lighting, view, and general aesthetics.[80]

As with houses, the preferred office usually is large and solidly enclosed enough to ensure control of access to the self. But not everyone has such an office, owing in part to the pervasive system of allocating office space on the basis of rank and seniority. Ideally, should offices be designed for isolation? The answer depends on the type of work, personal preferences, and social norms.

1. Not every job would be performed best in an office that offers complete solitude. Some work (such as writing textbooks) requires solitude, and other work is better suited to open office plans (brainstorming or interdepartmental communication). Therefore, the type of work being done is an important consideration.

2. Not every person *wishes* to work in a totally private office. Individual privacy preferences are another important consideration. Some writers work best as a team, and some brainstormers produce more alone than as part of a group.

3. Social interaction norms must be taken into account.[81] The type of interaction (such as informal banter versus financial decision making) is often linked to certain locations within offices. For example, informal conversation typically occurs in hallways and around water fountains, but financial decisions are usually

made by an individual or group in a physically isolated setting. Office arrangements should reflect these norms.

A study of performance and satisfaction in traditional one-person walled offices versus open four-person offices found that different kinds of persons performed best in different offices.[82] For example, male introverts performed simple tasks best in the open office. No single office design is best for all office employees.

Office design, then, should never be haphazard or based simply on tradition. Rather, it should be tuned to rank, type of work, personal preferences, norms, and even personality. Very little empirical research on work spaces has yet managed to consider all these factors. Furthermore, it is not easy to incorporate all these considerations into a design. In the meantime, the authors of one study suggest that the flexibility offered by modular furniture designs represent a good compromise between the tension created by our needs for solitude and interaction.[83]

Field studies in offices may try to take all these factors into account, but they usually lack experimental control. Consequently, some researchers have approached the office design problem by investigating one or two carefully controlled factors at a time in lab experiments. One such study focused on a work activity that comes before all other types of work—applying for a job.[84] Individuals who responded to a newspaper ad came to the laboratory, which had been furnished and decorated very much like a typical personnel office. They applied for one of four positions that students might really seek (community project officer, management trainee, research assistant, and clerk) and role-played the application and interview procedure.

To vary privacy during the interview, the researchers arranged for half the applicants to hear someone typing intermittently on the other side of a partition (low privacy); the other half heard no one else in the office except the interviewer (high privacy). Applicants in the low-privacy condition expressed significantly less satisfaction with the job interview. In particular, applicants interviewed in the low-privacy condition reported feeling significantly more inhibited in their answers than applicants in the high-privacy condition (see Figure 8–12).

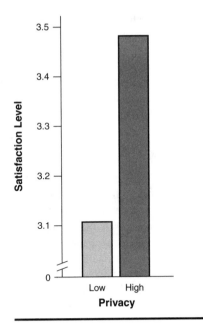

FIGURE 8-12 When job applicants believe that a third party can overhear their interview for a new job (low privacy), they are less satisfied than if they think no one can overhear the interview (high privacy).

◆ SUMMARY ◆

Privacy is a process in which we attempt to regulate interaction with others, including social interaction and information about the self that may be kept on file. It has largely been studied through questionnaires and interviews. Preferences, expectations, values, norms, and the behavior of individuals vary from person to person and from occasion to occasion as individuals attempt to manage their desires for solitude, reserve, anonymity, intimacy, and other forms of privacy. Privacy is intimately linked to other psychological processes, such as other space management mechanisms and control, communication, identity, emotion, adaptation, and growing up. The physical environment plays a key role in facilitating privacy regulation; it can either make the task easy or force those with few architectural resources to become creative in their search for privacy. Some persons who have little opportunity to regulate their privacy seem to adapt to these circumstances; whether that has harmful effects or represents successful coping is unclear. Sensitive designers can arrange architectural space in private and public spaces to maximize an individual's ability to regulate interaction with others.

Suggested Supplementary Readings

Altman, I. (1975). *The environment and social behavior.* Monterey, CA: Brooks/Cole.

Archea, J. (1977). The place of architectural factors in behavioral theories of privacy. *Journal of Social Issues, 33*(3), 116–137.

Haggard, L. M., & Werner, C. M. (1990). Situational support, privacy regulation, and stress. *Basic and Applied Social Psychology, 11,* 313–337.

Patterson, A. H., & Chiswick, N. R. (1981). The role of the social and physical environment in privacy maintenance among the Iban of Borneo. *Journal of Environmental Psychology, 1,* 131–139.

Stone, E. F., Gueutal, H. G., Gardner, D. G., & McClure, S. (1983). A field experiment comparing information-privacy values, beliefs, and attitudes across several types of organizations. *Journal of Applied Psychology, 68,* 459–468.

Sundstrom, E., Town, J. P., Brown, D. W., Forman, A., & McGee, C. (1982). Physical enclosure, type of job, and privacy in the office. *Environment and Behavior, 14,* 543–559.

Taylor, R. B., & Ferguson, G. (1980). Solitude and intimacy: Linking territoriality and privacy experiences. *Journal of Nonverbal Behavior, 4,* 227–239.

CHAPTER **9**

RESIDENTIAL ENVIRONMENTAL PSYCHOLOGY

> This is the true nature of home—it is the place of Peace; the shelter, not only from injury, but from all terror, doubt, and division. In so far as it is not this, it is not home. . . . It is then only a part of the outer world which you have roofed over.
>
> —John Ruskin[1]

*T*om *wandered aimlessly through his grandfather's big old house. He had spent so many childhood hours happily lost in its nooks, playing on the wonderfully smooth, worn, mahogany stairs and gazing at the titles of the heavy books on the shelves. His grandfather, weakening but still of sound mind, had just announced that, after his death, Tom would inherit the house.*

Tom loved its walls, the rooms, the pictures, the steep roof. Unfortunately, its formerly tranquil semirural neighborhood had been overtaken by the city. The house, which properly belonged on a small farm, now was stuck only a block from a busy six-lane road. The ills of the modern city lay just outside the door to the house that belonged to another, more peaceful century. The windows had been broken and Tom's grandfather had been the victim of three recent break-ins and one mugging.

Tom longed to show the house to Jane, but at the same time he was uncertain whether she would like it. For one thing, the house had been flooded several times in its lifetime; each time, Tom's grandparents had lost heavily. As he was about to abandon his dream of living with Jane in the old place, he remembered a few good points. The house was right on a bus line, close to downtown shopping and a great old park, and taxes were low.

And then there were the spacious rooms, the beautiful woodwork his grandfather had spent years carving, and the high ceilings that made you feel you were in a real house instead of one of those modern crackerboxes. Full of these thoughts, Tom set off to tell Jane of his coming inheritance—his new old home.

◆   ◆   ◆

Home is the most important place in our lives. This importance gives it great potential for helping us to thrive—or for threatening our very survival. In this chapter, the focus is on environmental psychology in the residence. The word *home* is used in this chapter to refer to small spaces, such as one's room, house, or apartment, or, in the next chapter, to broader areas, such as the immediate neighborhood, town, district, or city. Although *home* can refer to the nation, or the planet, these large-scale meanings will not be discussed in this book.

Home usually is the most important refuge from the stresses of work, school, and the street life. Unfortunately, many people live in residences that do not provide protection and rejuvenation, or have no home at all. When this primary territory does not serve our basic needs, it can become more hellish than the secondary and public territories we left for the peace of home. Three main concerns in this chapter on the environmental psychology of home are discussed.

We begin with a definition of home and then explore what makes residences preferable or satisfactory. The way we manage space in the home for work and relaxation is examined, as is the connection between home and self-identity. The positive and negative consequences of living in different residences are considered. Finally, four examples of the application of environmental psychology to the design of homes and communities are offered.

◆   WHAT IS HOME?   ◆

A house is not a home. A house (or apartment, condo, tipi or, in general, any residence) is a physical structure. Home is the rich set of evolving cultural, demographic, and psychological meanings we attach to that physical structure.[2] Thus, despite real estate advertisements to the contrary, you cannot buy a home. You can buy (or rent) a residence and, with luck, time, and effort, turn it into a home. Thus, two definitions are needed—one for residence and one for home.

What Is a Residence?

Although there are many forms of residences, their common element is that they are physical structures. Instead of trying to list every type of residence (e.g., longhouse, farmhouse, penthouse), which would lead to a very long list—particularly if we consider all the variations in housing around the world—it is preferable to discover a small number of key dimensions along which every type of residence may be located (see Figure 9–1). Adopting such an approach, Irwin Altman and colleagues have characterized residences along five dimensions: (1) permanent versus temporary, (2) differentiated versus homogeneous, (3) communal versus noncommunal, (4) identity versus communality, and (5) openness versus closedness.[3,4]

FIGURE 9–1 Residences take many forms and influence many of our most important interactions.

1. Residences vary from **permanent** to **temporary**. In industrialized countries, residents usually have permanent dwellings, although apparently this situation is not entirely satisfactory, because many householders also maintain temporary homes such as cabins, cottages, and recreational vehicles. In some less industrialized countries, residents move frequently and often construct temporary homes in new places.

2. Residences vary from **differentiated** to **homogeneous,** meaning the separation, or lack of it, in the functions of rooms. A highly differentiated residence has many rooms, each of which houses a specific activity; in a homogeneous residence, almost any activity may occur in nearly any room. Differentiation, of course, is partly a function of wealth. It is not easy to be poor and have a highly differentiated residence. Little research on the effects of differentiation is available, although it is must be an important environmental influence on our daily be-

havior. For example, privacy and territoriality, and perhaps crowding, must be strongly affected by the degree of differentiation in our homes.

3. Residences vary in **communality** and **noncommunality,** or the degree to which nuclear families live together or in different homes. In many Eastern cultures, several generations of a family live in one household. In some African and Native-American cultures, numerous unrelated families live in one home.

4. Dwellings vary in **identity** versus **communality**. Residences often reflect the personal touches of their occupants. Identity is the extent to which a residence depicts the unique interests and needs of its residents. Communality (the same word as in item 3, but with a different meaning here) is the extent to which a residence meets the common stereotype of a home in that culture. A tipi on a suburban lot in North America would be low on communality. The same tipi would be high on communality at a pow-wow on the open plains of the central United States.

5. Residences vary in their **openness** versus **closedness** to outsiders. This dimension varies both within and between cultures. In some places, houses typically are surrounded by walls or hedges; in others, they are not. Residents may be welcoming or cool or even hostile to casual visitors. Thus, dwellings and their occupants signal willingness or unwillingness to interact with neighbors or other visitors.

A fascinating panorama of residential variation may be observed across cultures.[5,6,7] Variation also occurs within any single culture, such as our own. Yet, the psychological effects of these variations are still largely unknown. We cannot ordinarily conduct field experiments by placing residents randomly in different kinds of homes, so we may never fully understand the effects of different home types. We can and should, however, conduct studies to monitor what happens when individuals move from one type of home to another, such as from the family home to a dormitory or nursing home.

In this culture, in which the ideal residence probably is permanent, differentiated, and noncommunal, many residents reside in homes that are temporary (dormitories, apartments, rented houses), homogeneous (a place that has space for the separation of dining from cooking, or hobbies from entertaining, or laundering from automobile storage is unaffordable), and communal (roommates are necessary to pay the rent).

Once Again, What Is Home?

Home is a set of meanings. Its earliest meaning probably was the village or community of one's origin; not until the sixteenth or seventeenth century did it refer to one's domestic dwelling.[8] Home is so different from the residence that some people may not even live at home, although they always live in their residences. Home really is where the heart is.

Home, like residence, may be described with a set of key dimensions. The dimensions of home are such that one end is *home* and the other end is *not a home* (as opposed to the residence dimensions, both ends of which describe residences, but of different kinds). Cer-

tainly not everyone who lives in a residence lives in a home, as the following dimensions of home will make clear.

Six dimensions of home are haven, order, identity, and connectedness, warmth, and physical suitability.[9,10,11,12]

1. Home is a **haven** that surrounds us with privacy, security, refuge, and protection from the slings and arrows of life outside it.

2. Home helps us to know our place in the world. It is a center from which we venture and return; it is one way that we **order** our existence in the world. This ordering is not only spatial but also temporal. Home is strongly related to our sense of continuity: childhood experiences, leaving and returning, and the patterning of our daily lives.

3. Home is central to our **identity**. As social creatures, home includes for us a sense of family or kinship, ethnic belonging, and socioeconomic status. Home is thus an important part of who we are. Through self-expression and personalization, the home comes to resemble or represent our selves. Home is a symbol of self,[13] "the articulation and confirmation of our very existence."[14] We give the physical structure identity as we transform it from a mere residence into a home, but we also derive our own identity in part *from* that home.

4. Through order and identity, home means **connectedness**.[15] The patterns of spatial and temporal order help us feel connected to certain people, to the place, to the past, and to the future. We feel part of a family or group, and part of a culture.

5. Home is **warmth**. It grows out of the preceding qualities, but goes beyond them. This warmth is like that of the hearth, but is symbolic and interpersonal.

6. Home is **physically suitable**. Obviously, this means more than the material physical aspects of the house. It means the form and structure of the house matches our psychological needs.

If we are fortunate to have a place that provides haven, order, identity, connectedness, warmth, and physical suitability, then home has great personal and social meaning for us, and we likely also experience be- longingness, happiness, self-expression, and good rela- tionships within the home.[16] To the extent that our residence does *not* have these meanings for us, we are homeless—even if we inhabit a palace.

Houselessness and Homelessness

We usually think of a homeless person as someone with- out a place to live, a houseless person. But it is possible to have a residence and yet be homeless. The place where such a person lives has little or no meaning to him or her, provides no sense of security, order, identity, con- nectedness, warmth, or suitability (see Figure 9–2). Some houseless persons have homes but are separated from them. Sometimes this is by choice (e.g., a person wants the street life or the gypsy life for a while); some- times it is not (e.g., the person was forced away from home, but that residence still has all the meanings of home). In short, homelessness is not necessarily the same as houselessness.

The houseless person probably becomes a homeless person in stages.[17] In the first stage, family support is lost. The person gradually loses the opportunity to rely on family for essential emotional or financial resources. In the second stage, the support of friends is lost. Some key elements of home can be provided by friends during

FIGURE 9–2 Houselessness and homelessness are major problems in many cities.

or after the loss of family, but once both family and friends are gone, houselessness is much closer to home- lessness. In the third stage, the person loses the support of the community. Some social benefits require an ad- dress or roots or connection to others in the commu- nity. Without these ties, financial or other supports from the community (even such minor but important items as a library card) may be lost.

Humane solutions to the problem of homelessness must focus on the provision of both housing and sup- port. Merely offering a place to sleep in a large, anony- mous shelter or in a horizontal barrel in a park is inadequate—so is merely providing hot lunches or emergency clothing allowances. When homeless people in shelters feel a greater loss of control, perhaps from having others both serve them and make the rules, they are more likely to give up looking for a way out of their homelessness.[18]

The homeless need an integrated plan aimed at the restoration of both housing and support. One city has generously funded a five-step program that offers:

- Basic services such as food, clothing, and showers
- Physical and mental health care
- Shelter
- Employment (including training and transporta- tion)
- Housing that is more permanent than shelters[19]

There will always be homeless people, but perhaps pro- grams like this one can reduce the number to those who *choose* to be homeless.

Measuring Home

How can a residence or a home be measured? In the case of a residence, one approach would be to classify it on each of the five physical structure-and-use dimensions used earlier in the definition of residence (how differen- tiated versus homogeneous its interior is, how commu- nal are the living arrangements are, etc.). A second approach would be financial: What is the monetary value of the dwelling? A third might be a lengthy listing of its attributes, such as its age, architectural style, size, rooms, and so on, such as one finds in a real estate ad- vertisement. No standard measuring system using these approaches is available, although it is known that trained real estate assessors can use their experience to reliably estimate the monetary value of houses.[20]

A fourth approach to measuring a residence or a home is to measure the *quality* of a residence for a particular purpose. One such purpose is child development. Several scales have been created to assess the quality of a residence for children.[21,22,23,24] These scales typically measure both the physical environment of the residence (e.g., its cleanliness, size, or form) and its social environment (e.g., positiveness of parents' vocal tone, number of stories read).

Because home is a set of meanings, a measure of it would attempt to assess the meaning of a residence as a home. Again, the best guide probably would be the set of dimensions outlined earlier. The more that a residence means to a person on each of the dimensions, the more the residence would be a home. However, no such measure has yet been devised. Maybe *you* should try!

◆ **IN SUM,** *a house is not home. Houses (or, more generally, residences) are physical structures that vary tremendously around the world. They can be described in terms of how open or closed they are, how similar to neighboring residences they are, whether they are permanent or temporary, or on any number of physical features such as number of bedrooms, size and age. Home is a set of meanings such as haven, order, connectedness, and meaningfulness that we bestow on a residence, which in turn becomes part of our own identity. Not everyone has a home; even some people who occupy a house are homeless. Houseless people may have a home—a residence with meaning that, for one reason or another, they are unable to live in. Houselessness is more than lack of a house; many other social negative social consequences follow. Individuals who are both houseless and homeless are extremely unfortunate.*

◆ **AN ORGANIZING FRAMEWORK** ◆

In order to make sense of residential environmental psychology, an organizing framework is needed (see Figure 9–3). The purpose of such a framework is to provide an overall picture of the causes and consequences of living in different dwellings. As in previous chapters, four main categories of influence will be considered: personal, social, physical, and cultural factors. The consequences fall into three general categories: attitudes, such as preferences and satisfaction; behavior, such as space management, leisure, and arrangement of furniture; and well-being, such as health, stress, fear of crime, and social support.

Figure 9–3 is presented as an organizing framework for this and other research. The framework is loosely patterned after Brunswik's lens model (see Chapter 2) and Craik's model of environment comprehension (see Chapter 3). Beginning at the left of the framework, note that each home has thousands of characteristics. Many of these might be unimportant, but others will be important in the understanding of residential satisfaction, behavior, and well-being.

Researchers must select for study some objective characteristics of the dwelling that they believe have some impact on satisfaction, behavior, or well-being. Some of these objective characteristics might be the type of housing (single-family dwelling, apartment, condominium), age, location, market value, lot size, and architectural style. Some (but obviously not all) of these objective features are perceived by the resident. But just how does the residence become known? A person may experience a dwelling over the span of a few minutes (as a prospective buyer who tours the house) or many years (in the case of long-term residents). The perception usually is "live," but if the residence happens to be still in its planning stages, it may have to be simulated. The observer's experience with the residence may be thorough, including an inspection of every corner, or cursory, merely viewing the place while driving by.

The next element in the model is the observer. Who is this person (which culture, personality, sex, age, occupation)? How much experience with different residences does this observer have? In evaluating a residence, will the observer compare it to an ideal residence, to past residences, or to standards of residential quality acquired from friends or from the media? Is the observer a resident of the dwelling in question, or a passerby, real estate agent, neighbor, or tax assessor?

So far, then, selected distal cues are perceived through two filters: the mode of presentation and the observer's personal characteristics. These interact and, presto, impressions emerge. "Aha," says the observer, "this house is cozy (or grimy, or gloomy, or functional)." These observer impressions are not, in themselves, con-

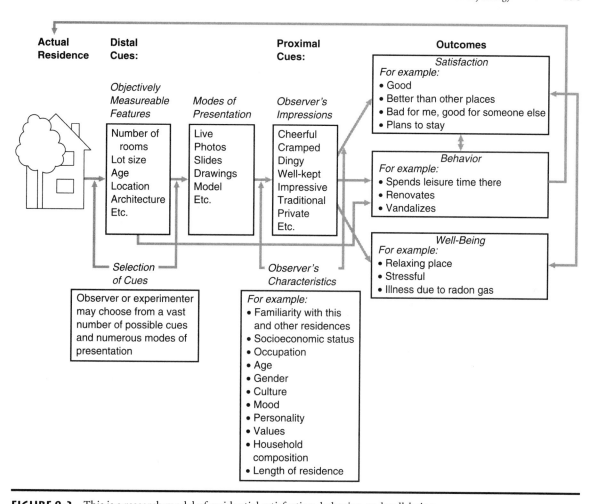

FIGURE 9–3 This is a research model of residential satisfaction, behavior, and well-being.

clusions about the ultimate value of the residence. For example, an observer may decide that a house is "traditional," but that does not tell us whether the observer values the house; some people like traditional houses and others do not.

Notice that the model also includes a direct path from the objective characteristics to the outcomes. This is because some effects of the house may occur without the resident's awareness. For example, if radon gas leaks into a house and the residents are not aware of it, their health may be seriously affected. Mode of presentation, observer characteristics, and impressions would be irrelevant.

◆ **RESIDENTIAL PREFERENCE, CHOICE,** ◆
AND SATISFACTION

What sort of residence would you prefer? Where are you actually living? If you gave different answers to these questions, you know the difference between residential preference and residential choice. If the difference between your preference and your choice is great, you may be unsatisfied with your residence and it may never develop into a home.

Many people prefer what they cannot have and so, for economic or other reasons, they must choose a less-preferred place to live. When we *can* choose what we prefer, we should be most satisfied. However, with tradeoffs, a less-preferred dwelling may not be terribly unsatisfying.[25] For example, many individuals would prefer to live in a single-family dwelling, but may be reasonably happy in a downtown apartment because it is closer to work, concerts, and friends. Researchers have examined just how much distance we are willing to trade off for our ideal dwelling.[26]

Both residential preferences and residential choices can be predicted.[27,28] Preferences are more predictable from personal and architectural factors (e.g., a person's values or the physical form of the residence); choices are more predictable from economic factors (e.g., income and cost of the residence).

Of course, there are some residences that would make *anyone* dissatisfied. They are so run-down, poorly maintained, or poorly located that almost no one would want to live there. And there are individuals who will not be satisfied by any residence. They are so fussy, cranky, neurotic, or perfectionistic that they would find fault with any residence. Between these extremes, however, are most homes and most residents. Different homes satisfy different residents.

Measuring Residential Satisfaction

To understand residential satisfaction, it must be adequately measured. But measuring it is not as simple as asking, "Do you like your apartment?" For example, satisfaction may vary depending on whether individuals are asked to compare their residences (e.g., to their previous residence or to their ideal residence) or not.[29] Satisfaction may vary for different sections of the residence, different qualities of it (e.g., spaciousness, beauty, or lighting), and the relation between these qualities and their use by the resident (e.g., lighting for a party versus lighting for washing the dishes).[30]

David Canter has described two cognitive processes related to residential satisfaction.[31] He believes that our evaluation of a residence's satisfactoriness is necessarily **purposive**. Purposive evaluations have several facets to them: the level, referent, and focus factors.

1. Satisfaction may vary in its specificity or **level**. Residents may be asked to evaluate a single part of the resi-

dence (e.g., the kitchen) or a larger portion of it (e.g., the bedrooms as a whole).

2. Residents may be asked to assess different qualities of the residence (e.g., its beauty, lighting, or spaciousness). These qualities are called **referents;** each one suggests a certain purpose the residence serves well or poorly. The lighting referent, for example, is important when the resident considers tasks such as reading or sewing that require good lighting.

3. Questions may take **focus** into account. The meaning of focus depends on the referent, but one way to think of it is to ask how broadly we are asking the resident to evaluate something. With reference to lighting, is it the ability of this particular lamp to light a study desk, or is it broader, such as lighting in the home as a whole?

The role of **purpose** emerges when we ask about the resident's relationship *to* the residence. Some feel as if they will live in the place forever, but others intend to move soon or are renting. This can make a huge difference in the resident's evaluation. Thus, in general, a resident's purpose in doing an evaluation is itself a crucial factor in satisfaction.

Another cognitive factor of interest is **comparison**. Whether we explicitly ask observers to compare a specific residence against a series of others or merely ask for a rating of the present one without explicitly pointing out others, they cannot help at least implicitly comparing the residence in question with others in their experience. This, of course, means that different observers will be comparing the present residence against different houses in their experience.

When the observer compares residences, a discrepancy between residences will appear. Some approaches to residential satisfaction focus on this discrepancy between present and past residences, or between present and ideal residences. *Perceived* physical qualities of a residence (such as its appearance and provision for privacy) are important predictors of satisfaction,[32] and so are *preferred* physical qualities. However, the *difference* between perceived and preferred qualities is a separate but important predictor of housing satisfaction.[33] Enough of these complexities. What do we actually know, based on research to date?

Personal Influences

Satisfaction and preference obviously depend, in part, on the resident. The characteristics of individuals that influence satisfaction include demographic factors, personality, values, expectations, comparisons with other housing, and hopes for the future. These psychological influences on housing satisfaction can be more important than the type of housing in which one lives.[34] Let's begin with some examples of demographic indicators of satisfaction.

Age and Stage of Life. First, differences in preferences for residences are associated with age or stage in the life cycle. Age-linked differences in satisfaction presumably are caused by changes in our needs, purposes, and position in society that usually accompany age. Over 85 percent of residents of all ages wish to own their dwelling,[35] but families with young children usually prefer the suburbs, whereas many older couples and single residents prefer to live downtown.

In an investigation of preferences for dwelling style, younger adults valued more ornate residences, and older adults preferred plainer ones.[36,37] Plainness may not sound attractive, but it does imply simplicity and clarity—attributes that are important to those elderly individuals who find mobility and perception more difficult than they once did. The younger adults liked a residence with mystery, but the older adults did not; they may prefer to find their mystery in a novel, where it would not make their lives more difficult.

Not much evidence is available on the residential satisfaction of individuals at the youthful end of the age range. However, one study of children's satisfaction reports that their views are quite similar to those of their parents.[38] One researcher asked 8- to 18-year-olds to draw their ideal homes.[39] Again, like adults, these residences tended to be single-family dwellings. However, they were larger than their current dwellings and had more leisure-oriented space in them.

The preference of many elderly people is to keep their current residence, particularly compared to the alternative of institutional housing. Most people over age 75 prefer to "age in place" and do not spend much time thinking about future residences; they generally want to keep things the same.[40] The elderly who are satisfied with their homes are less interested in new or different environments, travel less, and are happier with their lives than those who are less satisfied with their homes.[41]

Socioeconomic Status. Residential satisfaction is also related to socioeconomic status. In general, of course, wealthier individuals are better able to supply themselves with homes that meet their standards, and thus are more satisfied. However, wealthier and poorer members of society may be attuned to *different* features of their homes. One study found that wealthier individuals were sensitive to the aesthetic qualities of their homes, but poorer individuals were sensitive to safety, health, and family needs as well as aesthetics.[42] Presumably, the wealthier are less sensitive to the other concerns because their safety, health, and family are not in immediate danger, although other explanations are possible. Still, one implication of the results is that the poor must spend their energy attempting to satisfy a greater number of needs.

Sex and Social Role. Social role influences residential satisfaction. Husbands and wives often disagree on the suitability of a home. In a study of Canadian households that had recently moved, for example, husbands and wives were asked to list the things that made them happy about their new homes and apartments.[43] Among couples who moved to a downtown apartment, over 40 percent of the wives mentioned that they were satisfied with the quality of the home, but only 5 percent of the husbands mentioned this. On the other hand, among couples that moved to suburban apartments, over 50 percent of the husbands mentioned quality of the home as a source of their satisfaction, but only 5 percent of the wives did (see Figure 9–4).

As men increasingly enjoy cooking, similarities and differences in men's and women's preferences for kitchen designs become more important.[44] Both men and women prefer kitchens that open to dining and family room areas rather than kitchens that are separated from those areas.[45] However, women who work outside the home prefer open kitchens more than women who do not work outside the home. Despite their agreement on the open-closed aspect of the kitchen, men and women differ in many other kitchen spatial preferences.

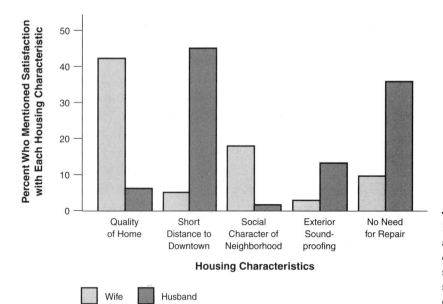

Housing Characteristics

☐ Wife   ■ Husband

FIGURE 9–4 Husbands and wives who moved to a downtown apartment report some different sources of satisfaction with their new dwelling.

A study in which men and women were asked to design houses found that women design smaller houses with more communal space and more curvature to the walls, and their designs were rated as more original.[46] When men and women designed houses together, the size was larger (like the males' designs) and had even more curvature than the women's designs.

Personality and Values. Some significant relations between personality and residential satisfaction have been reported. A study of satisfaction with army housing as a function of soldier personality found that aggressive soldiers were generally dissatisfied with their housing.[47] Those with a desire for structure in their lives particularly appreciated the physical features of their living environment, as did soldiers with more nurturant personalities. Soldiers whose personalities lead them to seek considerable social support expressed greater preferences for design features that would assist this need, such as more private visiting areas and more telephones.

Sociable individuals, given the choice, should select housing that maximizes social interaction. A study of first-year dormitory residents' preferences for their second year's housing showed that more affiliative students preferred, and actually selected, housing that offers the potential for more social interaction (e.g., a fraternity

versus living alone).[48] This trend even held up for housing choices in their third year, suggesting that personality is a reasonably long-term predictor of housing preference and choice.

Another key personal predictor of housing preference and choice is one's life values. We tend to favor residences that we believe will help us attain the goals implied by these life values.[49]

Comparisons. If you did not know that your friend lives in a mansion, you might be more satisfied with your hut. We compare residences, such as our own previous dwellings with our current one[50] and those of others with our own. Such comparisons can be an important source of satisfaction or dissatisfaction. In a study of army personnel living in mobile homes and apartments, comparison with other housing accounted for 30 percent of the variance in housing satisfaction—a very significant chunk.[51]

Dreams of the Future. Finally, time is important in residential satisfaction.[52] Whether one expects improvement in one's housing also affects satisfaction with one's current housing. Thus, several individuals can live in the same place, but some will be happier than others if they expect an improvement.[53] However, those who do not yet live in their dream house are not necessarily dissatisfied with their present dwelling. They seem able to tolerate its limitations as long as their aspirations seem possible. If, for some reason, the dream becomes impossible, however, dissatisfaction may grow.

Social Influences

Our interactions with other people—our ties to them, the norms we share, privacy versus independence, security—play an important role in residential preference, choice, and satisfaction. In fact, a key part of the definition of home is its social function. In a study of the reasons for satisfaction with dormitories, the main reasons given were independence (from parents, presumably), security (compared to off-campus housing), privacy (compared to sharing a house), and socialization (learning the customs of the school). The main reasons for dissatisfaction were visitor restrictions, curfew, and noise.[54] Note that every one of these reasons is essentially social; they all refer to interpersonal relations in one way or another.

Neighbors. Neighbors may be less important than they once were for housing satisfaction, but they still can be important, particularly if they are very good or very bad neighbors. A Spanish study of over 400 housewives found that neighbors and neighborhood attachment were the *most* important factor in residential satisfaction—more important than objective housing factors[55] (see Figure 9–5). Another social factor is the similarity of neighbors; residential satisfaction is greater when we believe our neighbors are similar to us.[56,57] A related factor is the seclusion-community dimension. We prefer housing that provides the balance of separation and togetherness with neighbors that suit us.

Norms. Most of us, when considering a place to live, pay at least some attention to what are "usual" housing arrangements for people like ourselves. For example, a study of the living arrangement choices of the elderly reports that social norms for privacy and independence are important factors when they select a living arrangement.[58]

Others' Preferences. Another social factor is living-group interaction. In any family or group that decides to

FIGURE 9–5 Social interaction among neighbors is a key factor in neighborhood success.

live together, considerable negotiation must be completed before a particular dwelling is selected for rent or purchase. We all know that such interpersonal politics over housing preferences and choices occur, but research on the topic is scarce.

The Shape of Privacy, Security, and Social Interaction. An interesting way to determine individual preferences for residences is to ask them to make a drawing or model. One study focused this question further by asking people to design a house to provide privacy (or security or social interaction).[59] Houses designed for privacy were more differentiated; they contained more rooms, and therefore more corridors and smaller average room sizes. Houses designed for security were the smallest. Smaller houses mean less territory to defend and they keep occupants closer together, which may aid in the defense of the house. Houses designed for social interaction had greater visibility among their interior spaces and more rounded walls; the latter may reflect sociopetal design tendencies.

Physical Influences

Obviously, the physical characteristics of dwellings also significantly affect our preferences and satisfaction with them. For example, smaller noisy dwellings with fewer rooms will generally be less satisfactory.[60] We will consider four kinds of physical features: housing form (e.g., single family, apartment, etc.), architectural style (e.g., farmhouse, saltbox, colonial, etc.), interior (e.g., size, room arrangements, colors, walls, etc.), and outdoor areas (gardens, patios, etc.).

Before describing specific research findings, it is worth stating that housing preference research supports two broad conclusions. One is that different housing will satisfy different people. Thus, the main question for researchers is: Who will be happy with which housing? The second conclusion is that some housing is satisfactory to almost no one (even those who live in it but who presumably have no choice)[61] or almost everyone (e.g., very expensive housing). Thus, another question is: Which physical characteristics of buildings will appeal to *most* people?

For example, a study of apartment preferences found considerable agreement in the ratings of 45 quite variable apartment buildings by residents of a town, even though the residents came from varying socioeconomic levels and neighborhoods.[62] If the residents agreed which apartments were preferable and which were not, which features swayed them one way or the other? In general, older apartment buildings were preferred over those that looked like multiple-family dwellings, and highly detailed designs were favored over plain and simple designs.

Thus, we reach two conclusions that sound contradictory: One is "to each his or her own" and the other says that most people agree about which housing is preferable. However contradictory they sound, the truth is that both statements are partly correct and neither is wholly correct. They are complementary rather than contradictory. With these thoughts in mind, let's examine the evidence concerning house form.

Housing Form. William Michelson was able to investigate housing type when he undertook a large-scale study of Toronto residents who moved.[63] Over 50 percent of those who moved to a single-family dwelling said they were "definitely satisfied," but less than 25 percent of those who moved to an apartment said they were "definitely satisfied." This general preference for the single-family dwelling has persisted in North America for many years.[64] Sometimes, condominiums or apartments are said to be growing in popularity, but often these reports occur because high cost forces the purchaser to rule out single-family dwellings, not because condos or apartments really are preferred.

Further evidence comes from the negative side of satisfaction. Mobile homes (as an example of a housing form that differs from the "standard" single-family form) are not generally popular, even though one could argue that mobile homes are environmentally preferable—they occupy less land and use less energy, for example. They are particularly dissatisfying to adolescents because schoolmates and others shun those who live in mobile homes, and this creates a climate of fear and passivity.[65] Of course, mobile homes may be satisfactory for other groups (e.g., the elderly, professionally mobile people, or some military personnel).[66,67]

Architectural Style. How about the style or design of the house? Casual observation suggests that when people have the means to convert a preference into an actual choice, they often choose housing that reflects their cultural backgrounds. Nevertheless, some trends are evident: In one study, farmhouse and tudor-style houses were preferred over saltbox and Mediterranean styles.[68] Preferences for style clearly change, in part, with changes in fashions.

Interior. Housing interiors have not been the subject of as much empirical research as you might think; much effort in interior design is concerned with shifting fashions and artistic statements rather than research as understood in environmental psychology. However, there is evidence, for example, that most individuals prefer higher (than the usual 8-foot) ceilings, flat or sloping ceilings (4:12 slope ratio [vertical:horizontal] but neither more than that nor smaller slopes), and walls that meet at 90 degrees or more (not walls that meet at smaller angles).[69]

Everyday experience suggests that the arrangement of rooms (floor plans) can be important in a purchaser's decision. Unfortunately, what little empirical data there is on this question is mixed. American university students preferred floor plans that showed the living room in the upper right-hand corner of a drawing.[70] However, when the study was repeated with Israeli students, less support was found for the right-hand preference idea.[71] A second study tried to assess the effect of other relevant variables, such as which room arrangement their subjects actually lived in, but was unable to clarify the differences between their results and those obtained in the first study. Much more study is required before we can reach any firm conclusions about which individuals prefer which room arrangements.

Even less evidence is available about the interiors of multiple-unit housing interiors. Presumably, the conclusions about single-family dwellings would apply inside an apartment or condominium, but location within the complex is an issue that does not pertain to single-family dwellings. Do people prefer the ground floor, middle floors, or the top floors? It seems they prefer end and corner units; at least one study of the elderly reports that they prefer end-of-corridor units.[72]

Color has been the subject of much research, but most of it has been based on preferences for small patches of color that resemble paint chips, in no particular context (i.e., subjects are not usually asked if they would paint their kitchen or bedroom that color).[73] These findings may not apply to choices in real-life situations.

A study in Japan tried to overcome these limitations by showing slides of living rooms that were painted different colors.[74] Preference is not merely a matter of hue (red versus blue versus green); it also depends on the hue's saturation (or denseness) and brightness (from light to dark). The study concluded that each of these three dimensions of color was related to a different aspect of preference. Hue was not strongly related to preference; instead, it was primarily related to perceived warmth (reds are warmer, blues and greens cooler). Saturation (regardless of hue) was most closely related to what we usually call preference: More saturated hues were evaluated as more elegant, more comfortable, and better. Brightness or lightness (regardless of hue) was related to how "active" the room seemed: Brighter colors were rated as fresher, lighter, and more cheerful than darker hues.

As an environmental psychologist, I have often been asked which color is best for a certain purpose. The questioner usually means which hue is best. As you can see, the answer is more complicated than the questioner thinks, but one important conclusion is that saturation

and brightness are at least as important, perhaps more so, than hue in people's preferences.

Outdoor Areas. The outdoor areas around a dwelling make a big difference in satisfaction. Some householders are gardeners and love the space and soil to work in. Others, like a former neighbor of mine, view gardening as being "too much like work." One does not have to be a gardener to appreciate nearby green spaces. A French study found that nearby green space was, with neighbors, the most important determinant of residential satisfaction[75] (see Figure 9–6).

Green spaces, in the sense of watered lawns and gardens, are not universally preferred, though. When the southwest United States began to grow rapidly after World War II, the ideal (brought from elsewhere) was a large green lawn. Recent realization that water is not an endless resource has gradually translated into a change of that ideal for many residents of the southwest. They now prefer a residential landscape that complements the dry, almost desert quality of the area to the grassy ideal.[76]

Cultural Influences

Housing varies tremendously around the world. I have seen earthen "beehives" in rural Iran, cedar longhouses

FIGURE 9–6 Gardening is an important source of satisfaction to many residents.

in British Columbia, and floating houses in Kashmir. Even within North America, culture-related variation in housing is large but not so dramatic: the bright pastel exteriors of Portuguese houses, the red-tile roofed villas of Italian suburbanites, the white farmhouses of mid-America, the adobe of southwesterners, and so on. The obvious assumption to make is that people prefer or are most satisfied with housing that matches their own cultural backgrounds. This is because residences that reflect one's culture are designed to complement behavior patterns typical of that culture.

Dwellings also match cultures in another way. An examination of house form across 73 cultures revealed that the extent of partitioning indoor space (differentiation) is related to the degree of sociopolitical complexity in the culture, (i.e., how much segmentation, specialization, and hierarchical ordering is typical of the culture).[77] Thus, a worldwide trend is for our dwellings to mirror the complexity of our society.

Even in such relatively similar cultures as England and Australia, house forms have significant differences.[78] In many English houses, cleaning the dishes, the clothing, and oneself are closely intertwined, so dishwashing, laundry, and (sometimes) bathing are traditionally done in one room or area. In Australia, these cleaning activities are seen as separate, so the laundry is usually separated from the dishwashing area. In fact, in Australian houses where the laundry *was* placed close to the kitchen, this was a significant source of dissatisfaction. Thus, in general, it would seem that residential satisfaction is greater when the residence matches the culture.

However, this is not always the case. In one study of housing preferences, Scottish and Australian architecture students were shown slides of Scottish and Australian residences.[79] The Scots tended to prefer the traditional bungalow house style typical of Australia, and the Australians tended to prefer the terrace or row housing typical of Scotland. This was true even though a later analysis of the data showed that the two groups comprehended the houses in a similar way.[80] Suddenly, the adage about the grass being greener on the other side of the fence seems relevant: Individuals do not *always* prefer housing that reflects their own culture.

◆ **IN SUM,** *residential preferences, choices, and satisfaction reflect what we would like in a residence, what we*

actually chose, and whether we are happy with it. Measuring these concepts is more complex than it sounds. We should know exactly which focus, level, and referents we are interested in; the answers we get from residents will have comparative and purposive bases of which we should be aware. Residential evaluations are influenced by many personal characteristics, including age, stage in the life cycle, socioeconomic status, personality, values, and hopes for the future. Social factors such as norms, others' preferences, and neighbors also influence these evaluations. Naturally, physical and architectural factors like house form, architectural style, floor plan and colors, and outdoor areas are also influential. Finally, cultural background strongly affects residential preferences, choices, and satisfaction.

◆ **ENVIRONMENT AND BEHAVIOR** ◆
IN THE RESIDENCE

It is much easier to study satisfaction with a home than to study behavior in the home. Satisfaction may be surveyed from any convenient public place where respondents may be found, but many of our beliefs and customs work against allowing researchers to monitor our behavior in the sanctity of our homes. For that reason, less research on this topic is available. Nevertheless, researchers have begun to acquire at least three categories of knowledge about behavior in the home: how different people arrange their home interiors, space management in the home and the effects of home design, and home-based leisure. Let's look at spatial arrangements first.

How Homes Are Arranged

Many residences look almost identical on the outside—think of apartment exteriors or tract houses, for example. However, there probably are no two house interiors exactly alike in the whole world. We personalize our living spaces in a billion wonderful ways. But do all these unique patterns of arrangement have *any* patterns to them? For example, do house arrangements vary by culture or resident personality?

In a study of cultural differences, French and Italian living room arrangements were examined.[81] Patterns were found: French living rooms could be described using three dimensions—decoration, functional organization, and structuring of space. For example, at one end of the decoration dimension were living rooms that were low on ambiguity and complexity. These living rooms tended to have velvet antique couches with armrests, copies of period wallpaper, and books for show (not use) in a wall unit that also included cupboards and a bar. Italian living rooms could be described using the same three dimensions, but they tended to be combined differently.

A second study examined only Italian living rooms, and found five major styles, labeled A through E.[82] These are arranged in a two-dimensional space characterized by richness versus poorness of the furnishings and symmetry versus asymmetry of their arrangements. Type A living rooms are asymmetric, eccentric, and unconventional; they include mixtures of modern designer furniture and tapestries, silkscreen paintings, and antiques. Type B is like Type A, but the objects are less expensive and a little more functional. Type C is the richest, containing expensive art objects, wooden floors, and antiques arranged in a ritualistic, ostentatious way. Type D living rooms are cheaper copies of Type Cs. The objects are of the same type and are arranged ritually, but they are reproductions rather than originals and are arranged more symmetrically. The Type E living room contains few valuable articles (a stereo is usually the only one); arrangements are symmetrical.

Owners of Types A and B dislike conspicuous consumption yet prefer artistic decor; the main difference between them is whether they can afford expensive objects. Owners of Type A and B living rooms tend to be older intellectuals and professionals. Owners of types C and D living rooms, who tend to be older successful businesspeople, prefer objects that show off their status and refer to the old symbolic order in society. Owners of Type E living rooms tend to be older, retired, working-class individuals.

Another study investigated California single-family dwellings.[83] The researchers began by describing a wide variety of homes on 38 different dimensions (such as cleanliness, number of books, need for repair). These factors were grouped into four factors using statistical procedures: disorder/functional complexity (the physical state and maintenance of the home), decorative complexity (material richness), warm/child oriented (number of child-centered items), and books (number and variety of books). Next, the researchers examined the connection between home type (based on the four factors) and several antecedent factors, such as family type (traditional nuclear family, unmarried parents, communal household, single mother), income, and lifestyle. The goal was to find which of these antecedent factors may have led homeowners to arrange their houses as they did.

The homes of unmarried parents had the highest scores on disorder/functional complexity. Their lawns were more overgrown and their houses more "funky" than those of traditional-marriage parents. The communal homes had more books than the traditional-marriage homes. Higher-income homes had lower scores on disorder/functional complexity. It is surprising that as women's incomes rose, the number and variety of books in the home dropped. Parents with natural/organic lifestyles had homes with higher scores on disorder/functional complexity (see Figure 9–7).

The Spatial Ecology of Home: Who Does What, Where?

Women, Men, Children and Territory. Certainly, the use of space within the home is not random. Some people spend more time in some rooms than others. For example, domestic space sharing does not reflect the presumed trend toward sexual equality. Data collected in 1980 on where and with whom almost 1,000 men and women spent time in the home found that fully employed women spent more time in the kitchen than fully employed men did. (They spent more than twice as much time *alone* in the kitchen.)[84]

In the living room, bathroom, and bedrooms, women spent more time than men in the company of others—usually children. Unless women have fewer privacy needs than men, or have territories of their own within the home that were not examined in this study, one could conclude that women are probably less satisfied with their privacy at home than men.

In living rooms, men spent more time than women engaged in passive leisure activities such as reading or watching TV. Women who are not employed outside the home spend almost seven times as much time as men on housework and child care. Fair enough, you say? Even when women are fully employed, they spend three times

FIGURE 9–7 Funky and trim dwellings reflect different lifestyles.

as much time as men on these activities.[85] (Do you think these trends have changed since 1980?)

The complex process of home privacy becomes especially intricate when children are around. As they grow up, children are taught which rooms are open to them at which times; later, they make privacy demands of their own. Privacy conflicts may occur depending on which activity a person is engaged in, which parent or child desires access, the size of the home, and the accepted child-rearing practices in the home.[86]

In a rare study that actually monitored behavior inside homes (as opposed to asking residents to report their activities), cameras were placed in New York homes (with the residents' permission).[87] The study found that although definite territories exist within the home, the degree to which the boundaries of these territories were respected varied considerably. For example, parents may feel they have the right to enter a teen's bedroom, but they do not think the teen should enter their bedroom. But both territories are sometimes intruded upon, which creates conflict.

Three strategies for dealing with residential space conflicts have been described.[88] **Time territory** strategies involve rotating a particular space (like the TV setting) among family members. **Space territory** strategies attempt to place conflicting activities in different parts of the home. **Cooperation-capitulation** arrangements occur when a dominant family member determines that everyone will engage in one activity, together, at the same time.

Consequences of Household Spatial Arrangements. Domestic spatial arrangements affect a variety of behaviors in the home. For example, they are related to family helpfulness and behavioral choices, as the next two studies show.

The traditional kibbutz in Israel took the radical step of separating parents and children. To discourage "privatism" and individualism in the socialist atmosphere of the traditional kibbutz, children lived in communal houses; parents visited the children's house for a few hours each day.

Recently, as political and social values have changed, some kibbutzim have altered this pattern so that children sleep in their parents' house. The differences between families using the two types of arrangements were compared.[89] Those using family-based sleeping arrangements reported that they helped, supported, and were more committed to one another than families using the communal arrangement. They also said they encouraged family members to act and speak more openly. Those whose children slept communally said they participated in more social and recreational activities and placed more importance on the planning and organization of family activities and responsibilities. These differences are traced in part by the authors to the different sleeping arrangements, but also to differences in values between families that have chosen one system or the other.

Child-rearing practices in a fixed amount of space (e.g., two-bedroom apartments) affect parents' behavioral freedom.[90] When parents subscribed to a permissive child-rearing approach, the children's activities usually spilled out into the living room and thereby restricted their parents' choices of things to do, simply because the limited space available was already covered with the children's toys and possessions. These more permissive parents also complained about noise and lack of privacy.

More restrictive parents, of course, were better off in these ways, but their children were required to keep their activities within their own rooms. This may be obvious, but it clearly illustrates how a particular behavior pattern (e.g., child-raising policies) can interact with the physical setting to have important consequences for all residents.

A series of large-scale examinations of mass housing in Russia and Estonia revealed many influences of constructing large numbers of high-rise apartments in cities.[91] This region has, on average, the tallest residential buildings in the world. However, compared to North America, most residents must cope with smaller, poorer-quality dwellings.

One survey question asked how residents would use an extra room if one became available; the answer generally depended on the current household density. When residents lived in apartments with two fewer rooms than residents, about 80 percent said they would use an extra room as another bedroom or private room. When the number of rooms and people were the same, one-third of the residents said they had no idea what they would do with an extra room and another one-third said they would use it for a study or work room. When space is short, the kitchen is used for more activities; the authors recommended that if economics dictates small apartments, kitchens should at least be made as large as possible to accommodate more activities.

Pleasant atmosphere is associated with the interior organization of homes.[92] By interviewing people about their own homes, one researcher found that pleasantness (or lack of it) was related to five themes: being able to communicate with one another, being accessible to one another, being free to do what one wants, being occupied rather than bored, and being able to relax after working. These themes were then shown to be related to the organization of the house itself. For example, the lack of or-

der (e.g., a messy table after preparing a meal) interferes for some people with the pleasantness of a meal eaten at the same table. That is, an unpleasant atmosphere results when the "relaxing after work" theme cannot be accomplished (the work in this case is cooking).

In another example, more walls were desired by one person because then she could "do more things" with them. Thus, more walls is seen as a way of being occupied rather than bored—in this case, occupied with decorating walls. In general, a positive or negative home atmosphere depends, in part, on how the arrangements in the residence support each of the five pleasantness themes for a particular resident.

These few studies offer only a hint of the relations between spatial arrangements and behavior in the home. Undoubtedly, much more remains to be learned about this important aspect of environmental psychology.

Home Leisure

One primary purpose of the residence is to provide a place for relaxation and entertainment. Over half our recreational time is spent inside the home,[93] so it is important to understand the role of the physical environment in residential leisure behaviors such as playing games, watching TV, gardening, crafts, reading, and just lounging.

Home-based leisure is strongly affected by the size and differentiation of the home. Those who live in singles apartments may feel driven away from their small space to find suitable recreation, but denizens of mansions wander from the billiards room to the indoor pool to the computer room to the bar. In relatively homogeneous homes, leisure is apt to conflict with other activities; in households where necessity or values favor work, leisure time and quality are likely to suffer. We may regard home-based leisure as too commonplace and unimportant for serious attention, yet its value in relieving stress and serving as an important vehicle for social bonds within the home seems clear.

This assertion is consistent with the results from a study of the home-based leisure activities of adolescents and their families.[94] A strong positive relation was found between the amount of time adolescents spent with their parents in recreational activities at home and their general sense of well-being.

Of course, not all leisure activities are equally valuable. Adolescents in the study who watched more television were found to be less oriented to intellectual and cultural activities. It is unfortunate that these hints from studies that home-based leisure can have important positive and negative effects on us remain to be verified, expanded, and refined by future researchers.

◆ **IN SUM,** *the environmental psychology of dwelling interiors is not very developed because studying behavior inside homes meets with a natural resistance. However, we know that residents arrange and decorate their interiors according to certain patterns that reflect such dimensions as simple/complex, conventional/unusual, rich/plain decor, and messy/tidy upkeep. These patterns are related to social class and marital or living arrangement differences. Men, women, and children use the interior dwelling spaces unequally. Changes in sex roles have not changed the traditional use of rooms much; women still spend more time in the kitchen and more time with children, and men spend more time in leisure activities.*

Children (until the teen years) have restricted territories: Parents generally can enter the children's space, but children generally cannot enter their parents' space. In limited space, residents use time territories, space territories, and cooperation-capitulation arrangements to manage household space. Half our leisure time is spent in the home, but it could be better spent. When teens spend more time sharing leisure with their parents, they report greater well-being. More TV time, however, is associated with less time spent on intellectual and cultural pursuits.

◆ STRESS AND WELL-BEING ◆ IN THE RESIDENCE

As indicated earlier in Figure 9–3, our residences can strongly influence our well-being. Housing is beneficial when it promotes the resident's physical and mental health. Many North Americans are fortunate to have such housing. In the world as a whole, however, experts estimate that one billion people have grossly inadequate housing and 100 million have no housing at all.[95]

Many dwellings fail to serve their most basic purpose: to shelter residents from ill health associated with exposure to the elements or to disease-causing organisms. Particularly in high-density houses that are poorly ventilated, the building serves to increase the rate of communicable diseases such as influenza, tuberculosis, and meningitis.[96]

Adapting to a New Residence

Adapting to a new residence may be relatively painless or very difficult. When the place is inadequate, one's choice is to actively deal with the problem (move, renovate, change activity patterns, or protest) or to be passive (change one's mind instead of the residence or not to adapt at all).[97]

Distress is a normal response to inadequate housing; well-being is seriously threatened when residents are blocked from changing their residences,[98] cannot move, fail to adapt, or attempt to adapt housing when the residents' efforts are doomed by forces beyond their control (e.g., a nonresponsive landlord or a crumbling house). Residents then may suffer physical or mental stress, live in fear, abuse drugs, have more accidents, or adapt poorly; children may not develop as quickly or as well as they otherwise might. Of course, moving itself can be a source of stress, which will be discussed later.

One group whose adaptation to new housing has been examined in some detail is the elderly, particularly when they must move to group settings. Besides the loss of privacy and control that results from a move away from one's own home, group settings have a tendency to produce **hyperhabituation**, or the overadaptation to routines.[99] Relocation of the elderly even may cause increased susceptibility to illness due to stress-induced suppression of the immune system.[100] Older people who face such a move may be helped by giving them a chance to air their feelings, supplying them with practical infor-

M. POWELL LAWTON *has extensively studied housing for older people, including ways to enhance the ability of seniors to control their lives through residential technology.*

mation about the new residence,[101] and encouraging **environmental proactivity**—the tendency to make active choices about, help create, and take control of their new housing.[102]

Many university students also must adapt to new residences. In one sample of students who left home for college, 31 percent experienced homesickness.[103] Those who experienced homesickness were more likely to be women and more likely to suffer some psychological disturbance. Those did not experience homesickness were more likely to have traveled or lived away from home before going away to college.

High Density at Home

High density in the residence has been shown to have many adverse effects. Crowding at home, where very important social interaction occurs, has more serious consequences than crowding in public environments.[104] Beginning with mere complaints, a study of Seattle residents showed that dissatisfaction was more strongly related to density than to such factors as income, financial value or age of the house, or family size.[105] When density was 0.4 person per room or less, residents made 7 percent of possible complaints on a survey; when density exceeded 1 person per room, residents made 33 percent of possible complaints.

High-density homes, as a whole, have more psychological distress and psychiatric illness[106,107] and have been associated with increased substance abuse,[108] juvenile delinquency, fertility and mortality rates,[109] and may lead residents to believe they have less social support.[110] However, when residents do have social support in a high-density household, it may protect them from these negative outcomes, at least in the short term[111] (see Figure 9–8).

Social support is also a factor at the other end of the crowding spectrum: living alone or being lonely. Loneliness is associated with greater residential mobility.[112] Living alone restricts one's social networks not merely inside the home but outside, too. This means that the person who lives alone has fewer social contacts who might provide support when personal adversity strikes.[113]

The physical environment of the residence also has important effects on children. In studies of preschool-

FIGURE 9–8   Living in a high-density residence, particularly without much social support, is psychologically risky.

ers, cognitive development was significantly slower when children lived in residences that were more densely populated and noisy.[114,115,116] These density influences are not equal for all children; for example, boys are more sensitive to household population density.[117] Interestingly, several seemingly important social variables—such as disciplinary practices, the number of adults, and adult activities—had no significant effect on the cognitive development of preschoolers in this study.

High density is even associated with differences in the temperament of toddlers. A case study found that high density predisposes toddlers to display less desirable qualities such as lower approachability, less adaptability, higher intensity, and more negative moods.[118]

In another series of studies, high density in homes was linked to school performance.[119,120,121] The homes of 12-month-old children were surveyed; those with higher indoor densities were found to have poorer physical organization and fewer play materials (even after various statistical controls were applied). Reading performance 5 years later was lower for children who had fewer play materials at home as 1-year-olds, even after their intelligence test scores were controlled for.

A number of studies focus on the effects of high-density living on parent/child relations. When the household is crowded, children may receive less attention of a constructive nature yet may be struck more often by their parents.[122] Thus, children from high-density homes may be forced outdoors more often, leading more of them into trouble on the street and in school.[123,124]

Crowding also affects children's sense of control. Children who lived with many other individuals exercised less control when they *were* given the power to make choices than did children from low-density homes.[125] Children who must live in high density may not learn to persist in tasks or to make active choices when given the chance. Perhaps children in high-density homes are less often given such opportunities to learn about or exercise choice and control than are children in lower-density homes.

These studies demonstrate that high density in homes has long-term effects on the development of important skills in children and that parent/child relations are disrupted by high indoor density. The negative effects of residential high density may appear smaller than they really are because families can, with effort, muffle the strain of high-density living through various coping strategies. However, this extra effort may cause stress that manifests itself in other ways.

It has been argued that the true cause of all these woes is poverty rather than high density; the two certainly do tend to occur together, however. Which is the true cause? In one study, researchers statistically controlled for poverty to find out whether density had any effect *apart* from the effect of poverty.[126] They found that mental hospital admission rates were predicted reasonably well by density alone, and that juvenile delinquency and fertility were also related to density alone, although not as strongly. They concluded that high density is hard to separate from poverty, but it does seem to have a moderate negative effect on its own. In another study, data from 65 countries showed that higher residential densities (persons per room) were correlated with higher murder rates,[127] which introduces our next topic.

Crime and Fear at Home

Further threats to residential well-being are crime and the fear of crime. Those fortunate enough to live in safe areas may have difficulty appreciating how stressful it is to experience a burglary or other in-house crime, or to live in fear of intruders.[128] The consequences of having one's primary territory invaded are long term, and cannot always be handled by the resident's own coping efforts.[129]

Not many studies have examined the psychological effects of home invasions by criminals, but one study compared fear of crime among elderly residents in low-rise versus high-rise buildings and found more fear in the low-rise buildings.[130] Perhaps low-rise buildings seem closer to, and more vulnerable to, crime that invades from the street.

House Form and Human Dysfunction

Some dwellings are not best for some residents, even if they may be suitable for others. One major architectural distinction is between single-family dwellings and multiple-unit dwellings. Many studies portray apartments as poor places for children to grow up and for adults to thrive.[131] Apartment living has been associated with numerous childhood afflictions, including retarded movement skills, more respiratory diseases, more aggression, insomnia, more nervous disorders, reduced social skills, and disrupted play. If all this is true, we may wonder how any child can survive in an apartment. However, many of these studies lack experimental rigor; their results must be questioned. Nevertheless, housing trends indicate that more and more of us will be living in apartments and that more and better research is needed on the effects of apartment living on children.

One form of apartments, the high rise, does seem to have negative effects, particularly on nuclear families. For example, one study compared the effects on adults of living in high-rise and low-rise multiple-unit residences.[132] High-rise and low-rise tenants of the buildings, part of a low-income project in New York, were of similar age, education, and other demographic indicators. However, residents of the high rises felt more socially overloaded, more anonymous, less safe, less satisfied with their building, and had more difficulty establishing supportive relationships with their neighbors. They also felt more powerless to change building policies and believed they had less privacy.

When families with young children live in high rises, parents find it difficult to allow children to go outside to play. When play is thereby confined largely to the apartment, tension and conflict in the family increase.[133] High rises are better for some people. For instance, in one study, people over 60 years old had higher morale, on average, in high-rise than in low-rise buildings.[134]

The architecture of the residence also affects early cognitive development. In a study of 1-year-olds, a key variable was view: Those who had no view outside the home were found to have slower cognitive development.[135] Residences that provide no "stimulus shelter" for escape, do not encourage exploration, do not offer a variety of play objects over time, and are not physically responsive also produce slower cognitive development.[136]

A Japanese study investigated the rate of development of over 1,000 infants who either lived in high-rise or low-rise buildings.[137] Those who lived in high rises were slower to develop independence than those who lived in low rises. The researchers speculate that this developmental delay occurred because high-rise mothers went outdoors less often and thereby grew overattached to their children, which slowed the growth of independence in their children.

Although one might think that a stimulus-rich environment would be good for toddlers, one study suggests the opposite. The availability and variety of objects (other than toys) in the toddler's home was measured. The more nontoy objects in the home, the more likely the toddlers were judged by their parents to be moody, intense, and lacking in persistence.[138] Perhaps too many objects frustrate rather than stimulate toddlers; it is also possible that parents supply toddlers who already display these qualities with more objects in an attempt to occupy or pacify them.

There are even more ways in which the child's own household may not be the most advantageous place to develop. A Swedish study of children's play at home and found that, in general, play at home often was restricted: Parents favored quiet over noisy play, fine motor activities over gross motor activities, and passive rather than active play.[139] Day care in private homes tends to restrict play in similar ways, whereas purpose-built day-care facilities usually are equipped to support all forms of play.

One study of economically disadvantaged children compared the intellectual performance of those who entered private homes for day care with those who entered purpose-built day-care centers.[140] The performance of both groups improved initially. But those in the purpose-built day-care facilities maintained their higher levels, whereas the performance of those in private homes actually declined after 18 months.

The architectural form of the residence is also related to the social conditions inside. A study in India, for example, compared the interpersonal climate in single-family dwellings, multistory apartments, and crowded small houses.[141] Cohesiveness, expressiveness, and active recreation orientation were highest in the single-family dwelling and lowest in the crowded small houses. Residents of the multistory apartments were loneliest. The residents in this study differed in other ways, such as income and whether members of the extended family lived in the same household. Thus, we cannot be sure that house form caused the differences found in the study. The authors note, however, that the results challenge the prevailing belief in India that living close together promotes cohesion and decreases conflict.

◆ **IN SUM,** *it is not always easy for the elderly and some college students to adapt to new dwellings. High densities in dwellings are associated with a very wide variety of negative outcomes for adults and children. Some of these are mitigated by social support, if the resident has any. Density appears to have negative effects apart from poverty. Very low densities (living alone) also cause problems for many people. High rises probably are not good for children, and one study suggests that young children are better off if they attend a good child-care center than if they stay at home.*

◆ **RESIDENTIAL MOBILITY** ◆

People move. In any given five-year period, about 45 percent of North Americans, 36 percent of Britons and Japanese, and 48 percent of Australians move.[142] They do so for many reasons, including stress or dissatisfaction associated with their current residence, positive or negative changes in their finances or occupation, and progression through the life cycle, such as going off to college, adding a child to the family, or downsizing after the children leave home.

Some moves have pleasant consequences and some do not, depending on whether the move was chosen or forced and whether it fits the resident's personality, needs, and values. In the earlier part of the century, some experts associated mobility with social problems and pathology. Gradually, researchers realized that residential mobility was not pathological, but a normal process often caused by life-cycle changes.[143]

Not all decisions to move are the result of social problems or dissatisfaction with previous housing. Nevertheless, some mobility is associated with a number of adverse outcomes. Mobility is not automatically bad for health, but it can be, depending on a person's residential history, present circumstances, and hopes for the future.[144] For example, among those who move less often, those with less choice about moving report more illness-related symptoms than those who have a greater choice about moving[145] (see Figure 9–9).

This stress is moderated by personal characteristics. Individuals in the study who were highly mobile and those who were generally less inclined to explore the environment reported more illness than those who were more inclined to explore the environment. This suggests that mobility is more damaging to those who move often but simply do not enjoy seeking out new places.

Mobility may be chosen or forced.[146] The poor and the elderly, whose mobility is often forced, typically become more crowded after a move. Also, displaced residents often pay more for their new housing than they did for their old housing. More illness is reported among residents who move less often but are unhappy with their present residence and feel they have little choice of residence.[147] Thus, a *lack* of mobility also can be damaging—when one's options for moving are restricted.

One group with restricted options is the family headed by a female single parent, which now comprises over one-quarter of all households in the United States. They are more mobile than other households[148] and, owing to higher rent costs (in relation to income) and relative lack of transportation, they face a more stressful housing search.[149] Even in a group that presumably does have some choice in leaving home—students leaving home for college—60 percent report being homesick.[150]

It might seem that preferences for the potential new residence may depend more on the characteristics of the proposed residence than on the resident's personal characteristics.[151] However, a more accurate observation is that the residence's characteristics predict housing preference best *when they support the resident's values.*[152] For example, that the proposed residence is located in a very sociable neighborhood predicts the resident's preference for it better if we know that neighborhood socializing is highly valued by the resident.

A change of residence often brings a change in the resident's pattern of activities. Some of these changes may have been planned and eagerly anticipated; others may not have been foreseen and come as unpleasant realizations. A study of homeowners who had recently moved from near and far to several Connecticut towns examined the impact of these changes in activity pattern.[153] Positive assessments of the move by residents were related to such changes as increased contact with friends and family, reduced commuting time, increased involvement in the church or community, and improved quality of the residence.

Remember, however, that movers might experience an improvement in some of these areas but suffer losses in other areas. One interesting finding was that women whose move resulted in more contact with relatives were especially likely to feel positive about the move. In general, however, residents considering a move should carefully consider the changes to the whole range of their activities. That way, a move does not result in one improvement at the expense of sabotaging many other important activities.

FIGURE 9–9 How are moving and illness related?

◆ RESIDENTIAL ENVIRONMENTAL ◆ DESIGN

Environmental psychologists have made many efforts to improve homes. Home may include a room in an institution, a single-family dwellling, or a multiple-unit dwelling. Here are two examples of environmental psychology applied to the design of homes.

Homes for Single-Parent Families

There are over 10 million single-parent families in the United States. Most of these families are headed by females and are poor; housing is a big problem for them. Usually, single parents must search for housing that was designed in a generic way to suit any group of people living together or housing that was meant for a nuclear family. However, the single-parent family is neither generic nor nuclear, and it has become a major residential category. It needs housing that takes its special needs into account.

Of course, not all single-parent families are the same; the number and age of children vary, for example, as does income, whether the single parent works, and the closeness or distance of the absent parent. How would you design a residence for a group that varies yet is different in some important ways from the nuclear family?

Numerous residences now have been specifically designed and constructed for single-parent families.[154] Based on an overview of these projects, Kathryn Anthony has reported that some of the most important specific design features of a good project, besides overall quality, are the following:

- On-site or nearby child-care facilities so parents feel better about working
- An open kitchen/living room area so parents can cook and watch their children at the same time
- Separate areas for children and parents
- Close proximity to public transportation (single parents often cannot afford cars)
- Classroom space (a crucial part of escaping the poverty cycle is education)
- Indoor as well as outdoor play space

From Building Blocks to a Home

Did you ever build forts or houses as a child? Younger children use building blocks and older children use scrap materials to build play residences. In Switzerland, there is a laboratory where people can build full-scale houses.[155] In the Laboratory for Architectural Experimentation (LEA) at the Federal Institute of Technology at Lausanne, there is a very large room with high ceilings where residents assemble their dream houses, full scale, using lightweight polystyrene blocks and walls. Even two-story simulated houses, complete with doors and windows, can be built and adjusted relatively quickly and easily.

Architects may learn to visualize spaces based on technical drawings, but most people find this difficult. As a researcher at LEA, Roderick Lawrence believes that the third dimension is an essential ingredient for the representation of architectural space to the public. If designers wish to involve residents and allow them to experience the building much as they would experience the real building, the LEA full-scale approach is valuable.

In one study at the LEA, houses that had been simulated were actually constructed later. Researchers then checked whether any changes had been made after the simulation process. The residents had made a few changes. Most concerned differences in furniture arrangement as envisioned during the simulation versus the way furniture was arranged in the finished house, often because at least some new furniture had been purchased. Architects made a few minor changes involving room sizes and layouts.

No design process is perfect, and the LEA experiments revealed a few problems. For example, because the simulation occurred in a lab, some aspects of windows and natural lighting were not well simulated. However, in general, the LEA approach might be tried more widely as designers try to build residences that better suit those who will live in them.

◆ SUMMARY ◆

Home is the most important physical setting for most of us. The physical structure (residence, dwelling, house, apartment) is distinct from the meaning structure (home). Individuals normally called homeless may properly be called houseless, although if their last residence loses its meaning, they truly are homeless. Residential satisfaction is complex to measure and has many determinants, including stage in the life cycle, socioeconomic status, personality, values, and hopes for the future. Norms, neighbors, and the preferences of others also influence these residential satisfaction. Physical features—such as house form, architectural style, floor plan and colors, outdoor areas, and one's cultural background—also affect residential preferences, choices, and satisfaction. We arrange our residential interiors in certain patterns, and these are related to our lifestyles. High density is hard on virtually everyone but it can be tolerable with social support. Adapting to new residences can be difficult. Moving can be stressful, depending on whether a person has some choice in doing so, likes to explore new settings, and likes the present residence.

Suggested Readings

Ahrentzen, S., Levine, D. W., & Michelson, W. (1989). Space, time, and activity in the home: A gender analysis. *Journal of Environmental Psychology, 9,* 89–101.

Anthony, K. H. (1991). Housing the single-parent family. In W. F. E. Preiser, J. C. Vischer, & E. T. White (Eds.), *Design intervention: Toward a more humane architecture.* New York: Van Nostrand Reinhold.

Evans, G. W., Palsane, M. N., Lepore, S. J., & Martin, J. (1989). Residential density and psychological health: The mediating effects of social support. *Journal of Personality and Social Psychology, 57,* 994–999.

Lawton, M. P. (1990). Residential environment and self-directedness among older people. *American Psychologist, 45,* 638–640.

Nasar, J. (1989). Symbolic meanings of house styles. *Environment and Behavior, 21,* 235–257.

Paulus, P. B., Nagar, D., & Camacho, L. M. (1991). Environmental and psychological factors in reactions to apartments and mobile homes. *Journal of Environmental Psychology, 11,* 143–161.

Peatross, F. D., & Hasell, M. J. (1992). Changing lives/changing spaces: An investigation of the relationships between gender orientation and behaviors, and spatial preferences in residential kitchens. *Journal of Architectural and Planning Research, 9,* 239–257.

Smith, S. G. (1994). The essential qualities of a home. *Journal of Environmental Psychology, 14,* 31–46.

CHAPTER **10**

COMMUNITY ENVIRONMENTAL PSYCHOLOGY

We must restore to the city the maternal life-nurturing functions, the autonomous activities, the symbiotic associations that have long been neglected or suppressed. For the city should be an organ of love.

—Lewis Mumford[1]

"What?" said Jane. "I can't hear you."
Tom laughed and repeated, louder, "What do you think of this awful noise?"
"You mean the jackhammers or the subway?"

"The whole thing. The whole rotten cacophony," Tom yelled.

"I think it's the price you pay for living in the city," Jane yelled. They were walking home from work, trying to discuss what to do that evening. In order to talk, they entered an espresso bar. It was jammed; they were jostled but at least they could hear each other.

"Are you sure you want to live in this neighborhood?" Jane asked. She was debating the wisdom of moving into Tom's grandpa's house, which was a block off the main avenue. Tom wanted to.

"It's as noisy as a buzz saw at rush hour," he said, "but there's a park close by and we can walk to concerts and the gallery. You can buy almost anything you want without using a car . . ."

"And get mugged if you don't do these things within a tiny window of time," Jane finished for him. "Or trip over a garbage bag or some wrecked person."

"Like you said, Jane, that's the price you pay. I don't know about you, but I already feel like I'm a part of this neighborhood. I've got genes here, memories of childhood visits. I'm coming home."

"I'm happy for you, Tom. Do you know anyone here?"

"Well, not exactly. But when I go for a walk, I see the same people over and over again. I feel like I know them."

"You feel like you know people that you don't even know? Tom, you have a lot of convincing to do if you want to share this neighborhood with this kid."

◆ ◆ ◆

This chapter explores person-environment relations in cities, public places, neighborhoods, the communities, and on the streets. Some of the questions to be addressed are:

- Are cities good for us?
- What constitutes a satisfying neighborhood?
- What are the effects of such community stressors as noise, heat, and air pollution?
- Under which environmental conditions will individuals in public places tend to help or hurt one another?
- What is the nature of social interaction in public places?
- How does the physical environment influence shopping?

A general model for this section is presented in Figure 10–1.

The physical aspects of the city (stressors and amenities) and personal factors are presumed to influence the way we think about our cities and neighborhoods (whether we feel satisfied or dissatisfied, fearful or safe, attached or unattached to them, mentally healthy or mentally unhealthy). The physical aspects of the city, personal factors, and these cognitions are presumed to affect our actual behavior in urban public places such as streets, parks, and stores.

These behaviors may be pro-social, anti-social, or neither; they include everyday behaviors, such as how fast we walk, kids playing in parks, or where we choose to sit in public areas. They also include behavior in retail settings such as our reactions to store music and displays. The model further states that these behaviors, in turn, are presumed to influence our cognitions (just as cognitions influenced behaviors) and the urban planning and design process.

The design process, to complete the cycle, will influence the physical shape of the city as zoning and other bylaws govern what sort of buildings, streets, and parks get built. The cycle then continues. Environmental psychologists have studied all phases of the general model in Figure 10–1.

◆ LIFE IN THE CITY: ◆ GREAT OR AWFUL?

There is a vast movement to the city. Earlier this century, most North Americans lived in rural settings; now, most live in cities. From 1970 to 1990, the population of Mexico City increased from 9 million to over 20 million; much of the increase has been due to migration from the country-

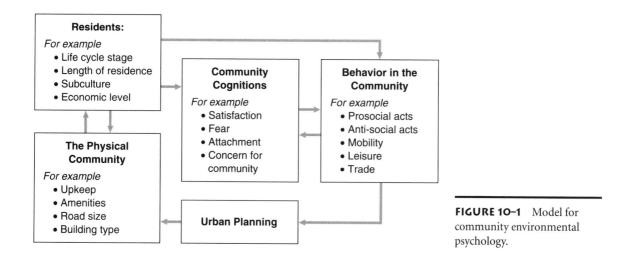

Residents:

For example
- Life cycle stage
- Length of residence
- Subculture
- Economic level

The Physical Community

For example
- Upkeep
- Amenities
- Road size
- Building type

Community Cognitions

For example
- Satisfaction
- Fear
- Attachment
- Concern for community

Behavior in the Community

For example
- Prosocial acts
- Anti-social acts
- Mobility
- Leisure
- Trade

Urban Planning

FIGURE 10–1   Model for community environmental psychology.

side rather than a dramatic increase in the birthrate. The rush to the city is a worldwide phenomenon; many other cities also have grown fantastically. What happens once nearly everyone lives so close together?

The Prosecution's Case

Cities can be very stressful: Noise, traffic, density, and pollution usually are much greater than in rural places. We humans have lived in such large agglomerations only for a tiny fraction of the time we have been a species; it is reasonable to say that cities are unnatural. Great ancient cities, such as Athens (the cradle of democracy and many of the ideas we hold dear) and Florence (the birthplace of great artists), had only about 25,000 people. Plato claimed that 40,000 was the upper limit to the size of an effective city. More recent experts claim that 150,000 is the ideal city size.[2]

Many people who live in large cities seem to agree that populations of multimillions are too much. Surveys indicate that 60 percent of New Yorkers, 48 percent of Los Angelenos, and 43 percent of Bostonians would leave their cities if they could.[3] Out of 192 U.S. cities with populations over 100,000, the average population of the 22 least stressful cities was 116,000.[4] In Canada, city dwellers are 67 percent more likely to be robbed and 44 percent more likely to be beaten up than rural residents.[5] The prosecution rests its case.

The Defense's Case

Some 5,000 pedestrians per hour jostle by each other at the corner of 59th Street and Lexington Avenue in New York. The street is "a collision of senses and sensibilities: shoppers lugging bags, workers toting briefcases, yuppies, beggars, vendors, pickpockets, all against a backdrop of honking horns and the smell of candied nuts." William Whyte, champion of the city's possibilities, says, "What a carnival!"[6] in an approving manner. He believes that people gravitate *toward* high density and thrive on it. According to Whyte, the vendors, performers, and screwballs make cities exciting.

Clearly, cities have benefits; besides the interesting street life, these include more cultural, educational, medical, leisure, social, and shopping resources, not to mention greater opportunity for jobs. The defense rests its case.

The scientific evidence will be presented later. First, we turn to that basic building block of cities—the neighborhood.

◆   **WHAT IS A NEIGHBORHOOD?**   ◆

The center of the model is based on the residents' thoughts about the community. This includes such topics as the residents' beliefs about what their neighborhood *is*, including its spatial extent, their confidence about its future, their safety fears,[7] their attachment to the neighborhood, and their overall satisfaction with it.

Is it obvious to you where your neighborhood's boundaries are or what your neighborhood means to you? The answers to such questions are not as simple as they may sound. Researchers have tried to answer them by examining residents' perceptions, cognitions, and definitions of their neighborhoods and communities.

Neighborhood is a psychological concept; not every physical or legal area (e.g., a school district or an electoral area) is a neighborhood. One psychological dimension of neighborhoods is their spatial-cognitive nature. For example, a Seattle study asked residents to describe the boundaries of their neighborhood.[8] Although not everyone agreed where the boundaries were, most respondents did think their neighborhood *had* boundaries. Within these boundaries, neighborhoods may be urban or suburban; may contain industrial, commercial, and/or residential development; may have undeveloped areas and/or developed parks; may be old or new, graced with quiet tree-lined streets or split by major roads; and will include varying percentages of high-rise, low-rise, single-family, and mobile homes as residences.

A study of downtown versus suburban neighborhoods found that the difference, in their residents' mental images, is that downtown neighborhoods contain more mixed land uses, traffic and parking problems, noise, crowding, stress, danger, pavement, and mess.[9] Despite these images, those who identified with downtown had more positive views of downtown (and those who identified with suburbia had more positive views of suburbia).

Residents live in such diverse settings that it may be difficult to imagine how different from one another neighborhoods can be. You can begin to realize the differences by asking yourself three questions: Is there much or little face-to-face interaction in my neighborhood? To what extent do the residents think of themselves as being *of* or *from* this neighborhood? Is there much or little contact between residents of this neighborhood and residents of other neighborhoods?

The answers to these questions may be combined to describe neighborhoods in a second major way; the answers yield six kinds of neighborhood in more social terms.[10] Three of these will be briefly described. The **integral neighborhood** has much face-to-face interaction, much cohesiveness from neighborhood support of local interest and values, and much participation in organizations outside the neighborhood. The **parochial neighborhood** is like the integral neighborhood except that it has fewer ties to outside organizations; it is inward facing and may even discourage participation in the wider community. The **anomic neighborhood** has little face-to-face contact, little identification, and few ties to the outside world.

A third view of neighborhoods is that they consist of three components: social interaction, symbolic interaction, and attachment to people and places.[11] **Social interaction** refers to the ways that neighbors give each other emotional support, supply one another with useful information, and help each other get things done.

Symbolic interaction refers to cognitions, such as cognitive maps of the neighborhood and the communication of status through symbols. A Boston study illustrates this role of status symbols in neighborhoods.[12] Status symbols are often viewed negatively, but if their meaning is widely shared, they serve to convey a shared sense of meaning in a neighborhood, even if that meaning is not especially positive for all residents. Students were shown photos of late-nineteenth-century Boston houses and asked which were residences of upper middle-, middle middle-, and lower middle-class people. Even 100 years after they were constructed, the houses still provided usable status cues. The students correctly identified the class of the owners. Agreement about the meaning of neighborhood symbols—in this case, the meaning of architectural details—is only one part of the psychological concept of neighborhood, but it is an important part.

Attachment refers to a resident's cognitive-emotional connection to the neighborhood. This component will be discussed in some detail later.

◆ NEIGHBORHOOD SATISFACTION ◆ AND ATTACHMENT

Once you are outside, on the streets near your home, are you satisfied with what you see and hear? Does your neighborhood make you feel proud or ashamed? Do you feel as if you would like to escape as soon as possible, or spend your whole life in such a great place?

One community cognition of special importance is confidence. When confidence about a neighborhood is high, residents will stay and improve it. When most residents are pessimistic about the future of their community, it is difficult to encourage residents to stay (if they have any choice), let alone renew, renovate, or revitalize it. One study of a government program that offered residents incentives to stay and fix up their homes found that neighborhood confidence was positively related to staying instead of moving and to greater social cohesion among residents.[13]

Neighborhood Satisfaction

Measuring Neighborhood Satisfaction. Personal, social, physical, and cultural factors influence satisfaction with a community. However, before each of these influences is described, we should consider how to assess community satisfaction. How would you measure neighborhood satisfaction?

The simplest approach is to ask a resident "Are you satisfied with your neighborhood?" However, recognizing that satisfaction and dissatisfaction have many sources, researchers prefer to measure satisfaction as an aggregate response to a range of questions. Certainly, if we hope to improve satisfaction with a particular neighborhood, we must determine which aspects of neighborhood satisfaction are most important and which are within the power of a government or a neighborhood to change.

Based on the definitions of neighborhood given earlier,[14] one way to measure satisfaction would be to ask about the extent of positive social relations, clear and symbolic interaction (clashing meanings lead to confusion and dissension), and strong attachment in the neighborhood. Another prominent view is that neighborhood satisfaction is composed of residents' satisfaction with the neighborhoods' physical conditions, political climate, convenience (e.g., access to schools, work, and shopping), and social relations.[15] This approach would assess satisfaction by asking residents about these four factors.

Not everyone is equally satisfied with a neighborhood; obviously, personal characteristics of the residents also play a role. The sections that follow will examine numerous factors that influence neighborhood satisfac-

tion; they are grouped into personal, physical, social, and cultural sources.

The general model (Figure 10–1) suggests that satisfaction may be a direct function of certain personal or physical variables, and it may depend on combinations of persons and physical features. For example, whether a skateboard park in the neighborhood increases satisfaction probably depends largely on whether the resident is 14 or 74 years old. Therefore, personal and physical influences will be discussed first, followed by combinations of the two.

Personal Influences. Most personal influences on neighborhood satisfaction are also based partly on the neighborhood in question, but some of them may be viewed mainly as personal because they are the cognitions of residents. For example, when residents believe their current neighborhood is an improvement over their former neighborhood, they will be more satisfied with their current neighborhood.[16] When the neighborhood has a higher interest level for them[17] and when they feel at home in it,[18] residents are more satisfied.

Some residents also value their own neighborhoods over others merely because they live in them. An Australian study found that residents, especially those who live in less prestigious neighborhoods, rated their neighborhoods as more prestigious than outsiders did.[19]

Adaptation to the level of neighborhood stimulation also affects satisfaction.[20] The large amount of stimulation found in cities may constitute an overload for some people, such as some new arrivals, but be just right for others. The adaptation-level approach may help predict who likes and does not like a city or neighborhood. Those who are adapted to quite low levels of stimulation—such as a villager—might find the sudden drastic increase in stimulation unpleasant.

Similarly, city dwellers who are adapted to a lot of action may find villages painfully boring. Harry Helson, the leading proponent of adaptation-level theory, suggested that *moderate* discrepancies from one's adaptation level are pleasing.[21] In the case of communities, this could mean that a villager would be pleased by a town but not a city, and that city dwellers would rather vacation in a small town than in a village or out in the wilderness.

The often-repeated specter of overload in the city is not true for everyone. After an initial period of actively coping with the admittedly higher levels of stimulation found in the city, most new residents are able to find a social and physical niche that protects them from undesirable levels of stimulation. Of course, this protection depends, in part, on one's resources; for example, it is often said that New York is a great place to live if you have plenty of money. Still, it is obvious that millions of urbanites lead satisfying lives that are sheltered from excessive stimulation.

Neighborhood satisfaction also depends on other personal factors, such as ownership versus renting (owners are more satisfied) and stage of life (e.g., houses for families and apartments for retired people).[22] Elderly observers prefer residential scenes that are open and well kept, and some prefer plain buildings to ornate ones.[23] They prefer more uniform scenes over more diverse ones, more organized scenes over more disorganized ones, and scenes with little mystery over others with more mystery.

Physical Influences. Satisfaction also depends, in part, on the physical characteristics of the neighborhood itself. Is it noisy, expensive, downtown, split by major transportation routes, smoggy?

Clearly, visual quality, aesthetics, and green spaces are key factors. One survey of research indicates that physical deterioration and lack of nearby green space are strongly related to dissatisfaction with the neighborhood.[24] Other research confirms the commonsense notion that satisfaction with a neighborhood depends largely on the aesthetic quality of the neighborhood.[25,26] Nearby nature is another important satisfier; neighborhoods with nearby trees, well-landscaped grounds, and places to walk have higher satisfaction levels.[27]

Researchers showed 60 residential scenes to design professionals and to adult laypersons. They preferred scenes that showed well-kept yards, ornate rather than plain buildings, scenes depicting single-use buildings (e.g., all residences as opposed to residential-commercial mixtures), and scenes that appeared open[28] (see Figure 10–2). These characteristics are typical of more expensive housing, which we would expect to be satisfying to many individuals. However, the value of such research is that we begin to learn which specific aspects of expensive housing are preferred. Certainly, houses have been constructed that are very expensive yet do not sat-

FIGURE 10–2 Contrasts in neighborhoods: Mixed residential-commercial development (*top*) is common in cities but is less preferable to most residents than purely residential districts (*bottom*).

isfy their residents; mere expensiveness does not guarantee satisfaction.

Project size is an important factor in satisfaction with public housing projects. Since the middle 1970s, the trend in the design of projects has been toward smaller size. Studies show that residents of these smaller projects that can fit into other neighborhoods are more satisfied with them.[29] Another important aspect of neighborhood satisfaction is access to schools, work, recreation, and shopping—or at least to public transportation that can move residents to these facilities.[30]

Almost everyone will be satisfied with a neighborhood with the physical attributes just described: beautiful, green, relatively small and natural, with good access to needed facilities and services. Other physical qualities, however, may be satisfactory to some residents but not others. Which *combinations* of personal qualities and physical features produce neighborhood satisfaction? One example is that older residents prefer outdoor places away from the sun's glare, where they can sit and watch people.[31] Not all age groups care about this particular combination of neighborhood features, however.

A clearer example comes from a study of Toronto families who had recently moved. Their satisfaction with physical aspects of the community is strongly influenced by availability of public transportation and parking facilities, appearance of the neighborhood, and distance to green spaces.[32] However, satisfaction is moderated by other factors, such as whether the resident lives downtown or in the suburbs and whether the residence is an apartment or a house. For example, distance to green spaces is a greater source of dissatisfaction for downtown residents than it is for suburban residents. Lack of public transportation is a bigger source of unhappiness for suburban apartment dwellers than it is for downtown residents.

Michelson reports a surprising source of dissatisfaction.[33] Noise is one of the most dissatisfying features of many communities. Because we think of urban areas as noisy, we might expect downtown residents to be most upset about noise. However, Michelson found that two or three times as many residents of suburban houses were dissatisfied with noise from the environment as were residents of downtown houses. Perhaps downtown residents have adapted to higher noise levels and no longer notice the noise, or maybe suburbanites expect their homes to be even quieter than they are.

Just what makes a noise annoying? It is not merely loudness. Annoyance depends, in part, on the noise-maker's perceived motivation and the degree of control felt by the listener. Annoying sounds tend to be those that—in addition to being louder—are less common, seem avoidable, and occur at night.[34] Such findings make the estimation of annoyance levels caused by particular sounds more predictable.[35]

The same level of sound also can be more annoying to people who associate it with other negative events. For example, one intriguing study tested the idea that aircraft noise annoyance is based in part on fears that planes may crash.[36] When annoyance in a community

that had recently experienced a plane crash was compared to that in a community with the same level of aircraft noise but no recent crash experience, annoyance indeed was higher in the community that had been through a crash.

Aircraft noise is a source of dissatisfaction in many neighborhoods. Near a busy southern California airport where air traffic alone created an average 65 decibels of sound all day, 84 percent of residents said aircraft noise was a problem.[37] However, annoyance was moderated by a personal factor: Residents with low perceived control over the noise were more annoyed than residents who believed they could have some control over it.

There may be an upper limit to the number of residents who become very annoyed by noise. A Swedish study found that the percent who reported being "very annoyed" rose steadily with the number of "noise events" (measured as the number of heavy vehicles passing by each day) until the 40 percent level was reached, at about 2,000 heavy vehicles per day. But the percent who said they were very annoyed did not increase beyond 40 percent, even when over 9,000 heavy vehicles per day passed by.[38]

Can a person get used to noise, so that it no longer bothers him or her? Some people who live near airports have sound-insulated their homes to protect themselves against exposure. This appears to reduce strong annoyance in the short term but not in the long term.[39] The evidence does *not* support the idea that people can get used to anything. In one study, the same residents were interviewed 4 months and 16 months after a major new highway opened in their community.[40] The new highway raised sound levels 16 to 20 decibels above that in similar neighborhoods with no highway. The residents' annoyance with the increased sound did not decrease in the 12-month interval between surveys. Residents became more pessimistic about their ability to adapt. This is one sample of individuals who do not believe that you can get used to anything!

Nevertheless, some individuals may be able to adapt to noise better than others. Some of us are more capable than others in screening out unwanted stimulation.[41] Another moderating variable may be anxiety level. A study of over 100 individuals' responses to traffic noise found that low-anxiety respondents appeared able to adapt to the noise but high-anxiety respondents did not.[42]

Individuals may, however, adapt to other community annoyances, such as air pollution. Long-time Los Angeles residents, for example, are equally *capable* of perceiving smog as newer residents, but they were significantly less likely to actually report a given day as smoggy.[43] It seems they were capable of seeing smog but, at lower smog levels, they no longer realized that what they saw was indeed smog. Presumably, then, long-term residents' satisfaction with their community would not be adversely affected by low levels of smog.

Social and Security Influences. What about the social environment of a community? Doesn't our satisfaction with a neighborhood depend on the quality of its social life? Surprisingly, social networks may be important sources of satisfaction in only a few communities. Marc Fried, who coauthored a classic study in favor of the crucial role of social ties for residential satisfaction,[44] later claimed that most residential satisfaction is largely due to the *physical* quality of the neighborhood.[45] Interviews with 2,500 residents of over 40 municipalities suggested that social ties are an important source of neighborhood satisfaction only to those who strongly value social ties.

The implication is that many of us simply no longer value the neighborhood as a source of friends. Instead, we look to work, school, and places other than neighborhoods for our social needs. Another study, which directly compared physical and social features of neighborhoods, found that the physical features predicted resident satisfaction better.[46]

Of course, the social aspects of the neighborhood are important in that we want our neighbors to be "good" people.[47] However, this does not always mean, in today's communities, that we actually want to socialize with these folks. Often, we just hope they are good in the sense that they will not harm us.

Safety fears are a key part of community satisfaction or dissatisfaction. These fears include parental concerns about possible traffic accidents involving children[48] and widespread fear of crime.[49] Fear of crime discourages older residents from leaving their homes to take the bus,[50] deters women from using downtown cores[51] and certain areas of college campuses,[52] and has even been shown to have adverse effects on the mental health of adults.[53]

It is not easy to feel good about a community if every time you go outside, you half expect to get mugged or raped. It is interesting that fear of crime does not heavily depend on the actual crime rate. It may be inflated by flashy media portrayals. In a study of Hong Kong and Toronto, fear of crime was more closely associated with population density than with actual crime rates.[54] This is an unresolved issue, however, because others have concluded that density is more associated with actual crime than with our fear of crime.[55]

Defensible space theory, introduced in Chapter 6, argues that certain arrangements of streets and other public territories create settings where space is easily given surveillance and clearly defined as to ownership.[56] Whether such designs really lower crimes is not proved (many other factors may play a role), but the designs do seem to make residents *feel* safer. For example, lighting designed to facilitate surveillance of public areas reduced the fears of individuals even though crime may not have been reduced.[57]

Crime and fear of crime do not have universally negative effects. For example, a Dutch study found that burglary victims did *not* develop strong negative feelings about their neighborhood.[58] However, an American study reported the more expected outcome that residents who believe their neighborhood to be safer are more satisfied with it.[59] Neighborhood physical decay may, by association, evoke fear of crime, but one study reported that this was true only for moderate-income residents, not for all residents.[60] Finally, the areas that residents *believe* to be dangerous are not always the areas that have the statistically highest rates of crime.[61]

Despite these exceptions, fear of crime is an exceedingly important and usually destructive cognition in many communities. It is based, of course, on legitimate concerns, but it unfortunately dampens exploration, activity, and the growth of interpersonal relations in affected neighborhoods.

Cultural Influences. Cities reflect the culture and eras in which they are embedded.[62] Within any single culture or era, we tend to overlook the ways in which neighborhood forms mirror our values in the same way that fish are said to be the last to discover water. Consider different eras within one culture, for example. Amos Rapoport described how a city on the U.S. East Coast has been remade several times.[63] First, it had an organic (irregular) street pattern. This pattern was replaced by a strict grid system that represented a modern point of view at one time. Now, the streets have become curves with many culs-de-sac, not unlike their original layout! Satisfaction with this and many other features of cities that vary with time and culture presumably is a function of congruence between residents' culture, the era with which they identify,[64] and the physical form of the community.

Cross-cultural diversity may characterize some features of communities, but other features seem to have a near-universal meaning.[65] For example, religious buildings from the cathedral at Chartres to temples in India to basilicas in Milwaukee to sacred buildings in Papua, New Guinea, all use height to express the idea of holiness. The idea of reaching toward the heavens with buildings seems to have occurred to most of the world's designers of religious buildings, reflecting a similar idea that is part of many cultures. Other features of communities also show widespread similarity across cultures. Satisfaction with community presumably is a function of whether these near-universal features are present in the buildings and forms of our own communities.

Earlier, I noted that the physical aspects of neighborhoods are more important to *most* residents than social features. One exception to this is a religious group that explicitly works toward building close physical ties (by buying or renting in one neighborhood) to facilitate close social ties.[66] This is a pattern many ethnic groups follow, especially among members who remain more oriented to the language and customs of the old country than to the dominant culture. However, many ethnic group members begin to seek housing outside the traditional ethnic enclave as soon as they have enough money and feel comfortable in the dominant culture.[67] This reinforces Fried's position that social ties are less important for most residents than the physical qualities of the community.

The Importance of Neighborhood Satisfaction. Satisfaction with one's neighborhood obviously is important in its own right, but its importance goes beyond that. Studies show that neighborhood satisfaction is closely related to crucial broader concepts such as a person's satisfaction with the city as a whole,[68] overall psycholog-

ical well-being,[69] and general satisfaction with life in general![70]

Place Identity and Place Attachment

Some places become an important part of our selves. **Place identity** refers to an individual's incorporation of place into the larger concept of self.[71,72] It is closely related to **place attachment,** the idea that we develop special bonds with certain settings that have deep meaning for us.[73] Although place attachment may sound similar to territoriality, research shows that they are distinct.[74]

What happens when we leave behind a place we are attached to, a place that has become part of our selves? We go away to college, we move, our old neighborhood gets redeveloped, the family home is sold. Place identity and place attachment research are concerned with the acquisition, interaction, and loss of relationships with places that are important to the individual sense of self.

Sources of Place Attachment. Place identity and attachment are processes that occur in individual persons, but they are established in us through a variety of cultural mechanisms. Setha Low reviewed the world literature on place attachment and determined that it has six cultural means of transmission: genealogy, loss and destruction, ownership, cosmology, pilgrimage, and narrative.[75]

1. Genealogy links persons with places through the historical identification of a place with a family. In some places, such as Spain and Japan, people's names and community names are the same, or houses occupied by generations have the same name as the family.

HAROLD PROSHANSKY *helped found the first graduate program in environmental psychology and produced valuable studies of place identity.*

2. Loss and destruction sometimes build or strengthen place attachment. Those who yearned for Israel, mourned the loss of redeveloped urban districts, and grieved for towns lost in earthquakes develop fierce attachments to places that might exist and even to places that never again will exist.

3. Ownership is a more familiar mechanism through which place attachment can be created. When we own a place for a long time, is becomes a part of us, and we of it. In one culture, people and their places are said to share blood.

4. Cosmological place attachment refers to a culture's religious and mythological views on person-place attachment. Many places are seen by their natives as the center of the universe. From a cosmopolitan, objective perspective may seem absurd (how many places can be the center?), but deep within the cultural meanings of each such place, the center of the town or village or shrine really is the spiritual center of the world.

5. We can be attached to places we merely visit; when a place is sacred to us and we make a **pilgrimage** there, we experience another kind of place attachment. This sort of attachment usually is religious (Mecca, Jerusalem, Banares) but it can be secular. Serious baseball fans feel an attachment to Cooperstown, New York, where the Baseball's Hall of Fame stores relics of their heroes; they literally make pilgrimages to the small town.

6. The term **narrative** refers to stories; place attachment can develop through stories that explain the important issues and questions of life in terms of people-place interactions. Stories tell residents how to interact with or respect their land and often include accounts of how the land strikes back if it is not treated properly.

In short, place attachment can develop many ways. The more mobile society becomes, the less place attachment is possible. The price we pay for placelessness has not yet been computed.

Studying Place Attachment. Place attachment emphasizes the manner in which we *personally construct* our notions of place. Humanistic researchers have long ar-

gued that individuals develop rootedness[76] or a sense of place.[77] Research into place attachment has often been phenomenological, based on the perceptions of the world-as-it-is to sophisticated observers.[78]

However, some place attachment researchers have surveyed or observed the behavior of everyday residents. A scale to measure sense of community, another related concept, has been developed.[79] The classic work is Fried and Gleicher's study of what happens to residents of neighborhoods that undergo redevelopment.[80] Before their work, planners generally assumed that residents of older neighborhoods would be pleased to move to newer, cleaner housing. Yet, Fried and Gleicher discovered that many relocated residents sat in their new apartments grieving for their lost homes. The old neighborhoods may have been physically run down, but they were the foundations for a complete way of life. When the neighborhoods were bulldozed, so was the way of life that permeated them.

Age, Time, and Place Attachment. Though relatively underresearched so far, place attachment is important throughout our lives. Apparently, boys and girls have different senses of the areas surrounding their homes.[81] The well-being of children[82] and adolescents[83] is crucially related to the form and content of their homes; leaving home to move, take a job, or go to college can be disastrous or fulfilling. In fact, residential mobility for families is stressful for most individuals.[84]

Place attachment seems to grow with length of residence and age,[85] but attachment probably is not merely a function of time. It grows through positive social interaction and the compatibility of the community with the residents' purposes in life.[86] Fear of crime or an influx of residents of another race or culture can damage place attachment for long-time residents.[87]

Physical Influences. What physical features of a community are associated with attachment? It has been argued that a key aspect is interaction with nature, either through the creation and maintenance of a garden[88] or access to a natural area.[89] Perhaps surprisingly, attachment is not necessarily reduced by the physical decay of a community.[90]

Interviews of women who lived on busy or quiet streets revealed that those who lived on quiet streets were more likely to have a sense of belonging to the neighborhood.[91] The researcher reasoned that a busy street discouraged belongingness by restricting space appropriation, the feeling that outdoor areas exist for the use of residents (as opposed to being the domain of strangers who are passing through). Similarly, residents of culs-de-sac seem to develop more attachment to the neighborhood than residents of through streets.[92]

Place Loss. One poignant form of community attachment occurs in dying towns. In the Midwest, literally thousands of communities have died in this century and many are barely surviving today.[93] Yet, attachment to such towns is often intense, perhaps because every factor that promotes place attachment is present. Only changes in the worldwide economy that favor massive urbanization prevent these communities from being successful. However, that many older residents cling to their dying towns is evidence that economic factors are not the most important aspect of community attachment.[94]

At some point, through divorce, conviction of a crime, mental disability, or pure exhaustion in old age, most of us eventually lose our places. The value of place is revealed most clearly when the settings we hold most dear are threatened or lost.

◆ *IN SUM, neighborhoods are psychological. Not everyone who lives in an area would even draw the same boundaries around the neighborhood, and certainly such official lines as census tracts do not define most residents' idea of their neighborhood. Neighborhoods have different characters—some more positive and some more negative—depending on the type of social contact, whether residents feel confident, whether they interact with outsiders ever (or always, by spending most of their time away from the neighborhood), whether they feel attached to or identified with the community, and whether they feel safe. Generally, the neighborhood's physical qualities are more important than its social qualities, unless (on the positive side) residents have special bonds with each other or (on the negative side) residents are at war, or nearly so. But a nice, green, natural, residential-only area is not everyone's favorite place; more important is whether the community fills a person's needs and whether the person is adapted to its pattern of stimulation. Place attachment is psychologi-*

cally important. It cannot be instantly attained; people need to spend time in a place, to hear stories, to be part of a spiritual quest centered there. Many people eventually lose the places to which they have become attached.

◆ COMMUNITY URBANIZATION ◆ AND STRESS

The growth of communities into city scale automatically means that fewer residents know one another. When more people are strangers, it is easier to treat others as objects or targets. Strength becomes an asset, both for aggressors and for potential victims. It is no wonder that most women find urban outdoor environments more threatening, or that these settings are more threatening in the evening and when no one else is around.[95] A rather broad spectrum of residents are now against community growth.[96]

Some evidence suggests that urbanization itself has a generally negative impact on mental health. For example, one investigation of selected years between 1880 and 1963 found a direct regional correlation between schizophrenia and urbanization in the United States.[97] Several explanations for this are possible. One is the **drift hypothesis**, which asserts that people who already have problems migrate (drift) into cities, as opposed to the hypothesis that stressors encountered in the city are the cause of their problems. Whatever the cause, however, cities have a greater per capita proportion of schizophrenics than rural areas, and this concentration itself causes problems.

If community stress is well represented by rates of crime, alcoholism, divorce, and suicide, then the drift hypothesis may apply to differences in stress among U.S. cities. The growing cities of the Sunbelt in Florida, California, Nevada, Texas, Arizona, and Oklahoma have 22 of the 25 most stressful cities out of 286 studied.[98,99] Only 1 city of the 25 least stressful cities is located in those states. The most logical conclusion is that stress is a product of migration. Either troubled people move and bring their troubles with them, or increased population causes disorganization and stress even among long-term residents of the destination cities, or both.

William Rohe has presented a model of the connection between community design and mental health.[100] He suggested that certain physical stressors may be especially important in promoting mental health problems: high density, through streets, poor upkeep of public places, a lack of community meeting places, and high-rise residences. As Rohe pointed out, such design elements are not equally stressful to everyone (in fact, high rises may even be less stressful for some residents), but most of these elements may be stressful to most residents.

◆ ANTI-SOCIAL BEHAVIOR IN THE ◆ COMMUNITY ENVIRONMENT

Drive-by shootings and carjackings are recent and serious manifestations of urban anti-social behavior. Less dramatic but equally disturbing incidents also occur frequently. A subway attendant reminds a patron that smoking is not permitted and the patron snarls, "OK, come here. I'll butt it out on your forehead!" A pedestrian, fed up with bicycles on the sidewalk, sticks an umbrella into the spokes of a passing bike. A few blocks later, the courier who was riding the bike hammers his fist into the fender of a car that approaches too close.

Community Design

Crime and vandalism are linked to or facilitated by certain aspects of the physical nature of a community. Let's begin with a small, everyday anti-social act: parking in spaces reserved for the disabled. The usual marking for such spaces is a symbol painted on the pavement. One study showed that merely adding an upright sign significantly deterred drivers without disabilities from parking in these spaces.[101]

Some of the research on crime and environment was discussed in Chapter 6, when defensible space theory was discussed. Further research at the community level (as opposed to the dwelling level) is appropriate here.

When an area seems more residential, with few through streets and little public parking, it usually will experience less crime than houses on the edges of such areas.[102,103] The general principle is to reduce passage by strangers through the area, which increases bonds among residents and helps everyone to spot suspicious activity.

Blocks with houses that have been burglarized have more street signs.[104] Possibly, streets with more signs in-dicate a more public area with less control by residents, which may be attractive to criminals. Apartments nearer parking lots and recreation areas are burglarized more, as are stores and residences near corners. Somewhat contrary to this overall picture, streets with heavier traffic may experience less crime—perhaps more cars mean more chance of being observed.[105]

More crime occurs in taller apartments and apartments with more than 5 units per floor or 50 total units.[106] This probably occurs because residents of larger buildings are less likely to know one another, tend to treat each other as strangers, and lose the ability to recognize who lives in the building and who does not. This makes entry by criminals easier.

A neighborhood in Dayton, Ohio, with a high crime rate incorporated some defensible space changes in 1991.[107] On the advice of Oscar Newman, many entrances to the neighborhood were closed, speed bumps were installed to slow down traffic, gates with the neighborhood logo were installed, and the community was divided into five mini-neighborhoods with physical barriers. By 1993, traffic was down 67 percent, violent crime declined by 50 percent, and total crime decreased by 26 percent.

This notion that more public areas are more vulnerable is confirmed by reports that more crimes are committed at the edges of central downtown districts.[108] Here, many people are not familiar with the darker areas near the main corners and are attacked as they leave or arrive for an evening's entertainment.

However, some areas that have defensible space characteristics still have serious crime problems. That is partly because *defensible* space (the physical layout) does not necessarily translate into *defended* space (residents actually acting against crime by keeping an eye out or reporting suspicious activity). This can happen, for example, if the neighborhood is not sufficiently cohesive to act together against criminal elements.[109]

Defensible space *sets the stage* for crime reduction by making it easier, almost automatic, for residents to fight crime through visual surveillance of outdoor areas. But if residents are unable or unwilling to act on what they see, crime will not be deterred.

A second reason that defensible space does not guarantee a crime-free neighborhood is that not all criminals pay attention to the environment. Less-experienced criminals, motivated by thrill seeking or social approval, use less rational criteria for choosing a target and may simply not pay attention to defensible space features of the setting.[110]

When the crime scene is a particular place (such as a convenience store) rather than an entire neighborhood, defensible space design principles may be more successful. One chain of stores incorporated a series of changes such as putting cash registers right in front of windows and removing window ads to make the interior more surveillable. Robberies declined 30 percent compared to other stores that were not redesigned.[111]

An analysis of bank robberies showed that bank robbers select locations in a bank that enable them to systematically control seeing and being seen during the crime. The study also analyzed the sales of stolen property in sting operations and found that stolen-property salespersons were more tense and left the scene more quickly when the transaction occurred in a setting with limited surveillability.[112] Burglars rate houses as likely crime targets or not depending largely on their visual surveillability.[113]

Another design factor is physical diversity in a neighborhood. In her influential book, *The Death and Life of Great American Cities,* Jane Jacobs speculated that diversity (defined as short blocks, mixed land use, old and new buildings, and concentrated use of space) increases public social interaction among residents, which thereby helps to discourage crime.[114]

A Toronto study of these ideas found support for the idea that more physically diverse districts do have more neighboring and less crime.[115] However, the connection between more neighboring and less crime was not significant. Thus, physical diversity may discourage crime, but for reasons *other* than the creation of more social interaction among residents.

Researchers in the Netherlands have developed a checklist for assessing the crime vulnerability of neighborhoods.[116] Six main elements comprise this checklist:

- The potential visibility of public areas (lines of sight)
- The actual presence of residents (to take advantage of these sightlines)
- Social involvement (residents care enough to maintain buildings and act against criminals)
- Access and escape routes (for both criminals and victims)
- Attractiveness (assuming that beauty evokes care in residents and decay informs criminals that the residents have little vigilance)
- The vulnerability of materials (locks, presence of easily vandalized walls, phone booths, etc.)

The checklist's primary aim is to identify areas that are susceptible to vandalism, but it may be further developed as a tool against other crimes, such as burglary and violent crime.

Vandalism is a widespread destructive behavior. Not every alteration of public territory is vandalism, of course. We can distinguish between vandalism and people's art.[117] Part of the distinction involves motive: The artist's goal is to beautify an ugly environment. Vandals are destructive or egocentric; instead of painting a mural that reflects a social concern, they break off a young tree or scrawl their own names on a subway wall. In contrast, public artists usually seek anonymity yet creatively enhance a bleak place.

The vandal's motive often may be revenge. **Equity theory,** the idea that social and other behaviors are based on each person's perception that social (or other) rewards and costs should be fair, views vandals as persons who feel unfairly dealt with.[118] Vandalism may be particularly likely when perceived unfairness is combined with a perceived lack of control—a feeling that the injustice cannot be rectified through normal channels. Whether potential vandals have a role model who engages in vandalism may also be important.[119]

Weather

Perhaps the most researched weather variable is temperature. A popular idea is that high temperatures, or, more precisely, heat discomfort,[120] causes riots and other social aggression. Police have subscribed to this notion for a long time,[121] but public awareness of the hypothesis was heightened by a report from the United States Riot Commission.[122]

The commission's figures indicated that all 1967 riots except one began when the temperature was at least 80°F. The commission did not intend this as proof that heat causes aggression. However, as sometimes happens when informal studies confirm an intuitively attractive idea, many readers accepted the data as proof that high temperatures cause riots. What is the empirical evidence?

Researchers studied riot and temperature records over a 4-year period and concluded that riots *did* increase with temperature—up to about 83°F.[123] A review of research concluded that some crimes (assault, burglary, collective violence, and rape) increase with temperature, up to about 85°F.[124] (A study of records showed a similar trend even in sports. Baseball pitchers hit twice as many batters when temperatures are in the 90s as when temperatures are cooler.)[125] However, at higher temperatures, crime seems to decrease. Researchers suggested that over this temperature, heat discomfort may be *too* high to promote riots.

This study sparked a hot (!) controversy. Other researchers reexamined the temperature and riot records and pointed out that riots decreased on very hot days mainly because there simply were not that many very hot days![126] They suggested that when this **base-rate problem** was corrected for, anti-social behavior does, after all, rise steadily with temperature.

Other field studies also show that, within the normal range of temperatures (up to about 95°F), the hotter it is, the more aggressive acts occur.[127,128] Another study replicated these findings and showed that they are particularly true for violent (as opposed to nonviolent) crimes[129] (see Figure 10-3).

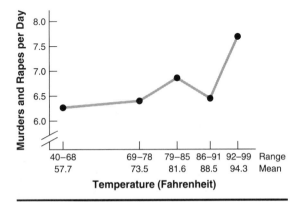

FIGURE 10-3 This shows the number of murders and rapes per day in Houston, Texas, as a function of the maximum temperature on the day of the crime. Violence generally increases across this temperature range rather than peaking at a moderately high temperature.

Thus, field studies support the linear hypothesis (more heat equals more aggression) rather than the curvilinear hypothesis (aggression peaks at moderately hot temperatures and declines in very hot temperatures). However, the original researchers' basic contention that anti-social behavior declines at very high temperatures must be true at sufficiently high temperatures.

My own experience with 113°F temperatures is that no one any longer wishes even to *move*, let alone run amok in a riot. However, and this is the important and ominous conclusion, the temperature at which aggression begins to decline because potential aggressors are too hot is so high that, for all *practical* purposes, aggression does increase with temperature.

Air Pollution

Some earlier lab studies suggest that bad odors negatively affect mood and attraction to others. For example, students exposed to a bad-smelling pollutant judged peers (shown in photographs) lower on a scale of well-being,[130] and a moderately bad odor facilitated aggression (giving electric shocks).[131]

This led environmental psychologists to search for links between air pollution and social pathology in community settings. In a couple of studies, higher levels of photochemical oxidants in the air were correlated with more domestic disputes and more instances of psychiatric disturbance.[132,133] Correlation does not imply causation, but the researchers were aware of this and were able to eliminate several alternative explanations for their findings, which suggests the link *may* be causal.

If these findings are confirmed by subsequent research, the implications are very important for two reasons. First, it is not terribly surprising to discover that high temperatures and loud noise harm social relations, but we usually do not think of air pollution as an anti-social agent. Air pollution may be a hidden cause of aggression. Second, activists committed to fighting air pollution could reasonably argue that it erodes more than paint, vegetation, and the pH balance of lakes. It erodes human relations.

◆ **IN SUM,** *personal safety is a very important urban problem. Some crime is caused by poverty and social breakdown, but defensible space principles combined with a* *take-back-the-streets community attitude can significantly reduce crime. Other physical forces facilitate aggressiveness, though. Hotter temperatures appear to increase the risk of violence. A less obvious aggression-causing problem may be air pollution; in addition to being a health risk, it may also trigger violence in some individuals.*

◆ **HELPFULNESS IN THE** ◆
COMMUNITY ENVIRONMENT

Environmental factors are linked with helpfulness (and the lack of it), not merely with actively anti-social acts.

Weather

A researcher asked individuals to help him with a questionnaire under different climatic conditions.[134] He found that temperature affected how much subjects were willing to help, but the effect was not the same in the summer as it was in the winter. In summer, people helped more on cooler days, but in winter, they helped more on warm days. He concluded that we help more when the weather is "nice" (warm winter days and cool summer days). The same researcher also discovered from waitresses that they received more tips on sunny days (in the spring). Assuming that most of us think of sunshine as pleasant, this supports the following nice-weather hypothesis: We are more willing to help when it is sunny (but not too hot).

Noise

Helping is not always facilitated by environmental variables. Loud noise reduces helping. If the noise is very loud, many of us try to escape it, rather than help someone in need. Also, loud noise may reduce helping because, in attempting to escape, our attention is narrowed. We walk faster and gaze straight ahead more.[135]

A moderating factor is the seriousness of the other person's predicament. If someone's life is in danger, we will probably risk noise loud enough to hurt our ears in order to render assistance. But if, as in some studies, the other person's only problem is a dropped book, we may not help. For example, construction noise (92 decibels as opposed to 72 decibels away from the construction) hindered individuals from giving a quarter to a person

who asked for one.[136] Panhandlers are advised to avoid noisy corners!

The seriousness factor was supported in a study in which researchers observed how many passersby helped a person who dropped an armload of books.[137] They arranged for a nearby lawn mower with no muffler to be running during the incident (87 decibels) or not (about 50 decibels). In addition, the person who dropped the books either was wearing a cast or not. Without a cast, the book dropper was helped by 20 percent of passersby under low noise and by 10 percent of them under high noise. A much larger difference occurred when a cast was worn. Under low noise, 80 percent helped, but only 15 percent helped under high noise.

Not every aversive environmental variable has this effect. Researchers conducted a study similar to the noise studies, but compared helping in hot, cold, and comfortable temperatures. This time, the needy case was someone on crutches. No temperature differences were found; over 95 percent of passersby helped in hot, cold, *and* comfortable temperatures![138] Apparently, then, there is a big difference between helping in extreme temperatures and helping in noise. Why should this be?

One possibility is that we can usually anticipate and dress for cold or hot temperatures, and thereby reduce the adverse effects of temperature. But when we encounter noise in public places, we cannot easily counter the annoyance, except by leaving. When the noise is localized (as with a lawn mower), we realize that a little fast walking, which incidentally carries us past the person who needs help, will carry us beyond the awful din.

Noise in the streets may even affect how we think about others. Researchers asked individuals to form impressions of others under low- and high-noise conditions. In the noisier conditions, these interpersonal judgments were more *extreme*. It seems that noise, perhaps because it acts as a general arousal agent, influences us to reach stronger conclusions about others than we might make under normal conditions.[139]

Number of People

Finally, the number of bystanders is related to helping. This idea was strengthened by the many studies stimulated by a 1964 episode in which a young woman, Kitty Genovese, was killed on a New York street while over 30 neighbors watched without helping her.[140] Subsequent research has found that, under most conditions, the more individuals who witness someone having a problem, the smaller the odds that any one of them will help.

In one field study, the experimenter appeared to lose her contact lens. Helping behavior was defined as the length of time that the subject helped her look for it. When the shopping mall where the study occurred was moderately full, subjects helped less than when it was moderately empty.[141] In another field study, density in the immediate vicinity of the person needing help was more closely related to helping (high density was associated with less helpfulness) than was density at the communitywide level.[142] At a broader level, as we saw in Chapter 7, city density is negatively correlated with helpfulness in many cities.[143]

Urbanites do, of course, help those in need under some conditions. Once again, moderating variables—such as a heavy workload,[144] where we are raised, and cognitive complexity—play an important and sometimes counterintuitive role. For example, in one study, those who were raised in the *city* helped more than those who were raised in the country.[145] Thus, high immediate densities may cause unhelpful behavior, but personal characteristics of the potential helper and certain circumstances other than the high density surrounding the event also affect helping behavior.

Cities sometimes are viewed as unrelenting sources of noise, crime, ugliness, and crowding. The overload approach suggests that urban stimulation is so great that individuals are *forced* to become apathetic and rude. Stanley Milgram's classic article, "The Experience of Living in Cities," was meant to defend urbanites by showing they had little choice in the face of an avalanche of stimulation.[146] They must select cues and pay attention only to the most important part of their environment, which means ignoring other sights that might seem important to outsiders. Milgram painted city dwellers as people doing the best they can in a place that was "deforming" them.

This perspective may have improved the image of city dwellers by arguing that they could not help being rude and unhelpful, but city dwellers are not always like that anyway, and it made *cities* look bad as well as city dwellers. On the first issue, it may be true that city dwellers are less friendly to neighbors and strangers than

are rural residents, but they are just as involved with family and relatives.[147,148]

Community Design and the Immediate Surroundings.
Helpfulness appears to depend, in part, on the complexity of a community setting. In one study, an experimenter asked for directions in complex street environments (many signs, more people, more noise, larger buildings) or simple street environments and in pleasant and less pleasant street environments.[149] Women helped more in the complex settings and men helped more in the simple settings.

Several explanations for this are possible, but one based on crowding research is that women are more likely than men to be cooperative and helpful when the population density is high. The pleasantness of the setting did not affect helpfulness. However, in a related study, pedestrians were more helpful in the same part of town after a shopping mall was constructed than before it was constructed.[150] The mall had improved the pleasantness of the district in the judgment of pedestrians, so the experimenter concluded that the improved environmental pleasantness promoted helpfulness. The conflicting results on the pro-social effects of street pleasantness require further research.

The immediate environment also affects helpfulness. When an apparently blind person dropped a glove, he was helped significantly more than when the same person appeared to be sighted, but only when the immediate area was free of cigarette smoke.[151] When cigarette smoke was present, help declined, particularly for the blind person, so that the blind person no longer received significantly more assistance.

◆ *IN SUM, acts of kindness occur more often in nice, sunny weather, when there is little noise to make us want to run away, on pleasantly designed streets, and when the presence of others does not make us feel as if our help is unnecessary.*

◆ EVERYDAY BEHAVIOR IN THE ◆ COMMUNITY ENVIRONMENT

Not everything we do on the streets of the community involves crime, vandalism, or even helping. In fact, most of the time in public spaces, we merely watch, sit, talk to others, or quietly enjoy life. This section deals with these simple but nevertheless important behaviors and their relation to the physical features of outdoor space (see Figure 10–4).

Watching

We spend much of our time in public places simply looking. What are we looking at? People and things. A more interesting question is: How are we looking? Donald Appleyard believed that when we are out in the community, we are looking in one of three modes.[152]

1. In the **responsive mode,** we look in a receptive, passive manner and see people and things as a sensory experience, almost as a form of entertainment or recreation. We see gardens, graffiti, and neon signs, but we are just looking, much as we look when we are window shopping or touring an art gallery.

2. In the **operational mode,** we look in a problem-solving way. Perhaps while we were walking around in responsive mode, we got lost; now we must pay attention to signs and look for familiar landmarks. When we look around us with a purpose, whether it is finding our way or looking for an address or playing treasure hunt, we are in operational mode. We look because we need something.

FIGURE 10–4 Most of the time, interaction on the street seems minimal. However, although "nothing" seems to be happening, we usually monitor others' behavior carefully.

3. In the **inferential mode,** we look at the community as a medium of communication. We are looking for messages, particularly social messages. Instead of objects, we see symbols or markers or indicators. Because all of us are different, we do not see the same messages; we infer contrasting messages from the same objects. I see an empty lot, the developer sees a building site. You see a book that you have to read, I see a project I worked on for years. In inferential mode, we all see meaning but we often see different meanings.

Walking

Walking is an important behavior, even if it is neglected by many people in this age of automated transport. As one psychologist argued,

> One goes for a walk to get the stuck, depressed state of mind . . . into an organic rhythm. . . . With the soul-calming language of walking, the dartings of the mind begin to form into a direction. . . . We may be driving, literally *driving* ourselves crazy by not attending to the fundamental human need of walking.[153]

So far, not a lot is known about walking and the environment, but we do know a little. It does not take a scientific investigation, for example, to know that many urban areas are not designed for walkers. In many places, walking is so unusual that pedestrians feel uncomfortable, concerned that passing motorists will think them odd or perhaps too poor to own a car.

However, there are still walkers out there. Many elderly walkers have taken to mall walking—that is, programmed early-morning walks in indoor shopping centers.[154] Despite their often negative image, malls do at least provide a place to walk. They have grown larger and increasingly connected to other malls and related structures until, in some places, they are like cities within cities. For example, Montreal has a weatherproof network of malls and tunnels over 14 kilometers (8 miles) long. One can wander past or into many apartment buildings, offices, theaters, over 1,000 stores, 100 restaurants, and subways without ever setting foot on a street.

What do we know from research? A fascinating pair of studies on simple walking speed demonstrate that average individual pedestrian velocity is strongly related to community size; the larger the population, the faster we walk.[155,156] This appears to be a culture-free trend; the data were collected in villages, towns, and cities in eight countries. The trend is so clear that the investigators proposed a precise mathematical formula for walking velocity: $V = .86 \log P + .05$, where V is velocity in feet per second and P is the population of the community.

When I first read about this research, I was skeptical. So, some students and I tested it in the town where I taught at the time.[157] We were amazed to find that the average walking velocity of individuals in our town was *exactly* that predicted by the formula.

Although the grand average of all individual pedestrian velocities conformed to the formula, the students and I found that pedestrian velocities reliably vary from the overall average under certain conditions. For example, groups walk slower than individuals. Pedestrians walk faster downhill and faster in the rain. Males walk faster than females. These effects are additive: A lone male walking downhill in the rain walks over 30 percent faster than a group of women walking uphill on a nice day! Other studies report that older people walk faster than younger people[158] and that people walk faster in cooler temperatures.[159]

Velocity is not everything: When people walk, they also make many decisions, most of which are hardly conscious. For example, they decide, but not very consciously, where and when to cross the street, how to interact with other pedestrians, and which route to take.[160]

A study in which adults and children were observed as they walked through a community and then were interviewed about their route choices found that pedestrians generally choose the shortest route (no surprise there!), but children select more complex routes than adults, and women select more complex routes than men.[161] When these pedestrians were asked why they took certain routes, the answer almost always referred to some physical feature of the neighborhood, such as the attractiveness of a route or the location of some building along the way.

For the most part, even though we would feel very strange if we were the only ones on the street, we try to avoid contact with most individuals in public. For example, commuters are less willing to make eye contact with a stranger in the city than they are with the same stranger in the suburbs.[162]

Urbanites operate according to a **mini-max principle:** Minimize involvement with others, and maximize social order.[163] A good example of this principle is provided by research on pedestrian behavior.[164] Films of urban pedestrians were analyzed, and researchers found they consistently followed certain rules, although not with much awareness. These rules promote noncontact and cooperation.

When pedestrians are headed on a collision course with one another, one of them will move aside when the distance between them is about 7 feet when the sidewalk density is low, and at about 5 feet when the sidewalk density is high. Other common patterns that pedestrians use as they make their way along a sidewalk full of strangers include the step-and-slide pattern, the head-over-the-shoulder pattern, and the spread effect.

Hanging Out

Young people gather with friends in the neighborhood. Hanging out often occurs in the so-called fourth environment (i.e., anywhere *except* home, playgrounds, and other places meant for kids).[165] This is another usually uneventful but important everyday activity. Although seemingly nothing is happening, the exploration of the neighborhood results in the development of spatial knowledge and competence, and is developmentally important.

In one study, the extent of the fourth environment was found to be larger for those who live in the country and for those with more money; in the suburbs, it was larger for boys and for older teens.[166] Teens prefer natural areas if they are available, away from people other than their friends.[167] Older teens gradually lose their social and activity ties to their neighborhood in favor of wider stomping grounds.[168]

Despite the developmental importance of playing or hanging out in the neighborhood, one historical study reports that, compared to earlier in the century, urban neighborhood environments are less supportive of children's play, and children use neighborhoods for play less than they once did.[169] This may be due to increased safety concerns and adult-supervised activities.

It is not only teens who hang out in public areas. Adults, children, and the elderly also gather in parks, in malls, and on street corners. One study that actually counted who hung out in two large malls discovered that, despite the stereotype of teens in the mall, the most frequent category of people to be found sitting around was elderly men.[170] In a city where people over age 65 represent about 9 percent of the population, they accounted for up to 50 percent of those sitting in the malls; teens were actually underrepresented based on their percent of the population!

Obviously, older people like to hang out, too. Active use of the neighborhood may be important and healthy for the elderly. Yet, old people's use of the neighborhood often is limited; this makes them "spatially disadvantaged."[171] Researchers have examined which characteristics of the elderly predict their use of neighborhood goods and services.[172] The ability to learn and remember locations was a better predictor than the degree of mobility or the length of time these individuals had lived in the neighborhood.

Homeless and poor people also hang out on the streets. In some cities, they also spend much time sitting in building lobbies. This form of hanging out annoys some building owners and middle-class individuals. In 1994, Seattle began enforcing a law that forbade sitting or lying on downtown sidewalks between 7 A.M. and 9 P.M.[173]

Familiar Strangers

Sometimes strangers become familiar. In an interesting article, Stanley Milgram described how some members of the anonymous mass confronting us become known quantities, even though we never talk to them.[174] Do you see the same people at the bus stop, the same jogger or skateboarder, the same man in the purple coat frequently? Even in a large city, certain individuals, both normal and odd, regularly cross our paths but we do not talk to them. Milgram calls such individuals our **familiar strangers**.

In one study, Milgram's students photographed groups of commuters waiting for the subway or bus. The photographs were then showed to some of the commuters in the picture, who were asked about the other individuals in the picture. About 90 percent of them recognized at least one person; the average person pointed out four others that he or she recognized but had never spoken to.

FIGURE 10–5 Some familiar strangers wait for a bus.

Many commuters said they often think about these familiar strangers, noticing when they get a new coat or trying to figure out what kind of life they lead. One of Milgram's respondents said she once helped a woman who had collapsed on the street (in New York, such assistance does not always happen). Why? The woman had been one of her familiar strangers for years (see Figure 10–5).

Sometimes the meanness and anonymity of city streets is overemphasized. There is crime and fear of crime, but the studies just discussed show that people definitely take each other into account, sometimes in a positive or helpful way.

◆ *IN SUM, we do a lot on city streets that seems close to nothing, perhaps because we do most of it automatically, without reflecting. However, upon closer examination, this "nothing" turns out to be a fascinating mixture of thoughts and activities. We monitor our progress through the city in responsive, operational, or inferential modes. We walk at a speed that reflects the pulse (or at least the size) of the city. Our walks follow planned patterns even when we are unaware of our plans. We carefully avoid interaction, but maximize social order. Elderly people hang out more than teens. Also, we know lots of people that we do not really know—our familiar strangers.*

◆ **THE ENVIRONMENTAL** ◆
PSYCHOLOGY OF SHOPPING

Shopping is an essential human activity. It has always had social and recreational aspects as well as the utilitarian function of obtaining the basic necessities of life.

Many forces shape our shopping habits; among these are physical setting influences such as location of the store, decor, lighting, weather, sounds, crowding, smells, and displays. Many unresearched or poorly researched claims about shopping environments have been made, but recently more and better studies are being done. Retailers have become conscious of environmental psychology.[175]

Location, Size, and Attractiveness

An adage in the retail trade is that the three most important keys to retail success are location, location, and location. Research tends to substantiate this claim, although, of course, location is not quite the entire story. When other factors are equal, most shoppers choose the closest store that stocks what they want to buy. Also, in general, shoppers will select the largest store. These two physical variables, size and location, explain much variance in consumer choice of stores.[176]

In an analogy to the physical laws of attraction among astronomical bodies, this approach is called the **gravitation model:** If all other factors are equal, consumers gravitate to larger stores and to closer stores. Another key variable in this gravitation model is the attractiveness of the product. For especially attractive products (usually the more expensive ones), the gravitational effect due to size and location is weakened and shoppers will travel farther.

For example, in a study of **outshopping**—the practice of leaving one's own community to buy goods—researchers found that 34 percent of furniture and 33 percent of cars were purchased away from a small city, but only 4 percent of food and groceries were.[177] One limitation to outshopping is age. Older people are more likely to confine their shopping to the home neighborhood—a finding that reinforces the gravitation model.[178]

Layout

Large stores may draw more shoppers, but not every shopper is happy with the usually impersonal environment in these retail settings. Researchers compared the social and physical qualities of supermarkets with those of farmers' markets. In farmers' markets, shoppers more

often arrive in groups and spend more time interacting with the sellers and with other shoppers.[179] The researchers observed that the spatial layout of supermarkets (block shape, aisle orientation, linear checkout arrangements) is a key factor in their sacrifice of friendliness in favor of traffic efficiency.

The length of aisles may affect buying behavior. One study found that when aisles are shorter, shoppers often just look down the aisle rather than walk down it.[180] Long aisles cannot be so easily surveyed, so shoppers walk down them and often fall victim to the impulse to buy an item they are attracted to but did not intend to buy before entering the store. As more of us register our dissatisfaction with settings that encourage alienation, shopping environment design will become more sensitive to the social needs of shoppers.

Emotional Impact

The emotional quality of retail environment is important. Store-induced pleasure and arousal were found in one study to have strong effects on shoppers' intended behaviors.[181] Based on Mehrabian and Russell's pleasure-arousal hypothesis (see Chapter 3), the researchers found that such shopping-related intentions as the time spent browsing, the tendency to spend more money than planned, and the likelihood of returning to the store all increased when pleasant stores were also arousing. When stores were neutral or unpleasant, arousal did not increase these intentions. One modifier of these findings may be the sex of the customer: The quality of shopping facilities apparently is more important to women than men.[182]

Density

Crowding in the shopping environment is another physical setting influence on consumer behavior. Objective density affects the shoppers' perceptions and cognitions about the store.[183] Feelings of crowding often ensue, which lead to adaptive strategies such as leaving the store earlier than planned. The shopper's attitude toward the store may then take a negative turn.

An interesting turn of the urban overload hypothesis compared the interactions between customers and staff in post offices and delicatessens that varied in location from urban to rural.[184] As predicted, the more urban locations were busier and the social interactions in them were briefer than in the more rural locations. However, even when the number of customers in the urban locations was relatively low, interaction was still less. Apparently, the low-interaction habits developed in busy times carry over to times when stimulus overload is not present.

Display

Purchasing is affected by how goods are displayed. Most research has been done in grocery stores. Shelf height, end-aisle placement, and location within the store all may affect normal buying as well as impulse buying.[185] For example, items placed on the end of an aisle will sometimes stimulate sales of that item. However, because shoppers searching for that product no longer need to travel down those long aisles where the item normally is located, overall stores sales may suffer (see Figure 10–6).

If the shopper does make the journey down the aisle, the height of an item affects its sales. One survey reports that sales of the same jars of applesauce increased fivefold when they were moved from waist level to eye level.[186] Basics such as dairy products are usually placed at the back of the store so the shopper is drawn past

FIGURE 10–6 Our cognition and behavior in retail settings is an important part of environmental psychology.

nonessentials; impulse purchases of these nonessentials often occur. Another key layout variable is store cleanliness; clean stores attract more customers.[187]

Music

Music has significant effects on behavior in stores and restaurants. In one study of supermarkets, fast music, slow music, and no music were played.[188] Shoppers walked significantly slower when slow music was played than when fast music was played. More important from a store perspective, shoppers bought more when the music was slow, presumably because they had more time to look at products.

Most interesting, perhaps, was the study's finding that when customers were asked as they left the store if they recalled whether music had been playing while they shopped, there were no significant differences in the three conditions. It may be, then, that shoppers can be induced to buy more without realizing that the key factor is environmental—the tempo of the music.

The volume of music also may be influential. Consumers in one study who shopped when loud music was playing finished shopping more quickly than those who shopped when the music was softer, but they spent the same amount of money.[189] Thus, it seems that the tempo of the music affects both the shopper's pace and the amount purchased, but the volume of music affects only pace.

Evidence suggests that music also affects eating and drinking. In one restaurant study, when the tempo was slow, customers stayed 25 percent longer and spent almost 50 percent more on bar purchases.[190] In another restaurant, fast music significantly increased the pace of eating (bites per minute), although total meal time was the same as for slower music.[191] Once again, a questionnaire showed that patrons were unaware of the music's effect on them.

◆ ***IN SUM,*** *the physical environment is not widely studied as a factor in retail behavior, but awareness of and research on its influence is growing. Well-known effects include location and store size. However, at the interior level, the way that shelves, aisles, and displays affect the emotions and behavior of consumers is gradually becoming clear. We even eat and shop to the beat.*

◆ **COMMUNITY ENVIRONMENTAL** ◆
DESIGN

Defensible Space in Row Housing

Oscar Newman's ideas about defensible space have been controversial for years. Many psychologists feel that Newman's thinking has some validity, yet the research supporting his concepts—like any field research—has been problematic. Here, we take a closer look at an actual project of Newman's: renovations of a low-income housing project adjacent to the south Bronx, in New York. Clason Point consists of rowhouse clusters housing from 12 to 40 families per cluster.

One of the goals of the renovations was to increase defensible space, thereby reducing both fear of crime and actual crime. Following defensible space principles, the renovations (1) assigned as much public space to the control of specific families, using both substantial and symbolic fencing; (2) reduced the number of pedestrian routes through the project and improved lighting along the paths; and (3) improved the project's image and encouraged a sense of personal ownership by resurfacing the dwellings, giving different colors to individual dwellings.

Newman reports that residents took new pride in their dwellings, planting grass, adding their own new modifications, and even sweeping the public sidewalks. According to Newman, maintenance costs and crime both were reduced significantly. Serious crimes such as burglary, assault, and robbery were said to have dropped by 61.5 percent. The number of residents who said they felt they had the right to question strangers in the project doubled. The results were not entirely positive,[192] but the renovations appear to have had a generally beneficial effect on Clason Point.

Plazas as Social Spaces

William Whyte has documented an increasing amount of positive social interaction (as opposed to carefully managed avoidance) in cities.[193] Some theorists, such as Oscar Newman, have concentrated on urban designs that minimize crime and insecurity, but Whyte has emphasized the pursuit of design features that promote positive social interaction in public places.[194]

In particular, Whyte has extensively studied urban plazas, searching for characteristics that distinguish beneficial plazas from useless spaces. Over several years, he and his coworkers observed and filmed 18 plazas in New York City. They counted how many individuals used each plaza on pleasant days and began to relate usage to various features of the plazas.

In general, plazas become more useful as the number of amenities rise. For example, many unused plazas simply have no place for people to sit. Sittable space is crucial.[195] Some features of successful plazas besides sittable space include water (fountains and pools), food stands, trees, accessible food outlets, and activities to watch (jugglers, mimes, and buskers). The siting of plazas is also important. Successful plazas have a sunny orientation (or a shady orientation in hot cities), provide shelter from wind, and are located on busy streets rather than hidden away (see Figure 10–7).

In 1961, the city of New York offered developers a deal: For every square foot of plaza they included in a new project, their new building could exceed normal zoning restrictions by 10 square feet. This deal certainly increased New York's supply of open space downtown. Unfortunately, the new plazas tended to be vast empty spaces devoid of most features just described. In 1975 and 1977, revised deals were offered. Perhaps as a result of Whyte's work, New York would give extra square footage away only if developers offered plazas that included many of the amenities identified by Whyte. New plazas are markedly improved social spaces that increase the city's pleasantness.

Bringing a Neighborhood to Life

Many neighborhoods are dead. Sure, people live there, but no one speaks to anyone except to complain, few people except troublemakers use the sidewalks or parks, and traffic moves quickly through the streets.

Sidney Brower has spent years developing and testing ideas for enlivening neighborhoods in Baltimore. His book, *Design in Familiar Places*, concludes with a list of guidelines for bringing communities to life.[196] Some of the guidelines require more time, capital, and energy than others, but all are attainable with community will. Some require city approval and therefore resident organization, but they are worth the effort. An overall plan helps, but it need not be implemented all at once. Here are some of Brower's guidelines.

FIGURE 10–7 How many of Whyte's recommended design elements are evident in this view of a large urban plaza?

1. *Keep the streetfront alive.* Take steps to encourage residents to walk, stroll, and play on the sidewalks. This encourages social interaction and enables natural surveillance over street activities. Find a legitimate use for every public space, so that people routinely visit all areas of the neighborhood and there are no dead spaces. Once some residents are outside, using public space, others will feel safe doing so; security and socializing go hand in hand. Ensure that every space belongs to or is managed by a specific person or group.

2. *Give residents things to do and places to be.* For some, this means benches; for others, it might be horseshoes or hopscotch or street vendors or library vans. Encourage use of the streetfront and street recreation by blocking off alleys, parking lots, or streets. Some areas, such as sidewalks themselves, must be preserved from fast, rough play for older people to enjoy walking or watching. Think of ways to incorporate recreation into a linked system of spaces between and around dwellings.

3. *Reduce the speed and number of cars.* Can the cars be rerouted at night, slowed with speed bumps, stopped at certain times with temporary barricades? Speed zones enhanced with speed bumps reduce traffic by up to 30 percent and accidents with injuries by about 25 percent. Residents accept them because they feel safer and the neighborhood is quieter and more suitable for walk-

ing.[197,198] However, do not ban cars completely; residents in cars help to maintain a street presence.

4. *Residences should open to the street, not from some central courtyard.* When buildings present their backs to the streets, the streets are ignored and street life shrivels.

5. *Make parks more attractive to adults.* Parks relegated to juvenile use operate at juvenile developmental levels. What might adults like to do in the park? Barbecues? Informal concerts? Mini-dramas? Where possible, incorporate all age groups in all activities, so that competition between the geriatric play reading and the kids' stickball game does not degenerate in intergroup hostility. Can some kids have roles in the play? Can some adults play, coach, or referee the stickball games?

6. *Distinguish between home-based recreation and park activities.* Parks are for noisier, louder activities (even when adults participate too). Don't put houses right next to houses if possible; have a buffer of stores or recreation centers or other semi-public structures.

These are guidelines that take much time and effort; form an organization to share the work. Get the city to help with money, advice, and equipment. Success is in all taxpayers' interest. Seek an equal partnership between officials and residents; don't expect or allow city officials to do it all. They need your local experience and your contacts with other residents to make it work.

◆ SUMMARY ◆

Neighborhoods are cognitive creations, not geographical entities. They have different personalities, depending on how their residents interact with each other and outsiders, and whether residents feel confident, attachment, and secure. The neighborhood's physical qualities are more important than its social qualities for most people, but neither suburbia nor urban communities are everyone's favorite. The key is whether the community satisfies its residents' needs and whether the resident is adapted to its pattern of stimulation. Place attachment is psychologically important, but it takes time to achieve and there a many paths to it. Urban dwellers face many stressors, but urbanization itself is a major one. Familiarity with these stressors encourages urbanites to overlook the major consequences.

Safety is a very important urban problem; city dwellers are so used to following many rules related to safety that they overlook the psychological costs of constant alertness. Defensible space, combined with an actively aware neighborhood, can decrease the threat. However, high temperatures and air pollution may increase the risk of violence. People are more helpful in quiet sunny weather on pleasantly designed streets when not too many others are around. On city streets, automatic behavior includes observing in particular modes, walking at a pace that matches the city's size, and avoiding interaction with strangers but becoming quite familiar with some of them. The environmental psychology of shopping includes the influence of store location, size, and layout. Basic and important behaviors such as spending, eating, and drinking are affected by the tempo of music.

Suggested Readings

Altman, I., & Low, S. M. (Eds.). (1992). *Place attachment.* New York: Plenum.

Altman, I., & Wandersman, A. (Eds.). (1987). *Neighborhoods and community environments.* New York: Plenum.

Cohn, E. (1990). Weather and crime. *British Journal of Criminology, 30,* 51–64.

Edelstein, M. R. (1988). *Contaminated communities: The social and psychological impacts of residential toxic exposure.* Boulder, CO: Westview Press.

Gaster, S. (1991). Urban children's access to their neighborhood: Changes over three generations. *Environment and Behavior, 23,* 70–85.

Krupat, E. (1985). *People in cities.* New York: Cambridge University Press.

Levine, R. V., Martinez, T. S., Brase, G., & Sorenson, K. (1994). Helping in 36 U.S. cities. *Journal of Personality and Social Psychology, 67,* 69–82.

Nasar, J. L. (1990). Patterns of behavior in urban public spaces. *Journal of Architectural and Planning Research, 7,* 71–85.

Proshansky, H. M., Fabian, A. K., & Kaminoff, R. (1983). Place-identity: Physical world socialization of the self. *Journal of Environmental Psychology, 3,* 57–83.

Whyte, W. H. (1980). *The social life of small urban spaces.* New York: The Conservation Foundation.

CHAPTER 11

EDUCATIONAL ENVIRONMENTAL PSYCHOLOGY

Nowhere else are large groups of individuals packed so closely together for so many hours, yet expected to perform at peak efficiency on difficult learning tasks and to interact harmoniously.

—Carol Weinstein[1]

*W*alking *through the woods to the university's field station where they had a lab for their forestry class, Tom and Jane started reminiscing about the schools they had attended. Jane's city-center school sat in the middle of an expanse of asphalt, surrounded by wire fences.*

"The windows were tall and narrow and the globe lamps hung down on long wires. In those ancient rooms with tall ceilings, I felt small and out of place," Jane recalled. "I can still see those big old oak desks with generations of initials carved upon initials."

"Sounds like doom itself to me," said Tom. He had grown up in a rural district that was being swallowed by suburbia. "My elementary school was certainly different. It was almost new—only one story and surrounded by grassy fields."

He thought for a minute. "There was something else quite different from yours—it was one of those open-plan schools. You know, with big spaces where the teachers could merge their classes or divide them up by subject instead of by age. I remember some of the teachers just couldn't handle it. They would try to fence out the rest of the school by using filing cabinets and bulletin boards."

"Sounds like chaos itself to me," said Jane, gently mocking him.

"You're right, actually. The noise level would steadily rise all day until you could hardly hear the bell at the end of the last period."

"That's strange—your whole school experience must have been so different from mine. Those old rooms were like caverns, huge and quiet. Your voice would sort of disappear into space." Jane actually shuddered as the sounds and smells came back to her. "Maybe the place seemed like that because our high school only had 1,100 students and the place was built for 2,000."

Tom was surprised. "Really? My schools were always too full. My high school was crowded the day it opened and by the time I graduated, it had 900 students—and it was built for 600."

Lost in these musings, they suddenly found themselves in front of the field station. "Well, back to forest ecology," said Jane.

◆   ◆   ◆

Learning is a central part of everyone's life. It often occurs even when we do not think of ourselves as learning, such as when we take a stroll through the woods or when we talk over the events of the day with friends.

We often associate learning with school, but of course much learning also occurs before we reach school age, outside school hours, and after we have completed school. Although only 12 to 14 percent of adults over age 44 and low-income earners have such experiences, virtually all children over the age of 2 receive some out-of-school learning, as do almost all higher-income earners and adults aged 18 to 25.[2]

Learning occurs in places where it is the designated purpose of the setting (school, seminars, practice fields, libraries, conservatories, museums, training grounds, etc.) and in places where learning is incidental to the primary purpose of the setting (playgrounds, street corners, parks, dinner tables, family rooms, offices, hallways, etc.).

This chapter is concerned with the role of the physical environment in learning, including such influences as architecture, noise, light, temperature, crowding, furniture arrangement, and room design. Most research focuses on the school setting, but some examines learning outside schools. In addition, we will discuss the nature of learning about the environment, the process of developing environmental competence (see Figures 11–1 and 11–2).

FIGURE 11–1 We spend years in schools; their physical environments have strong effects on our learning and other behaviors.

FIGURE 11–2 Learning also occurs outdoors and on nonacademic topics.

From the very large amount of attention psychology pays to nonphysical factors in learning, such as teaching style or educational philosophy, we might conclude that physical factors are not very important. Yet, many studies are now being conducted[3] and some of them do report dramatic changes in behavior. For example, Wollin and Montagne changed a typical, sterile, Introductory Psychology classroom into one with softer lighting, plants, posters, cushions, and rugs. Student exam scores after five weeks in the room were significantly higher than those of students who spent five weeks in a similar room that had not been modified. Physical factors *can* make a significant difference!

Vast sums of money are spent to educate individuals of all ages. Environmental psychologists believe that educational settings can and should make education both more efficient and more enjoyable. The physical setting may not make or break education on its own—to believe that would be a naive form of architectural determinism—but it can interact with nonenvironmental factors either to promote or to hinder the learning process.

The general framework for this chapter is presented in Figure 11–3. It proposes that the personal characteristics of students (past school experience, attitudes toward learning, age, gender, personality) interact with physical features of the learning setting (its size, noise level, climate, population density, and design) and the social-organizational climate (rules, curriculum, teaching style, progressive or traditional orientation) to produce learning-related attitudes (satisfaction with school, dissatisfaction with classroom, commitment to learning) and behaviors (class participation, attention to learning materials, questioning, appropriate or inappropriate activity, persistence, creativity, and, of course, learning and performance).

Generally, researchers cannot consider all these items in a single study, but most would agree that interactions among these factors should be considered where possible. Consider a typical study that included both personal and environmental factors and found important interactions.[4] The researchers sought to discover whether open-plan school designs were equally beneficial to students from urban and suburban neighborhoods. Suburban students achieved about as much in open-plan and traditional schools, but urban students achieved more in traditional schools than in open-plan schools.

This study shows that one cannot simply conclude that open-plan schools are better or worse. The interaction of a personal and an environmental variable suggests the more accurate conclusion that open-plan schools are better than traditional schools for certain students, but not better for other students.

Carol Weinstein has summarized four assumptions made by environmental psychologists who study learning and the physical environment.[5]

1. Although the setting usually does not teach directly, it can either facilitate or hinder learning, both directly and symbolically. Loud noise, for example, may directly interfere with the transmission of information from teacher to learner. In addition, a drab, untidy classroom may symbolize to learners that the school and teacher care little about their progress.

2. The effects of the physical setting on learning are not universal but are moderated by the social and instructional context. For example, open-plan schools

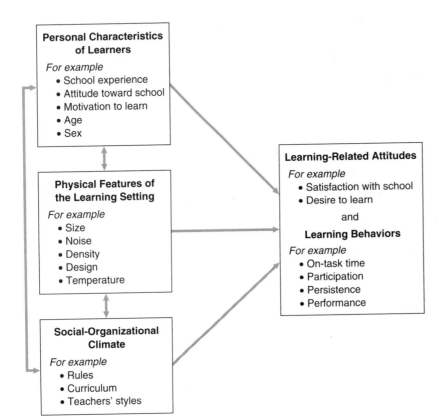

FIGURE 11–3 A framework for conceptualizing person-environment relations in learning settings.

work poorly when educators merely import their teaching methods from traditional schools with separate classrooms, but often work better when teaching methods suited to open space are used.

3. There is no single best learning setting. The best physical settings are those congruent with the type of material being learned, the goals of the class, and the characteristics of the learners. The very same setting, therefore, may produce wonderful results in one case and terrible results in another. This becomes dramatically obvious if we consider, for example, how well children could learn to play football in a hockey rink.

4. Learning is maximized when the physical setting is considered as carefully as are other aspects of the learning situation, such as the curriculum, the teacher's verbal ability, and other teaching aids. Unfortunately, most educational programs still pay little attention to the physical setting.[5]

The task of environmental psychologists who study learning is to identify conditions under which physical and nonphysical elements of the setting combine to result in improved learning. But what *is* learning? Usually, **learning** is defined as a relatively permanent change in behavior that occurs as a result of experience. This relatively narrow technical definition of learning excludes

CAROL WEINSTEIN
is a modern pioneer in educational environmental psychology.

important parts of the complex pattern of teacher and learner behavior that is part of the learning process.

This chapter examines the effects of the physical environment on four dimensions of learning, although the last of these has only very scantily been researched: learning itself, feelings about learning, social behavior related to learning, and the health and stress aspects of learning. Beginning with a look at how settings, as a whole, affect these dimensions of learning, the chapter will continue by examining the effects of more specific physical variables, including noise, light, color, temperature, crowding, and room arrangements.

◆ THE SETTING AS A WHOLE ◆

School buildings and grounds, as a group, are physically quite variable. Some are large, some small; some look like Monopoly hotels, some look like one-story geometric designs constructed of classroom "blocks"; some have large, grassy fields, some have 100 percent asphalt yards. How do such variations in the overall architecture of schools affect learning?

Size

Is there a relation between learning and the size of a school? Five high schools ranging in size from 35 to 2,300 students were compared.[6] Size did affect some aspects of learning. First, larger schools offer a wider variety of instruction to their students. Variety does not, however, increase as fast as size. Thus, a school that is much larger than another offers its students only a slightly greater choice of classes.

Second, participation in activities outside regular class hours was about the same for large and small schools. The important difference is that students in smaller schools participated in more kinds of extracurricular activities, and they much more often participated in central or responsible positions.

Third, in line with the last finding, students in large schools reported that their satisfactions were more often derived from vicarious experience (such as being *from* the school that won a championship). Students in smaller schools reported that their satisfactions came more from direct participation (such as being part of the newspaper staff).

Students from small schools more often believed their participation helped them to learn skills, be challenged, engage in important activities, be valued by others, and be involved in an active group.[7] On the other hand, students from large schools more often believed their participation helped them enjoy being part of the organization, learn about school activities, and gain credit for classes.

Because this research included only five schools, others have studied school size to determine whether these findings would be confirmed. In one study, the school activities of about 21,000 college-bound high school students were investigated.[8] Students from small schools reported more achievements (defined as public recognition of their efforts, such as getting a poem published or winning an election) than did students from large schools in writing, music, drama, and leadership.

Another study provided further support for the conclusion that students in small schools feel more involved and challenged than students in large schools, but it also demonstrated that these conclusions are not universally true.[9] A key factor underlying most of the school size findings we have discussed is that activities in small schools are chronically understaffed. Students in small schools are almost forced to accept a more active, central, and challenging role because there is often no one else to do the job.

But what about activities in small schools that happen to be overstaffed and activities in large schools that happen to be understaffed? When the staffing of activities was about equal in large and small schools, typical experiences (involvement, challenge, skill development, and being valued) were about equal, too. Apparently, the degree of over- or understaffing of a particular activity is the critical variable, rather than the size of the school, although school schools generally will have more understaffed behavior settings than large schools.

The effects of size in day-care centers have also been considered.[10] Larger day-care centers are more economical to the sponsoring agency, but problems arise when the number of students exceeds 60 or so. The necessary increase in programming leads to less freedom of choice in the child's activities and to fewer teacher/child interactions.

Plan and Facade

Another characteristic of the setting that affects learning is the overall plan of the school. A basic architectural distinction may be drawn between schools that are decentralized, with numerous smaller separate buildings, and schools that are centralized, with one or two large buildings.

Hundreds of students in three high schools that varied in centralization were interviewed.[11] Students in the decentralized campus needed more time to move from class to class. Apparently, time spent in transit restricts between-class student/teacher conversation: Students and teachers interacted 20 percent less in decentralized school classrooms. This suggests that learning itself is adversely affected in decentralized schools, although the researchers do not report evidence on this question.

The exterior of the school building, its facade, probably creates an impression on students and visitors. Consider the difference between an ivy-covered classical facade, a plain rectangular stucco facade, and a concrete tower, for example. A German researcher elicited reactions from students to a starkly simple modern facade and another that formed a colorful composite of styles, and found that students preferred the latter.[12] The researcher hypothesized that students care about facades and will be less likely to vandalize them.

Condition and Age

Does the physical condition of a school affect learning? The question is not easy to answer because the quality of a school's physical plant usually is tied to other relevant factors such as neighborhood quality and the socioeconomic status of its students. Nevertheless, it is reasonable to hypothesize that a dilapidated learning setting will harm the attitudes of both students and teachers, which will result in less learning.

Certainly, many schools are in poor condition. In 1989, officials estimated that it would take $30 billion to fix U.S. schools.[13] Even one of New York's best public high schools, the Bronx High School of Science, was operating with over 150 broken windows. A study of Canadian schools found that about $1 billion was needed to fix around 2,300 schools, but school boards would save about one-third of that amount each year if the schools

were fixed, so the repairs would pay for themselves in about three years.[14]

With the close of the Cold War, it has become more feasible—economically and politically—to use government funds to repair and improve schools. Is there any empirical evidence that doing so would have any effect on students and teachers? A British study investigated this question by interviewing teachers in both older and newer schools.[15] As might be expected, teachers in newer schools were generally more satisfied. However, teachers in older schools were not always dissatisfied with their buildings. Teacher satisfaction was a function of the number of changes and improvements to the physical plant. Alterations and improvements to an older building are associated with greater teacher satisfaction. This study investigated teacher satisfaction rather than student learning, but if satisfied teachers are better teachers, the results suggest that learning suffers in older buildings if they are not renovated or improved as they age.

◆ **IN SUM,** *physical features of the learning setting, as a whole, affect pupil performance. Many learning experiences are affected by school size, which is often linked to nonoptimal staffing of behavior settings. Students in large schools have an edge in the variety of things about which they can learn. Yet, partly because time at school is limited, students in large schools do not actually participate in more activities than students in small schools. Students in large schools more often learn and enjoy as spectators; students in small schools more often learn and enjoy as participants. In most areas of learning, students in small schools achieve more because they develop competence through direct involvement in activities. However, when activities in large schools are understaffed and activities in small schools are overstaffed, these outcomes may be reversed. Decentralizing school buildings may decrease student/teacher interaction. If satisfied teachers are better teachers, then construction or renovations should be undertaken when necessary.*

◆ INTERIOR ARCHITECTURE ◆ AND DESIGN

How do walls, ceilings, windows, and other elements of the school interior affect learning? You might think this was all worked out years ago by architects, but continuing changes in school design demonstrate that the elusive goal of an ideal classroom has yet to be achieved.

Walls

One interesting study examined the effect of walls and ceilings on distractions to teachers and students.[16] In 13 grade-school classrooms, the height of ceilings, the percent of permanent (versus nonpermanent) walls, and the percent of the classroom perimeter that was open (versus having walls) was measured. For teachers, classrooms with more nonpermanent walls and more open perimeters had more distractions from in-class noise and from visitors. Teachers were more satisfied with classrooms that had higher ceilings (see Figure 11–4).

For the students, distraction was related to nonpermanent walls: The more such walls, the less satisfied they were with reading in class. They were also less satisfied with the classroom, as a whole, when it had more open perimeter space. In general, this study supports the value of permanent walls to enclose the whole room and higher ceilings.

Walls are often taken for granted or used without much thought. Assignments, posters, and completed work are put up more on the basis of where there is an empty space than any better criterion. One educator be-

lieves that carefully designed classroom walls can have a strong impact on learning.[17] He argues that walls should do one of three jobs and that each kind of wall should be in a certain location within the classroom.

An **acquisition wall** should include the chalkboard and a bulletin board and be in the front of the room. Only material related to new concepts and concepts that students are struggling with should be placed on this wall; anything else interferes with the acquisition or learning function of this wall. The **maintenance walls** should be along the sides of the room where they may be seen but are less focal than the acquisition wall. As the name implies, maintenance walls should include material that helps students review and more fully understand material they already know fairly well. These walls serve to reassure students. Other material, such as students' work, notices about school activities, and so on, should not be on these walls to interfere with the maintenance function. Finally, the **dynamic wall** should be at the back of the room. It is so named because it should be changed often. It contains student work, school notices, holiday decorations, and other material important for organizational or social reasons.

The overall rationale of this system is to focus attention on learning materials. A small study that compared a typical classroom with one that used the

FIGURE 11–4 Classroom walls naturally affect what students see and learn; they should be carefully arranged.

system seemed to show increased learning in the three-wall system.

Equipment

Equipment and objects in the classroom are also of obvious importance. Few or old educational materials seem likely to create competition for resources and even aggression in younger students and apathetic or poor attitudes in older students. A study of day-care children showed that activities (such as type of play) are clearly affected by which kinds of equipment are available.[18] This is an obvious but sometimes overlooked facet of the classroom: What happens in the way of learning-related behavior is partly a function of what is available to students.

My Kind of Attractiveness

Having a classroom that is attractive, comfortable, and has interesting equipment is important. A study of over 1,500 high school science students found that those who perceived their classroom physical environment as better had better attitudes toward science and better science grades.[19]

Other researchers have directly asked young students what they would prefer in a classroom. In one study, kindergarten and first-grade pupils were shown simplified pictures of indoor and outdoor school settings.[20] The scenes systematically varied size, shape, color, complexity, texture, and lighting. The preferences of girls and boys were different: Girls preferred settings with more windows, color, texture, shapes, and lighting; boys preferred larger settings than girls.

Given that most boys and girls learn in the same schools, these results pose a challenge to school designers: how to design a single school that satisfies both sexes. This may not be a mere matter of taste: Some researchers present evidence that children actually learn better when various aspects of the learning environment match their preferences.[21]

Learning in Familiar Contexts

Over 50 years ago, a psychologist postulated that learning occurs "in a complex context of environing conditions not specific to it."[22] That is, learning is partially dependent on the background context in which it occurs. If this is true, this **familiar-context effect** means that our recall for material learned in a particular place is better in that same place than in a different place.

Indeed, several studies support the existence of the effect. For example, college students perform better on exams when they are tested in the room where they learned the material than when they are tested in an unfamiliar room.[23] In a dramatic field example, when divers are given a list of words to memorize either on dry land or underwater and then asked to recall them either on dry land or underwater, they recall more words in the same setting in which they learned them, whether that is underwater or on dry land.[24]

Apparently, placing the learner in the physical setting where the learning originally occurred produces optimal performance. Performance in a different room is more dramatically harmed when the learning room and the test room are quite different, as opposed to quite similar.[25] However, not every study supports this principle.[26] For example, distance estimation, a skill we all learn to some extent (although rarely in a formal learning setting), seems to be more accurate in novel environments than in familiar ones.[27]

Such nonconfirmations have stimulated researchers to distinguish the conditions in which the familiar-context effect works from those in which it does not. For example, distance estimation is a different cognitive activity than recalling memorized material. The effect seems to work for short-term but not long-term memory.[28] Other research suggests that it works better for recall memory than recognition memory.[29,30]

How does the familiar-context effect work, when it does work? One explanation is that people are distracted by the novel stimuli of the new context. New sights and sounds might distract from one's performance, whereas a familiar room is not so distracting. A second explanation is that the learned material is associated with the environmental context through a process like classical conditioning, even though that context had no direct role in the teaching/learning process.[31]

An interesting study supports this idea.[32] Subjects were asked to recall memorized words in a novel setting and in a familiar setting. When the subjects in the novel setting had their associations to the original learning setting strengthened (the experimenter asked them to vividly recall it or showed them slides of it), their performance was about as good as that of subjects who learned and recalled words in the same setting. Thus, the familiar-context effect works even when the learner actively remembers the room in which the material was learned, without even being in the room.

Of course, we learn only partly in the classroom; much reading and studying is done at home or elsewhere. This may be another reason for the inconsistency of the effect in field studies, especially those done with students past elementary school age, as opposed to lab studies.

◆ **IN SUM,** *interior school architecture has a variety of influences on students. Temporary or low walls increase distractibility. Acquisition, maintenance, and dynamic walls can be strategically used to match students' normal viewing patterns with current versus background educational information. Having a school one finds attractive is associated with better grades, but boys and girls may not find the same decor attractive. When we learn in a given setting, that material is better recalled in the same setting or in a vivid memory of that setting.*

◆ NOISE ◆

Does noise hinder learning? Common sense certainly suggests that it does. Teachers spend much time combating noise in the classroom, which suggests that they believe noise affects learning.

Squelching Noise

Behavioral psychologists have investigated methods of controlling noise, such as installing voice-activated relays. For example, in a home economics class, the teacher allowed students to listen to their favorite radio station as long as the sound level stayed below a certain level. When the sound exceeded this level, the relay automatically turned off the radio.[33] In another class, if a certain noise level was not exceeded for 10 minutes, students were given 2 extra minutes of gym and a 2-minute break from study period.[34] In an elementary school version of this anti-noise strategy, quiet periods in the classroom automatically lit up one light after another on

a smiling clown figure, but loud noise extinguished the lights.[35]

These efforts to quench noise are based on the premise that noise harms classroom performance. Yet, the scientific evidence on the question is not conclusive. Under some conditions, noise does not affect performance, and under certain conditions, it may even enhance it.[36]

Performance

The relation between noise and learning is complex because it depends on several factors:

- The properties of the noise itself (loudness, pitch, continuity, meaningfulness)
- The characteristics of the learner (sex, motivation, personality, intelligence, feelings of control)
- The nature of the task (reading, memorizing, problem solving, listening, motor)
- The situation (lab versus field setting, time of day, whether the noise is expected or unexpected)
- Learning versus performance (whether noise had its effect during the learning of the material or during the performance of material that had been learned)
- Individual differences (sex, personality)

With these complexities in mind, let's examine the available evidence concerning noise in educational settings.

Trains passed one side of a New York school frequently; classrooms on that side of the building were very noisy. The other side of the building was relatively quiet. The reading ability of children on both sides was measured, and the reading scores of children on the noisy side of the school were significantly lower.[37] The local government was persuaded to install rubber sound-reducing materials on the train tracks. The children's reading scores were measured again one year later and the differences in scores had disappeared.

In another study, the psychomotor performance of preschoolers whose day care was near or far from train noise was assessed; that of the children in the nearer preschool was worse.[38] Other schools are plagued by the noise of aircraft takeoffs and landings. The mathematics and reading achievement of third-graders in an area of

Los Angeles that experiences an overflight every 2½ minutes of the school day was measured.[39] Their scores were compared with those of students who worked in classrooms that had sound insulation (16 decibels quieter) and with those of children who went to schools out of the air corridor (22 decibels quieter). The reading scores of children in sound-insulated classrooms were significantly higher than those in noisy classrooms.

Oddly, the scores of children in the sound-insulated classrooms were even higher than those of children in the schools away from the air corridor. The schools away from the air corridor may have been different in some other way (such as poorer quality teaching), or perhaps the children in the sound-insulated classrooms were so glad to come into a relatively quiet classroom from the thunderous outdoors that they were happy to work on their schoolwork!

Under some conditions, performance is better when the noise is louder. In Nigeria, for example, university students were better able to recall words in 100-decibel noise than in 60-decibel noise.[40] The researcher notes that this may be due, in part, to the Nigerian cultural context, but better performance in higher noise also occurs for other groups, as we will see.

Interference During Learning or During Recall? Researchers try to identify specific conditions in which they hypothesize that noise will affect performance. For example, is it a hindrance during the actual learning of new material, or later, during recall (as on a test), or both? One relatively well-controlled study confirms the conclusion that noise during learning reduces later performance more than does noise at the time of recalling the learned material.[41] Students often, of course, are exposed to noise during both learning *and* performance of what they have learned.

Personal Influences. The effects of noise clearly vary with characteristics of the learner. One such individual difference is sex. For example, a study of adults doing arithmetic showed that noise slowed down women but not men.[42] Others hypothesized that boys and girls perform differently in noisy conditions.[43] First- to fifth-grade children worked at visual puzzles in somewhat noisy (70 decibels) or fairly quiet (40 decibels) classrooms. In the noisy conditions, boys solved more puzzles than girls, but in the quiet conditions, girls solved more puzzles than boys. It is important to note that if the performances of boys and girls in this study are lumped together (as they are in most noise studies), the data show no difference between noisy and quiet conditions.

A subsequent study of college students confirmed these results.[44] This is an important finding because statistical interactions (the pattern of results indicating that girls perform better in quiet and boys perform noise) often are not replicated in follow-up studies (see Figure 11–5).

Another example of the importance of individual differences is provided by a review of the evidence on noise and learning among exceptional children. It concludes that moderate noise actually helps hyperactive children learn, but not autistic children.[45] Apparently, rock music encourages hyperactive children to be less disruptive and less verbally aggressive, but autistic children often respond to noise by becoming even more passive and repetitive than usual in their actions.

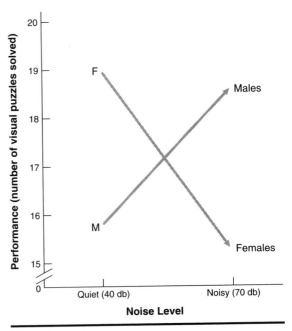

FIGURE 11–5 Performance of a moderately difficult task varies with noise and sex. Females, as a group, perform better when it is quiet; males, as a group, perform better when it is noisy.

Personality plays a role, too. One study of reading comprehension found that subjects with an internal locus of control performed better in noisy conditions and those with an external locus of control performed better in quiet conditions.[46] When the reading scores of 12-year-olds were compared in noisy and quiet conditions, those with higher intelligence test scores performed better in low noise, whereas those with lower test scores did better in higher noise.[47]

Introversion/extraversion also affects the noise-performance relationship. When introverts were asked to carefully watch certain stimuli, their performance improved over time when the noise level was lower, and worsened over time when noise was louder. This was reversed for extraverts. Their performance worsened over time in low noise but improved in louder noise.[48]

Finally, originality appears to affect performance, at least creative output. When university students were exposed to 60, 80, and 100 decibels and given creativity tasks, highly original (but not other) students were more creative at lower and higher noise levels than at the moderate noise levels.[49]

To integrate some of these results, imagine a class project in which pupils are asked to read through a story looking for details; imagine also that the room happens to be quite noisy. More intelligent boys with an external locus of control should do better than less intelligent girls with an internal locus of control. Furthermore, if the former also are extraverts, they may do better as time goes on, but if the latter happen to be introverts, they may perform worse as time goes on. Of course, this scenario has not been confirmed as a whole in an experiment, but it is what we could expect to happen based on the separate studies just described.

Individual differences also matter in terms of congruence (person-environment matching), which shows up in studies as statistical interactions. For example, a study of children in day care found that pupils who were used to noisy conditions performed better in noisy conditions and those who were used to quiet conditions performed better in quiet.[50] Similarly, sixth-graders who prefer a relatively noisy classroom perform better in a noisy room; those who prefer a quiet room perform better in a quiet room.[51]

The Task. The role of the material to be learned has not yet been emphasized yet. One review of the literature concludes that for difficult tasks, individual differences fade. For example, both ordinary and exceptional children perform difficult tasks less well in noisy conditions than in quiet conditions.[52] Notice that when studies are described, I usually point out that it involved memory, or vigilance, or psychomotor performance. This is because noise may affect one behavior in a given set of circumstances but not another. If someone asks you whether noise affects learning, you should ask in reply, "The learning of *what?*"

The Situation. A number of studies report that conditions besides the noise, the learner, and the task affect learning. For example, a study that examined how well visually presented words are remembered found that the result depended on whether the test occurred in the morning or the afternoon and whether the learners expected a recall or recognition test of memory![53] Instructions also matter. When college students were given instructions about solving a spatial puzzle on Rubik's cubes, verbal instructions produced better performance when it was noisy, and visual instructions produced better performance when it was quiet.[54]

Type of Noise. Noise, apart from being loud, can be continuous or intermittent, even pitched or variable, harsh or melodious, meaningful (as in speech or song) or not (as in mechanical noise). Type of noise affects learning. For example, college students were asked to recall numbers that had been shown to them.[55] They could recall the numbers better when noise in the background was not meaningful than when it was meaningful (speech).

Earplugs. Sometimes, for example during construction or where road traffic is close and loud, noise is unavoidable. What might be done? One investigator suggested people could put small foam noise reducers in their ears.[56] His study done in 13 high schools found that these inexpensive little foamies reduced the loss in performance due to noise on cognitive and motor tasks.

The Aftereffects of Noise. A few investigators have tried to determine whether noise affects learning *after* the noise has ceased. The Los Angeles air corridor study, for example, discovered learning decrements even when students are away from the noise they normally experience. The evidence is mixed, but the majority of studies support the conclusion that the effects of noise outlast the noise itself.[57]

In the best-known examination of this issue, third- to fifth-graders who lived in apartments built over a busy road were tested on their reading abilities.[58] All children were tested in quiet conditions, but those who lived in noisier apartments scored lower than those who lived in quieter apartments. In another study, children from homes their parents described as noisy performed more poorly in quiet conditions than children from homes described as quiet.[59]

How can noise harm a learner's performance after it is no longer present? There are at least four possible reasons.[60]

1. Noise during the learning process may interfere with moment-to-moment communication between student and teacher. The student may miss key instructions, or the teacher may be forced to repeat instructions often so that less material can be covered in a class period. A cumulative deficiency may then develop over the course of the school year that affects learning, even in quiet situations.

2. Noise may interfere with the development of a child's strategies for processing information. Learning is subsequently impaired, even in quiet surroundings, because the child uses inadequate strategies for thinking about the material to be learned.

3. When noise is beyond the control of a student—as it often is—his or her sense of personal control may be damaged. When the student attempts to master a new concept later, even in quiet, that sense of personal control, so important to learning, may not be there.

4. Continued loud noise raises the learner's blood pressure semi-permanently. This chronic increase in physiological arousal may interfere with learning, even in quiet periods. We have focused in this section on the effects of performance on noise, but this is evidence that noise affects the health of children as well as their learning performance.

Feelings

By definition, noise is unwanted sound. In classrooms, then, noise is nearly always unwelcome. Perhaps the single most common statement in public schools is "Quiet down, now, class." Nevertheless, the bothersomeness of noise varies with certain circumstances. For example, students in general (in both elementary and high school, and in both traditional and open-plan schools) report they are more distracted by social conversations than by schoolwork-related conversations.[61] Even when objective sound levels are the same, noise was reported to be more distracting in nonlaboratory settings than in laboratory settings and noise is considered more bothersome when classroom density is higher.

Teachers are as concerned about *potential* noise as they are about existing noise. Some teachers, especially in open-plan schools, modify their instructional methods to avoid creating noise. However, some effective methods of teaching naturally produce relatively high sound levels. Thus, teachers' fear of noise may lead them to avoid good teaching methods.[62]

◆ *IN SUM, evidence strongly suggests that noise interferes with learning both while it occurs and, if the learner is subjected to noise for long periods, even after the noise is gone. Noisy classrooms may impair the performance of girls more than boys, that of autistic children more than hyperactive children, and that of most children when the task is difficult. Noise may hinder performance by interfering with information processing, lowering the student's perception of control, and increasing blood pressure. Noise is more bothersome in nonlaboratory settings, high-density settings, and when it concerns social rather than schoolwork topics. To combat noise, instructors have changed their methods—sometimes sacrificing a good method for a quiet one—and successfully employed behavior-modification techniques such as sound-activated electrical relays that control reinforcers such as radio music and extra recess time.*

◆ **LIGHT AND COLOR** ◆

The human eye is remarkably able to adapt to various levels of light intensity. After a few minutes to adjust, students can read just as fast at 3 footcandles (very dim light) as they can at 53 footcandles (standard classroom lighting).[63] This is fortunate, because in surveying public classrooms, the light intensity at desktops varied from 8 footcandles to 1,000 footcandles (the latter is found when direct sunlight streams through a window onto a desk).[64] What is known about lighting and performance in educational settings?

Performance

Type of Light. Some research focuses on the relative effects of typical fluorescent lamps in comparison with full-spectrum daylight lamps. In one study, 98 first-graders in four classrooms were filmed during regular school activities.[65] All classrooms were windowless, to control for effects of sunlight. Two classrooms contained cool white fluorescent lamps and two contained daylight fluorescent lamps. The children in the daylight condition paid more attention to the teacher and were less fidgety. On reading and other tests, one daylight class scored better than both cool white classes, but the other daylight class scored worse than both cool white classes. It would seem that, on the whole, some learning and learning-related behaviors were affected by the difference in type of light; however, the study's methodology has been criticized.[66] It is worthwhile listing the criticisms because they apply to many studies, not only of lighting but of other environmental variables.

1. The children apparently were not randomly assigned to classrooms. Thus, the differences in behavior may have preceded the lighting experiment and had nothing to do with light.

2. The total amount of light was apparently not carefully controlled; the classrooms may have had not only different bulbs but also different intensities of light.

3. Teachers may have influenced the results through their teaching methods (they do not seem to have been randomly assigned either) or through their knowledge and expectations of the two kinds of lighting.

4. The experimenters did not explain exactly how they observed and scored the children's behavior. This makes it impossible for subsequent researchers to replicate the study.

5. The observers may have been aware of which lighting condition they were observing (we do not know because the researchers did not inform us). If they were, their own expectations about the outcome of the study may have influenced the results.

6. The experimenters report no estimate of the observers' reliability. We cannot be sure the behaviors were measured consistently between observers or consistently over time for the same observer.

7. It is not clear whether the observations were done at the same time in the four classrooms. If they were not, differences could be due to natural fluctuations in classroom activity, such as increased restlessness just before lunch and recess breaks.

These criticisms are not meant to disparage this study in particular; they are meant primarily as a partial list of concerns that every experimenter should have. The effects of lighting (and certain other environmental variables) are delicate and elusive; they require especially careful experimental procedures. An analogy to chemistry or physics might be drawn. If a chemist is searching for a rare but important compound, the failure to use perfectly clean equipment may contaminate a solution and lead to the false conclusion that the compound does not exist. A physicist searching for a new subatomic particle must use great care with the photographic records of nuclear collisions; careless observation or poor-quality film development could cause a particle that actually exists to be overlooked.

There are lighting studies that have carefully controlled most sources of error. In one of these, college women performed learning-related tasks under cool white and daylight lamps.[67] The experimenters even controlled for veiling reflection, a source of error not on the preceding list. **Veiling reflection** results when a light source bounces off a work surface into an individual's eyes. It becomes a factor in the outcome of lighting studies when the various lamps to be compared are installed in different kinds of fixtures—some that throw light directly onto a work surface and some that do not. If veiling reflection is not controlled for, a difference in results might be attributed to the difference between lighting types when the real cause is a difference in fixture design. The conclusion of this well-controlled study is this: Basic information processing related to decision making was better under daylight (full-spectrum) fluorescent lamps than under common cool white fluorescent lamps.

Another well-controlled study found that some effects of lighting require weeks of exposure before they appear.[68] Several tests and observations of elementary school children's behavior were made over 20 weeks under cool white and daylight (full-spectrum) bulbs. After 2 weeks, no significant differences were found. However, after 7 to 8 weeks, children exposed to daylight bulbs experienced a significant *decrease* in the strength of their grip and in the number of gross motor movements, and an *increase* in hand steadiness (see Figure 11–6). These findings are consistent with the hypothesis that cool

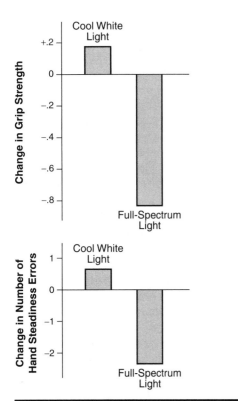

FIGURE 11–6 Lighting and elementary pupil performance are related. In a carefully designed study, children who worked for several weeks at school in full-spectrum lighting made fewer errors on a hand steadiness task than those who worked under fluorescent lighting. However, fluorescent lighting produced greater grip strength than the full-spectrum lighting did.

white bulbs are more physiologically arousing than daylight bulbs.

Amount of Light. As noted earlier, the human eye is very flexible in its light requirements. Although certain tasks require more light because the object is difficult to see, most classroom tasks are not in that category. In general, the amount of light in a learning setting may not be crucial.

However, different students may learn better under different levels of light. One such individual difference, the dark-interval threshold (DIT), has been shown to affect children's reading performance.[69] **DIT** is the shortest dark interval between the presentation of two bright images that a person can detect. Students with short DITs read more accurately in bright light than in dim light, but students with long DITs read more accurately in dim than bright light.

The amount of light students prefer also may affect their performance. Those who prefer bright light perform better in bright light and those who prefer dim light perform better in dim light.[70]

Hue (Color). Contemporary aesthetic standards seem to favor bright hues for learning settings. Whether this preference merely reflects today's fashions or actually helps children learn is not clear. One study reported in the popular press claimed that IQ scores measured in bright rooms (blue, orange, yellow) were 26 points higher than those in drab rooms (white, brown, black).[71] A 53 percent increase in friendly behaviors in orange rooms was also reported. Many of the problems with experimental control listed earlier were also present in this study, so these dramatic results must be classified as suggestive rather than conclusive.

A study that carefully controlled the properties of color in a specially constructed learning setting found that, contrary to conventional wisdom, red was no more arousing than blue or yellow. Performance of math, reading, and motor tasks did not significantly vary in red, blue, and yellow rooms.[72] Similar results have been found in other studies.[73]

Feelings and Beliefs

Lighting and color are important to many people. The popular press frequently carries stories connecting certain kinds of light with psychological and physiological disturbances. The focus of most research has been fluorescent lighting. Because it is undeniably more energy efficient and economical than traditional incandescent lighting, fluorescent lighting gradually has become standard in schools and most other public building interiors. Yet, few people find it aesthetically pleasing; many consider it a necessary evil rather than welcome progress.[74] A large percentage of people believe that fluorescent lighting is harmful to health.[75]

Several improved kinds of fluorescent lamps have been developed in response to this aesthetic criticism. One of the most popular alternatives is the daylight lamp, which radiates a spectrum of light closer to that of sunlight than does the older cool white lamp. A lamp that perfectly mimics sunlight is nearly impossible to invent, because the intensity and spectrum of sunlight itself changes through the day and across the seasons; also, fluorescent bulbs cannot avoid having spikes in certain wavelength bands that sunlight does not have.[76] Given that a truly natural indoor light does not exist, does fluorescent lighting affect health or stress?

Health and Stress. Light can affect health when people receive far too little natural light, but very few of us are that shielded from sunlight. It is important to determine whether any health problem is due to lighting type itself or perhaps to some other factor. Teachers in a school where sodium vapor lamps (the kind you see on highways, with a strong orange color) had been installed complained of eyestrain, nausea, and headaches.[77] Lighting experts who examined the installation reported that the lighting had been improperly installed; it was producing far too much glare.[78] According to them, the problem was glare rather than the type of light. Unfortunately, the experts were from a large lighting manufacturer. They did not perform a properly controlled study; their conclusions may well have been influenced by their unwillingness to believe that the lamps themselves could be harmful.

Two relatively well-controlled studies show that cool white fluorescent lamps increase the hyperactive behavior of children who are already prone to autism and other emotional disturbances.[79,80] In the first of these studies, most autistic children engaged in more repetitive behaviors under fluorescent lamps than under

incandescent lamps. The increases ranged from zero to a doubling of repetitive behavior, suggesting again that the effects of lighting vary across individuals.[81]

Some strange outcomes of exposure to fluorescent lighting have been reported. First-graders who spent 5 months under daylight fluorescent lamps have been reported to have fewer cavities than others who spent 5 months under cool white bulbs![82] This surprising result has not been substantiated and it is difficult to imagine the mechanism by which cool white lamps would cause cavities.

More plausible outcomes have also been reported. Several Russian studies indicate that a variety of health benefits result when ultraviolet light is added to fluorescent light.[83] Because sunlight contains ultraviolet light and fluorescent lighting normally does not, the addition of ultraviolet light makes the spectrum of indoor light more natural. One of these studies found that children in the supplemented light increased their height and weight more rapidly than children in the plain fluorescent light. Again, however, some controls may have been absent in these investigations.

A Swedish study with better controls found that students in windowless classrooms with full-spectrum lamps experienced two-month delays in the annual spring production of morning cortisol, a stress hormone that is associated with sociability and the ability to concentrate.[84] The authors believe their findings are sufficiently important to recommend that no child be placed in a classroom without windows or full-spectrum lighting.

Fluorescent lighting has demonstrated no dramatic, negative health effects. However, complaints sometimes are heard about fluorescent and sodium vapor lighting systems. Do these complaints merely reflect a nostalgic preference for the old familiar forms of light or are they really a menace to our well-being?

As is true for every aspect of the physical environment, the preferences of individuals who work or live in a building should be respected. In principle, it should not be necessary to demonstrate that something in the environment fries our brains or causes insanity before it is replaced. On the other hand, if one option costs significantly more than another, the space manager (the school board, in this case) may be forced to consider whether the cheaper alternative (fluorescent lighting) actually harms students and teachers or merely displeases them.

What about color? Many believe that greens and blues are calming and that reds and oranges are arousing. The evidence is not clear, partly because many studies that seem to support this were done by asking people to report how they would feel after looking at small colored cards such as those found in paint stores. One study in actual rooms found that blue was more calming than red or yellow.[85] However, another very careful study in real rooms found no differences in arousal, measured physiologically, among red, yellow, and blue rooms.[86] Maybe we merely *think* color affects us, perhaps because of our associations of colors with hot and cold objects in nature (cold blue waters and reddish-orange fires).

◆ *IN SUM, incandescent lighting is preferred by many, but it is more expensive than fluorescent lighting. Fluorescent lighting has not been shown to have dramatic negative effects on the performance or health of most students, although some odd claims have been made. Despite inadequate methodology in some studies, and the lack of significant differences in others, light does affect some kinds of performance, such as basic cognitive and motor activities. Short exposures to the different kinds of light in many studies may have led to incorrect conclusions that light has no effects. As with noise, the important effects may be on specific subgroups of individuals; when studies of whole classes or schools are done, large effects on a few learners may be obscured by an absence of effects on most learners.*

◆ CLIMATE ◆

Performance

Indoor climate—temperature, humidity, and air circulation—certainly affects learning. Climate is not an issue, however, in many schools where temperature and humidity are well controlled. Where climate does vary noticeably, learning is affected in complex and unexpected ways.

As an example, suppose that the most comfortable climate would produce the best performance. Several studies, however, refute this commonsense notion. For example, arithmetic and intelligence test scores were examined in British classrooms.[87] The best performance was found when the temperature was slightly *below* the optimal comfort level. Performance was also better when humidity was low and air circulated moderately. This study was correlational and not well controlled, so the findings must be considered tentative. Nevertheless, similar findings are reported in work settings (see Chapter 12).

A few studies report relatively simple relations between climate and performance. In the gymnasium, rising temperatures are correlated with poorer fitness and performance.[88] In a Swedish study, performance of language tasks by elementary school children was worse in warm than in moderate temperatures.[89]

The relation between climate and performance was investigated in suburban Portland, Oregon, schools.[90] Air-conditioned and non-air-conditioned schools, matched geographically and in the socioeconomic status of the students, were selected. Comparisons of performance in subjects ranging from spelling to languages to mathematics were made. In the schools with no climate control, the temperatures were higher and fluctuated more. When the temperature rose in these schools, the performance of students declined. These effects occurred only when the outdoor temperatures were relatively warm; in the cool fall of the year, performance was not correlated with temperature.

In a different study, children read in controlled temperatures ranging from 68°F to 86°F.[91] Their reading performance declined as the temperature rose, but at the highest temperature, performance rose again slightly! We might intuitively expect that performance changes steadily in one direction or the other as temperature changes, but the relation may not be linear after all. (Recall the temperature and aggression debate in Chapter 10.)

Feelings

Both teachers and learners want the atmosphere to be pleasant, of course, but there is no single set of conditions that is pleasant for everyone. Engineers have sought the perfect set of temperature and humidity parameters within which most people feel comfortable for many years. Such standards have been published. These are **thermal comfort envelopes** (*ranges* of temperature and humidity levels rather than precise numbers) within which most individuals prefer indoor climates.

Type of activity affects climate preferences. Clearly, students who are physically active (e.g., in the gym) will have different preferences than students who are reading at a desk. Another factor is the length of time spent in the classroom. Students, more than teachers, change classes or go outside for recesses. Teachers and students may develop preferences for different climates because they have different patterns of physical activity, and students change temperature and humidity levels more often as they move in and out of the classroom.[92]

◆ ***IN SUM,*** *we may conclude that there are few simple, direct relations between climate and educational behavior; some combination of person and setting variables may "mediate, transmit, modify, or resist" the variations of climate.[93] Research is difficult because climate is composed of many possible patterns of temperature, humidity, and air movement. Perhaps the most supported conclusion is that performance is best in slightly cool but not humid classrooms.[94] Even when care is taken in the control of indoor climates, there must inevitably be a compromise that considers individual differences in amount of clothing, type of activity, and indoor/outdoor movement. There may also be preferred temperature levels based on adaptation to one's home climate or cultural background.*

◆ **SPACE** ◆

The amount of space available and how that space is arranged in learning settings has been researched considerably more than indoor climate. Each major outcome is considered as a function of spatial density and spatial arrangements.

Performance

Density. Are high-density classrooms a hazard to student achievement? One study of 24 years' worth of school records showed that higher density was associated with *higher* achievement scores,[95] although class densities in this study were never very high. A famous meta-analysis of class size (which probably is strongly related to density) that examined 725 comparisons of larger and smaller classes in 77 different studies found that achievement increased as class size decreased.[96] However, this trend was most pronounced for class sizes in the 15 to 20 range, not for larger classes. When special education students worked in low or high social density, their on-task time was greater in low density.[97] Other studies find *no* effect of density. Clearly, high density harms learning under some, but not all, conditions.

Part of the confusion may be due to teachers' perceptions of larger classes. In a rare experimental study of actual classes, 62 fourth-grade classes and teachers were randomly assigned to class sizes of 16, 23, 30, or 37 for two school years in a row.[98] Student performance across numerous measures did not vary with class size. (One exception was that mathematics achievement was better in classes of 16 compared to 30 or 37). However, 81 percent of teachers *believed* that student performance in small classes was generally better.

Mobility is one harmful factor; density may cut into performance when the task requires mobility or physical interaction among individuals.[99] In a classroom, reading performance on a given afternoon is not necessarily affected simply because there are many students in the room. However, performance in a laboratory where students must move about from a supply counter to a work space to instruments might well be damaged by high density.

Similarly, one might expect that learning in a pure lecture format would not be affected by increasing density—as long as enough air to breathe and space to write are available. But learning that relies on discussion in groups might be harmed by increases in density. This is precisely what one study found.[100]

However, in keeping with our theme that density's effects depend on several factors, a laboratory study showed achievement depended not only on density and learning format but also on motivation.[101] The students read a long story in either high or low social density, studied it in lecture, discussion, or independent-study conditions, and either were motivated by possible monetary prizes or not.

Achievement on a multiple-choice test was, in general, greater in low density. However, achievement was also affected by learning format; it was lowest when students worked independently. The study showed that achievement can be greater in high density if certain other conditions apply—in this case, lower motivation and discussion group format.

The researchers explain the greater achievement in low motivation as an example of how they believe arousal mediates the relation between density and performance. Too much arousal (e.g., high motivation plus high density plus the stimulation from group discussion) can actually reduce performance. The trick in the classroom is to consider high density as one arousal agent, to consider what other arousing or calming influences are around, and to aim for moderate arousal.

Crowding may occur when a learner feels that the available space does not allow for appropriate distance between people; when a learner perceives a shortage of resources, such as the lack of needed equipment and materials; or when a learner has an individual history that leads to a definition of a certain combination of density, task, and other individuals present as crowded.[102] Consistent with the latter idea are the results of a study showing that only those students whose performance in a high-density room was below average found the room "crowded."[103]

Sometimes, it is unclear whether behavior is affected by density or by crowding. In a study of kindergartners, attentiveness to the teacher was measured under two conditions: when the children crowded round to listen to a story versus when they sat in separate, dispersed spaces.[104] Attentiveness was clearly greater when the children were not close together. There are at least four possible reasons for this. In the dispersed condition, (1) each child was able to see and hear better, (2) each child experienced less interference from other children, (3) fewer children defined the dispersed condition as crowded, or (4) having a space of one's own clarifies activities and reduces conflict between children.

To sort out such explanations, researchers systematically vary density and other relevant variables. In one study, density and the amount of materials available to children were carefully varied.[105] When density increased and materials were in short supply, behavior inconsistent with learning increased. As density and the amount of learning materials increased, so did learning-related behavior. The most learning-related behavior occurred when density was high and amount of materials was high; the least learning-related behavior occurred when density was high and amount of materials was low (see Figure 11–7). This study clearly shows that density should not be considered in isolation. We must

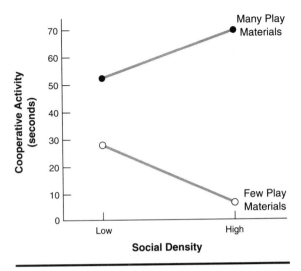

FIGURE 11–7 Cooperation among preschool children depends partly on social density and resource availability. More cooperation occurs when more play materials are available. As social density increases, children with more materials cooperate even more, but the cooperation of those with half as many play materials declines almost to zero.

also pay attention to how many resources are available to the learner.

In high-density conditions, learning complex concepts may be more difficult than learning simple concepts.[106] In one study, performance on concepts that are relatively complex for 10-year-olds (arithmetic) was examined as a function of density and territoriality.[107] Four classrooms of the same size that naturally varied in social density (32 students versus 22 students) were selected. In one high- and one low-density classroom, territoriality was encouraged; students were assured they would keep the same desks and they were given name tags to affix to their desks. In the other class, the normal policy of periodic desk switching was in force and students were discouraged from personalizing their desks.

Pre- and posttest scores on arithmetic tests over a 6-week period were administered. Students in low-density classes scored significantly better than students in high-density classes. In addition, there was a density-territoriality interaction. In high-density classes, students whose territoriality was encouraged learned more than students whose territoriality was not encouraged, but in low-density classes, students whose territoriality was encouraged learned less. Thus, low density is better for learning, but if a class is stuck with high density, encouraging students to feel that they have a secure place of their own helps.

An extensive investigation of preschoolers concluded that the chief effect of varying spatial density in the range of 25 to 75 square feet per child was to influence the amount and kind of activities they engaged in.[108] When given more space, the children engaged in more running, chasing, and vigorous uses of their play equipment. When given less space, there were more physical contacts among them and more use of equipment for climbing and sliding.

Teachers, of course, also spend much time in classrooms. How do they respond to higher density? One study compared two architecturally identical junior high schools; one experienced a 43 percent decrease in pupils, which we can assume decreased social density in many classrooms. In this school, teacher absenteeism significantly declined.[109] Other studies reported that teachers respond differently to high density than students do. In denser elementary school classrooms, teachers (but not students) said they experienced more restricted movement and crowding.[110] When we recall that in many classrooms, students sit while teachers circulate, this finding makes sense.

In classrooms with cluster seating, larger clusters make students feel more distracted and crowded than teachers, but small clusters make teachers feel more distracted and crowded than students.[111] This contrast in crowding presumably is also due to the different ways that students and teachers use classroom space.

This different perspective seems to affect crowding. When students, teachers, and administrators were asked to place figures in a model classroom to the point where one more figure would make the room crowded, students put in the fewest figures. Teachers put in more, and administrators put the most figures into the model classrooms.[112]

Spatial Arrangements. Can learning be facilitated by certain furniture arrangements or by improved decor? What are the effects of open classrooms? Do windowless classrooms harm performance? Can performance be

improved by selecting certain seat positions in the learning setting?

Little evidence is available about the effects of chair arrangements on learning itself, but the effects on learning-related behaviors, such as paying attention, participating, and using learning materials, and on grades have been studied.

Several comparisons of traditional rows versus the newer cluster-style seating have found that rows produce up to twice as much educationally oriented student activity and one-third as much disruptive activity.[113,114,115] However, one study found that cluster and single large-circle arrangements produced more on-task learning activity than rows.[116] Table arrangements may produce more interaction among students.[117]

Visual barriers, such as walls and partitions, appear to affect the social behavior of 2-year-olds. When toddlers are visually separated from adults, they behave in a more self-centered way and get into more conflicts.[118] Visual access to adults appears to encourage more friendly, cooperative play in this age group.

Will changing the overall design of the learning setting, rather than just the seating arrangement, affect learning-related activities? The soft classroom, mentioned at the beginning of the chapter, resulted in significantly better grades on Introductory Psychology tests. The researchers spent $450 on the alterations, but estimated that the alterations directly responsible for the improvements cost only about $75 to $100. The classroom was not vandalized, either, although some schools might be more vulnerable to this threat than others.

In a comparison of two third-grade classrooms that were similar in most respects, students in one class had longer attention spans, were more involved in their schoolwork, and were less noisy.[119] The comparison was not a proper experiment with random assignment and control of outside factors, but the researcher concluded that the differences in learning-related behavior were probably due to spatial arrangements:

1. In the better class, the teacher's desk was in a corner. She could not easily direct activities from there and therefore was forced to move throughout the room, which resulted in closer supervision of students. In the other class, the teacher's desk was in the middle of the room; she tended to sit there rather than move through the class to supervise students more personally.

2. Desks in the better class were arranged so that a maximum of two or three students could work together, but in the other class, up to 12 desks were placed in each cluster.

3. Different activities in the better class were separated by barriers (bookcases, etc.). In the other class, incompatible activities (such as ones that produce noise and others that require concentration) were not very well separated.

Another researcher attempted a more experimental approach to design changes (although because it does not meet all the criteria for a proper experiment, the study is more accurately called a quasi-experiment).[120] The changes were made to meet the teacher's specific goals: to increase use of certain classroom areas that students were not using much; to make each classroom area more versatile, so that a variety of activities could occur in each one; and to increase the students' use of learning materials that they could manipulate and rearrange themselves. The researcher attempted to meet these goals by rearranging furniture and by adding tables, shelves, and individual study carrels.

The children's behavior was carefully measured before the changes were made and some time was allowed to pass after the changes were made, so that behavioral changes could not be ascribed to the mere novelty of the design alterations. Then, the children's behavior was measured again; the design changes had indeed resulted in improvements in the learning-related behaviors desired by the teacher.

In a day-care center, children had difficulty staying involved in activities. Because one of the main ways that preschoolers learn is through involvement, researchers analyzed the spatial arrangements of the day care and recommended certain design changes.[121] Clear boundaries were established between different activity areas, traffic paths were rearranged so that children were not forced to cut through the playhouse to get to the blocks, and learning materials were placed in easy-to-reach, clearly organized arrangements. Again, comparing previous behavior with postdesign changes in learning-related behavior showed that chil-

dren spent more time involved in learning activities and in more constructive play.

In a major Canadian study involving over 1,000 preschoolers in 38 classrooms observed over three years, randomly arranged classrooms were compared with deliberately arranged classrooms.[122] (*Deliberately arranged* meant that five groups of educational activities were placed in specific locations within the classroom.) The rest of the program (time schedules, equipment, teacher/student communication) was similar in the random and deliberate classrooms. Children in deliberate classrooms had significantly better scores on creative productivity and creative skills, generalization of number concepts, language use, and utilization of prereading materials. Carefully planned locations for different kinds of educational activities appears to be an important, and often overlooked, factor in preschool development.[123]

Some researchers are concerned with the relation between classroom design and elementary school children's use of literature. In one study, over 130 classrooms were surveyed; few had special areas of the classroom for reading (library corners), but where library corners existed, students engaged in more literature activities.[124]

What about flooring and partitions? The effects of carpeting and thin screens that provide visual but not auditory privacy on the educational involvement of students and teachers were investigated in a nursery school.[125] Carpeting increased the amount of time the staff spent in direct, close, educational activities with the children. The screens led teachers to engage in more administrative, noneducational activities. Carpeted rooms with no visual screens produced the highest teacher/student involvement in the nursery school. Carpeting allowed more direct interaction because noise was lower, and the absence of screens discouraged teachers from going off to do paperwork because they were more visible by others.

Changes to the decor of the learning settings may even facilitate learning. Many educators today believe that classrooms should be decorated with many pictures, posters, illustrations, and other visual images. The educational effects of visual complexity (number of colorful pictures and posters on the wall) were examined.[126] Surprisingly, the 8- and 10-year-old children learned best in the plainest learning setting; the more background visual stimulation provided by the room's decor, the less children learned. We must be cautious about generalizing these results to actual classrooms, however, because the study took place in a trailer, the only persons present were the experimenter and one child at a time, and the time span of the study was short. Nevertheless, the study suggests that plentiful visual stimulation *may* interfere with learning.

Another study of decor investigated the persistence of children in rooms decorated with happy, neutral, and sad pictures.[127] Children in the happy settings persisted longest in their work. Perhaps few teachers would display sad pictures anyway, but the study underscores the idea that learning-related behavior can be affected by room decor.

Do windows in classrooms make any difference? Windowless classrooms have been built under the assumptions that costs will decline because the school offers fewer glass targets to vandals, fewer windows means lower heating and cooling costs, and windows distract students from classwork. Most studies, however, show that windowless environments have little positive or negative impact on the achievement of students.[128] This does not mean, however, that students *like* windowless classrooms, as we shall see later.

Is there a best place to sit in the traditional classroom? The center of the classroom has been called the **action zone.** A very large 1921 study of college students in which seating was more or less random (alphabetical) found that grades in the front rows was 3 to 8 percent lower than those in the middle rows, and grades then declined toward the rear, with a sharp drop in the last few rows.[129] One modern study showed a similar pattern when students could choose their own seats.[130]

Later research reported that students who sit in the action zone get higher grades[131] and participate more.[132,133] They are more attentive, spend more time in learning-related activities, and are absent less.[134,135,136] So, in that class you are having trouble with, all you have to do is move into the action zone, right?

Not necessarily. First, some studies have found no action-zone effect.[137] Second, perhaps students who sit in the action zone are those who already have considerable interest and talent in that subject. Their success may not be due to their choice of seats, but simply may reflect their penchant for that subject, age of the students, the educational format (e.g., lecture versus discussion group), and personality.

We do know, for example, that students who choose action-zone seating are zealous or even overzealous;[138] they also have higher self-esteem,[139,140] or at least have higher self-esteem about their schoolwork.[141] Women choose seats in the front more often and receive higher grades, at least in psychology.[142] Students are very aware of the implications of seating location for their social lives, their control over classmates and teachers, and their academic accomplishments.[143]

On the other hand, it could be that by choosing seats in the action zone, students are able see and hear better, become more involved in the course, begin to receive more attention from the teacher, and consequently feel better about themselves and school. In real classrooms, at least the first of these assertions is probably true. Students who like a subject and have a knack for it gravitate to the action zone, and from that vantage point, they see, hear, and are treated better than students outside the action zone. But the question remains: Can one benefit from this knowledge by moving into the action zone when one otherwise might have sat in a back corner?

Researchers have tried to answer this by randomly assigning some students to the action zone and others outside it. One researcher did this and also allowed students in an equivalent class choose their own seats.[144] Regardless of whether students were assigned seats or given their choice, those who sat in the middle got better grades than those who sat on the sides; they also liked the course more and liked the instructor more. This study found no front to rear differences, but that may be because the center rows were not separately considered as they were in the 1921 study.[145]

However, other studies have reached a variety of conclusions. One found that participation was higher in the action zone but only when students selected their own seats; grades were not higher either when students chose seats or when they did not.[146] Another simply found no relation between grades and seating position.[147] Yet another found higher grades in the action zone when students selected their seats but no differences in participation.[148]

Perhaps these conflicting results may be explained, in part, by taking the characteristics of individual students into account. One researcher examined the role of individual differences by randomly assigning students previously known to be vocal or quiet to the action zone and outside it[149] (see Figure 11–8). Vocal students who were assigned to the action zone participated much more than vocal students who were assigned to sit outside the action zone. However, students known to be quiet did not participate more after being assigned to the action zone. Once again, the environment affects some individuals more than it affects others.

One review of the action-zone literature concludes there is no good evidence of an action-zone effect on performance, but there is on attitudes and participation.[150] There are enough problems with existing studies, however, that more research is needed before we can draw a firm conclusion.

Besides furniture arrangement, wall decoration, and seat selection, one other major space factor may affect learning. This is the open-plan classroom, in which large spaces are shared by more than one class. Over the last three decades, many schools have been built "without walls," and many studies have examined their effectiveness.

The open-plan classroom has lost favor recently. One reason is the perception that student performance is affected by higher noise levels. Open preschools in Scotland sometimes reached 98 decibels and students received significantly less instruction in educationally valuable activities than did students in more traditional preschools with more separated spaces.[151] However, not every study of open space finds these decrements. Researchers who compared the reading performance of elementary students in open classrooms when the noise levels were naturally high and low found no differences in accuracy or speed either for good or poor readers.[152]

Probably the biggest single problem with open-plan classrooms is that teachers have not been adequately trained in their use. Many teachers try to apply teaching methods suited to traditional walled classrooms to open classrooms with very unsatisfactory results. When 21 open-space schools were examined, two-thirds did not have programs suitable for open space.[153] From a behavior-setting theory perspective, open space without an appropriate program is a violation of **synomorphy,** the principle that physical and social aspects of the setting should fit together well.

Teachers who use traditional methods in open-plan schools often try to create walls with whatever materials are at hand—bookcases, dividers, file cabinets, easels, and so on.[154] They are upset at noise distraction, which probably hinders their effectiveness as teachers. They may avoid useful but relatively loud activities in their own space in order to avoid bothering neighboring classes.[155] Open-plan schools, then, have decidedly negative implications for learning when the educational program is geared to the traditional, walled classroom.

Open-plan classrooms matched with open-plan teaching methods, which include team teaching and less frequent but more intimate contact with students, do produce certain learning-related behavior changes.[156] On the positive side, children seem to develop more initiative and autonomy. Because more activities occur simultaneously, children may learn to cope with distraction better than children in quieter, more focused traditional classrooms. If so, children educated in open-plan classrooms should be able to concentrate better, which

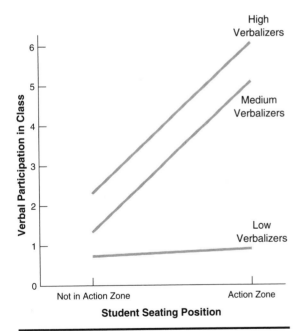

FIGURE 11–8 Participation in class depends on the students' preexisting tendencies to contribute to discussions and where the students sit in the room. High and medium verbalizers contribute more if they sit in the central "action zone," but quiet students do not.

should allow them to work more persistently. One study specifically tested this idea by giving puzzles to children from the two kinds of classroom. Those from open-plan classrooms worked more persistently on the puzzles than children from the traditional classroom.[157]

On the negative side, children in open-plan classrooms (even with appropriate programs) may spend more time in transition between activities and on off-task activities.[158] Additionally, they may spend less time than children in traditional classrooms actually engaged in educational activity.[159]

Overall, neither open-plan nor traditional classrooms produce clearly superior student achievement in general,[160] but the advocates of open-plan classrooms never really claimed they would produce higher achievement levels. Instead, open-plan schools are promoted as a more suitable arrangement by those who think of the learner as active, curious, and responsible.

When students are not motivated and responsible, open-plan classrooms may not be appropriate. Several studies report that children with socioeconomic, intellectual, or developmental problems perform worse in open-space classrooms.[161,162,163] The average student may score higher on standard achievement tests in a traditional setting[164,165] but the good student may score higher in open-plan classrooms.[166] The parents of creative children may prefer open classrooms because they have educational goals other than scoring high on achievement tests, such as developing their child's social or artistic skills.

Nevertheless, school administrators believe there are problems. As the open-plan classroom declines in favor, many schools are faced with the problem of reshaping large open spaces to fit today's teaching styles. Environmental psychologists have been involved in remodeling them. The addition and careful placement of sound-absorbent partitions can turn a poorly functioning classroom into one in which more relevant questions are asked of the teacher, traffic flows are separated from work areas, and privacy is increased.[167]

As I stress throughout the book, behavior is a product of the interaction of personal attributes, sociocultural context, and the physical environment. One study of open-space classrooms should be singled out because it paid particular attention to these interactions. Researchers used both the students' degree of

motivation and the type of classroom to predict achievement and other learning-related behavior.[168] They found that students who are self-directed but not academically inclined had more discipline problems in traditional classes than in open classrooms. The same students, however, had higher achievement scores in traditional classrooms than in open classrooms (see Figure 11–9).

The design of physical setting must not be considered separately from what ecological psychologists call the *program*.[169] In the case of the learning setting, the program is the social environment, including curriculum and teaching style. Again, a given physical setting might be very beneficial for one educational program but not for another. This means that much research that examines the value of particular physical arrange-

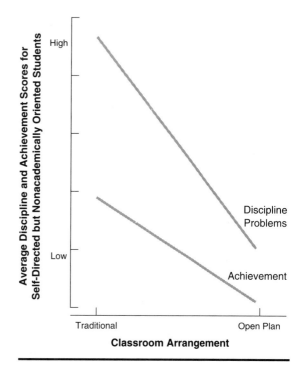

FIGURE 11–9 Classroom arrangements can produce mixed outcomes. Self-directed but nonacademically inclined students, for example, seem to have fewer discipline problems in open-plan arrangements compared to those in traditional arrangements, but they also demonstrate lower achievement in open-plan arrangements.

ments—in particular, educational programs—remains to be done, which might seem a formidable, even insurmountable, task. On the bright side, there are many similarities among educational programs that purport to be different, advanced, or new and improved. Thus, more research is needed to clarify the role of physical arrangements in different programs, but the task is not impossible.

◆ *IN SUM, the amount and arrangement of space in educational settings is very important for classroom performance and related behaviors. High density may affect learning when the activity involves physical movement around the classroom, when learning depends on some classroom resource that is not increasing as fast as the number of learners, when a particular situation seems crowded to a learner, and when the concept to be learned is complex.*

Among preschoolers, high density alters the child's choice of activities. Numerous classroom arrangement features have been linked to educational performance. Benefits appear to accrue in classrooms that have the teacher's desk in a corner, have different kinds of activities carefully arranged and separated, possess library corners, and are carpeted. Action-zone seating benefits some students. Open-space classrooms have positive outcomes when teachers use techniques suited to open-plan classrooms and students have fewer behavioral or other problems. They can be noisy but also can foster student autonomy. All these findings depend, in part, on grade level and teaching style.

Feelings

Our survey to this point has focused on classroom behavior. How do the physical features of learning settings affect the feelings of students and teachers?

Density. We have seen that increasing the number of individuals per unit of space (density) does not necessarily lead to increased discomfort (crowding). Nevertheless, high density in classrooms often does, in fact, lead to feelings of being crowded. Over 30 classes that met in the same college classroom were examined.[170] As the number of students in the class rose from 5 to 22, the number of complaints about room size and ventilation approximately doubled.

High density usually increases discomfort, but performance may not be affected if the task does not last very long. If all your classes are overenrolled, however, crowding discomfort may well lead to performance decrements. Elementary school pupils often must sit in the same class all day, yet the effect of high density in elementary school settings has received almost no study.[171]

Spatial Arrangements. Many students' feelings about the layout of schools may be represented by an individual in an interview:

> I'd like comfortable chairs . . . ones that have cushions so your back doesn't hurt and your bottom either. I'd like us sitting around . . . looking at each other, not in a line. . . . I'd like a sink, where you could get water to drink, and you wouldn't have to ask the teacher to go down the hall. . . . We could have our books in a bookcase, and we wouldn't have to sit in the same place all the time. . . . Most of all [a skylight, so I could] just look up and see the sky and the clouds and the sun . . . and you'd like it better, being in school.[172]

Years later, students are asking for some of the same design elements, but for some new ones too. British Columbia students were asked to write essays on "My School."[173] Besides skylights, they suggested that classrooms should have lofts, playhouses, refrigerators, and computers that allow them to access resources outside the school, such as libraries and museums. Classrooms should have emergency supplies, such as blankets in the case of earthquakes. They suggested that windows are not enough. There are too many awful or sterile views out too many windows. Playgrounds should include gardens, some suggested.

Many educators have wondered why architects and builders persist in making classrooms hard and linear when many students would prefer softer, rounded ones. Several possible reasons may be advanced:

- The burden of advocating and executing changes usually falls on an overworked teacher, who often ends up accepting the traditional classroom rather than pursuing change in addition to normal duties.
- Custodians often complain that such changes upset their work routines.

- Administrators resist offering financial support.
- Some educators, parents, and even students believe the hard, linear classroom is best for learning.

Whether or not any of these beliefs are valid, they usually triumph. Most classrooms remain relatively hard and linear. Some researchers have explored the roots of these preferences for the traditional classroom. Some teachers' support because it appears to be related, in part, to their need for control. In one study, teachers were asked to choose among a variety of classroom layouts. Those with a high need for control selected traditional formations in which the teacher was in a clear position of control, but those with a low need for control preferred formations where the teacher was not so obviously in a controlling position.[174]

Satisfaction with the classroom is also, in part, a function of its physical characteristics. When a room has fewer solid walls, teachers believe there are more visual and aural distractions.[175] When a room has lower ceilings, they reported more visual and movement distractions. Another study reminds us that satisfaction is a function of the congruence between program and setting. Teachers who use open-plan teaching methods and operate in open-plan environments are more satisfied than teachers in traditional classrooms.[176]

Students also differ in their spatial preferences. For example, deviant adolescents prefer larger interpersonal distances than nondeviant adolescents, and students prefer larger interpersonal distances in the morning than in the afternoon.[177]

Open-plan classrooms seem to cause greater anxiety about schoolwork among students than traditional classrooms do.[178] On the other hand, the same study found that traditional classrooms appear to produce more organizational problems for the student, such as not knowing what to do, being unsure of the rules, or getting into trouble.

Once again, these results suggest that no single classroom design is likely to be best for everyone. Is it possible, then, to build a school that makes most of its users happy? Probably not. But one solution is to create **pluralistic schools**—designs that accommodate differences in preference by providing several kinds of space within a single school.[179] When schools are built or remodeled, uniform designs might be avoided in favor of a variety of classroom plans that satisfy the needs of different users.

Consider the varying personal space needs of students. Class size and density in a pluralistic school might be arranged so that problem students are given a little more elbow room and so that students engage in more individual work in the morning and more interactive work, such as discussions and labs, in the afternoon.

Another feeling that many students express is a desire for more time alone, away from the harried life in the classroom. Open-plan classrooms, in particular, can be noisy and overstimulating.[180,181] Most people need to get away from it all at least briefly during the day, but public school children are given few opportunities to be alone. Of course, schools have the responsibility to preserve the health and welfare of their students, but must that imply constant surveillance? A few experimenters have offered students getaway spaces within classrooms; these efforts to meet privacy desires will be discussed later.

Windows have little impact on actual performance, but studies of student feelings about windows have reached mixed conclusions. An early investigation found generally positive feelings about windowless classrooms,[182] but later surveys report ambivalence or dislike of windowless classrooms.[183] Perhaps the reason for the mixed results is time: One study reported a preference for windowless classrooms at one new school turned into dislike after one year.[184]

The belief that students in windowless classrooms are deprived of something important received support in a study that asked children in both kinds of classrooms to draw pictures of schools.[185] Students in the windowless school included significantly more windows in their drawings than did students in schools with windows. A tentative conclusion may be: When students are deprived of windows, they are forced to compensate by creating mental images of a school that includes what their real school lacks.

We have not yet considered the feelings or perceptions of those who are neither students nor teachers: third-party observers such as principals, office staff, and visiting parents. Little is known about these observers' impressions of classrooms, but in one of the first studies, outsiders were shown slides of vacant classrooms that were either open plan or traditional, and were either neat or messy.[186] The observers judged that teachers in neat classrooms were significantly more organized, responsive, and creative than teachers in messy classrooms. The observers also felt that open-plan teachers probably were more responsive and creative than teachers in traditional classrooms. Another impression was that students in neat classrooms probably were happier and better behaved than students in messy classrooms. Classroom arrangements send messages to outside observers; the messages may or may not be valid, but they are certainly sent—and received.

Social Behavior

Density. What are the effects of high and low densities on social behavior in the classroom? In many places, fiscal restraint has meant even greater classroom densities than in the recent past (see Figure 11–10).

Research on classroom aggression has produced mixed results. Aggression among students sometimes increases with density and sometimes decreases with density. Gradually, environmental psychologists have realized that increases in social density are associated with increases in aggression, but increases in spatial density are not.[187] Why might this be?

1. Changes in density may or may not be accompanied by changes in the amount of resources (access to the teacher, toys, lab equipment) available to each student. When more children are added to the same room (an increase in social density), the result may be greater competition for resources that have *not* increased. However, when a class of children is moved from a larger classroom to a smaller one (an increase in spatial density), it is likely that they have access to about the same amount of resources. There is still one teacher for the same number of students, and often the new classroom has as many books, toys, and equipment as the old one.

This idea has been supported by research: Children in high-density situations with more resources are less aggressive than children in high-density situations with fewer resources.[188] However, when spatial density is increased, not by shifting to a smaller classroom but by slicing an existing classroom in half, aggression does increase.[189] In the latter case, many resources also were divided when the room was halved.

2. The effects of density are modified by the classroom's program. For example, high-density situations discourage students from selecting activities that require much concentration.[190] Teachers who are faced with large classes may modify their lesson plans to avoid confrontations among students.[191]

3. Architectural features such as ceiling height and perimeter space may modify the effects of density.[192]

FIGURE 11–10 High-density classrooms may harm academic performance and create dissatisfaction.

Imagine the difference in perceived crowding between a windowless basement room with one tiny door and a low ceiling and another one with the same floor size except that it is a second floor room with a panoramic view, high ceilings, and double sliding glass doors. When perceived spaciousness is increased by these architectural features, aggression and other anti-social behaviors may decrease.

Obviously, then, the number of persons present is only a starting point for considering the effects of density.[193] The type of density, the availability of key resources, the program and architectural features other than floor size are also important. Confusion in the findings of early studies on density and aggression is largely resolved when these factors are considered.

4. Classroom aggression may depend on the cognitive ability of the students. A study of preschoolers found that aggression increased when density reached one child per 15 square feet.[194] In a study of 72 classes of children with disabilities, more aggression occurred when social density was greater. When, in a second study, the social density was first increased and then decreased for another group of students with disabilities, aggression also increased and decreased.[195] When the immediate workspace of some second-graders was decreased, aggression increased 100 percent for boys and 130 percent for girls.[196] Yet, when the density in a college classroom was doubled, no aggression was reported, even though students reported being less comfortable, satisfied, and happy.[197] As we gain cognitive skills and are socialized against overt aggression, we feel worse but do not strike out against our fellow students.

Aggression is not the only social behavior affected by classroom density. Several studies have reported that students tend to withdraw and behave randomly, deviantly, or as spectators (rather than as participants) in high-density classrooms.[198] One study found low involvement both at very high and at very low densities;[199] another reported less social interaction when density rises to one student for every 15 square feet.[200] This implies that classroom involvement is greatest at moderate density; based on these studies, this would be about 30 to 40 square feet per student.

Unfortunately, little research on the relation between positive social behaviors and density has been re-

ported. However, one study does report that installing partitions to separate various activities increased cooperation.[201]

Spatial Arrangements. Classroom layout affects the social interaction of both teachers and students. Researchers have examined the effects of special booths that can provide privacy for elementary school students.[202] These **privacy booths,** where students could be alone during regular school hours, were very popular—for a while. For the first 10 days that the booths were installed, about 70 percent of the students visited the booths each day. Over the next two weeks, however, usage averaged about 15 percent, and after 25 days, less than 5 percent of the students used the booths each day.

The privacy booth experiment appears to be a surprising failure; the students seemed not to value the booths except as a novelty. However, the children in this study happened to be those who had abundant opportunities for privacy at home. Children without so much privacy at home might use privacy booths more. The study also found that some children consistently used the booth more than others. Boys rated by their teachers as more distractible, more aggressive, and less sociable used the booths more; girls who sought more privacy at home used the classroom booths more. Thus, privacy booths may benefit some children.

Unexpected findings also emerged from another study of student privacy.[203] Students in elementary school classrooms that allowed for privacy (separate rather than shared desks and secluded study areas within the classroom) reported that they had less privacy than did students in classrooms *without* amenities for privacy. This may have occurred because students were not allowed free access to the secluded study areas.

When one can see but not enter a desirable place, one may feel less privacy than if the desirable option was not available at all. The design lesson may be this: If expectations are raised by providing something desirable, but use of the new facility is restricted, discontent may be greater than if the desirable feature had never been built.

Social interaction is different in open-plan and traditional classrooms. Because classes in open-plan environments are often combined, teachers interact with one another more, students meet with teachers more, and students move around more than in traditional classrooms.[204] This increased interaction may, of course, create more noise and disruption than is found in traditional classrooms.[205] Open classroom space may be associated with more aggression, at least at the preschool stage.[206,207] Despite this image of barely controlled chaos, more students report being able to find an adequate place to study by themselves in open-plan classrooms than in traditional classrooms.[208]

In this section, we have reviewed several major environmental influences on the learning process. Is there a way to integrate this knowledge? If we could do so, such a framework might provide an overall set of guidelines for research and design of learning settings. One proposed framework is the **optimal stimulation** approach.[209,210] Its proponents suggest that all the influences we have discussed—noise, light, space, resources, and climate—may be characterized as presenting the learner with too little, too much, or optimal stimulation. Regardless of which modality the stimulation arrives in, the assumption is that teachers and learners perform better, feel better, and interact better when the total amount of stimulation is optimal. But what is optimal and how much stimulation is optimal?

The optimal level of stimulation is the amount required to produce an arousal level in the individual that produces the best work, the best feelings, and the best social interaction of which the individual is capable. But the question remains: How much stimulation is needed to produce the ideal amount of arousal? The exact numbers are not known, but researchers can make some relative statements about three considerations.[211]

1. *Individual differences.* Hyperactive children need more stimulation than typical children, who, in turn, need more stimulation than autistic children.

2. *Type of activity.* We all perform or feel better during certain activities when little physical stimulation comes our way (e.g., studying for an examination), but we also perform or feel better during activities when much stimulation is present (e.g., dancing).

3. *Length of time.* From the time a situation is new to us until it begins to fatigue or bore us, the optimal level of stimulation changes. Normally, the longer we are in the same setting, the more we adapt to the stimulation it offers, so that the optimal level of it rises with time.

Eventually, researchers might be able to identify quantities of stimulation that would be optimal when an individual's personal qualities, the nature of the activity, and the length of exposure to the activity are known.

◆ *IN SUM, the amount and arrangement of space in educational settings is very important for classroom performance and behavior. High density may affect learning when the activity involves physical movement around the classroom, when learning is dependent on some classroom resource that is not increasing as fast as the number of learners, when a particular situation seems crowded to a particular learner, and when the concept to be learned is complex.*

Space in classrooms also affects student and teacher feelings. Most students and teachers prefer lower-density classrooms because lower densities usually feel less crowded. Providing satisfying physical arrangements within schools is best accomplished by furnishing a variety of layouts. Softer, more homelike classrooms will not become common until attitudes change. School authorities must be willing to spend a bit more, janitors must be willing to deal with rooms that are probably harder to clean, and parents must be willing to believe that a real education is possible in a nontraditional classroom. Students probably wouldn't have to change their attitudes very much at all.

In terms of social behavior, increased social density leads to increased aggression and withdrawal when other resources, architectural features, and teaching style do not counteract it. Attempts to provide more privacy for most students in the classroom have so far not been very successful, but some students appear to benefit. Open-plan classrooms increase social interaction. Classroom arrangements should provide optimal stimulation. The proper amount in any given situation cannot yet be specified, but the student's need for stimulation, the type of activity, and the length of time spent in the activity must be considered.

◆ **ENVIRONMENTAL COMPETENCE** ◆

As noted at the outset of this chapter, not all learning occurs in classrooms. This section focuses on learning *about* the environment. **Environmental competence** is "people's ability to deal with their immediate surroundings in an effective and stimulating manner."[212] It includes many aspects of our interaction with the environment, such as wayfinding, sense of direction, knowledge of the best and worst parts of a city, familiarity with and appreciation for different architectural styles, awareness of the power structure of an organization so that design modifications might be lobbied for instead of merely commented upon, skill in navigation or wilderness hiking, outdoor skills, and the ability to personalize a setting quickly (see Figure 11–11).

People begin to develop environmental competence at birth and seek to increase it throughout their lives by traveling or paying special attention to local settings. Yet, little formal attention is given to the individual's development of environmental competence after early childhood. In youth and adulthood, people are often left to develop environmental competence on their own.

In parallel with this neglect, researchers have not yet investigated most forms of environmental competence very much. Nevertheless, enough work has been completed—and the topic is important enough—to devote this space to it. After discussing the nature of environmental competence, we will turn to methods for developing it further.

Varieties of Environmental Competence

Fritz Steele proposed three kinds of environmental competence.[213] The first includes one's personal style, atti-

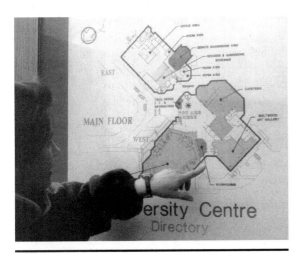

FIGURE 11–11 Learning definitely occurs outside the classroom, too. The physical environment, including you-are-here signs, influences this learning too.

tudes, and awareness. Thus, part of environmental competence is awareness of one's own environmentally relevant skills, abilities, needs, and values. Do you know where you stand on environmental issues? Have you ever actively assessed your own needs for space? Do you believe you could find your way out of a forest if you lost your way?

Skill in perceiving the environment without too much distortion or too many blind spots is another aspect of the personal dimension of environmental competence. Do you know anyone who consistently misjudges physical distances? Anyone who seems to be completely out of touch with the physical surroundings? Curiosity about the environment—the desire to explore new settings and learn more about familiar ones—is also very important. Someone who is not curious about the environment is unlikely to develop much competence in it!

A second kind of environmental competence concerns the individual's knowledge about the surroundings. This includes scientific knowledge relevant to environmental issues, knowing how to get around in a particular building or city or wilderness area, and knowing how to find out how to get around. Some students have acquired knowledge about how to get around that labyrinthine campus building; others have not, but at least they know who to ask or where to ask, and they feel comfortable about asking. Still others get lost in it even after months of trying and are too embarrassed to inquire.

Some psychologists have studied this problem with a view to better understanding how individuals get lost and which strategies they employ as they struggle to find their way back. For example, the behavior of hunters lost in the mountains has been investigated. Which medium (slides, videotapes, or walking) helps young children learn a route best has also been examined.[214] (Walking helps most.)

Steele says that technical knowledge of one's surroundings—for example, knowing the difference between fluorescent and incandescent lighting—is an important component of environmental competence because it provides design possibilities upon which to draw if one is faced with awful offices, classrooms, or airports. These design possibilities may then be offered to those charged with the maintenance and modification of the building. People do not always care enough to bother offering, pushing, petitioning, or politicking over design changes, but without some knowledge of design possibilities, they probably would never bother.

Knowledge about people in relation to settings is another aspect of knowledge about one's surroundings. From those who know little or nothing about any part of the environment to those who take their Ph.D.s in a specialized area, the range of environmental knowledge across individuals is immense. For example, a study that explored individual differences in knowledge about environmental issues found that natural science majors know more than social science or nonscience majors and that environmental studies students know more than those who are not environmental studies students.[215]

Knowledge about how our social system deals with the physical setting is the final aspect of environmental knowledge. What are the rules of the game governing remodeling? Who decides whether to move or who gets which office? When are the meetings about this held? What are the general norms in the organization concerning space, furniture, and other physical design features? Very often, space and design decisions are made by powerful managers who fail to consult with those who will be directly affected by the changes. The environmentally competent person will discover at least some of the answers to these questions and will perhaps try to exert some influence. The environmentally incompetent individual is likely to shrug and give up the quest almost before it begins.

The third kind of environmental competence described by Steele involves practical skills related to the environment. These practical skills include being able to scout a setting, match oneself with appropriate settings for different activities, personalize a setting, and use creative custodianship.

Scouting is the ability to get the feel of a place and to systematically canvass it through focused searching. As an example, I once hosted an eminent, much-traveled environmental psychologist. Lunchtime arrived and I could not think of restaurant suited to the occasion. We began scouting and within minutes, under the direction of my guest, who had no experience in my city but has great scouting ability, we found a very suitable restaurant.

Matching is the ability to find the right place for the right activity at the right time. Have you *actively* considered, for example, just where you work best? The difference between successful and unsuccessful students is often that successful ones discover the physical and temporal conditions in which they work well. Socially, some individuals seem to have a knack for selecting places for getting together that make the event worthwhile; others rarely think of the place to meet, focusing exclusively on the social aspects of the meeting.

The ability to personalize a setting well and quickly is another useful dimension of environmental competence. College students, for example, move relatively often. Some are able to transform a barren room into a glowing reflection of themselves, whereas others manifest no interest or ability in personalizing, sometimes preferring to complain about the plainness of the building.

At the public school level, one enlightened architect developed a service to provide inexpensive materials for teachers and students to personalize their classrooms.[216] It is amazing that some organizations still restrict or prohibit employees from personalizing their work spaces. Some organizations actively block the development of environmental competence in their employees. They seem to believe that environmental competence may lead to agitation for more democratic decision making on design questions.[217] They are probably correct!

Finally, **creative custodianship** is Steele's term for the skill involved in using a setting without unduly upsetting the place's essential character in the process. For example, some campers go to great lengths to leave no trace of their temporary habitation. A few vandals, on the other hand, go to great lengths to ensure their presence *does* leave an ugly and preferably permanent mark on the environment.

No one's environmental competence is perfect; many of us need to improve it in some or many areas. We turn now to ways of increasing environmental competence.

Developing Environmental Competence

Formal Education. Of course, many forms of formal environmental competence are taught in postsecondary schools, including architecture, landscape architecture, town planning, environmental studies and geography, as well as environmental psychology. Perhaps the most extensive training in environmental competence occurs in the military.[218] However, Steele asserts that high schools and colleges ought to teach courses in environmental competence in the broad sense of creating a citizenry interested in and knowledgeable about local everyday physical settings. This teaching would create ordinary citizens who are capable of responsible criticism of those settings, when criticism is needed.

In the rush of environmental activism that opened the 1970s, many traditional elementary school classes in biology and geography were suddenly transformed into environmental education classes. The emphasis shifted from the mere description of ecology to the stress on the fragility and limitedness of the planet Earth. New curricula were quickly developed, such as a series of so-called environmental encounters that were proposed for the whole public school-age range, from kindergarten to the end of high school[219] (see Figure 11–12). William Stapp, who devised these encounters, saw them as a way to develop awareness and knowledge of such concepts as the following:

- *A closed system.* Except for solar energy, we live in a closed and limited system.
- *An ecosystem.* Humans, other living organisms, and the nonliving environment are inseparably interrelated and vulnerable to sudden changes.
- *A land ethic.* Humans must develop an ecological conscience; we are not conquerors of the environmental community—we are citizens of it.

- *Population.* The whole system is threatened by the growth of human numbers; the problem is not so much a lack of space, but too many people for the available resources.
- *Environmental quality.* Too many people leads to contamination; we must develop concern for both the physical and psychological effects of pollution.
- *Environmental decisions.* We must rethink individual and collective behavior patterns; new policies and ethics must emerge and lead to decisions that are based on long-term environmental benefits.

These principles, so familiar to us now, were fresh ideas at the time Stapp sieved them from the ferment of late-1960s environmental activism. At that time, people were so impatient to learn more about the problems that they spontaneously attended environmental teach-ins.[220] Since then, environmental education has developed steadily. Evidence of its continuing vitality is the continuing stream of curriculum guides and manuals that fulfill the objectives set forth by Stapp and others.[221]

Some research has been concerned with the effectiveness of environmental education programs (see Chapter 3). The field trip, that hallowed and beloved institution, has been examined for its pedagogical value. Summer students aged 10 to 13 years old were taught two principles of plant ecology in their home school yard and in a natural setting (on a field trip).[222] Learning was significantly better in the home school yard than on the field trip. The novelty of a day out of school is pleasant, but it may interfere with the learning of concepts. On the other hand, students on a field trip may learn

FIGURE 11–12 In this environmental education class, students played representatives of a mining company and an environmental activist group to experience some of the dialog that occurs between developers and conservationists.

something different or more important other than the intended concepts. Educators must decide just what they hope to gain from a field trip.

How effective are different methods of teaching environmental competence? One survey indicated that teachers believe active-involvement instructional methods (e.g., debates, simulation games, field trips) are the most effective, but that most teachers actually use passive-involvement methods (e.g., lectures and readings).[223] Apparently, the effective teaching of environmental competence within the formal school system is hindered by a reluctance to relinquish the traditional forms of knowledge transmission—ones developed to teach classical disciplines such as philosophy and history.

The teachers' beliefs about the value of active involvement have been substantiated by research.[224] High school students who participated in a 6-day program received either instruction in environmental issues or instruction plus information on environmental action strategies.[225] As you might expect, those who received only instruction did not increase their environmental activities over the next two months, but those who were taught action strategies did.

Active-involvement alternatives do exist within formal educational settings. Over 35 university-based science programs that provide symbiotic links with the National Park Service in the United States have been established in the last decade or so.[226] Some students are being taught how to design settings, including their own classrooms. Children as young as age 8 have been taught enough architecture in hour-long, once-a-week sessions to produce good-quality designs for classrooms and other settings.[227]

Another alternative to the plain lecture is the simulation exercise. Instructors teach about such issues as resource depletion through games that show what happens when resources are used too quickly.[228] One such simulation exercise that concerned energy conservation was directly compared to the traditional lecture as a way of changing attitudes and behavior.[229] Students who took part in the simulation showed an increase in positive attitudes toward attitude change and a greater likelihood of taking action.

We must not forget that environmental problems can be frightening, particularly to younger students. People need to be more concerned, but an unintended

effect of some curricula is to unduly scare students—something that adds to the problems rather than ameliorating them. Environmental education programs should stress that problems exist but that with new skills we can overcome them.[230]

Informal Programs. A wide variety of programs promote environmental awareness in community settings. Some resemble school programs but are aimed at community adults. For example, a Texas program focused on water quality problems.[231] Five months after 51 adults had been in the program, they still reported greater awareness of the problems and felt confident about discussing them in public.

Robert Sommer described many awareness-enhancing programs that focus on the built environment in his book *Design Awareness.*[232] One school gave 4-year-olds the task of designing their own classroom. Another taught children about personal space and crowding by drawing circles on the floor and asking the students to squeeze into the circumferences of the circles.

Environmental psychologists have conducted workshops in schools and hospitals that serve to sensitize staff to the environment as it is experienced by their clients. Many physicians, for example, have never rolled down a hospital corridor on a gurney. When teachers are asked to sit in a student's desk for an hour without leaving it, they better understand why some children are fidgety and restless. The environmental competence developed in these workshops can help to create settings that reflect new respect for the needs of those who usually have little input into design decisions: students, patients, and clients.

Outdoor environmental competence, such as that gained through outdoor challenge programs and interpretation trails, also have received attention. One of the earliest empirical studies examined the effects of taking part in an outdoor challenge program. Adolescent boys spent two weeks in a primitive 17,000-acre forest, working on survival skills.[233] By their own account, the boys felt that the experience significantly improved a variety of skills, including their knowledge of the woods, map reading, compass use, food finding, and ecological knowledge.

The interpretation trail is an increasingly common feature of parks. Guides take individuals or small groups on short hikes, pointing out forest delights that might otherwise be overlooked. In one study, the merits of interpretations that emphasize a sensory approach (including many opportunities and exhortations to listen, touch, smell, and even taste the forest) were compared to a nonsensory approach (in which the emphasis was more on verbal information).[234] The sensory approach led to more expressions of enjoyment from the hikers, but the nonsensory approach led hikers to ask more questions and to engage in more social interaction. Investigations such as this one will help to fine-tune the process of developing environmental competence.

◆ *IN SUM, environmental competence involves learning about the environment. Three kinds include (1) personal style, attitudes, and awareness of physical settings; (2) knowledge of physical settings, including technical knowledge, how to unearth new information, knowledge about how social systems control space, and knowledge of person-environment relations; and (3) practical environmental skills such as scouting, matching, personalization, and creative custodianship. Programs in and out of school teach many different facets of environmental competence, from basic environmental ethics to campfire starting to architectural design. Although many subareas of environmental competence have received considerable attention, the concept, as a whole, so far has not received much attention.*

◆ LEARNING AND ◆ ENVIRONMENTAL DESIGN

Environmental psychologists have been involved in the design of many educational settings. Unfortunately, many other educational designs have been undertaken without any social science input either in the planning stages or in the evaluation of the design's effects on the behavior or feelings of students and instructors. In this section, two examples of educational design research by environmental psychologists are presented: efforts toward better kindergarten classrooms and college classrooms.

Kindergarten Classrooms

Recall from research described earlier that few classrooms have library corners, but where they do exist, students use them frequently. That study was correlational;

the use of library corners may have been due to other factors—such as teachers who stressed reading—as much as it was due to the library corners themselves.

To test the idea that having a library corner directly leads to increased literature activities when students have a choice of activities, Lesley Mandel Morrow and Carol Weinstein attempted a more experimental study of 13 kindergarten classrooms.[235] None of the classrooms already possessed special library corners or much preexisting literature activity. Each classroom was randomly assigned to one of four conditions: control (no changes), new library corner, library program, or both new library corner and program.

After allowing some time for the novelty of the changes to wear off, the researchers measured how often children used literature during their free-play periods. The number of children who used library materials during free play rose about twentyfold in the new library corner condition (from 0.28 user per free-play period to 5.75 users per free-play period). Introducing a new library program also raised the number of users (from 1.21 to 5.54). The combination of library corner plus program also produced more reading, but not more than a new library corner alone or a new library program alone. In the control classrooms, usage remained significantly lower than in all three experimental conditions.

Thus, the mere existence of a library corner in a kindergarten classroom increases children's literature activity. The results were moderated by gender differences: Girls used literature more than boys in all three experimental conditions. The challenge for future research in this area would be to design a library corner that will attract boys!

A College Classroom

Most of us have sat through classes in plain, boring, hard rooms. We can cope with such rooms; they probably do not cause brain damage or cocaine addiction. Nevertheless, they are not pleasant. If they could be made at least slightly more tolerable, would they help in any measurable way?

Robert Sommer and Helge Olsen redesigned a plain, 30-seat college classroom at the Davis campus of the University of California.[236] With a very small budget, they changed it into a soft classroom with semicircular, cushion-covered bench seating, adjustable lighting, a small carpet, and some mobiles (see Figure 11–13). Compared to traditional classrooms of similar size, student participation increased markedly in the soft classroom. The number of statements per student tripled and the percent of students who spoke in class approximately doubled.

The soft classroom, contrary to the expectations of some, was not damaged or vandalized, even though some of its components were vulnerable to vandals. Besides the dramatic increase in participation, students using the room wrote many glowing comments about it in a logbook placed in the soft classroom. This research, together with Wollin and Montagne's[237] work (described at the start of the chapter) showing that soft classrooms for introductory psychology improved performance, suggests a tentative conclusion: College classrooms need not be plain and hard. In fact, the early evidence suggests that inexpensive changes to make classrooms more pleasant have very tangible benefits.

◆ SUMMARY ◆

Educational activities—including learning, participation, classroom social interaction, and feelings about school settings—are affected in important ways by the physical school setting, in conjunction with other factors such as teaching style and age of the learner. The size, plan, and condition of the setting, as a whole, is one set of influences. Noise has a larger effect than light and climate, but this may be because in the typical school the latter two are usually provided at reasonably acceptable levels, whereas noise often varies widely from classroom to classroom. Budget crunches have created space crunches. The resulting larger class sizes (increased social density) are linked with numerous difficulties in the learning process. Open-plan classrooms can work well when teachers are appropriately trained and students are able to handle the flexibility they provide. Aggression and withdrawal accompany greatly increased social density.

Environmental competence refers to learning about environments ranging from a classroom to the great outdoors. It involves a personal dimension (one's orientation toward learning more about the environment), technical and social knowledge of specific settings, and practical skills. All forms of environmental competence may be developed through programs in and out of schools. Examples include lessons in resource conservation, field trips, and workshops for adults. Two design

FIGURE 11–13 This is the original soft classroom at the University of California, Davis.

research interventions are described in which the use of books was increased in kindergarten and participation in college classes was increased through design changes.

Suggested Supplementary Readings

Ahrentzen, S., Jue, G. M., Skorpanich, M., & Evans, G. W. (1982). School environments and stress. In G. W. Evans (Ed.), *Environmental stress.* New York: Cambridge University Press.

Bronzaft, A. L. (1981). The effect of a noise abatement program on reading ability. *Journal of Environmental Psychology, 1,* 215–222.

Cohen, S., & Trostle, S. L. (1990). Young children's preferences for school-related physical-environmental setting characteristics. *Environment and Behavior, 22,* 753–766.

Gump, P. V. (1978). School environments. In I. Altman & J. F. Wohlwill (Eds.), *Children and the environment.* New York: Plenum.

Kuller, R., & Lindsten, C. (1992). Health and behavior of children in classrooms with and without windows. *Journal of Environmental Psychology, 12,* 305–317.

Montello, D. R. (1988). Classroom seating location and its effect on course achievement, participation, and attitudes. *Journal of Environmental Psychology, 8,* 149–157.

Ramsey, J. M., & Hungerford, H. R. (1989). The effects of issue investigation and action training on environmental behavior in seventh-grade students. *Journal of Environmental Education, 20*(4), 29–34.

Rivlin, L. G., & Weinstein, C. S. (1984). Educational issues, school settings, and environmental psychology. *Journal of Environmental Psychology, 4,* 347–364.

Steele, F. (1980). Defining and developing environmental competence. In C. P. Alderfer & C. L. Cooper (Eds.), *Advances in experimental social processes, 2,* 225–244.

CHAPTER  **12**

WORKPLACE ENVIRONMENTAL PSYCHOLOGY

Facilities planning tends to be delegated to accountants or office management people whose training and experience are almost exclusively in dealing with figures. It is therefore not surprising that the quantifiable costs—construction costs per square foot, cleaning costs per week—are weighted heavily and that the less quantifiable factors—decreases in stimulating contacts, lack of identification with the system—tend to be ignored when decisions are made.

—Fred Steele[1]

*T*om *struggled into consciousness as the clock radio dribbled out the dreary 7 A.M. news. After dragging himself through the bathroom and kitchen, he went outside—only to discover that his car had a flat. "What do I do now?" he moaned to himself.*

If he wanted to make it to work on time, the only choice was to take the bus. The bus schedule was in a drawer somewhere, but of course he couldn't find it. Tom stood in drizzling rain for 20 minutes before the bus pulled up. The driver tossed out a cheery, "Morning, there! Wet today, isn't it!" All this for a part-time job, Tom thought.

After the bus dropped him off, Tom passed a machine shop as he waded his way to his office. Even if he were in a good mood, he muttered to himself, he couldn't understand how those people could stand all that noise of machinery and yelling. He sat down at his desk, wishing he could just quietly let his clothes dry and his emotional health improve. Unfortunately, the open plan of his office made him the center of attention and he felt compelled to pretend the whole situation was humorous. This did not improve his emotional health.

Throughout the day, Tom waited for the moment when his coworkers were all away from their desks so he could call Jane for a little sympathy, but there was not one minute that he was left alone. However, most of them didn't seem to mind calling to place bets, arrange parties, or talk to their friends.

Between his own desire for a moment's solitude and the steady stream of distracting conversations that he couldn't help overhearing, Tom was a wreck by the end of the day. He was determined to ride off into the sunset, even if it was on a bus. Then he remembered that his place was east of the office.

◆　◆　◆

Working can provide some of the best and some of the worst experiences in life. For Sigmund Freud, it was one of the two major paths to fulfillment (the other one was love). Many factors determine a person's productivity, stress, and satisfaction at work, but for decades, psychologists have realized that the physical environment is an important influence on employee productivity and satisfaction (see Figure 12–1).

Early researchers assumed that environment-behavior relations operated according to simple environmental determinism. The famous Hawthorne studies included a dozen years of work on the effects of the environment on the productivity and satisfaction of assembly-line workers at the Hawthorne plant of the Western Electric Company, near Chicago.[2] Many separate studies were completed, and the meaning of the voluminous results is still debated, six decades later.

Certain basic conclusions from the Hawthorne studies are widely accepted, however. For example, in some early studies, it was hypothesized that changing the level of lighting on an assembly line would affect productivity. This is a straightforward hypothesis that anyone new to environmental psychology might reasonably propose. If workers can see better, they probably will be able to assemble more items, and production will rise. But the researchers were surprised to discover, in several separate studies, that production did *not* reliably vary with lighting level. At one stage, the amount of light was even reduced by 70 percent without a loss of productivity. The researchers became convinced that something very odd was happening when they replaced

a set of lights with bulbs *of the same wattage* and found that the employees expressed satisfaction with the "increased illumination."

FIGURE 12–1 Adults spend much of their lives in factories and offices. The effects of these settings deserve close study.

Some observers took these results as evidence that the physical environment was not important. Because the Hawthorne studies were one of the first large-scale investigations of environment and behavior, this conclusion may have set back the development of environmental psychology by as much as three decades. Unfortunately, the conclusion was wrong. A more accurate view is that employee/environment relations are complex.

Three important findings of the Hawthorne studies were overlooked by those who concluded the environment was unimportant.

1. The findings refute an assumption that is itself faulty. The simplistic notion that lighting directly affects work output is a form of naive environmental determinism. Environmental psychologists believe that physical setting influences are buffered by employee perceptions, beliefs, preferences, experience, and personality. For example, the behavior of employees in the Hawthorne studies was clearly affected by their *perceptions* of the work environment. In the bulb-changing study, for example, employees probably assumed that a bulb someone took the trouble to replace was deficient; a new bulb must be an improvement.

2. The conclusion focuses on one environmental variable when a *different* environmental variable—more subtle but perhaps more important for that very reason—was operative.[3] Employees in some of the Hawthorne studies were moved to a different room, away from most employees. This room made the employees feel special and its physical and social characteristics may have affected performance more than the environmental variables examined by the researchers.

3. The layout of the room facilitated social contact among employees. This probably encouraged the employees to form and maintain informal norms about how much to produce in a given day.

In general, the Hawthorne studies disconfirm naive determinism, but confirm that physical settings have important influences on work behavior. However, these influences are more complex than previously thought. They involve broader, more subtle aspects of the setting, which, in turn, are moderated by employee characteristics (see Figure 12–2).

The work environment can be considered not only as a collection of physical stimuli (noise, light, temperature, etc.) but also as a physical structure (size, furniture, hallways, etc.) and as a symbolic artifact (the meaning or image of the work setting).[4] Employees are experienced or not, noise sensitive or not, senior or junior. Fundamental psychological processes are invoked by employee/environment interactions: arousal, overload, affect, adaptation, personal control, and so on. This leads to outcomes that, in general, may be categorized as performance or productivity, health or stress, satisfaction or morale, and interpersonal relations.

One example of the modern approach to environmental psychology on the job examined how an employee's private self-consciousness moderates the effects of an unpleasant physical workplace.[5] **Private self-consciousness (PSC)** refers to the tendency to compare one's desired condition with one's actual condition; some of us monitor this difference between our ideal and reality frequently and some of us do not. When the work environment is worse (more dangerous, high or low temperature, air pollution, noise), high-PSC employees experience more distress than low-PSC employees.

More generally, the physical environment at work affects some employees more or differently than others. Another illustration is provided by a study that showed that overloaded employees report fewer adverse reactions to hotness and high density than employees who are not overloaded.[6] Overworked employees cannot or will not allow environmental problems to intrude into their consciousness. Whether this is wise or healthy is another matter, of course.

This chapter considers research on the complex relations between the physical environment and performance, feelings, social behavior, health and stress at work, and getting away from work (travel).

◆ ENVIRONMENTAL PSYCHOLOGY ◆
ON THE JOB

The physical environment at work is crucial to employees' performance, satisfaction, social relations, and health. Over the 40-year life cycle of an office building, only about 2 to 3 percent of all expenditures are on the initial costs of the physical environment; in contrast, about 90 percent is spent on salaries and benefits.[7]

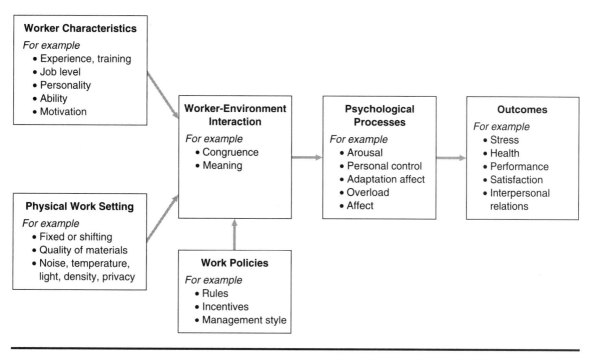

FIGURE 12-2 A model for workplace environmental psychology.

If the 2 to 3 percent is well spent, very large savings on the 90 percent might be achieved. If it is poorly spent, many employees will suffer (and, as a consequence, so will their organization). Good workplace design begins with knowledge of person-environment relations in workplaces. This section surveys what is known on this topic.

We must remind ourselves of the tremendous variety of job activities. Psychologists have long sought a simple classification system to make the huge number of tasks in different workplaces more manageable. We will rely on a taxonomy adapted from earlier ones.[8,9] Most work outcomes fall into one of four major categories: performance (productivity itself, but also such indicators as resignation rate, time spent in the office, and attendance), feelings (satisfactions, evaluations, attitudes, emotions, and perceptions), health and stress (negative changes in body or mind), and social behavior (space, interaction, privacy, and status).

What affects these four kinds of work activity? Five major aspects of the physical setting that can affect employees include: sound (noise, music), temperature (heat, cold), air (pollution, freshness), light and color (sunlight, incandescent, fluorescent, windows, views), and space (amount of it, arrangement of work stations).

Let us stroll through the known relations between the five major environmental aspects of workspaces and the four major categories of work behavior. We will proceed by covering the effects of each environmental aspect, beginning with sound, on all the work behavior categories.

Sound, Noise, and Music

On the job, sound may come from jackhammers, typewriters, background music, coworkers talking, and many other sources. Some of these sounds may be expected, natural, or even desirable—silence is not always pleasant—but others may be unwanted and annoying. Fancy formulas exist for specifying the conditions under which sound is likely to be labeled noise,[10] but here is the most straightforward way to define it: **Noise** is unwanted sound. Desirable, beautiful sound, on the other hand, is called **euphony**.

Whether a particular sound is heard as noise or euphony depends on the individual and the situation. One person's euphony may be another person's noise: A whisper at 2 yards (30 decibels) may be euphonic but a rocket lifting off at 300 yards (200 decibels) may be noise. However, to the workers who labored long and hard to enable the rocket to lift off, the 200 decibels may be euphonious (see Figure 12–3). Noise levels in typical offices average about 45 decibels and range from about 40 to 60 decibels.[11]

Performance. Early noise research focused on hearing damage from industrial sounds that were too loud. Even today, many industrial workers are exposed to sound levels that can cause either temporary or permanent hearing damage. More workers today use hearing protection devices, but a recent study found that manufacturers' ratings of the degree to which these devices reduce sound are substantially overestimated; they may not provide as much protection as they claim.[12]

Usually, individuals do not go deaf suddenly; instead, the lowest level of sound that one can detect at a given frequency gradually rises—that is, there is a shift in the hearing threshold. **Temporary threshold shift (TTS)** is defined as a threshold shift that reverses itself within 16 hours (about the length of time between leaving the noise source at work and returning to it the next day.) If a threshold shift repeatedly is allowed to last into the next workday, it may become a **permanent threshold shift (PTS).** This process may easily go unnoticed and the victim may gradually lose considerable hearing ability.

TTS can occur after only 10 minutes of 100-decibel sound,[13] a sound level that may be found in very noisy factories and in many concerts and nightclubs. TTS can also occur after 90 minutes of 90 decibels, a sound level

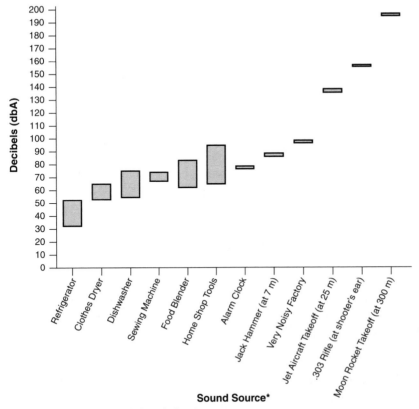

FIGURE 12–3 The loudness of some familiar sound sources. The measure dBA is a weighting of the objective sound pressure that approximates human perception of loudness.

*All distances are 1 m unless indicated otherwise.

found in many factories; it is about the loudness of noisier kitchen waste disposers and electric lawn mowers at a distance of 3 feet.[14]

For these reasons, occupational health and safety standards are set in terms of length of exposure to a given level of sound. For example, in one jurisdiction, workers may be exposed to 105 decibels, but for no more than 15 minutes, whereas they may be exposed to 99 decibels for an hour or 90 decibels for 8 hours.[15]

Sound levels in offices rarely reach levels that endanger hearing, but that does not mean sound is unimportant in offices. The sound level in most offices ranges from about 40 to 60 decibels, but other factors (such as the source, meaning, controllability, and predictability of the sound) may be more important than the volume of the sound. As the source of the sound becomes more relevant to an employee, as its meaning grows, and as its controllability and predictability decrease, sound is more likely to be perceived as noise and will negatively affect work behavior.

Whether noise affects actual productivity at realistic sound levels in actual offices is not yet clear.[16] Many employees and researchers *believe* that noise interferes with performance, but the evidence itself is contradictory. In fact, noise occasionally has even been shown to improve performance.[17,18]

Noise-performance relations remain unclear partly because of inadequate research funding. Government funding on the topic in the late 1970s was less than one-twentieth of the amount spent on noise-induced hearing loss.[19] This is unfortunate because sound itself and research on sound effects on behavior are both extremely complex.[20] A good example of the complex relations between noise and productivity is provided by the results of a study in which subjects were asked to proofread in a room that either was quiet or received intermittent bursts of teletype sound at 70 decibels.[21] The subjects could detect just as many spelling errors and they could recall the passages they had proofread just as well in the noisy condition as they could in the quiet condition.

First conclusion: Performance is not affected by noise. However, the subjects could not detect as many grammatical errors when it was noisy. Second conclusion: Performance *is* affected by noise. When the room was noisy, subjects started working more slowly and

they worked less steadily. Once more, performance was found to be affected by noise. Yet, in the noisy room, subjects worked *more* accurately. Third conclusion: Performance is affected, but in the opposite-from-expected direction!

Don't throw up your hands in exasperation yet. This study illustrates five common outcomes in noise research that lead us to some tentative conclusions and help clarify these apparently conflicting results (although no one can claim that noise effects are simple). The nature of the task, the employee, the sound, combinations of these, and other environmental factors all play a role.

First, the task matters. The work we do may be grouped into four broad types of tasks: cognitive (reading, writing, reasoning, creative), vigilance (monitoring people, a machine, or a production line), motor (manual manipulation of tools), and social (meetings, evaluations of employees). For a particular employee, such tasks may be familiar and well learned or not. Tasks may be relatively simple or complex. We may be asked to engage in one task at a time or several. The task may be an expected part of one's routine or the boss's idea of a surprise.

Given these distinctions, one leading noise researcher, Donald Broadbent, reviewed numerous similar studies to reach the relatively straightforward conclusion that performance will not be affected by continuous loud noise when an employee (1) performs a routine task, (2) merely needs to react to signals at certain definite times, (3) is informed when to be ready, and (4) is given clear visual signals.[22] Examples of work fitting this description include servicing a machine one knows well or writing a routine letter.

Tasks that are often affected by noise include those that ask the employee to pay attention to multiple sources of information or to perform more than one task at a time.[23] If an employee must monitor several other employees or machines, or think carefully while performing, performance is more likely to be affected.

The effects of noise on performance differ for simple versus complex tasks. A typical finding is that noise hinders the performance of complex tasks more than it hinders the performance of simple tasks.[24] In fact, noise sometimes *improves* the performance of simple tasks.[25] For example, if you work in a skateboard factory and have assembled the model skateboard a thousand times, some noise that is not too irritating might arouse you enough to speed up your work on this very well-learned task.

This is an extension of the **Yerkes-Dodson hypothesis,** which states that performance is better at moderate levels of arousal than at either low or high levels of arousal. A little arousal "pushes" performance of a simple task up toward the peak of this inverted-U-shaped function, but a further dose of arousal may push performance over the peak and down (see Figure 12–4).

When one of several tasks is more important, noise tends to increase the effort expended on less important tasks.[26] Consider, for example, the difference between finding spelling errors and finding grammatical errors. For some people, spelling errors almost leap off the page; performance on this almost automatic task may not be affected for them. On the other hand, the detection of grammatical errors requires more thought, and performance is more likely to suffer.

Motor (manual) tasks are not as easily affected by noise. Some research supports the idea that the performance of manual labor is not affected much by noise, but that employees *believe* they are working harder. In fact, they may be working harder at the cognitive level in order to maintain the expected level of performance at the objective level.[27,28]

Second, employee characteristics matter. Most research on this has examined sex, age, and personality differences. For example, in a study of arithmetic performance under noisy conditions, women slowed their work pace but men did not (accuracy was the same for both sexes).[29] Another study showed that men and women perform better in different combinations of noise and time of day.[30]

When it is noisy, performance is also affected by age. Noise slows reaction time and harms the memory of older people more than younger people.[31,32] However, older people may perform some tasks better. One study showed that under noisy conditions, young and middle-aged men responded less accurately than older men to nonobvious events that occurred during the task.[33]

Personality also modifies work performance in noise, and does so in complex ways. As you would expect, the performance of noise-sensitive workers is adversely affected by noise.[34] Extraverts prefer more stimulation, in general (and sound, in particular), than introverts;[35] noise harms the reading comprehension of introverts but not of extraverts.[36] The performance of introverts is more affected than that of extraverts by distractions that resemble stimuli important to the task.[37] Introverts seem to perform tasks under noisy conditions better in the evening; extraverts perform the same tasks better at midday.[38]

Under low-noise conditions, persons with an external locus of control comprehend reading material better than persons with an internal locus of control.[39] Some individuals appear to be able to screen out unwanted stimuli better than others.[40] Possibly, screeners can tune out noise because they have developed coping strategies that nonscreeners do not have. The performance of creative employees appears to follow the Yerkes-Dodson law (better performance at moderate levels of noise or arousal), but the performance of less creative employees does not.[41]

Third, characteristics of the sound itself are important. Sound may be loud or soft, high or low, continuous or intermittent, familiar or novel, meaningful or not, musical, mechanical, masked by other sounds, natural, or human. One of the clearest research findings is that *novel* sounds reduce performance.[42] Of course, novelty wears off; the same sound may not affect performance shortly after its introduction. Loud and uncontrollable noise causes people to remember more negatively toned trait words and to worsen their moods,

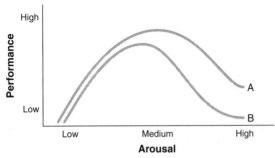

A: Easy, simple, or well-learned task
B: Difficult, complex, or novel task

FIGURE 12–4 According to the Yerkes-Dodson hypothesis, performance is better for easier tasks (naturally), but this difference is greater when a worker is more physiologically aroused.

but this does not happen either in loud controllable noise or quieter uncontrollable noise.[43] Cognitive tasks may not be affected by continuous white noise, but mixtures of sounds heard in many offices (keyboards, background speech, and music) do interfere with the performance of cognitive tasks.[44]

Donald Broadbent suggests that intermittent noise often causes temporary setbacks in performance during the noise. However, some employees can compensate with increased efficiency during quiet periods, so that overall performance is similar to that under uniformly quiet conditions.[45] A recent study that specifically varied the amount of effort put into the task supported this idea.[46] When noise is unpredictable, coping strategies are more difficult to implement and performance may suffer more than when the noise is intermittent but at predictable intervals.

Some of the complexity is resolved by assuming, as Broadbent does, that noise is a general arouser. Arousal benefits performance of some individuals in some circumstances, but impairs performance on other occasions. When noise is masked (not reduced in volume, but "covered" with white noise so that its distinctive elements are reduced), performance of some tasks improves.[47] A safe, general conclusion is that performance is *variable* in noisy conditions.

Fourth, certain employee-noise combinations *affect performance.* For example, employees may perform better when the sound level matches their preferred sound level.[48] Those who have had more time to adapt to noise may learn faster.[49] Employees who have control over sound probably are less affected by it than are employees who do not have control over the type of sound or whether it is on or off.[50] Employees who can turn on the radio when they believe it will not affect their present task and turn it off when it bothers them will probably accomplish more than employees who have no choice in the matter.

Fifth, the relation between noise and performance is affected by other *aspects of the environment, and not always in expected ways.* One study, for example, examined how noise and vibration affect a cognitive task (mental arithmetic).[51] You might think that performance would decline as noise and vibration increase. The study found, though, that performance equaled that in a control condition (no noise or vibration) when

noise and vibration were present in subjectively equal amounts but actually *declined* when either noise or vibration was subjectively lower than the other.

Finally, noise can affect performance after the noise ends! So far, we have concentrated on the effects of concurrent noise—that is, noise that occurs during the employee's attempt to do a job. Environmental psychologists learned two decades ago that noise also can have negative effects on performance *after* it stops,[52] and more recent studies have confirmed this.[53,54] The pattern of performance after exposure to noise may or may not be uniformly worse, however.[55] One study suggests it is relatively better when moderate noise is followed by an easy task *or* when loud noise is followed by a difficult task than when conditions are intermediate (e.g., loud noise is followed by an easy task or moderate noise is followed by a difficult task).[56]

Music and Performance. What about the effects of music on performance? A widespread belief is that music can speed up production or slow it down. This is an idea that suppliers of planned indoor music systems would like people to believe. However, the effects of music are not that simple. They depend on the kind of music, the type of work, and the characteristics of the individual employee.

A fair number of studies support the idea that music improves productivity,[57] but there are three problems with this research. First, most research on music was performed decades ago. It often supported the basic notion that music improves productivity, but research methods in those days often left much to be desired. For example, control groups were not often used. Second, music on the job was a novelty and, in those days, a rare privilege. Positive effects might have been due to these factors, rather than to the music itself.

Third, most researchers examined the effect of music on simple, repetitive tasks, which leaves open the question of its effects on cognitively demanding work. In general, early research of questionable quality did show that productivity could be enhanced by music, at least for simple tasks, although novelty and gratitude for the granting of a privilege may have played a crucial role.

One modern reviewer nevertheless concludes that light music will help even in modern workplaces with greater cognitive demands.[58] But he points out that a great variety of results have been found, including studies showing that music harms performance. When one considers the vast variety of tasks people undertake at work, combined with the vast variety of musical styles, tempos, and volumes, the only reasonable summation is that no general conclusion is possible.

Presumably, music *may* increase (or decrease) productivity, but the conditions that lead to one outcome or the other still have not been clearly identified. Employees' *feelings* about noise and music are clearer than are performance effects, as we see next.

Feelings. Noise is, by definition, unwanted sound. If you ask industrial or office workers their opinions about noise, they quite likely will tell you they do not like it and wish it would go away, and probably that noise adversely affects their own productivity. Of course, not all noise is equally aversive; for example, noise that an employee feels is relevant is less annoying than irrelevant noise.[59] Nevertheless, in a typical survey, over 1,000 office workers rated the "opportunity to concentrate without noise and other distractions" as the single-most desirable office characteristic (out of 17 choices).[60] But in rating their own work spaces, all but 2 of the 17 office characteristics were rated *more* satisfactory than "the opportunity to concentrate without noise."

In another survey of employees at 58 sites, job satisfaction declined as noise from people talking and telephones ringing increased.[61] In short, office employees believe that noise is a serious problem. As with noise, not all employees are the same; those with neurotic tendencies may experience the same noise as more annoying.[62] Nevertheless, there is a clear gap between the results of the productivity studies and the attitude studies. To date, research indicates that actual performance is often unchanged by noise, although it is *sometimes* changed.[63,64]

Some employees clearly feel noise detracts from their work. Who is right? One answer may be that researchers have not yet examined sufficiently sensitive measures of productivity. That is, perhaps productivity really does decline in noisy conditions, but so far, measures of productivity that are sufficiently sensitive and appropriate to demonstrate this decline have been overlooked. Also, many studies have examined only very short exposures to noise; at work, some employees are subjected to years of it. The effects of noise on productivity may be gradual and cumulative.

On the other hand, perhaps employees do not really know themselves. Employees do not usually keep objective counts of their own productivity, so it is possible that their opinions about noise and productivity are formed in good faith but are simply inaccurate. One study, for example, demonstrated that subjects *believed* noise hurt their performance even when it did not.[65]

Another possibility is that, in a sense, both viewpoints are correct. Because employees whose work slows in noisy periods are often able to work faster and better during quiet periods, their overall performance could appear unaffected. However, to struggle during noisy periods and to compensate during quiet periods in order to achieve the same overall level of performance requires greater effort and more effective coping strategies than does performance during uniformly quiet work sessions.

Thus, employees' dissatisfaction with noise and their beliefs that performance is affected may stem from their knowledge that they worked harder to produce what turns out to be the same amount of work. Because more work was required to produce the same amount of work, it is easy to feel both dissatisfied and to believe that less work was produced.

Perhaps what employees who labor in noisy settings really mean to say is that they could have produced *more* work for the amount of effort they expended. Therefore, in a sense, they produced less than they are *capable* of producing. If what they mean to say is that noise makes their work harder, they should be congratulated for producing as much as they do under difficult conditions (see Figure 12–5).

The noisiest work settings are in industry, but industrial work tends to include those types of tasks that are least affected by noise. In fact, in industrial settings, hearing damage is a bigger problem than reduced productivity. In offices, where there are more tasks that are easily affected by noise, the worst settings appear to be open-plan offices.[66] Noise in open-plan offices is largely a function of spatial arrangements, which will be discussed later.

Music and Feelings. Employee attitudes toward music are relatively clear. Most like it and *believe* that it improves

FIGURE 12–5 One very noisy job.

their productivity. However, up to 10 percent of employees definitely do *not* like music at work. Sometimes, this is a function of the type of music played and sometimes employees find that it interferes with their work. Music should be introduced to the workplace very carefully. As we discovered earlier, it may raise or lower productivity. But because 90 percent or more of employees prefer music, removing it once it is installed is likely to cause bad feelings among the vast majority of employees.

Health and Stress. Physiological changes due to sound in workplaces are limited, for the most part, to hearing loss. However, some studies suggest that sound may have other health effects. The strongest possibility is that exposure to some kinds of sound increases one's chances of cardiovascular disease. A review of 40 studies concluded that employees who are exposed to unpredictable noise for at least three years and whose work involves mental concentration have at least a 60 percent higher chance of cardiovascular disease than other employees.[67] Unfortunately, in many of the studies reviewed, the investigators were unable to separate noise effects from other aversive factors that were present at the same time. Nevertheless, the study's conclusion is consistent with the idea that employees who must expend extra effort coping with loud noise suffer long-term consequences.

Noisy factories seem to have another side effect— less critical but certainly undesirable: more laryngitis

and sore throats! All that yelling required to make oneself heard on a noisy factory floor seems to increase the frequency of these throat problems.[68]

Social Behavior. The key social effect of noise is to impair employee privacy. The ideal workplace should be quiet enough to permit concentration and communication without too much difficulty, yet open-plan offices should be suffused with enough sound to allow for conversational privacy.[69] Existing open-plan offices are very often deficient in acoustical privacy, with up to 90 percent of employees unhappy about the lack of opportunity to converse confidentially.[70,71]

Even when office employees are generally satisfied with the physical aspects of the office, mechanical noise (e.g., telephone, heating and ventilation equipment) and human noise (overheard conversations) are associated with increased tension, depression, anger, and fatigue.[72] Office privacy is greatly influenced by spatial arrangements. Generally, walls and partitions provide a greater sense of privacy.[73,74,75] Open-plan offices, which are increasing in popularity, are often deficient in sound insulation.

In addition to depriving employees of privacy, noise may make them less helpful. Subjects exposed to 85 decibels were less likely to help another person who had just dropped something than were subjects exposed to 65 decibels or less.[76] The implications for jobs in which the primary function of employees is to help clients, customers, or coworkers are obvious.

Noise may even influence employees' judgments about their coworkers. In one study, students playing the role of managers were given the resumés of five newly hired applicants.[77] The student-managers were asked to consider the qualifications of the five new employees and then to recommend a starting salary for each one. Student-managers made their recommendations after reading the new employees' resumés either in a room where the sound level was about 53 decibels (normal office sound level) or a room where the sound level was about 75 decibels (loud but realistic office sound level).

Student-managers from the noisier room recommended starting salaries that were significantly less than those made by student-managers in the quieter room! This result, which the authors replicated in a follow-up study, has enormous implications not only for pay recommendations but also for other kinds of recommendations made at work and for interpersonal attitudes among coworkers.

◆ **IN SUM,** *noise has many effects on work behavior. In industrial settings, it can cause serious hearing loss. Loud noise is particularly dangerous when employees do not realize that deafness comes slowly and almost imperceptibly. Despite the suspicion that noise affects performance, research in natural settings shows (1) how complex the issue is and (2) that performance decrements depend on the task, the person, and the type of noise. Noise harms performance when certain combinations of employee, task, and type of noise occur simultaneously, but not under other circumstances. For certain tasks, noise may even arouse a person enough to improve performance. Music may improve performance, but research on the topic is suspect. Once again, no universal effect is to be expected: Performance effects, if any, will be a function of person, task, and music.*

Employees dislike noise but, for the most part, like music on the job. They generally think noise hinders and music helps their performance. Noise is a serious problem

in modern open-plan offices. Employees find sound a problem both coming and going: Sound entering their work space is annoying and when their own words escape over partitions too easily, their privacy is compromised. Office noise may even affect important interpersonal behavior, from mere impressions of others to important judgments regarding them. There is some suggestion that long-term exposure to loud sounds has serious physiological effects beyond hearing loss.

Indoor Climate

Heat and cold can affect most work behavior but, like those of sound, the effects are complex. Temperature itself is multifaceted. The temperature of the air alone does not help us understand its influences on work behavior very well. A hot dry atmosphere is quite different from a hot humid one, and the degree of air movement further affects the character of the atmosphere. **Effective temperature**—an index composed of air temperature, humidity, and air movement measures—has replaced that of simple temperature in most research (see Figure 12–6).

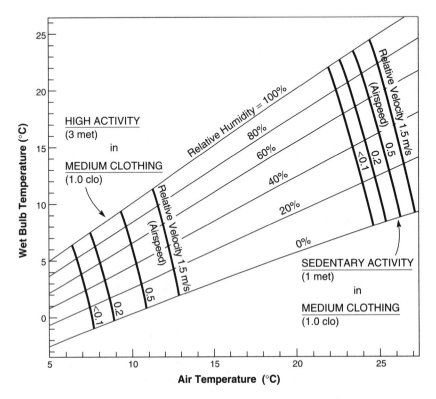

FIGURE 12–6 Comfort zones that simultaneously take into account temperature, humidity, air speed, activity level, and amount of clothing have been developed.

The effects of temperature depend on the type of work being done, the amount of clothing worn, and the length of time spent in high or low effective temperature. My sister, who sometimes lives in the countryside, tells me that firewood warms her twice—once when she cuts and splits it and again when she burns it. As I sit writing this, and as you sit reading it, very little heat is generated; a higher effective temperature obviously is necessary for our comfort when we are writing or reading than for my sister when she is chopping wood.

The effect of temperature on our work depends in part on how much clothing we wear. Researchers have even invented a scale (the unit is called the **CLO**) to measure exactly how much each piece of clothing helps to keep us warm[78] (see Figure 12–7).

Another complexity in temperature research is that our **core body temperature** is sometimes more important than effective temperature. Core body temperature takes some time to change, so short-term exposure to a wide variety of effective temperatures may not affect work behavior.

Finally, the length of time an employee is exposed to heat or cold has an effect. Cognitive performance is essentially unaffected up to 100°F, if the employee must only work 30 minutes. However, if the employee must work three hours, the maximum temperature before cognitive performance is affected is 87°F.[79]

Most of us, most of the time, are not seriously affected by cold or heat. When the ambient temperature is low or high, we often can adjust it or at least adjust our clothing. We may not be perfectly comfortable, but neither are we often as distressed as we are, for example, by uncontrollable noise at work. Nevertheless, there are some consequences of heat and cold in most of the work behavior categories.

Performance. Every possible outcome has been reported for heat and cold—performance declines when it is hot and when it is cold; performance increases when it is hot and when it is cold; performance is unchanged when it is hot and when it is cold. There are even studies that report increases *and* decreases in performance at the same time![80] Participants whose body temperatures were high were asked to detect certain signals. Compared to those whose body temperatures were lower, they detected more signals correctly (better performance) but they also made more false detections (worse performance).

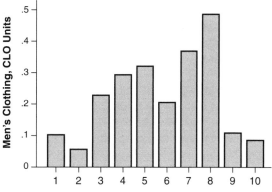

(1) T-Shirt. (2) Briefs. (3) Light, long-sleeve shirt.
(4) Heavy, long-sleeve shirt. (5) Heavy trousers.
(6) Light sweater. (7) Heavy sweater. (8) Heavy jacket.
(9) Ankle-length socks. (10) Oxfords, shoes.

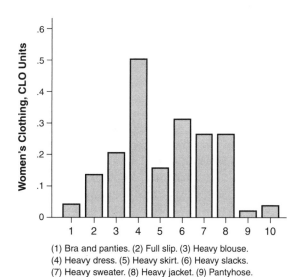

(1) Bra and panties. (2) Full slip. (3) Heavy blouse.
(4) Heavy dress. (5) Heavy skirt. (6) Heavy slacks.
(7) Heavy sweater. (8) Heavy jacket. (9) Pantyhose.
(10) Pumps, shoes.

FIGURE 12–7 A CLO is a measure of the capacity of each clothing article to insulate us.

Nevertheless, there are some general patterns to the research findings. For example, as temperatures rise into the very hot range, productivity definitely drops, especially for heavy manual labor.[81] Another relatively consistent result is that cold temperatures negatively affect the performance of work that requires fine movements and sensitive touch from an employee's hands.[82,83] Interestingly, it seems that the performance of such tasks does not gradually slip as the temperature drops, but holds up well until hand-skin temperature reaches a certain point (about 57°F), then drops off quickly.

Cool (not cold) offices, however, may *improve* the performance of officelike cognitive tasks and reduce postwork fatigue, even though employees may prefer warmer temperatures.[84] In general, the more complex the task, the more that performance will worsen with heat or cold. Dual tasks and tasks that require vigilance appear to be performed best in moderately warm temperatures (80 to 88°F), but tracking tasks and learning tasks are performed best at slightly lower temperatures.[85]

The great variety of findings that do not conform to these basic trends are probably due to factors that determine performance besides temperature itself. Examples include which task is being performed and whether the employee is acclimatized, believes the temperature is controllable to some extent, has few or many coping strategies, and is motivated.

One simple coping strategy, for example, is to adjust the amount of clothing we wear. One study examined performance of office work at cool (65°F) versus warm (78°F) temperatures with the same degree of humidity.[86] Lightly dressed men performed both simple and complex tasks best in the warm conditions and worst in the cool conditions. Heavily dressed men performed best in cool and worst in warm conditions.

Dressing appropriately, of course, is a very simple coping strategy. You may be able to think of other, more complex ways of overcoming inappropriate temperatures. The point is that coping strategies, where they exist and are used, make the question about how temperature affects performance obsolete. A better answer is that performance is affected by the way individuals cope with, or fail to cope with, temperature.

When the factors already mentioned (body temperature, clothing, duration of work, humidity, air movement) are all taken into account, the modern study of temperature effects becomes very technical. The experimenter must specify a whole range of conditions that were present at the time of testing in order to draw conclusions about the effects of temperature on work productivity.

Feelings. Feelings about temperature are usually considered in terms of stated comfort. Much engineering

research has been devoted to finding the ideal effective temperature. Obviously, no single temperature is best, but the modern approach has been to identify **comfort envelopes**. These are specific ranges of effective temperatures under which most individuals report feeling comfortable, depending on how much clothing they are wearing and what activity they are engaged in. For example, an office employee working at a desk while wearing light clothing in a room with 45 percent humidity will be comfortable when the temperature is between 75 to 80°F. A field study showed that the limits of comfort under typical humidity and clothing conditions are 70 to 80°F[87] (see Figure 12–8).

Feelings about temperature are affected not only by the actual temperature but also by what the individual *thinks* the temperature is and by room decor. Individuals report feeling warmer, at equal temperatures, when the heaters in a room are pointed out to them, the decor is more luxurious, and thermometers are fixed to report higher than actual temperatures.[88]

In another study, college students were asked how comfortable they were when an actual increase of 5°F occurred and when they were led to believe that such an increase had occurred.[89] The students reported similar changes in comfort for the real and the fake temperature increases. The fake heating strategy may be unethical as an energy conservation tactic, but it once again illustrates the Hawthorne principle: One's *perception* of a sit-

FIGURE 12–8 This freezer worker spends hours on end at 30°F.

uation is often more important than the objective characteristics of the situation.

Perceived control affects satisfaction with temperature. When we believe we have some control over the room temperature, our satisfaction with the actual temperature is greater.[90] Interestingly, however, *having* that control also has its drawbacks; the effort implied by being responsible for the temperature seems to cause some dissatisfaction. Thus, people seem to want control but not to have the responsibility that comes with control.

One might think environments that are ideal in terms of comfort would be ideal in terms of performance—that a comfortable employee is a productive employee. Unfortunately, research suggests that this commonsense hypothesis is not true. A careful study found that performance of work similar to that usually done in offices was significantly greater in temperatures about 18°F below the comfort envelope standard.[91] Subjects reported being cooler than they might prefer, but they nevertheless performed better at the lower temperatures. Despite feeling too cool, subjects in the cool conditions also reported feeling more energetic at the end of an hour's work than at the beginning of the session! (In warm conditions, reported energy dropped during the hour.)

Health and Stress. Temperature stress depends on effective temperature, duration of exposure, and the amount and type of protective clothing. Lasting physiological changes from high or low temperatures take a long time to develop, unless the temperatures are extreme (e.g., touching a flame or falling through the ice into a freezing lake). Apart from these extremes, the human body is wonderfully able to adapt to a wide range of environmental conditions. The Inuit (formerly referred to as Eskimo) have adapted quite well to very cold conditions. Adults work and children play outdoors in temperatures that would make those of us who live farther south scurry for warmth. On the hot side of the temperature spectrum, while visiting India, I saw hodcarriers who literally ran, all day, in the summer, with very heavy loads of bricks on their backs.

Clearly, individuals can adapt to severe conditions, but physiological changes, or **temperature stress,** will occur as they acclimatize, and may occur even after they are acclimatized. For example, fishermen who work the cold northern Atlantic waters actually undergo semipermanent physiological changes in their hands that allow them to avoid discomfort and frostbite longer than nonacclimatized individuals.[92] Both heat and cold as long-term stressors appear to have acute effects on cardiovascular disease.[93]

There are individual differences in acclimatization—some individuals seem to adapt better than others—but they are less important in determining temperature stress than is length of exposure.[94] That is, most individuals who have the time to adapt to a large temperature change can do so, but some never acclimatize. A study of behavior in very cold conditions found that those who were older, more depressed, and had no previous cold-caused injury were less likely to engage in preventive actions than others.[95]

Social Behavior. Quite a number of laboratory studies have examined the effects of temperature on social behavior. For example, students who were exposed to fairly hot temperatures (91°F) wrote endings to stories.[96] When the first part of the stories contained potential cues to aggression, students in the hot conditions completed their stories with material that contained more references to aggression. Whether these conclusions would generalize to typical work settings is not clear. In addition, we should recall that many work settings have well-controlled temperatures. Heat or cold sufficiently deviant from the comfort envelope to affect social behavior is uncommon for many employees.

We might assume that moderately hot temperatures always influence employees to be more aggressive toward their coworkers. However, a series of studies suggest that the relation between heat and aggression can vary, depending on such factors as the length of exposure, whether a person has access to fluids, and even whether those fluids are alcohol-based drinks or not.[97] Until these influences are sorted out, we must be cautious in our conclusions about how heat affects aggression.

Let's turn briefly to the positive side of social behavior. Several studies have shown that moderate variations in temperature do not increase or decrease helping behavior.[98] If temperature does affect helping behavior less than noise does, employers in client-serving organizations should pay more attention to noise problems than to temperature problems. This is a tentative conclusion, however, because a direct comparison of noise and temperature on helping has not yet been attempted.

◆ **IN SUM,** *indoor climate is measured by effective temperature, which includes humidity and air movement as well as temperature. Relatively extreme effective temperatures do not affect many work behaviors unless core body temperature is altered. The effects of temperature are also usually muffled by access to heavier or lighter clothing. The amazing variety of temperature effects reported partly are the result of these measurement and clothing factors, as well as many others, including degree of acclimatization, knowledge of coping strategies, motivation, and type of work. Engineers have found well-described comfort envelopes, but environmental psychologists have discovered that comfort depends on perception as well as actual effective temperature and that optimal performance may be found outside the comfort envelope. Stress occurs when individuals are initially subjected to effective temperatures farther outside the comfort envelope, but many can adapt to these more extreme temperatures after longer-term exposure to them.*

Air

The ingredients of air can play an important role in work behavior and health. Recently, considerable concern has been expressed over the effects of air pollutants in offices. Many newer buildings are tightly sealed for energy conservation; equipment designed to filter and recirculate air have replaced the openable window. Sometimes the equipment malfunctions, is not maintained properly, or sucks in tainted air and then distributes it. In one famous case, air from a government health building's lab was circulated to offices. The air contained viruses that had been sent to the lab for testing. Ironically, many employees got sick in a building devoted to the promotion of health!

Performance. Does air affect actual performance at work? It is known that commuters trying to *reach* work occasionally have problems, such as when carbon monoxide levels on roads are high enough to affect driving ability.[99] However, employees engaged in normal amounts of manual labor are essentially unaffected by

moderate doses of carbon monoxide.[100] But most studies so far have studied only short-term performance (a few hours) and have used healthy young males. Carbon monoxide and other pollutants may yet be found to affect performance in more sensitive groups or over longer time periods.[101]

Some kinds of work are affected by carbon monoxide and other air pollutants that restrict the oxygen-carrying capacity of the blood. For example, when a job calls for prolonged alertness but generally involves low stimulation, performance may be affected by moderate levels of carbon monoxide.[102] Such concentrations may be found in buildings close to major roadways.

Some air pollutants (e.g., carbon monoxide) are poisonous but odor free. Bad-smelling air seems to have its own effects. One study reports that malodorous air impaired performance of a relatively complex task (proofreading) but not in a relatively simple one (arithmetic).[103]

Another aspect of air that has been suspected of affecting performance is the level of air ionization. Clean rural air contains about 1,200 positive and 1,000 negative ions per cubic centimeter of air; modern urban air-conditioned offices contain about 150 positive and 50 negative ions.[104] On the assumption that modern industrial cities and workplaces are deficient in negative ions, some individuals have become convinced that negative ion generators are valuable. (I know two reputable environmental psychologists who have the machines in their offices.)

The popular press and manufacturers of ion generators have made so many exaggerated claims about the alleged benefits of negative air ions that many environmental psychologists scoff at any mention of air ions (except, of course, my two acquaintances!). The U.S. Food and Drug Administration even prohibited the sale of ion generators in the mid-1950s. However, some well-controlled studies do indicate that very high ion concentrations affect performance. One, for example, tested individuals (who did not know the study was about ions) on several simple tasks.[105] When negative ion concentrations were over 4,000 per cubic centimeter, participants' reaction times were significantly faster and they had better motor coordination. Another study found significant improvements in basic perceptual-motor tasks, compared to performance under normal levels, when very high levels of negative ions were present.[106] However, other studies have reported no beneficial effects of high levels of negative ions on performance.[107,108]

The mixed results may occur because individuals differ in their sensitivity to ion concentration. This hypothesis has been tested, although the study examined positive ion concentrations, which are supposed to be harmful, rather than negative ions.[109] The performance of individuals, in general, was not adversely affected by high positive ion concentrations. However, the performance of ion-sensitive subjects (individuals predicted to be more susceptible to the harmful effects of positive ions, based on physiological tests) was worse than that of subjects who were less ion sensitive.

The case of air ionization is a good illustration of an environment-behavior link that is strongly moderated by individual difference factors. Other research on air ions has reported effects for men but not women, for example.[110] Thus, air ion effects seem to differ depending on the sex and physiological sensitivities of individuals (see Figure 12–9).

Further evidence that air ion influence is moderated by personal characteristics comes from a study of ions and aggression.[111] Participants were asked to train others to reduce their heart rate using biofeedback. Participants were to deliver bursts of heat when trainees failed to reduce their heart rates. The trainees, who were actually confederates of the experimenters, pretended to be poor learners. Type A participants (irritable, consistent sense of urgency, strong reactions to stress) exhibited more aggression (delivered more heat to trainees) when high levels of negative ions were present than when low levels of negative ions were present. These results are puzzling because negative ions generally are thought to produce beneficial outcomes. The study's authors speculate that negative ions act as arousers, magnifying one's natural tendencies. For Type A individuals, this may cause an increase in aggressiveness.

A later study provided evidence for this magnification effect of ions. Higher levels of negative ions produced more arousal and seemed to intensify either positive or negative feelings about other people.[112] More negative ions caused subjects to make more errors on a simple cognitive task, as if they were too aroused to be

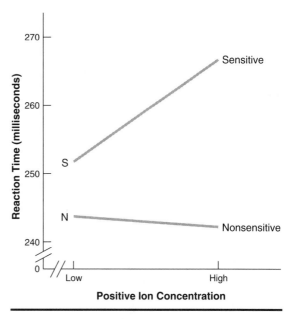

FIGURE 12–9 A simple behavior (reaction time) that is important in many tasks such as driving and operating equipment is harmed by high concentrations of positive air ions for those who are ion-sensitive (i.e., have low autonomic lability) but not for those who are not ion-sensitive.

accurate. Perhaps the important point here is that ions have complex effects that vary with different individuals and may not affect many individuals at all.

Another moderating variable is perceived control. A study of malodorous air found that when the air smelled bad *and* participants believed they could not avoid the smell, their persistence at working on puzzles declined significantly.[113]

Recently, researchers have investigated the possible benefits of artificial fragrances on work performance. Some reports in the popular press have claimed performance increases of 54 percent, but these studies have not been published in scientific journals. A few well-controlled studies have shown that fragrances improve performance on certain tasks, such as monitoring simple displays on a computer screen and completing word puzzles.[114,115] Probably there is no particular magic fragrance; rather, any odor that a person finds pleasant will work. Also, the effects of fragrances appear to decline over the course of an hour or so.

ROBERT A. BARON'S
research on air ionization, scents, and other workplace social and physical features have illuminated workplace environmental psychology.

Feelings. The quality of air at work is a growing concern of employees. As speculation and knowledge about potentially harmful fumes from office machines and building materials increases, workers have become more aware of the possible harmful effects of air in their own work spaces. We will focus on two aspects of feelings about air: complaints about perceived inadequacy of air, and changes in emotion that apparently occur without employee awareness that the air has changed.

Among office workers, air quality is one of the most important factors in the environment.[116] Even so, many more office workers feel like complaining about air quality than actually do so.[117] Complaints about air quality depend, in part, how the question is asked. If employees are asked, "What are some of the problems in your workplace?" fewer complaints about air will be registered than if employees are asked, "Is the air in your workplace good quality?"

A story about air in a factory illustrates how important employee perception of atmospheric conditions can be.[118] Many complaints about the stuffiness and lack of movement of the air in the factory were received. The ventilation system was thoroughly checked and found to be working perfectly. Many of the factory's employees had worked outdoors most of their lives, and they felt that buildings *must* be stuffy and breezeless. Then someone devised the idea of attaching streamers to the ventilation outlets near the ceiling. When the employees could see the streamers flying, complaints about air movement stopped.

In everyday offices, drafts and temperature are common problems. If the air moves too quickly, some employees will complain. Researchers now have experimented with various combinations of temperature and air movement and developed a formula to predict how many employees will complain about drafts.[119] For example, at 72°F and air movement of 0.2 meters/second, around 20 percent will complain of drafts, but at the same temperature and air movement of 0.3 meters/second, around 40 percent will complain.

One study attempted to determine the amount of dissatisfaction in everyday buildings.[120] Over 1,000 employees in 9 buildings with no reputation for "building sickness" were surveyed. Some 75 percent reported that too little air circulated "sometimes" or "often." Also, 77 percent said the temperature was too cold and 72 percent said it was too hot "sometimes" or "often." These are very high rates of dissatisfaction, especially among buildings with no reputation for building illness. The statistics suggest that facilities managers and engineers have much work to do to improve conditions for employees.

At least one component of air appears to change people's feelings even when they are unaware of it. That component is the controversial negative ion. Two double-blind studies in Great Britain report improvements in feelings when more negative ions are present. One, in the offices of a large insurance company, found that employees working in greater concentrations of negative ions felt warmer and more alert; they also judged the environment as fresher.[121] In the other, students reported feeling more relaxed and stimulated and less irritable and depressed after six hours of negative ion exposure.[122]

Finally, it appears that changing the air by infusing it with artificial fragrances is risky: Some individuals may be alienated while others may be impressed. Mock job interviews were conducted in one study; applicants wore scents or did not.[123] Female interviewers gave more positive evaluations to applicants who wore perfume or cologne than those who did not. Male interviewers, however, gave more positive evaluations to applicants who wore no scent than they gave to those who did wear some.

Of course, the use of artificial scents is a complicated issue (evaluations probably also depend on how much scent is worn, what sort of clothes are worn with the scent, customary behavior in each workplace, etc.). But it seems that altering local airspace may be perceived as air pollution or air enhancement, depending on the sex of the person making the evaluation.

Health and Stress. Air quality can have drastic effects on health, as the relatives of many legionnaires who attended the fateful convention in 1976 that killed 29 people, made 182 others ill, and gave birth to a new phrase (Legionnaires' disease) will testify. Modern ventilation systems are capable of moving air very efficiently, but if an airborne disease agent gets into the system, the same efficiency becomes a severe liability.

Besides disease-causing microorganisms, air can carry other agents that make people ill, including ozone (emitted by copy machines), tiny airborne particles from asbestos (found in most office buildings dating from the late 1960s), cigarette smoke, and organic solvents such as benzene (found in stencil fluids, copy machine toner, and rubber cement). Most of these agents have been linked to serious diseases, such as cancer, and to a wide variety of troublesome minor problems, including eye irritation, respiratory tract problems, allergies, thyroid disturbance, gastrointestinal cramps, and others.[124]

Both white- and blue-collar workers are exposed to bad air. One survey found that more than 50 percent of factory workers say they are exposed to hazardous air pollution in their work.[125]

Sick buildings are structures that contain airborne health-threatening substances. **Sick building syndrome** refers to the collection of health problems linked to these substances. One study carefully examined the different kinds of building-related problems and concluded that two syndromes exist: **building-related illness** (a cluster of symptoms found in all office buildings to differing degrees) and **building-specific illness** (a cluster of symptoms that occurs only in air-conditioned buildings).[126]

Sick building syndrome is very common. The Environmental Protection Agency (EPA) estimates that 20 to 30 percent of all U.S. office buildings cause health problems—including at the EPA itself.[127] Precisely what causes sick building syndrome is unclear, perhaps because there are multiple causes and multiple symptoms in employees. Modern chemicals, tight sealing, poor ventilation, noxious fungi, bad duct design, a history of smoking, physiological susceptibility, mass psychogenic illness (workers frightening one another into illness), and "complaining personality" have all been offered as possible causes.[128,129]

The sick building phenomenon has become so widely known that one advertisement for an office building to rent sported this headline: "Enjoy Fresh Air! You can open our office windows." Of course, how fresh that outdoor air is depends on where you live; in some cases, the filtered indoor air may be cleaner than outdoor air. Also, two virtues clash when windows open: The fresh air is usually nice, but heated (or cooled) air simultaneously leaves, which is not very good energy conservation.

Whether any particular employee is affected by air quality depends on the concentration of the hazardous agent, the coping strategies of the employee, the employee's basic physiological sensitivity, and whether the employee has control of temperature and ventilation. In general, sick building syndrome is partly explained by environmental factors and partly by personal factors.[130] Relatively low levels of oxygen in a tightly sealed building, for example, may affect only those workers who do not get outside for a break or those who require larger amounts of oxygen (such as employees engaged in heavy labor). But when oxygen levels sink very low, nearly everyone will be affected.

A few years ago, the trading floor of the Toronto Stock Exchange had to be cleared when many employees and traders began to faint, speak incoherently, and complain of numbness in their chests. Apparently, all the doors and windows had been closed and the busy traders simply used up all the available oxygen! Some evidence suggests that air conditioning alone (without any airborne pathogens) may cause increases in the frequency of eye, nose, and throat irritation.[131]

Control over the controls is also related to employee health. In a survey of 1,100 employees, those who could not control the air conditioning in their work space were three times as likely to report building illness symptoms such as headaches, fatigue, and respiratory irritation as employees who could control the air conditioning.[132]

Air ions have been implicated in health as well as performance. In three offices, researchers compared the frequency of headaches reported when negative ion generators were on and off (without the knowledge of the employees).[133] When they were on, headache reports dropped by about 40 percent.

Social Behavior. Air in a workplace can even affect social relations. Most relevant studies have focused on cigarette smoke and bad odors. In one study, enlisted army personnel were asked to sit in pairs and work on a manual task.[134] After the session, during which their smoking had been observed, participants were asked to indicate how much they liked each other. (They were strangers before meeting for the session, so previous experience was not a factor.) Nonsmokers liked coworkers who did not smoke more than they liked coworkers who did smoke. Those who normally smoked but did not in the session preferred others who smoked courteously (i.e., made attempts to blow the smoke away from the other person). Those who normally smoked and did so in the session preferred partners who smoked *discourteously* (i.e., blew smoke in their faces)! Another study produced a compatible result. When nonsmokers were faced with smoke, they reported feeling aggressive.[135] It appears we like others who share our smoking preferences.

The findings relevant to bad odors are less straightforward; research indicates that attraction toward others under smelly conditions depends on whether we have attitudes similar to those of the other. If we think alike, the bad smells seem to *increase* attraction.[136] Sharing an odorous disaster with someone similar to ourselves apparently causes us to draw together, possibly against some other person in the vicinity who is not like us (and might even be the source of those bad smells!).

Moderately bad odors may even cause aggressiveness toward unfamiliar others. In a laboratory study, participants in another study decided to shock another person more when the room smelled bad.[137] Once again, these effects are probably moderated by personal characteristics of the individuals involved. For example, when subjects in one study were highly motivated to work, their annoyance with cigarette smoke was relatively small. When they were not very motivated to work, however, they were much more annoyed by cigarette smoke.[138]

◆ **IN SUM,** *several components of air—including carbon monoxide, air ions, and bad odors—may affect performance, but the effects are not striking under normal conditions. Extremely low concentrations of negative ions may affect some basic cognitive processes and extremely high concentrations may facilitate them, but for the average person these effects are not strong. However, long-term exposure, differential physiological sensitivity, and psycho-logical mediators such as perceived control help to explain why the performance of some individuals is affected but that of others is not. When it carries chemical impurities or disease-causing organisms, air can seriously impair health. Air quality is a growing concern of employees. Lack of control over it when air is noticeably bad may affect persistence at work and, in some circumstances, foster negative feelings among employees.*

Light, Color, and Windows

Light is essential to work, of course. Without it, few industrial or office jobs can be performed at all. However, natural or artificial light is nearly always available. Research on light primarily involves comparisons of different light:

- Sources (sunlight, incandescent, fluorescent, sodium vapor)
- Fixtures (ceiling, desk, floorlamp)
- Amounts (illuminance)
- Arrangements (angle at which it strikes the work surface, uniform versus nonuniform)

The light sources vary in which parts of the visible spectrum are emphasized, which means they have different color tones. Color is less essential than light in the workplace, but is still important for safety coding and wayfinding.

Lighting primarily has been studied from an engineering standpoint, using specialized equipment and terminology. Often, in the search for optimal lighting from a purely technical point of view, the human dimension has been lost (see Table 12–1). For example, one of the main reasons for the widespread installation of fluorescent tubes is their energy efficiency. An incandescent bulb transforms about 10 percent of the electricity it uses into light; the other 90 percent is transformed into heat. The ratio for a typical fluorescent bulb is about 20 percent light to 80 percent heat. Thus, although fluorescent bulbs are about twice as efficient at producing light, many people simply do not like them. Recently, considerable attention has been focused on full-spectrum lamps, which are fluorescent bulbs that roughly mimic the spectral distribution of sunlight.

TABLE 12-1   Illumination Ranges Recommended for Different Activities

I. Illuminance Categories and Illuminance Values for Generic Types of Activities in Interiors

Type of Activity	Illuminance Category	Ranges of Illuminances		Reference Work-Plane
		Lux	Footcandles	
Public spaces with dark surroundings	A	20–30–50	2–3–5	General lighting throughout spaces
Simple orientation for short temporary visits	B	50–75–100	5–7.5–10	
Working spaces where visual tasks are only occasionally performed	C	100–150–200	10–15–20	
Performance of visual tasks of high contrast or large size	D	200–300–500	20–30–50	Illuminance on task
Performance of visual tasks of medium contrast or small size	E	500–750–1000	50–75–100	
Performance of visual tasks of low contrast or very small size	F	1000–1500–2000	100–150–200	
Performance of visual tasks of low contrast and very small size over a prolonged period	G	2000–3000–5000	200–300–500	Illuminance on task, obtained by a combination of general and local (supplementary lighting)
Performance of very prolonged and exacting visual tasks	H	5000–7500–10000	500–750–1000	
Performance of very special visual tasks of extremely low contrast and small size	I	1000–1500–20000	1000–1500–2000	

II. Illuminance Categories for Selected Commercial, Institutional, Residential and Public Assembly Interiors

Area/Activity	Illuminance Category	Area/Activity	Illuminance Category
Auditoriums		**Barber shops and beauty parlors**	E
Assembly	C	**Club and lodge rooms**	
Social activity	B	Lounge and reading	D
Banks		**Conference rooms**	
Lobby		Conferring	D
General	C	Critical seeing (refer to individual task)	
Writing area	D	**Court rooms**	
Tellers' stations	E	Seating area	C
		Court activity area	E
		Dance halls and discotheques	B

How does light affect performance, feelings, social behavior, health, and safety? Let's look first at performance.

Performance. Within the normal range of lighting, from slightly dim to quite bright, performance of office tasks increases with more light.[139,140] However, this statement requires several qualifications.

1. Optimal light level depends on the task. Proofreading fine print requires much more light than a round table discussion.

2. The work surface is important. If the surface is shiny, higher light levels—especially from undiffused sources such as a bare bulb—will cause glare, which definitely cuts into the performance of many tasks. A particularly important problem is glare from video display screens.

3. The angle of the light is important. For some tasks, performance is enhanced when light is very diffused. Surgery and assembly-line work are examples. For other tasks, the definition of surfaces provided by shadows means that carefully angled lighting is best. Examples of such tasks include searching for flaws in fabrics or other manufactured objects that should have uniform surfaces.

For these reasons, one conclusion on which engineers and environmental psychologists generally agree is that lighting should be tailored, if possible, to each task and individual. If implemented, this policy would probably result in much greater use of immediate or local lighting and decreased use of lighting intended to serve everyone working in a large area. In general, a positive effect of more localized lighting would be energy savings realized from the reduced use of light in work areas that do not require their current, probably excessive, levels of light.[141] Energy-efficient lighting does not seem to harm work performance.[142]

The full-spectrum lamp has received much attention, primarily because of its effect on some forms of clinical depression (seasonal affective disorder). From such reports, some observers have assumed that it must have a broad range of benefits, such as improved performance for typical (nondepressed) office employees. In one study, full-spectrum lamps were compared with regular cool-white and warm-white lamps.[143] Over a broad range of cognitive tasks, no performance increment could be found for full-spectrum bulbs.

A follow-up study investigated the possibility that *belief* in the full-spectrum lamp produced performance increases.[144] As before, no performance-enhancing qualities of full-spectrum lamps were found, but when subjects were *told* that full-spectrum lamps had benefits, their reading performance increased. Oddly, however, reading performance also improved when they were told that claims about the benefits of the lamps were highly exaggerated!

Increased light appears to expand arousal level. A clear demonstration of this came in an investigation of the alertness of shift workers.[145] After working one night under quite dim light, employees worked the next night under dim, moderate, or bright illumination. Those who worked in the brightest condition were the most alert and their cognitive performance was significantly enhanced.

Alertness is a problem with shiftwork; another study assessed the possibility of adjusting employees' biological clocks so they became more alert at night and less alert during the day.[146] A light was used as a "pacemaker" to gradually adapt the employees to brightness at night and darkness during the day; the experimenters claim this was effective.

In another study, four methods of lighting graveyard shifts were compared.[147] Special skylights were used that could keep illumination high, low, increase it across the shift, or decrease it. High and decreasing light levels improved performance on complex cognitive tasks, compared to the other light conditions. Presumably high levels of light physiologically arouse employees; decreasing levels appear to work because high levels of light at the start of a shift are enough to counteract the normal sleepiness at that time of day. Apparently, once aroused at that time of day, employees do not need continuing stimulation from light.

Light levels may influence the amount of time employees spend in the office. A study of office lightness found that, in general, when offices are darker, employees are more likely to leave when they have the choice, such as eating lunch out of the office versus eating at their desks.[148]

In general, giving employees control over their work environment and other aspects of their job is thought to be good and to produce better performance.

Is the same true for lighting? A laboratory study that simulated office work conditions gave some subjects control over the type of lighting they could use to work and denied control to other employees.[149] Unexpectedly, those who were given control performed worse on creativity tasks than those denied control. This is consistent with the idea (introduced earlier during the discussion of temperature) that control is desirable but carries with it the cost of being responsible and having to make decisions. Perhaps this cost affects creative work.

As noted earlier, little quality research on color has been conducted that directly relates to workplaces. Color has three dimensions: hue, saturation, and brightness. **Hue** is the proper name for what people call color in everyday language (i.e., red, blue, green, etc.). **Saturation** refers to the purity of the hue (i.e., the extent to which it is the only hue present). **Brightness** refers to the luminance or light/dark aspect of the color.

One recent study illustrates how color may have unexpected effects.[150] Do you think office workers type faster in offices with red or blue walls? Subjects in the study typed in red or blue office settings, then typed again either in the same-colored setting or the other-colored setting. Subjects made no more errors in one color setting or the other, but they made more when they moved to a different-colored setting.

Feelings. Some surveys indicate that most employees are generally satisfied with lighting,[151] but others report that complaints are frequent.[152] The resolution of this contradiction probably rests with the type of work an employee does. Those who perform visually demanding work often believe lighting is inadequate, but those whose work is not visually demanding believe their light is adequate. In addition, the importance of lighting varies with office type. Employees in enclosed offices rate lighting as more important than employees in open-plan offices.[153] In general, darker offices and factories may be less satisfying.[154,155]

Some of the newer kinds of artificial lamps produce dissatisfaction because they render colors strangely. Most everyone has had the experience of buying clothing that appears apricot in the store but looks more like carrot at home.

At work, poor lighting can do the same to skin color. Researchers asked subjects to judge the acceptability of a familiar face (their own) under several different light sources.[156] Incandescent and warm-white incandescent lamps were the most acceptable, followed by cool-white and "improved" mercury lamps. At the bottom were two kinds of high-pressure sodium lamps. The importance of semipermanent off-color appearance at work has not yet been demonstrated, but it would not seem to be conducive to good interpersonal relations on the job. John Flynn, a pioneer in light research, demonstrated with his colleagues that individuals find a variety of light sources and types more interesting than single-source lighting or repetitive use of one kind of fixture.[157]

Employee feelings about another source of light are clear: Light from outdoors is very desirable.[158] Although sunlight has high potential for glare, employees would like to be located near a window. Those who are located farther from a window are more often unhappy about lighting. Too much sunlight penetration, however, is not relaxing.[159] Windows, of course, also offer views, which contribute to satisfaction.[160] Windows offer the opportunity to stay in touch with conditions in the outside world—weather, time of day, and the action on the street. No evidence suggests that windows improve work performance,[161] but windows do reduce boredom and increase overall job satisfaction.[162]

Employees in windowless offices appear to compensate; they put twice as much visual material—especially nature themes—on their walls as occupants of windowed offices.[163] Workers even want inside windows (from room to room), especially if the room being viewed has a window to the outdoors.[164] Given that employees definitely prefer windows, researchers now examine more specific questions, such as the nature of preferences for different room sizes and tasks. Apparently, we prefer proportionately larger windows in smaller rooms, for example, and smaller windows for a computer work room than for an office.[165]

So far, we have concentrated on feelings *about* lighting. What sort of feelings are created *by* light? Lighting designers certainly believe that different arrangements of light create different moods, but evidence concerning this belief is not abundant. When the relevant studies are carefully examined, the claim that lighting changes mood is not strongly supported. One recent study, however, shows that the *amount* of light may affect mood.[166] Subjects rated literary passages under bright (1,830 lux), normal (502 lux), or dim (114 lux) light. (Ten **lux**, the metric measure, are about equal to one footcandle.) Subjects gave these passages more intense or extreme emotional ratings under bright *or* dim light than under normal light. This suggests that emotion is heightened by lighting that strongly differs (in amount) from the level we are used to.

Health, Aging, Stress, and Safety. Light is important for health. Ultraviolet light, rare indoors, assists in the formation of vitamin D and in the body's processing of calcium. More broadly, the advent of artificial lighting has changed the biological rhythms of most industrialized peoples. Glare causes eyestrain. Glare is found in a surprising variety of places in the typical office, from shiny pages in a book (indirect glare) to sunlight streaming into our eyes from behind someone we are talking to (direct glare).

Nevertheless, as noted earlier, most recent complaints about glare have come from video display terminal (VDT) operators. This problem has arisen because offices and VDTs originally were not well designed for each other. For example, office lighting is normally from the ceiling; indirect glare caused by the reflection of the lights from the screen causes eyestrain for the VDT user. Offices and VDTs gradually are accommodating one another. Now, of course, computers come with coated screens and swivel heads so the operator can orient the screen to minimize glare. Localized lighting, placed at the side or rear of the VDT, can eliminate glare.

As we age, the ability of our eyes to gather light diminishes; we need more light to experience the same level of environmental illumination. People 60 years old, on average, need about three times as much illumination as people 20 years old.[167] Thus, workplace lighting must take into account the age of employees. But merely increasing the level of light is not effective; the possible increase in glare must also be considered.[168] In addition, high illumination levels from fluorescent lamps, especially full-spectrum lamps, make offices seem less desirable in social terms, increase visual discomfort, and physiologically arouse people.[169]

Control over lighting at work might may even affect health beyond eyestrain. Employees in one large-scale survey who personally could change their lighting conditions were three times less likely to report building illness symptoms.[170]

Employee safety, particularly in industrial settings, is obviously threatened by inadequate lighting. Considerable research, for example, has been devoted to the reduction of glare from dangerous areas such as the surface of the saw bed in the vicinity of the saw blade. Proper illumination in transit areas of a building also prevents accidents. In European factory studies, increases in illumination from 150 to 1,000 lux resulted in accident rate reductions of 50 percent.[171]

Social Behavior. Can light affect social behavior on the job? This does not seem like a promising avenue of research, but lighting occasionally prompts discussions about how bad or good it is or makes employees literally look bad or good to others. Unfortunately, apart from the just-mentioned study that examined the acceptability of one's own face under different lights, only one study examined whether others look more or less attractive. It found no evidence that full-spectrum or regular fluorescent lamps make any difference.[172] However, different *amounts* of light may affect appraisals of other employees' work.[173] When the lighting level in the study was quite low (150 lux), performance appraisals were more positive and subjects were more willing to donate volunteer time than when the lighting level was quite high (1,500 lux).

According to an arousal model, increased illumination should produce more activity in general and more communication in particular. However, only two studies have examined this question. One found that brighter light produced *less* "conversational energy" than soft light, contrary to theory.[174] The other found that when participants wrote letters to one another, they wrote more intimate things and they wrote for a longer time in brighter light, which is consistent with the arousal view.[175]

Different spectral qualities of light (slightly different color tones) may affect certain other judgments at work. Warm-white fluorescent lamps, which look slightly more orange-red, may produce greater desire to resolve conflicts through collaboration and to donate more time; cool-white lamps may produce a desire to resolve conflicts through avoidance.[176]

◆ *IN SUM, light affects work behavior primarily when it is quite insufficient (leading to low productivity and accidents) or improperly placed (leading to glare and eyestrain). Office lighting often is excessive. Many employees dislike fluorescent and other newer forms of lighting, some of which distort color. Carefully placed local lighting could resolve some of these problems. Access to natural light and views is psychologically important.*

Space: Density and Arrangements

How does space—the amount of it and how it is arranged—affect employees? This chapter emphasizes research in office and shop settings, which comprise most contemporary work settings. However, the growth of computers and related telecommunications systems is now increasing the feasibility of working away from the traditional workplace. This totally different use of space for work will be briefly discussed first.

Working Away from Work. The trend of working away from the work office has been called **computer-assisted work decentralization (CAWD)** or **telecommuting**.[177] In the popular media, articles about CAWD depict a smiling employee sitting in a den at home, working at a computer terminal in front of a large picture window looking over an idyllic scene. Some suggest that soon most of us will be working at home. However, a more thoughtful analysis shows that CAWD is not for everyone. It may promise an end to commuting and a reduction in the cost of working (such as clothing costs), but it has more potential for employees whose work is based on information than for those in manufacturing, it can conflict with home life, it may create social isolation, and it can pose supervisory problems. Even some employees whose jobs *could* largely be accomplished at home (e.g., stockbrokers) prefer the office as a place that is specifically set aside for work, keeps them in touch, and sustains their motivation.[178]

Nevertheless, CAWD may be right for some employees. In one study of female insurance claims processors, a high level of satisfaction was found, along with a 69 percent drop in absenteeism and a 10 percent increase in productivity.[179] One experiment with a "halfway house"—a workplace between the office and the home—will be described later in this chapter.

FRANK BECKER'S *studies of quality work environments and telecommuting have been influential.*

Traditional research on work spaces emphasizes the study of **human factors,** or **ergonomics**. Volumes of information have been produced on how machines ought to be designed to suit human needs in the immediate workstation—for example, how best to lay out the controls in a fighter plane cockpit or how chairs for secretaries ought to be designed.[180]

Research at a broader level of analysis—that is, how best to arrange the office or industrial floor as a whole—is more directly relevant to environmental psychology. Some individuals work in very cramped spaces, such as submarines; others work in spaces that are too wide open for them (there is a basis for all those lonesome cowboy songs). In some offices and industrial settings, space may be almost entirely open, such as in an airplane manufacturer's hangar or the old office bullpen, or it may be so private that employees must pass several guardian secretaries to gain the ear of the big boss. What *is* known about the effects of spatial arrangements?

Performance. Few studies have compared actual performance of a job in different work space arrangements. One difficulty is in measuring performance accurately, particularly in white-collar jobs, although some useful beginnings have been made.[181] Somewhat indirect measures of performance, such as withdrawal (leaving the workplace or not when you have a choice) and turnover (the rate of resignations), have been used in a few studies. When an office has fewer barriers (walls or partitions), withdrawal rates are higher.[182]

If we can generalize from laboratory studies, offices with high employee densities (i.e., little space for each person) jeopardize performance, especially if the work involves physical mobility and interaction.[183] People literally may trip over each other as they try to do their jobs. The amount of space and how it is arranged have joint effects. When less space is available, when employees are closer together, *and* when fewer barriers or enclosures are present, higher turnover and withdrawal rates are found.[184] Employee performance ratings decline when people work in offices with a combination of higher density and closer interpersonal distances, and when they have difficulty screening out unwanted stimulation.[185]

In many organizations, performance depends on good communication. Open-plan arrangements are said to facilitate communication, which *sounds* as if they increase productivity. Unfortunately, it seems that this does not follow, mainly because the increased communication is very often not work oriented. Open-plan offices seem to produce more social communication but not more productive communication.[186]

Attitudes about spatial arrangements may not correspond to performance-related behaviors in spatial arrangements. One research team investigated the possibility that open-plan offices would drive employees away.[187] College professors usually can choose to spend parts of their workdays in their offices, at libraries, or in their homes. Researchers counted the actual number of occupied and unoccupied faculty offices in colleges that had open-plan and private offices. Even though faculty in the open-plan arrangements expressed dissatisfaction with working there, they were present in their offices just as often as were faculty in private offices.

Are interviews conducted in offices affected by privacy or sound level? Low privacy and high sound levels produced dissatisfaction in one interview study, but participants did not speak less with the interviewer under those conditions.[188]

These and other studies suggest that employees strive to achieve a certain amount of work in spite of negative environmental influences. They may often be successful in doing so, but the cost of coping with an inhospitable setting over the long term may be high.

Feelings. When spatial arrangements are inadequate, employees sometimes are quite willing to say so. Too often, however, employees adapt to bad situations or do not realize that the surroundings could be better. I call this unfortunate form of adaptation **environmental numbness**.[189] In such cases, employees do not spontaneously report their feelings about the workplace. Overloaded employees may be even more environmentally numb than others; overworked clerical employees complain less than others about temperature and density problems.[190]

On the other hand, many surveys have shown that if employees are asked their opinions and feelings about their workplace, they will respond quickly and fully. Where I teach, for example, we sent out to campus employees a long survey regarding the office environment. In only a few days, with no reminders, over 80 percent of the surveys were returned—an exceptionally high return rate for mass-distributed surveys.

The biggest issue in workplace arrangements at present is whether open-plan offices are beneficial. The majority of employee reactions to open-plan offices are negative.[191] A few positive responses come from employees who have very recently moved from dingy, cramped former offices into bright new ones (a novelty effect) or from employees who enjoy the social aspects of work more than they enjoy the work itself. Those whose work requires confidentiality and supervisory-professional employees are especially unhappy with open-space designs.[192]

Further evidence that various groups of employees are affected differently comes in a study of professional, managerial, and clerical employees who moved from traditional enclosed offices to open-plan offices.[193] Professionals were affected least; clerical and managerial employees were affected the most. Clerical staff experienced an increase in privacy and the adequacy of their work area; managers reported that their privacy and work area worsened.

Despite overwhelming evidence of employee rejection, the percentage of all offices that are arranged in open plans continues to increase. Why do open-plan arrangements continue to grow in popularity? One reason is that employee resentment has taken a long time to be documented, collated, and fed back to organization heads. A second reason is that organization heads are still being sold very effectively on the alleged advantages of open-plan offices, including better tax breaks on furniture. For example, a marketing manager for open-plan systems will argue that carpeting costs can be cut by 20 to 30 percent because installers do not have to cut around walls and partitions.[194]

What are the long-term consequences of choosing tax breaks and a 20 to 30 percent savings on carpet costs over the considerable dissatisfaction of employees? One study, typical of many reporting employee unhappiness with open-plan offices, discovered that not only are individuals merely dissatisfied with open-plan offices but they also begin to feel their jobs are less significant.[195] Another study found that employees in more accessible desks reported their tasks to be less significant and they spent less discretionary time (during coffee breaks and lunch) in the office.[196]

A few organizations have begun to respond to these problems. One computer company, for example, has implemented a "neighborhood" concept—small groups of employees in an open area with walls between the neighborhoods. Whether the open-plan office can be adapted to fit human needs remains to be demonstrated; its research record, to date, is generally poor.

One study did report that increasing employee density, a common by-product of moving to open-plan offices, *increased* job satisfaction. However, many other aspects of the environment were changed at the same time that density was changed, so it was difficult to conclude that density caused more satisfaction.[197] When employees of another organization were moved from a fully open (no partitions) space to another fully open office with lower density or to an open plan (with partitions), they felt less crowded, more private, and more satisfied.[198]

Open plans may not be the worst form of spatial arrangement. When clerical employees in a health organization moved from a totally open (bullpen) arrangement to an open-plan arrangement with low partitions, their performance improved.[199] Thus, open offices are not necessarily unsatisfactory, but if (as often happens), they do not allow enough space for each employee, they will not be satisfactory.

Is the problem with open-plan offices caused by a lack of privacy or the sheer number of others one can see? One study examined the effect of working with a large or small *number* of coworkers, rather than spatial density or arrangements.[200] This perspective, based on behavior setting and staffing theories, hypothesizes that when too many or too few staff members operate behavior settings, performance and feelings are affected.[201,202] You may recall from Chapter 11 how students were affected by attending large versus small schools.

Researchers studied 22 bank branches that varied in size. The researchers assumed that branches with many employees were relatively overstaffed and that branches with few employees were relatively understaffed. Employees in small branches did report greater **setting claim**—the sense that they are needed, perform important jobs, and work hard. In turn, greater setting claim was significantly related to greater job satisfaction, greater identification with the bank, and less tardiness. Thus, space in the sense of staffing level is another important component of feelings about work.

Researchers have begun to examine combined influences. For example, employees are more dissatisfied when they work in offices with higher densities and closer interpersonal distances, *and* have difficulty screening out unwanted stimulation.[203] When offices have few enclosures, place employees close together, are relatively dark, and are occupied by larger numbers of employees, dissatisfaction is, not surprisingly, higher.[204]

A few researchers have investigated another dimension of feelings in offices—the reactions of visitors. Have you ever entered someone's office and quickly developed an impression of the person who works there? Or have you wondered what your office or your organization's reception area may be communicating to visitors? One study reports that desk placement, display of status symbols, and tidiness were related to visitors' feelings and their perceptions of the office occupant[205] (see Figure 12–10).

Some findings were obvious. A tidy office creates the impression that the occupant is organized, a display of status symbols (such as diplomas and awards) makes visitors believe the occupant is higher in rank, and a messy desk makes them think the occupant is busy and rushed. Other findings were not quite so obvious. An office with neat stacks of papers—as opposed to an office that is messy or extremely tidy—makes visitors feel comfortable and welcome. Visitors also seem to think that occupants of such offices are high achievers. Desk placement may be open (placed against a wall so that the office occupant has no barriers between self and visitor) or closed (placed between self and visitor). Open arrangements make visitors feel welcome and suggest to them that you are extraverted and have confidence in dealing with others.

FIGURE 12–10 Office appearance creates impressions. What sort of impression would you develop about this office's occupant?

Of course, the observer's own character makes a difference, too. Not everyone prefers tidy offices; sensation seekers seem to prefer messier offices than nonsensation seekers.[206] Whether or not the office's occupant is present also seems to matter: A messy office without an occupant produced favorable ratings of the occupant, but these impressions were lessened or even reversed when the occupant was seen in the midst of the messy or tidy office.[207]

In another investigation, informal seating positions (kitty corner or side by side) elicited more positive evaluations of the office occupant's concern for visitors than did a more formal seating position (directly opposite).[208] When the office occupant chose to sit at a small conference table in the office rather than at a desk, the host was seen as more friendly, caring, helpful, and open minded, but less authoritative. Thus, the mere arrangement of one's office can have a variety of important influences on the impressions of visitors.

The impression made by the organization as a whole depends, in part, on visitor impressions of reception or lobby areas. Most organizations are aware of this and make some effort to create a positive impression with their reception areas. But what is a positive impression, exactly?

One view is that such areas vary in two important ways: the amount of control and the amount of consid-

eration that is implied by the decor of the lobby or reception area.[209] The message that control (order, stability, rigidity) is important to an organization is conveyed by the display of flags, official seals, logos, and emblems. The message that consideration (warmth, comfort, ease, and goodness of communication) is important is conveyed by plants, art, magazines, and furniture arranged in a sociopetal manner.

These control and consideration dimensions are not salient to everyone. In a study of reception areas, students differentiated reception areas only on the basis of high versus low consideration, whereas executives differentiated them on the basis of both dimensions.[210] Thus, in general, visitors' perceptions of organizations are based, in part, on the design and decor of reception areas.

Health and Stress. Might the very arrangement and amount of space in an office affect employee health? That health might be affected by poor air quality, extreme temperatures, or even noise seems likely, but space itself? In one study, office employees who worked with fewer enclosures surrounding them and with more coworkers reported more fatigue and psychosomatic complaints, particularly if they were nonscreeners.[211] In another, 1,200 employees who worked in enclosed versus open-plan offices were surveyed.[212] In open-plan offices, about 40 percent of employees said they "frequently" suffered from headaches, whereas only 20 percent of employees in enclosed offices said they "frequently" had headaches. These findings that employee health may be compromised by open-plan arrangements are serious and warrant further investigation. Satisfaction, productivity, and interpersonal relations all will suffer if employees are often tired or feeling sick at work.

Social Behavior. Open-plan offices are supposed to facilitate communication. Most, but not all, research supports this view. The mixed results may be explained by realizing that different kinds of communication may increase or decrease in open offices. As I said earlier, necessary and desirable communication may decrease, but unwanted and interfering communication increases.[213] In open-plan offices, compared with enclosed offices, supervisory feedback and communication with other departments is greater, but confidential communication is less.[214] A study of two high-technology firms showed that more enclosures actually was associated with increased communication—having a door or walls or higher partitions was correlated with increased time spent working with others.[215] Thus, open-plan offices may increase communication, but this is not always desirable; in fact, enclosed office arrangements may encourage more useful forms of communication.

Another dimension of social behavior—status—is related to office arrangements. Supervisory employees typically have different kinds of space than nonsupervisory employees. They have more space, more freedom to personalize, more expensive furniture, and more means (such as walls and doors) of regulating the access of others to their space.[216] Space and furnishings are very important to employees; the best way to show just how important is to suggest that it be taken away from them. This threat of **environmental deprivation** even makes normally soft-spoken executives turn red and turn up the volume.[217]

When privacy becomes an issue in the office, how do employees try to achieve it? They can use verbal means (e.g., "I'm busy, please come back later"), nonverbal means (e.g., a sign on the door), or environmental means (e.g., closing the door) for regulating

interaction. A study of school administrators showed that they avoided using privacy mechanisms that required direct rejection of others (e.g., asking them to call back or to schedule an appointment with a secretary).[218] Instead, the administrators tended to use indirect forms of rejection (e.g., avoiding others by coming in early or staying late). They also favored combinations of mechanisms that all give the same message, especially when this could be justified by a heavy workload or confidential meeting.

By choosing an open-plan arrangement, the organization saves money, but the new arrangements often mean that employees lose a private office and gain a partitioned space in the midst of peers and subordinates. The pursuit of status is often considered hollow and vain, but status symbols can help to create and develop the impression among employees that a sense of order guides the organization's allocation of resources (such as space). The larger, more private or better-furnished office may also serve as a way to recognize and reward achievement.[219] Status seeking becomes an end in itself for some individuals, but when work space arrangements are carefully managed, larger and better work spaces may be a reasonable way to concretely inform employees that the organization values their work.

Besides the physical qualities of a space—size of the office, desk, couch, or plant; whether the office is in a corner, has closable doors, or a private washroom—another important dimension of work space arrangement is the employee's freedom (or not) to personalize the immediate work area. Some organizations forbid any posters, pictures, or other employee contributions to the decor, fearing that an expensive overall interior design scheme will be compromised.

However, such edicts may backfire. When employees are heavily restricted, they lose a feeling of personal control over their work, which increases stress, decreases satisfaction, and, perhaps, decreases productivity.[220] Facility managers are faced with a choice. Are the aesthetic values of a uniform design scheme more important than the dissatisfaction of their employees?

At present, the vast majority of workplaces are designed *for* employees, rather than *with* them. Recently, movement in this direction has resulted in tentative or even token efforts to involve employees, but they are not yet sufficient in most cases. Designers undoubtedly have good intentions, but without fully involving those who know themselves and their work best—the employees—their designs usually will suffer, often in important ways.

Employee performance, feelings, and social behavior are importantly affected by spatial arrangements. Employee participation in design will be covered in detail in a later chapter. The important point for now is simply that much more needs to be done to involve employees in the shaping of the spaces in which they will spend many of the best years of their lives.

◆ *IN SUM, naturally occurring spatial arrangements have few documented effects on performance, but employees are very sensitive to space and unhappy with many existing arrangements. Many open-plan arrangements reduce desirable communication and increase undesirable communication. Office arrangements lead visitors to form impressions of the character and status of the person in the office. Yet, many organizations restrict the degree to which employees may arrange or personalize their offices and fail to adequately consult employees when offices are planned.*

◆ TRAVEL: GETTING AWAY ◆ TO A NEW ENVIRONMENT

For most employees, the time for a vacation eventually arrives. Over the last century, the amount of time the average person spends at work has been shrinking; we have more and more time for leisure. We may choose to leave our everyday surroundings for any of a vast array of destinations. Leisure-related behavior has been under increasing scrutiny by a variety of social scientists, including environmental psychologists[221] (see Figure 12–11).

This section examines the environmental psychology of travel, which includes the study of tourist behavior, cognitive images of exotic destinations, choice of travel mode, and related phenomena.[222,223] Touring has a life cycle of its own. Its five temporal stages are:

- Anticipation
- Travel to the destination
- On-site behavior
- Return travel
- Recollection[224]

FIGURE 12–11 One classic destination.

A similar model (see Figure 12–12) provides a framework for research on travel behavior that is congruent with the general approach to environmental psychology described in this book.[225] Persons who differ in motives, personality, age, sex, and so on consider traveling. In the choice phase, they may choose *not* to travel because of some barrier (more on travel barriers soon). If they choose to travel, they select an activity and a destination, which may be nearly automatic (e.g., "We always go to the mountains in the spring") or be the subject of much discussion and study.

Once a place and activity are selected and the trip begins, the traveler enters the experience phase. This includes all the events and occurrences from departure to return, such as the travel itself, the weather, interactions with people, and the on-site activities that were the reason for the trip. These events lead to outcomes, such as whether the motives for going were fulfilled, general satisfaction or dissatisfaction, and safety or harm.

The return phase includes the trip home and subsequent trip-related thoughts and actions. Is the traveler rested, relaxed, a better person, broke? Do travelers tell others positive or negative things about their trips? Do they force slides and pictures on unsuspecting friends? Do they plan to repeat the trip?

Travel is part of environmental psychology for two main reasons. First, by traveling to environments away from their usual haunts, individuals alter themselves, sometimes radically. But not everyone travels. Who

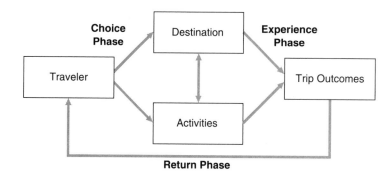

FIGURE 12–12 A basic model for the environmental psychology of tourism.

travels and who does not? Why travel and why not? What do travelers *do* in their temporary environments? What are the effects of destination environments on travelers? Second, travel has a significant impact on destination environments. In what ways are destinations harmed by tourism? Are they enhanced in any way?

The topic of travel is discussed in this chapter because work finances most travel and because travel is frequently seen as the *yang* to work's *yin* (that is, the two form an integral whole). One such connection is the development of **incentive travel,** the practice of rewarding productive employees with trips. Perhaps $2 billion a year is spent on incentive travel in North America and Western Europe; one Hawaiian hotel derives 40 percent of all its income from it. Many employees will work harder for a free trip than for cash or merchandise of equal value.[226] Let's begin with the traveler; later, the focus will be on the destination.

Who Goes (and Who Doesn't)?

Some people go on vacation every chance they get; others work years without taking a vacation. Personal experience suggests that one reason for traveling or not is whether a person's job satisfaction and involvement are high or low. Some people's jobs are everything to them; others cannot wait to get away. Sometimes, a job that once was almost everything is now almost nothing.

Apart from this, researchers speak of barriers to leisure or travel, such as lack of time, lack of money, lack of desirable places to go, and crowding.[227] A **barrier** is any factor that precludes or limits an individual's travel.[228] In general, barriers may be personal (fear of travel, no interest in exploring, love of home), environ-

mental (poor sites or destinations), interpersonal (poor social relations either at the destination or during the process of deciding where to go or whether to go, no one to go with), or resource problems (not enough money or time, too great distances).

But, of course, many employees *do* go on trips. Travel decisions result in the interesting concept of **travel careers.**[229] When you think of it, each of us has a travel history: We have traveled much or little, to many or few places that are exotic or conventional. As we shall see later, one's travel career influences the outcome of one's next trip. The mix of travel motives, travel careers, and such demographic variables as age, sex, and whether children are going on the trip results in certain identifiable clusters or groupings of travelers. These groupings are called **segments** by marketers, who study them in order to promote travel to particular destinations.

Numerous segments have been described, but one set of segments developed to understand the main kinds of travelers to outdoor recreation destinations will serve as an example.[230] These five groups are the excitement-seeking competitives (one likely destination would be white-water rafting), the get-away actives (sightseeing), the fitness driven (walking for pleasure), the health-conscious sociables (picnicking), and the unstressed and unmotivated (driving for pleasure). Many segments, like this one, are based on the reasons or motives for travel. We turn now to that topic.

Why Go?

Individuals who have unfulfilling jobs may find this question ridiculous; obviously, you go away to escape from a workplace that offers little except a means of supporting the parts of your life that are more pleasant than work. Individuals lucky enough to love their work ask the question seriously. Many individuals, however, even in cultures that are well known for devotion to work, currently believe there is more to life than job satisfaction. A large survey of German employees found that about half preferred their leisure time to their work time, whereas 20 years earlier, only one-third preferred leisure to work.[231]

Many studies have examined the motives for leisure and travel; researchers have reported from 4 to 48 different motives. A typical survey of the reasons for taking vacations yielded the following responses: to rest and relax (63 percent), to escape routine (52 percent), to visit friends and relatives (45 percent), and to explore new places (35 percent).[232] To some extent, of course, motives on the longer lists overlap with each other. Seven motives that are found in most studies, however, are:

- *Social.* To interact with family and friends away from one's usual setting
- *Escape.* To get away, find peace and quiet, avoid routine and others' expectations
- *Play.* To have fun, be entertained, seek pleasure
- *Nature.* To enjoy the unbuilt environment
- *Growth.* To improve oneself, learn, explore
- *Challenge.* To test oneself, be fit, hone skills, be competitive or alert
- *Recognition.* To be known for taking this trip, to increase status

Obviously, different motives fuel different trips to different places by different persons. For example, one researcher examined the leisure motives of masculine versus feminine persons.[233] Biological sex was not related to motives, but sex-role orientation was. Feminine individuals were more likely to seek an escape from reality; masculine individuals were more likely to seek challenge or competitiveness. Even a single destination may have several motives; more specialized hikers, for example, seek autonomy, exercise, achievement, and nature more than less-specialized hikers.[234]

Another view considers travel as a trade-off of contrasting motives.[235] This trade-off may be viewed as an optimizing process. We try to balance two motives: the desire to leave the familiar parts of our lives behind (e.g.,

to achieve growth or to escape) and the desire to retain certain rewarding aspects of our lives at home, such as our safety and health. When we leave home, we gain novelty and, we hope, pleasant experiences in the sun, among ruins, in museums, on the water, or in the wilderness. But we leave behind some or all family and friends, sure knowledge of our surroundings, and a tried and tested pattern of living. We take a chance on airplanes, roads, unfamiliar places, unknown systems of medicine, law, economics, and daily customs.

Some find this trade-off decision very easy to make; others experience difficulty deciding what to do. But most of us eventually are willing and eager to fly away. Each person must solve the tension between the need for novelty and the need for familiarity in order to achieve optimal experiences. If the decision is to go, then we must decide where.

Go Where?

Most recreational travel destinations are:

- The homes of family or friends
- Resorts (often in sunny places)
- Rural or wilderness locations
- Cities worth touring
- Planned leisure developments (e.g., theme parks)
- Religious shrines

Some destinations, of course, offer more than one attribute. For example, Athens is a sunny place that has great touristic value and a religious shrine in a pleasant rural setting. In the choice phase, we weigh our images of the places we are considering as one factor in the selection of a destination. Our images of places are based on a mix of personal experience (if we have been there before), word of mouth, advertisements, and stories about the place in the media. One outcome of a visit is that our image of the destination often changes.

Because it would take centuries to study every travel destination, researchers have tried to classify destinations into types. The assumption is that if we can discover something important about one kind of destination, it might well apply to other destinations of the same kind, which would save studying every destination individually.

One such distinction is between authentic and staged destinations.[236] **Authentic destinations** offer experiences that travelers feel are genuine. Such places usually are natural (like wilderness) or, in the case of built-up areas, places that have not been specifically altered to attract travelers. **Staged destinations** are those that, although they may be pleasurable, do not provide a sense of genuineness. They typically include elements designed for travelers, the epitome of which are theme parks, which do not even have residents—only employees trained to enact fantasy roles.

In one study, authentic destinations generally were preferred, but not equally by everyone.[237] Travelers with more extensive travel careers especially liked authentic destinations, and those with less extensive travel careers considered more staged destinations more satisfying.

Destinations must balance tourism value with other considerations. For example, wilderness areas derive income from timber and tourism. These two sources of income clash; research shows that tourists do not intend to visit forest areas with even small clear-cuts, but they are especially negative about visiting areas with large clear-cuts.[238]

Do What?

Travelers engage in many forms of behavior, of course. One important activity is seeking and developing knowledge about one's new surroundings. An example of knowledge-development research is a study of tourists visiting Oxford, England.[239] First-time visitors were asked to draw cognitive maps of Oxford to determine how much they had learned about it. As expected, tourists who had been in the city longer drew maps that included more landmarks, streets, and districts, and that were more accurate. Tourists whose accommodations were on the periphery of the city also seemed to understand the city better, presumably because they traveled more widely during their stay.

Philip Pearce, a leading researcher in this field, has also studied another common behavior while traveling: asking for help.[240] In 120 U.S. bus terminals from Portland, Oregon, to New Orleans, Louisiana, Australian and U.S. tourists asked fellow passengers and total strangers for information. Travelers more often received a helping response from fellow passengers than from to-tal strangers, and the longer the subjects had been fellow passengers, the more likely they were to offer help. Female travelers were helped more than male travelers. The male Australian traveler received more help than the male U.S. traveler. Pearce suggests that subjects perceived the Australian male as a foreign tourist, legitimizing his requests for help; the male tourist from the United States was not seen as foreign and therefore subjects viewed his requests as less legitimate.

Surprisingly little research has been done on just what travelers do once they reach their destinations. Most research is motivated by marketing and promotion goals and is aimed at getting travelers to choose a certain destination. Much of this research is comprised of surveys rather than studies about what travelers actually do.

Managers of national parks and commercial theme parks are concerned about the flow of tourists through their settings. Commercial operators wish to design their settings to maximize flow and minimize traffic pathways and customer discomfort. In national parks, the rationing of entry in the busy summer season encourages research into tourist activities such as length of stay and rate of travel through the park.[241]

Just as with travelers and motives, there are many travel activities. One distinction among activities (again, the purpose is to investigate *classes* of activities because studying every form of travel activity is impossible) is that between appreciative and consumptive travel activities (see Figure 12–13). As the terms imply, **appreciative activities** are those in which the goal is to see or experience something without taking or destroying the object of admiration (e.g., photography, sightseeing, birdwatching), whereas **consumptive activities** involve removing at least some of that which one goes to see (e.g., hunting, fishing). Those who prefer these two kinds of activity differ in certain ways. For example, those who choose appreciative activities tend to have stronger proenvironmental attitudes than those who choose consumptive activities.[242]

With What Outcomes?

The Impact of Destination Environments on Travelers.
Traveling, of course, usually has multiple effects on the traveler. Knowledge and experience may be enriched,

FIGURE 12-13 Appreciative versus consummatory recreation: The people in the top picture are appreciating nature (just looking); those in the bottom picture are consuming it (drying seaweed to eat).

one's circle of friends may enlarge, and one will likely be refreshed and ready for a return to the familiar life. The traveler may also have experienced anxiety, discomfort, illness, theft, exhaustion, loss, and stress. The traveler's image of the destination changes. Travel usually has both positive and negative outcomes that depend partly on the experience and partly on the traveler.

If we begin on the positive side, travel has many potential benefits. One researcher claims there are 44 psychological benefits that may be derived just from outdoor leisure activities.[243] Among these are improvements in physical and mental health, life satisfaction, and personal growth.

Some trips may be better than others. A study that compared the effects of wilderness backpacking with

nonwilderness vacations found that those who chose nature were more restored by their vacation than those who did not.[244] Another reports that extended time in the wilderness results in greater self-actualization.[245] A third found that after a wilderness experience, life seemed less cluttered and travelers were more mindful of those close to them and more focused on activities that were important to them.[246]

Recent research suggests that when tourist personality matches the type of destination, the vacation will have more restorative benefits.[247] Vacationers who scored higher on the Urbanism scale of the Environmental Response Inventory (ERI) did not experience as great a reduction in occupational strain after a nature holiday as vacationers who scored lower on the Urbanism scale.

Another kind of outcome is satisfaction with the trip or destination itself. Whether every traveler to the wilderness experiences the beneficial changes previously described is not clear, but it is clear that travel satisfaction depends on both the person and the environment. For example, some campsites are satisfactory or dissatisfactory to most campers, but any given campsite has some features that appeal to some campers and other features that appeal to other campers.[248] This, of course, is probably the case for all types of destinations and travel activities.

Which characteristics of travelers make a difference? One is experience with an activity or a destination. For any given activity, experience tends to make one's preferences more specific, which usually means harder to satisfy.[249] For instance, on one's first trip to Paris, just *being* in the fabled Left Bank is exciting. One's tenth trip to Paris may not be satisfying unless more particular events occur, such as meeting a certain kind of person in a certain kind of Left Bank bistro.

Similarly, a study found that a tour of a national wildlife refuge that featured wild birds was more satisfying to visitors who knew less about birds. More knowledgeable birdwatchers require more exotic birds to be as satisfied as those who know little about wild birds.[250] Studies of inner-tube floaters report that some like floating when many other floaters are near by, whereas others dream of being the only floater on the river.[251] Specialization or experience help to explain why satisfaction varies when the density of floaters is identical.[252]

One issue is whether traveler satisfaction is related more to the traveler's preferences or expectations. When the two are *not* in conflict (let's say you prefer hot sun for your beach trip and also expect hot sun, based on the season or a weather forecast), there is no issue. However, what if you prefer museums in places you visit, but end up visiting a place that you expect (maybe because it is a sleepy little town) has no museums? Will you be more satisfied if it turns out to have a museum (your preference) or turns out not to have any (your expectation)? A study found that campers' *preferences* for various features of a campsite were more predictive of satisfaction than their *expectations* of the site.[253]

Pilgrimages are an ancient travel practice that continues today. The traditional pilgrimage involves a journey to a religious site to fulfill a spiritual goal or to be healed. At the healing sites, the physical condition of pilgrims is often studied, but one researcher investigated whether a pilgrimage to Lourdes, the French site that over 3 million Christians visit every year, has a beneficial effect on the emotional state of pilgrims.[254]

The anxiety and depression of pilgrims was measured 1 month before their trip, 1 month after their trip, and 10 months later. Anxiety and depression significantly declined after the pilgrimage and stayed significantly lower for the 10 months after the pilgrimage. Of course, it is not clear whether Lourdes itself or some other aspect of the journey caused the emotional improvement, but presumably the pilgrims do not care; for them, the trip had a positive effect.

Unfortunately, there are also negative experiences in traveling. Philip Pearce has suggested that many tourists react to their new situation, with its lack of familiarity and routine, by going into **environment shock**.[255] He found that the moods of visitors to a resort on a tropical island noticeably worsened on the second and third days of their stay. Minor health complaints also peaked in this period, lending credence to the environment shock notion.

Getting away from it all can have even worse complications. Hawaiian authorities recognize the "coconuts and bananas syndrome," which refers to the myth believed by some stray wanderers that life is so easy in the tropics that one can simply pick food off the trees.[256] The study found that "coconuts and bananas" tourists (who tend to be young, unmarried, and unemployed) often have psychiatric breakdowns when they discover that life is not that easy, even in Hawaii.

Tourists who hold such unrealistic expectations (such as seeing grass huts at Waikiki and wanting to get back to nature) had about 10 times the psychiatric admission rate of other tourists. The broader message, of course, is that tourist destinations can be stressful if the tourist believes the destination will solve most of life's problems.

Finally, visiting a destination can change the traveler's image of that destination. An Australian study compared the ideal images that travelers believed to be true of the wet northern tropics in that country and the actual image they developed as a result of visiting the area.[257] Both positive divergences (i.e., ways in which the area was better than expected, such as roads being less crowded than expected and seeing more wildlife than expected) and negative divergences (i.e., the climate and road conditions were worse than expected) were found.

Similarly, the images of British Columbia changed for Japanese exchange students as a result of a study visit.[258] The climate was better than they expected and the pace of travel was less hectic than they expected. However, it was more difficult to reach natural surroundings than the students had expected. These examples suggest that experience in a destination very often changes one's image of the place, usually in both positive and negative ways.

The Impact of Travelers on Destination Environments. So, travelers have growth experiences and sometimes go bananas. What happens to the environments they visit? We are familiar with the economic and sociocultural effects of visitors. They bring needed revenue but also sometimes import unpleasant attitudes and behaviors. The environmental impact of travelers is now recognized: the beer cans on top of Old Smoky, the use of scarce groundwater in dry resort areas, land development pressures, and litter (see Figure 12–14).

The famous prehistoric paintings in the caves at Lascaux, France, were so damaged by the mere breathing of tourists that the French government has closed them. Crime rates are affected, too. Compared to places with few tourists, tourist centers have significantly more crimes of certain types.[259] However, the negative impact of tourists can be reduced.[260] The design of English stately houses that are open to the public serves as an example.

In one, trees and gardens are arranged so that numerous tourists do not detract from the aesthetic experience of visiting the home. It has always had a public

FIGURE 12–14 The impact of travelers on one destination: Resident anger.

nature and would look odd deserted. The other's garden is designed for the contemplation of nature in solitude; when many tourists are present, the whole effect is ruined. In general, we may have to discourage **romantic tourism,** in which the ideal vacation consists of a lone individual or pair of lovers in an uninhabited tourist destination—whether that's a famous garden, unspoiled wilderness, or tropical beach.

Given the limited number of undeveloped wild beaches and wilderness areas, romantic tourism eventually can lead only to disappointment and unmet expectations on the part of travelers. It fosters the relentless development of ever-more-remote beaches and wildernesses to satisfy romantic tourism. Much better use of existing tourist areas could be made. For example, the provision of more extensive signs and maps could educate travelers about appealing places off the beaten track in established tourist areas.

The environmental psychology of travel is young; the studies discussed here represent the first in an area that will grow. Too many studies rely solely on surveys and are done for marketing and advertising purposes.[261] The study of travelers' actual behaviors is important and interesting in its own right. The topic may seem frivolous, but travel has important impacts on both the traveler and the destination. Nevertheless, we still have much to learn about traveler-destination transactions. This knowledge, once gained, will be invaluable in designing highly adapted destinations (e.g., amusement

parks and resorts) and planning for the survival of more vulnerable destinations (e.g., wildernesses, heritage buildings, and archeological sites).

◆ **IN SUM,** the environmental psychology of travel is a new but growing area. Travelers affect destinations and are affected by them. Anticipation, travel, and recollection of travel involve environmental perception and cognition. Recreational travel is an environmental trade-off, but as society is able to provide employees with more disposable income and time, it is a trade-off many are pursuing. Destination selection, acquisition of knowledge about destination, and behavior along the road are a few areas of developing research. Some destinations bring relief from anxiety; others throw travelers into environment shock. Travelers ruin some physical settings and enhance almost none; romantic tourism is an undesirable luxury. More careful planning of destination sites might spread the impact of visitors, offer more authentic experiences, and educate travelers while offering them solace from the working world.

◆ WORK, TRAVEL, AND ◆ ENVIRONMENTAL DESIGN

Environmental psychologists have been involved in the design of many work settings, from basic noise and light consultations to complete office designing. Better office designs not only are a basic right of employees but they also save money for organizations. A very comprehensive study found that improved layout and enclosure in offices would lead to productivity increases of 15 percent for managers and professional-technical employees, and 17.5 percent for clerical workers.[262] Similar studies report 10 to 50 percent increases with better workplace designs.[263]

In this section, two settings are selected as examples of applied research that illustrate the major parts of this chapter: an example of an entirely new type of work setting and a design for acoustic privacy in an open-plan office.

Loosely Coupled Work Settings

In an earlier section, computer-assisted work decentralization (CAWD) was discussed. **Loose coupling** is a concept that assumes that things are less interdependent than we normally think. An architectural implication is that there is less need than previously believed to place all units of an organization under one roof.

An early loose-coupling solution was to encourage or even force employees to work at home, but that only works for a few employees. Yet, CAWD does allow for working outside the office and there are certain good reasons to decentralize work if possible. (One would be to help solve the problem described in the last section by essentially replacing many commuting vehicles with communications cables.)

A compromise solution has been tested in Sweden: One works neither at home nor at the office, but in a **neighborhood work center** (NWC).[264] The experimental NWC was opened in a small town about 30 miles from Stockholm from which many residents commute daily to the city. The NWC occupied space in a shopping center. Employees from a variety of organizations work in the same place and share equipment. Their reasons for trying out the NWC concept included being closer to their families, crowding at their main office, cutting commuting costs, and the availability of equipment at the NWC that was unavailable in their main offices (see Figure 12–15).

Like any experiment, the NWC experienced both success and failure. Some employees who simply would not be able to work otherwise, because of the difficulty of commuting, were able to work. Others benefited

FIGURE 12–15 A loosely coupled setting: Telecommuting offices in a suburban mall save employees most of their commuting.

from the special equipment, and some benefited from being able to work with spouses. On the other hand, the NWC was unsatisfactory for some employees because confidential documents were not entirely secure, they were too isolated, or they lacked commitment to the NWC concept.

The neighborhood work center is an interesting idea. Further experience will yield a profile of the kind of employee and organization for which it is well suited. The question is not whether work settings are loosely coupled or not; it is *which* work settings and employees are sufficiently loosely coupled to benefit from NWCs.

Acoustic Privacy in Open-Plan Offices

As we saw earlier, open-plan offices are increasingly common. However, a big problem with them is acoustic privacy—employees are concerned about their conversations leaking to others and about unwanted speech floating into their work areas. Nevertheless, if open-plan offices are carefully designed, acoustic privacy can exist.

L. W. Hegvold decided to create a "ready reckoner" procedure that would allow designers to assess the level of acoustic privacy between any two desks in an office.[265] This, of course, allows designers to create offices that maximize acoustic privacy without wasting space. (One *could* create excellent acoustic privacy by simply placing desks very far apart, but space is expensive.) Hegvold's procedure involves measuring (1) the distance between workstations, (2) the prevailing background machine noise, (3) the level of conversational sound, (4) whether there are any partitions between the speaker and the listener, and (5) speaker/listener orientation (e.g., back to back or face to face). The combination of these factors determines the **articulation index,** or the percentage of spoken words understood by a listener. Acoustic privacy is worse when the articulation index is high.

In general, acoustic privacy will be worse when employees are closer together, background noise is low, the speaker and listener face each other, and the situation calls for louder speech (e.g., in conferences as opposed to two-person conversations). Here are two examples using Hegvold's "ready reckoner." When the employees are 9 feet apart from chair to chair, with no partitions between them, with the background noise level at 45 decibels and the speech level at normal (60 decibels), and the speaker faces 180 degrees from the listener (back to back), the articulation index is .14 (about 1 word out of 7 can be understood), which Hegvold says is "acceptable." When the employees are 15 feet apart, with no partitions, 45 decibels of background noise, a 60-decibel speech level, and the speaker and listener face *toward* each other, the articulation index is .57, which Hegvold describes as "nil" acoustic privacy.

◆ **SUMMARY** ◆

Working as well as getting away from work are fertile fields of study for the environmental psychologist. Noise—unwanted sound, by definition—has complex effects on work performance. Some conditions under which it is likely to improve or harm performance have now been tentatively identified. In industrial settings, noise often impairs hearing without the victim's awareness; it has also been linked to health problems. Noise in offices, where work often involves considerable cognitive processing and sensitive social interaction, is an important problem. Few performance effects have been documented, but privacy complaints are widespread in typical open-plan offices.

Most employees can sufficiently control temperature through clothing or other protective devices so that it has no strong effects on performance. In experimental situations where temperature is varied strongly, the same pattern of complex effects observed for noise are reported. Temperature swings can be annoying in buildings with inadequate heating and cooling systems. Performance may be optimal at temperatures below typical comfort zones, which may create conflict between the goals of creating pleasant work settings and creating efficient ones. Long-term extreme temperatures are stressful, but humans have considerable adaptive capacity for temperature.

Airborne disease agents can cause health problems, but ions and malodors have weak effects on most individuals. Certain employees, however, have ion sensitivities or other qualities that make them more susceptible than most people. Lighting is a problem primarily when it is too bright or placed inappropriately for a task. Lower levels of more localized light, and more sunlight where possible, would increase employee satisfaction.

Spatial arrangements should reflect the employee's need for interaction with others, which varies with the task and the employee. As with noise, the problem is essentially one of privacy.

Recreational travel involves most areas of environmental psychology; the difference is that the setting is typically unfamiliar but desirable. Little research about the traveler's perceptions, cognitions, social interactions, and learning have yet appeared, but what has surfaced offers tantalizing glimpses of an interesting new area of research. Environmental design in this chapter is illustrated by describing a new kind of work setting, the neighborhood work center, and acoustic privacy in an office.

Suggested Supplementary Readings

Baron, R. A. (1994). The physical environment of work settings: Effects on task performance, interpersonal relations, and job satisfaction. *Research in Organizational Behavior, 16,* 1–46.
Becker, F. D. (1981). *Workspace: Creating environments in organizations.* New York: Praeger.
Broadbent, D. E. (1979). Human performance and noise. In C. M. Harris (Ed.), *Handbook of noise control.* New York: McGraw-Hill.
Fridgen, J. D. (1984). Environmental psychology and tourism. *Annals of Tourism Research, 11,* 19–39.
Harris, L., & associates. (1989). *The Steelcase office environment index 1989.* Grand Rapids, MI: Steelcase Inc.
Hedge, A. (1987). Office health hazards: An annotated bibliography. *Ergonomics, 30,* 733–772.
Katzev, R. (1992). The impact of energy-efficient office lighting strategies on employee satisfaction and productivity. *Environment and Behavior, 24,* 759–778.
Mazumdar, S. (1992). "Sir, please do not take away my cubicle." The phenomenon of environmental deprivation. *Environment and Behavior, 24,* 691–722.
Oborne, D. J., & Gruneberg, M. M. (Eds.). (1983). *The physical environment at work.* New York: Wiley.
Pearce, P. L. (1982). *The social psychology of tourist behavior.* Oxford: Pergamon.
Roberts, J. T. (1993). Psychosocial effects of workplace hazardous exposures: Theoretical synthesis and preliminary findings. *Social Problems, 40,* 74–89.
Steele, F. I. (1973). *Physical settings and organizational development.* Reading, MA: Addison-Wesley.
Sundstrom, E. (1986). *Work places.* New York: Cambridge University Press.
Sundstrom, E., Town, J. P., Osborn, D., Rice, R. W., Konar, E., Mandel, D., & Brill, M. (1994). Office noise, satisfaction, and performance. *Environment and Behavior, 26,* 195–222.

CHAPTER 13

NATURAL ENVIRONMENTAL PSYCHOLOGY

Nature's peace will flow into you as sunshine flows into trees. The winds blow their own freshness into you and the storms their energy, while cares drop off like autumn leaves.

—John Muir[1]

Poor naked wretches, wheresoe'er you are,
That bide the pelting of this pitiless storm,
How shall your houseless heads and unfed sides,
Your looped and window'd raggedness, defend you
From seasons such as these?

—Shakespeare, *King Lear*

*J*ane lifted her head and peeked out the tent flap. Dawn had not yet arrived, but she could see light anyway. Even though the night was crystalline cold, she crawled out of her sleeping bag to see more of the horizon. Once outside, she saw Venus huge and low in the sky. It seemed almost as big and bright as a full moon. Entranced, she silently stared, wonderstruck, for several minutes.

"Tom," she finally said, "You have to see this."

Mumble.

"Tom, wake up. Come see." Tom dragged himself into consciousness. He had been in the middle of a bad dream, watching his new old house he had inherited from his grandfather being swept away in a flood. He and Jane were about to move in, but already the house had become a part of them; to see it floating away, tilted at a crazy angle, was terrifying.

"Jeez, I'm glad you woke me up," he said. "You wouldn't believe what happened to the house in my dream."

"Look," said Jane, distracted. "Isn't it amazing? Do you think Venus really affects love on earth?"

"I don't know. But I remember once when we were sitting outside in the dark last July, it made a great conversation piece. I've never seen it this big though."

Tom made breakfast and as the sun rose, he and Jane sat next to the fire, talking and soaking up its heat like the ancients. Jane remarked how she felt like a new person after a few days in the woods. Tom noticed that this was in marked contrast to her initial comments, which were more along the lines of how she was going to get behind at work.

"I think I'm hard to get outdoors, but now I'm going to be hard to drag back to work," she said.

◆ ◆ ◆

This is a chapter about the great outdoors. It covers a lot of territory—from cosmic rays to local weather patterns, from wilderness to floods. Nature is a huge force on our behavior, thoughts, and feelings; a victim of our unsympathetic actions; a wondrous restorative agent for our stressed-out souls; and an awesome source of power to disrupt our lives (see Figure 13–1).

The first part of the chapter, on extraterrestrial and atmospheric environmental psychology, examines influences from far away (deep space) to near at hand (weather and climate)—influences over which we have

FIGURE 13–1 Many people bring as much of nature indoors as possible.

little control. Next, we will consider the hypothesis that nature provides an enhancing, restorative tonic for the mind and body. We will then focus on the immense "hit" that nature can deliver with a mere shrug of the shoulders—natural disasters. Also, we will examine technological hazards.

◆ **EXTRATERRESTRIAL AND** ◆
ATMOSPHERIC FORCES

Is our behavior or fundamental nature affected by forces beyond earth? This may seem unlikely to skeptics, but the answer is yes—in some ways. First, current views of cosmology argue that the whole planet is spun-off star matter. Thus, not only the earth, but all upon it is highly developed star dust. You are star dust. Second, all that happens on the earth is powered by the sun, either directly through solar power or indirectly through the use of stored solar power. (Coal, gas, and oil are plant-stored solar power; hydro power is based on the sun lifting water into the atmosphere so it can rain; most of our food is produced through photosynthesis.)

Sure, sure, you say—but what about our everyday actions, tendencies, hopes, and beliefs? In some very basic ways, the sun influences those too. Prolonged sunny weather induces us to garden, go to the beach, to play summer sports; the lack of the sun creates good conditions for staying indoors or for engaging in winter sports. Yes, you say, but we do not need studies to prove that. Other, more subtle, influences will be discussed in the weather section here. Perhaps you are asking, Are there any more mysterious, exotic deep-space influences on us?

Deep Space and Heavenly Bodies

Cosmic Rays. Some research reports connections between outer space phenomena and earthly actions. For example, cosmic ray activity has been associated with psychiatric hospital admissions and behavioral disturbances in schizophrenics.[2] In this study, hospital admissions increased with cosmic ray activity; behavioral disturbances increased for some schizophrenics but decreased for other schizophrenics. Possibly, although much more research is necessary, the flow of neutrons from cosmic rays somehow affects schizophrenics.

Planets: Is Astrology Valid? Another study examined the relation between the positions of planets at birth and later personality; essentially, it was a test of astrology's validity.[3] Among eminent French people, a significantly high proportion of introverts were born when Saturn had just risen or just passed overhead, and extraverts were more likely to be born when Mars or Jupiter had just risen or passed overhead. As the researchers admit, there is a major problem in that although the data are reasonably clear, no causal mechanism for these findings is available. *How* could planetary position possibly affect the personality of a child who is being born?

The Moon: Is Lunacy Real? The belief that the moon influences strange behavior goes back at least to 400 B.C. and has had prominent supporters through the centuries.[4] One study showed that 49 percent of undergraduates agreed with the statement, "Some people behave strangely when the moon is full."[5] Even higher percentages of police officers believe the full moon affects people.[6] What does the evidence say?

Numerous studies do report significant connections between phases of the moon and such behaviors as calls to counseling centers, admissions to psychiatric hospital admissions, and homicides.[7] However, critics

of this research say these results probably are due to Type I errors and the file-drawer problem.

A **Type I error** occurs when a researcher accepts a significant result as true when actually it is untrue. Type I errors can occur when an investigator computes many statistical tests and finds a few significant results. For example, if 20 tests are computed at the .05 level of significance, one will appear significant purely by chance. If a researcher reports that one result, particularly if the other 19 negative outcomes are not reported, that published article will help create the false impression that a genuine effect has been found.

The **file-drawer problem** occurs when a researcher finds no significant relationships in a study. Null findings are not favored by scientific journals, so they tend to get filed away rather than reported in journals. Thus, studies with Type I errors may appear in scientific journals; those with null results do not. The innocent inquirer who then searches the published scientific literature will find mainly significant results.

The lunacy hypothesis—the moon affects bad and crazy behavior—has been declared dead,[8] but it still lives for some researchers who believe it has not been fairly evaluated.[9] However, as with the planetary-position study described earlier, a major problem is the lack of a plausible causal mechanism for the lunacy effect.

One theory that seems reasonable at first glance suggests that the moon's gravitational influence on bodily fluids causes tides like those caused by the moon in oceans, and somehow these "biological tides" result in lunacy behaviors.[10] Unfortunately, the moon's gravitational force on humans is over 5,000 times weaker than that of the earth; even a large building such as the campus library tugs on your bodily fluids harder when you walk by it than the moon does.[11] The moon's gravitational effect is far too weak to affect our bodily fluids. A subsequent analysis examined eight other possible causal mechanisms and concluded that none was credible.[12]

Nevertheless, James Rotton and I. W. Kelly took the trouble to assemble every lunacy study they could find (117 data sets in 37 studies) and performed a meta-analysis on them.[13] In a **meta-analysis,** the investigator mathematically combines the results of different studies to estimate the magnitude of an effect. **Effect sizes** computed in meta-analyses are usually expressed, like correlation coefficients, as a value that ranges from 0 to 1,

JAMES ROTTON'S

work on the effects of air pollution and lunar influences have shown that the former may be more important than we thought and the latter may be less important than we thought.

where 0 indicates no (0 percent) relationship and 1 indicates a complete (100 percent) explanation of an outcome by the hypothesized influence on that outcome. Rotton and Kelly's meta-analysis yielded an effect size of 0.01; lunar influences explain less than 1 percent of the variation in behaviors usually associated with lunacy.

Earthly Forces

Let's move a little closer to home—the atmosphere. What effects do climate, the weather, and the seasons have on us?

Weather, Climate, and Seasons. Influences from specific meteorological components (e.g., sunshine, rain, wind, temperature, and humidity in different seasons and climates) are impossible to examine in field experiments because these components of weather cannot be separated from one another or controlled in everyday life. Investigators cannot special-order different combinations of outdoor weather variables.

To compensate, a few researchers use special climate chambers to do just that; thus, laboratory experiments are possible. However, as with all lab experiments, a certain element of realism is lost when a study is done in a sealed chamber! Also, subjects in labs may perceive the experimenter's purpose and respond to conditions as they think the experimenter wants them to.[14] Other researchers use special statistical procedures to control for the unwanted influence of some variables (e.g., temperature and rain) when studying the effects of another (e.g., wind). Unfortunately, some researchers do neither, which leaves their purely correlational conclusions highly suspect.

Everyday experience suggests that weather does influence us. One street survey, for example, found that 71 percent of people asked said that their mood was affected by that day's weather, and 39 percent said it affected their mood "strongly" or "very strongly."[15] So, millions of people *believe* their mood is influenced by the weather, but what about their behavior?

Let's begin with temperature. Based on many studies, temperature clearly influences human behavior; the only question, as we will see in a moment, is the "shape" of this influence. The main influence of higher temperatures is on aggressiveness. As the temperature moves from comfortable to hot, collective violence (such as riots, domestic violence, assaults, and rape) increase.[16] Higher temperatures seem to increase crimes against persons, but not property crimes.[17] Evidence from field studies clearly supports the conclusion that heat causes aggression.[18]

If high temperature does cause aggression, do even higher temperatures cause even more aggression? As we saw back in Chapter 10, the answer is that aggression increases with temperature to a certain point and then decreases when the temperature becomes too hot for people to function. The only issue is the exact temperature at which aggression reaches its maximum.

Some "cool" studies have tested these ideas in real-world settings. In Phoenix, Arizona, researchers in cars were deliberately slow to move after a stoplight turned green.[19] They counted the rate of horn honking in cars stuck behind them. Especially among drivers who appeared not to have air-conditioned cars, there was a direct linear increase of horn honking with increased temperature. Horn honking increased right up to 118°F.

But *why* does heat cause aggression? Does it have a direct effect, or does it trigger some other process or interact with social or cultural factors, or both?[20] At least five distinct models of the heat-aggression relation have been proposed, but three seem most likely.[21,22]

1. The **negative affect escape model** proposes that increasing discomfort from heat causes aggression up to a point. But in very hot temperatures, the motive to escape the heat becomes stronger than the motive to aggress. This model is the basis of the idea that the heat-aggression relation is curvilinear (it rises and then falls).

2. The **excitation transfer/misattribution model** proposes that when the temperature rises, we experience a general increase in physiological arousal. We look for a reason for this increased arousal; if we do not realize it is due to the temperature, we look for other causes. If this search happens to focus on another person who seems annoying, we are more likely to decide that our arousal actually must be anger at this person and we become aggressive.

3. The **cognitive neoassociation model** states that, over time, we learn to associate uncomfortable conditions (such as extreme temperatures) with aggressive thoughts and emotions. Aggression may occur even when no one who seems particularly annoying is around.

So far, the emphasis has been on heat; less research has examined the effects of cold temperatures. Cold also may lead to aggressiveness, but of a different sort.[23] Whereas high temperatures increase aggression slowly and produced aggressive acts that are not particularly specific to ambient events (such as insults), cold temperatures produce aggressive acts that are swift and more specifically directed toward ambient events. Cold temperatures are not strongly related to crime patterns, except for robbery;[24] this may represent a survival strategy for people who desperately need food or shelter.[25]

Temperature is also associated with emergency room visits and calls to suicide prevention lines, but probably in an indirect manner.[26] Warm weather brings people outside to work and play, and they injure themselves more often than in cold weather. People stay indoors more when it is cold, which induces "cabin fever" and depression and leads to more calls to help lines.

Sunshine obviously is related to temperature, but not always (e.g., cold, sunny days do occur), and it seems to elicit a somewhat different set of behaviors. One researcher examined generosity in relation to sunshine in two interesting ways.[27] First, he asked people to help with a questionnaire and told them they could answer as many questions as they wished. Second, he measured the amount of tips received by waitresses. On sunny days, people volunteered to answer more questionnaire items and gave more tips. Probably not incidentally, the moods of waitresses were also better on

sunny days! Apparently, sunlight can improve the spirits too much for some people, however: The incidence of mania rises in the long days of summer.[28]

Other weather variables—such as relative humidity, wind, rain, and barometric pressure—have not received much research attention and have not been strongly linked to human behavior. However, one extraordinary effect of wind is worth recounting. In 1968, the world long jump record was 8.37 meters. In the Mexico City Olympics that year, Bob Beamon jumped 8.90 meters and broke the record by over half a meter. The record lasted for over 20 years. Some observers attributed the astounding jump to the high altitude, but the wind helped too. Several scientific analyses of the jump have been published; the most sophisticated shows that altitude contributed 15 cm and wind 16 cm to the jump.[29] Thus, although wind (and altitude) lengthened the famous jump, it would have broken the world record by 22 cm (over 8 inches) at sea level with no wind.

Another meteorological component, ozone level, is worth mentioning because it is less obvious yet may be an important factor in human behavior if one study's results are replicated. This study showed that higher levels of ozone in the atmosphere were associated with more family disturbances severe enough to result in calls to the police.[30] The same study illustrates the valuable point that weather *combinations* may be more important than levels of individual weather variables. Assaults and family disturbances tended to occur just after days that were warmer and drier with lower winds.

The proper analysis of weather variable combinations requires sophisticated statistical analyses that were not available to early researchers. Consideration of long-term weather combinations, or climate, did lead to some rather grand theories of climate in the first decades of the century. The most notable of these was Huntington's **cyclonic theory**, which argued that people born in the northern temperate zones (northern Europe, North America) attained the highest level of technology and civilization because of the moderate but very changeable weather in those latitudes.

The idea was that people in these zones learned to work hard during good weather because the weather might turn bad at any time. This theory was very influential in the first half of this century but it has fallen into disfavor because of its questionable assumptions about whose civilization is "highest," a lack of empirical support for the theory, and its determinist tone.

Another kind of weather combination is "bad" weather, which usually means cold, wet, and windy weather with fluctuating barometric pressure; "good" weather is warm, dry, and calm with stable barometric pressure. Preschoolers' play may be affected by these weather patterns. Good weather and weather changing from good to bad was associated with more playing with objects than other children; bad weather and weather changing from bad to good was associated with more playing with other children than objects.[31]

Such weather will obviously curb some outdoor activities, but it may (indirectly) have less obvious, more sinister effects. A number of studies report a greater-than-expected number of psychiatric problems among people born in the first quarter of the year (January through March).[32] This may be especially true for females, for whom the risk in one large study was 28 percent higher in February than in July.[33]

The authors present evidence that bad weather may—indirectly—cause schizophrenia. More severe winters and winters with larger outbreaks of influenza are followed by higher rates of first-quarter babies who later develop schizophrenia. Bad weather increases the chances of getting the flu, and the anti-bodies produced by the mother to combat influenza during a crucial stage of pregnancy may also harm the developing child's brain.

The earth's geomagnetic field varies, sometimes more than others. Strong variations are called *geomagnetic storms*. Over a 10-year period, admissions to psychiatric hospitals of depressive-phase manic-depressive individuals rose by 36 percent in the second week following geomagnetic storms.[34]

Electromagnetic Forces. Do electric power lines and other sources of electromagnetic power have any effect on human behavior or well-being? There are over 2 million miles of power lines criss-crossing the United States. One review concludes there are no important effects,[35] but another reports that several independent studies show an association between electrical power distribution and childhood leukemia, with possible health effects to adults.[36]

Of more immediate psychological importance may be differing *perceptions* of power lines' potential effects.

Technical experts are baffled by the public's continuing concerns in the absence of any hard evidence that power lines cause physiological or psychological damage. Some members of the public are equally baffled why the experts dismiss their concerns.[37] Clearly, as we saw in Chapter 3, one useful approach is to understand the bases of experts' and laypersons' beliefs; the two groups literally are thinking about different things as they arrive at their views. As just one example, experts may be thinking that power lines have not been clearly shown to harm human health, but laypersons may be thinking that power lines will reduce property values.

◆ **IN SUM,** *a few studies suggest that extraterrestrial forces from cosmic rays, planets, and the moon may be associated with human behavior, but these results probably are Type I errors. In any case, no one has suggested a reasonable mechanism by which such forces would wield their influence. Weather influences our behavior in many obvious ways and in some less-obvious ways. Aggressiveness rises with temperature to a point and then declines. Ozone levels may influence violence. Electromagnetic radiation may affect public fears more than it affects our health.*

◆ NATURE AS A RESTORATIVE AGENT ◆

People have believed for a long time that nature is good for them. Even back in the days when the world's largest cities were small towns by today's standards, the hanging gardens of Babylon and the walled gardens in Mesopotamia were nurtured so those early urbanites could maintain some contact with nature. Ancient Romans brought trees into the city and built prized mansions that looked over open fields.

As we saw earlier in the book, in general, people much prefer to look at nature scenes than urban scenes. The question here is whether this preference translates into benefits such as improved health, recovery from stress, or superior psychological functioning. The most famous early American landscape architect, Frederick Law Olmsted, created Central Park in New York City and other urban parks explicitly because he (and those who funded his work) believed that nature is beneficial to the emotional and physiological health of people.[38] Modern surveys confirm that most people today feel the same way.

RACHEL KAPLAN

was among the first to investigate the psychological benefits of nature.

A study in British Columbia found that over half of the population over age 18 considers outdoor recreation to be "very important" to them, compared to their other interests; 84 percent report that it is of at least "some" importance to them.[39] Even though about three-quarters of Canadians live in cities, 70 percent participate in wildlife-related activities and 22 percent take special trips to watch, study, feed, or photograph wildlife in a given year.[40]

Even when nature is potentially dangerous, many people want to experience it. In one survey, 42 percent of those who visited the outdoors responded positively to the idea of hiking in an area that was posted with a sign warning of bears in the vicinity. Some 86 percent said they would like to see a grizzly bear in the wild from a safe distance.[41]

Some observers believe that nature is even more important to people today than it was in ancient days. As people are increasingly cocooned in an industrial, urbanized environment, they are increasingly alienated from nature.[42] People go to nature to be restored and refreshed. But what, exactly, does this mean?

What Needs Restoring?

Environmental psychologists and others have tried to identify, in more precise terms than everyday phrases such as "to recharge my batteries," why people seek out nature. Until the motives and presumed outcomes of experiencing nature are clearly spelled out, testing the hypothesis that nature is good for us is impossible. Some researchers have explicitly hypothesized that exposure to nature improves our health or speeds recovery. Others have identified experiences that nature provides—presumably experiences we need but cannot easily obtain in heavily built-up environments.

Many authors have attempted to list all the reasons, experiences, motives, or benefits that people associate with nature or outdoor recreation. These lists have included up to 40 or 50 items and there is considerable repetition within lists and from list to list. To simplify things, I examined all previous lists in order to create a complete but relatively short, nonoverlapping set of motives or benefits associated with nature.[43]

Following is that study's list, integrated with proposals that were either made since that study was completed or omitted from it. Not everyone seeks or finds all of these 10 experiences and benefits, but many people believe they can experience at least several of them in natural settings.

- Cognitive freedom
- Escape
- Experience nature
- Ecosystem connectedness
- Growth
- Challenge
- Guidance
- Social
- Health
- Self-Control

One such experience is **cognitive freedom**.[44] Being out in nature provides a sense that we have the freedom to pay attention to whatever we like and to do what we choose to do, *when* we choose to do it. This cognitive freedom is possible, in part, because nature also allows for a sense of **escape**—the chance to be relatively free from the rules and constraints of society (e.g., bosses, traffic, bills, Keep Off the Grass signs, etc.). Of course, one is not truly free in nature and there are still rules, but for many people, the rules and constraints are sufficiently different and less demanding in a natural setting that they experience considerable cognitive freedom and escape.

However, we go to nature for reasons other than to escape everyday life. We may need to be in nature for its own sake; that is, we may have a basic need to **experience nature**. The fourth reason for being in nature goes beyond the immediate experience of trees and streams.

It is to sense **ecosystem connectedness,** the awareness that we are part of the immensity of nature and the cosmos.[45,46]

This sense of connectedness is often associated with the fifth reason: People seek **growth** when they are in the great outdoors. It is an opportunity to develop themselves and learn what the natural environment has to teach them. This growth can be in skills, knowledge of the woods, self-knowledge, self-actualization, or in one's spiritual domain.

Sixth, some people go to nature for the **challenge,** or what has been called the *adrenaline experience*[47]—the excitement that emerges in potentially dangerous situations such as white-water rafting, encountering a bear, or rock climbing. Of course, one can have an adrenaline experience crossing a busy street in any big city, but the difference is that in nature, one often *chooses* the experience (recall cognitive freedom).

Seventh, when the challenge involves responsibility for others (such as being a scout leader), a person may seek a **guidance** experience. The chance to lead a group may be particularly important to someone whose city occupation involves little opportunity for leadership.

Most of the experiences already described involve a **social** dimension that is different from social life in the city. One spends time with different people in different activities; even being in nature with your family or friends is a different social experience than being with them in the city. Thus, we can be socially restored by nature. The ninth reason for being in nature is that it is often said that nature improves our **health,** both mental and physical, through the fresh air and exercise it offers.

Tenth, nature can provide a therapeutic experience by giving its visitors a chance to exert **self-control**.[48] This is not the same as perceived control, which would be difficult to attain in the wilderness, but a kind of self-confidence in which one feels able to accept whatever comes and adapt to it.

Does Nature Restore Us?

Casual experience suggests that all these experiences and benefits occur, at least for some people some times. That is, nature restores us by facilitating cognitive freedom, ecosystem connectedness, escape, challenge, growth, guidance, a renewed social life, and health. However, ca-

sual experience is not always borne out in carefully done studies. Research on the restorative capacity of nature has asked two basic questions: Does being out *in* nature restore us? Can nature benefit people in a building who merely have a *view* of nature? Let's begin with the latter issue.

Views of Nature. Merely looking at nature may well help to restore us. In one study, surgery patients who had a view of nature out their hospital room windows (as opposed to a view of a brick building) recovered faster. They had shorter hospital stays, fewer problems noted by nurses, and fewer postoperative medical problems.[49] In two studies of prisoners, those with nature views were less likely than those without nature views to make sick calls[50] or to report stress-related minor illnesses such as headaches and upset stomachs.[51]

In a more controlled laboratory study, students were shown a stress-inducing film about workplace accidents and then shown one of six short films that depicted natural or urban settings.[52] Students who were shown nature films recovered from the stressful experience faster, according to both self-report and physiological measures.

Not every study confirms the idea that nature views are beneficial, however. A study of nursing-home patients found that a nature view was related to a significant *decline* in mental status one month after admission to the home.[53] More research may be needed to clarify who benefits, under which conditions, from nature views.

Being in Nature. One would think that actually being in nature would have more beneficial effects than merely viewing it. However, before we deal with that issue, we should remember that nature is not always benign. Natural hazards will be discussed at length in the next section of this chapter. Nature can be dangerous in other ways, too. As I write this, a cougar recently attacked and nearly killed a boy walking to school on the island where I live; most summers, in fact, cougars are sighted in my community. People drown in lakes and fall off mountains. Nature is not always beneficent.

But are safe nature outings good for us? One study compared the feelings and performance of backpackers who took a wilderness vacation, a nonwilderness vacation, or no vacation.[54] The backpackers felt better and performed better on a proofreading task after they returned. Interestingly, the backpackers actually felt *worse* immediately after returning, but better some time later. Possibly they were a bit depressed at first about the return to society! These findings were confirmed in a second, more experimental study by the same scientists; the difference was that stressed subjects took a walk in a park (versus a walk in a built-up area or staying indoors).

Wilderness experiences may foster **self-actualization,** the fulfillment of one's potential for personal growth and psychological health. In a large-scale survey, individuals who spent time in wilderness areas were more self-actualized than those who did not.[55] A follow-up study found that among campers, those who appreciated wilderness more were slightly more self-actualized.[56] These correlational data do not *prove* that going into the wilderness causes self-actualization, but they are consistent with that hypothesis.

How Does Nature Restore Us?

The evidence is clear that nature usually helps people recover from stress associated with modern industrial life. But what is the mechanism by which this is accomplished?

Some theories argue that the benefits do not derive from nature itself, but from aspects of nature that may be found in other settings, too. One of these theories, the **affective-arousal approach,** asserts that nature's benefits derive from the positive emotions it elicits in us and that any calm, peaceful setting will have similar benefits.[57] A similar idea is that we get overloaded by stimuli in the built environment, and nature usually provides a reduction in stimulus level, which is restorative.[58] However, the study just described in which stressed students took a nature walk or sat in a calm room does not support this view.

Another proposal asserts that nature itself is not the main factor; culture is. This idea is that we learn through our family and culture to love nature and to dislike cities; thus, nature's benefits result more from being in a loved place than from nature's inherent qualities.[59] The cultural approach could be tested by determining whether nature experiences help people who are neutral

or negative toward the great outdoors, but such a test has not been made yet.

Two other theories argue that nature itself is the cause of nature's restorative abilities. One of these, advocated by Rachel and Stephan Kaplan, may be called the **mental fatigue approach**.[60] Nature, the authors believe, is inherently fascinating; that is, it compels our involuntary attention. This involuntary attention requires little or no effort; we simply take in the scene without trying. This is restorative because, ordinarily, in our workaday world, we are required to actively focus our attention most or all the time. Focused attention is taxing; we get tired. Nature provides a setting for nontaxing involuntary attention and we are gradually refreshed by being there.

The other theory that requires nature is the evolutionary approach taken by Roger Ulrich and colleagues.[61,62] This theory takes an even firmer position that nature is necessary for restoration (see Figure 13–2). Nature may be one of the few settings that is fascinating, but there are others—beautiful art, one's child or lover, for example. However, the basic thesis of the evolutionary or **biophilia approach** is that humans have evolved for two or three million years in natural environments, and we have only lived in cities for a tiny fraction of that time. Thus, genetically, we are much more

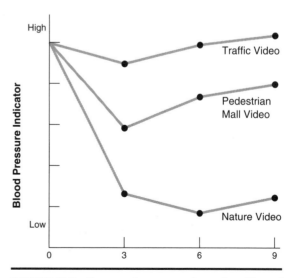

FIGURE 13–2 Recovery from stress after seeing videos of nature versus videos of malls.

adapted to natural than built settings. Being in nature is like going home, genetically. We are where we belong, where we fit in, and this is very restorative.

The Kaplans' approach is based on the recharging of our capacity for attention—a cognitive approach. Ulrich's approach assumes that nature makes us feel good—an affective approach. This difference reflects a larger issue in psychology about the relative primacy of affect and cognition.[63] But both theories agree that nature itself provides restorative benefits to people.

◆ **IN SUM,** *people have always believed that nature is restorative, even though it can be destructive, too. Different benefits or ways in way nature can be restorative are by facilitating cognitive freedom, escape, experiencing nature, ecosystem connectedness, growth, challenge, guidance, a renewed social life, health, and self-control. Being in nature, even merely viewing nature, can have restorative effects, although some researchers maintain that the same effects might be gained by features of nature that also may be found in civilization. The two main mechanisms by which nature restores us are through refreshing our attentional capacity and improving our moods by being "home."*

◆ NATURAL (AND TECHNOLOGICAL) ◆ HAZARDS

Big Trouble

A primary human goal is to forestall the possibility of violent death and destruction from fire, storm, flood, explosion, meltdown, avalanche, earthquake, and other major hazards. Despite these efforts, the annual death toll from such hazards is increasing. Each year, about 250,000 people are killed by extreme events of nature.[64] The number of technological accidents and catastrophes seems to be increasing.[65]

Hurricane Andrew destroyed about 28,000 residences and caused more than $25 billion in damage.[66] The 1994 earthquake in Kobe, Japan, killed over 5,000 people. In July 1976, the huge Tangshan earthquake killed between 250,000 (official estimates) and 800,000 (unofficial estimates) people in China. The 30-year average deaths caused by tornadoes is 82 per year; for hurricanes, 28 per year.

Disasters do not strike people equally. Fate appears to be kind to North America, which appears to receive fewer great natural blows than other continents. Within North America, some groups face greater risks than others. For example, the elderly make up about 12 percent of the U.S. population but comprise 29 percent of annual deaths by fire.[67] Blacks are more likely than whites to live near hazardous waste sites.[68] Naturally, then, we need to learn more about human response to the threat and the reality of environmental hazards. This section covers human preparation and response to these environmental disasters. Unfortunately, it also must cover human failure to prepare for and respond to them.

Definitions and Distinctions

As a preliminary step to organizing knowledge about hazards, efforts to classify them are still preliminary.[69] Environmental hazards may be easier to characterize by listing common types than by attempting a formal definition, but the following one is reasonably accurate and comprehensive (see Figure 13–3).

Environmental hazards are events of unusually large magnitude, often unpredictable and allowing little or no preparation, that cause death or injury to many people, destroy much property, and disrupt many social and economic activities. Sometimes, they are nonevents—for example, droughts. *Nonevents* are hazards that have no single low point, no particular "crunch" time. Sometimes,

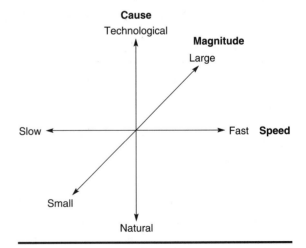

FIGURE 13–3 A way to classify environmental hazards: natural versus technological in origin, slow versus fast in speed, and large versus small in impact.

as with spring floods, environmental hazards are somewhat predictable and greater preparedness is possible.

Nearly everyone's home is threatened by one or more possible disasters. Some of these are **natural hazards:** flood, fire, storm, earthquake, heat or cold wave, volcano, drought, tsunami, avalanche, and so on. **Technological hazards,** in contrast, result from human works: nuclear plant accidents, radioactive or chemical spills and seepages, nuclear bombs, falling space debris, large explosions, floods due to broken dams, and so on. Of course, combinations are possible—such as when heavy rains cause a dam to break or an earthquake causes a nuclear power plant disaster.

Apart from their natural or human origins, these two kinds of environmental hazards differ in other ways, although some experts believe these differences are not always clear.[70] According to one view, technological catastrophes are more likely than natural ones to have direct long-term effects, to have effects far beyond the original place of impact, and to threaten us differently than natural hazards do.[71] For example, the 1979 nuclear accident at Three Mile Island is likely to have physical and psychological effects that spread farther and last longer than those from a tropical storm.

Both technological and natural hazards may have important *indirect* long-term effects, not all of which are bad. For example, the eruption of Santorini ruined the Minoan civilization, which stimulated the rise of Greek culture—the basis of our own civilization. Most large disasters spark legislation, which governs building codes and zoning for many subsequent years.[72]

Natural hazards usually occur rather suddenly (drought is one exception), but technological hazards often act slowly (explosions are one exception). One problem in the poorer areas of many urban areas, for example, is lead contamination. Lead occurs in some paints, in soil and air near smelters, in printing factories, in foundries and other industrial plants, and in traffic fumes. It has been associated with mental retardation, hyperactivity, and a variety of illnesses.[73]

Preparation and response to environmental hazards may be divided into three phases. *Before* the calamity, individuals who differ in age, education, and attachment to the community have (1) more or less knowledge about hazards and differing perceptions of the risk from a given hazard, (2) more or less experience with previous hazards, and (3) more or less education about hazards. *During* a calamity, individuals obviously experience a great deal of stress. They may be killed, injured, extremely frightened, stressed, lose friends or relatives, and see their property destroyed. *After* the calamity, victims must somehow cope with the experience. They seek a variety of solutions to future occurrences as well as compensation for their losses. Let us begin at the beginning—before calamity strikes.

Before the Calamity

Awareness: Knowing What Is Possible. Before disaster strikes, most of us are engaged in our normal routines. We may be aware that disaster is possible, our disaster plans may be in place, but unless someone refreshes our memory, we pay little attention to the possibility. After all, environmental disasters are relatively rare, most of us have never experienced one, and many other causes of death kill people more frequently. However, just one eruption, tornado, meltdown, hurricane, bomb, quake, flood, or fire easily can end your life. Take a moment to consider which disasters might strike *your* community.

Attitudes: Thoughts and Feelings about Hazards. Given that you are aware of potential hazards, what do you think and feel about them? Attitudes about environmental hazards are important to understand because they are related to the degree of preparation that people engage in, and preparation is often the key to survival. Attitudes include the following:

- How much knowledge individuals have about the possibility of a disaster
- How risky people perceive a hazard to be
- Whether people favor or oppose hazardous technological developments such as nuclear power or pesticides
- How much individuals trust authorities who dispense information or warnings
- People's beliefs about the costs and benefits of technological developments
- People's feelings such as fear or anxiety
- Individuals' behavioral tendencies such as coping style or whether they move away from the site of the calamity

Attitudes are related clusters of thoughts and feelings. Thus, for example, higher levels of concern, less trust in officials, greater perceived risk, increased fear and anxiety, greater opposition to hazardous technology, and environmentalism tend to go together.[74,75,76,77,78,79] Some hazards are feared more than others; for example, nuclear power plants generally are less acceptable than oil developments.[80] However, people who are fearful or concerned about one hazard are likely to be concerned about other hazards.[81] These clusters of thoughts and feelings are even similar across cultures.[82]

One important attitude concerns the favorability (or not) toward the planning, development, and use of hazardous technologies. Those who favor such technologies tend to be less worried about them and less willing to prepare for natural hazards; those who oppose these technologies tend to be more fearful, concerned, and willing to prepare for natural hazards.

Furthermore, those who favor dangerous technological developments such as nuclear power or hazardous waste disposal plants assign more credibility or weight to the project's benefits than to its costs. Nuclear plants provide power and jobs; waste disposal sites provide jobs. These are immediate and tangible benefits. The risks to health, the landscape, property values, and the social fabric of the community usually are less tangible, would occur later, and are more difficult to prove.

Naturally, part of the reason for favoring or opposing hazardous technology sites is related to direct outcomes from and associations with the sites. For example, individuals opposed to an arsenic-emitting smelter believed they were more vulnerable to its effects and have less choice about being exposed to the emissions.[83] Immigrant Mexican farm workers believe the risk to themselves from pesticide exposure is greater if they have experienced harm previously and believe exposure to the pesticide is unavoidable.[84]

However, other important bases for favoring or opposing dangerous technologies are less directly connected to the hazard itself. Attitudes toward environmental hazards are rooted in such antecedent factors as individual differences (e.g., sex, age, education, and personality), past experience with disasters, proximity to the potential disaster site, and exposure to media reports.

In general, women fear or oppose such hazardous technical developments more than men;[85,86,87] they also have greater concerns about such natural hazards as tornadoes[88] and earthquakes.[89] As usual, these differences appear to be more learned than genetic.[90] Married people and those with children at home are more concerned than nonparents.[91,92] Younger people usually report being more concerned or fearful.[93,94]

Attitudes toward environmental hazards can be influenced by media coverage.[95] The **heuristic** (inferential rule) used by individuals to estimate their probability of being harmed can be unduly influenced by the availability of **fallible indicators,** such as the high degree of **memorability** and **imaginability** of the event due to extensive media coverage.[96] TV documentaries can significantly shift attitudes about nuclear power,[97] although not every study agrees that TV programs can change a person's perception of risk.[98]

The primary purpose of documentaries usually is to inform rather than warn people; other research has examined the effects of media presentations meant to warn. For example, one study compared four public service ads designed to warn about earthquakes.[99] The images either contained a picture of earthquake damage or not, and contained estimates of the likelihood of a future quake or not. Subjects rated the images with pictures more likely to motivate them to prepare for an earthquake than those without pictures; the estimates of quake likelihood had no effect.

Officials must be careful with warnings; one prediction of a quake that did not happen produced mild but widespread stress disorders in children.[100] Another reason that warnings must be carefully planned is that people respond differently, depending on which medium carries the warning to them,[101] probably because warnings carried by radio, newspapers, and TV vary in memorability, vividness, and imaginability.

Closeness to the site of the environmental hazard also affects concern. Three kinds of closeness may be identified: physical proximity to the actual site, place attachment or length of residence in the community where the site is located, and experiential closeness (having experienced that hazard before).

Let's start with living physically close. You would expect that living close would lead to greater concern and opposition to an environmental hazard and less trust of official warnings, and this is often the case.[102,103] In accordance with this idea, social scientists have begun to create **risk perception shadows**—maps that show the degree of perceived risk as a function of distance from a hazard.[104]

However, concern does not always rise directly with closeness; in fact, the reverse sometimes occurs. For example, a study of northeastern U.S. residents whose community had *more* radon gas—that is, they were literally closer to it—found that residents tended to *under*estimate its health risks, whereas those whose community had *less* radon tended to *over*estimate its risks.[105]

As that study implies, sometimes—particularly if a hazard is difficult to control—residents deny or downplay a hazard, even when it is inside their own homes. Students who lived in a dormitory with very poor seismic safety ratings were significantly more likely to deny the seriousness of the situation than students who lived in dorms with good seismic ratings.[106] Teens who live 3 miles from a nuclear power plant were less fearful of it than teens who live 64 miles away.[107] Agricultural workers who believe that finding an alternative occupation would be difficult also believe their risk from pesticides is less.[108]

The second form of closeness is place attachment or length of residence in the community. Studies of proposed nuclear power plants, coal liquification plants, and arsenic-emitting smelters show that permanent community residents (as opposed to temporary residents such as students) tend to favor such proposals more than short-term residents.[109,110] For technological hazards, at least, familiar risks—assuming familiarity grows with length of residence—appear to be more tolerable than unfamiliar risks. However, for natural hazards, residents who have lived in an area longer believe the probability of a future earthquake is higher.[111]

The third form of closeness is experience or familiarity with hazards. Experience with hazards obviously affects people's attitudes toward them; in one study, for example, people who had experienced an earthquake were more concerned about future quakes than those with no experience.[112] Once again, however, attitudes toward natural and technological hazards is not always the same. Residents of a community that already had a nuclear power plant were *more* favorable to a new plant than residents of other communities in the area.[113] Pre-

sumably, as the benefits of the plant accrued and no costs were salient, acceptance grows. Furthermore, a study was made of the fears of Washington State residents 5 months before and 1 month after the Chernobyl accident. People thought about and discussed a nearby nuclear plant more, and their expectation that they would develop cancer or suffer genetic changes actually declined.[114]

Attitudes toward hazardous technology also can depend on the importance that individuals place on previous problems they have experienced with it. For example, individuals who downplayed the importance of Three Mile Island's problems were more accepting of a local nuclear power plant.[115] Thus, denial can lead to apparently positive attitudes.

Social interaction can influence attitudes. When people in an affected area discuss natural or technological hazards, risk may be **socially amplified;**[116] that is, one's risk estimates can be increased, decreased, or shaped by the social, cultural, psychological, and institutional context in which risk is discussed. Simply put, people can alarm *or* assure one another. Perhaps because we tend to discuss hazards with others who share our views, we have a tendency toward **false consensus,** the belief that more others have the same beliefs as ourselves than actually is the case.[117,118]

Personality also plays a role in hazard perception. As you would expect, persons who are typically or dispositionally more anxious or less trusting are more likely to be concerned[119] and to expect that there will be greater risk of death and damage.[120,121] Specific risks cause dispositionally anxious persons more anxiety.[122] It does not help these people, with their usually higher state of anxiety, that they are more likely to deny the importance of an actual disaster warning when it arrives.[123]

Individuals with an internal locus of control are more likely to be aware that there is a hazard,[124] and perhaps because they are accustomed to thinking they can change things, internals experience more stress when an environmental threat that is very difficult to change is near their home.[125] Similarly, people who tend to cope with stressors in a problem-solving manner (as opposed to those who fight stress by working on their own emotions) experience more stress when the threat is a hazardous waste dump that is already in place, and therefore very difficult to change.[126]

Personality is an interrelated set of dispositions or behavior tendencies. One research team examined the statements made by residents who live near a large chemical-industrial complex in the Netherlands and found that many showed one of four major patterns,[127] which we might call **hazard response personalities.** Each pattern to be described next shows more anxiety and concern about environmental hazards than the previous one.

The least anxious pattern is the Secure personality, whose attitude is, "What hazard? Is there a hazard around here?" Next is the Accepting personality, who tends to say, "Well, it's not good, but life is a trade-off—if we want modern goods, we have to accept some risks." Then comes the Defensive personality, who claims, "It isn't all that bad, you know; people exaggerate these risks." Finally, and most anxious, is the Vigilant personality, who believes "They don't tell you everything; reality is probably worse than they or anyone knows."

More educated people tend to have fewer fears and concerns about hazards.[128,129,130] This is consistent with older research that shows that more sophisticated individuals are less vulnerable to threats of other kinds.[131] This does not mean that more educated people think hazards are less likely—in fact, they even may believe hazards are *more* likely[132]—but simply that they are less fearful about hazards.

This educational difference parallels a very widespread and important difference between two groups: experts (who presumably have technical education on the topic) and laypersons (who presumably do not).[133] Compare, in Table 13–1, the risk rankings (out of 30 risks presented) of some technological hazards by League of Voters members, college students, and experts.[134] Such disagreements reflect the serious policy, planning, and expenditure conflicts among environmental activists, middle-class citizens, and experts. They also create an ominous potential for chaos in the event of large-scale disaster, because the biggest difference is between experts and laypersons (students and women voters). There are several possible reasons for these disagreements.[135]

1. Experts and the rest of us speak different languages when it comes to hazard risks. To experts, for example, the very word *risk* tends to mean average fatalities per

TABLE 13–1 Ratings of the Risk from Selected Environmental Hazards by College Students, League of Women Voters Members, and Experts

	League of Women Voters	College Students	Experts
Nuclear power	1	1	20
Pesticides	9	4	8
Motor vehicles	2	5	1
Hunting	13	18	23
Skiing	21	25	30
Mountain climbing	15	12	29
Electric power	18	19	9

Raters judged the risk of 30 hazards (low ranking signifies high risk).

year. To nonexperts, however, *risk* often means fatality rate plus other factors, such as the evenness with which the risk is spread through the community.

2. Experts and nonexperts may be trying to solve different problems. When faced with a particular risk, the two groups may perceive different sets of possible solutions and different sets of potential consequences of the risk. They may think they are struggling with the same threat, but their differing conceptions of that threat mean that they often are not really on the same track.

3. Experts and laypersons often disagree about which solutions are feasible. In considering what should be done about a risk, experts often are aware of a greater variety of possible technological solutions, but they also feel constrained to limit their actions to a certain policy mandate or budget. Concerned citizens, on the other hand, tend to see political action as a solution—that is, changing the policy or budget rather than being constrained by it.

4. Experts and others may actually see the facts differently. This may arise because experts withhold some key information, because nonexperts fail to do their homework, because the mass media distort facts, or because the two groups gained their facts from different sources.

5. Experts try to consider risks and benefits separately, but most laypersons do not separate the two. For example, if people are given more information about the *benefits* of

pesticides, they begin to associate fewer *risks* with pesticides, even though nothing was said about the risks.[136]

Officials and experts often describe lay estimates of risk as unreasonable or even irrational because they differ from their own estimates, based on technical and quantitative analyses. However, unreasonable or irrational risk perceptions would make no sense; in reality, the risk perceptions of laypeople make considerable sense when the context of their perceptions is understood.[137] That is, laypeople view risks in quite understandable ways that reflect their personal, cultural, political, and economic situations.[138,139]

Put another way, experts employ a **technical model** for estimating risk and making decisions that places more value on rationality, efficiency, and expertise. However, laypersons base their risk estimates on a **democratic model** that places more emphasis on personal, experiential, and social values.[140] In England, for example, many people were opposed to a new nuclear plant who were not anti-nuclear in principle (e.g., they were not worried about health or safety), but they opposed it because it posed a threat to the landscape, in their view.[141]

So who is right in these disagreements—experts or laypersons? You might assume that the experts are correct. However, for at least some technologies, the experts themselves disagree with one another, so they cannot always be correct. Furthermore, experts are not always confident about their assessments of the effects of environmental hazards on people.[142] In many instances, there really may be no correct answer—at least until much later, when time and experience show who was right.

Laypersons misperceive risks, too, and their tendency to think unclearly about the hazard has even been given a name: **bounded rationality**.[143] For example, many people incorrectly estimate the odds that a particular environmental hazard will affect them. In one study, individuals were asked the odds of a lightning strike in comparison to another hazard, botulism, a potentially fatal form of food poisoning.[144] The average response was that botulism was 3.33 times more likely; actually, lightning is 52 times more likely!

Another example of risk misperception is provided in a study of a technological hazard—the falling of *Skylab* in July 1979.[145] On the day before the expected crash,

Israelis were asked what their chances of being injured by falling debris were, on a scale of 0 to 100 percent. Over half the respondents gave answers of over 1 percent, which itself is a very large overestimate. One expert calculates that the odds of *Skylab* striking any specific person were about 1 in 200 billion.[146] These misperceptions were related to several personal characteristics: Younger individuals, women, less educated individuals, and more anxious individuals overestimated their chances of being struck by *Skylab*.

Can anything be done about the differences in lay and expert risk perception? Certainly. Many procedures have been identified that should help bring experts and laypersons closer together in a joint effort to combat hazards.

1. The mental models used by laypersons and experts should be identified and compared. In a study of lay versus expert opinion about the use of nuclear power in space, investigators literally mapped out models of how each group thinks about the hazard.[147]

2. Concepts and terminology must be agreed upon. There cannot be a fruitful discussion unless the definitions of key concepts are the same. For example, does the word *risk* refer solely to the odds of being injured, or can it include other forms of harm?

3. Gaps in technical knowledge should be eliminated. Laypeople must recognize they need to learn factual material, even though the discussions probably need to go beyond facts.

4. Alternative solutions and possible consequences must be clarified. The feasibility of technical and political strategies for nullifying hazards must be discussed.

5. All pertinent facts, including the sources of those facts, must be disclosed and recognized.

6. The similarities and differences of the mental models (exactly what is believed to cause what) should be made clear to everyone.

7. Ideas and issues that really should be outside the discussion should be recognized.

Preparedness. When environmental psychologists assume their usual role as problem solvers, the problem to be solved in this context is to get people who are threatened by an environmental hazard to prepare. Obviously, it is important to know who is likely to be prepared and what sort of influences can be used to increase preparedness among individuals who are not prepared.

Preparedness comes in several varieties. A person might call the local emergency preparation office for a pamphlet on how to upgrade the house to withstand a hurricane; stock the cellar with food, first-aid supplies, and radio batteries in case of a tornado; wear protective clothing when using pesticides; or organize a meeting to oppose a proposed local hazardous waste dump. More generally, we can say that preparation can take four forms: information seeking, household readiness, self-protective behavior, and political involvement. Examples of each of these will be given.

The residents of a certain community were threatened by water contamination.[148] Those who sought information about how to reduce their risk from contaminated water tended to be those who perceived their personal risk to be greater and those who trusted the experts' ability to solve the problem less. As expected, the information seekers knew more about how to combat the water problem, and thus were more prepared.

The second form of preparedness is household readiness. The goal is to get everyone who might be struck by an environmental hazard to prepare their residences as much as possible and to learn what to do if disaster strikes. To achieve this goal, it helps to know who in a large community is likely to have already prepared and who has probably has not; efforts to improve preparedness can then be targeted more efficiently.

The value of preparation is shown by the outcome of a study done on building damage caused by hurricanes in Texas and North Carolina. About 70 percent of the damage was the result of poor building code enforcement.[149] In areas where building codes were strictly enforced, only 3 percent of affected dwellings suffered major structural damage. Residents either must induce local authorities to enforce building codes, even retroactively, or upgrade their residences themselves. In the case of Hurricane Andrew, the building codes are excellent—but enforcement was lax. Experts say that 4 to 6 billion dollars could have been saved by improved enforcement of building codes.

Typically, attempts to predict who will and who will not ready their households are based on such person- and situation-based factors as sex, age, proximity to the danger, and environmental concern. For example, a study of which residents in a flood-threatened area had taken out flood insurance yielded the unsurprising result that those who were employed and were better educated were more likely to have done so.[150]

However, some less obvious variables also can help to improve prediction. For example, consider the **theory of reasoned action**. What others *expect* you to believe (such as that nothing can be done about flooding, or that something *can* be done) and your belief that a given behavior *will* have consequences (such as that fastening bookshelves to walls will—or will not—prevent injury during an earthquake) are important predictors of preparedness.[151,152]

Bounded rationality can affect whether we do or do not prepare for disaster.[153] We tend to perceive and adopt a narrower than necessary range of **adjustments** (preparations) to the possibility of a disaster. Often, of course, *no* adjustments are made—we simply wait for disaster to strike. Even when we do make adjustments, such as taking out insurance or stocking emergency food, we tend to make fewer of adjustments than we know about. We also tend to be aware of fewer adjustments than are actually available.

We also seem to prefer **crisis response**—that is, to wait until disaster strikes before preparing for the *next* one. We routinely misperceive risks from environmental hazards.[154] Some of us erroneously believe that hazards occur in cycles and "it isn't time yet," others place too much faith in such protective devices as dams, and some of us deny that the hazard exists at all. One flood victim, when asked why he had not prepared, answered that he

PAUL SLOVIC'S

research concentrates on expert and layperson assessments of environmental hazards, and on the attempt to reconcile the differences.

didn't prepare because floods don't happen in his town—only "high water."

The third form of preparedness is to engage in self-protective behavior. When the threat comes from some slow-acting but nearby source such as air pollution or pesticides, individuals may (or may not) adopt preventive measures. Self-protective behavior is most likely to occur in persons who know about the risk, believe they have some control over their own health and job, and believe that precautions really work.[155] Women, in one study, took more steps to avoid exposure more than men.[156]

Those who already suffer from an ailment related to the hazard—such as lung-diseased people who live in an area with serious air pollution—may take *fewer* precautions.[157] Perhaps these people believe the damage has already been done and it will not worsen, or perhaps whatever influenced them to endanger themselves in the first place continues to influence them even after their health has been damaged.

For some, the fourth but best form of preparation for potential disaster is political involvement. When hazardous waste facilities are proposed in one's community, some people donate time or money, or organize or attend meetings. A study of a rural community near Phoenix, Arizona, showed that persons who got involved were more likely to use **problem-focused coping** (trying to solve problems by changing the source of their stress) rather than **emotion-focused coping** (trying to solve problems by changing their own emotional reactions to the source of their stress).[158] An Australian study of residents facing another proposal to place a hazardous waste facility nearby found that residents who become slightly involved politically (e.g., signing a petition or attending a meeting) tend to be those who have lived longer in the neighborhood or who have children. Those who become more seriously involved tend to be those with a greater financial stake (e.g., greater property value).[159]

Obviously, many other residents never become politically active. The town with the "number one toxic waste dump" in the United States has a "conspicuous absence of . . . sustained and forceful protest" about the dump.[160] The town's residents, in general, have a high level of trust in government, which apparently reduces their perceived need to protest. The minority of residents who did become involved tended to be those who believe they can make a difference, have more education, and are married.

The experimental study of *how* individuals become politically involved is in its infancy, although we know that certain demographic factors such as socioeconomic status are correlated with political involvement. In one study, however, the effect of graphic images as a motivating force was examined.[161] Students were shown a set of slides depicting serious water pollution—such as images of police officers collecting medical refuse on a beach and poisoned fish washed up on a shore—or were shown a set of control slides that did not depict water pollution. When asked for help, the former group offered significantly more verbal commitment to a local water pollution activist group and they backed up their verbal commitment with more donations than the latter group.

Some research on disaster preparations focuses on how to get more people more prepared. One influence that *ought* to be facilitating our preparations for environmental hazards, but is *not* doing that very well, is education. Educational programs about disaster often are fragmented and, as a consequence, so is individual knowledge of local potential disasters.[162] Publicity about disaster plans can be surprisingly poor at raising community awareness.[163]

Where disasters have not occurred recently, preparations for them are rare. Where they are frequent, preparations are more often incorporated into daily living. Thus, education in the absence of any recent disaster may be ineffective, but frequent or recent experience is a great teacher. For example, those who live in Bangladesh's delta country experience frequent storms and floods. They are very poor, yet they still invest much effort in small levees, elevated platforms for themselves and their livestock, and special anchoring devices. Of course, the larger cyclonic storms overcome these preparations, killing many people and destroying agricultural lands.

The lack of preparation for uncommon disasters means that the most dangerous environmental hazards are the rare but large ones. Most of us are aware that cataclysmic events may occur, but this does not often lead to action.[164] For effective action on the part of potential victims, vague warnings will not suffice. Where warnings are possible, they must:

- Be clear and contain specific directions
- Come from a credible source
- Be reinforced socially at the local level
- Use an appropriate medium of communication

Experts warn of a pervasive myth that may be expressed as follows: If we educate, we will change attitudes, which, in turn, will change behavior.[165] Research to date indicates that this sequence simply does not occur in most environmental hazard situations.

What about warning threatened residents (see Figure 13–4)? If you received a letter describing a possible earthquake or hurricane in your community, would you actually take steps to increase your household readiness? Based on a study of Los Angeles-area individuals, it depends on what the letter says.[166] Altogether, 16 different forms of a warning letter were sent. Each letter included material that emphasized one side or the other of four themes: the quake is highly likely (or not), the severity of the quake was likely to be great (or not), being prepared is likely to reduce damage (or not), and getting prepared is easy (or not).

Merely receiving this letter (regardless of which version) made little difference in the residents' preparedness, but certain forms of it were effective. In particular, letters asserting that the probability of a quake was high and that preparation does help to reduce the damage caused by the quake significantly increased preparedness.

Awareness of a hazard threat may lead to better preparation if that awareness is grounded in experience.

FIGURE 13-4   Hazard warnings are not always heeded.

Some 22 years after a tornado ripped through Flint, Michigan, residents who lived near the path of the tornado were interviewed.[167] The investigators discovered that residents who were aware of the 1953 tornado were more likely to make preparations such as taking shelter upon hearing a tornado warning and having tornado insurance than residents who had actually experienced the 1953 tornado.

These findings are encouraging in that they suggest better preparedness need not result only from bitter experience; if individuals can be made aware of the specific hazard possibilities, they may be better prepared for disaster. Disasters, simulations, and field exercises clearly improve preparedness.[168]

During the Calamity

Until this point, the disaster has not happened. This section deals with what happens when the potential hazard becomes an actual hazard. What do we know about people's behavior, thoughts, and feelings as the disaster unfolds?

The First Moments: Stand Up and Protect. The first question concerns panic. When the disaster strikes, do people panic? Most individuals do *not* panic during disaster. There are many well-documented cases of victims acting as calmly, rationally, and effectively as possible under the circumstances.[169,170] If people are not panicking, then, just what *are* they doing?

John Archea asked Japanese people who underwent a 1982 earthquake that measured 7.1 on the Richter scale exactly what they did during the 30-second quake.[171] The average person engaged in five separate actions and moved 27 feet. About half turned off gas valves or gas flames (good idea), over a third grabbed freestanding cabinets to keep them and their contents from falling (bad idea), about a quarter went outside (often a bad idea), and about a fifth helped others (usually a good idea).

Archea followed this up with a study of earthquake behavior among people who lived in the town of Aptos, near the center of the 1989 Loma Prieta earthquake in California. This quake was the same strength as the earlier Japanese one, but its main shock was shorter (10 to 12 seconds). Virtually everyone responded first by standing up (if they were not already standing) and walking (bad idea). About 93 percent were in position to be hit by flying debris. However, by the end of the shock, about half had assumed a more protected position (good idea).

The average person moved about 14 feet and engaged in four distinct actions. Half sought a protected place for shelter. A fifth did nothing; they just stood or sat there waiting for the quake to cease. Another fifth helped someone else. Only 7 percent went outside, but of course there was less time to get outside during the Loma Prieta quake than during the Japanese quake.

Not everyone responds the same. The Aptos residents mostly were middle-class Anglos, and about half were retired. Archea also interviewed a sample of Hispanic agricultural workers who generally were younger, poorer, and had more children at home. They had the same initial reaction (stood up), but they then moved around more, tried to help others (their children, especially) more, and went outside more.

Thus, the immediate response to sudden disaster has some similarities and some differences depending on economic status, stage of the family cycle, and culture. (Archea says that in Latin America people are told to go outside during quakes.) Archea speculates, quite reasonably, that after the first seconds of shock, people move to protect what is most dear to them (see Figure 13–5).

Some people, of course, do collapse completely or act in ways that endanger their own and others' lives. Other common soon-after reactions to disaster include confusion, irritability, lethargy, withdrawal, and crying.[172] How these stress reactions may be ameliorated will be discussed later, but panic behavior is immediately important because it is dangerous. Therefore, some research goals are to discover who is likely to panic, under what specific circumstances, and to find ways to reduce panic in future situations. For example, a study of flood victims showed that the calmer individuals were those who knew more about the flood hazard in their area.[173] Presumably, knowledge about a hazard helps a person feel more control or certainty, even when the water is rising.

A special case is the person at the center of a disaster, such as someone who works at a nuclear plant when things start to go wrong. These employees may experience even more stress than others because they have the same fears as everyone else, but they also feel responsible for causing the problem, solving it, or both. During the Three Mile Island nuclear incident, employees naturally

FIGURE 13–5 A rare photo of what individuals do *during* earthquakes.

felt significantly more tension than employees at other, nearby nuclear plants.[174] In particular, they felt overloaded and they experienced considerable conflict about what to do because of the uncertainty at the plant and how this might affect their families.

The Immediate Aftermath: Evacuation and Therapeutic Communities. Immediately after disasters strike, many survivors leave the building or the community. Building evacuation is a crucial process because it can be done very successfully (no injuries) or very unsuccessfully (many deaths). Evacuation from the community is a big decision that may have benefits (safety from further exposure to the hazard) as well as costs (possible looting of one's home, the expense of traveling, traffic jams).

Building evacuation depends, in part, on the design of the building, such as whether there are enough doors, stairs, and exit signs. Terrible disasters in which trapped people died have helped refine building design rules into most building codes; safety legislation is in place and safety equipment is available.[175] But the human element is still not fully understood; evacuation may be unsuccessful even when the building design follows the design rules set forth in building codes.

In England, researchers examined what shoppers and staff did as they became aware of an existing large fire that ultimately killed 50 people in a store.[176] Designers of escape routes assume a **physical science and complementary panic model**, which predicts that when people realize they are in danger, they will head for emergency exits, assuming the exits are nearby and visible. The **affiliative model**, in contrast, predicts that people will move toward their companions first. What happened?

Interviews revealed that shoppers mainly conformed to the affiliative model, but staff mainly conformed to the physical science model. Of course, shoppers were much more likely than staff to be accompanied by friends or family. Thus, it appears that the affiliative model holds when loved ones are near, and is the model of choice when people could follow either model, but the physical science model holds when loved ones are not nearby.

Pro-active approaches to evacuation do not assume that good signs and exits will be enough to get everyone out safely. For example, a Japanese study compared the Follow Directions method, in which leaders tell people where to go with loud voices and vigorous gestures, with the Follow Me method, in which leaders actually take a few people where they should go.[177] The results showed that the Follow Me method worked best when each leader had a few (four or so) people to guide, but the Follow Directions model worked better when each leader had to guide many more people.

Evacuations also occur at the community level. Typically, authorities call for everyone to leave, but not everyone does. One famous case was the man who had lived on Mount St. Helens for a long time; he was told that an eruption was imminent and was asked to leave, but he did not. A study of who evacuated, who did not, and why, after the Three Mile Island nuclear incident, is instructive.[178] Nearby residents received conflicting information and had to decide for themselves what was best.

About a third of the 660,000 residents within 20 miles of the plant decided to leave. About two-thirds later said they left after hearing the governor's call for evacuation. About half returned after a week, and almost everyone returned within two weeks. About 60 percent said they left out of fear for their children or their health. Evacuation rates varied depending on one's situation: Residents were more likely to leave if they lived closer to the plant, were younger, if the household was larger (usually when small children were involved), and if they had neighbors who also left.

However, about 40 percent said they left because of the uncertainty caused by conflicting reports and unclear leadership. Because of the costs of evacuation, it is important to evacuate only when it is necessary. This study shows that many residents left out of uncertainty; that should not be the reason for leaving. Residents should hear clear, uniform calls to stay or to leave, and obviously the calls should be correct—no false positives (go when it is not necessary) or false negatives (stay when you should have evacuated). Evacuation rates should not differ by age or household size. At the same distance from the disaster everyone is equally at risk. Therefore, calls to evacuate should pay particular attention to groups who are less likely to heed the call to leave.

One frequent immediate postdisaster phenomenon is the **therapeutic community,** when even unrelated people work hard together during the disaster or very soon afterward. Therapeutic communities often develop in response to fast-acting natural disasters, but how about technological disasters? Case studies of two technological hazards—aerial pesticide spraying and the disposal of asbestos—indicate that therapeutic communities are not likely to develop in response to technological hazards.[179] This may be because the hazard's effects unfold slowly, because of confusion about who is or is not a victim, and because of community conflict about whether a hazard really exists at all.

After the Calamity

The study of environmental hazards harks back to 1917, when a Red Cross supply ship collided with another ship loaded with 3,000 tons of TNT and other explosive materials in the harbor at Halifax, Nova Scotia. The resulting explosion was the largest ever recorded until the first atomic bombs were dropped. It killed about 2,000 people, injured about 8,000, and flattened many homes in Halifax and the neighboring town of Dartmouth. One can still see pieces of the ships embedded in the walls of surviving buildings. The social-psychological responses of the victims were studied and recommendations were made for methods to avoid future disasters and to improve community relief efforts if they did recur.[180]

Thus, the most compelling reason for postdisaster research is that the postdisaster phase also happens to be the period preceding the next disaster. This may be divided into knowledge about what happens soon after a disaster and knowledge about how society and individuals go about mitigating future disasters.

Soon Afterward: Cognition, Behavior, and Mental Health. What happens a little later? In the case of natural disasters, this means what happens after the immediate worst, sometimes called the **low point**? In the case of technological hazards, this means what happens soon after people realize that a serious threat exists? What do people typically think and do? What are the effects on their mental health?

In terms of thoughts, people respond to disaster with worry and appraisals of blame and support. Who is to blame? Who will pay? Will it happen again? Who will help? *Will* anyone help? Sadly, survivors receive much

less help than they expected they would before the disaster.[181] Even after an incident such as the Three Mile Island nuclear plant accident, which caused no deaths and few injuries, or death, worry soars. It rises to the point where worries about nuclear energy equal worries over money, health, and friendship.[182] Clearly, when the disaster is greater, worry will be greater and, as will we see later, may cause mental health problems.

Women, on average, worry more than men in such situations, and this may cause them to cope more actively than men. This may occur because men, on average, show more trust in technology.[183] Of course, some people deny the reality of a threat that is real but that has not yet had a clear impact on them. Fishers in a Puerto Rican estuary that was contaminated by mercury were aware of the threat, but they denied that it was important or believed that the "real" contamination was elsewhere in the estuary.[184] These thoughts enabled them to keep eating the fish they caught in the estuary.

Who is to blame? Who should pay? Survivors of disasters typically want *someone* to pay. In natural disasters, they expect the government to help; in technological disasters, they expect both the government and any company involved to pay. The issue of who should pay how much in technological disasters is complex and depends on whether the company or organization was following safety guidelines and using the best available technology when the accident happened.[185] For example, in a hypothetical flood scenario, the more severe the flood, the more that women blamed an official in charge of levee maintenance. Men, in contrast, were more likely to check whether the official had been doing the job properly, and based their blame on that criterion rather than on the severity of the flood.[186]

Unfortunately, many people who are unaffected by the disaster see the *victims* rather than the government or a company as blameworthy,[187] a tendency known as **blaming the victim**. The reasoning for such thinking is usually, "Well, they shouldn't have been living in that area, anyway. They knew that floods happen there."

Before a disaster happens, many individuals believe they will be able to control dangerous events—an **illusion of control**. When fate spares a person, even when neighbors are struck, this illusion is strengthened.[188] Thus, if a disaster injures or kills only a fraction of the people in a community, many other residents will tend to believe, *more than before,* that they can handle future disasters. This can be a big mistake.

Some technological disasters affect not so much *what* people think as *how well* they can think. Czech children who lived in a heavily polluted area could not remember things as well as a matched group who lived in an unpolluted area.[189]

Will the disaster happen again? Will there be serious aftershocks, new flooding, another emission of radioactivity? In the case of technological hazards, this depends, in part, on previous beliefs: Those who supported a technology before it caused a problem tend to think the disaster will not happen again, yet opponents think it will.[190] In the case of natural hazards, those who feared the disaster more than others before it happened are more likely to fear that it will happen again.[191]

So much for thoughts soon after the calamity. What sorts of behaviors are seen soon after? Here, we are mainly interested in whether residents move out of the area, what happens in their close relationships, and whether they protest or organize against the causes of the disaster.

Unless a disaster is extreme, most residents do not move; ties to jobs, family, friends, and the physical setting result in place attachment, which tends to keep people in a place even after a disaster. After the Three Mile Island nuclear incident, for example, only about 2 percent of residents who lived within five miles had moved away a year later.[192] One study of the movers suggested that those who leave fear the threat more and those who stay have more faith that experts can ease the threat.[193] However, another study found that the rate of moving (2 percent) was the same *before* the incident, and even though movers *said* they moved because of the incident,

their attitudes toward Three Mile Island were no different from those who did not move.[194] However, people who moved *into* the neighborhood tended to have favorable attitudes toward Three Mile Island.

If most people do not leave, do they remain passive or become active in fighting the source of the disaster? In a fascinating study of people who lived in a flood-stricken area, researchers traced the steps that led to activism or not (see Figure 13–6).[195] The results of the study are described in some detail because the same pattern may apply to activism in the face of other environmental threats.

First, residents must perceive the flood as controllable. You might think floods cannot be controlled, but when a system of levees and dams has been constructed to prevent flooding, some people will believe the flood could have been controlled by a *better* system of engineering. (Such disasters show how the distinction between natural and technological hazards is not always clear.)

Residents who believed floods are *not* controllable tended to deal with the disaster through emotion-focused coping—going inside themselves to cope. Those who believed the flood was controllable tended to see floods as a future threat. Seeing floods as a future threat was associated more strongly with problem-focused coping—the tendency to deal with a stressor by attacking it. Finally, problem-focused coping was strongly associated with activism.

Unfortunately, disasters may split communities when activists committed to different perceptions of and solutions to the problem argue with each other, try to recruit other residents, and sometimes clash with residents who believe there is no real problem. In Centralia, Pennsylvania, an underground coal fire has burned for 30

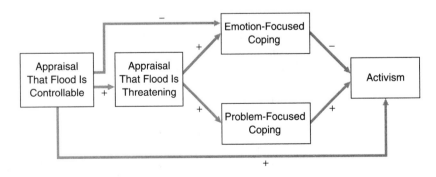

FIGURE 13–6   Research suggests this causal model for predicting who will engage in activism and who will not.

years; as many as seven groups exist to fight the problem, and some residents believe the whole thing is a hoax.

As many as 100,000 sites in the United States alone are threatened by toxic waste dump sites. When a community becomes aware of this problem, ties to the community are weakened both by knowing that you live in a contaminated place and by struggling over the best solution or form of activism.[196] Of course, having a reduced sense of community leads to greater distress in the wake of the disaster.[197]

Other postdisaster behavioral changes that have been documented include the rate of marriage among survivors. Although a U.S. study of six large-scale disasters could find little evidence that disasters affected marriage or divorce,[198] the huge 1976 Tangshan earthquake in China had an important effect. Remarriage after the death of a spouse is traditionally discouraged in China, but 2,000 of 3,000 widowed people in Tangshan remarried within a few years, primarily to provide economic security and to ease personal suffering.[199]

This leads to the third major outcome of disasters: stress and other mental health problems. Survivors, of course, suffer considerable stress from the losses they suffer and the shock of experiencing an overwhelming event (see Table 13–2).

Some psychologists focus on the mental health outcomes of disasters to individuals. Immediately, many survivors show signs of **posttraumatic stress disorder** (**PTSD**), but depression, phobias,[200] and medically unexplained symptoms such as abdominal pain, vomiting, nausea, fainting, amnesia, and even paralysis[201] are also seen. In many ways, victims avoid the overwhelming reality facing them. For example, those who survived the November 1985 volcano and mudslide that killed about 22,000 people in Armero, Colombia, often did not want to know the full extent of the tragedy and resorted to primitive ("magical") thinking styles.[202]

The stress reactions of residents living near Mount St. Helens were assessed after the eruption of 1980.[203] By comparing the rates of various social and personal pathological behavior before and after the event, researchers documented increases in alcohol abuse, family stress, illness, and violence. One ray of positive light emerged when the researchers discovered a 90 percent decrease in child abuse; unfortunately, other domestic violence rose by almost 50 percent.

After the Exxon oil spill in Alaska, traditional social relations in the area declined, people engaged in less fishing and hunting, and residents believed their health declined and that drug use, alcohol use, and domestic violence increased.[204] After a large Australian bush fire, families experienced more conflict, withdrawal, and irritability, and mothers tended to overprotect their children.[205] After the 1989 earthquake near San Francisco, college students had many more nightmares than students in another (unaffected) town.[206]

Residents living near Three Mile Island at the time of the nuclear reactor accident were examined for stress and sense of control.[207] Residents reported feeling less control over their lives and performed more poorly on tasks measuring persistence. Those reporting more loss of their sense of control also had more symptoms of stress. Nearby residents, particularly men, showed elevated levels of biochemicals associated with stress for at least 17 months after the accident.[208]

Many similar studies have been conducted after major natural and technological disasters. The results of 52 carefully done studies were quantitatively summarized in a meta-analysis.[209] It found that, compared to normal conditions, a 17 percent increase in the rate of psychopathology is found in the wake of disaster. Of course, this figure is averaged across all the studies and disasters in the meta-analysis. Naturally, mental health problems are greater when more people are killed. For example, in the Armero disaster, major depression and posttraumatic stress disorder affected about 50 percent of the survivors.[210] Women appear more strongly affected by disaster. Adolescent girls report more nightmares and fear of being alone than adolescent boys.[211]

A study of tornado victims found that younger people experienced more physical stress, anxiety, and disruption to their social lives than older people, possibly because older people have learned more coping mechanisms.[212] Distress is also greater when victims mistrust authorities.[213] One study reports the surprising finding that among people struck by Hurricane Hugo, those who had taken part in disaster education and other preparedness activities manifested *more* physiological and psychological stress than those who had not![214]

The amount of stress caused by the disaster partly depends on one's circumstances before it strikes. People who were already showing signs of stress before the dis-

TABLE 13-2 Foster's System for Assessing the Impact of Environmental Hazards and Some Stress Scores for Selected Large Events

Infrastructural Stress Values

Magnitude	Designation	Characteristics	Stress Value
I	Very minor	Noticed only by instruments.	0
II	Minor	Noticed only by sensitive people.	2
III	Significant	Noticed by most people including those indoors.	5
IV	Moderate	Everyone fully aware of event. Some inconvenience experienced, including transportation delays.	10
V	Rather pronounced	Widespread sorrow. Everyone greatly inconvienenced; normal routines disrupted. Minor damage to fittings and unstable objects. Some crop damage.	17
VI	Pronounced	Many people disturbed and some frightened. Minor damage to old or poorly constructed buildings. Transportation halted completely. Extensive crop damage.	25
VII	Very pronounced	Everyone disturbed; many frightened. Event remembered clearly for many years. Considerable damage to poorly built structures. Crops destroyed. High livestock losses. Most people suffer financial losses.	65
VIII	Destructive	Many injured. Some panic. Numerous normal buildings severely damaged. Heavy loss of livestock.	80
IX	Very destructive	Widespread initial disorganization. Area evacuated or left by refugees. Fatalities common. Routeways blocked. Agriculture adversely affected for many years.	100
X	Disastrous	Many fatalities. Masonry and frame structures collapse. Hazard-proofed buildings suffer considerable damage. Massive rebuilding necessary.	145
XI	Very disastrous	Major international media coverage. Worldwide appeals for aid. Majority of population killed or injured. Wide range of buildings destroyed. Agriculture may never be reestablished.	180
XII	Catastrophic	Future textbook example. All facilities completely destroyed; often little sign of wreckage. Surface elevation may be altered. Site often abandoned. Rare survivors become life-long curiosities.	200

Examples of Event Magnitude

Event	Location	Date	Magnitude
Plague (Black Death)	Europe/Asia	14th century	10.9
Spanish Armada	British coastal waters	July 21–29, 1588	7.2
Black Hole of Calcutta	Bengal, India	1756	5.0
Eruption of Mt. Pelée	Martinique	May 8, 1902	7.3
Landslide	Frank, Alberta, Canada	April 29, 1903	5.1
Titanic sunk by iceberg	South of Newfoundland Grand Banks	April 14–15, 1912	6.1
World War I	Europe	1914–1918	10.5
Munitions ship explosion	Halifax, Nova Scotia, Canada	1917	7.1
Train derailment in tunnel	Modane, France	Dec. 12, 1917	5.2

TABLE 13-2 (*Continued*)

Event	Location	Date	Magnitude
Great Purge	USSR	1936–1938	10.2
World War II	World	1939–1945	11.1
Atomic Bomb	Hiroshima, Japan	Aug. 6, 1945	8.2
Tsunami	Hawaiian Islands	April 1, 1946	5.8
USS Thresher lost	Off Cape Cod, Mass.	April 10, 1963	4.7
Glacier avalanche	Yungay, Peru	May 31, 1970	8.1
Mass poisoning from fungicide-treated grain	Iraq	1971	7.4
Flood	Rapid City, S.D.	June, 1972	6.6
Earthquake	Managua, Nicaragua	Dec. 23, 1972	7.9
Tornado	Xenia, Ohio	April 3, 1974	6.4
Cyclone (Tracy)	Darwin, Australia	Dec. 25, 1974	6.6
Bus skidded into lake	Japanese Alps	Jan. 1, 1975	4.1

Foster developed a formula to estimate total community stress (Magnitude, above) from the number of casualties, damage to the infrastructure (Stress Value, opposite page), total population affected, and whether the disaster occurred in a developing or developed nation.

aster tend to experience more stress afterward.[215] In the case of Hurricane Hugo, for example, victims who had higher levels of stress because of financial, family, and physical problems before the hurricane exhibited more psychological stress afterward than other victims.[216] Child victims of Hurricane Andrew reported more stress when they had parents who were in conflict; this was particularly true of Hispanic children.[217] Children whose academic achievement had been higher experienced less stress from the same hurricane.[218]

Findings such as these led to the creation of a formula to approximate the amount of distress after disasters:[219]

$$\text{Distress} = \frac{\text{Exposure to Stressors} + \text{Vulnerability}}{\text{Psychological Resources} + \text{Social Resources}}$$

Fortunately, mental health problems appear to decline with time after the disaster.[220] However, this does not occur always or very rapidly. Among victims of the large Armero earthquake and mud slide, the rate of emotional distress over a four-year period declined from 65 percent to 31 percent.[221] One could say that stress declined by 50 percent, but one could also say that after four years, almost a third of the population was still suf-

fering. Psychological testing more than a dozen years after the great Tanshan earthquake showed that survivors were still affected.[222]

The last statement assumes that the disaster does subside; not all do. Certain natural disasters (such as drought) and technological hazards (such as pollution) can continue for a long time. People in these circumstances really are stuck: Their home, which once had all the positive qualities of a home, now becomes a "place of danger and defilement."[223]

Furthermore, when the disaster becomes widely known, no one else wants to live in that area either, and the value of the residences plummets. The residents have lost their home in the psychological sense that their identity, security, and place attachment are damaged, but they also lose in a material, financial sense.[224] This is very stressful and it can last a long time if moving is unaffordable.

Which is more stressful, natural or technological disasters? In some studies, technological disasters cause more stress and mental health problems than natural hazards,[225,226,227] but the meta-analysis found that natural hazards caused more mental health problems. Apart from any difference in the *magnitude* of a disaster, which obviously can account for differences in stress levels, the primary psychological difference between natural and

ANDREW BAUM

led the study of psychological and physiological outcomes of the Three-Mile Island nuclear incident.

technological disasters may be the potential for blame. It is easier to blame someone for a nuclear plant meltdown than it is to blame someone for an earthquake.

Evidence from nondisaster clinical situations suggests that stress tends to be lower when the survivor has someone else to blame. Perhaps this is why stress is greater after natural rather than technological disasters.[228] However, if the blame is assigned to *oneself* (or a group to which one belongs), the stress might be greater, not less.[229] This can happen, for example, if community residents blame themselves for allowing a hazardous waste dump site or other environmental threat in their community.

Nevertheless, technological disasters may cause more total stress because their effects, or the effects that people worry about, persist much longer than that of most natural disasters, and the disaster has no particular worst moment that passes.[230] A tornado may rip your roof off, but the repairs are done relatively soon; the threat to your health from the toxins in a nearby hazardous waste dump may continue for years.

Given that both natural and technological hazards are stressful, how can stress be relieved? Survivors must cope somehow. Some do so by using problem-focused coping and some use emotion-focused coping. Still others use denial to reduce the reality of disaster stress. Each style may help, depending on the nature of the disaster.

When the problem is very difficult to change, a problem-focused approach may increase one's distress: It is like trying to solve an insoluble problem. The Three Mile Island incident apparently was handled better by people who used an emotion-focused coping style,[231,232] although younger residents in the area who used a more problem-focused approach to the restart of the nuclear plant seemed to experience less stress.[233]

Some survivors are helped by friends or family; social support would seem to be a key element in recovery from disaster stress. However, research indicates that the matter is not as simple as one may think—having the support of friends and family eases the pain but does not necessarily stop the pain. Social support may help more in some ethnic groups than others.[234] In one Three Mile Island study, having at least moderate social support after the nuclear incident helped those who experienced stress,[235] but another Three Mile Island study reported that women were *not* helped by social support.[236]

A third Three Mile Island study showed more specifically where social support helps and where it may not. It helps more when the person experiences lower rather than higher levels of stress and it helps when it comes from one's supervisor (as opposed to one's peers). Surprisingly, social support sometimes may *worsen* stress.[237] This occurred when supervisors were offered support from other supervisors and when nonsupervisors were offered help from other nonsupervisors.

Among the survivors of a flood, disaster made people believe the social support available to them was reduced.[238] This makes sense when we recall that some sources of support may be incapacitated or have their own problems. However, the study also showed that having the support of family members did *not* reduce stress, but having the support of (nonfamily) others *did* reduce stress.[239,240] In general, social support helps survivors of disasters, but it may help only some—such as (according to one study) men who have not been severely stressed and are offered support by nonfamily members who are their seniors.

Apart from coping style and social support, survivors appear to follow a three-part **social stage model** of coping.[241] After the disaster, survivors openly talk and think about it for approximately two weeks. In the next stage, lasting about six weeks, they inhibit talking about the disaster but continue to think about it. During this inhibition stage, some indicators of distress increase—perhaps because survivors are thinking but not talking. Finally, an indefinite adaptation stage arrives, during which survivors neither talk nor think about the disaster. This certainly does not mean all the disaster's effects are over; symptoms may be under the surface for years or forever.[242]

After some disasters, mental health professionals have banded together to provide relief for the survivor's typical feelings of grief, guilt, isolation, anger, depression, and anxiety.[243] Special response teams have been organized in the United States,[244,245] Mexico,[246] Australia,[247,248] and other countries after major disasters. The concept of mental health rescue teams to complement traditional rescue workers has grown; after the big Kobe earthquake in early 1995, I saw an e-mail note from Japan pleading for U.S. mental health rescue teams to come over and help survivors.

When the impact is strong and swift, the usual outcome is many persons with moderate to severe cases of posttraumatic stress disorder (PTSD). After a tornado, team members have found people mowing lawns that were not there any more or trying to glue together chairs in the midst of completely destroyed homes.[249] Obviously, such people need psychological first aid, but even a few years ago, the ratio between traditional Red Cross volunteers and volunteers doing mental health work was 25,000 to 20.[250] (This is, by the way, the International Decade for Natural Disaster Reduction.[251]) In 1991, a Disaster Relief Network was created in the United States to help; today, it has over 1,200 members.[252]

Later: Mitigating Future Hazards. Over the years, a large and well coordinated international effort toward improving society's response to disasters has evolved. These efforts have sought to:

- Assess the extent of human occupancy of hazard zones.
- Identify the full range of possible human adjustment to the hazard.
- Study how individuals perceive and estimate the occurrence of the hazard.
- Describe how damage-reducing strategies are adopted.
- Estimate the optimal set of adjustments, taking social and cultural consequences into account.[253]

A considerable body of knowledge and many organizations have developed since the Halifax explosion of 1917 to implement these goals. These include (1) research on how best to warn and communicate with people faced with a disaster, (2) attempts to model behavior

during disasters in order to better anticipate how officials and ordinary individuals will respond when the "big one" comes, and (3) contributions to public policy concerning natural and technological disasters.

The first of these kinds of postdisaster contributions by psychologists has been to study what and how to communicate risks and warnings.[254] In some disasters, residents have received conflicting information and false comforting words. On the other hand, information should not alarm residents to the point that they cannot act in a manner that helps themselves and others. Clearly, the information should be expert and credible,[255] and should use plain language and reflect goals shared by authorities and residents.[256]

Second, psychologists have tried to model or simulate the ways that authorities and victims will behave during a disaster. Just as one might study how a new jet design might react by using a wind tunnel, social scientists work at predicting behavior during disasters. In one such study, 60 families participated in a simulation of the personal and family decisions they would make if faced with a volcanic disaster like Mount St. Helens.[257] In another, the goal was to understand international negotiation over ozone-depletion issues among scientists and diplomats.[258] Although findings from such simulations need to be checked against the reality of behavior in real disasters, knowledge gained in them is still very useful as a way of approximating what people will do without having to wait for a disaster (see Figure 13–7).

Third, psychologists have assisted in formulating government policy on environmental hazards. Elected and appointed officials must make many decisions that have an impact on if and how people prepare for or respond to disaster. But psychologists are better qualified to investigate the stressfulness of living near a toxic waste dump or who in a community is likely to test their home for radon gas.[259] For example, research on which ethnic groups are more likely to adopt safety measures when dealing with pesticides can have a significant positive impact on government policies concerning pesticide use.[260] In general, government policy does alter human behavior, and psychologists who study natural and technological hazards can help develop policy that should reduce both the risk and the magnitude of a disaster's impact when it comes.

FIGURE 13–7   The aftermath of the Mount Saint Helens eruption is shown for one local residence.

Let's turn back now to the actions of individuals, rather than organizations and scientists. Faced with possible loss of life and/or property and strong increases in stress, what can individuals do? One might think survivors would take a great number of actions to prevent recurrence of their losses. However, the loss of a sense of control over one's destiny suggested by the Three Mile Island study casts doubt on one's ability to vigorously act against future loss.

Most investigations have examined individuals' adjustments (short-term responses) to hazards, rather than their adaptations (long-term responses) to them. **Adaptations** include more basic changes throughout the social fabric or even the biology of the species, and are perhaps best studied by anthropologists or biologists. **Adjustments** include purchasing insurance, devising warning systems, constructing dams and levees (for floods) or shock-resistant buildings (for earthquakes, storms, and bombs), or simply bearing the cost of the disaster. These adjustments naturally group into three types: reducing one's vulnerability to the hazard, accepting losses by bearing them (alone or by sharing), and leaving a hazardous location.

The latter adjustment, moving away, may seem the most logical, but it is rare. Why don't individuals, especially those who are repeatedly subjected to hazards, simply move away? A few do; but most do not. A study of Los Angeles residents confirmed that neither objective earthquake hazards (e.g., living near a fault) nor perceived hazards (e.g., fear of quakes) related to residents' intentions to move away.[261]

Instead, moving was related to a group of variables that may be called **attachment to community.** Older individuals, those with children, those who own a home, and those who were satisfied with their community did *not* intend to move, but those who were less attached to the community *did* intend to move. The earthquake hazard is just too remote and ambiguous to be a factor; in fact, researchers discovered that, if anything, residents who were more afraid of earthquakes were *less* likely to move! In an area of Hamilton, Ontario, that is subject to multiple hazards, residents do not move primarily because of community attachment and the relatively low housing costs there.[262]

If residents will not move, what should be done? A number of studies suggest that catastrophe victims in developed countries generally favor technological and engineering solutions to environmental hazards.[263] Interviews of flood plain residents in Australia showed that they are very aware of the flood hazard, yet most residents make few adjustments, favoring the construction of dams, levees, and other public works to solve the problem.[264]

In general, individual response to environmental hazards is not very impressive. Despite occasional heroics during a calamity, the larger scenario is one in which many of us fail to prepare for disaster, deny or underestimate the probability of being victimized (except when the hazard is highly publicized, in which case we often ridiculously overestimate our chances), fail to move away from hazardous locations, yet expect to be protected from the hazard by engineers paid for largely by other taxpayers, and hope to be compensated by the government when disaster strikes! (Incidentally, the latter is not a good bet; in major disasters, aid rarely covers more than one-third of actual losses).

I will close with a challenge: Can you construct a defense against this unflattering portrait? That is, are there any justifiable reasons for the apparent lack of self-protective behavior? By the way, what preparations have *you* made for those hazards that might strike your area?

◆   *IN SUM, a person's attitudes about environmental risk—including awareness of a hazard's existence, assess-*

ments of a disaster's likelihood, evaluation of hazardous technologies as desirable or not, and trust or distrust of authorities—are related to numerous antecedent factors, such as sex, education, proximity, disaster experience, and media exposure. However, once formed, those attitudes toward hazards are, in turn, related to the level and type of each person's preparedness for disaster.

We may be aware of a threat; we may have complex attitudes toward it and the experts and authorities; we may perceive the risk as high or low and may well assess it differently than the experts do; we may be breathing toxins but have no symptoms yet; we may or may not have prepared ourselves and our residences; we may be apathetic or politically active. Still, the fears have not been realized.

Most homes are subject to one or more serious environmental hazards, some natural and others technological. Before the calamity occurs, governments attempt to reduce risk through engineering and education, but when neither of these are effective, many lives can be lost. Specific warnings and awareness-raising simulations can help, but effective personal action is often blunted by the human tendency to bounded rationality, inadequate preparation, crisis response, and risk misperception. During disaster, losses may be high but individuals generally act in relatively rational ways. The outcome of disaster is stress in many forms. Some ways of coping reduce stress better than others. Community attachment and economic factors often prevent residents from vacating high-risk areas; they would rather see governments engage in massive public works to protect their homes.

◆ NATURE, ENVIRONMENTAL ◆ HAZARDS, AND ENVIRONMENTAL DESIGN

Supportive Hospitals

Hospital. The very word conjures up images of institutional green walls, sterile trays, gleaming instruments, and cold, inward-looking interiors. Health-care workers do their best to help, but the building usually offers all the reassurance, warmth, and naturalness of an oil tanker. Hospitals do not have to be that way, though. They need to be clean and functional for medical procedures, but not all areas need to be sterile, either figuratively or literally. What *should* they be like?

For one thing, hospitals should be psychologically supportive.[265] To the extent that architecture can facilitate healing, it should. According to Roger Ulrich, architecture can be supportive and foster health by reducing stress, which is an impediment to recovery.[266] In general, this can be accomplished in two ways. First, the building should not cause patients (or visitors or staff) any *further* stress than they already must face. It should not be crowded or noisy, be difficult to find one's way, spread noxious air, or have bad lighting. Second, it should provide exposure to physical features of the environment that reduce stress. The first of these is obvious from previous chapters; what about the second?

According to Ulrich, the designed environment can reduce stress by enhancing social support, providing a sense of control, and offering access to positive distractions in the physical surroundings. Social support can be enhanced by increasing the potential for social interaction through flexible, sociopetal seating arrangements in patient rooms and lounges. Sense of control can be improved by giving patients easier control over temperature, drapes, television, their beds, and their privacy.

Based on the research described earlier about the health-related consequences of viewing nature, Ulrich advocates giving patients and staff more pleasant, natural views or art in their hospital spaces. These might be views of nature, water, animals, fish in an aquarium, or caring human faces.

Housing of Survivors of Disasters

Emergency housing is needed at many sites around the world each year. The art and science of providing shelter for disaster survivors is relatively new and is developing rapidly. Probably no donations of emergency shelter by outside countries occurred before World War II, yet within 10 days of a large 1976 quake in Turkey, over 6,500 tents had been delivered.[267]

Many technologically advanced solutions to post-disaster housing have been devised, including parachutes that turn into freestanding tents ready for immediate occupancy upon landing, polyurethane igloos, and instant floating marina-type shelters for flood victims. The United Nations and other agencies have sponsored competitions for emergency housing designs that are very low in cost, very lightweight, collapsible, easy to erect, and sturdy.

Yet, surprisingly, this may not be at all what is required. Ian Davis, who has extensive experience with international agencies that provide disaster shelter, has listed seven unsupported beliefs about emergency housing.[268]

1. "After disasters there is a need for many new shelters." Actually, most families go to official shelters only when all else has failed.

2. "Survivors show no clear patterns of housing preference after a disaster." Actually, a clear order of preferences usually emerges: Go to (a) the homes of friends and family, (b) locally improvised shelters, (c) converted buildings such as school gymnasiums, and finally (d) officially provided shelter.

3. "Compulsory evacuation is an effective policy." In fact, attachment to community is so strong that no such evacuation in the last 40 years has been successful.

4. "Tents make an effective shelter." Actually, despite stockpiles of up to 10,000 tents in various places around the world, tents tend to be late in arriving and underused once they arrive.

5. "Emergency shelter is a matter of life and death." Actually, it usually is not; local coping mechanisms take care of most serious threats.

6. "In disastrous circumstances people will be prepared to live in unusual housing." In fact, novel housing is often rejected as culturally alien (remember, the need for *any* official housing is lower than we often think).

7. "In a disaster, people are willing to live communally." In fact, people usually become more conservative, clutching to their family unit where possible.

Four more myths pertain to the reconstruction phase.

1. "Temporary housing is needed prior to reconstruction." Actually, reconstruction of regular dwellings starts—at least in the Third World—immediately, ignoring temporary housing.

2. "An important priority is clearing rubble." In fact, except for clearing access roads, the rubble is often best left in place, to be recycled into new homes.

3. "Crash programs by agencies and governments are an effective way of solving postdisaster housing needs." In fact, local people respond faster and better in rebuilding.

4. "Community relocation is ideal." So far, most attempts to relocate entire communities have been unsatisfactory.

Given all this negativity, what does Davis suggest? One prime goal of those who would like to help in some way should be to train local people how to rebuild their own houses with safer materials and, if possible, in a safer site in the same area. The safer design should, of course, respect local cultural traditions.[269] These efforts should be at the grass-roots level, rather than persuading governments to institute new building codes that often have no practical influence on house construction. Meetings in villages and comic-book depictions of safe construction techniques are more likely to change the house construction techniques that are passed down the generations.

◆ **SUMMARY** ◆

Some research reports that extraterrestrial forces from cosmic rays, planets, and the moon may affect human behavior, but these results probably are false-positive errors. No one has suggested a plausible mechanism by which such forces would influence people. Aggressiveness rises with temperature to a point and then declines. Ozone levels may influence violence. Electromagnetic radiation may affect public fears more than it affects our health. Most of us think that nature can restore us, but obviously it can be very destructive, too. Nature can be restore us by facilitating cognitive freedom, ecosystem connectedness, escape, challenge, growth, guidance, a renewed social life, and health. Being in nature, even merely seeing nature, apparently is restorative. The two main ways that nature restores us are by refreshing our attentional capacity and improving our moods.

Our attitudes about environmental risk—including awareness of a hazard's existence, assessments of a disaster's likelihood, evaluation of hazardous technologies as desirable or not, and trust or distrust of authorities—are related to sex, education, proximity, disaster experience, and media exposure. Once formed, those attitudes toward hazards are, in turn, related to the quality of our preparedness for disaster. We perceive risk differently than the experts do; efforts toward mutual understanding are necessary. In the pre-calamity phase, governments attempt to reduce risk through engineering and education, but when neither of these is effective, many lives are lost. Specific warnings and awareness-raising simulations can help, but effective personal action is often blunted by our bounded rationality, underpreparation, crisis response, and risk misperception. During disaster, losses may be high but individuals generally act in relatively rational ways. The outcome of disaster is stress in many forms. Some forms of coping reduce stress better than others. Community attachment and economic factors often prevent residents from vacating high-risk areas; they would rather see governments engage in massive public works to protect their homes.

Suggested Readings

Altman, I., & Wohlwill, J. F. (Eds.). (1983). *Behavior and the natural environment.* New York: Plenum.

Baum, A., & Fleming, I. (1993). Implications of psychological research on stress and technological accidents. *American Psychologist, 48,* 665–672.

Travis, C. B., McLean, B. E., & Ribar, C. (1989). *Environmental toxins: Psychological, behavioral, and sociocultural aspects, 1973–1989.* Washington, DC: American Psychological Association.

Ulrich, R. S. (1993). Biophilia, biophobia, and natural landscapes. In S. R. Kellert & E. O. Wilson (Eds.), *The biophilia hypothesis.* Washington, DC: Island Press/Shearwater Books.

MANAGING LIMITED RESOURCES

Freedom in a commons brings ruin to all.

—Garrett Hardin[1]

*I*t was moving day. Tom and Jane at last were able to move into the house Tom's grandfather had given him. The excitement of having so much space and being together in it was almost too much. They sat among the cardboard boxes in the kitchen with friends who had helped them move, sipping tea.

"Well," asked one friend, "What are you going to do with this place after you're settled in? Build a swimming pool?"

"You're kidding, I hope," Jane replied. "We have barely enough money to heat the place. And now—well, you heard the mayor's speech, didn't you?"

The town's reserves of water were virtually depleted in the drought and the mayor had appealed to residents not to use any *water except for drinking, cooking, personal hygiene, and one weekly bath. "We couldn't very well justify a private pool now," Jane said.*

"One thing we will have to do," Tom broke in, "is put some insulation in the walls. I looked inside one wall and there was absolutely none there! I don't know how Gramps lived through the winter."

"Someday I'd like to investigate solar heating," said Jane. "We have a good southern exposure in the back."

"I guess you two will just have to keep each other warm until you save up a little!" a friend replied.

After a moment's reflection, one of their friends brightened. "I saw enough bottles in the basement that if you took them all to the recycling place, you'd probably have enough to pay for solar heating," he laughed.

◆ ◆ ◆

After years of public debate, environmental issues are familiar to all of us. We are quite aware that on one hand, some vital natural resources are being depleted quickly, while on the other hand, there is an oversupply of undesirable by-products from our use of those same natural resources (e.g., automobile fumes and litter).

This chapter considers the psychological processes involved in managing environmental resources. What is meant here by the word *managing?* As a society, we extract, refine, use, and dispose of many natural resources. As individuals, our role in this process is primarily as users and disposers of processed natural resources. Few of us would seriously advocate an absolute halt to this process, except perhaps in the case of such nearly depleted resources as endangered species. This implies that we will continue to use and dispose of or recycle most resources. The term *management* here refers to the *rate* and *quality* of an individual's use of natural resources, including manufactured products made from natural resources. The rate of this process is often quantifiable; the quality of the process is often debatable (see Figure 14–1). For example, if a resident of a drought-threatened town decides to water a newly seeded lawn, it would not be difficult, using a water meter, to identify the quantity of the resource used. Whether the resident is wrong to use the water, however, is not easily decided.

Another aspect of managing concerns *who* will be doing the managing. Certainly, much environmental management is done by governments, corporations, and other organizations. Such management is performed at the societal level, or *macrolevel*. Environmental psychologists usually are more interested in the resource management behavior of individuals and small groups—resource management at the *microlevel*. Of course, both macrolevels and microlevels are important, but environ-

FIGURE 14–1   Recycling center in a multiunit residential development.

mental psychologists generally prefer to work from the microlevel upward, rather than from the macrolevel downward.

As individuals, we are faced with our own resource management problems. To varying degrees, we monitor our personal use of resources, observe the effects that our usage has on the environment, and are aware of the usage patterns of other individuals. Our resource management decisions are based on all three of these considerations, and more. The crucial aspect of microlevel resource management is that it sums to the macrolevel in mysterious, irrational, yet all-important ways. One subject of this chapter is this interplay between an individual's own resource management and the individual's perception of others' resource management.

After defining the commons and some key related concepts, the chapter will examine some of the research strategies used by environmental psychologists to understand resource management. Then the factors that promote different management styles and strategies will be surveyed and some of the theories about resource management will be described. The latter part of the chapter is devoted to three important cases of resource management: pollution, energy conservation, and recycling. The basic question guiding that discussion is this: If we are all so *aware* of environmental resource problems after 15 years of information bombardment, why is there still so much pollution and energy wastage and so little recycling?

◆ RESOURCE MANAGEMENT ◆ AS A COMMONS DILEMMA

Originally, the **commons** was a central open space in the heart of a settlement. The land was owned by all the citizens of the settlement and therefore by no citizen in particular. Today, we would probably call such spaces parks. Any citizen is welcome to use the space for picnics, sports, or just strolling. In the old days, when economies were more agriculturally based, people also grazed their animals on the commons.

As long as there is room and grass enough for everyone, the commons is a tranquil place. In most commons, however, the day eventually arrives when someone's frisbee sails into someone else's softball game, a cyclist on a narrow path knocks over a child, or an er-

rant football lands in someone's potato salad. In the ensuing discussions, the rate and quality of the offender's management of commons space often will be a hot topic. The offender may counter with the opinion that "it's a free country, isn't it?" The issue becomes freedom in the commons[2] (see Figure 14–2).

Commons are established on the assumption that the supply of the resource can meet the demands of the community. In fact, eighteenth-century economists such as Adam Smith did not see the boundaries or limits that are inherent in commons. Each individual was therefore free to exploit resources as much as possible, because in exploiting the resource for his or her own benefit, the individual was allegedly guided by an "invisible hand" to benefit the whole community. If a farmer could grow enough wheat to make himself rich, he would also employ people to assist him, buy equipment, send his children to the university, and in other ways aid the economy.

An early nineteenth-century economist, William Lloyd, was one of the first to see a problem with Smith's logic. He wrote:

> If a person puts more cattle into his own field, the amount of the subsistence which they consume is all deducted from that which was at the command of his original stock [of cattle]; and if, before, there was no more

FIGURE 14-2 This is what happens when "harvesters" have the mechanical power to take resources faster than the resource can regenerate itself.

than a [bare] sufficiency of pasture, he reaps no benefit from the additional cattle, what is gained in one way being lost in another. But if he puts more cattle on a common, the food which they consume forms a deduction which is shared between all the cattle . . . that of others as [well as] his own . . . and only a small part of it from his own cattle. . . . Were a number of adjoining pastures, already fully stocked, to be at once thrown open and converted into one vast common . . . the stock [of cattle] would be increased and would . . . press much more forcibly against the means of subsistence.[3]

The essential difference between the ideas of Smith and Lloyd is that Lloyd recognized that many resources are limited. According to Garrett Hardin, in a desirable but limited commons, individuals act in self-interest. Hardin asserted that a process called the "tragedy of the commons" begins. "Each man is locked into a system that compels him to increase his herd without limit—in a world that is limited. Ruin is the destination toward which all men rush, each pursuing his own best interest."[4]

Social scientists and philosophers now recognize that grazing land, as in the Lloyd-Hardin example, is just one of many resources that are limited and held in common. The same basic ideas apply to overpopulation, air pollution, oil, whales, buffalo, energy brownouts, water shortages, congested radio bands, food supplies, and many other resources. Thus, a *commons* is any desirable resource held jointly by a group of individuals, from an office lottery pool to the oceans. Some of these resources renew themselves relatively quickly (such as grass for grazing or river water for electric power), others not so quickly (such as trees), and some very slowly or not at all (for instance, oil and endangered species).

I chose the commons dilemma as a metaphor for discussing the problem of scarce natural resources because it seemed vivid and appropriate. Now there is evidence that the basic story is more memorable than other environmental messages.[5]

Despite the knowledge that natural resources are being depleted rapidly, people do not seem to be able to stop. In fact, we people are depleting natural resources *faster* since we became aware of ecological shortages back in the 1970s. According to a United Nations agency, tropical forests were being harvested 40 percent faster in 1993 than in 1983.[6]

Hardin believes that it is difficult or impossible for us to reverse our tragic path toward ruin. For example, he rejects such technical solutions to the population problem as exporting people into space. The only thing that can save us, according to Hardin, is a "fundamental extension of morality." By this assertion, Hardin means that we must abolish the freedom of the commons and institute "mutual coercion, mutually agreed-upon." That is, society must agree, through laws and regulations, to severely limit individual freedom to exploit the commons. Hardin does not seem optimistic that society can accomplish this limitation because the individual's freedom to exploit resources is so deeply valued by many members of society. Hardin's provocative pessimism has spurred much debate and research.

Self-Interest and the Public Interest

What is a commons *dilemma*? It is the difficult choice whether to act in self-interest or in the public interest. To paraphrase Hamlet: To get ahead or to cooperate, that is the question! In times of plenty, we might be able to choose both, but when times are lean, we must choose between two undesirable outcomes.

Environmental psychologists have not accepted Hardin's argument that people will always act in self-interest at face value; they consider the issue of how individuals will behave in a limited commons to be an empirical question. For example, it is known that sometimes individuals do act in the public interest rather than in self-interest. Many individuals will walk out of their way to deposit litter in a garbage can, voluntarily limit the number of children they have, or turn down their thermostats. On the other hand, everyone can recall occasions when someone did act selfishly. Laboratory studies show that stealing from others in the commons is frequent.[7] Thus, the key question is: *Under what conditions* do individuals act in self-interest?

Each member of a limited commons has the choice of acting in self-interest or in the public interest. One can act in self-interest in two basic ways: by *taking* (drinking a cup of coffee from the office pot without paying, cutting down a protected redwood tree, or filling the swimming pool during a drought) or by *giving* (not installing a pollution control device on the car, deciding to have a third child in a densely populated country, or dumping household garbage along a country road).

In each case, it is easier or more rewarding, at least in the short run, to engage in the self-serving behavior than it is to behave in the public interest. In a limited commons, the public-spirited act is often more expensive, difficult, or time consuming and less immediately rewarding than the self-serving act. This observation has led some observers to conclude that self-serving behavior is natural. If by "natural" these observers mean "unchangeable part of human nature," then most environmental psychologists would disagree. They assume that certain influences promote self-serving behavior and others promote public-interest behavior.

Before surveying the research on which conditions lead to self-serving or public-interest behavior, a discussion of several types of dilemmas is warranted.

Commons Dilemmas, Social Traps, and Social Dilemmas

Psychologists have approached the problem of resource management from two directions. One group became involved through their interest in choice, decision making, and rationality. Such processes are often studied using carefully devised games. The most famous such game, prisoner's dilemma, goes like this:

> Two people rob a bank. They are apprehended by the local district attorney, who knows they have committed the robbery but who does not have sufficient evidence to convict them. The district attorney puts the two prisoners in separate rooms and makes an identical proposition to each. If either prisoner confesses and the other does not, the one who confesses will go free for supplying state's evidence and the other will be sent to jail for 10 years. If they both confess, they will both go to jail for 5 years. If neither confesses, they will both go to jail for a single year on some minor charge such as carrying a concealed weapon. The district attorney informs each prisoner that the same proposition was made to the other, and then the prisoners are left in separate rooms to think.[8]

What you would do in such a situation? You might also wonder what the prisoner's dilemma has to do with the commons dilemma. One difference is that the prisoner's dilemma has two participants, whereas commons dilemmas have more than two participants. Second, the prisoner's dilemma mainly deals with interpersonal trust, whereas the commons dilemma is concerned with shrinking resources. Third, in prisoner's dilemma research, the same scenario is offered repeatedly to subjects, whereas in the commons dilemma, the scenario changes because the pool of resources grows or shrinks after each choice made by the subjects.

Nevertheless, the prisoner's dilemma is, in terms of the mathematics of decision making, a special (simplified) form of the commons dilemma.[9] Psychologists interested in human decision making came upon the resource management problem while searching for a more general and realistic instance of decision making. The second group of researchers became interested from their direct environmental concerns; these psychologists were looking for ways to study the self-interest and public-interest choices made by individuals in managing limited commons. Three identifiable streams of this second group are reflected in the terms *commons dilemma, social trap,* and *social dilemma.*

Commons dilemma refers to the overuse of natural resources such as land, energy, or endangered species as a result of conflict between individual and group interests. The term, inspired by the thought of Lloyd and Hardin, was first used by Robyn Dawes.[10] **Social trap** emphasizes the temporal trap caused when individuals (or society) succumb to immediate rewards that have some built-in and gradual cost that eventually becomes very large.[11] On the individual level, classic social traps are overeating and smoking. At the societal level, the use of DDT is a social trap if it kills mosquitoes but gradually erodes the ability of birds to lay viable eggs. Although the individual and societal varieties may be found in the same social trap (overeating may harm the individual as well as deprive members of the Third World of food), they need not be. One may distinguish between *temporal* traps, meaning an individual falls victim with little consequence to the commons, and *social* traps, referring only to individual versus group conflicts with consequences to the commons.[12]

Dawes suggested the term **social dilemma** to encompass commons dilemmas, social traps, and even the

ROBYN DAWES'S

thinking and research forms much of the basis for research in commons dilemmas and resource management.

prisoner's dilemma.[13] The defining characteristics of a social dilemma are that (1) each participant receives more (or is penalized less) for a self-interest choice than for a public-interest choice and (2) the participants, as a group, benefit more if they all choose to act in the public interest than if they all choose to defect, or act in self-interest.[14] In some social dilemmas, frequent defections result in the destruction of the resource.

Research Strategies

Social dilemmas may be studied from several perspectives.[15] In one sense, behavior in the commons may be characterized as cooperative (oriented toward mutual gains), individualistic (oriented toward self gain), or competitive (oriented toward self's gain *relative* to others' gain).[16] Second, social dilemmas may also be viewed as a form of group problem solving.[17] Third, some researchers have focused on the formation of coalitions and the use of power in managing the commons.[18] And last, some see social dilemmas as a set of behaviors governed by reinforcements and learning processes.

Field Experiments and Studies. Social dilemmas certainly are complex situations that include each of these dimensions. How can the social dilemma be studied? Field approaches are attractive but difficult and rare. They require that the experimenter have control of the resource and the situation, which, of course, can be very difficult to obtain. When a resource is in limited supply, the experimenter simply becomes one individual among many who wish to control it. Gaining a corner on the market in order to perform an experiment is even harder than merely obtaining a piece of the action! Field studies do not require the same degree of control over the resource and the situation. But the price of this relaxation of the scientific rules is that a variety of explanations for the results must be entertained, because the lack of control allows many variables to potentially influence behavior in the commons.

Simulations. Without ruling out the possibility of undertaking more field experiments and studies in the future, environmental psychologists also study social dilemmas by using simulations.[19,20,21,22,23,24,25,26] Just as there are many variations in everyday social dilemmas, there have been many experimental simulations of social dilemmas. The rules and values of the resources in both real and simulated social dilemmas vary considerably. The number of participants, the amount of the resource, and many other factors are systematically changed to determine each factor's importance. However, most social dilemmas share the following characteristics.

1. If one participant acts in self-interest while others act in the public interest, the self-interest participant (called a **defector**) will receive the highest payoff.
2. If everyone acts in the public interest (cooperates), everyone will receive a higher payoff than if everyone defects.
3. If everyone defects, the commons will be destroyed.

Thus, defection is the most attractive choice, but each participant is best off if no one else defects, next best off if everyone cooperates, and worst off if everyone defects.[27]

Consider a simple representative simulation.[28] A number of participants sit around a large, shallow bowl. The bowl contains a dozen walnuts. The walnuts may be traded at the end for something valuable—money, concert tickets, food, or whatever. The experimenter explains that participants may take as many walnuts out of the bowl as they wish at any time; there is no turn taking. However, before the participants knock each other over grabbing the walnuts, the experimenter adds one more piece of information: "If any walnuts remain in the bowl 10 seconds after the start, I will place that many more walnuts in the bowl." How would *you* proceed?

Cooperation in this simulation may be defined in several ways. It can be defined as the number of trials (i.e., the number of times the group leaves at least one walnut in the bowl) the group keeps the pool of resources from extinction. It can be defined as the total **harvest**, the sum of walnuts garnered by all participants. It can be defined as the amount of resource left at any given time. These measures of cooperation usually, but not always, are highly correlated. As an exercise, you might consider the possible outcomes if the participants adopt defecting, mixed, or cooperative strategies.

An obvious problem with simulations is the suspicion that behavior will not match behavior in everyday commons. For example, if the exercise is to be a valid indicator of behavior in a real-world commons, the walnuts or other symbolic objects should have enough value that harvesters take the simulation seriously. Most studies conducted so far have offered very limited payoffs. At present, there is little evidence either for or against the validity of simulations.

Observations of research participants suggest, however, that even small payoffs can produce behavior that *seems* quite similar to that which could be expected in a real, valuable, limited commons. For example, in a study in which participants could win no more than $10.50, participants were so caught up in the dilemma that defectors were sworn at and unrequited cooperators cried, stormed out of the room, and told defectors they "would have to live with their decisions for the rest of their lives."[29]

Other researchers with similar payoffs have reported equally strong responses. Some participants have threatened ("jokingly") to beat up defectors, to destroy their reputations, and even to kill them![30] In my own lab, subjects have said such things as, "You greedy pig!" and "You die!" and "I could have smashed some heads."[31] Thus, despite the lack of field investigations, the research using simulations of commons dilemmas may have reasonable validity.

◆ **IN SUM,** *each of us manages a steady supply of natural resources that have been converted into products we use every day. Some of these resources come from limited sources called commons. A commons is a pool of desirable materials that may be harvested by a number of individuals or organizations that all have access to it. Commons dilemmas occur when harvesters can extract natural re-*

sources faster than the resource can regenerate; individuals then must decide whether to maximize their own gain or the gain of the group, including themselves. Social traps are similar, but emphasize the time dimension; we are trapped as a result of the eventual outcome of repeatedly yielding to short-term rewards while ignoring long-term costs. Social dilemma is the general term for these conflicts.

Field experiments on social dilemmas are nearly impossible and field studies are uncommon. Many laboratory simulations have been done instead. Social dilemmas are very complex; some simulations take into account a large number of the many dimensions in everyday social dilemmas. Judging from participants' reactions, these may not be as unrepresentative of everyday behavior as one might think.

◆ **WHAT INFLUENCES** ◆
PUBLIC-INTEREST
RESOURCE MANAGEMENT?

A great variety of social dilemmas have been studied, but in most studies, the fundamental question remains similar: Under which conditions will group members cooperate—that is, act in the public interest? What influences individuals to harvest much or little from a shared, limited, slowly regenerating resource? The influences may be placed into four categories (see Figure 14–3).

1. *The resource.* Is it important to the participants? Is it nearly depleted or relatively plentiful?
2. *The participants as individuals.* Are they old or young? Experienced or not? Do they hold cooperative values or not?
3. *The participants as group members.* How many are there? Do they trust or know each other? Are they friends or strangers?
4. *Structure of the dilemma.* What are the relative payoffs for cooperation and defection? May the participants communicate with one another? Are their choices made public? Are they told something about the nature of social dilemmas or left to their own ability to understand? Is there a leader or not?

The Resource

There is no dilemma if the resource is not desirable. There is no dilemma—only regret—if the resource is

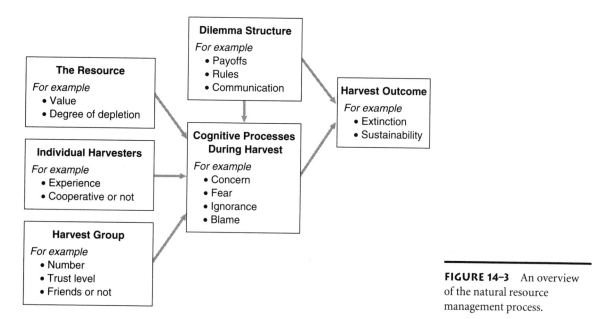

FIGURE 14–3 An overview of the natural resource management process.

extinguished. Resource amount is often not precisely known. These three characteristics of the resource (importance, abundance, and certainty) all affect rates of cooperation among harvesters.

As the importance or value of the resource increases, the rate of cooperation decreases.[32] This has been formally demonstrated only for resources with small values, but is consistent with everyday experience and laboratory evidence that individuals become quite seriously involved over very inexpensive resources. In a classic simulation study, groups of 15 to 21 individuals were asked to pull small metal cones from a narrow-necked bottle using strings that were attached to the cones.[33] The resource in this case is space in the neck of the bottle. When there was no reward or punishment for removing cones, no "traffic jams" occurred. However, when there were rewards of only 10 to 25 cents for getting a cone out and fines of 1 to 10 cents for failure to get cones out, traffic jams occurred frequently.

Whether cooperation *always* is low when the resource is valuable remains to be seen. Incidents in which moviegoers are crushed as they attempt to leave burning theaters suggest that cooperation declines tragically when resources (cool, fresh air, and space) become very important. On the other hand, there may have been many occasions in which moviegoers cooperated and safely left burning theaters, but because no deaths occurred, the item was not news. Or, if the rewards for cooperation or the punishment for acting in self-interest are high, individuals may work together even when harvesting very valuable resources. Diamond miners, for example, usually work as a team.

Abundant resources mean there is no dilemma. If the resource is almost gone, will participants cooperate more than when it was relatively plentiful, or will they scramble to get what they can before the resource is totally exhausted? Early "give some" studies compared behavior in commons that were pure or half ruined. The experimental situation was analogous to decisions to pollute (giving is the self-interest choice) rather than decisions to harvest (where taking is the self-interest choice). If a group of individuals builds cottages around a lake that is either entirely unpolluted or about halfway ruined, will they pollute the lake further or not? The participants cooperated significantly more in the half-degraded situation[34,35] (see Figure 14–4).

These results are grounds for optimism; when we inherit partly polluted surroundings, it seems that we will cooperate. Unfortunately, another implication is

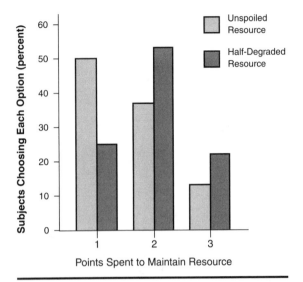

FIGURE 14-4 As the environment is degraded, it is treated with more respect. Swedish teenagers in this simulation spent more money to maintain the resource if they were given a half-ruined resource than if they were given an unspoiled resource.

that when we inherit pure surroundings, we will act selfishly *until* things get bad.

Another study examined a harvest situation (as opposed to the pollution situation) in which students worked for course credits.[36] When fewer course credits were available in the commons, fewer cooperative responses occurred than when many course credits were available. This finding conflicts with earlier studies. Perhaps the difference lies in whether the social dilemma is framed as a "give some" dilemma or a "take some" dilemma. Apparently, individuals cooperate more in half-*polluted* commons (those that have gone halfway from purity to death from the donation of pollutants, such as a lake suffering from acid rain) but act in self-interest more in half-*harvested* commons (those that have gone from a full complement halfway to extinction, such as an endangered animal species).

Resources may decline at different rates. Does it matter how quickly the water, trees, or fish are disappearing? According to one study, that depends, in part, on whether the harvesters are trusting individuals.[37] Generally, when the resource depleted slowly, harvesters increased their take as time went on. Less trusting par-

ticipants harvested at about the same rate regardless of how fast the resource disappeared, but more trusting participants harvested more when the resource was depleting slowly and less when the resource was rapidly disappearing. Thus, trusting harvesters seem to be sensitive to the speed of resource depletion, but distrusting harvesters seem not to be.

Resources may disappear for different reasons, and this affects cooperation, too. What is the difference in cooperation if the fish or trees are being depleted by human overharvesting versus some natural cause, such as disease or a climate shift? Generally, more harvesting occurs when a resource is abundant than when it is scarce, but this difference is magnified when the cause of depletion is natural rather than when it is human.[38] Apparently, if we think other *people* are depleting the resource, we want to get some too, but if *nature* is depleting the resource, we are more willing to restrain our harvests.

What about the certainty of the resource? In the real world, we are often unsure exactly how much of a resource is available for harvest. No one knows exactly how many whales or salmon are in the sea, or how much oil remains in the earth. Most early simulations of commons dilemmas presented exact amounts to harvesters; recently, however, researchers have examined resource uncertainty as a factor in cooperation. Low levels of uncertainty may not affect cooperation,[39] but higher levels do. When uncertainty is at least moderate, harvesters increase their take.[40,41] Given that the amount of many resources is not precisely known, this is a disturbing finding. It may occur because harvesters, when faced with a range of possible harvest amounts, optimistically but often incorrectly assume the larger numbers are accurate.

Uncertainty can focus on resource replenishment rates as well as their actual amounts. We cannot be sure how fast whales will reproduce, or how long trees will take to reach maturity, or how many fish will spawn; we have only estimates. Once again, as uncertainty grows, we seem to believe the more optimistic estimates and harvest more.[42]

Characteristics of the Participants as Individuals

Personal qualities that harvesters bring to the dilemma (e.g., their age, sex, personality, and social values) affect cooperation. Often, however, the effects of these factors depend on some aspect of the dilemma as it unfolds. For example, men and women, as a whole, cooperate about equally, but men cooperate more (and women do not) when group members trust one another and can communicate with each other.[43]

Age. The ability to work together toward sound management of the commons generally increases with age, at least up to the late teens. Nursery school children are primarily "own-gain oriented."[44] One study employed the commons dilemma simulation described earlier to study groups of children from age 3 to 16.[45] As age increased, cooperation increased. By age 14, groups were harvesting up to 85 percent of the maximum possible points while maintaining the health of the commons. At age 16, however, a drop in cooperativeness was observed. The researcher (me) remarked, half seriously, that maybe we should turn over the management of natural resources to 14-year-olds, especially in light of the following study's results (see Figure 14–5).

An earlier study using a similar simulation showed that 18- to 20-year-olds showed quite *low* levels of cooperation.[46] But another study reported a slight increase in cooperation across the 18 to 40s age range.[47] It appears that up to age 5 or so, most children are unable to grasp the idea that one may have to give up an immediate gain for a long-term gain. However, from age 5 to 14, chil-

dren are increasingly able to understand the value of cooperation. After age 14 or so, cooperative behavior probably depends largely on factors other than age.

Sex. Several studies have tried to determine whether males or females cooperate more in commons dilemmas. In North America, females probably receive more socialization to cooperate than do males. In reasonably similar commons dilemma simulations, one study found that females consistently cooperated more than males.[48] However, another found no differences between males and females.[49] The only study to examine sex differences as its central concern found no differences in actual cooperation, although women gave more moral reasons for their actions than men.[50] Gender, like age after the mid-teens, is probably less influential than other factors.

Personality and Social Values. Early social dilemma researchers suggested there are three basic personality types: the person who consistently tries to cooperate, even when that strategy results in losses; the person who quickly settles into a noncooperative stance and refuses to budge even when others try to cooperate; and the person who falls in between these extremes.[51]

A later study began by postulating the existence of a $1/n$th personality—the tendency to cooperate or adopt public interest strategies.[52] In this study, $1/n$th personalities did indeed act in the public interest more often than non-$1/n$th personalities, and there were no overall differences between men and women. However, the *combination* of sex and personality also affected harvesting. Males who were high on the $1/n$th personality dimension cooperated no more or less than men who were low on it. However, high $1/n$th females cooperated much more than did low $1/n$th females. Thus, gender and personality interact to predict who will act in the public interest.

Social values also influence behavior in the commons. Three common social value orientations are *cooperativeness* (when I believe that I should maximize my profit *and* your profit), *competitiveness* (I maximize my profit *relative* to yours), and *individualism* (I maximize my profit with no particular concern for your profit).[53] Less common orientations include *altruism* (I maximize *your* profit relative to mine) and so-called *murder-suicide* (I minimize my profit *and* your profit).

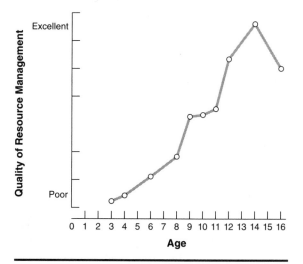

FIGURE 14–5 Quality of resource management in a simulated resource management task by groups of children from ages 3 to 16.

Generally, as would be expected, persons who hold cooperative values do restrain their harvests in commons dilemmas.[54,55] However, other factors can modify this. For example, cooperative participants who hear a message promoting cooperation cooperate more than those who do not hear such a message, but this further depends on other participants' cooperativeness.[56]

Experience and Knowledge. Harvesters' prior experience and knowledge also affect the outcome of social dilemmas. Managers new to the commons dilemma may have only a vague idea how their actions affect the commons as a whole. If so, giving members prior experience with the commons might improve performance in a later commons. Evidence supports this hypothesis; better understanding of the commons dilemma is associated with more cooperation.[57] In another study, prior experience as a one-person manager of a commons was better than prior group experience in subsequent commons management situations.[58] Presumably, in the simpler context of one-person management, individuals learned more about how their actions affected the commons. Experience in the sense of knowledge about environmental issues is also associated with more responsible environmental behavior.[59]

Characteristics of the Participants as Group Members

Once individual harvesters are formed into a group, a complex mix of interactions begins to occur among the members. Researchers have examined the importance of objective group characteristics (e.g., its size and interpersonal cognitions and behaviors (e.g., trust, conformity, friendship, sense of community, and differences in the amount harvested).

Conformity. The commons can be confusing, particularly to new participants, when several or many others harvest from a pool of resources that constantly changes in size. One way to deal with this problem is to play it safe by simply doing what others do.[60,61] When this tendency was examined in one study, conformity influenced harvesting even when verbal warnings were issued, the probability of punishment was present, and conformist harvesting was against the harvesters's own

best interests![62] Inexperience in a complicated situation seems to produce strong conformity as harvesters desperately try to figure out the best course of action.

Number of Harvesters. Group size affects harvesting. Nearly every study of group size has found that behavior in resource management tends increasingly toward self-interest as group size increases.[63] Cooperation declines both as the number of harvesters rises and as the number of groups *within* a commons with a constant total membership rises.[64] There are some good reasons for this.

1. As group size increases, the harm from any one participant's defection is spread thinner among the other participants; no single other is badly hurt.
2. Defection often is less visible to others in larger groups.
3. The effect of the harm done is less visible to the defector[65] (it is easier to inflict pain if one does not have to watch the victim experience the pain).
4. Negative feedback to the defector is more and more difficult to sustain in larger groups. (Unfortunately, most commons in the everyday world involve large or very large groups.)

The upper population limit for a well-functioning (cooperative) commons may be as low as 150 members.[66] One study showed that trust—a key component of cooperation—affects cooperation in groups of three but not seven harvesters, suggesting that trust helps only in very small groups.[67] This implies that in larger commons (such as towns, cities, and the earth as a whole), Garrett Hardin's pessimism may be well justified unless other, more positive, factors can improve management of the commons.

Friendship. The quality of relations among the harvesters can be one positive factor. As might be expected, as friendship grows, cooperation grows.[68] Friends know one another's needs; they may draw on past experience that probably includes some give and take; they have a stake in continuing their good relations, which favors cooperation over self-interested harvesting. Harvesters do not require preexisting friendship before they cooperate; when they know strangers have attitudes identical to their own, they cooperate more.[69]

Trust. Another potentially positive factor is trust. It would be quite reasonable to expect that trust is associated with cooperation in commons dilemma. However, when Donald Hine and I tested this idea through meta-analysis, we were surprised to find that the research literature shows that trust has little effect on cooperation.[70]

The reason appears to be that the effect of trust depends quite heavily on certain other factors, so that its effect, *in general,* is weak, although it is associated with cooperation in some circumstances. For example, as noted earlier, trusting participants cooperate more only in smaller groups[71] and only when they know how much others are cooperating, not when others' harvest behavior is not known to the group as a whole.[72] Again, as noted earlier, cooperation increases for men but not women when group members trust one another and can communicate with each other.[73] The effect of trust also depends on how quickly the resource is being depleted. Those who do not trust others much harvest about the same amount regardless of how fast the resource is going, but those who do trust others harvest more when the resource pool is full and less when it is almost empty.[74] Thus, interpersonal trust may be important only in concert with other factors.

Sense of Community. Another factor, a sense of community or group identity, can provide a positive glow in the dilemma. Apparently, not much is required to create enough group identity to improve cooperation. In one study, the only difference between high-identity and low-identity participants was that the high-identity participants came to the lab and received their instructions together, yet the high-identity harvesters cooperated more.[75] When harvesters think of themselves more as individuals than as group members, they overharvest more.[76]

Equality. The degree of equality among harvesters affects cooperation, too. What happens when harvesters find out that others all harvest about the same amount or that some harvesters take much more than others? They harvest more when the others' harvests are more variable.[77] This may occur because of the conformity effect mentioned earlier ("Oh, that's what everyone's taking; I may as well do the same") or it may occur because harvesters view the largest harvest as self-rewarding but

acceptable ("Oh, if you can take *that* many, I may as well do so too").

Note that the latter reasoning is also a form of conformity, but conformity to the most self-rewarding option observed. The idea is consistent with the results of another study in which harvesters were found to increase their harvests when they found out that others were overharvesting.[78] Conformity to a self-rewarding pattern of harvesting may be another way of defining competitiveness.

Conformity's effects depend, in part, on other factors. Participants in another study were provided with various impressions about others' harvesting.[79] When told that others were *under*using the commons, participants increased their own use of it; this sounds like nonconformity. However, when told that although most others were underusing the resource, a few were overharvesting, they overharvested; this is conformity to a selfish model. When told that the commons was being *over*used by others, participants increased their own harvests (conformity; "get it while you can!") when they had little trust in the other participants, but decreased their own harvests (nonconformity) when they trusted their cohorts.

The Structure of the Dilemma

The customs, norms, ground rules, and circumstances of social dilemmas vary. Whatever the qualities of the harvesters or the resource itself, these variations in the structure of the dilemma itself will, in part, determine the quality of resource management. Some of these variations include the pattern of rewards and punishments for harvesting, whether or not harvesters are educated about the dilemma, whether they may communicate with each other, whether the resource is partitioned into territories, rules about who may harvest how much at in which order, and the effect of different ways of governing dilemma situations (see Figure 14–6).

Payoffs, Rewards, and Punishments. What is the effect of changing the payoffs or delivering actual rewards or punishments, instead of merely asking harvesters to cooperate? One way to induce cooperation is to increase the financial gain for cooperating or the penalty for defection so much that there is no point in not cooperat-

FIGURE 14-6 Commons already are governed in various ways. Do you think this sign will effectively protect this resource?

ing. But that is cheating: If the reward for cooperation is high enough, the dilemma simply is no longer a dilemma.[80] Managers of everyday commons dilemmas often do not have enough money or policing power at their disposal to transform them into nondilemmas. For example, rhino horns bring thousands of dollars to poachers; governments cannot afford to pay every potential poacher the same amount *not* to poach or to hire enough park rangers to be certain that no poaching occurs. Within a payoff structure that retains the essence of the dilemma, smaller rewards will lead to less harvesting, and higher rewards (as in the large sums paid for small amounts of rhino horn) lead to more harvesting, just as might be expected.[81] Punishment will reduce defection.[82]

One key question with a less obvious answer is whether rewards or punishments are more effective in producing cooperation. One study found that positive incentives evoked more cooperation than negative incentives,[83] but another found that rewards and punishments were equally effective.[84] Other research showed that overconsumption decreased as the probability of punishment rose, but positive incentives were not exam-

ined.[85] Because of its important implications for how to manage real-world resources, this question needs more research.

The absolute size of a reward is not always its most important aspect. Sometimes, the key is the *relative* size of the reward (e.g., baseball players have sulked when they make "only" $3 million a year because another player makes $5 million). One study separately varied the size of the harvester's own gain (high or low) and the size of the gain for all harvesters (high or low).[86] Varying the harvester's own gain affected cooperation much more than varying the common gain. This result does not always occur, however. In other studies, harvesters who were told that the group's total winnings would be divided equally among the participants produced more cooperation than the usual payoff structure in which each individual wins as much as possible.[87,88]

Such discrepancies may be caused by the complexity of the dilemma's rules.[89] When the rules are very complex (as they were in the first study), harvesters may act selfishly not because they do not care about others, but because they could comprehend just enough of the rules to understand what might happen to themselves as the dilemma progressed. When the rules are too complex, harvesters may give up trying to discover how to serve the public interest and simply look after themselves as best they can. When the rules are simpler (as in the other studies), cooperation does increase when others' welfare is at stake.

Incidentally, the reinforcers do not have to be monetary. Verbal reinforcement such as "Good choice!" after a cooperative harvest was sufficient to improve cooperation in two studies.[90,91]

The rewards and punishments discussed so far are administered by an external authority (the researcher, taking the role of government). Paul Bell and colleagues have asked what happens when rewards and punishments are administered by the harvesters themselves. In one such study, harvesters were given the opportunity to punish those who acted in self-interest.[92] After every set of five choices, they could vote to penalize others; if two of the five group members voted to sanction a third participant, the latter lost 5 points; if three voted to sanction a fourth, the loss was 10 points; if four participants all voted to punish a fifth, the fifth participant lost 15 points. Not surprisingly, cooperation was higher when

PAUL BELL

has investigated many factors that affect cooperation in commons dilemmas.

punishment by "armed cooperators" was part of the dilemma's structure than when it was not.

Unfortunately, sanctioning systems are not free in the real world. Harvesters may be quite willing to fine others who are greedy, but a policing system requires money to establish and operate. In one study that allowed harvesters to sanction others but charged for policing services, the sanctioning system did not improve the overall functioning of the dilemma.[93]

Enlightenment. Before the action begins, one might attempt to persuade harvesters to "do the right thing." One experimenter tried to *induce* morality by delivering a short "sermon" to the participants, mentioning the benefits of cooperation, public-interest ethics, resource exploitation, the sad case of whales, and so on. Compared to a group that received no sermon, the participants cooperated more.[94] Another study demonstrated that advocating either the Golden Rule or altruism produced greater cooperation than if no moral guidelines were advocated.[95] It appears that morality can be produced, at least temporarily, by an appeal for cooperation.

Communication. Communication among harvesters is a crucial aspect of social dilemmas. In everyday life, communication may not occur because the participants choose not to, because communication is forbidden by superiors or governments, or because harvesters are unable to communicate because they rarely encounter one another. The choice not to communicate may result from self-interest in combination with good fortune, as when an old prospector discovers a gold mine or when a whaler finds one last pod of blue whales. In fish wars, an increasingly common social dilemma, governments may

forbid fishers from divulging the size of their catches to avoid international diplomatic trouble. Those who poach orangutangs in Borneo may not communicate because they rarely meet one another during their poaching forays.

In general, when communication occurs, management of the commons improves.[96,97,98,99,100] Communication among group members serves a number of beneficial functions:

- Clarifying the payoffs (which, in some studies and in the real world, can be complex)
- Reaching agreements on harvesting (such as taking turns)
- Reducing distrust
- Enhancing group identity
- Encouraging public commitment to cooperation[101] (fewer members, in a public discussion, are likely to advocate defection strategies)
- Devising penalties for not following agreements
- Eliciting promises to cooperate (as long as all group members make the promise)[102]

The development of these "group-regarding motives" may be a necessary and nearly sufficient condition for good management of the commons and group harvesting success.[103] Communication in the commons may have other side effects, too. Group discussion may not only increase cooperation in the immediate situation but also the individual's tendency to cooperate in other situations.[104]

Group cooperation may also may overcome the "bad apple" effect. When researchers inserted a confederate into the harvest group who was instructed to act in self-interest and other participants were allowed to communicate, the selfish confederate's presence did not reduce cooperation. However, when communication was not permitted, the selfish confederate's presence led to significantly more self-interest behavior on the part of others.[105] When group members think they will be meeting and communicating in the future, cooperation is better.[106]

Communication is not always beneficial, however. For example, communication may lead to cooperation only among better-adjusted individuals.[107] It may facilitate the performance of trusting males but not trusting females.[108] In the real world, communication is not free—someone must invest time, effort, or cash to establish and maintain communication. When communication is not free, its benefits are reduced (but not eliminated).[109]

Public Disclosure. Information is also crucial. One important form of information is the harvest totals for participants: Are they made public or kept private? Intuitively, we expect a greater number of public-interest harvest choices when participants must tell others what they are doing. In a nondisclosure situation, the resource itself declines but the participants cannot determine who among them is acting in self-interest and who is trying to cooperate.

One study used computer terminals to display the state of the commons to groups of four participants. When participants could see (by pressing a key on their terminal keyboards) how each of the others was acting, two out of three measures of cooperation rose significantly[110] (see Figure 14-7).

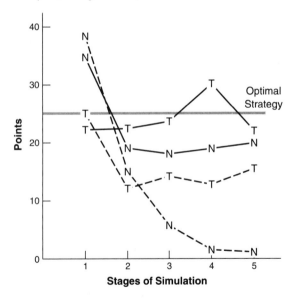

Stages of Simulation

- – N – – No public disclosure/No territory condition
- — N — Public disclosure/No territory condition
- – – T – – No public disclosure/Territory condition
- — T — Public disclosure/Territory condition

FIGURE 14-7 The effects of resource visibility and territories on harvesting. As harvesting rate deviates from the optimal rate, the outlook for the resource worsens. Across several stages of this simulation, the most favorable harvesting rates occurred when the resource was visible and territories existed.

Other studies have also reported that public disclosure increases the number of public-interest choices.[111,112,113] Public disclosure and trust are related; without knowing what others are taking, trust may diminish. The positive effect of trust on cooperation occurred only when harvesters knew others' harvest totals and, more importantly, when harvesters knew that others knew what they were doing.[114]

Harvest Alternatives. Researchers have begun to explore the usefulness of several variations on the standard harvest rules. For example, what is the effect of putting a limit on the maximum harvest each round? In one study, the effect was that harvesters cooperated more at the beginning than later in the exercise.[115]

What if harvesters are allowed to donate resources back to the pool? This would be analogous to a wealthy lumber baron financing a tree-planting project, or a poor but generous wood-cutter volunteering time to plant trees. One laboratory study supports the idea that when donations are possible, the resource is depleted less quickly.[116]

Although some harvesters are greedy, others are not; to permit donations is to allow generous harvesters to "give something back." A few harvesters do not even wait for an authority to tell them they can donate. One of the most touching moments in my own research career occurred when a 4-year-old girl in one of my studies saw that the resources (walnuts that could be traded later for cookies) were disappearing from the bowl that held them. She looked at the bowl, looked at her own stash, looked at me, and then put some of her own walnuts back.

What if harvesters are allowed to steal from other harvesters? Thiefs are not popular, but perhaps if harvesters take resources from each other, they will take less from the source, which will help to preserve the resource pool. In a study that punished overharvesting but allowed theft, theft did increase and the resource was better preserved.[117] When stealing was punished, then overharvesting occurred and the resource was more rapidly depleted. Given that neither stealing nor overharvesting is desirable, which policy would you implement if you were in charge of a commons dilemma?

Resource Partitioning. If the commons is divided into portions, each of which is managed by a separate participant, will management of the entire commons be better than if no subdivisions are made? One of the few field studies of social dilemmas examined two kinds of lobster fishing arrangements in Maine.[118] In one arrangement, the commons is open; all fishers who operate out of a given harbor have equal access to the lobsters in the vicinity of the harbor. In the other, fishers are organized into groups. Each group holds a clearly defined territory from which other groups are barred. In the subdivided commons, lobster management is better. There are more lobsters, the lobsters are larger, and each fisher makes more money.

Of course, this study was done in the field; one cannot be sure, for example, that lobster stocks were equal for the subdivided and undivided commons *before* the researcher began collecting data, and other circumstances may be different in the two arrangements. However, controlled laboratory studies also support the value of subdividing the commons.[119] Harvesters in these studies use the resource in a manner that simultaneously earns them more and leaves more of the resource in the commons. This is the very definition of good resource management. These results might be applied to energy distribution. If the total pool of electricity, natural gas, or gasoline could be divided into small pools controlled by neighborhoods or apartment blocks, there might be fewer brownouts and gasoline shortages.

Subdividing the commons may make external reinforcements, such as rewards and punishments, less necessary. In a study that compared subdivision versus no subdivision and reinforcements versus no reinforcements, subdivision improved management of the commons, but reinforcements did not bring *further* improvement.[120] One problem with subdivided commons, however, is equality: In the real world, some harvesters have big or choice territories while others have smaller or less desirable territories. Next is a discussion about this issue of equality or equity, not only in territories but in rewards.

Equity. In the real world, some harvesters enter commons dilemmas with more resources than others (e.g., a lobster fisher may inherit a prime territory from a parent, or a rich kid may decide to enter the poaching business and starts out by buying the best equipment money

can buy). Some harvesters reap more than others through greater effort, skill, greed, or persistence.

These differences are of two types: **Inequality** is a difference in the *actual* amount of resources, and **inequity** is a difference in the *perceived fairness* of the amount of resources. If Bill fishes 12 hours every day and Kim fishes 8 hours a day, Bill is likely to catch more fish (harvests unequal), but many people would say their harvests were equitable because Bill worked harder than Kim.

What happens when harvesters are told that at the end of the dilemma, no matter what happens to the resource, all harvests will be split equally? In one study, cooperation was better in the sense that all harvests were larger.[121] In other studies, inequality or inequity in the harvest or distribution of resources has led to decreased cooperation.[122,123]

Equal outcomes may produce the greatest cooperation, but not all harvesters are happy with the practice. Some participants in both simulated resource management exercises[124] and in real-world energy conservation[125] do not feel that forced equality is fair. These, of course, tend to be individuals who prefer the individual-gain orientation to the justice-for-all orientation, or those who are operating as individuals as opposed to a group of friends or family. Cohesive (friendly) groups seem to use equality as the basis of distributing the resources they harvest, whereas noncohesive groups seem to use equity as the basis.[126]

Governance. In the standard commons dilemma, the rules are set by the experimenter, who may be said to represent the government, and they are fixed for that particular dilemma. However, some researchers have begun to investigate which **structural solutions**—forms of government—harvesters prefer. The obvious reason for these studies is eventually to recommend how commons dilemmas ought to be run.

In an early governance study, harvesters who experienced an overused resource were more likely to vote in favor of eliminating free access to the resource and electing a leader who would regulate harvests than were harvesters whose resource was not overused.[127] Wanting to vote for a leader is particularly popular when the resource is overused, when harvesters are allowed to take more of the resource (as opposed to being limited in their harvests), and when the amount of others' harvests varies more.[128,129] Harvesters are more likely to vote for a leader to run the commons when they believe the cause of noncooperation is that the task is difficult rather than that other harvesters are greedy.[130] Finally, cooperative harvesters are more likely than noncooperators to vote for an elected leader when the commons is overused; noncooperators are against having elected leaders regardless of the state of the resource.[131] These self-interested persons presumably do not want any leaders slowing up their harvesting and presumably do not care about the resource itself. Voting for a leader is more popular than forced-equal outcomes.[132]

Once leaders are elected in the commons, how can they maintain support among the harvesters? Little research has been done, but one thing is clear: Leaders' support will vanish if harvesters see leaders allocate relatively more of the harvested resource to themselves and other harvesters.[133]

Does leadership actually improve management of the commons? Unfortunately, one study found that voluntary leaders in simulated commons dilemmas did not produce more cooperation than was found in leaderless groups.[134] Generally, one would expect leadership—at least high-quality leadership—to improve management of the commons. Further research will clarify just what a leader needs to do to improve cooperation in commons dilemmas.

What to Do?

In everyday life, some commons are managed well; since trouble-free commons receive little attention, it is not easy to think of examples. However, in some places, hunted wildlife such as ducks and deer are managed relatively well by systems of permits, seasons, and hunting rules. The list of commons that are poorly managed is long, and these problems have stimulated the research just surveyed. The important question is whether commons that are now managed poorly can be managed better. What, if anything, can be done?

Garrett Hardin's classic article that stimulated much research on the topic is fairly pessimistic.[135] Early on, some psychologists suggested there is more hope for solutions than Hardin thought, but others were more skeptical.[136,137] The many studies conducted in the last 25

years place people in a better position to resolve this dispute. Each real-world commons needs its own analysis, but from the results of studies, a tentative set of general recommendations that might lead to more socially responsible management of the commons might be constructed. (In fact, such a list is given in the In Sum section.)

In general, what might be done? Some have suggested that a dictator should be appointed, with the hope that the dictator would use power in a wise and benevolent way.[138,139] Others might advocate a sort of environmental Walden Two (a fictional utopia invented by B. F. Skinner) where public-interest behavior in the commons is positively reinforced. Third, the existing governmental framework might be used to lobby for legislative enactment of rules that enforce cooperation in the commons. Finally, some would advocate that friendship, trust, and communication be encouraged, perhaps in a more decentralized and territorialized system than now exists.[140]

Central to the issue is an ancient problem: how to allocate resources in the first place.[141] This is, in the broadest and deepest sense of politics, a political question. If we think of society as, in part, a system for distributing resources, how should society be run? A marketing professor has suggested that the main barriers to increased cooperation are (1) the desire to maintain one's own freedom, (2) the desire to avoid being a sucker (cooperating when no one else does), (3) self-interest, and (4) mistrust of others.[142] He described some ways that cooperation might be sold to "me-firsters" using marketing strategies originally developed for conventional retail products such as soap. Can we use marketing techniques to convince selfish people to be cooperative?

Another approach to understanding social dilemmas (which, of course, is a beginning toward overcoming them) is in the arena of theory. If people can view social dilemmas from the vantage point of a coherent framework, perhaps other solutions will become apparent. After this summary, those theories will be discussed.

◆ *IN SUM, the quality of resource management depends on the resource itself, the characteristics of participants, and the rules of the game. Cooperation seems to decline as the importance of the resource increases and to improve as the resource is depleted—two ominous signs. As children develop, their ability to manage commons dilemmas increases. One might advocate that, when a commons dilemma exists, part of the resource should be allocated to each participant to manage, that friendship and trust should be encouraged among the participants, and that the total number of participants be kept small. In addition, one might advocate that participants should communicate, make public choices, and be subject to punishment for selfish decisions, although positive incentives for cooperation are even more effective. Further, individuals should be given experience operating the commons, and the benefits of altruism in the commons should be pointed out. Last, but certainly not least, the payoff for cooperation should be increased, if possible.*

◆ THEORIES OF SOCIAL DILEMMAS ◆

Some of the major influences on individual choice in the commons have been discussed, but the larger perspectives that attempt to integrate knowledge about social dilemmas still need to be examined. This section briefly reviews six theories of social dilemmas: biosocial theory, tragic-choice theory, social-trap and reinforcement theories, limited processing theory, structural/goal expectation theory, and three-motive theory. Each theory offers a different perspective, some broader and some narrower.

Biosocial Theories

The first approach to social dilemmas is really several approaches that share the broad view that behavior in the commons is largely a function of the genetic or biological makeup of humans.[143] The biosocial theories agree that competitiveness or selfishness dominate human action, but vary in the degree to which these tendencies are expressed in aggression.

The competitive but less aggressive view, espoused by Wynne-Edwards, holds that animals manage commons by establishing territories, perhaps with some initial violence, but that these territories are subsequently maintained with little serious violence.[144] The territories serve several integrated functions, but in terms of commons management, resources are preserved by spreading the animals out in space and limiting new

population, both of which reduce consumption of food resources in any particular territory.

An extension of this theory argues that in humans, the competitiveness for territory reaches more aggressive levels, emerging as violence, fraud, and deceit.[145] No one would deny that these behaviors occur in humans; the controversial tenet of this theory is that a competitive urge for territory, rooted in our genes, is the cause of it. Territories, this theory asserts, are the basis of the social hierarchy in society, which in turn controls the distribution of resources, which is where the management of the commons comes in. Inequality is seen as the natural basis of society, and the most resources go to people highest in the hierarchy.

Both forms of the theory believe that altruism exists, although perhaps only for competitive reasons. At best, wealthy people give money (let's say a scholarship or student loan) to poorer people (students) so the wealthy people can later employ the better-trained people to help the wealthy get even richer. At worst, wealthy individuals give money to the poor merely so the poor will survive to comprise a group of people to which the wealthy individuals can feel superior!

The third biosocial approach, articulated by Dawkins, differs in that it believes altruism directed at society, in general, simply does not exist.[146] The **selfish gene theory** proposes that aid and assistance occur *only* where a gene might ensure its own survival. Thus, one shares resources with one's children, but not with those who do not carry one's genes.

All these theories have some scientific support in nonhuman animal populations, but they are difficult or impossible to formally test in humans. They may sound plausible or not, depending on your view of human nature, but scientific evidence for (or against) them in humans is virtually nonexistent.

Tragic-Choice Theory

Most of us would prefer a world without social dilemmas. The dream of sufficient food, land, and energy for everyone is very attractive. Yet, when we look around, we see that whether or not there are actually enough resources for everyone, existing resources clearly are not equally allocated. Tragic-choice theory, as proposed by Calabresi and Bobbitt, is largely phrased in terms we have called macrolevel, or societal-level, decision making.147 However, many of the concepts in it may be extended to the micro, or individual, level.

The theory begins with the fundamental assumption that this inequality and the resulting scarcity and suffering is natural and therefore nearly impossible to change. In this way, it is similar to the biosocial theories. Tragic-choice theory offers an explanation of social dilemmas that is controversial and not pleasant to hear. In fact, the theory itself predicts that people will not be receptive to it because, according to the theory, some widely held ideals are simply incompatible, such as freedom and equality.

Most of us support the ideals of freedom *and* equality, but tragic-choice theory maintains that the two goals are fundamentally incompatible. Freedom means the opportunity to get ahead—that is, to be "more equal" than others.[148] It also claims that democracy does *not* lead to equal allocation.[149] Tragic-choice theory maintains that equal or more nearly equal allocation of resources is possible, but that it could only be accomplished by a much more powerful central authority than most of us would tolerate.

The theory posits that scarcity originates in a **first-order determination**—that is, a conscious decision *not* to produce as much as could be produced.[150] One of the clearest examples of a first-order determination is the sometimes profitable decision not to produce as much food (e.g., dairy products, grains) as *could* be produced. Such decisions are reached in the interests of stabilizing prices, but, in fact, they serve to assist or enrich producers at the expense of other members of the commons.

These decisions to create scarcity are followed by **second-order determinations**—decisions about how to distribute the insufficient supply of goods. In contrast to the cry of "All persons are created equal," tragic-choice theory says it is unfortunate but true that our allocation policies clearly show that we do not value every person equally (see Figure 14–8). To disguise the conflict between the ideal of equality and the fact of nonequality, various devices support second-order determinations.[151]

One such device is to offer many and much-publicized resources to a few of the needy but not to offer resources to most of the needy most of the time. (Examples of this are when a wealthy philanthropist selects one worthy charity to benefit while ignoring other

FIGURE 14–8   Second-order determinations lead to the familiar spectacle of poor persons against rich backdrops.

equally worthy causes or when we give the homeless turkey on Christmas, but on no other day of the year.) The allocation problem is also avoided through political devices (we relinquish decision-making power—and our guilt—to someone else), the free market device (if those people really wanted a slice of the pie, they would work harder), and custom (we have always done it this way).

At the individual level, tragic-choice theory predicts that people will engage in self-interest behaviors because they accept one or more of these devices as justifications for getting ahead by overusing the commons. The only way out, according to the theory, is to be more honest and aware of our relationships to the suffering of others. No specific technological or legislative solution is offered.

Social-Trap and Reinforcement Theories

John Platt's social-trap theory is based on reinforcement.[152] The problem in a social dilemma, from his point of view, is that too many of us reward ourselves too immediately. For example, if you are holding a fast-food package and do not see a trash can nearby, it is immediately rewarding to litter (your hands are free of a burden), but, of course, when you or others repeatedly litter, the whole area eventually is visually ruined by litter.

The social-trap theory solution is to examine the reinforcement structure of the social dilemma and to re-arrange the timing and the value of reinforcements to reverse the pending disaster. In some commons, this is not only a workable solution but it is a solution that is already working. Most fish and game laws work reasonably well, for example.

In general, in a social trap or applied behavior analysis approach, the antecedent conditions (events that lead up to the harvest choice, including education, prompting, goal setting, and commitment) and consequence procedures (postchoice events such as reinforcement and punishment) must be carefully considered if more cooperation is to be elicited in larger-scale, longer-term everyday commons dilemmas[153] (see Figure 14–9).

As another example, subways in Moscow are very tidy places compared to those in some other cities. In part, this is because subway attendants who see someone dropping a cigarette butt will gently but firmly and, perhaps most important, *immediately* suggest to the litterer that such acts are anti-social and must be rectified.

A primary reason that commons are mismanaged, according to social-trap theory, is that not only are reinforcements for public-interest acts smaller than those for self-interest acts but they also are often not *contingent* on the public-interest behavior; that is, they are offered long after the occurrence of the public-spirited act. Our only material reward for not littering, for example, is a tiny reduction in taxes (because fewer trash collectors and landfill sites are needed) at some distant future time.

However, many social dilemmas are harder to resolve than littering, because the *values* of citizens differ.[154] Even those who litter will admit that it is not a good idea. But when not everyone agrees on values, de-

E. SCOTT GELLER'S *work provides a blueprint for improving the state of the environment.*

livering those immediate reinforcements can produce sparks. In a Victoria, British Columbia, aquarium, five Orca whales died in recent years. When the aquarium applied to capture more, the community was split on the value of displaying captured whales. The ensuing debate made it clear that there was no general agreement on whether capturing and displaying whales (presumably of some educational value) or leaving them in their open-ocean habitat (the natural thing to do) was the public-interest choice. (Postscript: The aquarium eventually closed completely.)

One common solution is to place control of the resource in government hands. There are two obvious problems with this solution. First, if individuals relinquish absolute control to a government, who controls the controllers?[155] Second, if individuals democratically elect a government and the government begins to force public-interest behavior (by restricting the harvesting of fish or trees), it may be voted out of office in favor of a government that promises the freedom to harvest. Once again, if the commons is limited, defection will occur and disaster may ensue.

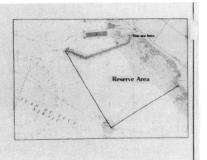

FIGURE 14–9 Commons managers sometimes simply freeze access to resources, which results in economic losses and poaching. Better management of resources before closures are necessary would be preferable.

Platt and Hardin believe the root problem is that there are too many people, rather than too few resources. However, some proposals for reducing the population are quite ominous (witness the Holocaust). Even relatively benign approaches to population control are sometimes seen as morally unacceptable or as attempts by the First World to control the Third World.

However, if the world population cannot be reduced, then Platt and Hardin believe we must dispense with either the ideal of equality (in resources) or the ideal of freedom. Influenced as he is by B. F. Skinner (the author of a book appropriately titled *Beyond Freedom and Dignity)*, Platt suggests we should sacrifice freedom. Beyond freedom (in a benevolent but authoritarian political climate) lies the possibility of justice and equality.

Limited Processing Theory

Robyn Dawes, who proposed limited processing theory, also believes that individuals do not, in many situations, behave in a rational manner.[156] By this, he does not mean that people act irrationally in the sense of derangement. Rather, they often coolly and calmly act nonrationally.

There are two basic modes of nonrationality. First, people sometimes simply do not pay much attention to what they are doing. For example, a person may litter, catch a fish, or leave a light on after he or she leaves a room without any thought about the resource management consequences of the act. Thus, in a social dilemma, defection with no conscious choice may occur.

Second, people may act nonrationally even when they have a basic understanding of social dilemmas and an awareness that they are making choices. This can happen when the structure of the social dilemma is too complex to understand or when no one has explained that a particular behavior happens to be a defection. Consider the African villager who poaches rare rhinoceros in order to sell the horn for its alleged medicinal properties. This is defection from our point of view, but the villager may not understand or agree with our assessment that taking the rhinoceros constitutes defection; rather, it is seen as a way to feed a family.

Dawes has suggested that much defection can be explained in terms of limited processing theory, and the way to overcome it is obvious, although not easy, to

overcome. We must increase awareness that certain behaviors constitute defection and that alternative behaviors will result in positive long-term outcomes. That is one major purpose of this chapter.

However, a complication is that defection sometimes harms one commons but helps another. The African villager who poaches rhino contributes to the demise of an endangered species, but the money gained probably enriches the villager's family and community. This complication ultimately leads to moral and political dilemmas, rather than strictly economic or psychological ones. Some social dilemmas have relatively simple solutions—such as more education—but others are true dilemmas.

Structural/Goal Expectation Theory

As proposed by Yamagishi, structural/goal expectation theory asserts that a certain set of conditions is required for cooperation to occur.[157] First, the harvesters must agree that mutual cooperation is desirable. This occurs when harvesters realize they are interdependent and that defection cannot continue for long. Second, the harvesters must realize that harvest cooperation based on individual, voluntary decisions does not work. Third, they must agree that a "structural" change (i.e., an elected leader who controls behavior in the commons) is necessary and will be effective (e.g., the leader would make or receive the harvest and then allocate it to each harvester).[158]

Structural/goal expectation theory, then, requires that harvesters change their belief that free access to the commons is desirable to the belief that a leader-controlled system will work, if cooperation is to occur. Obviously, this does not always happen, which is why—according to this theory—cooperation does not always happen.

For example, if harvesters believe the cause of bad management is a personal quality of other harvesters (e.g., greediness), they may be less likely to accept the third condition (that leadership would be effective) than if they believe the problem is that the management of the commons is very complex (but which a talented leader could handle). Although evidence reviewed earlier shows that depleted commons generally lead to acceptance of the leader idea, one study shows that that is not enough. Harvesters must also believe the problem is one that a leader *could* solve.[159]

This theory is not clear on whether cooperation might be achieved in any other way, but it implies there *are* no other ways. So far, the theory focuses on predicting which conditions are necessary for cooperation, but it says little about how to get harvesters to alter their beliefs.

Three-Motive Theory

Finally, David Messick and colleagues offer a theory about the motives involved in commons dilemma behavior.[160] This proposal assumes that a harvester's decision is based on three motives: self-interest (greed, or the desire to get ahead), the desire to act responsibly (not to deplete the resource too much), and conformity (to make decisions not very different from what others are doing).

Depending on many circumstances, any of these motives might be paramount. Thus, under some circumstances (e.g., being told that "everyone" is harvesting heavily), conformity might be the strongest motive and the harvesters might act to deplete the resource. Under other circumstances (e.g., when self-interest is not especially strong), they might act more cooperatively.

◆ *IN SUM, six theories of social dilemmas have been described. Biosocial theories claim that self-interest is genetic; two forms of the theory differ about whether this self-interest is accompanied by aggressiveness. Tragic-choice theory maintains that self-interest cannot be overcome except by the creation of a very strong central authority; this is unpleasant but necessary for the survival of the commons. Without such a central authority, the production and distribution of resources will be organized so as to benefit the wealthy at the expense of both the poor and the commons. Social-trap theory applies a reinforcement perspective to social dilemmas. It suggests that better management of the commons would follow from a restructuring of reinforcement timing. Like tragic-choice theory, a centralized authority appears necessary.*

Limited processing theory postulates that most individuals act selfishly, not because they are evil, but because the dangers of defection simply do not occur to them. Its solution is clear: Make more individuals aware of the consequences of overusing resources that are in limited supply. Structural/goal expectation theory again asserts the need for a central authority. This leader should be elected, and the harvesters must believe that mutual cooperation is necessary. Three-motive theory proposes that harvesters balance the desires to enrich the self, to take care of the resource, and to do what everyone else is doing.

◆ **DEFECTION: SHORT-TERM,** ◆
SELF-INTEREST BEHAVIOR

Focus now turns to three examples of human behavior that represent everyday responses to everyday social dilemmas: air pollution, energy conservation, and recycling. In the terminology of this chapter, the act of polluting is a defecting response. Most of us think of pollution as something produced by large, anonymous organizations, certainly not by ourselves. Some pollution is, indeed, produced from large plants and factories where no one person may be fairly described as a defector. However, a surprising amount of pollution is traceable to the decisions and acts of individuals. That is why pollution may be described as a behavioral problem, why it is reasonable to include pollution in a discussion of individual resource management strategies, and why so much research directed at pollution control involves attempts to change the behavior of individuals.

At the individual level, one kind of pollution that is very important is automobile exhaust. However, environmental psychologists have also studied noise as a form of pollution and visual pollution, the imposition of ugliness on the landscape, as well as litter (see Figure 14–10).

◆ **AIR POLLUTION:** ◆
A SOCIAL DILEMMA

The by-products of civilization that are released into the air constitute a type of "give some" social dilemma. Although there is a large pool of fresh air, it can be reduced in specific locations through the addition of smoke and chemicals to a level that is fatal for some people, animals, and plants. That is the "give some" equivalent of removing all the fish or trees in a "take some" social dilemma.

FIGURE 14-10 A "give some" form of bad resource management, as opposed to the "take some" form exemplified by overfishing or clear-cutting practice in the lumber industry.

Myths about Air Pollution

The following are myths about air pollution.

1. *Air pollution is a big-city problem.* A study that examined air pollution residues in the blood of blood donors in many rural and urban settings found that overexposure to carbon monoxide is common even in rural areas.[161] For example, the worst air pollution in Canada occurs in a fairly small town in the far north.[162] The cause: extensive wood burning for heat, combined with a valley location and climatic tendency toward inversions.

2. *Air pollution is a relatively new problem.* Although it is worsening in some places, air pollution is considerably less now than it was 100 years ago in some industrial cities, such as London. This is partly because coal and wood are not used as often as they used to be in cities for home heating and cooking. Although air pollution is not new, pollution from smoke recently has become a serious problem again in parts of North America. Particularly in areas with a reasonable supply of firewood, so many residents burn wood for home heating that some neighborhoods have a real problem. My own town just passed a bylaw that controls the amount of smoke that may leave our chimneys; it has had outdoor burning regulations for years.

3. *Air pollution is an outdoor phenomenon.* It is easy to forget that outdoor air is drawn into homes and workplaces; we normally do not notice the pollution inside because it is not dense enough to see. Also, the psychological study of indoor air pollutants is increasing.

4. *Air pollution may affect health but not behavior.* Obviously, air pollution can have drastic effects on health. In one especially bad month (December 1952), the deaths of about 3,500 individuals in London were attributed to air pollution. An extensive catalog of health problems that may be caused by air pollution has been assembled.[163] However, many studies also have shown that air pollution has distinctly *behavioral* effects in addition to the much-publicized effects on health.

5. *Air pollution is caused by factories, not people.* Over 80 million tons of carbon monoxide alone are released into the atmosphere each year in North America from transportation sources; most transportation still involves one or two individuals driving a car.[164] Incidentally, these pollution figures, mind-boggling as they are, do not include other common air pollutants such as sulfur dioxide, nitrogen dioxide, and particulates (tiny particles produced during combustion).

6. *Incineration destroys toxins.* When wastes are burned, the particulates go into the air. However, in many incinerators, ash or finer particles still contain dangerous compounds. Even state-of-the-art incinerators with the latest "scrubbers" do not entirely destroy toxins. Many are left in the ash inside the incinerator after the waste is burned and must be put *somewhere* afterward.

If these are the myths, what are the facts? What is known follows.

Air Pollution and Behavior

True experimental studies of air pollution are relatively rare. There are ethical problems; subjects who are willing to inhale carbon monoxide to advance scientific knowledge are understandably difficult to find. The existing evidence indicates that common air pollutants affect the range of our behavior, basic psychological processes, and, perhaps, attraction, aggression, and schizophrenia.

Restriction of Activities. When I was 13 years old, I attended a school in an area that was so polluted that students were sometimes required to wear gas masks whenever they went outside. Try playing your favorite sport in a gas mask! Clearly, the first behavioral effect of air pollution is that one's behavior sometimes is *constrained* to a narrower range than is desirable.

Cognitive Performance. The second behavioral effect of air pollution is that excessive levels of carbon monoxide negatively affect such basic cognitive activities as reaction time and arithmetic ability,[165] the ability to judge time,[166] and the ability to detect changes in light intensity.[167] These alterations of basic behavior may not sound exciting to anyone except experimental psychologists with specialized interests in them. However, these basic behaviors are the essential building blocks of such important behaviors as driving and problem solving.

Researchers have attempted to discover whether high but realistic levels of carbon monoxide (e.g., levels characteristic of traffic rush hours) are associated with increased accident rates. People do not *feel* any different when they are exposed to levels of carbon monoxide high enough to affect performance. Because of this lack of awareness, people often fail to avoid either the carbon monoxide or the affected behavior.

The evidence concerning driving accidents is not clear; some studies report no relation and others show small but significant correlations between accident rates and levels of carbon monoxide on the road or at the place of work just left by the driver.[168] The lack of clarity in this applied research should not be taken as proof that air pollution does *not* affect complex behaviors; the problems of conducting research on this complicated but everyday phenomenon may obscure its subtle effects on key everyday behaviors.

Social Behavior. Air pollution may affect social and interpersonal processes, as discussed in earlier chapters. Subjects in one study who were exposed to cigarette smoke were more aggressive than those who were not.[169] A correlational study of air pollution in relation to psychiatric emergency room visits reports that the amount of air pollution is related both to the total number of visits and to the number of schizophrenia-related vis-

its.[170] Correlational data do not *prove* that air pollution drives people crazy, but the data do suggest that individuals who are having difficulties even in clean air may find that the slight performance decrements caused by air pollution are enough to throw them off balance.

Adapting to Air Pollution. Given its unpleasant aesthetic qualities and its effects on health and behavior, environmental psychologists have wondered why public outcries against air pollution have not been louder. For example, in preparation for the 1984 Olympics, Los Angeles tried to implement strict controls in an attempt to improve its Smog City image. But why did it take an event such as the Olympics for the city to implement the controls?

There are two general answers: adaptation and perceived costs. It has been said that humans can get used to anything. This assertion, however, is not true. In an earlier chapter, evidence was presented, for example, that people do not adapt to community noise pollution. In most instances, air pollution increases gradually. This allows time for a population to get used to the decrease in visual quality, the increase in eye irritation, and the small decrements in cognitive performance.

The **Weber-Fechner law** of psychophysics says that noticeable differences in the level of a stimulus change with the overall intensity of the stimulus. This laboratory-derived law may be applied to everyday air pollution: When little pollution is present, a small increase will be apparent to an observer, but when much pollution is present, the same increase will no longer be noticed.[171]

The same principle may apply to all resource management situations. When the pool of resources is large, a few defections will go unnoticed, but when the pool is nearly depleted, a defection is very obvious. One piece of litter in a spotless hallway stands out, but one piece of litter added to many others will not be noticed.

A study of smog perception demonstrates this adaptation process in an interesting but unfortunate way.[172] Long-term Los Angeles residents and newcomers were shown scenes that differed in the amount of smog present. The long-term residents were less likely to perceive smog in any given scene. They had become so used to air pollution that they were no longer sure when it was present and when it was not.

A second reason for inaction is the perceived cost of action. If someone's job depended on air pollution, that person would be reluctant to struggle against air pollution. For instance, what if one of the costs of installing expensive "scrubbers" in the smokestacks includes your own layoff?[173]

If the cost of cleaning up the atmosphere to a commuter is bicycling six miles to work through all kinds of weather, is it worth it? Public-interest choices are desirable, but how many immediate comfort losses will individuals absorb? Let's say our commuter, in a fit of public spiritedness, decides that bicycling is, in the long run, worth it. "The grandchildren will thank me for giving them cleaner skies," says our newly converted cyclist, puffing as the rain begins to soak through. Just then, an office-mate who lives down the street drives by, hits a puddle and splashes mud on the cyclist's damp clothes. Equity theory predicts that our admirable commuter will decide that the burden of environmental responsibility is not being shared equally. Tomorrow, the cyclist may take the car.

To both the adaptation and perceived cost problems, the concerned environmental psychologist has an answer. Implied in both equity and limited processing theories, the answers are to increase awareness of the long-term costs of defection and to find ways to increase equity. The drastic long-term costs of acid rain, for example, have been dramatized in a National Film Board of Canada film that received much publicity when exhibitors of the film in the United States were forced to label the films as "foreign propaganda." It is true that changing behavior may require Herculean efforts on the part of concerned citizens.

◆ **IN SUM,** *air pollution is a "give some" form of social dilemma. Individuals or organizations cleanse their own hands but dirty the commons. Air pollution is an old problem caused by individuals as well as industry that occurs in both rural and urban areas, indoors and outdoors, and affects people's behavior as well as their health. Its behavioral effects are subtle but probably include constraining the kinds of activities we engage in, mildly impairing cognitive processing, and increasing interpersonal and psychiatric problems. Efforts directed against air pollution have been blunted by our tendency to adapt to it and by the high perceived cost of correcting it.*

◆ ENERGY CONSERVATION: ◆ A SOCIAL DILEMMA

Two researchers were walking through a campus married-student housing complex one day. They were studying energy conservation practices and had decided to have a look around the real world. Although it was a cold day, they noticed the distinctive sound of an air conditioner coming from one apartment. Upon knocking and asking a few questions, they discovered that the resident did not like the high temperatures in the apartment produced by the furnace, which was running full blast. To adjust the temperature, he had turned on the air conditioner![174]

Because most energy we use comes from natural resources, energy conservation is a social dilemma.[175] In commons dilemma terms, many energy resources (e.g., oil, coal, natural gas, and wood) renew themselves so slowly (how much new natural gas will be created by nature during our lifetimes?) that they usually are called *non*renewable energy sources. Although hydroelectric power on a given river renews itself whenever rain falls, no new rivers are being created.

Energy conservation was an important public issue in the 1970s when oil price hikes caused shortages. Then, a gradual relaxation of prices made many people complacent about the issue. However, the recent resurgence of general environmental interest has brought with it renewed interest in energy conservation.[176] The price of energy certainly is not the only important motive for energy conservation.[177] Nevertheless, we still use energy much faster than it is being created, and not everyone uses it equitably. The amount of energy used in the United States for air conditioning *alone* is nearly equal to the *total* amount of energy used in China; the

PAUL STERN *has investigated the important psychological and technical factors that influence energy conservation.*

per-capita use of energy in developing countries is only about 1 percent of per-capita use in Canada.[178]

Government and industry are the biggest energy users,[179] but residential users also have control over the disposition of many resources; behavior in the home can significantly affect energy conservation.[180] In the 1970s, it was estimated that energy costs for typical existing houses and apartments could be reduced by up to 50 percent.[181] The savings could, of course, be used for many purposes: to reduce the cost of energy to the consumer, to finance deserving social programs (how about more student loans at lower rates?), and to ease national dependence on distant, tenuous sources of energy.

These savings may be accomplished partly by technological advances, partly by changing the behavior patterns of residents, and best by integrated programs that include both.[182] A comprehensive study of the energy crisis concludes that changing residential energy conservation by changing behavior has been largely overlooked and holds great promise.[183] Many studies in the last decade support this view.

This is not to imply that changing behavior is easy. For example, perhaps the most important variable under the immediate control of householders is thermostat setting. One study found that for high-frequency resource management behaviors such as turning down the thermostat each evening, the best predictor of future behavior is past behavior: Those who *have* been doing it will continue to do it.[184] One challenge for psychologists, then, is to get homeowners *started* in conservation so that they will continue to help conserve. High-energy use is tied to self-esteem for some people; to cut back implies giving up on their vision of a better life.[185]

Another challenge is posed by the recognition that home energy conservation is affected not only by simple daily choices such as whether to turn the thermostat down but also by larger choices such as where to live and other demographic characteristics. A nationwide study of actual energy consumption in Canada found that energy use was well predicted by climate, house characteristics (fireplace, fuel source, single family versus multiple family), resident characteristics (bigger, wealthier families with more members use the most energy) and attitudes (beliefs that energy conservation is important).[186]

Further challenges occur when behavior-change programs are viewed by residents as infringements on

their freedom. The programs do not always fit easily into residents' lifestyles, and they can be quite labor intensive and costly. Despite these problems, residential energy conservation holds great potential for easing pressure on diminishing supplies of nonrenewable resources. The environmental psychologist's challenge is to discover inexpensive ways to improve energy consumption patterns in homes and to help preserve the home as a haven from excessive outside pressures.

Technological solutions to the energy problem receive more attention than psychological approaches. In many instances, however, all the technology in the world will not save one kilowatt-hour if consumer behavior does not change. Some of the methods used to promote energy conservation include appeals from authorities, educational campaigns, providing feedback about rates of energy use, and reinforcing conservation practices with money or rebates.

Before we try to change behavior, however, it helps to know who already conserves, and when. Then we know where to aim energy conservation programs.

Who Conserves, Under Which Conditions?

Although everyone has become aware of energy shortages, not everyone adopts energy conservation measures. Environmental psychologists have begun to construct models to predict who will engage in energy-saving behavior and who will not.[187] This section examines some of these factors (see Figure 14–11).

Attitudes, Knowledge, Values, and Norms. Four attitudes are strongly related to energy use: whether or not you think energy use is important for comfort and health, whether or not your energy savings are worth the effort of conserving, whether or not your efforts as an individual can make any difference, and whether or not the energy crisis is real.[188] These four attitudes predict over half of the variance in actual electricity usage by households.[189]

Nevertheless, the remainder of the explanation lies outside one's attitudes, and people who hold pro-conservation attitudes or values do not always engage in pro-conservation behaviors. Favorable attitudes toward conservation do not necessarily lead to actually turning

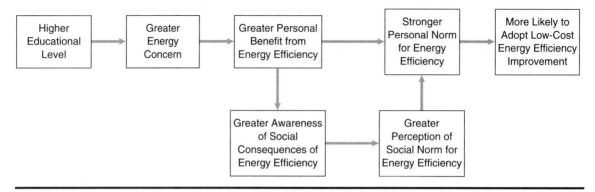

FIGURE 14–11 The more important causal influences on who will (and who will not) acquire low-cost energy efficiency devices.

down the thermostat, changing furnace filters, or caulking,[190] or even having a commitment to do such things.[191] Even concerned citizens tend to adopt only conservation behaviors that are familiar and easy to engage in.[192] Sometimes, energy conservation practices are adopted for a brief period, then abandoned.[193] People do not accurately report which conservation actions they have taken.[194]

Worse yet, people's attitudes often are based on overconfidence about what they know. A survey of California residents found that *claimed* knowledge about particular energy-saving programs was much greater than *actual* knowledge of them.[195] When asked to rank the energy requirements of various machines, people tend to group them by function or size and to believe that larger machines use more energy than smaller ones, even though that is not always the case.[196] How can you save energy if you think you know more than you do?

Consider a simple process such as how a thermostat works. Interviews with householders show that one-fourth to one-half of us think thermostats work like valves (you turn the knob up to produce more heat or turn it down to produce less heat) instead of as feedback devices (you set a temperature; the thermostat then senses the current temperature and turns the furnace on or off to maintain that temperature).[197]

Furthermore, many people who *say* they have undertaken some action to save energy really have not done so.[198] Even individuals who attended an intensive energy conservation workshop and generally emerged with increased concern about conservation and opti-

mism that they could make a substantial difference in overall savings usually did not actually change their behavior or their homes.[199] In a subsequent home check, only 11 percent of the workshop attendees had installed a water flow restrictor and only 1 of 70 had lowered the water heater thermostat as a result of the workshop.

Unfortunately, it seems, people often confuse what they *believe* with what they *think* they know and what they *think* they have done with what they have *actually* done. And, of course, actions are what really conserve energy, not intentions or beliefs. Therefore, we must be particularly skeptical of research that is based only on attitudes or unconfirmed verbal reports of energy conservation behavior.

Not all the attitude research is negative. Although energy-related attitudes are not great predictors of actual behavior, they do help. For example, in a study that tried to predict thermostat-setting behavior, knowing a person's attitudes helped to predict who turned thermostats down and who did not, even *after* such as variables as the dwelling's physical characteristics, the person's demographic characteristics, and economic data were used as predictors.[200]

Furthermore, knowledge of attitudes can be used to guide energy policy. For example, individuals whose attitudes include an acceptance of personal responsibility for the energy crisis are more likely to be in favor of individual-level solutions (e.g., thermostat setbacks and a reduction of travel). Those who assign the cause of energy crises to causes outside themselves (e.g., oil companies and government) are more likely to favor outside solutions.[201] Pro-environmentalists tend to favor "soft" solutions such as solar power and reduction in energy use, whereas nonenvironmentalists tend to favor "hard" solutions such as nuclear power or new dams.[202]

Pro-conservation attitudes are best promoted by a strategy that emphasizes the desirable consequences of conservation rather than one that focuses on negative issues such as whether an energy crisis really exists or not.[203] Attitudes do not predict conservation behavior very well, but pro-conservation attitudes are a necessary first step (who will save energy if no one even thinks it is a good idea?). Finally, merely being in favor of conservation may not be a great predictor of doing something about it, but believing that one is competent or able to make the necessary changes to one's dwelling is important.[204]

Income and Status. Relatively high and very low income earners conserve more. Consumers with relatively high incomes are better educated and better able to afford the initial start-up costs of some alternatives.[205] Solar energy, for example, is relatively expensive to begin with and its costs take several years to repay through energy savings; it is not very feasible for low-income or mobile consumers.[206] In telephone surveys, higher-status persons *report* (for what it is worth!) that they adopt conservation practices more.[207]

Very low income groups in North America and in developing countries already conserve more, partly because they have much less money to spend on basic energy costs (heating, cooling), let alone energy-gobbling gadgets. Thus, one prime target of conservation programs is higher-income individuals who have not yet changed their lifestyles. These individuals are especially ripe because they use more energy at present, but usually believe conservation is desirable.

Ownership and Building Type. Homeowners take more actions than renters to make their dwellings energy efficient, but they do not reduce energy-using activities any more than renters.[208] Residents who live in multiple-unit dwellings with a single electrical meter tend to conserve less. In many such buildings constructed before energy prices rose dramatically, only one gas or electric meter was installed for the whole building; energy was not expensive, but installing separate meters in every unit was. Many landlords are thereby forced to include the cost of utilities in the rent because they cannot easily compute how much each resident uses.

When someone else pays for utilities, the temptation to defect is strong. If the air conditioner controls are closer than the furnace controls, why not just cool off one's overheated place with the air conditioner? In the case of residential energy, the cost is largely passed on to one's neighbors in a manner that is directly analogous to William Lloyd's parable of the villagers and their cattle.

Lifestyle, Age, and Experience. As might be expected, people who tend toward lifestyles characterized by "voluntary simplicity" engage in more conservation than do those whose lifestyle is not so characterized.[209] Those whose lives have been directly touched by energy shortages, or who believe their health and comfort are threatened by shortages, are more likely to take action.[210] Understandably, people who are home during the day use more energy and those with small children use more heat at night.[211] The elderly use more heat at night[212] and during the day,[213] probably because they are more worried about their health. Older people are slower to adopt other conservation techniques, too.[214] This may be because conservation programs have not yet been designed for the needs of older people.

Provoking Energy Conservation

Now that we have a sense of who tends to conserve under which conditions, we can discuss how to increase conservation.

Appeals from Authorities. In the scenario that opens this chapter, the mayor of a town facing a water shortage appeals for citizens to use less water. How well do such appeals work?

In the United States, the best-known appeal was one made on national TV by President Carter in 1977. Two studies seized this opportunity to evaluate the effect of the appeal. One surveyed over 400 residents and found that 27 percent of the households had reduced their thermostats to the recommended 65°F.[215] Unfortunately, those who had not even heard the appeal had lowered their thermostats too, so that the appeal itself appeared not to be the reason for lowered thermostats.

In another study, an energy conservation program was already underway when Carter's appeal came.[216] A plea from the governor came at about the same time. The investigator was thus able to compare the existing program, which was behaviorally oriented, and the two appeals. President Carter's appeal was much more effective than the behavioral program. The behavioral program was then refined to include group meetings and more incentives. The refined program was more effective than the gubernatorial appeal.

Others have noted that energy conservation behavior is partly spurred on by simple economic factors.[217] Appeals and other strategies to induce behavior changes in consumers must be evaluated against the change due simply to price increases. A comparative review concluded that appeals from authorities are useful over and above economic considerations, but not universally so.[218] The response varies with climate and type of energy used in the home. Presumably, the appeal's effectiveness will vary with the attractiveness of the leader.

Educational Campaigns. The most widely used strategy to promote energy conservation is to distribute pamphlets, letters, flyers, stickers, and booklets describing how one might conserve energy around the home. This approach is relatively inexpensive and seems rational: If consumers are told how they can save money, surely they will take advantage of the information.

Unfortunately, as noted earlier, the nearly unanimous results from numerous studies are that the distribution of energy conservation literature alone does *not* have a significant impact on behavior.[219,220] Researchers and energy agencies both have sent out millions of colorful informative items without, apparently, changing much behavior. These educational aids are not necessarily worthless, however. They may serve to *prime* consumers so that other intervention strategies will work better.

Perhaps we need to start earlier, when consumers of energy are still in school. The U.S. government placed about 140 Energy-Environment Simulators in schools.[221] The simulators compress 100 years into 1 minute; students try to maintain viable sources of energy under a variety of conditions such as a cutoff of Mideast oil, the development of new technology for producing energy, or an increase in population. These simulators and other

realistic games should help raise awareness of the problems involved in energy conservation and may foster increased conservation behavior.[222]

Another educational approach is to use the power of the media, which some see as the best method of achieving significant energy savings.[223] Based on social-psychological principles, a media campaign should (1) come from a believable source, such as an admired person; (2) contain a specific message; (3) be presented in a vivid manner; and (4) let people know what they are losing by not conserving.[224] An Australian study measured the effectiveness of a 30-second commercial that advocated conservation of gasoline.[225] It found that after 4 weeks of intensive airplay, the commercial had a small but significant effect on self-reported conservation of gasoline.

Commitment. Individuals who have in some way made a public commitment to energy conservation conserve more than those who have not.[226,227] Obviously, if I have announced to my neighbors that I am careful to turn off lights in rooms I am not using, I feel pressure not to have my neighbors pass by and notice that every room in my house is lighted.

The logical extension of this idea was tested. If public commitment leads to conservation, will stronger public commitment lead to even more energy conservation? Researchers invited 24 small businesses to participate in a conservation program.[228] All businesses were told that there was a community relations component to the program. They might be assigned, randomly, to a mild commitment condition (their business listed in a newspaper advertisement thanking firms in the small town where the study occurred for their participation), a strong commitment condition (nearly the same ad, except that newspaper readers could tell just how much each business had conserved or not), or a control condition (no ad exposure). The control condition produced the least conservation, as expected. However, the strong commitment condition produced *less* conservation than did the mild commitment condition.

Perhaps this happened because the strong-commitment firms were placed under too much pressure and felt trapped. Whether these results might have been different with another form of strong commitment—perhaps one where firms had a chance to volunteer to be in a strong commitment condition—is difficult to determine. If such an experiment were to be conducted, it would be open to the criticism that those who volunteered were already, before the study began, set to conserve more than were those in a mild commitment condition. Public commitment leads to conservation, but care must be taken with the level of public commitment requested so that the participant's motivation is not stifled.

Feedback. Assuming that a consumer is inclined toward saving energy, a basic principle is that providing feedback about rate of energy use will facilitate behavior change. Of course, consumers already receive feedback every month or two in the form of a bill. However, this information is often ineffective as a behavior-change agent because it arrives long after the behavior in question and it is too diffuse. Consumers are usually unaware just which appliance or heater was used, on which days they used energy extravagantly, or whether an increased bill reflects increased usage or increased utility prices.

Environmental psychologists who have investigated the effectiveness of feedback have offered energy-use information to the consumer much more frequently—sometimes even an immediate, continuous readout of how much energy is being used. In a typical study, householders were told four times a week how much electricity they had used in comparison to an amount predicted for them on the basis of outdoor temperature and other factors.[229] Compared to a no-feedback control group, the informed residents used 10.6 percent less electricity. Other studies of feedback have reported savings in the range of 5 to 15 percent[230,231] (see Figure 14–12). These savings do not sound very dramatic until they are multiplied by the number of residential units in a whole country; then, the potential value of frequent feedback is clear.

Feedback may have even greater potential when it is more immediate. In pilot programs, this approach has evolved from one that hand delivers a written record of use to one that installs a digital readout on the wall of the consumer's living room. British Columbia Hydro, for example, has tested a device that offers a continuous display of the ongoing electrical use. Because the consumer may lose track of the overall meaning of a continuous display, usage rates for the past day and week are

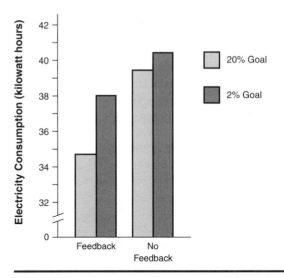

FIGURE 14–12   Daily average electricity consumption (adjusted for prestudy consumption rates) of townhouse residents in four conditions. Giving residents moderately difficult goals and feedback produces the most savings.

also displayed. A California study found that continuous displays, combined with different rates for peak versus off-peak electricity use, did not manage to reduce overall energy consumption, but at least caused consumers to shift their electricity use to off-peak periods.[232]

Goal Setting. Energy savings are easier to achieve when individuals are also asked to meet relatively difficult, but voluntarily chosen, goals—such as a 20 percent saving.[233] When strategies are combined, savings are better. A Dutch study reports that daily feedback plus a commitment to save resulted in significant natural gas conservation.[234]

Modeling. People learn from watching others. This principle has been shown to increase energy conservation behaviors in studies of university showering practices and home energy conservation. In the shower study, despite printed signs of instructions to the contrary, only 6 percent of students soaped up with the water off and took short showers. A larger sign increased compliance to 19 percent, but the sign was a target for aggressive remarks and minor vandalism. When one student (a confederate of the experimenter) modeled the desirable behaviors, half of the others soaped up with the water off and took shorter showers. When two students modeled, 67 percent of others complied.[235]

Monetary Rewards. For many, the most effective behavior-change agent is money. An obvious strategy is to offer grants, loans, or rebates for saving energy. The early studies of this strategy were full of promise: Individuals responded extremely well. However, if a conservation program based on financial reward is to have wide-ranging potential, it must be cost effective, at least in the long run. Fortunately, research shows that careful planning of rebates (the size of rebates in relation to the season and peak usage rates), grants, and loans can make monetary payoffs cost effective.[236,237,238]

Home Audit Programs. Energy utility companies and governments also have tried to provoke conservation through programs in which a company representative visits the house and examines its energy-wasting capacity. Typically, the auditor points out problems, suggests that repairs be done, offers an attractive grant or loan for major refits, and suggests reputable contractors.

The success of such programs is variable; a national average might be about 15 percent of householders who go on to make the necessary changes to weatherproof their houses. Psychologists have improved that success rate by training auditors in how to communicate with householders.[239] For example, auditors were told to use vivid examples, such as saying, "If you were to add up all the cracks under these doors, it's the same as if you had a hole the size of a basketball in your wall." The auditors were told to focus on loss rather than gain, such as saying, "If you don't fix cracks, it's your hard-earned cash going right out the window." The auditors were also trained to induce investment or commitment in the audit process by getting householders to follow them around the house, help take measurements, and actually look at the cracks. Together, these changes to the auditor's style produced a cooperation rate of about 60 percent, roughly four times the usual.

Designing for Energy Conservation

Energy-use patterns are relatively resistant to change. One study indicates that major Western countries re-duced their demand for oil only about 2 percent from 1973 to 1980.[240] High rates of usage are part of the lifestyle of many consumers. They may not wish to change; if they do, they may find it difficult to maintain interest in an energy conservation program. This leaves a great deal of potential for increased conservation.

The weather remains the single largest predictor of what consumers will do with their heating and cooling machines. Educational campaigns are convincing more and more consumers that conservation is worthwhile in the long term. Feedback and tailored rebates to individual consumers may help increase conservation by many small percentages that add up to large national savings. Research into newer aspects of energy conservation—such as field studies of adjustment to nonoptimal temperatures, modeling, and peak-load management—are just a beginning.[241] Research into the personal, social, and cognitive aspects of energy conservation is needed.[242] The promised savings of "up to 50 percent" may not be realized until (1) behavioral and cognitive approaches (2) hardware improvements, and (3) economic considerations are integrated.[243,244]

One way to integrate these items is to build a small community composed of energy-conscious individuals and energy-saving houses. Michael and Judy Corbett, developers in Davis, California, have gone beyond merely adding solar panels to the houses in their project, Village Homes.[245] Davis can be very hot in the summer; the Corbetts' designs take advantage of natural ventilation patterns to reduce the need for air conditioning. One ambient source of excess heat in some developments comes from broad expanses of pavement; in Village Homes, the pavement area is reduced by narrowing streets and clustering homes.[246]

Village Homes incorporates these energy conservation features into an overall plan aimed at ecological soundness. There are water conservation features, defensible space features, and a community-constructed playground. Parts of a preexisting orchard were retained; income from it goes into the homeowners' association coffers. The Corbetts reside in the development, so that assistance with technical problems is close at hand.

Energy conservation is not merely turning the thermostat down. It is part of a pattern of living that includes voluntary lifestyle simplicity[247] and environmental designs that make it easy to conserve.

◆ *IN SUM, energy use is a social dilemma when it is easier to waste energy, particularly from nonrenewable sources in the service of short-term goals, than to conserve it for the future. Up to 50 percent savings could be achieved in ideal conditions, which would include an integration of psychological, economic, and engineering contributions. Conservers include those with enough money to purchase energy-saving devices so they can save over the long haul; those who must conserve because they cannot afford much gasoline, air conditioning, or fuel oil; those who have adopted a voluntarily simpler lifestyle and feel a personal responsibility for energy problems; those who are willing to make moderate public commitments toward energy conservation; and those whose energy use is* not *monitored with a shared meter.*

 Conservation may be enhanced by some appeals from authorities. Educational campaigns seem to change attitudes, priming individuals for changing behavior, but energy-use habits are relatively difficult to change. Feedback and goal setting have achieved 20 percent savings. Monetary approaches have a cost-benefit problem: They sometimes cost more than they save. The case of a housing development that integrated several design innovations with a group of ecologically oriented residents was described as an important step toward the the upper limit of 50 percent energy savings.

◆ RECYCLING: A SOCIAL DILEMMA ◆

In April 1983, *National Geographic* featured a story full of garbage. Instead of the usual exotic and beautiful scenes for which the magazine is famous, its pages were filled with pictures of human beings scuttling over mountains of trash. In many countries, whole classes of people are engaged full time in processing garbage. They sort out the valuable materials, fight over rights to the garbage of the wealthy, and often live at the dump. This is hardly an attractive scene. Yet, the only difference between these people and you, is that they work near the end of a disposal process and you work at the beginning (see Figure 14–13).

 Each of us is curator of a steady stream of natural resources that has been transformed into usable goods. Of course, most of us do not realize this; we simply think we are throwing out the garbage. Yet, it remains true that many times daily, each of us decides how to manage the

FIGURE 14–13 "Dumpster divers" may be found even in well-off places. They search for food and they help recycle cans and other materials that others find too much trouble to recycle.

flow of paper, glass, metal, food, water, and oil that comes to us so routinely. In North America, most of these products are discarded into unsorted general garbage, to be collected, transported, crushed, burned, and bulldozed at a cost of over $6 billion each year.[248]

 In the language of this chapter, the public-interest choice is to find ways to *reuse* resources, not to toss them into messy unsorted piles. The key to managing resources in the public interest is to change this common practice of having a single bag or can for throwing away anything no longer wanted.

 There are two forms of what is technically called **resource recovery**: Recycling occurs when waste material is processed to re-create the original product, and **reclamation** occurs when the waste material is processed to create a different product.[249] Recycled paper may go from being a sheet of paper to being a shopping bag. Reclaimed tires have recently been used as an ingredient in paving mixes for airport runways and for streets. Apparently, bits of tire help prevent cracking during cold weather.

Technical Problem or Human Problem?

Resource recovery may be viewed as a technical problem or as a behavioral problem, or both. The pure technical approaches tend to allow consumers to send in mixed garbage in the present manner; the separation and recovery of materials is done at a central plant. Such high-technology solutions tend to maximize both consumer convenience and expense.[250] However, the expense (high-technology plants can be very expensive) is unfortunately remote in time and it forms an indeterminate part of the consumer's tax bill. Thus, in the short run, the technical solution is often more attractive.

The alternative, to consider resource recovery as a behavioral problem, focuses on persuading consumers to reduce their original use of materials, to separate, to prepare, and sometimes to deliver their discarded items at the beginning of the waste disposal process. This can be bothersome. Yet, because the high-tech solution is often more expensive (sometimes more so than the old bulldozing-for-landfill approach it is supposed to replace), the public-interest choice is probably the low-tech, consumer-based form of resource recovery.

Recycling is a commons dilemma and a key part of natural resource management. One community of about 200,000 people, with a recycling rate of about 68 percent, saved 70,000 trees in one year.[251] However, even this level of recycling diverts only about 4 percent of the material from that community's traditional garbage stream; the national U.S. average is about 2.5 percent. Part of the reason that recycling rates are not greater is that, as of 1992, only one-third of single-family dwellings in the United States had access to curb-side recycling programs.[252] Another reason is that some individuals recycle more than others, as will be seen in the next section.

Who Recycles and Who Does Not?

Most people say they recycle; by 1991, 81 percent of college students and 58 percent of community householders said they recycle.[253,254] However, not everyone recycles yet, and, as usual, self-reports may not be entirely accurate. A study that asked who recycled and then checked who *really* recycled found that higher-income households claimed they recycled more than lower-income households, but they actually did not.[255]

Not surprisingly, individuals with greater environmental knowledge, awareness, or commitment tend to recycle more[256,257,258,259] and homeowners recy-

cle more.[260,261] Recyclers tend to have higher incomes and more education.[262] There are ethnic differences in recycling (whites most, blacks and Asians next, Hispanics least), but these may be more a matter of differences in access to recycling facilities than to ethnicity itself.[263] For example, residents with access to a structured recycling program and ample room to store their materials before recycling are much more likely to recycle.[264] These access barriers probably are stronger influences *against* recycling than environmental attitudes are as *pro*-recycling forces.

The Recycling Program. Features of the recycling program influence rates of recycling. For example, a program that accepts **commingled** materials (all recyclables are placed in one container, rather than separate materials in separate containers) achieved very high participation rates, although the method was not directly compared with separated-materials programs.[265] The location of containers and user-friendliness of the system were important in another study, and, as in the previous study, the more different kinds of containers, the less recycling was done.[266]

As with littering, recycling occurs more (or less) when individuals' beliefs about recycling are salient: If I am reminded that I am in favor of recycling, I am more likely to recycle than if I am in favor of recycling but I am not especially aware of that belief at the moment I am deciding whether or not to recycle.[267]

How to Encourage Recycling

Many people now recycle, but millions still do not. How can the holdouts be encouraged to responsibly manage the valuable resources passing through their households?

Educate, Prompt, Reward. Some answers are, by now, familiar: Educate, prompt, and reward recycling behavior. Increasing awareness through speeches, personal communication, and pamphlets works;[268,269,270] reminding people to recycle with signs and labeled receptacles works;[271] and using positive reinforcement works.[272] One study reports the intriguing finding that positive appeals had the greatest effect on recycling *attitudes*, and a negative message had the greatest effect on recycling *behavior.*[273] Some researchers see the problem as a marketing issue: The same arsenal of techniques should be used to sell recycling as to sell commercial products.[274]

One study of recycling was done in a Virginia university. The campus already had an educational campaign on recycling, but the researchers prompted recycling by delivering a flyer that encouraged paper recycling once a week to every resident of two dormitories. Less than 3 percent of the residents responded, but even this small number of recyclers produced about 45 pounds of paper a week.[275]

The researchers also tried two reward systems. They created a competition between dorms by offering a $15 prize to the dorm that recycled the most paper. This strategy produced about 544 pounds of paper a week— 10 times as much as the flyer-only strategy. Participation rates also doubled. In the other reward system, the researchers offered raffle coupons for $80 worth of prizes for each pound of recyclable paper brought in. This yielded about 820 pounds a week and participation was four times greater than in the flyer-only condition. Even though dormitories are not great sources of paper for recycling in the first place, these strategies certainly increased the amount of paper recovered.

This study illustrates both the advantages and disadvantages of the low-technology behavioral approach to recycling. Prompts and rewards increased recycling over the flyer-only baseline, but when they were discontinued, recycling fell back to baseline levels. Thus, reward strategies must be continued in order to promote recycling in the long run.

One curiosity in the study's findings suggests there is hope for long-term changes in behavior. In the prompt condition, recycling actually was higher in the weeks after prompting ended than during the prompting phase. Mere prompts may not be as immediately effective as monetary rewards, but their effect may last longer. One way to prompt recycling in the longer term is to use signs. These prompts increase recycling, but their placement is very important. Placing signs very close to the containers can dramatically increase the rate of recycling.[276]

A major disadvantage of the reward approach is cost. As noted in discussing residential energy conservation, programs must be cost effective to have potential for widespread usefulness. In this study's contest, a total

of $45 in prizes was distributed and about 3,250 pounds of paper were collected. The paper was sold for about $20. In the raffle, prizes worth $240 were given away, but the paper (4,900 pounds) was sold for less than $40. The prizes were donated by local merchants, so, in a sense, they cost nothing. However, to implement the program more widely, merchants would have to keep giving prizes away; this seems unlikely to happen. Even if it did, their customers would have to pay for the donations through increased prices.

Behavioral approaches have great value, but their advocates must discover ways to make the payoffs cost less than the public-interest gains achieved by their programs.[277] An even greater threat to the usefulness of the behavioral programs is that labor costs are rarely counted. In the study just described, research assistants invested many hours of work receiving and weighing the recycled materials for no return except course credits. In the real world, workers will demand real wages. In the Virginia study, the bottom line was that the prompt-only strategy produced the smallest increase in recycling, but it did so with by far the cheapest outlay, and thus was the most cost-effective approach.

All is not lost. The behavioral approaches will discover cost-effective strategies. Lotteries are one promising technique; individuals are willing to contribute much more to a cause than would be predicted from their mathematical odds of winning when an attractive lottery prize is offered for recycling.[278]

Block Leaders. A different strategy is to locate individuals on each block (or equivalent) who might encourage their neighbors to recycle.[279] When these block leaders each approached several of their neighbors, recycling increased significantly; it even increased compared to recycling by other neighbors who received the same plea in written form instead of in person.[280] In a similar approach, recycling also will increase when "significant others" are depicted recycling.[281]

Commitment and Feedback. Asking people to make a commitment to recycle also works.[282] In a retirement home, residents were asked to make the commitment as part of a group; their recycling increased 47 percent.[283] In a follow-up study with college students, the researchers found that students who made a *personal* commitment kept recycling at a higher level longer than students who made a commitment as a group. Incidentally, the effect of personal commitment lasted longer than the effect of a token reward for recycling. This is encouraging, given the disadvantages of paying people to recycle, because obtaining commitments costs less.

Which works better—an educational approach or feedback? Over five months, Michigan university students in dormitories were educated about the need for recycling or given posted feedback once per month about the actual amount they had recycled. The feedback group recycled significantly more.[284]

Laws. It has been said that morality cannot be legislated. In general, though, the same cannot be said for recycling. First, although there are some people who react against being forced to recycle, most people accept bottle refund laws, for example.[285] Second, the laws are effective in cleaning up the streets. Before and after a bottle bill was enacted, the number of cans and bottles observed each day dropped from 47 per block to 2 per block![286] The law had a tremendous effect, but the researcher noted that the recycling of bottles and cans may have been done mostly by street people rather than the original purchasers of the bottles and cans. Nevertheless, one way or another, the law alone reduced the number of cans and bottles by 96 percent.

Integrated Approaches. Overall, the most effective approach is an integrated program combining these strategies and factors. Together, two studies found that several factors play important roles in recycling:

- How much awareness and information people have about recycling
- Who the potential recycler is, in demographic terms
- How convenient recycling is
- The economic payoff
- Attitudes toward recycling
- Local norms about recycling
- The operating policies of the recycling agency[287,288]

All these factors are important, but for different locales and materials to be recycled, different factors are *more* important. That is why other researchers stress that re-

cycling programs should offer potential recyclers a variety of reasons to recycle; the idea is that everyone will find one or more of the reasons persuasive.[289]

Designing for Recycling

Educational campaigns and prompting have value in easing a social dilemma, but clever environmental design can have an important impact, too. In general, the key is to make cooperation physically easy.

In large offices, huge amounts of wastepaper are generated. If this paper could be sorted into the different categories, *as it is generated,* recycling would be greatly facilitated. Many offices have now tried this; a few studies have taken a close look at how it works.

In the administration offices of a large university, three sort-as-you-toss designs were compared: (1) two wastebaskets, one for recyclable paper and one for nonrecyclable garbage, (2) divided wastebaskets with one section for recyclable paper and one for nonrecyclables, and (3) a personal wastebasket for recyclables and a central (public) wastebasket for nonrecyclables.[290] The first two designs resulted in over 92 percent of paper properly recycled in the 10 weeks of the study. (Proper recycling was measured as the absence of nonrecyclables in wastebaskets designated for recyclables.) Even the less convenient (but presumably cheaper) alternative of a centralized contained for nonrecyclables resulted in 84 percent proper recycling.

Employees in half the 16 locations of the study received personal prompts on two occasions during the study. The prompts had only a small effect; they increased proper recycling from 88 to 92 percent. The vast bulk of the recycling was due to placing the recycling containers in the office—a very simple design feature. More recent research confirms that nearby containers in offices produce dramatically increased recycling rates, compared to centralized containers.[291]

One company has created a slightly more sophisticated sort-as-you-toss system.[292] This is a desktop system that places the paper separation process even closer to the point at which mail or old drafts of memos become garbage. This system is recommended by the U.S. Environmental Protection Agency (EPA), which lives up to its recommendation by using it in its Washington headquarters. The desktop system, used by about 2,700 people in the building, manages to outperform the divided wastebasket: Proper recycling reaches 97 percent. In the first year, the EPA recovered 150 tons of high-grade paper. Designing the environment so as to encourage "mindless" recycling may be an important key to the promotion of recycling in the future.

◆ **SUMMARY** ◆

Many natural resources are commons: desirable commodities that many individuals or organizations can harvest. When the rate of harvesting exceeds the rate at which the resource replenishes itself, a commons dilemma exists. Harvesters must decide whether to get rich or comfortable quickly, or, through restraint, to benefit all harvesters more moderately with the crucial consequence that the commons is preserved for the future. Through field studies and laboratory simulations, environmental psychologists have identified which characteristics of the resource and its harvesters and which rules of the game promote cooperation rather than defection.

Theories of social dilemmas offer political solutions, systematically consider the many dimensions of social dilemmas, propose reinforcement strategies, and note that most individuals are basically unaware of social dilemmas. The theories, therefore, raise important questions as they provide a way of understanding behavior in the commons. For example, *should* individuals cooperate—choosing in broadest terms justice over freedom? If forced to choose, it seems that many people choose freedom—the freedom to burn fossil fuels, to "harvest" forests, to turn up the heat or air conditioning, to throw out unwanted paper and tin cans.

This chapter has reviewed the case for justice. Simulation research clearly shows that freedom—that beautiful word—easily can lead to ruination. Some theorists believe we are already too far along the defection trail to reverse our tragic course; most environmental psychologists believe it is not too late. We begin with educational campaigns and by searching for individuals who already take personal responsibility for management of the commons. But one of the great lessons learned so far is that changed attitudes do not lead to changed behavior often enough. Pollution, energy conservation, and recycling are everyday instances of social dilemmas.

Many strategies for behavior change are evolving: appeals from respected leaders, moral arguments for justice, prompts, feedback, goal setting, obtaining public commitments from consumers, changing payoffs to favor conservation instead of exploitation, public disclosure of defections, increased communication among commons members, careful arrangement of the physical setting, provision of smaller resource territories for which individuals feel more responsible, and last (but most important), the fostering of trust and friendship. Friendship is the most important because it may allow us a little of that almost unaffordable luxury: freedom. Julian Edney observed that friendship, with its "sympathetic and mutual awareness of each others' condition, needs, and feelings," may be the vehicle by which we achieve both justice *and* freedom.[293]

Suggested Readings

Cone, J. D., & Hayes, S. C. (1980). *Environmental problems: Behavioral solutions.* Monterey, CA: Brooks/Cole.

Dawes, R. M. Social dilemmas. (1981). *Annual Review of Psychology, 31,* 169–193.

Edney, J. J. (1984). Rationality and social justice. *Human Relations, 37,* 163–180.

Fox, J. R. (1985). Psychology, ideology, utopia and the commons. *American Psychologist, 40,* 48–58.

Geller, E. S., Winett, R. A., & Everett, P. B. (1982). *Preserving the environment.* New York: Pergamon Press.

Hardin, G. (1968) The tragedy of the commons. *Science, 162,* 1243–1248.

Messick, D. M., Wilke, H., Brewer, M. B., Kramer, R. M., Zemke, P. E., & Lui, L. (1983). Individual adaptations and structural change solutions to social dilemmas. *Journal of Personality and Social Psychology, 44,* 294–309.

Samuelson, C. D. (1990). Energy conservation: A social dilemma approach. *Social Behavior, 5,* 207–230.

Shrum, L. J., Lowrey, T. M., & McCarty, J. A. (1994). Recycling as a marketing problem: A framework for strategy development. *Psychology and Marketing, 11,* 393–416.

Simmons, D., & Widmar, R. (1990). Motivations and barriers to recycling: Toward a strategy for public education. *Journal of Environmental Education, 22*(1), 13–18.

Stern, P. C. (1992). What psychology knows about energy conservation. *American Psychologist, 47,* 1224–1232.

Stern, P. C. (1992). Psychological dimensions of global environmental change. In M. R. Rosenzweig & L. W. Porter (Eds.), *Annual Review of Psychology, 43.*

Winkler, R. C., & Winett, R. A. (1982). Behavioral interventions in resource management: A systems approach based on behavioral economics. *American Psychologist, 37,* 421–435.

CHAPTER  **15**

DESIGNING MORE FITTING ENVIRONMENTS

I am firmly convinced that architecture . . . can be considered an art only when it reflects an understanding of the perceptions of the consumers of the designed environment.

—Kiyo Izumi[1]

Tom and Jane were spending a leisurely Saturday afternoon at their local library, which had opened a few weeks earlier. Tom had checked out a book on renovating old homes. They were reading the paper, trading small talk on current issues and the bizarre story of the day ("10-year old girl, discovered by Indians, lives with pack of panthers and goes about on all fours, fighting with panthers for food and trying to leap into trees").

A young woman approached them. "Excuse me," she said, "I am conducting a study of this library and I wonder if you would mind telling me your opinions of it?" Tom and Jane agreed, but groaned silently. They had responded to more than their share of questionnaires that year at school. "Now they're even invading public territories," Tom thought to himself.

The questionnaire covered various aspects of the library, such as spatial layout, lighting, windows, and noise. It asked their reasons for coming to the library and for any special gripes or compliments they wished to offer about it.

The woman returned in a few minutes for their completed questionnaires. She explained that similar questionnaires had been distributed in the old library, for comparison purposes.

"I have to tell you, too," she said somewhat hesitantly, "that I have been watching you for the last half hour." Tom and Jane looked at each other quickly, then back at the researcher. "In our evaluation, we want to see how people actually use the library as well as how they feel about it. You see, our study of the old library showed that people were afraid to talk aloud to each other and that it took a long time for people to find the books they were looking for.

"This new design is supposed to make you feel more like talking because we've separated the study area from the light-reading area. All those maps and signs, together with a carefully planned arrangement of the card catalog and stacks are supposed to help you find things faster. Do you realize that it took you only 38 seconds to find the book you're holding?"

This long speech took Tom and Jane a bit by surprise. They stared for a minute, then Jane stammered, "I guess your project seems like a good idea. . . ."

The woman leaned closer. "I have to ask," she said, "what were you reading in the paper that was so hilarious?"

◆ ◆ ◆

We have surveyed research and theory across the broad domain of environmental psychology. For some of you, this is enough; to understand something of how and why individuals interact with environments satisfies your curiosity about the field. The application of this knowledge is not particularly important. For you, I have tried to present some *principles* of environmental psychology. Others of you may yet be hoping for something more. Examples of design applications were offered in earlier chapters, but we have not yet directly examined the process of designing environments or the role of social science in the design process. This chapter is especially for those of you who have been waiting patiently for a fuller treatment of the *practice* of environmental psychology in architectural design—about putting environment-behavior knowledge to work to improve buildings.

The chapter begins with a description of social design, a process that can improve the habitability of buildings. Next, the goals, problems, and advantages of including social science in architecture are considered. The social design process is described, with a focus on its two most important phases: programming and post-occupancy evaluation. The chapter closes with descriptions of several examples of programming and post-occupancy evaluations.

◆ SOCIAL DESIGN ◆

There is a way to design more humane buildings. This process, developed over the last two decades under a variety of names, might best be called **social design**[2,3] or social design research. Most generally, it involves studying how settings can best serve human desires and requirements. It must be distinguished from technical design research (such as the performance of building materials).

A Definition

Robert Sommer, a social design pioneer, characterized social design as follows:

> Social design is working with people rather than for them; involving people in the planning and management of the spaces around them; educating them to use the environment wisely and creatively to achieve a harmonious balance between the social, physical, and natural environment; to develop an awareness of beauty, a sense of responsibility, to the earth's environment and to other living creatures; to generate, compile, and make available information about the effects of human activities on the

biotic and physical environment, including the effects of the built environment on human beings. Social designers cannot achieve these objectives working by themselves. The goals can be realized only within the structures of larger organizations, which include the people for whom a project is planned."[4]

This definition includes some topics that have been discussed elsewhere; in fact, it might almost suffice as a definition of environmental psychology as a whole.

Social design may be distinguished from formal design (the traditional approach).[5] **Formal design** favors an approach that may be described as large scale, corporate, high cost, exclusive, authoritarian, tending to high-tech solutions, and concerned with style, ornament, the paying client, and a national or international focus. In contrast, social design favors an approach that may be described as small scale, human oriented, low cost, inclusive, democratic, tending to appropriate technology, and concerned with meaning and context, the occupant as well as the paying client, and a local focus.

Although these distinctions provide the flavor of social design, they may not all apply in every design project. For example, social design may cost more at least initially, but it may save more over the life of the building. Social design techniques may be applied to large-scale projects as well as small-scale projects. The difference between social design and formal design is that in a large-scale project, the social designer often pays more attention to specific behavior settings within the large project. In a large office complex, for example, the individual needs and activities of employees are more likely to be researched and incorporated into the building design.

The Need

Architecture as a Limited Discipline. Certainly there are portions of the built environment that need improvement. One well-publicized example is a large St. Louis apartment complex that was completed in 1954. The Pruitt-Igoe project was designed with the admirable intention of replacing deteriorating inner-city housing. The complex, containing 43 11-story buildings for about 12,000 people, was praised in an architectural journal for having no wasted space, vandal-resistant features, and individualistic design.[6]

The Pruitt-Igoe design saved space, in part, by having elevators stop only at every third floor, so most residents would walk up or down one flight of stairs to their apartments. Altogether, Pruitt-Igoe cost about $1,000 less per unit than comparable buildings of the time. The design changes were considered so admirable that the architect even applied for a patent on the design.

But problems appeared soon after it opened. The failure to carefully examine its design in relation to human behavior contributed to high rates of fear, vandalism, vacancy, and serious crime. A particular problem was crime in the stairwells that residents were forced to use because of the innovative elevator savings plan. The situation was so bad that, after only 18 years, the city demolished the entire complex. Whether the architect received his patent is unknown.

Pruitt-Igoe is the most dramatic example of building design failure—part of the demolition was shown on national television—but many other buildings also pose problems for their users (see Figure 15–1).

What causes these problems? For three reasons, we must assume that architects do their best: They have personal standards of excellence and ethics, they are legally responsible for the design of their buildings, and they want to enhance their reputations and win recognition. Two reasons for failure stand out: Architects view their designs differently from those who will occupy the designs, and there is a misguided process by which architects win recognition. Research that supports the first reason were described in Chapter 3. Further research shows that not only do architects view buildings differently but, partly because of their training, they categorize and interpret buildings differently. Buildings quite literally *mean* different things to architects and nonarchitects.[7]

Recently, researchers have begun to examine just how and why architects develop their design skills. For example, during the course of architecture school, the immersion of students in architectural style builds into them an increasingly complex cognitive structure about styles[8]—as it should. Studies have tried to describe the cognitive processes involved in design process, to get inside the architect's head.[9,10] Unfortunately, architecture schools often subtly create values that promote the ideas that good architects are male creative geniuses or stars who will or should operate in a patriarchal, hierarchical, power-oriented, competitive fashion.[11]

FIGURE 15–1 An example of hard architecture. These benches cannot easily be destroyed, but neither does anyone choose to sit on them!

The differences in meaning lead to differences in design preferences. When architects and nursing home residents were shown a series of alternative designs for nursing homes, many differences were found.[12] Generally, architects preferred designs that promoted social interaction, whereas residents preferred designs that promoted privacy. This illustrates a key point: Architects act in good faith but often misjudge client needs. In this case, they think social interaction is desirable for the residents, but the residents have other ideas.

This leads to the second reason for failure—the drive for recognition. One key to success for many architects is to win prizes. Virtually all prizes are awarded by committees of architects. Thus, a prize-winning architect is one who has impressed other architects. Does that mean everyday folks are impressed, too?

One study of a design competition for an actual building compared the rankings that architectural experts made of the five entries with rankings of the same entries made by 65 nonarchitects who were even given the criteria used by the architectural experts.[13] The experts' first choice was ranked fourth out of the five entries by the nonarchitects. Another study of design awards compared evaluations of new housing projects by a design competition jury, a trained but independent observer, and residents of the projects.[14] The observer's ranking of the projects was exactly the reverse of the design jury's. One reason was the use of different criteria:

The design jury relied heavily on attractiveness or aesthetics, judged mainly from drawings and photos, whereas the observer and the residents used two further criteria—the quality of construction and livability.

Obviously, designers must learn to see the built world through the eyes of their clients so they can appreciate their needs and perceptions. (You may wish to glance again at the quote that opens this chapter.) This does not mean, however, architects should throw out all their training and expertise and design buildings exactly as a group of unsophisticated users wants them to. Instead, designers must be **enabling practitioners**—that is, experts who actively listen to, and collaborate with, building users.[15] But because architects often have more than enough trouble dealing with many technical aspects of a design, and because most architects have little training in social science, they usually cannot perform an adequate social design of a building. They need the assistance of a professional social designer.

Another reason for poor buildings pertains to *standards*. Although the word sounds official, some standards are questionable.[16] First, they vary—standards for classroom size, for example, range from 600 square feet in some states to 1,100 square feet in others. Second, standards often are not based on research, but on someone's opinion or on historical precedent. Third, they sometimes are meant as the *minimum* criterion, but often are used as (quite) *acceptable* criteria, so buildings designs are barely adequate. Finally, when accepted un-critically, architects can create buildings that are unacceptable for individuals who are unusual or special in some way.

Architecture as Art

Design education and design competitions encourage designers to emphasize the aesthetic dimension of architecture at the expense of the setting's functional value. Environments should, of course, be both beautiful and functional for their occupants. Unfortunately, attempts to create fashionable works of art dominated architecture for a long time—and still do. Architectural magazines still use expensive photography and glossy paper to show off buildings, but often no people are even visible in the scenes.

It is tempting to conclude that these unpeopled buildingscapes accurately reflect many designers' interests. One of the most influential architects in the world, Philip Johnson, said, "The job of the architect is to create beautiful buildings. That's all."[17]

In an advertisement placed in my local newspaper by the company he founded, a tribute to a retiring architect states that he "is certainly not discarding his brush or his palette. His keen interest in Architecture as a Fine Art remains intense." These architectural formalists think of buildings more as paintings or sculpture than as habitats.[18] Commenting on the way children's spaces are designed, for example, one observer noted that designers think more about such visual qualities as the geometry of the space, perspective, and vista than about children's preferences or developmental needs.[19]

Growing Collaboration. But the times *are* changing. Many architects and designers now recognize the importance of designing for human use of buildings, without necessarily sacrificing technological or aesthetic considerations. For example, two decades ago, the American Institute of Architects sponsored a conference that served as an early summit meeting between social scientists and designers.[20] The Coolfront Conference outlined several key roles that social scientist consultants might play, including evaluating building habitability, defining the psychological needs of occupants, and training occupants in the optimal use of buildings.

While architecture was mesmerized by the aesthetic properties of geometric space, psychology neglected the physical context of behavior. In the growing collaboration, real people were imagined in designed spaces—a concept that might be called **placemaking**.[21,22] To make a place, architects and social designers work together to create a space with a human face, or an envelope for behavior.

Even the social versus formal design dispute need not be adversarial. If formal designers try to make beautiful buildings *for* the multisensory pleasure *of the building's users,* then aesthetic pursuits serve at least part of the social designers' goals.[23] Beautiful buildings may improve our perceptions of each other, facilitate social interaction, and assist occupants in some less direct ways, such as enhancing tourism or a city's reputation.

Actually, consultation with building users was not even new in the early 1970s, but perhaps it had been forgotten by many designers. Back in 1914, at least one office design team "spent several months in consultation, asking advice, and studying the needs of every department and of every individual,"[24] although these consultations primarily concerned one aspect of design—the physical distance between employees.

Nevertheless, in the late 1960s, entire organizations (e.g., the Environmental Design Research Association and the International Association for the Study of People and Their Physical Surroundings) devoted to the cooperation of designers and social researchers sprang up and have been active through the present. The Appendix at the end of the book offers a more complete list of these organizations.

A growing number of social design researchers make their living from their contributions to the design process. Most practitioners operate as one- or two-person offices, much like clinical psychologists or physicians. A few of these offices employ up to 20 researchers. Some individual collaborations between psychologists and architects have lasted 15 years or more.[25]

When and How Social Design Helps. Social design is not *always* needed in the design process. It is not required, for example, in times and places where buildings are constructed by small communities in which everyone works together in accordance with a time-tested architectural tradition. These traditions, called **preindustrial**

vernacular,[26] evolved an architecture that already fits community and cultural norms, individual interests, local climate, geography, and materials quite well. When community members are both builders and occupants, the design process does not need separate financiers, architects, boards of directors, and construction firms (see Figure 15–2).

In the developed nations of the world, division of labor has produced material benefits for all of us. However, in the design professions (as in other occupations), it has produced considerable role specialization. As work is split more narrowly and each person's entire career is reduced to just one phase of a fundamental process in society—such as the creation of buildings—there is a tendency for communication among the principal players in the design process to diminish. The **principal players** in building include the client (who puts up the money), the designer (architect, planner), the engineer (on larger projects) and, most important, the everyday building user, occupant, or visitor.

Therefore, social design research has become necessary in industrial and postindustrial societies. Two of its major roles are to reestablish and to facilitate communication among the principal players in the design process. A third role is to remind everyone involved that the everyday building user *is* one of the principal players.

After the rise of industrialism and before the advent of environmental psychology, the building user was almost forgotten in architecture. The dazzling technology produced by the industrial revolution provides a vast array of design possibilities (in building materials, construction principles, and international communication among designers). The design of some buildings requires so much attention to technical factors that the future occupants were forgotten.

◆ ***IN SUM,*** *some buildings are human disasters; others are merely persistent nuisances to those who occupy or use them. Social design is a way of creating buildings that fit occupants and users better by involving them in the planning process. Social design is needed in societies that have splintered the building creation process into many specialist roles. It is a remedy for the malady in which architects saw themselves primarily as artists, ignoring the basic needs and activities of occupants. This malady is now widely recognized, yet many buildings are still constructed without significant user involvement.*

◆ SOCIAL RESEARCH ◆ IN THE DESIGN PROCESS

Before delving into a stage-by-stage examination of our primary concern—the design process—we will take a step back to consider the goals, advantages, and problems of the social science contribution to environmental design.

The Goals

Social design researchers and practitioners have six goals, some broader than others, some overlapping with others.

1. Create physical settings that **match** the needs and activities of their occupants. This goal, which is probably the most important of all, sometimes is variously called *habitability, congruence,* or *goodness of fit.*

2. Satisfy the building users. Occupant satisfaction is important because occupants must spend significant parts of their lives working, residing, or relaxing in the setting.

3. Change behavior. Such changes might include increasing office-worker productivity, enhancing social

FIGURE 15–2 An example of vernacular architecture: A longhouse of the Kwakiutl people of Vancouver Island.

ties among institutionalized elderly people, reducing aggression in a prison, or increasing communication among managers in an administrative office. As we shall see, the behavior change goal can be both difficult to attain and controversial.

4. Enhance the occupant's **personal control.**[27] The more building users are able to alter the setting to make it suit their needs, the less stressful that setting will be.

5. Facilitate **social support.**[28] Designs that encourage cooperation, assistance, and support are desirable primarily for building occupants who are disadvantaged in one way of another, but also for active and successful individuals.

6. Employ **imageability.** This refers to the ability of the building to help occupants and (especially) visitors and newcomers to find their way around without getting lost or confused.

Let's examine each of these goals more closely.

Matching. Matching refers to how well the occupants' activities and needs are met by the setting. Ideally, of course, buildings should perfectly match their occupants' needs and behavior. Whether the degree of match is high or low sometimes depends, in part, on whose viewpoint is considered.[29] You may recall the difference between alpha and beta press, a distinction made by the personality theorist Henry Murray between actual and perceived influences on human behavior. Similarly, there are alpha and beta forms of matching. Alpha matching, **congruence,** refers to how well the setting fits the person from an objective point of view. Beta matching, or **habitability,** is "environmental quality as perceived by occupants of buildings or facilities."[30]

All the principal players in the design process hope, of course, that both perceived and actual matches are good. The possibility remains, however, that a team of design experts could *declare* that congruence had been achieved when the occupants believe that it has not. Unfortunately, significant disagreements between experts and users have indeed been demonstrated in several studies of residential environments.

For example, one study found that professional planners believed a high-quality neighborhood was re-

lated to how open, interesting, and pleasant it was. However, neighborhood residents believed high quality was related only to how pleasant it was.[31] Such clashes mean that efforts must be made not only toward improving the fit between users and their environments but also toward reducing differences between designer and occupant definitions of good design. Because users' actual activities are sometimes easier to document than their needs, clashes may be resolved if data on activities are collected.

When alpha and beta press are the same—such as when a building user has a clear-cut need that everyone perceives—the design implications are clear, but the design still does not always meet this need. For example, persons with physical disabilities often have obvious, clear-cut needs, such as smooth ramps for those in wheelchairs. Yet, there are still too many buildings used by people in wheelchairs that lack ramps. Similarly, aged people whose perceptual and cognitive abilities have marked declined have specific design needs that are often not provided.[32,33,34]

Nevertheless, building guidelines for people with specific characteristics are a good idea, and many lists of guidelines have been prepared. For example, some have considered the proper design for relatively able-bodied older people.[35] Recommended design features for mental patients were among the first to receive attention from social designers,[36] and continue to be issued.[37,38,39,40] Another setting that has been the focus of many recommendations is the children's day-care center.[41,42] A set of design guidelines has also been created to reduce a drastic behavior—suicide—among jail inmates.[43]

Satisfaction. Habitability corresponds to occupant satisfaction; congruence is the expert's opinion that the occupant is satisfied. But principal players *other* than the occupant may or may not be satisfied with the project. Some architects, for example, hope their buildings will work as statements of minimalist or postmodernist aesthetic design principles. The paying client might be primarily satisfied if the project is completed within its budget. Most social researchers would be happy if their work contributed to a habitable structure.

Behavior Change. Many projects implicitly or explicitly embody someone's hope that occupant behavior will change for the better. When all principal players, including occupants, agree that a certain pattern of behavior needs encouragement or discouragement from the design, the design process may steam merrily ahead. In a New York psychiatric hospital, the violent behavior of some severely regressed psychotic patients was one target when renovation designs were considered.[44] The new design significantly reduced this violence.

Sometimes, quite simple design changes can change behavior. By merely adding table-top "distractor shields" (partitions) between pairs of students with profound retardation, researchers were able to increase the amount of on-task behavior of the students by a significant amount.[45]

Unfortunately, principal players sometimes disagree about who should change which behaviors. Clients who pay for new or renovated workplaces, for example, often expect that the new design will increase employee productivity. When faced with this expectation, the social researcher is in the uncomfortable position of being asked to use the environment to squeeze productivity out of employees. The very thought of attempting to manipulate employees for the benefit of an organization is unpleasant for many practitioners.

Occupant satisfaction, on the other hand, is usually the goal of practitioners and other principal players who are particularly sympathetic to the needs of the building user. Some social designers see the process as part of a worldwide concern for human rights; social design began with attempts to provide the benefits of design to the unfortunate (such as mental patients) and to the poor.[46] This activist tradition still fuels the efforts of many environmental psychologists.

Regardless of one's party affiliation, social design is necessarily political in the original sense of discussing and debating policy. Some observers contend that design programs reveal and confirm the nature of social power in the organization that will occupy the building.[47] Some argue that designers and evaluators of designs *cannot* be objective (even if they think they are) because they always conclude their work by endorsing—implicitly if not explicitly—a set of values concerning social relationships and social power that would be embodied in their building plans.[48,49] Building design almost necessarily implies tradeoffs.

Tradeoffs usually cannot be decided by quantitative or purely objective means. That means values must en-

ter the design process. Different building users naturally will have different preferences that the environmental psychologist will encounter without even trying. However, practitioners will have to examine their own values, too, as they relate to the project, the clients, and the negotiation process.[50] After deciding who their values allow them to represent, practitioners try to discover and advocate the most advantageous set of tradeoffs, based on the best obtainable information.

What happens, then, when work efficiency is promoted as more important than other goals, such as employee satisfaction? Clients who bring in a social researcher do often expect productivity gains in return for their investment. Robert Sommer agonized over these questions for years. In his book *Social Design*, several answers to the productivity question are offered.[51]

To begin, Sommer believes the research evidence demonstrates that design *can* sometimes raise productivity. However, because design-behavior relations are so complex and influenced by so many other factors, one cannot be sure when building design boosts productivity. Alternatively, we could take a leap of faith and *assume* that careful social design must produce some gains in productivity, even though the gains are hard to prove.

Another response to the productivity question is that social research is, in a modern democracy, a basic right of those who must occupy buildings for large parts of their lives. Social research, from this point of view, is valuable in its own right and should not have to be justified in productivity terms.

Finally, one might question why some clients are so productivity conscious in the first place. "Those who ask the productivity question would like to put dollar signs on positive experiences."[52] Thus, productivity and satisfaction sometimes are conflicting goals, with some principal players stressing one more than the other. Of course, both goals are desirable. Sadly, many situations arise where productivity and satisfaction goals are in conflict. When this happens, practitioners are forced to decide what their own political and economic values are.

Personal Control. If possible, social design will provide occupants with real options to control their proximate environment. What does this mean in specific terms?

Consider, for example, children in hospitals. It is bad enough being there, but if all the furniture and equipment is adult-sized, the place is that much more intimidating. To increase children's independence and sense of control, one researcher published body measurement data for people from 0 to 19 years old in the hope that hospital designers would use it.[53]

A second example is publicly funded residential space for students (dormitories) or poor people (housing projects). Some buildings, high rises in particular, seem designed to overload the resident with social stimulation. Too few elevators and long, narrows hallways, for example, result in the sense that people are everywhere and inescapable. Residents develop the feeling that they cannot control the number of social contacts—especially unwanted social contacts—they must face daily.

Two other common examples of low-control settings are crowded retail stores and traffic jams. Crowding is caused, in part, by social and informational overload, which, in turn, leads to the sense that one has lost control. Designing *against* crowding is, in part, designing *for* personal control. Again, simple design changes can be effective. By merely adding a few entrances to a mental health center, clients' sense of freedom was increased and the units within the center experienced a greater sense of identity.[54] A sense of freedom is important to a person's sense of control.

Stress is often related to lack of personal control over physical and social input. Noise, unwanted social contact, and congestion are primary sources, yet social design can anticipate and attempt to overcome them or at least buffer the building user from them.

Social Support. Personal control is an individual process; social support is a group process. Many social problems would be eased if more and better social support were available.[55] Common psychological problems such as depression and anxiety have been shown to increase when social support is absent or inadequate. Social support may be seen as an anti-stress process.[56]

What can social design do for social support? At the smallest scale, furniture arrangement, studies show that sociopetal arrangements can foster more interaction.[57] At the building level, open-space areas may be arranged to facilitate social interaction.[58] Of course, if the personal control goal as well as the social support goal is to be met, the increased social interaction must be controllable; occupants should be able to find social interaction when and if they want it, but not be faced with unwanted encounters.

In office buildings, social support may be fostered through the provision of high-quality lounge space for employees. The mere existence of such space does not guarantee that valuable social support will be available, but with inadequate space for employees to share coffee and conversation, the likelihood of social networks declines.

Finally, social support may result from a design that provides optimal privacy (being able to filter one's interactions). Consider shelters for survivors of domestic violence. A study of alternate designs for such shelters found that designs characterized by anonymity and safety were most preferred.[59] Sometimes, social support is maximized when a shelter resident simultaneously can be near a helper and far from an abuser.

Imageability. Buildings should be imageable, or clearly understandable or legible, to their users.[60] When someone walks into a building, that person should immediately be able to find his or her way around, or, in more technical terms, be capable of *purposeful mobility*. In negative terms, the person should not get lost.

I find it astounding how often I enter a building—even a new building—that is unfamiliar to me, and I cannot figure out where to go next. Unless we realize that buildings *should* be imageable, there is a tendency to blame ourselves ("I never did have a good sense of direction"). Sometimes, observation reveals that you are not the first to have problems: Perhaps you see handmade signs tacked up that occupants have made either to be helpful or to save themselves answering the same question about where such-and-such is for the hundredth time.

The Problems

The Gap. Designers in our society are almost completely separated from those who will actually use their buildings. You use numerous buildings every day and will spend the vast majority of your life in one building or another. But when was the last time you sat down with an architect to discuss any building that you have ever used (see Figure 15–3)?

The paying client (or clients; often a board of directors) is the missing link between the designer and the occupant. Architects communicate extensively with board members or facility managers who work for the board. However, neither architect nor board member nor facility manager is very likely to spend much time in the building after the opening-day ceremonies. If paying clients do use the building, they are likely to occupy a special area or floor of the building. In general, there is a serious gap between designer and occupant.

Resistance. Not everyone involved in the design process sees the advantage of social research. In the absence of legal requirements for social design research, many designers and clients view it as an unnecessary or extravagant part of the building process. Because some principal players do not want their lives "complicated" by new information—even valuable new information—the social design researcher's entry into a project can be difficult.[61] In general, resistance to social design comes primarily from five sources: some designers, some clients, some members of the public, government, and some building users.

First, designers who are wholly concerned with architecture as a fine art obviously see little need for social design research. They tend to subscribe to some or all of the following views:

- If a building is beautiful, it must be useful.
- Beauty is so much more valuable than function that social design research on building function is not worth the effort.
- If the building is beautiful, occupants will be so awestruck, impressed, or happy with it that function will somehow take care of itself.
- Designers are capable of placing themselves in the shoes of occupants and therefore can create a building that is functional, satisfying, and beautiful for occupants without consulting or studying them.
- People are very adaptive and malleable, making it unnecessary to try matching the building to their needs and activities.

Fortunately, of course, many designers do not subscribe to these views. But resistance does come from designers who are unaware of, or do not understand, social design research.

A second source of resistance to social research comes from some paying clients. The client is already paying a substantial fee for the design of a new building; social design research is likely to appear as an unnecessary extra. Some clients cannot see the long-term benefits of social research, often merely because they still do not know very much about it. Even some designers who appreciate social design nevertheless do not budget for it in their design proposal because they fear the additional initial costs will cause them to lose their contract to a lower bidder.

Without a clear explanation of how the expenditure may be beneficial to their organization, clients are naturally wary of spending the extra money and time necessary for social research. So far, the most progressive clients appear to be governments and nonprofit service agencies, many of which support social design research in the construction of administration buildings, subsidized housing, prisons, and other public- or service-oriented construction projects.

Third, some members of the public resist social design. When a design proposal, for example, suggests a solution quite different from conventional practice,

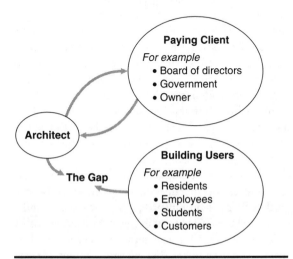

FIGURE 15–3 The gap between architects and building users.

public resistance sometimes appears. For example, in the neighborhood where I grew up, a house was built with no front picture window and a "stone carpet" instead of a front lawn. Every other house had a picture window and a lawn. Some neighbors actually started a petition to force the owners of the unusual house to install a picture window and a lawn.

The fourth source of resistance to social or innovative design is the government. A San Francisco architect saw the need for shelter among the homeless, so he designed a lockable structure about the size of a small truck camper.[62] It was just large enough to sleep in (in San Francisco's climate, body heat could keep it warm at night) and safely store essentials. But when he supplied one to two homeless people, the State of California subpoenaed him. As the architect says, "Those are the things that start to happen when you start to play with the prevailing ethic."

Finally, even some building users may resist social design. A standard bathroom is not the most functional bathroom; better but nonstandard bathroom designs encounter resistance.[63] In one of the earliest attempts to employ social science to make a setting more habitable, a psychologist who worked in a mental hospital rearranged the tables and chairs in a hospital ward for elderly women.[64] The chairs were originally placed around the edge of the room in straight rows; this arrangement made it difficult for some of the women to turn to one another for a decent conversation. When the psychologist arranged the furniture to resemble a cafe (four chairs around a table) to facilitate conversation, the women moved the chairs back to their former positions. It seems one could no longer tell whose chair was whose and this territorial ownership was very important in a setting where residents could lay claim to little else but their own chair.

The psychologist eventually convinced the women to give his idea a try. They did converse with one another much more than previously. This social interaction may have provided some much-needed stimulation to aging residents. The moral of the story, however, may be that practitioners as well as architects must not forget to consult with users before implementing design changes.

Unrealistic Expectations. Some clients and designers are overly optimistic about the power of social design

(see Table 15–1). They naively believe that this right design can solve nearly any problem the organization is experiencing.[65] The common belief in **architectural determinism**—that building design strongly controls behavior—has led listeners in my public talks to ask what color the kitchen should be painted to make people more sociable. Every social design researcher has been asked analogous questions: How big should prison cells be? How loud can a classroom get before students stop learning? Which music should be played to improve office productivity?

The environment is important, but we know that it is not all-important. The social environment is also important for productivity, learning, health, stress, and sociability. Individual characteristics, too, lead occupants to respond differently to the same setting. The social researcher must educate clients and designers to the complexity of environment-behavior relations and remind them that significant but not magical results may be expected from social research in the design process.

There are at least two alternatives to architectural determinism.[66] The first, **environmental possibilism,** began as an extreme anti-determinist point of view, suggesting that people's behavior is not at all determined. A more moderate version asserts that the environment sets certain limits on human behavior, allowing a finite range of behavior. Another alternative is **environmental probabilism**. In many areas of science, from quantum mechanics to human perception, theories have evolved that argue for a statistical point of view. That is, a given combination of circumstances sets up certain odds that an event will occur. Events are never certain and never impossible; their odds are merely very high or very low. It is even possible for a chair to jump off the ground unassisted—if all its atoms happen to vibrate in the vertical direction at the same time. Of course, the odds against this actually happening are vanishingly small.

In everyday settings, the various environmental and other factors that operate set up certain odds—according to the environmental probabilist—that an individual will be affected by noise, begin to socialize with a neighbor, or benefit from a negative ion generator. Depending on the number, strength, and direction of these influences, the odds of the individual behaving in these ways vary from quite low to quite high. Social design's

TABLE 15–1 Heimsath's Designer Fallacies

The architect Clovis Heimsath has outlined six fallacies that designers commonly believe. Note that some fallacies are incompatible with others. Different fallacies may be believed by different designers, but it is surprising how often a designer will offer a second, incompatible fallacy after one has explained the weaknesses of the first one offered.

1. Designer fallacy. "The building directly determines behavior in it." This is a form of architectural determinism. Things are just not that simple. Actually, behavior is determined by personal, social, cultural, and economic factors, as well as by the form of the building.

2. Genius fallacy. "Designs created by great architects have universal value; they may be applied easily in other times and places." Actually, because every set of building users is unique, each new building design should be at least slightly different to take their needs into account.

3. Common person fallacy. "Architecture has no important effect on behavior; people will do what they want regardless of building design." After the 14 previous chapters, I hope this one requires no further comment!

4. Open society fallacy. "Good design is not really necessary because good people will survive and overcome even slums to become successful." But how difficult did awful buildings make the life of the few who made it? What about the many who did not overcome bad design? Why make life harder for either group?

5. Manipulation fallacy. "Designing for human behavior is a veiled form of totalitarianism and behavior control." Design already exerts influence on human behavior; we just do not understand all the mechanisms yet. Also, design can be aimed at giving more control to building users.

6. Know-nothing fallacy. "It is all so complicated that let's forget about the behavioral implications of design and just get this building built!" The holder of this burned-out position no longer has the energy required for good design. Social design certainly can be complicated, but the situation is not hopeless. Careful adherence to the design process as outlined in this chapter can produce useful information.

---

goal is to increase the probability of selected activities and feelings.

Conflict. Social design research may bring to light disagreements among the principal players. This may sound like a reason for *not* undertaking design research, but it is not so. Sometimes, architects and social designers must risk collaboration by questioning some of the basic assumptions that are widely accepted within their own professions in order to develop a shared and improved approach to design problems.[67] The following evaluation of a residence for senior citizens suggests the value of revealing conflicts.

The residence is new, spacious, and lovely. The general quality of construction and furnishings is at least equal to that in most private, middle-class, single-family dwellings. Yet, a common complaint of residents is that they are too cold. One of the first things that was noticed in touring the residence was that every room has its own thermostat, but every one of them is enclosed in a clear plastic cover (see Figure 15–4). The covers have keys, but only the staff have keys.

The staff claim that residents merely need to ask, and the setting on their thermostat will be changed. Some residents say this is not true; they are told that their requests are unreasonable. The staff admits this, claiming that some residents would overheat themselves because they would turn the thermostat up and forget to turn it down later. Residents scoff at this claim.

Regardless of who is correct, the plastic covers in this residence are a source of conflict between the building's staff and its occupants. That residents can see the

FIGURE 15–4 This thermostat covered with a clear plastic shield tells occupants that personal control over their environment is possible, but not by them!

control lever through the plastic but are unable to alter it themselves seems to me a perverse form of torture, although the staff does not see it that way. Energy bills can be a problem, but in this new and presumably well-insulated building, it would seem that slightly higher temperatures would not be financially serious. Perhaps a few residents are endangering themselves, but those who are could be identified. At present, *no* residents control their own thermostat.

Conflict may also occur among building users, both as individuals and as groups. Differing preferences among individuals need little description (different strokes for different folks). But differences among groups are more serious and more interesting. Consider the design of a hospital.[68]

Patients, visitors, physicians, nurses, and office and maintenance staff all use the building differently and therefore want it to look different in many ways. For example, physicians prefer signs that use medical terminology (e.g., oncology) but patients and visitors prefer signs that use everyday words (e.g., cancer).

When building users and architects meet in planning groups, conflict sometimes is suppressed. In one case, a new psychiatric facility was being designed.[69] A

number of design faults that left in-patients at risk were not anticipated by the planning group, and were part of the new building. This happened for six reasons that are very frequently the case when planning groups include no social designer:

- There was pressure to finish the building quickly.
- Those who worked hard to identify design problems were viewed as troublemakers who were spoiling the party ("We're lucky to be getting a new building—don't be causing trouble by raising difficult issues!").
- The architects knew little about psychiatry and the medical staff knew little about architecture.
- Neither side wanted to admit it knew little about the other's profession.
- Both sides subscribed to the leader myth ("They must know what they're doing—they're paid experts!").
- The precise task of the planning group was unclear—were they merely to advise, to pass judgment, or to make final decisions on design features?

Conflict among principal players can be fruitful, but it requires the mediating, neutral role of a good social designer to be turned into an advantage. The conflict was present anyway; the social designer merely brings it to the fore and uses it constructively. Conflicts that are not unearthed remain vague but potent sources of discontent. Conflict cannot be resolved until it is identified. Once identified, conflicts have a chance of resolution.

In the case of the senior citizens' residence, most residents might be given keys to their thermostats, or the covers might simply be removed. Or, perhaps, the energy bill was seriously underestimated by planners and it really is necessary for everyone to bundle up a bit more until better economic times. In that case, many occupants would probably feel better having the difficult situation explained to them, even if it remains unchanged. However, if the conflict fails even to reach the discussion stage, it may fester and someday become part of a larger eruption.

Thus, one problem of social design research is that it often reveals conflicts among principal players. But, with skillful consultation and mediation, this problem becomes one of the key *advantages* of doing social design research. Next, some other advantages offered by social design research are discussed.

The Advantages

To Users. When design research is successful, the occupant receives a more habitable place to live, work, or relax. Three specific benefits of a habitable environment to occupants are that the building mirrors their aesthetic and behavioral tendencies, which thereby reduces their stress, which in turn supports or enhances their ability to accomplish their goals.

Mirroring means the building suits the occupants' customary living or working habits, social patterns, and cultural backgrounds. A very simple example is the office building window. Many office employees prefer to work in conditions that are refreshed by the occasional breath of fresh air. Yet, most new office buildings do not allow the simple freedom of opening a window. This is a minor irritant that, over time and combined with other failures to mirror, can become a significant source of stress. When occupants are stressed, they must either expend extra energy to overcome the shortcomings of their work space or simply yield to an unsupportive environmental structure, working less effectively and with less enjoyment.

Participation in the design process gives users a sense of control that has its own intrinsic value. It helps to satisfy the need to create, it brings community members together, it demonstrates concern by management, and it can produce positive public relations.[70] For example, one hospital that asked nurses to participate in the design of a new addition received newspaper coverage that praised the new project as a "nurses' special." Presumably, the opportunity to provide design input and the favorable publicity will make nurses proud and even more ready to serve their patients.

To Designers. Designers can benefit from social design research, too. Evaluation of their work can

- Provide feedback for improvement in the design of the next building's design.
- Extend and create more contracts.
- Save them undue criticism.[71]

- Save them time.
- Improve communication with other principal players.
- Offer a useful external perspective on the project.[72]

Let's consider these six advantages one at a time. Many architects specialize in certain types of buildings. The care and consideration that goes into any one of them is enormous. Clearly, much could be learned about how each new building design succeeds and fails by studying the opinions and behavior of the building's users after it is occupied. However, as an early environmental psychologist once said, not very kindly, architects are like cuckoos who lay their eggs and then leave the scene.[73] By staying around to learn how the building works in practice, an architect could easily become more skillful (and successful) than competing architects who reinvent the wheel time after time.

Some designers turn design research into a more extensive contract. In one case, pedestrian pathways at a certain zoo were imperfectly arranged; some interesting exhibits were missed by zoo visitors who overlooked the walkway leading to them.[74] A study of the problem revealed the reasons for the problem. This research impressed the client, who asked the researchers to do much more design work at the zoo.

In another project, a new headquarters building, the design was generally successful but there were many complaints about temperature. Most of the blame fell on the architects. Had the architects not followed up their work with an evaluation, they might never have discovered these complaints; meanwhile, their reputation was suffering. The evaluation brought these complaints to light and led to an investigation, which found that the heating and ventilation system had been improperly installed. When this was corrected, the temperature problems disappeared and so did the continuing threat to the designer's reputation.

Social design work can be very inefficient for design professionals who are not trained in social science methods. The interviews with clients and various user groups necessary for fulfillment of the goals espoused in this chapter are not within the time budget, experience, or skill of most designers. In fact, this is true of survey development, behavior mapping, and most other social design methods. Thus, the involvement of an outside research consultant can save the designer much time and effort.

Designers think and talk in a special way that is strongly oriented toward the pictorial. Some architects are almost mute without a sketch pad. Nondesigners, such as clients and building users, are likely to be less visual in their thinking. Some may not be very articulate. A good social design practitioner, with some experience in the visual world of the designer and some in the verbal world of clients and users, may serve as a translator among the principal players.

Finally, most people who spend immense effort on a project feel, near the end of it, that they can no longer see the project objectively. In the design process, endless small and large revisions to floorplans and facades produce this experience. Input from external sources, such as users or the social design researcher, can help place the project into a realistic semblance of how others will perceive it.

To Clients. Social design research can even benefit the paying client, who often is concerned with costs and assumes that research is a net cost to the project. Instead, social research may cost less than other planning methods; studies have documented direct savings to building projects that may be attributed to social design research.[75]

An Australian study suggests that information provided by social design research can help the paying client avoid mistakes that would cost considerable money indirectly over an extended period of the building's life.[76] These include chronic inefficiency in building maintenance, duplication of effort, user ignorance of building capabilities, overspending, and, of course, a design that is inappropriate for the activities housed by the building.

◆ ***IN SUM,*** *social design has numerous goals, problems, and advantages. It aims to match settings to their occupants, to satisfy a variety of principal player needs, to promote personal control in the building, and to encourage social support. Under some circumstances, another goal may be to increase productivity or otherwise change behavior. The problems include a frequent lack of communication between those who pay for a building and those who use or occupy it, resistance to the extra effort of involving users and occupants, unrealistic expectations that socially*

designed buildings will directly cure various evils, and inevitable conflict among principal players. Social design usually means serving the needs of building occupants first, but it also offers benefits to architects and paying clients.

◆ STAGES IN THE DESIGN PROCESS ◆

Construction follows a series of stages that, in general terms, is the same whether the project is a new building, renovation of an older building, or the development of an outdoor setting such as a park. Social design can play a role in every stage of this process, but usually is most prominent in the programming and postoccupancy evaluation phases.

John Zeisel suggested a model of the design process (see Figure 15–5) on which the present discussion is based.[77] An important feature of Zeisel's model is its cyclical nature. Social designers all agree that knowledge gained from one project ought to be used for the next similar project. This has always occurred, but as noted earlier, to an unfortunately limited extent.

In one example of truly cyclical improvement in design, however, behaviorally based evaluations were used to inform the design evolution of three generations of correctional facilities.[78] The whole cycle of participatory planning and subsequent evaluation has been completed in numerous other design projects.[79] These studies suggest that participatory planning does increase the likelihood of a positive evaluation later.

Traditionally, when an architectural firm builds numerous structures of a given type, it acquires a store of information. Two problems with these private stores of information are that they come from select and limited sources and they are not widely shared. The architect's primary feedback comes from the paying client, a few members of the community who make comments in a guest book on opening day, fellow architects, and perhaps an architecture critic. If future designs are to improve, these are necessary but not sufficient sources of information. Systematic input from the building's users is conspicuously absent.

Whatever information that does get collected may not be widely shared because it constitutes, to some extent, the secrets of the trade. If there are principles of design that are not immediately evident in the actual

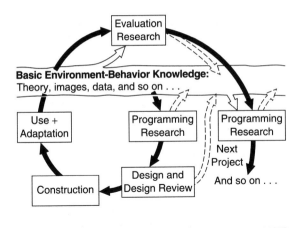

Basic Environment-Behavior Knowledge:
Theory, images, data, and so on . . . .

Five Steps in the Design Cycle

1. Programming	(Analysis)	Identifying design objectives, constraints, and criteria
2. Design	(Synthesis)	Making design decisions that satisfy criteria
3. Construction	(Realization)	Building the project and modifying plans under changing constraints
4. Use	(Reality Testing)	Moving in and adapting the environment
5. Evaluation	(Review)	Monitoring the final product in terms of objectives and use—ideally to be translated into future design criteria

FIGURE 15-5 One prominent view of the design cycle.

structure, architects may be understandably reluctant to divulge them. If the building is found to have serious problems, the architect will not be keen to publicize them.

An improved design process would expand the sources of information about each building type and tactfully but widely disseminate knowledge of its strengths and weaknesses. Designers already act as one-person data banks on the design of various types of buildings.[80] Several observers have called for clearing-house accumulations of useful design information on successful and unsuccessful social design solutions. These could be stored and retrieved through a computer network, supplemented by drawings available on micro-film. Small-scale clearinghouses already exist in some design circles, but a vastly enlarged system could be extremely useful to prevent design disasters and reduce the time and effort required to produce successful designs.

Step one in the design process is the decision to build. This begins with an original plea for space from a group that has outgrown its old space or feels the need for refurbished, expanded, or new facilities. The plea for new space may originate with a formal or informal evaluation of the current setting. The pleading group lobbies the paying client, who may be a board of directors, a government agency, or a wealthy individual. Undoubtedly, there are other calls for funds; the group must impress the paying client with its need for new or renovated facilities in competition with other groups.

Programming

Once tentative approval for the project is given, the next step is **programming**: the planning of the building that occurs before blueprints are drawn up. Programming has both a technical side and a social side. On the technical side, preliminary studies of possible sites, costs, sources of outside funds, and regulations are conducted. In general, it consists of determining the technical and financial constraints to the project.

The social side of programming sometimes is treated very lightly. However, because it is crucial to both matching (congruence and habitability) and to valued outcomes (satisfaction, productivity, personal control, and social support), social design practitioners treat it as one of the most important phases in the design cycle. Social programming involves three steps: understanding occupants, involving them in the design process, and setting design guidelines.

Understanding Users. The first segment of social programming includes two activities that may occur simultaneously: clarifying the social rationale of the new space and analyzing the needs and wants of its future occupants. Clarifying the social rationale means deciding what the organization's goals are. Prison administrators, for example, should decide whether the institution's goal is to deliver punishment, to offer privacy, to support rehabilitation, to be a warehouse, to encourage integration with the outside world, or some combination of these goals.[81] In a new housing complex, is the goal to promote a sense of community or to bolster privacy? The organization should decide which outcomes it expects the new structure to encourage.

The second activity, analysis of user needs (sometimes called needs assessment), begins with basic questions such as: Who will use the structure? How many people will use it? How many will be visitors, as opposed to eight-hours-per-day users or full-time residents? Which activities will these users be engaged in? Needs assessment will also include more difficult questions such as: How much space is required for each user? How can the customs and values of the occupants be expressed in the building?

The answers may seem obvious when North Americans design buildings for other North Americans, but how should a building look when it is designed for, say, Arabic peoples?[82] This problem can be compounded when such a culture is undergoing rapid change: Arab society has been strongly affected by oil wealth. Cross-cultural researchers have begun to attack this problem, although it is massive. For example, a study of houses in 73 societies found that as sociopolitical complexity or segmentation increases, there is typically more segmentation of house interiors into separate spaces.[83]

Sometimes, a distinction between user *needs* and user *wants* is important.[84] This distinction implies that building users will ask for things they do not really need. If users seem to be doing this, practitioners must ask tactful probing questions that allow users to give answers that permit the practitioner to justify the request as a real need. Needs are much more marketable to paying clients than are mere wants.[85]

User needs analysis should involve multiple methods. **Surveys** and **interviews** of occupants are the most common ways of determining needs, but these self-report methods have shortcomings. Occupant responses may be inaccurate due to their honest but mistaken memories of their behavior patterns, their lack of knowledge of architectural possibilities, or their unfortunate attempts to tell the interviewer what sounds right rather than offer their true opinions.

However, interviewing can be useful. In Sweden, the dining room of a geriatric hospital was redecorated based on interviews with patients.[86] The interviews revealed that the sterile hospital environment would best be replaced with one that resembled the patients' homes. The redecorated dining room was constructed to resemble a typical Swedish home of the 1930s or 1940s—the prime era of the patients' lives. The redecoration was very popular with the residents, confirming the value of the interviews. Yet, sadly, the hospital administration required the social researchers to return the dining room to its former design after 16 weeks. Apparently, administrators viewed staff needs for efficiency as more important than patient needs for an appealing setting.

Another questionnaire study of the elderly found that their high-priority activities were sleeping, watching TV, preparing food, relaxing, and eating.[87] Once a group's high-priority activities are clarified, the adequacy of the design to meet these needs can be assessed.

Some studies focus on one element or another of the design. For example, one research group has concentrated on the kinds of lighting and windows preferred by undergraduates.[88,89] In different settings (classroom, room at home, library, computer lab), which level of lighting and type of windows (if any) do you prefer?

There are four major alternatives to the self-report methods (surveys and interviews).[90] In two of these (**behavior mapping** and **behavior tracking**), researchers systematically observe the daily activities of the occupants. Watching what individuals actually *do* may be a better guide to a useful design program than what occupants *say* they do.

One researcher extensively observed the behavior of pedestrians in subways, concert halls, and airports.[91,92] Some of his findings are not surprising; subway patrons usually keep to the right side of walkways and they tend to seek the shortest path. Other discoveries, however, are less obvious—for example, 85 percent of parcels are carried in the left hand. This led to the overuse of one vending machine (resulting in high maintenance costs) while another machine was underused.

Subways usually have banks of turnstiles. In one bank of six turnstiles, 43 percent of the subway riders used one of the turnstiles but only 2 percent used another. Such behavior patterns are unlikely to be uncovered through interviews, yet knowledge of them would be valuable in the design of a new subway station.

In a third alternative to interviews, researchers observe **physical traces** of occupant activities. Traces include evidence of **erosion** (wear) or **accretion** (something added to the setting). These cues might include worn carpet (indicating a heavy traffic path), graffiti and posters (indicating the degree to which occupants want to personalize their own space), or walls built of filing cabinets (indicating a need for more privacy). A major advantage of studying traces is that thousands of hours of behavior observation may be compressed into a few minutes. Physical traces are the environmental psychologist's foray into archeology.

One example of a design oversight revealed by the observation of accretion occurred in Chandigarh, a modern city in India. The famous architect who designed Chandigarh did not take into account the residents' longstanding practice of hanging clothes out to dry. He was greatly dismayed to find, on a visit to the city, that his beloved design for a high-rise residential complex was largely covered up by clothes drying in the wind off nearly every apartment balcony.

The fourth alternative is **simulation**. Researchers may construct a mock-up of a space station, house, or office, and let potential users try it out. Simulation studies usually include an element of self-report afterward (e.g., "Did you like it this way?").

One study, for example, focused solely on stairs.[93] Some 19 different combinations of stair width and height were built and 66 people tried them out. The most widely satisfying stairs were 7.2 inches high and 11 to 12 inches deep. Of course, simulations are not limited to specific design elements such as stairs; they have included full-scale mock-ups of entire dwellings.[94] More futuristic forms of simulation—such as holographs, computer imaging, and virtual reality—are on the way.[95,96]

Each of these there methods has its advantages and its disadvantages. Interviews allow the social researcher to query the user's opinions, feelings, and perceptions, but they may produce a distorted picture of the user's actual behavior. Behavior mapping and tracking may be time consuming and expensive, but they can provide an accurate image of user behavior. Physical traces provide

a capsule history of building use, but they may be insensitive to the needs or behaviors of individuals who use the building atypically. Obviously, the practitioner who aims to achieve the best program will employ multiple methods rather than rely solely on any one of them.

Two studies of libraries have used multiple methods in this way.[97,98] Both studies found that the whole (of the three methods) was greater than the sum of its parts; that some things were learned that could *only* have been learned by using all three methods. For example, in a study done in a public library (see Figure 15–6), it was learned that patrons of a public library believed there were not enough tables.[99] Yet, behavior mapping showed that many tables were unused. Instead of recommending to the library board that more tables be acquired, which would be logical had the researchers merely interviewed the patrons, it was recommended that the library be rearranged. Reality was that there were enough tables, but too many popular activities were located in the same area of the library, so there was a shortage of tables *in that area.*

Sometimes, the actual occupants of a setting that is being designed are not yet known. During the design phase of a new university residence hall, recreation center, or park, those who will be using the facility when it is complete are (at present) scattered across the community or nation. In their absence, **surrogate users**[100] or **consumer input**[101] must be studied. The practitioner must find the most nearly equivalent group of accessible individuals. In the case of the residence hall, residents of other dormitories on campus are probably a good approximation of next year's first occupants of the new dormitory.

User needs must be considered within the context of the new setting's social rationale. Knowing the future users and their needs will clearly produce more habitable structures. Knowledge of needs is more useful than other kinds of knowledge about building users. For example, an Australian study found that when architects knew future occupants' spatial needs, they designed more appropriate houses for them than when they were armed with knowledge of the future occupants' lifestyles.[102]

Involving Users. Another programming goal is **user activation**. Occupants may protest that they do not know

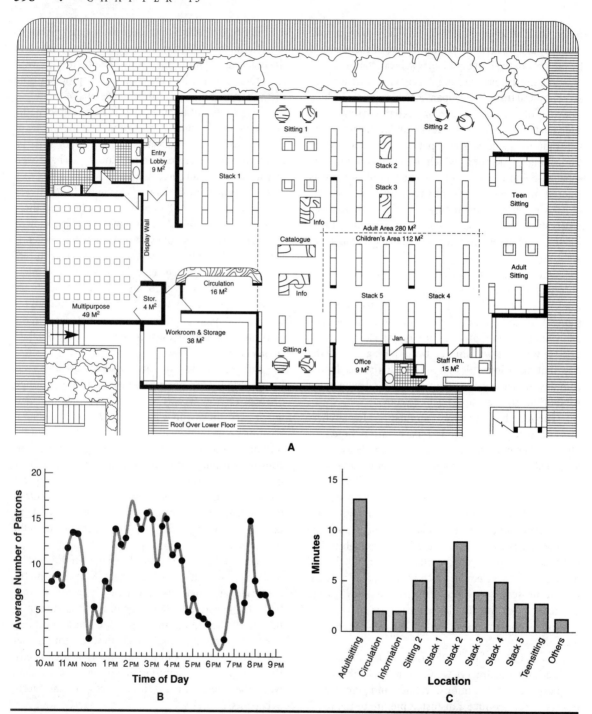

A

B

C

FIGURE 15–6 Multiple methods in the postoccupancy evaluation of a new library. By combining information from the knowledge of the library's floorplan (*A*), the patron flow rate (*B*), the time spent in each location (*C*), and other information such as a user survey and the time patrons spend in each kind of library activity (not shown), the environmental psychologist can pinpoint trouble spots and recommend changes that might alleviate the problems.

anything about architecture or design. Some of them may initially care little about devoting time to the design process. The practitioner's job includes demonstrating to occupants that they need not be professional designers to participate in the planning of the new setting and that there are good reasons to become involved in the design of their next work or living space. How can user activation be accomplished?

The practitioner can present building users with examples of how others participated in the design of their own facilities. Seeing that other nonprofessional designers were able to make valuable contributions can be a strong confidence-builder for those who think design is only for the experts. Building users who already believe they can successfully participate become more excited about their own chance to contribute.

Another way to encourage user participation is for the practitioner to become an **advocate designer**.[103] In this role, the social designer's goal is to actively serve the educational and political needs of occupants. This means supplying them with technical knowledge, teaching them how they might create their own designs and representing their interests to the rest of the design team.

Some even see the advocate designer as a vehicle to remove the authoritarian character of the architect. Ultimately, this would help return the design process to the preindustrial vernacular model, discussed early in this chapter, in which everyone in the community works together on a project with little role specialization. This is unlikely to occur in technological societies but it expresses the democratic, user-oriented direction that some designers favor.

Design assistance often is available in inverse proportion to users' need for it. The wealthy, who already occupy less stressful settings, can afford to hire consultants to improve them. Social design is "in part an attempt to reallocate design services to improve the housing and neighborhood needs of the poor."[104]

User activation includes user education. This does not usually mean classroom-style lectures on design. It may include writing articles that speak directly to users, urging them to actively undertake design projects. One such article, written for office employees, describes "the six basic steps in the design process" in straightforward, positive language.[105] Another, presumably aimed at administrators, is titled "Employees Need Role in Design of Work Space."[106]

Design education can even be successful with elementary school children. Children ages 8 and 9 were taught enough about design to produce an ideal classroom that was significantly better than children who did not receive design training.[107]

User education may also involve expanding the horizons of users by presenting them with a variety of workable design solutions. Generally, participants find it much easier to provide useful decision information if they are presented with easily understood choices, rather than by being asked "What do you want?"[108] Or it may involve workshops in which occupants and designers literally walk through a typical day's activities to experience or relive the successful and unsuccessful features of the present design.

Mock-ups of proposed designs are yet another possibility. In one such mock-up, social researchers investigating a design for a hospital room discovered a life-threatening flaw.[109] During a drill simulating a cardiac arrest situation, a design research team found that one of two beds in the room could not fit past the other one; a patient who experienced a heart attack might lose valuable time while being transferred to intensive care. As a result of the drill, the designers enlarged the room to prevent the problem. In Switzerland, the Laboratory for Architectural Experimentation allows for the full-scale simulation of buildings. Using large but lightweight blocks, families working with designers can easily construct and revise life-size plans for their houses.[110]

One exciting possibility for involving future users of a building is virtual reality. In these computer-based simulations, with a metal helmet over the user's head and an interactive device in his or her hand, a building can be simulated to the degree that the user can walk through it and even look to the left, right, and rear if desired. In fact, a computer lab in North Carolina *was* designed with the help of virtual reality simulation. The architect was convinced to change the position of some walls after experiencing the design in virtual reality.[111]

Another programming activity is facilitation of direct user participation in the design process. User participation varies widely. One view is that there are three kinds of programming in common practice.[112] In **traditional planning**, a manager makes a few sketches and tells someone to draw them up and "make it happen" or the organization's architect/planners decide what the users' requirements are for them and then work out a design. Users themselves are rarely consulted directly. In **direct planning,** corporate managers hire social designers to do the programming. Users are consulted more often, depending on the mandate provided by the corporation and the values and styles of the programmers. In **joint planning,** all phases of programming are accomplished by a coalition of professionals (architects and social designers) and users.

Another view of the range of user participation is as follows:[113]

- Users are not consulted at all.
- Users provide information to a designer who then creates the design.
- Users choose among already completed designs.
- Users select and arrange forms provided by the designer.
- Users create the project themselves.

When setting users have preexisting or newly enhanced enthusiasm for and confidence in the design process, they are ready for something more than the first of these options. A basic assumption is that informed, motivated occupants can make significant contributions toward solving the puzzle of how to translate a social rationale and differing user needs into an actual plan.

In one example of direct user participation, the design of a hospital courtyard was studied.[114] A table-sized model of the courtyard was constructed so that it could be taken apart and reassembled in different patterns. After showing many possible variations of the courtyard to over 200 patients and visitors, the social researchers concluded the courtyard should have densely planted trees, colorful plants, and seating arrangements that allowed for privacy or social interaction. (Which level of participation is this, based on the two hierarchies of participation just described?) Many users who are offered the opportunity to express their preferences among choices are pleased that someone cares enough to ask and even happier when some element of the final design reflects their choices.

User participation patterns are quite variable; they may, for example, fall between the levels or types of participation described earlier. Some users may be involved but not others. In one project, for example, a landscape architect, a child psychologist, social design researchers, and the staff (but not the children) of a day-care center worked together throughout the programming phase of an outdoor learning environment for preschoolers.[115]

In another example of user participation, the emphasis was on setting design priorities in the context of financial and social constraints.[116] In the Truax housing complex in Madison, Wisconsin, low-income residents were guided through a set of procedures for designing their ideal apartment. They were also faced with the necessity of trade-offs ("If the costs of your ideal apartment rose, which features would you sacrifice?"). Using models, the residents were asked to begin the design process by assessing how their present apartment met their needs. The ideal apartment grew out of needs unmet by their present apartment.

The notion of trade-offs is central to an approach that emphasizes the user as an active design agent who is capable of adapting to some building features and changing others.[117] Merely determining the users' needs and preferences is to regard users as passive, unable, or unwilling to actively interact with the building.

User participation has valuable side effects. Apart from the usefulness of the suggestions and contributions made by users, the *process* seems beneficial to them. Users who were involved in the design process report more satisfaction than, for example, equivalent users who were not involved.[118] The positive glow from participation even seems to affect perception of the environment. Some office employees who received new offices that were smaller than their old ones were so pleased with their participation experience that they believed they had more space in their new offices.[119]

Programming, in practice, takes on a variety of emphases depending on the size and nature of the project and the orientation of the programmer. The focus may be on persons as individuals, aggregates, or groupings, or on spaces, individually, aggregated, or grouped, although actual projects often combine some of these six approaches.[120] Concentrating on individual persons' needs or on the design of individual spaces is much easier when few persons or spaces need attention. Programming for aggregates occurs when there are many people or spaces of a given type, such as secretaries or faculty offices. Programming for groupings occurs when the people are not merely the same in some characteristic function, such as their occupation or age, but share values, norms, and meaning—as in a cultural group. Space groupings are similarities in terms of the meaning of the space groupings to the architect. Programmers must be aware that adopting an approach that is inappropriate for a project can lead to problems, or even render the program counterproductive.

Formulating Design Guidelines. The next major part of the programming process, although it overlaps with the activities just described, is the formulation of design guidelines. This phase of the process identifies, based on the foregoing analyses and various constraints, specific objectives that the design should make more likely to achieve.

Obviously, these guidelines are unique to each design problem; no comprehensive list will accurately reflect the needs identified by users and designers of any individual building project. Nevertheless, some needs are more frequently identified than others and it is possible to list the most frequently identified guidelines. One such list was provided by one of the pioneers of social design, Fritz Steele.[121] Here are six workplace design guidelines:

- *Shelter and security*. Adequate filtering of weather elements (e.g., natural light without too much glare, fresh air without an office gale, etc.), adequate space, territorial control
- *Social contact*. A balance between too much and too little communication: privacy
- *Task instrumentality*. Person-machine and microspatial arrangements that facilitate work performance
- *Symbolic identification*. Appropriate workplace symbols to convey employee status in a positive manner
- *Growth*. The opportunity to explore and to learn
- *Pleasure*. Comfort, convenience, aesthetic appeal, varied but controllable stimulation

Steele offers these guidelines as a way to specifically answer questions such as: Is this a quality environment for people? If not, what alterations would help? Many organizations treat physical space only as a factor that harms employee morale. Steele's guidelines include some that are concerned with positive notions such as

growth, identification, and social contact. The guidelines were developed from Steele's own observations of many offices and inspired by Abraham Maslow's theory of basic human needs. The goal was to create a broad manageable set of design guidelines.

A few examples of projects in which some of these guidelines have been established may be instructive. (In most projects, several to many guidelines are identified but I will focus on just one guideline for each example.)

Inadequate privacy is a very common problem to be solved. Chapter 8 described the programming for a low-income housing project in Peru that revealed privacy to be the key issue for residents.[122] The architect, Christopher Alexander, designed a **privacy gradient** into the new houses. The long narrow dwellings were arranged so that casual and formal visitors were restricted to the front rooms of the house, leaving the deeper sections of it for family and close friends.

Safety and security as a guideline is illustrated in a hospital design. Architects planned to surface parts of the courtyard with brick.[123] Brick is attractive and other hospitals had used it frequently. But interviews at these hospitals revealed that patients with recent injuries or surgery found it painful to be wheeled over brick surfaces, which are often bumpy. Although the decision was not popular with aesthetics-minded designers, portions of the courtyard over which wheelchairs were expected to pass were redesigned with a smoother surface.

Comfort, physical or psychological, is another possible guideline. For example, in the Swedish geriatric hospital project discussed earlier, the dining room decor taken from the 1930s and 1940s was familiar and psychologically comforting to the elderly patients.

Clear communication, or imageability, is a seventh guideline (in addition to Steele's six). The building should automatically inform visitors and regulars where all its key elements are. When the building itself cannot or does not do so, signs must be used. But many signs are inadequate or even misleading. The clarity of signs can, of course, be studied experimentally. In settings used by people who speak many different languages, the search is on for pictorial representations that communicate well to everyone.

In a series of studies in Canada, symbolic representations of public information messages were compared.[124] Pictorial symbols for washrooms, the lost and found, car rental information, and other places were presented to subjects. Measures of legibility, comprehension of the sign's meaning, and preference were used; because they were highly intercorrelated, an overall measure called *efficiency* was created from them. The efficiency index scores for the various competing signs were computed, allowing the researchers to make recommendations about which symbolic representation of each message was best.

An eighth common guideline is the provision of control to building occupants. One form of control—an important design guideline in some situations—is personalization. An issue in the design of dormitories, for example, is the provision of opportunities for residents to personalize their rooms with pictures, posters, and other personal articles.[125] If control is deemed an important design guideline, dormitories can be designed to facilitate personalization. Nameplates on doors, walls lined with surfaces that can be taped, pasted, or tacked without damage, and movable rather than built-in furniture are a few ways to enhance a resident's sense of control in a dormitory room.

Control is also important in other settings. For example, in day cares, one key design guideline is that children have the opportunity to change and influence their surroundings, where this is feasible.[126]

Design

In the design phase, the guidelines must be transformed into building plans. Because the design stages are not entirely separable, a few examples of design solutions to the problems of creating settings that fulfill design guidelines have already been discussed in the last section.

It is important to remember that building plans must reflect many considerations in addition to the design guidelines established by the social researcher. Constraints imposed by financial limitations, building codes, and siting problems are a few of these obstacles. Also, some design guidelines fail to survive the political process.

Every setting includes a variety of user groups with different and often conflicting needs and goals. To produce a final building plan that successfully integrates design guidelines, constraints, and competing user needs, a designer needs great skill and creativity.

The social researcher's job is to advocate as many design considerations that benefit users as possible. In large Michigan hospital project, over 500 design and policy changes were recommended.[127] Had these research-based suggestions not been made, the architect would have been forced to make intuitive decisions. As it happened, because of constraints and the political aspect of design, the social research team managed to get only about 60 percent of its recommendations adopted. However, that means about 300 social research-based improvements were made to a hospital that will play a crucial, if brief, role in the lives of thousands of people over the next several decades.

Construction

Social researchers play their smallest role in the construction phase. The architectural plans are turned into wood, concrete, glass, and steel. The designer oversees construction, ensuring that the plans are faithfully executed and that the plans do not reflect any gross oversights. Legends of rooms with no doors, stairwells with enough headroom for children only, and floors from different sections of the building that do not match keep architects vigilant. Minor problems are often corrected as the building is constructed.

The construction phase is not, however, totally without interest from the social researcher's point of view. One social design-oriented architect saw an opportunity for participation even in the construction phase.[128] In a medical school project, he insisted that construction workers be given a role in design. Rather than merely follow the plans in every detail, which can be an alienating, stultifying experience, the architect asked the workers to take a more active role.

For instance, they were asked to pick up beautiful rocks or other materials on their way to work and to line the concrete forms with them. Masons were given only a rough idea of the architect's plans for the brickwork and encouraged to do the masonry their own way. Happy, enthusiastic construction workers were bringing their families down to the project evenings and weekends to show them their personal contributions to the project!

Use and Adaptation

The building is finally occupied. The smell of new paint and furniture greets curious and optimistic new users. Very often, the first days and weeks in the life of a new building are happy ones. The occupants usually have moved from older, perhaps cramped quarters with cranky heating or cooling systems. The new building is a pleasant novelty.

Gradually, however, strange events occur. A middle manager who moved from small but enclosed offices to spacious open-plan settings is grouchy. A receptionist who brought in a poster of Greece to put up near her desk is forbidden to do so because the poster does not fit the new image of the organization that the decor is supposed to communicate to clients. A clerk notices that windows do not open; his allergies are acting up inside the building. Cynical graffiti about the wonderful new building begins to appear on the bathroom walls. Top management, sensing problems, begins to think of the employees as ungrateful for the large expenditure represented by the construction of the new setting (see Figure 15–7).

This is, for the designer, the period of reality testing.[129] Building programs are unlikely to anticipate all the needs of all the users. However, the social researcher may observe the extent to which the building is used as the program intended, and adapted by users in unexpected ways. Programs should be sufficiently explicit to be tested.[130]

If the program was successfully incorporated into the building's plans, patterns of behavior that indicate achievement of the desired goals should be evident. Generally, odd adaptations of the building reflect a failure of the plans to embody the program goals, or indicate that user needs never were included in the program itself. One example would be the teacher who, without training in open education, is placed in an open classroom. The teacher may harness all available materials (such as bookcases, desks, and filing cabinets) to construct makeshift barriers against neighboring classes in the open space.

Research in this phase of the design process is not common, although perhaps it is more accurate to say it usually is lumped together with the next phase, postoccupancy evaluation. Strictly speaking, research in the

FIGURE 15–7   When buildings are inadequate because their original designs were unsuitable or because technology has outstripped them, employees must improvise adaptations. This woman has fashioned a shield for her video display terminal to cut glare. In the background, a noisy office machine is covered with a blanket to reduce its noise.

use-and-evaluation phase is a nonevaluative look at how occupants use their building. However, it is difficult to observe behavior without drawing conclusions about whether the building successfully achieved the goals of the program. Because evaluation is an important explicit or implicit aim of many social design research projects, many more postoccupancy evaluation studies have been done.

Postoccupancy Evaluation

The final stage of the design process is postoccupancy evaluation (POE). Of course, due to the cyclical nature of the process, this "final" stage may be the prelude to the design of another building.

What POEs Are and Are Not. A **postoccupancy evaluation** is "an examination of the effectiveness for human users of occupied designed environments."[131] It must be distinguished from the practice of architectural criticism, which emphasizes aesthetic criteria and is usually done by architectural experts alone or in design juries. These evaluations are based on the expert's own reading of the design and views on artistic quality.[132] In contrast, the social design research approach uses the program as the criterion by which the building is judged, and bases its conclusions on user impressions and behavior in the working setting.

POEs must be distinguished from appraisals of buildings that each of us makes on an informal basis every day.[133] We have ways to voice our appraisals, for example, by avoiding a certain fast-food restaurant that we dislike or by seeking out a coffee shop with an atmosphere we like. The POE, in contrast, is much more careful in that it should include all user groups, all important activities occurring in the building, and rigorous methods of collecting and analyzing data.

The POE also differs from most social science experiments, even though both aim for valid results. As POE experts state,

> Whereas social science strives to control extraneous factors, evaluation often *describes* those factors; whereas social science is most concerned with discovering *causes* for behavior, evaluation looks at *influences* on behavior . . . whereas social science aims to reduce the number of factors, evaluation often examines complex systems.[134]

Dimensions. Postoccupancy evaluations vary along four dimensions.

1. Size. Some POEs are small in the amount of resources invested (one student spends a few hours interviewing a few users); others are large, involving teams of researchers operating over several years, with six-figure budgets.

2. Generality. Many POEs are designed specifically for one building; the social design researchers do not expect the results to be applicable to any other building. Other POEs are done on representative schools, prisons, hospitals, or housing developments with the explicit expec-

tation that the knowledge gained from the effort will apply to other buildings with similar functions.

3. Breadth of focus. Some evaluations aim to study only one or two building characteristics, such as noise, space, privacy, or lighting. Other POEs attempt to study more characteristics of the building or even "all" important ones. These broader POEs often aim to capture the whole complexity of the building as an interrelated system.

4. Application timing. The purpose of some POEs is to provide useful information for a renovation that is scheduled to begin next month. Others may have no known date when the results are needed. The POE is performed as part of a program to collect information over the building's lifespan so that one day, when the building needs replacement, a wealth of valuable data is available to guide the designers.

POEs usually are considered tests of *building* effectiveness, but they may also be tests of *program* effectiveness.[136] When construction follows a clear, testable program, the evaluation is essentially a determination of whether the program successfully identified the needs of users. Sometimes, no program was done or it cannot be found. In this case, the evaluation researcher must try to find the architect and, from an interview, determine what the architect intended to accomplish.[137] If the architect also is unavailable, the social researcher should attempt to discern which values are represented by the building's layout to obtain a very rough idea of the program that guided the designer.

Methods. The focus now turns from the nature of postoccupancy evaluations to methods of doing them. How can someone determine whether a building is effective for its users? The major methods are similar to those used in other areas of environmental psychology: surveys, interviews, observations of behavior as it occurs, observations of behavior traces (the physical effects of behavior on the environment, such as worn pathways or posted signs), and analysis of archives (records pertaining to building use). These unobtrusive methods, first discussed in a classic book,[138] have been adapted to environmental psychology.[139,140,141]

In addition to these general approaches, some environmental psychologists have worked on comprehensive assessment instruments designed for specific types of buildings. For example, extensive measures of the physical and social environment of sheltered care environments have been developed and used to show how design changes affect the behavior of institutionalized individuals.[142] Others have created standardized sets of evaluation tests for correctional institutions,[143] schizophrenia treatment facilities,[144] or, more generally, for any building.[145]

Great care, of course, must be taken to ensure that appropriate and valid methods are used. This means that multiple methods are better than a single one, that building users should be involved in the development of the methods to be sure that important issues receive attention, that methods imported from other research areas are not used uncritically, and that features of the experimental and quasi-experimental methods, such as control groups, should be used where possible.

Each POE is unique; questionnaires, surveys, and other methods borrowed from elsewhere must be scrutinized and revised where necessary to fit the requirements of the current study. One error, for example, might be to use a survey developed for secondary schools in a POE of a new elementary school. Although they may respond in good faith, the younger children may simply be not sufficiently developed to answer some questions about their needs or their behavior in the school accurately.[146] Of course, when a series of quite similar buildings is to be evaluated, a standardized questionnaire or interview may be valid, and has the added value of helping to build up a bank of easily compared design data.

Some postoccupancy evaluations are like traditional scientific experiments in that specific goals were identified in the design program, and the POE takes these goals as its hypotheses. For example, one could redesign a ward for patients who are severely mentally disturbed, with the goal of reducing violence and improving patients' self-image,[147] or to reduce the frequency of repetitive behaviors and change where patients hang out.[148] The POE examines the changes in these variables before and after remodeling to evaluate the success of the remodeling.

◆ *IN SUM, the design process includes programming, design, construction, use and adaptation, and postoccu-* *pancy evaluation. Programming consists of three phases: understanding the needs of building users, involving them in the possibilities of design, and translating their needs into design guidelines—goals the actual design should achieve. The first phase involves discerning user needs through surveys and interviews, observing their behavior, and studying the traces they leave. If the actual users are unavailable, a surrogate group should be studied.*

The second phase, direct user participation in the design process, increases steadily from traditional to directed to joint planning. It includes encouraging, activating, and educating users, and involving them directly in the planning process. Social researchers often find themselves in a strong advocacy position, arguing for the interests of the average building user against the interests of other principal players.

The third phase, formulating design guidelines, requires that specific goals be set. These vary from building to building, but a widely useful group of them includes the provision of shelter and security, appropriate social contact, positive symbolic identification, task instrumentality, pleasure, and the opportunity for growth. Turning these guidelines into plans and reality is the job of architects and construction companies. The environmental psychologist returns later to monitor user behavior and adaptation of the new building. Postoccupancy evaluation examines the effectiveness of the program and design, using a variety of social science tools. As illustrations of this process, some examples are described next.

◆ A SELECTION OF DESIGN PROGRAMS ◆ AND POSTOCCUPANCY EVALUATIONS

Hundreds of programs and POEs have been completed; of course no single example gives a complete sense of programs or POEs. In this section, a variety of programs and POEs have been selected as illustrations because they show the diversity of sites, methods, and results that may be found.

Shelter for Survivors of Domestic Violence

Tragically, over 800 shelters for survivors of domestic violence have had to be created in recent years. Domestic violence is not new, but buildings to shelter those in need are a relatively recent development. If you could start from scratch and design a building especially for this purpose, how would it look? This is a question that Ben Refuerzo has tried to answer for years.[149]

Many such shelters are hastily adapted from existing residences and other buildings by well-meaning but underfunded groups. The shelters are often overcrowded, with little privacy. Refuerzo has used a variety of methods to improve the design of shelters. One of his studies tried to specify the preferred attributes of shelters by showing pictures of 48 potential shelter buildings to 100 shelter residents and staff members and asking for many different kinds of reactions to each one.

After analyzing the answers, Refuerzo produced a set of 11 design guidelines for the ideal shelter. Some of these pertain to the neighborhood in which the shelter is to be located, some are related to the building site and landscaping, and some concern the building itself.

Four design guidelines fell into the first category. They were:

1. Ensure there are resources such as stores, schools, parks, and clinics within walking distance. The trip to these resources should have as safe a path as possible (short and public), to minimize exposure to further violence from angry spouses.
2. The shelter should fit into the neighborhood architecture and reflect the shelter's philosophy, which may tend toward anonymity or toward being a widely recognized landmark.
3. The shelter should *not* look like an institution, with high walls, no windows or landscaping, and so on. The structure should provide a sense of security without looking like a fortress.
4. Shelters often are located in urban areas, which are noisy. However, residents are often under unusual stress, so shielding from urban noise is important.

Two guidelines pertained to the site and landscaping:

5. Screen the shelter with trees and other vegetation, but do so in a way that avoids the creation of hiding places on the premises.
6. Try to provide safe outdoor places for reflection and privacy. Shelters are often crowded, so such outdoor spots are very useful in the healing process.

Five guidelines for the building and its siting are offered:

7. The entry should be "serialized"—that is, created as a series of transitional spaces so that visitors can be observed as they approach the shelter.
8. The entry zone should be arranged so that a receptionist can view visitors as they approach the building, both directly and through a video monitoring system, if possible.
9. Create a courtyard with shelter units surrounding it, if possible. This permits spaces (see guideline 6) that are safe but add space to the shelter as a whole.
10. Include play areas for children that meet the security provisions mentioned in earlier guidelines.
11. Include indoor "viewing stations" that allow parents to watch children outside. Ensure that these stations are not vulnerable to invasion by hostile spouses.

Hospital

Frank Becker and Donald Poe were involved in the renovation of a hospital wing.[150] They had helped hospital users of all types (patients, staff, and visitors) to participate in the renovation decision making. The changes made to the building (see Table 15–2) represented those agreed upon through a consensus-seeking process, although financial and administrative constraints restricted the changes slightly. The effects of the changes were measured, using three methods, and the renovated hospital wing was compared with two similar but unchanged wings. Thus, this is an example of a postoccupancy evaluation rather than a program.

One method of evaluation was to measure changes in **organizational climate,** or attitudes toward the hospital. The mood and morale of the hospital staff on the renovated wing improved dramatically after the design changes, in comparison to the mood and morale of staff who worked on the control wings. The mood and morale of the patients and visitors showed smaller and more variable changes in response to the renovations. The visitors even seemed to dislike the renovations. However, staff opinions may be more important in this case because they must spend the most time on the wing. Readers who are concerned about patient welfare will be

TABLE 15–2 Changes in the Environment of the Hospital Studied by Becker and Poe (1980)

Location	Changes
Corridor	paint walls and ceilings wallpaper sections of corridor remove diffusers from fluorescent lights paint room numbers on doors signs for nurses' stations and other rooms railing along corridor
Visitor's waiting area	paint stretched fabric mural rearrange seating different (used) furniture
Solarium (porch)	remove partition wall remove equipment stored behind partition put shelves in existing closet paint area rug rearrange furniture different (used) furniture change type of phone booth stretched fabric murals
Nurses' station	carpet shelves tack board paint
Nurses' kitchenette	paint stretched fabric mural storage shelves rearrange furniture different (used) furniture remove unused equipment
Alcove outside nursing unit	directional graphics paint relocate phone booth add (used) chairs and magazine table

glad to hear that the mood and morale of patients also increased, although less so than that of the staff.

A second evaluation method used by Becker and Poe was a questionnaire to directly assess the environment. All user groups were asked to rate various features of the renovated and control wings. All user groups rated the changed features of the renovated wing as better than comparable features of the unchanged wings, although once again, the staff was most favorably affected.

Finally, Becker and Poe observed behavior in the hospital. The ward area receiving the most renovation was the solarium. Behavior mapping showed that on the renovated wing, the solarium was used significantly more than before the renovations, but solaria on the control wings were used slightly less than before. Users were also observed in conversation; postrenovation conversation increased in the renovated wing, but was essentially unchanged in the control wings.

The postoccupancy evaluation by Becker and Poe is a good example of an intervention that began with programming and ended with evaluation of design changes. The results were enlightening because they showed which user groups seemed to benefit and which did not. Some results were unexpected, such as the negative reaction of visitors after they had been consulted about the changes. But that is how one turn of the design cycle goes. Anyone contemplating a hospital renovation should be able to benefit from Becker and Poe's work to make the next turn of the cycle even more useful.

Office

Robert Marans and Kent Spreckelmeyer evaluated a government office building that won architectural awards for excellence.[151,152] What they learned from questioning three user groups reflects one of the most fundamental findings in environmental psychology: The perceived value of a setting often depends on the evaluator's relation to the building (e.g., employed in it, visitor, passerby).

Marans and Spreckelmeyer believe that a POE should focus not only on the value of a building's nuts and bolts (such as lighting, noise, and parking space) but also on its overall architectural quality or aesthetics. They therefore asked employees to rate the functional aspects of the building, but they also asked employees, visitors, and members of the public to judge its overall architectural quality.

The three groups disagreed on the merits of the office building. Residents of the community and visitors were asked to judge both the interior and the exterior of the building. Their average judgment was that the building was fairly attractive, or about 3 on a scale of 1 to 4. Employee judgments of architectural quality were less positive, averaging about 4 on a scale of 1 to 7.

Closer examination of employee judgments showed that lower ratings were given by employees who had worked in the building longer (familiarity seemed to breed contempt). Also, ratings of interior features of the building such as spatial arrangements were lower than ratings of general or exterior features.

This pattern of appreciation by judges with weak links to a building (visitors, passersby, and tourists) and dislike by judges with strong links to a building (employees and frequent users) has been found before. My own doctoral dissertation dealt with the architectural merits of a university campus that had won international awards and fame for its designer.[153] Sunday visitors, strolling through its striking buildings, write adoring comments in the visitor's book. Photos from helicopters on sunny days depict the university's bold exteriors, which remind many viewers of Egyptian or Mayan temples. But students and staff, who frequently endure fog, rain, and drips in the grey concrete edifice, often find the campus cold, inhuman, and depressing (see Figure 15–8).

In addition, as Marans and Spreckelmeyer point out, evaluations of all sorts, including architectural evaluations, are often influenced by external factors. When local newspapers report that a building has won awards, community residents are likely to believe, *a priori*, that the building must be good.

In contrast, employees whose jobs may be unfulfilling, boring, or worse—which is unfortunately the case for many office employees, especially in the lower echelons—may be inclined to negatively evaluate almost anything placed before them. To produce a good POE, the evaluator must be aware of these possible biases. Another possibility is that a building is a chief cause of user dissatisfaction, so the possible existence of biases must not necessarily be interpreted as a reason for ignoring user evaluations.

Furthermore, building users usually prefer some features over others, even when a generally negative pall surrounds their evaluations. In the office building studied by Marans and Spreckelmeyer, the single-most important predictor of employee satisfaction was the amount of space in the employee's workstation, regardless of whether it was open plan, bullpen, or conventional (walled in). When workstation size was equivalent, however, employees preferred conventional offices to open-plan offices.

In conclusion, postoccupancy evaluation is a necessary and growing part of the building process. With increasing experience, the methods employed by social researchers are being refined; gradually, a knowledge base is accumulating that will be used to create more habitable buildings.

FIGURE 15-8 The glorious exterior versus one inglorious interior of a famous building. Visitors love the exterior and the building has won several international awards. Its architect was awarded the Gold Medal of the American Institute of Architects in 1985. However, those who actually use the building frequently complain because they experience interiors like this more than the building exterior.

Some problems remain. Observers have suggested that social researchers sometimes spend too much effort on data gathering and too little on ways to actually apply the knowledge.[154] Presumably, as design research teams are better supported, more time and effort can be devoted to all phases of the design cycle, including even more direct application of the research findings.

◆ **SUMMARY** ◆

Social design is a building-creation process that emphasizes the active involvement of building users. The specialization of modern society has separated designers from occupants; some designers view architecture

purely as an art. If buildings are to be very habitable, these tendencies must be overcome. Because it requires some extra effort at the beginning of a building's life and because it calls for input from more principal players, the social design process has met some resistance. Some expect too much in the way of behavior change. The process unavoidably leads to some conflict, although this can be useful conflict. However, social designers believe the effort is worthwhile; benefits to users, designers, and paying clients outweigh the costs—particularly in the long run. Social design is most active in programming (understanding and involving users and formulating design goals) and in postoccupancy evaluation (examining the program and design in action). POEs of a shelter for survivors of violence, a hospital, and an office are described.

Suggested Readings

Davis, G., & Ventre, F. T. (Eds.). (1990). *Performance of buildings and serviceability of facilities.* Philadelphia: ASTM.

Friedmann, A., Zimring, C., & Zube, E. (1978). *Environmental design evaluation.* New York: Plenum.

Hatch, C. R. (Ed.). (1984). *The scope of social architecture.* Toronto: Van Nostrand Reinhold.

Marans, R. W., & Stokols, D. (Eds.). (1993). *Environmental simulation: Research and policy issues.* New York: Plenum.

Preiser, W. F. E., Vischer, J. C., & White, E. T. (Eds.). (1991). *Design intervention: Toward a more humane architecture.* New York: Van Nostrand Reinhold.

Priorities for research on human aspects of the built environment. (Special Issue). (1993, March). *Architecture et Comportement/Architecture and Behavior, 9.*

Sommer, R. (1983). *Social design: Creating buildings with people in mind.* Englewood Cliffs, NJ: Prentice-Hall.

Steele, F. I. (1973). *Physical settings and organization development.* Don Mills, ON: Addison-Wesley.

Zeisel, J. (1981). *Inquiry by design: Tools for environment-behavior research.* Monterey, CA: Brooks/Cole.

UTOPIA VERSUS ENTOPIA

It has been a long journey—an entire term for you and four years for me: 15 chapters packed with brief descriptions of books and research projects that took months and years of work by hundreds of environmental psychologists and kindred spirits. In this brief look back, I will avoid recounting new studies and more facts. Instead, I will attempt to give a perspective on what it is all about.

◆ THE ESSENTIAL, ◆ CHALLENGING DISCIPLINE

The first fundamental truth is that every human activity occurs in a physical context. Whether one is interested in environmental psychology itself, in another area of psychology, or in a different discipline, all the action occurs in offices, labs, outdoors, studios, residences, vehicles, institutions, or factories. The second fundamental truth is that mutual influence of person and setting usually is neither sudden nor dramatic (some natural disasters are exceptions). Because these influences are often cumulative and subtle and because people often adapt even to bad settings, they often go unnoticed.

Because of these truths, the vital importance of person-environment transactions often is overlooked. But when by reflecting on the previous 15 chapters, one will realize that environmental psychology is an essential human endeavor. You may already agree, but it is well to remember that not everyone else did, or does.

In its early days, psychology focused on mental dynamics. Later, it began to realize the importance of interpersonal and social forces. Except for the lonely voices of a few pioneers, the role played by the physical environment was recognized only three decades ago. Even today, if your experiences are like mine, you must often field questions about what environmental psychology is. Someone hears that you are studying it and they say, "That sounds interesting. But what is it?" I try to take great care in giving an answer, because the public at large still is generally unaware of this field; its opinion about environmental psychology depends, in part, on what it hears from you and me.

Of course, you must develop your own assessment of the field to offer the curious. Years of work in the field have convinced me that environmental psychologists have bravely undertaken a task that is ultimately more difficult than that undertaken by any other branch of science. This book never offered to provide simple recipes for solutions to practical problems, and I doubt there are any simple answers to the problems that environmental psychologists try to solve. While knowledge is growing so fast that it fairly bulges out of the book, it still provides illumination of theoretical issues and broad research questions more like that offered by the full moon than that offered by the noonday sun.

At this stage, my hope is that you have learned the real strengths of environmental psychology: having the courage to struggle with complex problems and refining the methods needed to understand and overcome these problems in local community settings. At present, reading about research and theory in environmental psychology requires more tolerance for uncertainty than a willingness to master a set of established laws. However, the techniques and procedures needed to conduct applied research that can significantly improve the habitability of built and natural settings in one's own local community are already well developed and ready for use.

This is all that may reasonably be expected, in my view, after only 30 years of sustained effort. Given another few decades, resources like those allocated to other areas of science, and a growing understanding of the individual, social, and societal processes, environmental psychology will compare very favorably with progress in older disciplines.

One reason for this lies in the degree of dedication of most environmental psychologists who, in my experience, are even more driven than most others in the knowledge business. They seem to derive extra energy from knowing their work forms an integral part of their everyday lives; that they can affect the world around them; and that they are always in a physical setting that affects them, is affected by them, and might be improved by their efforts.

◆   WHY ARE WE DOING THIS?   ◆

This sense of improving the community provides considerable fuel. In this spirit, I had hoped in this finale to explore what environmental psychology might say about utopia. There is not enough space for that. Nevertheless, I cannot resist offering a few observations and suggestions. Then you can pursue the matter if you wish with some friends over a glass of your favorite thirst quencher. You may even wish to pursue the matter further by looking at some of the suggested readings provided later.

Which Topia?

Topia is Greek for "place." Environmental psychologists hope to help create better places. *Utopia* is word coined by Sir Thomas More for his famous 1516 book. It has no precise meaning; *u* is not a Greek word. In Greek, *eutopia* would translate as "good place" and *outopia* as "no place." Perhaps More meant utopia as a pun or a combination of the two meanings. One way to interpret utopia is as a good place that cannot be realized; this may be why most people today think of utopia as nothing but castles in the air.

Utopia emphatically is *not* what we environmental psychologists aim for. We have a different topia in mind: **entopia,** which roughly means "achievable place." This conveys the important idea that better settings *can*, with effort, be brought into existence. The search for better places is not a hopeless or even foolish search for utopia.

Architectural Entopia

Most utopian visions have a static quality to them—a certain set of rules that are presumed to enhance life, a certain architecture that will support the visionary's philosophy. Yet, it seems to me that entopic settings must have flexibility, if not guaranteed change. Even a supposedly perfect place would get boring if it did not change. This raises an ancient paradox: How can an ideal setting remain ideal if it must change?

Entopia should change, even if it is constructed for one person, but it would very likely be home for many individuals. Human personalities will always vary; how should an entopia be designed to fit them all? One major challenge is how to build a setting for different individuals who will use it.

Another challenge is to create settings that suit human cognitive, perceptual, and social tendencies that are relatively *similar* across people. Some features of entopia must do the same things for everyone. For example, settings are needed that help promote the fulfillment of human potential instead of limiting or even squashing it. To that end, the major settings of life—homes, schools, and workplaces—must be revamped in an entopia.

All three of these settings often are saddled with traditions that make them far short of entopic. Classrooms are still set up in rows, many homes have open brick fireplaces that owners rarely use but that are very energy inefficient, and poorly designed offices still plague employees. Even prison buildings go beyond their purpose of denying freedom; they encourage violence and illness.

What will it take to change the design process so that user needs are more often taken into account? The process described in Chapter 15 still is not yet in widespread use. One answer is to educate policymakers and the public to the need for humane programming and careful postoccupancy evaluation. For certain kinds of buildings, perhaps those built for members of the public, it may be desirable to seek legislation that ensures consideration of users.

Natural Entopia

What about the natural side of entopia? Some would claim that nature *is* entopia, but victims of nature's awesome forces would not. What *should* we think about nature? At least since biblical times, when the author of Genesis said that everything was put upon the earth for people to use, we have almost blindly espoused this utilitarian view. Trees are there for us to make lumber from, animals exist for eating and hunting, water for washing, stones for building.

Now we see the growth of another view—one that sees nature as a being of its own. In this view, nature deserves the same sort of love and respect we would accord a person we love. More radical views envision nature as an entity that is living, breathing, and evolving just like us.[1] Ecocentrists see nature as worthy of respect and benign treatment *for its own merits*, as opposed to utilitarian environmentalists who believe we should treat the earth kindly *so we will have a nice place to live and play*. This difference between viewing nature as a resource pool to enrich human life versus seeing it as worthy of care and respect[2] independent of human needs is a crucial issue.

For example, if nature lives and breathes, it could either grow more healthy or die. As many have pointed out, we humans will not get far on a dead planet. A more intriguing idea is that a living, breathing nature may be capable of both beneficent love and malevolent destruction. If we treat nature well, will it grow more trees and food for us? If we treat nature poorly, will it respond with natural disasters? Does nature experience a mine shaft as a stab wound? Is a garden like a massage?

In case these philosophic musings are too exotic for you, I turn now to more familiar environmental problems. I believe there are both good and bad trends. One bright spot is that awareness of environmental issues is now extremely widespread. Positive actions may be seen everywhere in anti-litter, conservation, and recycling campaigns. Where curbside recycling is available, over 80 percent of residents recycle. Although automobile manufacturers always say that new emission control regulations cannot be achieved, when the laws are enacted, they have never failed to meet those standards by the time the deadline arrives.[3]

Nevertheless, there is a growing number of cars, the total distance driven keeps increasing, and the amount of greenhouse gases emitted from cars and trucks has doubled since 1980.[4] On the positive side, acid rain has been cut by 50 percent. More forests are being made into parks, but at the same time, the world's forests are shrinking. It seems that no forest is simply left alone—either it becomes a shrine or it is cut down. Contrary to the predictions of opponents, strict air pollution regulations have not hurt the economy, at least not that of the Los Angeles area, where the number of smog alerts has declined 86 percent.[5]

Still, the gap between awareness and reality hurts. Those who try hard are often frustrated by negative trends that seem too strong to change. Environmental depression is a real possibility, yet some therapists tell their clients who have tried to explain this to focus on their "real" problems.[6] A previously unknown group of nomads was recently discovered in South America. They were wandering in search of a "painless place" they had heard about. We all seek a better world—entopia. What can *you* do to help?

Suggested Readings

Fox, D. R. (1985). Psychology, ideology, utopia, and the commons. *American Psychologist, 40,* 48–58.

Leff, H. R. (1978). *Experience, environment, and human potentials* (Chapter 7). New York: Oxford.

Moos, R., & Brownstein, R. (1977). *Environment and utopia: A synthesis.* New York: Plenum.

Porter, P., & Lukerman, R. (1976). The geography of utopia. In D. Lowenthal & M. Bowden (Eds.), *Geographies of the mind.* New York: Oxford.

Sommer, R. (1969). *Personal space: The behavioral basis of design* (Chapter 10). Englewood Cliffs, NJ: Prentice Hall.

Zimmerman, M. E., Callicot, J. B., Sessions, G., Warren, K. J., & Clark, J. (1993). *Environmental philosophy: From animal rights to radical ecology.* Englewood Cliffs, NJ: Prentice Hall.

APPENDIX

PUBLICATIONS, GRADUATE SCHOOLS, AND ORGANIZATIONS

My students frequently ask me where to look for information about particular topics, graduate schools, and organizations for those interested in environmental psychology. This appendix is for those who wish to pursue their interests in environmental psychology and to be aware of the primary institutions in the field. It provides a brief guide to the organizations, journals, publications and graduate schools associated with the field. It is as accurate as I could make it in mid-1995, but be aware that information in it can change.

◆ PUBLICATIONS ◆

Handbook

Handbook of Environmental Psychology (1987) was edited by Daniel Stokols and Irwin Altman and published by Wiley. It is a massive, 43-chapter compendium of knowledge about person-environment relations. The *Handbook* is indispensable for the serious researcher, but very expensive. Try your library!

Journals

Environment and Behavior. Established in 1969, *E&B* is one of the primary journals in the field.

Journal of Environmental Psychology. Established in 1981, *JEP* is the other major journal known for its international emphasis.

Journal of Architectural and Planning Research. Established in 1984, its emphasis is true to its title, but with a fair amount of behavioral research.

EDRA Proceedings. Volumes of papers presented at the annual meetings of the Environmental Design Research Association are included. See your library's card catalog under EDRA.

Children's Environment Quarterly. CES was established in 1984 and focuses on settings for children.

Architecture and Behavior—Architecture et Comportement is a French-English journal established in 1980.

Population and Environment is the journal of Division 34 of the American Psychological Association. Roughly half its articles are on environmental psychology.

Journal of Environmental Education focuses on research related to efforts to improve environmental behavior through educational courses and programs.

You will also find scattered articles of interest in many other other journals. An indispensable tool for the modern researcher is *Psychological Abstracts* on CD-ROM, which allows keyword searching. Environmental psychology research is interdisciplinary, so useful articles that one could never otherwise find may be found with this tool in widely scattered journals.

Book Series

Every discipline needs in-depth reviews of particular topics at the professional level. There are many such books available; here, I will only introduce those forming part of established series. These books consist of chapters reviewing the latest developments in environmental psychology.

414

Human Behavior and Environment: Advances in Theory and Research, edited by Irwin Altman and others since 1976, is published by Plenum Press. The first two volumes were on general topics. Since then, the volumes have focused on children (3), culture (4), transportation (5), the natural environment (6), the elderly (7), home (8), neighborhood and community (9), public places and spaces (10), emergence of intellectual traditions (11), and place attachment (12).

Advances in Environmental Psychology, published by Lawrence Erlbaum Associates since 1981, has volumes focused on urban life (1), personal control (2), energy conservation (3), health (4), research methods (5), and exposure to hazardous substances (6).

Advances in Environment, Behavior, and Design, from Plenum Press, has published 4 volumes since 1986. Each volume contains chapters on advances in theory, research with building users, and applications.

Annual Review of Psychology, published each year by Annual Reviews, Inc., presents volumes that summarize recent developments in psychology and other fields. Environmental psychology has been the the subject of a chapter in the *Annual Review of Psychology* in 1973 (by Kenneth Craik), 1978 (by Daniel Stokols), 1982 (by James Russell and Lawrence Ward), 1986 (by Charles Holahan), 1990 (by Susan Saegert and Gary Winkel), 1992 (by Paul Stern), and 1996 (Eric Sundstrom et al.).

Community Development Series, from the publishers Dowden, Hutchison and Ross, contains over two dozen books and the EDRA Proceedings. The emphasis is on community planning and design.

◆ GRADUATE SCHOOLS ◆

Those of you who wish to specialize in environmental psychology will need a master's or doctoral degree. Many universities offer formal or informal programs in psychology departments, other social science departments, schools of architecture, and certain other departments. Some of these programs are listed here. Further details are available in most university libraries that collect calendars from other universities, by writing to the university itself, or by consulting *Graduate Programs in Psychology,* published by the American

Psychological Association. The latter may be available in your psychology department office or the campus counseling center.

The oldest continuing program is the Ph.D. program in environmental psychology at the the Graduate Center of the City University of New York, founded in 1968 by William Ittelson and Harold Proshansky. Some other graduate programs in *psychology departments* are active but vary in size and formality, from lone but eager faculty members who provide individualized programs up to full programs with numerous faculty members. The smaller programs tend to concentrate on particular areas of research, such as lighting or territoriality. Investigate Arizona, Arizona State, British Columbia, California (Berkeley, Davis, and Irvine), Carleton (in Ottawa), Claremont Graduate School (Los Angeles area), Colorado State, Manitoba, Rutgers, Surrey (in England), Utah, and Victoria.

In *architecture or urban planning departments,* consider California (Berkeley and Los Angeles), Georgia Tech, Michigan, Montreal, Ohio State, and Wisconsin (Milwaukee). In *sociology departments,* look into Kansas, Michigan State, Rutgers, and Washington State. In *geography departments,* consider Nebraska, California (Santa Barbara), Toronto, and Victoria. In *natural resources departments,* there are Arizona and Michigan.

If you believe the field can best be studied from an interdisciplinary perspective, consider social ecology at California (Irvine), design and environmental analysis at Cornell, or family and consumer studies at Utah.

◆ PROFESSIONAL ORGANIZATIONS ◆

For most of you, the first two organizations listed here would be the most important. But depending on where you live or what your particular interests are, other groups may be closer to your heart.

Division 34 (Population and Environment). This group, part of the American Psychological Association, is for environment-minded psychologists. Contact APA at:
750 First Street NE
Washington, D.C. 20002-4242
Telephone: 202-336-5500

Environmental Design Research Association. EDRA is a large association of designers and researchers (about 30 percent psychologists, 30 percent architects, and 40 percent others) that has held annual meetings since 1969. For more information, contact EDRA at:

> P.O. Box 24083
> Oklahoma City, OK 73124
> Telephone: 405-843-4863

Section on Environmental Psychology. Part of the *Canadian Psychological Association*, this is a small, hardy group in Canada. Contact CPA at:

> 151 Slater Street, Suite 205
> Ottawa, Ontario K1P 5H3
> Telephone: 613-237-2144

International Association for People and Their Surroundings. IAPS is based in Europe. Contact:

> Dr. David Uzzell
> Department of Psychology
> University of Surrey
> Guildford, Surrey, England GU2 5XH

Division of Environmental Psychology. This group is part of the *International Association of Applied Psychology*. Contact:

> Professor Gary Evans
> College of Human Ecology
> Cornell University
> Ithaca, New York 14853

Man-Environment Relations Association. MERA is based in Japan. Contact:

> Professor Toshihiko Sako
> Department of Human Health Sciences
> Waseda University
> 2-579-15 Mikajima, Tokorozawa City 359 Japan

People and Places Environment Research. PAPER is based in Australia and New Zealand. Contact:

> Professor Ross Thorne
> Department of Architecture
> University of Sydney
> N.S.W. 2006, Australia

Society for Human Ecology. This interdisciplinary group investigates human-behavior transactions from an ecological perspective. Contact the Society at:

> College of the Atlantic
> 105 Eden Street
> Bar Harbor, Maine 04609

Environmental Design Technical Group. This is part of the *Human Factors Society*, for those who lean toward an engineering approach. Contact:

> P.O. Box 1369
> Santa Monica, CA 90406

American Planning Association. This large group is oriented toward planning and design on the urban scale.

> 1776 Massachusetts Avenue NW
> Washington, D.C. 20036

REFERENCES

Chapter 1

1. Chein, I. (1954). The environment as a determinant of behavior. *Journal of Social Psychology, 39,* 115–127.

2. Brunswik, E. (1943). Organismic achievement and environmental probability. *Psychological Review, 50,* 255–272.

3. Lewin, K. (1943). Defining the field at a given time. *Psychological Review, 50,* 292–310.

4. See note 1.

5. Barker, R. G., & Wright, H. (1955). *Midwest and its children.* New York: Row and Peterson.

6. This week's citation classic. (1980). *Current Contents, 12*(26), 10.

7. Morgan, J. J. (1916). The overcoming of distraction and other resistances. *Archives of Psychology, No. 35, 24*(4), 1–84.

8. Vernon, H. M. (1919). *The influence of hours of work and of ventilation on output in tinplate manufacture.* Industrial Fatigue Research Board, Report No. 1. London: HMSO.

9. Griffith, C. R. (1921). A comment upon the psychology of the audience. *Psychological Monographs, 30*(136), 36–47.

10. Snow, C. E. (1927). Research on industrial illumination. *The Tech Engineering News, 8,* 257–282.

11. Maslow, A. H., & Mintz, N. L. (1956). Effects of esthetic surroundings: Initial effects of three esthetic conditions upon perceiving "energy" and "well- being" in faces. *Journal of Psychology, 41,* 247–254.

12. Sommer, R. (1969). *Personal space: The behavioral basis of design.* Englewood Cliffs, NJ: Prentice Hall.

13. Osmond, H. (1957). Function as the basis of psychiatric ward design. *Mental Hospitals* (Architectural Supplement), 8, 23–30.

14. Sommer, R. (1959). Studies in personal space. *Sociometry, 22,* 247–260.

15. Ittelson, W. H., Proshansky, H. M., & Rivlin, L. G. (1970). The environmental psychology of the psychiatric ward. In H. M. Proshansky, L. G. Rivlin, & W. H. Ittelson (Eds.), *Environmental psychology: Man and his physical setting.* New York: Holt, Rinehart, and Winston.

16. Wohlwill, J. F. (1966). The physical environment: A problem for a psychology of stimulation. *Journal of Social Issues, 22*(4), 29–38.

17. Helson, H. (1964). *Adaptation-level theory.* New York: Harper and Row.

18. Berlyne, D. E. (1960). *Conflict, arousal and curiosity.* New York: McGraw-Hill.

19. Mehrabian, A., & Russell, J. A. (1974). *An approach to environmental psychology.* Cambridge, MA: MIT Press.

20. Cohen, S. (1978). Environmental load and the allocation of attention. In A. Baum, J. E. Singer, and S. Valins (Eds.), *Advances in environmental psychology* (Vol. 1). Hillsdale, NJ: Erlbaum.

21. Milgram, S. (1970). The experience of living in cities. *Science, 167,* 1461–1468.

22. Suedfeld, P. (1980). *Restricted environmental stimulation: Research and clinical applications.* New York: Wiley.

23. Suedfeld, P., Landon, P. B., & Ballard, E. J. (1983). Effects of reduced stimulation on divergent and convergent thinking. *Environment and Behavior, 15,* 727–738.

24. Selye, H. (1976). *Stress in health and disease.* Woburn, MA: Butterworth.

25. Stokols, D. (1979). A congruence analysis of human stress. In I. Sarason and C. Spielberger (Eds.), *Stress and anxiety.* Washington, DC: Hemisphere Press.

26. Campbell, J. M. (1983). Ambient stressors. *Environment and Behavior, 15,* 355–380.

27. Evans, G. W. (Ed.). (1982). *Environmental stress.* New York: Cambridge University Press.

28. Lazarus, R. (1966). *Psychological stress and the coping process.* New York: McGraw-Hill.

29. Buttimer, A., & Seamon, D. (Eds.), (1980). *The human experience of space and place.* London: Croom Helm.

30. Barnes, R. D. (1981). Perceived freedom and control in the built environment. In J. H. Harvey (Ed.), *Cognition, social behavior and the environment.* Hillsdale, NJ: Erlbaum.

31. Brehm, J. W. (1966). *A theory of psychological reactance.* New York: Academic Press.

32. Seligman, M. E. P. (1975). *Helplessness.* San Francisco: Freeman.

33. Altman, I. (1975). *The environment and social behavior: Privacy, personal space, territoriality and crowding.* Monterey, CA: Brooks/Cole.

34. Barker, R. G. (1968). *Ecological psychology: Concepts and methods for studying the environment of human behavior.* Stanford, CA: Stanford University Press.

35. Wicker, A. W. (1979). *An introduction to ecological psychology.* Monterey, CA: Brooks/Cole.

36. See note 35.

37. Wicker, A. W. (1987). Behavior settings reconsidered: Temporal stages, resources, internal dynamics, context. In D. Stokols &

I. Altman (Eds.), *Handbook of environmental psychology*. New York: Wiley.

38. See note 1.

39. de Rivera, J. (1986). The "objective-behavioral" environment of Isidor Chein: In memory of a humanistic scientist. *Environment and Behavior, 18*, 95–108.

40. Stokols, D., & Shumaker, S. A. (1981). People in places: A transactional view of settings. In J. H. Harvey (Ed.), *Cognition, social behavior and the environment*. Hillsdale, NJ: Erlbaum.

41. Altman, I., & Rogoff, B. (1987). World views in psychology and environmental psychology: Trait, interactional, organismic and transactional perspectives. In D. Stokols & I. Altman (Eds.), *Handbook of environmental psychology*. New York: Wiley.

42. Wapner, S. (1981). Transactions of persons-in-environments: Some critical transitions. *Journal of Environmental Psychology, 1*, 223–239.

43. Geller, E. S. (1987). Environmental psychology and applied behavior analysis: From strange bedfellows to a productive marriage. In D. Stokols & I. Altman (Eds.), *Handbook of environmental psychology*. New York: Wiley.

44. Stokols, D. (1990). Instrumental and spiritual views of people-environment relations. *American Psychologist, 45*, 641–646.

45. Demick, J., & Wapner, S., (1990). Role of psychological science in promoting environmental quality. *American Psychologist, 45*, 631–632.

46. Strathman, A., Baker, S., & Kost, K. (1991). Distinguishing the psychologies of the sociophysical and the natural environment. *American Psychologist, 46*, 164–165.

47. Roszak, T. (1994). The greening of psychology. *The Ecopsychology Newsletter, 1*, 1, 6.

48. Zeisel, J. (1981). *Inquiry by design: Tools for environment-behavior research*. Monterey, CA: Brooks/Cole.

49. Bechtel, R. B., Marans, R. W., & Michelson, W. (1987). *Methods in environmental and behavioral research*. New York: Van Nostrand.

50. Craik, K. H. (1977). Multiple scientific paradigms in environmental psychology. *International Journal of Psychology, 12*, 147–157.

51. Saegert, S., & Winkel, G. H. (1990). Environmental psychology. *Annual Review of Psychology, 41*, 441–447.

52. Fuhrer, U. (1983). Oekopsychologie: Some general implications from a particular literature. *Journal of Environmental Psychology, 3*, 239–252.

53. Chapman, D., & Thomas, G. (1944). Lighting in dwellings. In *The lighting of buildings (Post war building studies*, No. 12). London: HMSO.

54. See note 8.

55. Yamamoto, T. (1984, August). *Current trends in Japanese psychology*. Paper presented at the annual meetings of the American Psychological Association, Toronto.

56. Inui, M. (1982). Environmental psychology in Japan. *Journal of Environmental Psychology, 2*, 313–321.

57. Kobayashi, S. (1961). *An introduction to architectural psychology*. Tokyo: Shokokusha Publishing.

58. Funabashi, T., Shimizu, M., & Sekida, H. (1978). A study on approach space to shrines. *Proceedings of the Annual Convention of the Architectural Institute of Japan*, 1713–1714.

59. Abe, K. (1982). *Introduction to disaster psychology*. Tokyo: Science Publishing.

60. Heron, W., Doane, B. K., & Scott, T. H. (1956). Visual disturbances after prolonged perceptual isolation. *Canadian Journal of Psychology, 10*, 13–18.

61. Sommer, R., & Ross, H. (1958). Social interaction on a geriatrics ward. *International Journal of Social Psychiatry, 4*, 128–133.

62. Garling, T. (1982). Swedish environmental psychology. *Journal of Environmental Psychology, 2*, 233–251.

63. Garling, T. (1969). Studies in visual perception of architectural spaces and rooms. *Scandinavian Journal of Psychology, 10*, 250–256.

64. Hesselgren, S. (1967). *The language of architecture*. Lund: Studentlitteratur.

65. Berglund, B., Berglund, U., & Lindvall, T. (1976). Psychological processing of odor mixtures. *Psychological Review, 83*, 432–441.

66. Berglund, B., Berglund, U., & Lindvall, T. (1976). Scaling loudness, noisiness, and annoyance of community noises. *Journal of Acoustical Society of America, 60*, 1119–1125.

67. Wyon, D. P., Lofberg, H. A., & Lofstedt, B. (1975). Environmental research at the climate laboratory of the National Swedish Institute of Building Research. *Man-Environment Systems, 5*, 107–200.

68. Acking, C. A., & Sorte, G. (1973). How do we verbalize what we see? *Landscape Architecture, 64*, 470–475.

69. Kuller, R. (1972). *A semantic model for describing perceived environment* (sic). Unpublished doctoral dissertation, Lund Institute of Technology, Lund, Sweden.

70. Niit, T., Kruusval, J., & Heidmets, M. (1981). Environmental psychology in the Soviet Union. *Journal of Environmental Psychology, 1*, 157–177.

71. Kremer, A., & Stringer, R. (1987). Environmental psychology in the Netherlands. In D. Stokols & I. Altman (Eds.), *Handbook of environmental psychology*, New York: Wiley.

72. Churchman, A. (1984, August). *Environmental psychology in Israel*. Paper presented at a symposium on "International Developments in Environmental Psychology," annual meetings of the American Psychological Association, Toronto.

73. Jodelet, D. (1987). Environmental psychology in France. In D. Stokols & I. Altman (Eds.), *Handbook of environmental psychology*. New York: Wiley.

74. Thorne, R., & Hall, R. (1987). Environmental psychology in Australia. In D. Stokols & I. Altman (Eds.), *Handbook of environmental psychology*. New York: Wiley.

75. Pamir, A. H. (1981). An overview of Turkish research and education in environmental social science. *Journal of Environmental Psychology, 1*, 315–328.

76. Sanchez, E., Wiesenfeld, E., & Cronick, K. (1983). Environmental psychology in Venezuela. *Journal of Environmental Psychology, 3*, 161–172.

77. Perussia, F. (1983). A critical approach to environmental psychology in Italy. *Journal of Environmental Psychology, 3*, 263–277.

78. Diaz-Guerrero, R. (1984). Contemporary psychology in Mexico. *Annual Review of Psychology, 35,* 83–112.

79. Al-Soliman, T. M. (1991). Societal values and their effect on the built environment in Saudi Arabia: A recent account. *Journal of Architectural & Planning Research, 8,* 235–254.

80. van Staden, F. J. (1987). A decade of environmental psychology in South Africa. *South African Journal of Psychology, 17,* 72–75.

81. Setala, M., & Syvaneen, M., (1988). Environmental psychology in Finland. *Journal Environmental Psychology, 8,* 315–323.

82. Suedfeld, P. (1990). Groups in isolation and confinement: Environments and experiences. In A. H. Harrison, Y. A. Clearwater, & C. P. McKay (Eds.), *From Antarctica to outer space: Life in isolation and confinement.* New York: Springer-Verlag.

83. Clearwater, Y. (1985). A human place in outer space. *Psychology Today, 19*(7), 34–43.

84. Harrison, A. A., Struthers, N. J., & Putz, B. J. (1991). Mission destination, mission duration, gender, and student perceptions of space habitat acceptability. *Environment and Behavior, 23,* 221–232.

85. Rothblum, E. D. (1990). Psychological factors in the Antarctic. *Journal of Psychology, 124,* 253–273.

86. Ellis, P. (1980). Review of Designing for therapeutic environments. *Bulletin of the British Psychological Society, 33,* 325–326.

87. Altman, I. (1981). Reflections on environmental psychology: 1981. *Human Environments, 2,* 5–7.

88. Stokols, D. (1982). Environmental psychology: A coming of age. In A. Kraut (Ed.), *The Stanley Hall Lecture Series* (Vol. 2). Washington, DC: American Psychological Association.

89. Canter, D. V., & Craik, K. H. (1981). Environmental psychology. *Journal of Environmental Psychology, 1,* 1–11.

90. Baird, J. C., & Berglund, B. (1989). Thesis for environmental psychophysics. *Journal of Environmental Psychology, 9,* 345–356.

91. Willems, E. P. (1974). Behavioral technology and behavioral ecology. *Journal of Applied Behavior Analysis, 7,* 151–164.

Chapter 2

1. Ross, H. E. (1974). *Behavior and perception in strange environments.* London: George Allen and Unwin.

2. Ittelson, W. H. (1978). Environmental perception and urban experience. *Environment and Behavior, 10,* 193–213.

3. Gifford, R., & Ng, C. F. (1982). The relative contribution of visual and auditory cues to environmental perception. *Journal of Environmental Psychology, 2,* 275–284.

4. Ittelson, W. H. (1970). Perception of the large-scale environment. *Transactions of the New York Academy of Sciences, 32,* 807–815.

5. Ittelson, W. H. (Ed.). (1973). *Environment and cognition.* New York: Seminar Press.

6. See note 2.

7. McGill, W., & Korn, J. H. (1982). Awareness of an urban environment. *Environment and Behavior, 14,* 186–201.

8. Sommer, R. (1972). *Design awareness.* New York: Holt, Rinehart and Winston.

9. Gifford, R. (1976). Environmental numbness in the classroom. *Journal of Experimental Education, 44*(3), 4–7.

10. Leff, H. (1978). *Experience, environment, and human potential.* New York: Oxford University Press.

11. Marans, R. W., & Stokols, D. (1993). *Environmental simulation: Research and policy issues.* New York: Plenum.

12. Hetherington, J., Daniel, T. C., & Brown, T. C. (1993). Is motion more important than it sounds? The medium of presentation in environment perception research. *Journal of Environmental Psychology, 13,* 283–291.

13. Appleyard, D., & Craik, K. H. (1978). The Berkeley environmental laboratory and its research program. *International Review of Applied Psychology, 27,* 53–55.

14. McKechnie, G. E. (1977). Simulation techniques in environmental psychology. In D. Stokols (Ed.), *Perspectives on environment and behavior: Conceptual and empirical trends.* New York: Plenum.

15. Coeterier, J. F. (1983). A photo validity test. *Journal of Environmental Psychology, 3,* 315–323.

16. Sirikasem, P., & Shebilske, W. L. (1991). The perception and metaperception of architectural designs communicated by video-computer imaging. *Psychological Research/Psychologische Forschung, 53,* 113–126.

17. Wood, W. (1972). *An analysis of simulation media.* Unpublished Graduation Project, School of Architecture, University of British Columbia, Vancouver.

18. Stamps, A. E. (1993). Postconstruction validation of photomontage simulations (Part 2). *Perceptual and Motor Skills, 76*(3, Part 2), 1335–1338.

19. Bateson, J. E., & Hui, M. K. (1992). The ecological validity of photographic slides and videotapes in simulating the service setting. *Journal of Consumer Education, 19,* 271–281.

20. Lowenthal, D. (1972). Research on environmental perception and behavior: Perspectives on current problems. *Environment and Behavior, 4,* 333–342.

21. Brunswik, E. (1944). Distal focusing of perception. *Psychological Monographs, 56,* 1–48.

22. Lynch, K., & Rivkin, M. (1959). A walk around the block. *Landscape, 8,* 24–34.

23. Feimer, N. R. (1984). Environmental perception: The effects of media, evaluative context, and observer sample. *Journal of Environmental Psychology, 4,* 61–80.

24. Wagner, M., Baird, J. C., & Barbaresi, W. (1981). The locus of environmental attention. *Journal of Environmental Psychology, 1,* 195–206.

25. Stevens, S. S. (1975). *Psychophysics: Introduction to its perceptual, neural, and social prospects.* New York: Wiley.

26. Reed, C. F., Lehberger, P. F., & Haase, R. F. (1980). Application of psychophysical scaling to measurement of complexity of houses. *Perceptual and Motor Skills, 50,* 655–660.

27. Coren, S., Porac, C., & Ward, L. M. (1984). *Sensation and perception.* Toronto: Academic Press.

28. Nasar, J. L., Valencia, H., Omar, Z. A., Chueh, S., & Hwang, J. (1985). Out of sight further from mind: Destination visibility and distance perception. *Environment and Behavior, 17,* 627–639.

29. Hershberger, R. G. (1968). A study of meaning and architecture. *Man and His Environment, 1*(6), 6–7.

30. Kaplan, R. (1973). Predictors of environmental preference: Designers and clients. In W. F. E. Preiser (Ed.), *Environmental design research*. Stroudsburg, PA: Dowden, Hutchinson and Ross.

31. Valadez, J. J. (1984). Diverging meanings of development among architects and three other professional groups. *Journal of Environmental Psychology, 4*, 223–228.

32. Payne, I. (1969). Pupillary responses to architectural stimuli. *Man-Environmental Systems, 1*, S-11.

33. Edney, J. J. (1972). Place and space: The effects of experience with a physical locale. *Journal of Experimental Social Psychology, 8*, 124–135.

34. See note 28.

35. Smith, C. D. (1984). The relationship between the pleasingness of landmarks and the judgement of distance in cognitive maps. *Journal of Environmental Psychology, 4*, 229–234.

36. Turnbull, C. (1961). Some observations regarding the experiences and behavior of the Bambuti Pygmies. *American Journal of Psychology, 74*, 304–308.

37. See note 27.

38. Wohlwill, J. F. (1973). The environment is not in the head! In W. F. E. Preiser (Ed.), *Environmental design research* (Vol. 2). Stroudsburg, PA: Dowden, Hutchinson and Ross.

39. Thiel, P. (1970). Notes on the description, scaling, notation, and scoring of some perceptual and cognitive attributes of the physical attributes. In H. Proshansky, W. Ittelson, & L. Rivlin (Eds.), *Environmental psychology: Man and his physical setting*. New York: Holt, Rinehart and Winston.

40. Pederson, D. M., & Topham, T. L. (1990). Perception of enclosure effects of architectural surfaces in a large scale interior space. *Perceptual and Motor Skills, 70*, 299–304.

41. Thiel, P., Harrison, E. D., & Alden, R. S. (1986). The perception of spatial enclosure as a function of the position of architectural surfaces. *Environment and Behavior, 18*, 227–245.

42. Dainoff, M. J., Sherman, R. C., Miskie, D., & Grovesnor, J. (1981). Perceived enclosedness of schematic architectural space. *Journal of Experimental Psychology, 7*, 1349–1356.

43. Lloyd, R. E. (1989). Color sensation and the realizations of color on exterior architecture: An archival and experimental study of color perception, preference, and meaning. *Dissertation Abstracts International, 49*(11–A), 3186.

44. See note 1.

45. Okabe, A., Aoki, K., & Hamamoto, W. (1986). Distance and direction judgement in a large-scale natural environment: Effects of a slope and winding trail. *Environment and Behavior, 18*, 755–772.

46. Sadalla, E. K., & Magel, S. G. (1980). The perception of traversed distance. *Environment and Behavior, 12*, 65–79.

47. Sadalla, E. K., & Staplin, L. J. (1980). The perception of traversed distance: Intersections. *Environment and Behavior, 12*, 167–182.

48. Sadalla, E. K., & Oxley, D. (1984). The perception of room size: The rectangularity illusion. *Environment and Behavior, 16*, 394–405.

49. Cadwallader, M. (1979). Problems in cognitive distance: Implications for cognitive mapping. *Environment and Behavior, 11*, 559–576.

50. Sadalla, E. K., Burroughs, W. J., & Staplin, L. J. (1980). Reference points in spatial cognition. *Journal of Experimental Psychology: Human Learning and Memory, 5*, 516–528.

51. Hirtle, S. C., & Jonides, J. (1985). Evidence of hierarchies in cognitive maps. *Memory and Cognition, 13*, 208–217.

52. See note 48.

53. Korte, C., & Grant, R. (1980). Traffic noise, environmental awareness, and pedestrian behavior. *Environment and Behavior, 12*, 408–420.

54. Maslow, A. H., & Mintz, N. C. (1956). Effects of aesthetic surrounding: I. Initial effects of three aesthetic conditions upon perceiving "energy" and "well-being" in faces. *Journal of Psychology, 41*, 247–254.

55. Wilmot, D. (1990). Maslow and Mintz revisited. *Journal of Environmental Psychology, 10*, 293–312.

56. Brunswik, E. (1956). *Perception and the representative design of psychological experiments*. Berkeley: University of California Press.

57. Brunswik, E. (1957). Scope and aspects of the cognitive problem (p. 5). In H. Gruber, K. R. Hammond, & R. Jessor (Eds.), *Contemporary approaches to cognition: A symposium held at the University of Colorado*. Cambridge, MA: Harvard University Press.

58. Craik, K. H., & Appleyard, D. (1980). The streets of San Francisco: Brunswik's lens model applied to urban inference and assessment. *Journal of Social Issues, 36*(3), 72–85.

59. Gibson, J. J. (1966). *The senses considered as perceptual systems*. Boston: Houghton Mifflin.

60. Gibson, J. J. (1979). *The ecological approach to visual perception*. Boston: Houghton Mifflin.

61. Gibson, J. J. (1976). *The theory of affordances and the design of the environment*. Paper presented at the annual meetings of the American Society for Aesthetics, Toronto.

62. Kaplan, S., & Kaplan, R. (1982). *Cognition and environment: Functioning in an uncertain world*. New York: Praeger.

63. See note 61.

64. Berlyne, D. E. (1972). *Aesthetics and psychobiology*. New York: Appleton-Century-Crofts.

65. Berlyne, D. E. (Ed.). (1974). *Studies in the new experimental aesthetics: Steps toward an objective psychology of aesthetic appreciation*. New York: Halsted.

66. Rapoport, Am., & Kantor, R. E. (1967). Complexity and ambiguity in environmental design. *Journal of the American Institute of Planners, 33*, 210–221.

67. Venturi, R. (1966). *Complexity and contradiction in architecture*. New York: Museum of Modern Art.

68. Wohlwill, J. F. (1976). Environmental aesthetics: The environment as a source of affect. In I. Altman & J. F. Wohlwill (Eds.), *Human behavior and environment* (Vol. 1). New York: Plenum.

69. See note 68.

70. See note 68.

71. Russell, J. A., & Mehrabian, A. (1978). Approach-avoidance and affiliation as functions of the emotion-eliciting quality of an environment. *Environment and Behavior, 10*, 355–387.

72. Russell, J. A., & Pratt, G. (1980). A description of the affective quality attributed to environments. *Journal of Personality and Social Psychology, 38*, 311–322.

73. Russell, J. A., Ward, L. M., & Pratt, G. (1981). Affective quality attributed to environments: A factor analytic study. *Environment and Behavior, 13,* 259–288.

74. See note 62.

75. Heidegger, M. (1971). *Poetry, language, and thought.* New York: Harper and Row.

76. Seamon, D. (1982). The phenomenological contribution to environmental psychology. *Journal of Environmental Psychology, 2,* 119–140.

77. Korosec-Serfaty, P. (1984). The home from attic to cellar. *Journal of Environmental Psychology, 4,* 303–321.

78. Jacobs, J. (1961). *The death and life of great American cities.* New York: Random House.

79. Seamon, D., & Nordin, C. (1980). Marketplace as place ballet: A Swedish example. *Landscape, 24,* 35–41.

80. Tuan, Y. F. (1974). *Topophilia.* Englewood Cliffs, NJ: Prentice-Hall.

81. Relph, E. (1976). *Place and placelessness.* London: Pion.

82. Buttimer, A., & Seamon, D. (Eds.). (1980). *The human experience of space and place.* London: Croom Helm.

83. Norberg-Schulz, C. (1980). *Genius loci: Towards a phenomenology of architecture.* New York: Rizzoli.

84. Relph, E. (1981). *Rational landscapes and humanistic geography.* London: Croom Helm.

85. Livingstone, D. H., & Harrison, R. T. (1983). Reflections on a phenomenological approach. *Journal of Environmental Psychology, 3,* 295–296.

86. Sixsmith, J. (1983). Comment on "The phenomenological contribution to environmental psychology " by D. Seamon. *Journal of Environmental Psychology, 3,* 109–111.

87. Seamon, D. (1983). Response to Sixsmith's comments on the phenomenological contribution. *Journal of Environmental Psychology, 3,* 199–200.

88. Low, S. M., & Ryan, W. P. (1985). A methodology for the integration of architectural and local perceptions in Oley, Pennsylvania. *Journal of Architectural Planning and Research, 2,* 3–22.

89. Hendrick, C., Martyniuk, O., Spencer, T. J., & Flynn, J. E. (1977). Procedures for investigating the effect of light on impression: Simulation of a real space by slides. *Environment and Behavior, 9,* 491–510.

90. Kaye, S. M., & Murray, M. A. (1982). Evaluations of an architectural space as a function of variations in furniture arrangement, furniture density, and windows. *Human Factors, 24,* 609–618.

91. Kitchin, R. M. (1994). Cognitive maps: What they are and why study them? *Journal of Environmental Psychology, 14,* 1–19.

92. Downs, R. M., & Stea, D. (1977). *Maps in minds: Reflections on cognitive mapping.* San Francisco: Harper and Row.

93. Bostrom, A., Fischhoff,B., & Morgan, M. (1992). Characterizing mental models of hazardous processes: A methodology and application to radon. *Journal of Social Issues, 48*(4), 85–100.

94. Taylor, J. G., Stewart, T. R., & Downton, M. (1988). Perceptions of drought in the Ogallala Aquifer region. *Environment and Behavior, 20,* 150–175.

95. Brown, R. S., Williams, C. W., & Lees-Haley, P. R. (1994). The effects of hindsight bias and causal attribution on human response to environmental events. *Journal of Environmental Psychology, 14,* 661–674.

96. Cherulnik, P. D. (1991). Reading restaurant facades: Environmental inference in finding the right place to eat. *Environment and Behavior, 23,* 150–170.

97. Chawla, L. (1986). The ecology of environmental memory. *Children's Environments Quarterly, 3,* 34–42.

98. Peron, E. M., Baroni, M. R., Job, R., & Salmaso, P. (1990). Effects of familiarity in recalling interiors and external places. *Journal of Environmental Psychology, 10,* 255–271.

99. Schiavo, R. S., & McWalter, S. (1990, August). *Building renovation and memorableness.* Paper presented at annual meetings of the American Psychological Association, Boston.

100. Hammitt, W. E. (1987). Visual recognition capacity during outdoor recreation experiences. *Environment and Behavior, 19,* 651–672.

101. Lynch, K. (1960). *The image of the city.* Cambridge, MA: MIT Press.

102. Aragones, J. I., & Arredondo, J. M. (1985). Structure of urban cognitive maps. *Journal of Environmental Psychology, 5,* 197–212.

103. Magana, J. R. (1978). *An empirical and interdisciplinary test of a theory of urban perception.* Doctoral dissertation, University of California, Irvine.

104. Downs, R. M. (1981). Maps and metaphors. *Professional Geographer, 33,* 287–293.

105. See note 62.

106. Chase, W. G., & Chi, M. T. H. (1981). Cognitive skill: Implications for spatial skills in large-scale environments. In J. H. Harvey (Ed.), *Cognition, social behavior, and the environment.* Hillsdale, NJ: Erlbaum.

107. O'Neill, M. J. (1991). Evaluation of a conceptual model of architectural legibility. *Environment and Behavior, 23,* 259–284.

108. Golledge, R. G. (1976). Methods and methodological issues in environmental cognition research. In G. T. Moore and R. G. Golledge (Eds.), *Environmental knowing: Theories, research, and methods.* Stroudsburg, PA: Dowden, Hutchinson and Ross.

109. Aadland, J., Beatty, W. W., & Maki, R. H. (1985). Spatial memory for children and adults assessed in the radial maze. *Developmental Psychobiology, 18,* 163–172.

110. O'Neill, M. J. (1992). Effects of familiarity and plan complexity on wayfinding in simulated buildings. *Journal of Environmental Psychology, 12,* 319–327.

111. Hart, R. (1979). *Children's experience of place.* New York: Irvington.

112. Evans, G. W. (1980). Environmental cognition. *Psychological Bulletin, 88,* 259–267.

113. Blades, M. (1990). The reliability of data collected from sketch maps. *Journal of Environmental Psychology, 10,* 327–339.

114. Magana, J. R., Evans, G. W., & Romney, A. K. (1981). Scaling techniques in the analysis of environmental cognition data. *Professional Geographer, 33,* 294–301.

115. Sonnenfeld, J. (1985). Tests of spatial skill: A validation problem. *Man-Environment Systems, 15,* 107– 120.

116. Holahan, C. J., & Dobrowolny, M. B. (1978). Cognitive and behavioral correlates of the spatial environment: An interactional analysis. *Environment and Behavior, 10,* 317–333.

117. O'Neill, M. (1991). A biologically based model of spatial cognition and wayfinding. *Journal of Environmental Psychology, 11,* 299–320.

118. Sherman, R. C., Croxton, J., & Giovanatto, J. (1979). Investigating cognitive representations of spatial relations. *Environment and Behavior, 11,* 209–226.

119. See note 49.

120. Waller, G. (1986). The development of route knowledge: Multiple dimensions? *Journal of Environmental Psychology, 6,* 109–119.

121. Downs, R. M., & Siegel, A. W. (1981). On mapping researchers mapping children mapping space. In L. S. Liben, A. H. Patterson, & N. Newcombe (Eds.), *Spatial representation and behavior across the life span.* New York: Academic Press.

122. Moore, G. T. (1979). Knowing about environmental knowing: The current state of theory and research on environmental cognition. *Environment and Behavior, 11,* 33–70.

123. Bryant, K. J. (1984). Methodological convergence as an issue within environmental cognition research. *Journal of Environmental Psychology, 4,* 43–60.

124. Bryant, K. J. (1991). Geographical/spatial orientation ability within real-world and simulated large-scale environments. *Multivariate Behavioral Research, 26,* 109–136.

125. Webley, P. (1981). Sex differences in home range and cognitive maps in eight-year-old children. *Journal of Environmental Psychology, 1,* 293–302.

126. Rovine, M. J., & Weisman, G. D. (1989). Sketch-map variables as predictors of way-finding performance. *Journal of Environmental Psychology, 9,* 217–232.

127. Nasar, J. L. (1984). Visual preferences in urban street scenes: A cross-cultural comparison between Japan and the United States. *Journal of Cross-Cultural Psychology, 15,* 79–93.

128. Karan, P. P., Bladen, W. A., & Singh, G. (1980). Slum dwellers' and squatters' images of the city. *Environment and Behavior, 12,* 81–100.

129. Herman, J. F., Miller, B. S., & Shiraki, J. H. (1987). The influence of affective associations on the development of cognitive maps of large environments. *Journal of Environmental Psychology, 7,* 89–98.

130. Coshall, J. T., & Potter, R. B. (1987). Social psychology variations in the distance cognitions of urban consumers in Britain. *Journal of Social Psychology, 127,* 611–618.

131. Janowsky, J. S., Oviatt, S. K., & Orwoll, E. S. (1994). Testosterone influences spatial cognition in older men. *Behavioral Neuroscience, 108,* 325–332.

132. Sako, T., Ando, T., & Fukui, I. (1990). Effects of orientation on direction judgment of places. *Proceedings of the 54th Annual Convention of the Japanese Psychological Association, 54,* 533.

133. Hart, R. A., & Moore, G. T. (1973). The development of spatial cognition: A review. In R. M. Downs & D. Stea (Eds.), *Image and environment: Cognitive mapping and spatial behavior.* Chicago: Aldine.

134. See note 133.

135. See note 112.

136. Spencer, C., & Darvizeh, Z. (1981). The case for developing a cognitive environmental psychology that does not underestimate the abilities of young children. *Journal of Environmental Psychology, 1,* 21–31.

137. Acredolo, L. P. (1988). From signal to "symbol": The development of landmark knowledge from 9 to 13 months. *British Journal of Developmental Psychology, 6,* 369– 372.

138. Biel, A. (1982). Children's spatial representation of their neighbourhood: A step towards a general spatial competence. *Journal of Environmental Psychology, 2,* 193–200.

139. Matthews, M. H. (1985). Young children's representations of the environment: A comparison of techniques. *Journal of Environmental Psychology, 5,* 261–278.

140. Conning, A. M., & Byrne, R. W. (1984). Pointing to preschool children's spatial competence: A study in natural settings. *Journal of Environmental Psychology, 4,* 165–175.

141. Neisser, U. (1976). *Cognition and reality.* San Francisco: Freeman.

142. See note 124.

143. Ohta, R. J., & Kirasic, K. C. (1983). The investigation of environmental learning in the elderly. In G. D. Rowles & R. J. Ohta (Eds.), *Aging and milieu.* New York: Academic Press.

144. Pearce, P. L. (1981). Route maps: A study of traveller's perceptions of a section of countryside. *Journal of Environmental Psychology, 1,* 141–155.

145. Aubrey, J. B., & Dobbs, A. R. (1989). Age differences in extrapersonal orientation as measured by performance on the Locomotor Maze. *Canadian Journal on Aging, 8,* 333–342.

146. Kirasic, K. C., Allen, G. L., & Haggerty, D. (1992). Age-related differences in adults' macrospatial cognitive processes. *Experimental Aging Research, 18,* 33–39.

147. Aubrey, J. B., & Dobbs, A. R. (1990). Age and sex differences in the mental realignment of maps. *Experimental Aging Research, 16,* 133–139.

148. McCormack, P. (1982). Coding of spatial by young and elderly adults. *Journal of Gerontology, 37,* 80–86.

149. Kirasic, K. C. (1991). Spatial cognition and behavior in young and elderly adults: Implications for learning new environments. *Psychology and Aging, 6,* 10–18.

150. Georgemiller, R., & Hassan, F. (1986). Spatial competence: Assessment and topographical memory in normal aging. *Clinical Gerontologists, 5,* 19–38.

151. See note 149.

152. See note 149.

153. See note 150.

154. See note 146.

155. See note 148.

156. See note 144.

157. Evans, G. W., Smith, C., & Pezdek, K. (1982). Cognitive maps and urban form. *Journal of the American Planning Association, 48,* 232–244.

158. Porteous, J. D. (1977). *Environment and behavior: Planning and everyday life.* Don Mills, Ontario: Addison-Wesley.

159. Evans, G. W., Brennan, P. L., Skorpanich, M. A., & Held, D. (1984). Cognitive mapping and elderly adults: Verbal and location memory for urban landmarks. *Journal of Gerontology, 39,* 432–452.

160. See note 144.

161. Kirasic, K. C., & Mathes, E. A. (1990). Effects of different means for conveying environmental information on elderly adults' spatial cognition and behavior. *Environment and Behavior, 22,* 591–607.

162. Pearson, J. L., & Ialongo, N. S. (1986). The relationship between spatial ability and environmental knowledge. *Journal of Environmental Psychology, 6,* 299–304.

163. Pearson, J. L., & Ferguson, L. R. (1989). Gender differences in patterns of spatial ability, environmental cognition, and math and English achievement in later adolescence. *Adolescence, 24,* 421–431.

164. Simon, S. L., Walsh, D. L., Regnier, V. A., & Krauss, I. K. (1992). Spatial cognition and neighborhood use: The relationship in older adults. *Psychology and Aging, 7,* 389–934.

165. See note 124.

166. Weisman, J. (1981). Evaluating architectural legibility: Wayfinding in the built environment. *Environment and Behavior, 13,* 189–204.

167. Garling, T., Lindberg, E., & Mantyla, T. (1983). Orientation in buildings: Effects of familiarity, visual access, and orientation aids. *Journal of Applied Psychology, 68,* 177–186.

168. Schouela, D. A., Steinberg, L. M., Levelton, L. B., & Wapner, S. (1980). Development of the cognitive organization of an environment. *Canadian Journal of Behaviourial Science, 12,* 1–16.

169. Giraudo, M., & Peruch, P. (1988). Spatio-temporal aspects of the mental representation of urban space. *Journal of Environmental Psychology, 8,* 9–17.

170. Foley, J. E., & Cohen, A. J. (1984). Mental mapping of a megastructure. *Canadian Journal of Psychology, 38,* 440–453.

171. See note 110.

172. Kirisic, K. C., Allen, G. L., & Siegel, A. W. (1984). Expression of configurational knowledge of large-scale environments: Students' performance of cognitive tasks. *Environment and Behavior, 16,* 687–712.

173. Garling, T., Book, A., Lindberg, E., & Nilsson, T. (1981). Memory for the spatial layout of the everyday physical environment: Factors affecting rate of acquisition. *Journal of Environmental Psychology, 1,* 263–277.

174. Cohen, R., Weatherford, D. L., Lomenick, T., & Koeller, K. (1979). Development of spatial representations: Role of task demands and familiarity with the environment. *Child Development, 50,* 1257–1260.

175. Moeser, S. D. (1988). Cognitive mapping in a complex building. *Environment and Behavior, 20,* 21–49.

176. Carr, S., & Schissler, D. (1969). The city as a trip: Perceptual selection and memory in the view from the road. *Environment and Behavior, 1,* 7–36.

177. See note 144.

178. Orleans, P. (1973). Differential cognition of urban residents: Effects of social scale on mapping. In R. M. Downs & D. Stea

(Eds.), *Image and environment: Cognitive mapping and spatial behavior.* Chicago: Aldine.

179. Windley, P. G., & Vandeventer, W. H. (1982). Environmental cognition of small rural towns: The case for older residents. *Journal of Environmental Psychology, 2,* 285–294.

180. Karan, P. P., Bladen, W. A., & Singh, G. (1980). Slum dwellers' and squatters' images of the city. *Environment and Behavior, 12,* 81–100.

181. Ward, S. L., Newcombe, N., & Overton, W. F. (1986). Turn left at the church, or three miles north: A study of direction giving and sex differences. *Environment and Behavior, 18,* 192–213.

182. See note 147.

183. Webley, P., & Whalley, A. (1987). Sex differences in children's environmental cognition. *Journal of Social Psychology, 127,* 223–225.

184. See note 124.

185. See note 173.

186. See note 172.

187. See note 112.

188. See note 163.

189. Webley, P. (1981). Sex differences in home range and cognitive maps in eight-year-old children. *Journal of Environmental Psychology, 1,* 293–302.

190. Matthews, M. H. (1986). Gender, graphicacy and geography. *Educational Review, 38,* 259–271.

191. Matthews, M. H. (1986). The influence of gender on the environmental cognition of young boys and girls. *Journal of Genetic Psychology, 147,* 295–302.

192. See note 170.

193. See note 179.

194. Orleans, P., & Schmidt, S. (1972). Mapping the city: Environmental cognition of urban residents. In W. J. Mitchell (Ed.), *Environmental design: Research and practice.* Los Angeles: University of California.

195. See note 181.

196. Antes, J. R., McBride, R. B., & Collins, J. D. (1988). The effect of a new city traffic route on the cognitive maps of its residents. *Environment and Behavior, 20,* 75–91.

197. Byrne, R. (1979). Memory for urban geography. *Quarterly Journal of Experimental Psychology, 15,* 157–163.

198. See note 112.

199. Sadalla, E. K., & Montello, D. R. (1989). Remembering changes in direction. *Environment and Behavior, 21,* 346–363.

200. Montello, D. R. (1991). Spatial orientation and the angularity of urban routes: A field study. *Environment and Behavior, 23,* 47–69.

201. Stevens, A., & Coupe, P. (1978). Distortions in judged spatial relations. *Cognitive Psychology, 10,* 422–437.

202. Allen, G. L., & Kirasic, K. C. (1985). Effects of the cognitive organization of route knowledge on judgements of macrospatial distance. *Memory and Cognition, 13,* 218–227.

203. See note 101.

204. Appleyard, D. (1976). *Planning a pluralistic city.* Cambridge, MA: MIT Press.

205. Tzamir, Y. (1975). *The impact of spatial regularity and irregularity on cognitive mapping* (Technical Report). Haifa, Israel:

Technion-Israel Institute of Technology, Center for Urban and Regional Studies.

206. Canter, D., & Tagg, S. K. (1975). Distance estimation in cities. *Environment and Behavior, 7*, 59–80.

207. Holahan, C. J., & Sorenson, P. F. (1985). The role of figural organization in city imageability: An information processing analysis. *Journal of Environmental Psychology, 5*, 279–286.

208. See note 196.

209. Hart, R. A., & Moore, G. T. (1973). The development of spatial cognition: A review. In R. M. Downs & D. Stea (Eds.), *Image and environment: Cognitive mapping and spatial behavior.* Chicago: Aldine.

210. Siegel, A. W., & White, S. H. (1975). The development of spatial representations of large-scale environments. In H. W. Reese (Ed.), *Advances in child development and behavior* (Vol. 10). New York: Academic Press.

211. See note 204.

212. See note 101.

213. Evans, G. W., Marrero, D. G., & Butler, P. A. (1981). Environmental learning and cognitive mapping. *Environment and Behavior, 13*, 83–104.

214. See note 173.

215. See note 112.

216. Weisman, G. D. (1979). *Wayfinding in the built environment: A study in architectural legibility.* Doctoral dissertation, University of Michigan, Ann Arbor.

217. Garling, T., Book, A., & Lindberg, E. (1986). Spatial orientation and wayfinding in the designed environment: A conceptual analysis and some suggestions for postoccupancy evaluation. *Journal of Architectural Planning and Research, 3*, 55–64.

218. See note 166.

219. O'Neill, M. J. (1991). Effects of signage and floor plan configuration on wayfinding accuracy. *Environment and Behavior, 23*, 553–574.

220. Peponis, J., Zimring, C., & Choi, Y. K. (1990). Finding the building in wayfinding. *Environment and Behavior, 22*, 555–590.

221. Hunt, M. E. (1985). Enhancing a building's imageability. *Journal of Architectural Planning and Research, 2*, 151–168.

222. Wolkomir, R. (1987). It is easy to get bushed when you're threading a maze. *Smithsonian*, 109–118.

223. See note 204.

224. See note 157.

225. Wohlwill, J. F. (1966). The physical environment: A problem for a psychology of stimulation. *Journal of Social Issues, 22*(4), 29–38.

226. Helson, H. (1964). *Adaptation-level theory.* New York: Harper and Row.

227. Suedfeld, P., Landon, P. B., & Ballard, E. J. (1983). Effects of reduced stimulation on divergent and convergent thinking. *Environment and Behavior, 15*, 727–738.

228. Kalish, N., Landon, P. B., Rank, D. S., & Suedfeld, P. (1983). Stimulus tasks and environmental characteristics as factors in the cognitive processing of English sentences. *Bulletin of the Psychonomic Society, 21*, 1–3.

229. See note 22.

230. See note 107.

231. See note 204.

232. See note 157.

233. Bartram, D. J. (1980). Comprehending spatial information: The relative efficiency of different methods of presenting information about bus routes. *Journal of Applied Psychology, 65*, 103–110.

234. Garland, H. C., Haynes, J. J., & Grubb, G. C. (1979). Transit map color coding and street detail: Effects on trip planning performance. *Environment and Behavior, 11*, 162–184.

235. Bronzaft, A. L., Dobrow, S. B., & O'Hanlon, T. J. (1976). Spatial orientation in a subway. *Environment and Behavior, 8*, 575–594.

236. Wright, P., Hull, A. J., & Lickorish, A. (1993). Navigation in a hospital outpatients' department: The merits of maps and wall signs. *Journal of Architectural and Planning Research, 10*, 76–89.

237. See note 122.

238. Pick, H. L. (1976). Transactional-constructivist approach to environmental knowing: A commentary. In G. T. Moore & R. G. Golledge (Eds.), *Environmental knowing: Theories, research, and methods.* Stroudsburg, PA: Dowden, Hutchinson and Ross.

239. See note 238.

240. Golledge, R. G., Smith, T. R., Pellegrino, J. W., Doherty, S., & Marshall, S. P. (1985). A conceptual model and empirical analysis of children's acquisition of spatial knowledge. *Journal of Environmental Psychology, 5*, 125–152.

241. Leiser, D., & Zilbershatz, A. (1989). The traveller: A computational model of spatial network learning. *Environment and Behavior, 21*, 435–463.

242. Coucleis, H., Golledge, R. G., Gale, N., & Tobler, W. (1987). Exploring the anchor-point hypothesis of spatial cognition. *Journal of Environmental Psychology, 7*, 99–122.

243. Sadalla, E. K. (1988). Landmarks in memory. Conference on Landmarks in Spatial Cognition and Spatial Development. *British Journal of Developmental Psychology, 6*, 386–388.

244. Presson, C. C., & Montello, D. R. (1988). Points of reference in spatial cognition: Stalking the elusive landmark. *British Journal of Developmental Psychology, 6*, 378–381.

245. See note 242.

246. Gotts, N. M. (1989). Unplanned wayfinding in path-networks: A theoretical study of human problem solving. *Dissertation Abstracts International, 50*(4–B), 1670.

247. Mutter, L. R., & Westphal, J. M. (1986). Perspectives on neighborhoods as park-planning units. *Journal of Architectural Planning and Research, 3*, 149–160.

248. Cornell, E. H., & Heth, C. D. (1984). Report of a missing child. In S. H. White (Chair), *Human development in the real world.* Symposium at the annual meetings of the American Psychological Association, Toronto.

249. Taylor, B., & Taylor, A. (1993). Wayfinding training for the severely mentally ill. *Families in Society, 74*, 434–440.

250. Saisa, J., & Garling, T. (1987). Sequential spatial choices in the large-scale environment. *Environment and Behavior, 19*, 614–635.

251. Halperin, W. C. (1986). Spatial cognition and consumer behavior. *Dissertation Abstracts International, 46*(11-A), 3458.

252. Garling, T., Book, A., & Lindberg, E. (1984). Cognitive mapping of large-scale environments: The interrelationship of action

plans, acquisition, and orientation. *Environment and Behavior, 16,* 3–34.

253. Russell, J. A., & Ward, L. M. (1982). Environmental psychology. *Annual Review of Psychology, 33,* 651–688.

254. Gauvain, M. (1993). The development of spatial thinking in everyday activity. *Developmental Review, 13,* 92–121.

255. Ward, L. M., Snodgrass, J., Chew, B., & Russell, J. A. (1988). The role of plans in cognitive and affective responses to places. *Journal of Environmental Psychology, 8,* 1–8.

256. See note 254.

257. Passini, R. (1984). Spatial representations, a wayfinding perspective. *Journal of Environmental Psychology, 4,* 153–164.

258. Smith, C. J., & Patterson, G. E. (1980). Cognitive mapping and the subjective geography of crime. In D. E. Georges-Abeyie & K. D. Harries (Eds.), *Crime: A spatial perspective.* New York: Columbia University Press.

259. Brantingham P. L., & Brantingham, P. J. (1993). Nodes, paths and edges: Considerations on the complexity of crime and the physical environment. *Journal of Environmental Psychology, 13,* 3–28.

260. Pyle, G. F. (1980). Systematic sociospatial variation in perceptions of crime location and severity. In D. E. Georges-Abeyie & K. D. Harries (Eds.), *Crime: A spatial perspective.* New York: Columbia University Press.

261. Canter, D., & Larkin, P. (1993). The environmental range of serial rapists. *Journal of Environmental Psychology, 13,* 63–70.

262. O'Keefe, J., & Nadel, L. (1974). Maps in the brain. *New Scientist,* 749–751.

263. O'Keefe, J., & Nadel, L. (1978). *The hippocampus as a cognitive map.* Oxford: Clarendon.

264. Tolman, E. C. (1932). *Purposive behavior in animals and men.* New York: Century.

265. Tolman, E. C. (1948). Cognitive maps in rats and men. *Psychological Review, 55,* 189–208.

266. Beatty, W. W., & Bernstein, N. (1989). Geographical knowledge in patients with Alzheimer's disease. *Journal of Geriatric Psychiatry and Neurology, 2,* 76–82.

267. De Renzi, E. (1982). Memory disorders following focal neocortical damage. *Philosophical Transactions of the Royal Society of London, 298,* 73–83.

268. Kritchevshy, M. (1988). The elementary spatial functions of the brain. In J. Stiles-Davis, M. Kritchevsky, & U. Bellugi (Eds.), *Spatial cognition: Brain bases and development.* Hillsdale, NJ: Erlbaum.

269. Neisser, U. (1976). *Cognition and reality.* San Francisco: Freeman.

270. Kosslyn, S. M. (1975). Information representation in visual images. *Cognitive Psychology, 7,* 341–370.

271. See note 112.

272. Lieblich, I., & Arbib, M. A. (1982). Multiple representations of space underlying behavior. *The Behavioral and Brain Sciences, 5,* 627–659.

273. Levine, M. (1982). You-are-here maps: Psychological considerations. *Environment and Behavior, 14,* 221–237.

274. Levine, M., Marchon, I., & Hanley, G. (1984). The placement and misplacement of you-are-here maps. *Environment and Behavior, 16,* 139–157.

275. Warren, D. H., Rossano, M. J., & Wear, T. D. (1990). Perception of map-environment correspondence: The roles of features and alignment. *Ecological Psychology, 2,* 131–150.

276. Warren, D. H., & Scott, T. E. (1993). Map alignment in travelling multisegment routes. *Environment and Behavior, 25,* 643–666.

277. Butler, D. L., Acquino, A. L., Hissong, A. A., & Scott, P. A. (1993). Wayfinding by newcomers in a complex building. *Human Factors, 35,* 159–173.

278. Evans, G. W., Fellows, J., Zorn, M., & Doty, K. (1980). Cognitive mapping and architecture. *Journal of Applied Psychology, 65,* 474–478.

279. Carpman, J. R., Grant, M. A., & Simmons, D. A. (1983–84). Wayfinding in the hospital environment: The impact of various floor numbering alternatives. *Journal of Environmental Systems, 13,* 353–364.

Chapter 3

1. Hume, D. (1757). Of the standard of taste (An essay). *Four Dissertations.* Modern reference: Miller, E. F. (Ed.). (1987). Of the standard of taste. *Essays: Moral, political and literary* (p. 230). Indianapolis: Liberty Classics.

2. Craik, K. H., & Zube, E. H. (Eds.). (1976). *Perceiving environmental quality.* New York: Plenum.

3. Heberlein, T. A. (1989). Attitudes and environmental management. *Journal of Social Issues, 45*(1), 37–57.

4. Kinnear, T. C., & Taylor, J. R. (1973). The effect of ecological concern on brand perceptions. *Journal of Marketing Research, 10,* 191–197.

5. Larsen, K. S. (1994). Attitudes toward the transportation of nuclear waste: The development of a Likert-type scale. *Journal of Social Psychology, 134,* 27–34.

6. Maloney, M. P., & Ward, M. O. (1973). Ecology: Let's hear from the people. *American Psychologist, 28,* 583–586.

7. Maloney, M. P., Ward, M. O., & Braucht, C. N. (1975). A revised scale for the measurement of ecological attitudes and knowledge. *American Psychologist, 30,* 787–790.

8. Weigel, R., & Wiegel, J. (1978). Environmental concern: The development of a measure. *Environment and Behavior, 10,* 3–15.

9. Dunlap, R. E., & Van Liere, K. D. (1978). The "New Environmental Paradigm." *Journal of Environmental Education, 9*(4), 10–19.

10. Noe, F. P., & Snow, R. (1990). The New Environmental Paradigm and further scale analysis. *Journal of Environmental Education, 21*(4), 20–26.

11. Schahn, J., & Holzer, E. (1990). Konstruktion, validerung und anwendung von skalen zur erfassung des individuellen umweltbewu. (Construction, validation, and application of scales for the measurement of individual environmental concern). *Zeitschrift fur Differentielle und Diagnostische Psychologie, 11,* 185–204.

12. Banerjee, B., & McKeage, K. (1994). How green is my value: Exploring the relationship between environmentalism and materialism. *Advances in Consumer Research, 21,* 147–152.

13. Sohr, S. (1994). Ist es schon "funf nach zwolf"?—Entwicklung einer skala zu "okologischer hoffnungslosigkeit." (Is it "five past twelve" already? Development of a new instrument to measure "ecological hopelessness.") *Praxis der Kinderpsychologie und Kinderpsychiatrie, 43,* 203–208.

14. Larsen, K. S., Groberg, D. H., Simmons, D. D., & Ommundsen, R. (1993). Authoritarianism, perspectives on the environment, and work values among social science students in former socialist and Western societies. *Social Behavior & Personality, 21,* 251–263.

15. Bowler, R. M., & Schwarzer, R. (1991). Environmental anxiety: Assessing emotional distress and concerns after toxin exposure. *Anxiety Research, 4,* 167–180.

16. Brown-Allen, B. P. (1992). The development of the Test for the Environmental Attitudes of Children. *Dissertation Abstracts International, 52*(12–A), 4200–4201.

17. Simmons, D. D., Binney, S. E., & Dodd, B. (1992). Valuing "a clean environment": Factor location, norms, and relation to risks. *Journal of Social Behavior and Personality, 7,* 649–658.

18. Thompson, J. C., & Gasteiger, E. L. (1985). Environmental attitude survey of university students: 1971 vs. 1981. *Journal of Environmental Education, 17*(1), 13–22.

19. Arcury, T. A., & Christianson, E. H. (1990). Environmental worldview in response to environmental problems: Kentucky 1984 and 1988 compared. *Environment and Behavior, 22,* 387–407.

20. Krause, D. (1993). Environmental consciousness: An empirical study. *Environment and Behavior, 25,* 126–142.

21. See note 17.

22. Gigliotti, L. M. (1992). Environmental attitudes: 20 years of change. *Journal of Environmental Education, 24*(1), 15–26.

23. Herrera, M. (1992). Environmentalism and political participation: Toward a new system of social beliefs and values? *Journal of Applied Social Psychology, 22,* 657–676.

24. Dodds, J., & Lin, C. (1992). Chinese teenagers' concerns about the future: A cross-national comparison. *Adolescence, 27,* 481–486.

25. Mukherjee, B. N. (1993). Public response to air pollution in Calcutta proper. *Journal of Environmental Psychology, 13,* 207–230.

26. Srichai, N. K. (1988). A study of environmental perceptions and attitudes of selected university students in Thailand. *Dissertation Abstracts International, 50*(4–A), 833.

27. Smythe, P. C., & Brook, R. C. (1980). Environmental concerns and actions: A social-psychological investigation. *Canadian Journal of Behavioral Science, 12,* 175–186.

28. Van Liere, K. V., & Dunlap, R. E. (1981). Environmental concern: Does it make a difference how it's measured? *Environment and Behavior, 13,* 651–676.

29. Painter, J., Semenik, R., & Belk, R. (1983). Is there a generalized energy conservation ethic? A comparison of the determinants of gasoline and home heating energy conservation. *Journal of Economic Psychology, 3,* 317–331.

30. MacGregor, D. (1991). Worry over technological activities and life concerns. *Risk Analysis, 11,* 315–324.

31. Verplanken, B. (1989). Beliefs, attitudes, and intentions toward nuclear energy before and after Chernobyl in a longitudinal within-subjects design. *Environment and Behavior, 21,* 371–392.

32. Midden, C. J., & Verplanken, B. (1990). The stability of nuclear attitudes after Chernobyl. Special Issue: Psychological fallout from the Chernobyl nuclear accident. *Journal of Environmental Psychology, 10,* 111–119.

33. See note 25.

34. Gutteling, J. M., & Wiegman, O. (1993). Gender-specific reactions to environmental hazards in the Netherlands. *Sex Roles, 28,* 433–447.

35. Zhang, J. (1993). Environmental hazards in the Chinese public's eyes. *Risk Analysis, 13,* 509–513.

36. Gifford, R., Hay, R., & Boros, K. (1982–1983). Individual differences in environmental attitudes. *Journal of Environmental Education, 14*(2), 19–23.

37. Arcury, T. A., & Christianson, E. H. (1993). Rural-urban differences in environmental knowledge and actions. *Journal of Environmental Education, 25*(1), 19–25.

38. Stern, P. C., Dietz, T., & Kalof, L. (1993). Value orientations, gender, and environmental concern. *Environment and Behavior, 25,* 322–348.

39. Schahn, J., & Holzer, E. (1990). Studies of individual environmental concern: The role of knowledge, gender, and background variables. *Environment and Behavior, 22,* 767–786.

40. Grieve, K. W., & Van Staden, F. J. (1985). Environmental concern in South Africa: An attitudinal study. *South African Journal of Psychology, 15,* 135–136.

41. Arcury, T. A., Scollay, S. J., & Johnson, T. P. (1987). Sex differences in environmental concern and knowledge: The case of acid rain. *Sex Roles, 16,* 463–472.

42. Honnold, J. A. (1984–1985). Age and environmental concern: Some specification of effects. *Journal of Environmental Education, 16*(1), 4–9.

43. See note 35.

44. See note 37.

45. Szagun, G., & Mesenholl, E. (1993). Environmental ethics: An empirical study of West German adolescents. *Journal of Environmental Education, 25*(1), 37–44.

46. See note 42.

47. Palmer, J. A. (1993). Development of concern for the environment and formative experiences of educators. *Journal of Environmental Education, 24*(3), 26–30.

48. Eiser, J. R., Hannover, B., Mann, L., Morin, M., et al. (1990). Nuclear attitudes after Chernobyl: A cross-national study. *Journal of Environmental Psychology, 10,* 101–110.

49. Schultz, P. W., & Stone, W. F. (1994). Authoritarianism and attitudes toward the environment. *Environment and Behavior, 26,* 25–37.

50. Eckberg, D. L., & Blocker, T. J. (1989). Varieties of religious involvement and environmental concerns: Testing the Lynn White thesis. *Journal for the Scientific Study of Religion, 28,* 509–517.

51. Greeley, A. (1993). Religion and attitudes toward the environment. *Journal for the Scientific Study of Religion, 32,* 19–28.

52. Newhouse, C. H. (1986). An investigation of the relationship between environmental behaviors and personality factors in church members and environmentalists. (Doctoral dissertation,

Michigan State University, 1986). *Dissertation Abstracts International, 46*, 3884A.

53. Hand, C. M., & Van Liere, K. D. (1984). Religion, mastery-over-nature, and environmental concern. *Social Forces, 63*, 555–570.

54. Balderjahn, I. (1988). Personality variables and environmental attitudes as predictors of ecologically responsible consumption patterns. Special Issue: Marketing research. *Journal of Business Research, 17*, 51–56.

55. Howard, G. S., Delgado, E., Miller, D., & Gubbins, S. (1993). Transforming values into actions: Ecological preservation through energy conservation. *Counseling Psychologist, 21*, 582–596.

56. Ray, J. J. (1981, March). Are environmental activists middle class? *Tableaus*, pp. 6–7.

57. Howard, G. S. (1993). Thoughts on saving our planet: Political, economic, cultural, and bureaucratic impediments to ecological activism. *Counseling Psychologist, 21*, 597–617.

58. See note 49.

59. Borden, R. J., & Francis, J. L. (1978). Who cares about ecology? Personality and sex differences in environmental concern. *Journal of Personality, 46*, 190–203.

60. Swearingen, T. C. (1990). Moral development and environmental ethics. *Dissertation Abstracts International, 50*(12–B, Part 1), 5905.

61. Axelrod, L. J., & Lehman, D. R. (1993). Responding to environmental concerns: What factors guide individual action? *Journal of Environmental Psychology, 13*, 149–159.

62. Kinnear, T. C., Taylor, J. R., & Ahmed, S. A. (1974). Ecologically concerned consumers: Who are they? *Journal of Marketing, 38*, 20–24.

63. See note 61.

64. Thompson, S. C. G., & Barton, M. A. (1994). Ecocentric and anthropocentric attitudes toward the environment. *Journal of Environmental Psychology, 14*, 149–157.

65. di Nenna, P. M., Paolillo, V., & Giuliani, M. M. (1987). Le convinzioni ambientaliste dei cacciatori Italiani: Indagine conoscitiva per mezzo dell' "I.C.A. test." (Environmental values of Italian hunters: A cognitive study based on the ICA test). *Movimento, 3*, 104–110.

66. Ostman, R. E., & Parker, J. L. (1987). Impact of education, age, newspapers, and television on environmental knowledge, concerns and behaviors. *Journal of Environmental Education, 19*(1), 3–9.

67. Lyons, E., & Breakwell, G. M. (1994). Factors predicting environmental concern and indifferences in 13- to 16-year-olds. *Environment and Behavior, 26*, 223–238.

68. Greenwald, J. (1993). Environmental attitudes: A structural developmental model. *Dissertation Abstracts International, 53*(12–B), 6550.

69. Synodinos, N. E. (1990). Environmental attitudes and knowledge: A comparison of marketing and business students with other groups. *Journal of Business Research, 20*, 161–170.

70. McKnight, M. D. (1991). Socialization into environmentalism: Development of attitudes toward the environment and technology. *Dissertation Abstracts International, 52*(1–A), 301.

71. See note 36.

72. Hausbeck, K. W., Milbrath, L. W., & Enright, S. M. (1992). Environmental knowledge, awareness and concern among 11th-grade students: New York state. *Journal of Environmental Education, 24*(1), 27–34.

73. See note 66.

74. See note 37.

75. See note 67.

76. Elliott, S. J., Taylor, S. M., Walter, S., Stieb, D., Frank, J., & Eyles, J. (1993). Modelling psychosocial effects of exposure to solid waste facilities. *Social Science and Medicine, 37*, 791–804.

77. Baldassare, M., & Katz, C. (1992). The personal threat of environmental problems as predictor of environmental practices. *Environment and Behavior, 24*, 602–616.

78. Keen, M. (1991). The effect of the Sunship Earth program on knowledge and attitude development. *Journal of Environmental Education, 22*(3), 28–32.

79. Bull, J. N. (1993). The effect of participation in an environmental action program on empowerment, interest, and problem-solving skills of inner city students. *Dissertation Abstracts International, 53*(10–B), 5481.

80. Leeming, F. C., Dwyer, W. O., Porter, B. E., & Cobern, M. K. (1993). Outcome research in environmental education: A critical review. *Journal of Environmental Education, 24*(4), 8–21.

81. Ramsey, J. M., & Hungerford, H. (1989). The effects of issue investigation and action training on environmental behavior in seventh grade students. *Journal of Environmental Education, 20*(4), 29–34.

82. Ramsey, J. M. (1993). The effects of issue investigation and action training on eighth-grade students' environmental behavior. *Journal of Environmental Education, 24*(3), 31–36.

83. Jordan, J. R., Hungerford, H. R., & Tomera, A. N. (1986). Effects of two residential environmental workshops on high school students. *Journal of Environmental Education, 18*(1), 15–22.

84. Yount, J. R., & Horton, P. B. (1992). Factors influencing environmental attitude: The relationship between environmental attitude defensibility and cognitive reasoning level. *Journal of Research in Science Teaching, 29*, 1059–1078.

85. Gillett, D. P., Thomas, G. P., Skok, R. L., & McLaughlin, T. F. (1991). The effects of wilderness camping and hiking on the self-concept and the environmental attitudes and knowledge of twelfth graders. *Journal of Environmental Education, 22*(3), 33–44.

86. Shepard, C. L., & Speelman, L. R. (1985–1986). Affecting environmental attitudes through outdoor education. *Journal of Environmental Education, 17*(1), 20–23.

87. Newhouse, N. (1990). Implications of attitude and behavior research for environmental conservation. *Journal of Environmental Education, 22*(2), 26–32.

88. Boerschig, S., & de Young, R. (1993). Evaluation of selected recycling curricula: Educating the green citizen. *Journal of Environmental Education, 24*(3), 17–22.

89. Dresner, M. (1989–1990). Changing energy end-use patterns as a means of reducing global-warming trends. *Journal of Environmental Education, 21*(2), 41–46.

90. Monroe, M. C. (1992). The effect of interesting environmental stories on knowledge and action-taking attitudes. *Dissertation Abstracts International, 52*(11–A), 3867.

91. Hine, D. W., & Gifford, R. (1991). Fear appeals, individual differences, and environmental concern. *Journal of Environmental Education, 23*(1), 36–41.

92. Riesenberg, R. D. (1991, August). *Was Earth Day a moving experience? Pre- and post-environmental attitudes in a midwestern suburban population sample?* Paper presented at the 99th Annual Convention of the American Psychological Association, San Francisco.

93. O'Riordan, T. (1976). Attitudes, behavior, and environmental policy issues. In I. Altman & J. F. Wohlwill (Eds.), *Human behavior and environment: Advances in theory and research* ((Vol. 1). New York: Plenum.

94. Scott, D., & Willits, F. K. (1994). Environmental attitudes and behavior: A Pennsylvania survey. *Environment and Behavior, 26*, 239–260.

95. Dispoto, R. G. (1977). Interrelationships among measures of environmental activity, emotionality, and knowledge. *Education and Psychological Measurement, 37*, 451–459.

96. Borden, R. J., & Schettino, A. P. (1979). Determinants of environmentally responsible behavior. *Journal of Environmental Education, 10*(4), 35–39.

97. Syme, G. J., & Nancarrow, B. E. (1992). Predicting public involvement in urban water management and planning. *Environment and Behavior, 24*, 738–758.

98. Manzo, L. C., & Weinstein, N. D. (1987). Behavioral commitment to environmental protection: A study of active and nonactive members of the Sierra Club. *Environment and Behavior, 19*, 673–694.

99. Diekman, A., & Preisendorfer, P. (1992). Personliches umweltverhalten: Diskrepanzen zwischen anspruch und wirklichkeit. (Ecology in everyday life: Inconsistencies between environmental attitudes and behavior). *Kolner Zeitschrift fur Soziologie und Sozialpsychologie, 44*, 226–251.

100. Heberlein, T. A., & Black, J. S. (1981). Cognitive consistency and environmental action. *Environment and Behavior, 13*, 717–734.

101. Weigel, R. H., & Newman, L. S. (1976). Increasing attitude-behavior correspondence by broadening the scope of behavioral measure. *Journal of Personality and Social Psychology, 33*, 793–802.

102. Lynne, G. D., & Rola, L. R. (1988). Improving attitude-behavior prediction models with economic variables: Farmer actions toward soil conservation. *Journal of Social Psychology, 128*, 19–28.

103. Verplanken, B. (1989). Involvement and need for cognition as moderators of beliefs-attitude-intention consistency. *British Journal of Social Psychology, 28*, 115–122.

104. Gill, J. D., Crosby, L. A., & Taylor, J. R. (1986). Ecological concern, attitudes, and social norms in voting behavior. *Public Opinion Quarterly, 50*, 537–554.

105. Syme, G. J., Beven, C. E., & Sumner, N. R. (1993). Motivation for reported involvement in local wetland preservation: The roles of knowledge, disposition, problem assessment, and arousal. *Environment and Behavior, 25*, 586–606.

106. Hines, J. M., Hungerford, H. R., & Tomera, A. N. (1986–1987). Analysis and synthesis of research on responsible environmental behavior: A meta-analysis. *Journal of Environmental Education, 18*(2), 1–8.

107. See note 54.

108. Sivek, D. J., & Hungerford, H. (1989–1990). Predictors of responsible behavior in members of three Wisconsin conservation organizations. *Journal of Environmental Education, 21*(2), 35–40.

109. Nemiroff, L. S., & McKenzie-Mohr, D. (1992). Determinants and distinguishing variables of pro-disarmament behavior and responsible environmental behavior. *Journal of Social Behavior and Personality, 7*, 1–24.

110. Etzioni, A. (1972). Human beings are not very easy to change after all. *Saturday Review,* June 3.

111. Geller, E. S. (1992). Solving environmental problems: A behavior change perspective. In S. Staub & P. Green (Eds.), *Psychology and social responsibility: Facing global challenges.* New York: New York University Press.

112. Dwyer, W. O., Leeming, F. C., Cobern, M. K., Porter, B. E., & Jackson, J. J. (1993). Critical review of behavioral interventions to preserve the environment. *Environment and Behavior, 25*, 275–321.

113. de Young, R. (1993). Changing behavior and making it stick: The conceptualization and management of conservation behavior. *Environment and Behavior, 25*, 485–505.

114. Craik, K. H. (1968). The comprehension of the everyday physical environment. *Journal of the American Institute of Planners, 34*, 29–37.

115. Feimer, N. R. (1984). Environmental perception: The effects of media, evaluative context, and observer sample. *Journal of Environmental Psychology, 4*, 61–80.

116. Canter, D. (1985). Intention, meaning and structure: Social action in its physical context. In G. P. Ginsburg, M. Brenner, & M. von Cranach (Eds.), *Discovery strategies in the psychology of action.* Orlando, FL: Academic Press.

117. Ward, L. M. (1977). Multidimensional scaling of the molar physical environment. *Multivariate Behavioral Research, 12*, 23–42.

118. Osgood, C., Suci, G., & Tannenbaum, P. (1957). *The measurement of meaning.* Urbana: University of Illinois Press.

119. Canter, D. (1968). *The measurement of meaning in architecture.* Unpublished manuscript, Building Performance Research Unit, Glasgow.

120. Canter, D. (1969). An intergroup comparison of connotative dimensions. *Environment and Behavior, 1*, 37–48.

121. Cass, R. C., & Hershberger, R. G. (1973). *Further toward a set of semantic scales to measure the meaning of designed environments.* Paper presented at the annual meeting of the Environmental Design Research Association, Blacksburg, VA.

122. Collins, J. B. (1969). *Perceptual dimensions of architectural space validated against behavioral criteria.* Unpublished doctoral dissertation, University of Utah, Salt Lake City.

123. Hershberger, R. G. (1972). *Toward a set of semantic scales to measure the meaning of architectural environments.* Paper presented at the annual meeting of the Environmental Design Research Association, Los Angeles.

124. See note 121.

125. Sancar, F. H., & Matari, H. (1988). *A situational research approach for discovering the meaning of city image.* Paper presented at the 19th annual meetings of the Environmental Design Research Association, Pomona, CA.

126. Sonnenfeld, J. (1966). Variable values in space and landscape: An inquiry into the nature of environmental necessity. *Journal of Social Issues, 22*(4), 71–82.

127. Bernaldez, F. G., Gallardo, D., & Abello, R. P. (1987). Children's landscape preferences: From rejection to attraction. *Journal of Environmental Psychology, 7,* 169–176.

128. Verderber, S., & Moore, G. T. (1977). Building imagery: A comparative study of environmental cognition. *Man-Environment Systems, 7,* 332–341.

129. Gifford, R. (1980). Judgments of the built environment as a function of individual differences and context. *Journal of Man-Environment Relations, 1,* 22–31.

130. Lyons, E. (1983). Demographic correlates of landscape preference. *Environment and Behavior, 15,* 487–511.

131. Pedersen, D. M. (1986). Preferred city size by ruralists and urbanites. *Perceptual and Motor Skills, 63,* (2, Part 1), 441–442.

132. Canter, D., & Thorne, R. (1972). Attitudes to housing: A cross cultural comparison. *Environment and Behavior, 4,* 3–32.

133. Nasar, J. L. (1984). Visual preferences in urban street scenes: A cross-cultural comparison between Japan and the United States. *Journal of Cross-Cultural Psychology, 15,* 79–93.

134. Nasar, J. L. (1984, June–July). *Cognition in relation to downtown street-scenes: A comparison between Japan and the United States.* Paper presented at the annual conference of the Environmental Design Research Association.

135. Yang, B., & Brown, T. J. (1992). A cross-cultural comparison of preferences for landscape styles and landscape elements. *Environment and Behavior, 24,* 471–507.

136. Duffy, M., Bailey, S., Beck, B., & Barker, D. G. (1986). Preferences in nursing home design: A comparison of residents, administrators, and designers. *Environment and Behavior, 18,* 246–257.

137. Stamps, A. E. (1991). Comparing preferences of neighbors and a neighborhood design review board. *Environment and Behavior, 23,* 618–629.

138. Nasar, J. L., & Purcell, T. (1990, July). Beauty and the beast extended: Knowledge structure and evaluations of houses by Australian architects and non-architects. In H. Pamir, V. Imamoglu, & N. Teymur (Eds.), *Culture, space, history.* Ankara, Turkey: Sevki Vanh Foundation.

139. Nasar, J. L. (1988). *Architectural symbolism: A study of house-style meanings.* Paper presented at the 19th annual meeting of the Environmental Design Research Association, Pomona, CA.

140. Devlin, K. (1990). An examination of architectural interpretation: Architects versus non-architects. *Journal of Architectural Planning and Research, 7,* 235–244.

141. James, K. (1989). Family-role salience and environmental cognition. *Journal of Environmental Psychology, 9,* 45–55.

142. Srinivasan, T. (1987). A study of mental health of the adolescents in relation to geographical environments. *Child Psychiatry Quarterly, 20,* 55–60.

143. Kaplan, R. (1977). Patterns of environmental preference. *Environment and Behavior, 9,* 195–215.

144. Iwata, O. (1990). The relationship of social evaluation and subjective sensitivity to environmental evaluation. *Psychologia: An International Journal of Psychology in the Orient, 35,* 69–75.

145. Gifford, R. (1980). Environmental dispositions and the evaluation of architectural interiors. *Journal of Research in Personality, 14,* 386–399.

146. See note 145.

147. Im, S. (1984). Visual preferences in enclosed urban spaces: An exploration of a scientific approach to environmental design. *Environment and Behavior, 16,* 235–262.

148. Kaye, S. M., & Murray, M. A. (1982). Evaluations of an architectural space as a function of variations in furniture arrangement, furniture density, and windows. *Human Factors, 24,* 609–618.

149. Nasar, J. L. (1981). Responses to different spatial configurations. *Human Factors, 23,* 439–446.

150. Baird, J. C., Cassidy, B., & Kurr, J. (1978). Room preference as a function of architectural features and user activities. *Journal of Applied Psychology, 63,* 719–727.

151. Butler, D. L., & Steuerwald, B. L. (1991). Effects of view and room size on window size preferences made in models. *Environment and Behavior, 23,* 334–358.

152. Frewald, D. B. (1990). Preferences for older buildings: A psychological approach to architectural design. *Dissertation Abstracts International, 51*(1–B), 414–415.

153. Pedersen, D. M. (1986). Perception of interior designs. *Perceptual and Motor Skills, 63*(2, Part 1), 671–676.

154. Nasar, J. L. (1983). Adult viewers' preferences in residential scenes: A study of the relationship of environmental attributes to preference. *Environment and Behavior, 15,* 589–614.

155. Nasar, J. L. (1990). The evaluative image of the city. *Journal of the American Planning Association, 56,* 41–53.

156. Nasar, J. L. (1987). Environmental correlates of evaluative appraisals of central business district scenes. *Landscape and Urban Planning, 14,* 117–130.

157. Wong, K. K. (1990). Scenic quality and cognitive structures of urban environments: The role of scene attributes and respondent characteristics. *Dissertation Abstracts International, 51*(5–B), 2269.

158. Nasar, J. L. (1987). Physical correlates of perceived quality in lakeshore development. *Leisure Sciences, 9,* 259–279.

159. Kuller, R. (1980). Architecture and emotion. In B. Mikellides (Ed.), *Architecture for people.* London: Studio Vista.

160. Wohlwill, J. F. (1982). The visual impact of development in coastal zone areas. *Coastal Zone Management Journal, 9,* 225–248.

161. Nasar, J. L. (1987). The effect of sign complexity and coherence on the perceived quality of retail scenes. *Journal of the American Planning Association, 53,* 499–509.

162. Stamps, A. E. (1991). Public preferences for high rise buildings: Stylistic and demographic effects. *Perceptual and Motor Skills, 72*(3, Part 1), 839–844.

163. Devlin, K., & Nasar, J. L. (1989). The beauty and the beast: Some preliminary comparisons of "high" versus "popular" resi-

dential architecture and public versus architect judgments of same. *Journal of Environmental Psychology, 9,* 333–334.

164. Stamps, A. E. (1993). Public preferences for residences: Precode, code minimum, and avant-garde architectural styles. *Perceptual and Motor Skills, 77,* 99–103.

165. Purcell, T., & Nasar, J. L. (1990, August). *Australian architect and non-architect students experiences of American houses.* Paper presented at the Conference of the International Association of Empirical Aesthetics, Budapest, Hungary.

166. Nasar, J. L. (1994). Urban design aesthetics: The evaluative qualities of building exteriors. *Environment and Behavior, 26,* 377–401.

167. Miller, P. A. (1984). *Visual preference and implications for coastal management: A perceptual study of the British Columbia shoreline.* Unpublished doctoral dissertation, University of Michigan, Ann Arbor.

168. Kaplan, R., Kaplan, S., & Brown, T. (1989). Environmental preference: A comparison of four domains of predictors. *Environment and Behavior, 21,* 509–530.

169. Herzog, T. R., & Bosley, P. J. (1992). Tranquility and preference as affective qualities of natural environments. *Journal of Environmental Psychology, 12,* 115–127.

170. Appleton, J. (1975). *The experience of landscape.* New York: Wiley.

171. Ruddell, E. J., & Hammitt, W. E. (1987). Prospect refuge theory: A psychological orientation for edge effect in recreation environments. *Journal of Leisure Research, 19,* 249–260.

172. Peterson, G. L., & Neumann, E. S. (1969). Modeling and predicting human response to the visual recreation environment. *Journal of Leisure Research, 1,* 219–237.

173. Abello, R. P., Bernaldez, F. G., & Galiano, E. F. (1986). Consensus and contrast components in landscape preference. *Environment and Behavior, 18,* 155–178.

174. Yi, Y. K. (1993). Affect and cognition interface in aesthetic experiences of landscapes. *Dissertation Abstracts, 53*(8–A), 3015–3016.

175. Kaplan, S., & Kaplan, R. (1982). *Cognition and environment: Functioning in an uncertain world.* New York: Praeger.

176. Kaplan, S. (1987). Aesthetics, affect, and cognition: Environmental preference from an evolutionary perspective. *Environment and Behavior, 19,* 3–32.

177. Ulrich, R. S. (1983). Aesthetic and affective response to natural environment. *Human behavior and environment: Advances in theory and research, 6,* 85–125.

178. Balling, J. D., & Falk, J. H. (1982). Development of visual preference for natural environments. *Environment and Behavior, 14,* 5–28.

179. See note 130.

180. Butler, D. L., & Biner, P. M. (1989). Effects of setting on window preferences and factors associated with those preferences. *Environment and Behavior, 21,* 17–31.

181. Lindberg, E., Garling, T., Montgomery, H., & Waara, R. (1986). Preferences for housing aspects: A study of underlying beliefs and values. *Umea Psychological Reports,* No. 184.

182. Carmichael, B. A. (1991). *Tourist image and ski resort choice: An analysis of the Victoria, B.C. skier market.* Unpublished doctoral dissertation, University of Victoria, Victoria, British Columbia.

183. See note 175, p. 80.

184. Herzog, T. R. (1984). A cognitive analysis of preference for field-and-forest environments. *Landscape Research, 9,* 10–16.

185. Herzog, T. R. (1985). A cognitive analysis of preference for waterscapes. *Journal of Environmental Psychology, 5,* 225–241.

186. Herzog, T. R. (1989). A cognitive analysis of preference for urban nature. *Journal of Environmental Psychology, 9,* 27–43.

187. Herzog, T. R., & Smith, G. A. (1988). Danger, mystery, and environmental preference. *Environment and Behavior, 20,* 320–344.

188. Scott, S. B. (1990). Preference, mystery and visual attributes of interiors: A study of relationships. *Dissertation Abstracts International, 50*(11–A), 3386.

189. See note 168.

190. Friedman, C., Balling, J. D., & Valadez, J. J. (1985). *Visual preference for office buildings: A comparison of architects and non-architects.* Paper presented at the Annual Meeting of the Environmental Design Research Association, New York City.

191. Gimblett, H. R. (1990). Environmental cognition: The prediction of preference in rural Indiana. *Journal of Architectural Planning and Research, 7,* 222–234.

192. Finlay, T. W. (1990). The prediction of preference evaluations of zoo exhibits: A comparison of the informational and psychophysical theories of environmental preference. *Dissertation Abstracts International, 51*(1–B), 427.

193. Herzog, T. R. (1992). A cognitive analysis of preference for urban spaces. *Journal of Environmental Psychology, 12,* 237–248.

194. See note 191.

195. See note 184.

196. See note 185.

197. See note 186.

198. See note 193.

199. See note 184.

200. Fenton, D. M. (1985). Dimensions of meaning in the perception of natural settings and their relationship to aesthetic response. *Australian Journal of Psychology, 37,* 325–339.

201. Ruddell, E. J., Gramann, J. H., Rudis, V. A., & Westphal, J. M. (1989). The psychological utility of visual penetration in near-view forest scenic-beauty models. *Environment and Behavior, 21,* 393–412.

202. Hull, R. B., & Revell, G. R. (1989). Cross-cultural comparison of landscape scenic beauty evaluations: A case study in Bali. *Journal of Environmental Psychology, 9,* 177–191.

203. Thornton, J. A., McMillan, P. H., & Romanovsky, P. (1989). Perceptions of water pollution in South Africa: Case studies from two water bodies (Hartbeesport Dam and Zandvlei). *South African Journal of Psychology, 19,* 199–204.

204. Bourassa, S. C. (1990). A paradigm for landscape aesthetics. *Environment and Behavior, 22,* 787–812.

205. Kuller, R. (1980). Architecture and emotions. In B. Mikellides (Ed.), *Architecture for people.* London: Studio Vista.

206. Mehrabian, A., & Russell, J. A. (1974). *An approach to environmental psychology.* Cambridge, MA: MIT Press.

207. Mehrabian, A., & Russell, J. A. (1975). Environmental effects on affiliation among strangers. *Humanitas, 11,* 219–230.

208. Russell, J. A., Ward, L. M., & Pratt, G. (1981). Affective quality attributed to environments: A factor analytic study. *Environment and Behavior, 13,* 259–288.

209. See note 206.

210. Daniel, T. C., & Ittelson, W. H. (1981). Conditions for environmental perception research: Comment on The psychological representation of molar physical environments by Ward and Russell. *Journal of Experimental Psychology: General, 110,* 153–157.

211. Russell, J. A., & Ward, L. M. (1981). On the psychological reality of environmental meaning: Reply to Daniel and Ittelson. *Journal of Experimental Psychology, 110,* 163–168.

212. Gold, J. R., & Burgess, J. (Eds.). (1982). *Valued environments.* London: George Allen & Unwin.

213. Tuan, Y. F. (1974). *Topophilia.* Englewood Cliffs, NJ: Prentice-Hall.

214. Sixsmith, J. (1986). The meaning of home: An exploratory study of environmental experience. *Journal of Environmental Psychology, 6,* 281–298.

215. Hershberger, R. G. (1970). Architecture and meaning. *Journal of Aesthetic Education, 4,* 37–55.

216. Espe, H. (1981). Differences in the perception of National Socialist and Classicist architecture. *Journal of Environmental Psychology, 1,* 33–42.

217. Jencks, C. (1978). Post-modern history. *Architectural Design, 1,* 13–58.

218. Groat, L. (1982). Meaning in post-modern architecture: An examination using the multiple sorting task. *Journal of Environmental Psychology, 2,* 3–22.

219. Cherulnik, P. D., & Souders, S. B. (1984). The social contents of place schemata: People are judged by the places where they live and work. *Population and Environment: Behavioral and Social Issues, 7,* 211–233.

220. Cherulnik, P. D., & Bayless, J. K. (1986). Person preception in environmental context: The influence of residential settings on impressions of their occupants. *Journal of Social Psychology, 126,* 667–673.

221. Sadalla, E. K., & Sheets, V. L. (1993). Symbolism in building materials: Self-presentational and cognitive components. *Environment and Behavior, 25,* 155–180.

222. See note 139.

223. Nasar, J. L., & Julian, D. (1985). Effects of labelled meaning on the affective quality of housing scenes. *Journal of Environmental Psychology, 5,* 335–344.

224. Groat, L., & Canter, D. (1979). Does post-modernism communicate? *Progressive Architecture, 12,* 84–87.

225. Prak, N. L., & van Wegen, H. B. R. (1975). *The influence of cognitive factors on the perception of buildings.* Paper presented at the annual meeting of the Environmental Design Research Association, Lawrence, KS.

226. Genereux, R. L., Ward, L. M., & Russell, J. A. (1983). The behavioral component of the meaning of places. *Journal of Environmental Psychology, 3,* 43–55.

227. Ampofo-Boateng, K. (1989). Children's perception of safety and danger on the road. *Dissertation Abstracts International, 49*(10–B), 4567–4568.

228. Shaffer, G. S., & Anderson, L. M. (1985). Perceptions of the security and attractiveness of urban parking lots. *Journal of Environmental Psychology, 5,* 311–323.

229. Loewen, L., Steel, G. D., & Suedfeld, P. (1993). Perceived safety from crime in the urban environment. *Journal of Environmental Psychology, 13,* 323–331.

230. Macdonald, J. E., & Gifford, R. (1989). Territorial cues and defensible space theory: The burglar's point of view. *Journal of Environmental Psychology, 9,* 193–205.

231. Shaw, K. T., & Gifford, R. (1994). Residents' and burglars' perceptions of defensible space cues. *Journal of Environmental Psychology, 14,* 177–194.

232. Flynn, J., Slovic, P., & Mertz, C. K. (1993). Decidedly different: Expert and public views of risks from a nuclear waste repository. *Risk Analysis, 13,* 643–648.

233. Barke, R. P., & Jenkins-Smith, H. C. (1993). Politics and scientific expertise: Scientists, risk perception, and nuclear waste policy. *Risk Analysis, 13,* 425–439.

234. Vaughn, E., & Nordenstam, B. (1991). The perceptions of environmental risks among ethnically diverse groups. *Journal of Cross-Cultural Psychology, 22,* 29–60.

235. Vaughn, E. (1993). Individual and cultural differences in adaptation to environmental risks. *American Psychologist, 48,* 673–680.

236. Pilisuk, M., Parks, S. H., & Hawkes, G. (1987). Public perception of technological risk. *Social Science Journal, 24,* 403–413.

237. Prince-Embury, S., & Rooney, J. F. (1987). Perception of control and faith in experts among residents in the vicinity of Three Mile Island. *Journal of Applied Social Psychology, 17,* 953–968.

238. Larrain Navarro, P., Simpson-Housley, P., & deMan, A. F. (1987). Anxiety, locus of control and appraisal of air pollution. *Perceptual and Motor Skills, 64,* 811–814.

239. Mehta, M. D., & Simpson-Housley, P. (1994). Trait anxiety and perception of potential nuclear power plant disaster. *Psychological Reports, 74,* 291–295.

240. Pedigo, S. K. (1986). The risks of radiation: A study of the attitudes of a select sample of residents of southeast Tennessee. *Dissertation Abstracts International, 47*(3–B), 1016.

241. Maharik, M., & Fischhoff, B. (1993). Contrasting perceptions of the risks of using nuclear energy sources in space. *Journal of Environmental Psychology, 13,* 243–250.

242. Sjoberg, L., & Drottz-Sjoberg, B.-M. (1991). Knowledge and risk perception among nuclear power plant employees. *Risk Analysis, 11,* 607–618.

243. Vaughan, E. (1986). Some factors influencing the nonexpert's perception and evaluation of environmental risks. *Dissertation Abstracts International, 47*(3–B), 1332.

244. Freudenburg, W. R., & Pastor, S. K. (1992). NIMBYs and LULUs: Stalking the syndromes. *Journal of Social Issues, 48*(4), 39–61.

245. See note 244.

246. Renn, O., Burns, W. J., Kasperson, J. X., Kasperson, R. E., et al. (1992). The social amplification of risk: Theoretical foundations and empirical applications. *Journal of Social Issues, 48*(4), 137–160.

247. Cvetkovich, G., & Earle, T. C. (1992). Environmental hazards and the public. *Journal of Social Issues, 48*(4), 1–20.

248. Brown, P. (1992). Popular epidemiology and toxic waste contamination: Lay and professional ways of knowing. *Journal of Health and Social Behavior, 33*, 267–281.

249. MacGregor, D., Slovic, P., Mason, R. G., Detweiler, J., et al. (1994). Perceived risks of radioactive waste transport through Oregon: Results of a statewide survey. *Risk Analysis, 14*, 5–14.

250. Chess, C., & Salomone, K. L. (1992). Rhetoric and reality: Risk communication in government agencies. *Journal of Environmental Education, 23*(3), 28–33.

251. Wandersman, A. H., & Hallman, W. K. (1993). Are people acting irrationally? Understanding public concerns about environmental threats. *American Psychologist, 48*, 681–686.

252. Maharik, M., & Fischhoff, B. (1992). The risks of using nuclear energy sources in space: Some lay activists' perception. *Risk Analysis, 12*, 383–392.

253. Winder, A. E. (1992–1993). Risk assessment—Risk perception: Who shall decide? *International Quarterly of Community Health Education, 13*, 405–410.

254. Bord, R. J., & O'Connor, R. E. (1992). Determinants of risk perceptions of a hazardous waste site. *Risk Analysis, 12*, 411–416.

255. Kunreuther, H., Easterling, D., Desvouges, W., & Slovic, P. (1990). Public attitudes toward siting a high-level nuclear waste repository in Nevada. *Risk Analysis, 10*, 469–484.

256. Craik, K. H. (1971). The assessment of places. In P. McReynolds (Ed.), *Advances in psychological assessment* (Vol. 2). Palo Alto, CA: Science and Behavior Books.

257. See note 256.

258. Moos, R. H. (1973). Conceptualizations of human environments. *American Psychologist, 28*, 652–655.

259. Rowe, R. D., & Chestnut, L. G. (1983). Introduction. In R. D. Rowe & L. G. Chestnut (Eds.), *Managing air quality and scenic resources at national parks and wilderness areas.* Boulder, CO: Westview Press.

260. Yuhnke, R. E. (1983). The importance of visibility protection in the national parks and wilderness. In R. D. Rowe & L. G. Chestnut (Eds.), *Managing air quality and scenic resources at national parks and wilderness parks.* Boulder, CO: Westview Press.

261. Christensen, D. L., & Carp, F. M. (1987). PEQI-based environmental predictors of the residential satisfaction of older women. *Journal of Environmental Psychology, 7*, 45–64.

262. See note 2.

263. See note 261.

264. Zube, E. H. (1980). *Environmental evaluation: Perception and public policy.* Monterey, CA: Brooks/Cole.

265. Anderson, T. W., Zube, E. H., & MacConnell, W. P. (1976). *Predicting scenic resource values: Studies in landscape perception* (Technical report). Amherst: Institute for Man and Environment, University of Massachusetts.

266. Moos, R. H., & Lemke, S. (1984). *Multiphasic environmental assessment procedure.* Unpublished manuscript, Stanford University, Social Ecology Laboratory, Palo Alto, CA.

267. Craik, K. H. (1983). A psychology of large scale environment. In N. R. Feimer & E. S. Geller (Eds.), *Environmental psychology: Directions and perspectives.* New York: Praeger.

268. See note 2.

269. Moser, G. (1984). Water quality perception, a dynamic perspective. *Journal of Environmental Psychology, 4.*

270. See note 266.

271. Zube, E. H. (1984). Themes in landscape assessment theory. *Landscape Journal, 3*(2), 104–110.

272. Zube, E. H., Sell, J. L., & Taylor, J. G. (1982). Landscape perception: Research, application and theory. *Landscape Planning, 9*, 1–33.

273. Daniel, T. C. (1990). Measuring the quality of the natural environment: A psychophysical approach. *American Psychologist, 45*, 633–637.

274. Kaplan, S., Kaplan, R., & Wendt, J. S. (1972). Rated preference and complexity for natural and urban visual material. *Perception and Psychophysics, 12*, 354–356.

275. Ulrich, R. S. (1981). Natural versus urban scenes: Some psychophysical effects. *Environment and Behavior, 13*, 523–556.

276. Hull, R. B., & Buhyoff, G. J. (1983). Distance and scenic beauty: A nonmontonic relationship. *Environment and Behavior, 15*, 77–91.

277. See note 276.

278. Patsfall, M. R., Feimer, N. R. Buhyoff, G. J., & Wellman, J. D. (1984). The prediction of scenic beauty from landscape content and composition. *Journal of Environmental Psychology, 4*, 7–26.

279. See note 271.

280. Hamilton, W. G. (1985). The Okanagan Valley, British Columbia: Visual landscape assessment and planning policy. *Environments, 17*, 46–58.

281. Dearden, P. (1980). Landscape assessment: The last decade. *Canadian Geographer, 24*, 316–325.

282. Zube, E. H., Pitt, D. G., & Anderson, T. W. (1975). Perception and prediction of scenic resource values of the Northeast. In E. H. Zube, R. O. Brush, & J. G. Fabos (Eds.), *Landscape assessment: Values, perceptions, and resources.* Stroudsburg, PA: Dowden, Hutchinson and Ross.

283. See note 282.

284. Craik, K. H. (1983). A role theoretical analysis of scenic quality judgments. In R. D. Rowe & L. G. Chestnut (Eds.), *Managing air quality and scenic resources at national parks and wilderness areas.* Boulder, CO: Westview Press.

285. Zube, E. H., & Pitt, D. G. (1981). Cross-cultural perceptions of scenic and heritage landscapes. *Landscape Planning, 8*, 69–87.

286. Zube, E. H., Pitt, D. G., & Evans, G. W. (1983). A life-span developmental study of landscape assessment. *Journal of Environmental Psychology, 3*, 115–128.

287. Carp, F. M., & Carp, A. (1982). Perceived environmental quality of neighborhoods: Development of assessment scales and their relation to age and gender. *Journal of Environmental Psychology, 2*, 295–312.

288. Carp, F. M., & Carp, A. (1982). A role for technical environmental assessment in perceptions of environmental quality and well-being. *Journal of Environmental Psychology, 2*, 171–191.

289. Fried, M., & Gleicher, P. (1961). Some sources of satisfaction in an urban slum. *Journal of the American Institute of Planners, 27,* 305–315.

Chapter 4

1. Jung, C. G. (1921/1971). *Psychological types.* Princeton, NJ: Princeton University Press.

2. Guilford, J. P. (1959). *Personality.* New York: McGraw-Hill, p. 5.

3. Allport, G. W. (1961). *Pattern and growth in personality.* New York: Holt, Rinehart and Winston, p. 28.

4. Gormly, J. (1983). Predicting behavior from personality trait scores. *Personality and Social Psychology Bulletin, 9,* 267–270.

5. McKechnie, G. E. (1974). *ERI Manual: Environmental response inventory.* Berkeley, CA: Consulting Psychologists Press.

6. Veness, A. (1987). Place and personality. *Social Science, 72,* 29–33.

7. Campbell, C. M. (1934). *Human personality and the environment.* New York: Macmillan.

8. Murray, H. A. (1938). *Explorations in personality.* New York: Oxford University Press.

9. See note 8, p. 121.

10. See note 8.

11. Lewin, K. (1951). *Field theory in social science: Selected theoretical papers.* New York: Harper and Row.

12. Allport, G. W. (1955). *Becoming: Basic considerations for a psychology of personality.*

13. Brunswik, E. (1943). Organismic achievement and environmental probability. *Psychological Review, 50,* 255–272.

14. Sommer, R., & Amick, T. L. (1984). *Action research: Linking research to organizational change.* Davis, CA: Center for Consumer Research, University of California.

15. Driver, B. L., & Knopf, R. C. (1977). Personality, outdoor recreation and expected consequences. *Environment and Behavior, 9,* 169–193.

16. Altman, I. (1975). *The environment and social behavior: Privacy, personal space, territoriality and crowding.* Monterey, CA: Brooks/Cole, p. 73.

17. Eddy, G. L., & Sinnett, R. (1973). Behavior setting utilization by emotionally disturbed college students. *Journal of Consulting and Clinical Psychology, 40,* 210–216.

18. McElroy, J. C., Morrow, P. C., & Ackerman, R. J. (1983). Personality and interior office design: Exploring the accuracy of visitor attributions. *Journal of Applied Psychology, 68,* 541–544.

19. Hensley, W. E. (1982). Professor proxemics: Personality and job demands as factors of faculty office arrangement. *Environment and Behavior, 14,* 581–591.

20. Miller, S., Rossbach, J., & Munson, R. (1981). Social density and affiliative tendency as determinants of dormitory residential outcomes. *Journal of Applied Social Psychology, 11,* 356–365.

21. Osborn, D. R. (1988). Personality traits expressed: Interior design as behavior-setting plan. *Personality and Social Psychology Bulletin, 14,* 368–373.

22. Gifford, R. (1982). Projected interpersonal distance and orientation choices: Personality, sex, and social situation. *Social Psychology Quarterly, 45,* 145–152.

23. Craik, K. H. (1975). Individual variations in landscape description. In E. H. Zube, R. O. Brush, & J. G. Fabos (Eds.), *Landscape assessment: Values, perceptions and resources.* Stroudsberg, PA: Dowden, Hutchinson and Ross.

24. Feimer, N. R. (1981, August). Personality and sociodemographic variables as sources of variation in environmental perception. In H. M. Proshansky (Chair), *Environmental cognition.* Symposium conducted at the meeting of the American Psychological Association. (ERIC Document Reproduction Service No. ED 211 393.)

25. Bryant, K. J. (1982). Personality correlates of sense of direction and geographical orientation. *Journal of Personality and Social Psychology, 43,* 1318–1324.

26. Eysenck, M. W., & Graydon, J. (1989). Susceptibilty to distraction as a function of personality. *Personality and Individual Differnces, 10,* 681–687.

27. Shigehesa, T., & Gunn, W. J. (1979). Annoyance response to recorded aircraft noise: IV effect of intensity of illumination in relation to personality. *Journal of Auditory Research, 19,* 47–58.

28. Duke, M. P., & Nowicki, S., Jr. (1972). A new measure and social learning model for interpersonal distance. *Journal of Experimental Research in Personality, 6,* 119–132.

29. Heckel, R. V., & Hiers, J. M. (1977). Social distance and locus of control. *Journal of Clinical Psychology, 33,* 469–474.

30. Sundstrom, E. (1978). Crowding as a sequential process: Review of research on the effects of population density on humans. In A. Baum & Y. M. Epstein (Eds.), *Human response to crowding.* Hillsdale, NJ: Erlbaum.

31. Verbrugge, L. M., & Taylor, R. B. (1980). Consequences of population density and size. *Urban Affairs Quarterly, 16,* 135–160.

32. Ruback, R. B., & Pandey, J. (1991). Crowding, perceived control, and relative power: An analysis of households in India. *Journal of Applied Social Psychology, 21,* 315–344.

33. Lepore, S. J., Evans, G. W., & Schneider, M. L. (1992). Role of control and social support in explaining the stress of hassles and crowding. *Environment and Behavior, 24,* 795–811.

34. Sims, J. H., & Baumann, D. D. (1972). The tornado threat: Coping styles of the North and the South. *Science, 176,* 1386–1391.

35. Evans, G. W., Jacobs, S. V., & Frager, N. B. (1982). Behavioral responses to air pollution. In A. Baum & J. E. Singer (Eds.), *Advances in environmental psychology.* Hillsdale, NJ: Erlbaum.

36. Sia, A. P., Hungerford, H. R., & Tomera, A. N. (1985–1986). Selected predictors of responsible environmental behavior: An analysis. *Journal of Environmental Education, 17*(2), 31–40.

37. Pettus, A. M., & Giles, M. B. (1987). Personality characteristics and environmental attitudes. *Population & Environment: Behavioral & Social Issues, 9,* 127–137.

38. Huebner, R. B., & Lipsey, M. W. (1981). The relationship of three measures of locus of control to environmental activism. *Basic and Applied Social Psychology, 2,* 45–58.

39. Tucker, L. R. (1978). The environmentally concerned citizen: Some correlates. *Environment and Behavior, 10*, 389–418.

40. Arbuthnot, J. (1977). The roles of attitudinal and personality variables in the prediction of environmental behavior and knowledge. *Environment and Behavior, 9*, 217–232.

41. Trigg, L. J., Perlman, D., Perry, R. P., & Janisse, M. P. (1976). Anti-pollution behavior: A function of perceived outcome and locus of control. *Environment and Behavior, 8*, 307–314.

42. Propst, D. B., & Kurtz, M. E. (1989). Perceived control/reactance: A framework for understanding leisure behavior in natural settings. *Leisure Studies, 8*, 241–248.

43. Ruback, R. B., & Patniak, R. (1989). Crowding, perceived control, and the destruction of property. *Psychological Studies, 34*, 1–14.

44. Palinkas, L. A. (1985). *Sociocultural influences on psychosocial adjustment in Antarctica.* U.S. Naval Health Research Center Report No. 85–49, 17.

45. Juhasz, J. B., & Paxson, L. (1978). Personality and preference for architectural style. *Perceptual and Motor Skills, 47*, 241–242.

46. Salling, M., & Harvey, M. E. (1981). Poverty, personality and sensitivity to residential stressors. *Environment and Behavior, 13*, 131–163.

47. See note 17.

48. See note 25.

49. See note 19.

50. See note 17.

51. See note 40.

52. Miller, A. (1985). Cognitive styles and environmental problem-solving. *Journal of Environmental Studies, 26*, 21–31.

53. Cotgrove, S. (1982). *Catastrophe or cornucopia.* New York: Wiley.

54. Miller, A. (1982). Environmental problem-solving: Psychosocial factors. *Environmental Management, 6*, 535–541.

55. Gifford, R., & Gallagher, T. M. B. (1985). Sociability: Personality, social context, and physical setting. *Journal of Personality and Social Psychology, 48*, 1015–1023.

56. Cottle, W. C. (1950). A factorial study of the Multiphasic, Strong, Kuder, and Bell inventories using a population of adult males. *Psychometrika, 15*, 25–47.

57. Thurstone, L. L. (1946). Factor analysis and body types. *Psychometrika, 11*, 15–21.

58. Little, B. R. (1968). Factors affecting the use of psychological versus non-psychological constructs on the Rep Test. *Bulletin of the British Psychological Society, 21*, 113.

59. Little, B. R. (1972). Psychological man as scientist, humanist, and specialist. *Journal of Experimental Research in Personality, 6*, 95–118.

60. Little, B. R. (1976). Specialization and the varieties of human experience: Empirical studies within the personality paradigm. In S. Wapner, S. B. Cohen, & B. Kaplan (Eds.), *Experiencing the environment.* New York: Plenum.

61. Friedman, S. (1974). Relationships among cognitive complexity, interpersonal dimension and spatial preferences and propensities. In S. Friedman & J. B. Juhasz (Eds.), *Environments:*

Notes and selections on objects, spaces and behavior. Belmont, CA: Wadsworth.

62. Kelly, G. A. (1955). *The psychology of personal constructs.* New York: Norton.

63. See note 60.

64. See note 60.

65. Sonnenfeld, J. (1969). Personality and behavior in environment. *Proceedings of the Association of American Geographers, 1*, 136–140.

66. See note 65.

67. Sivek, D. J., & Hungerford, H. (1989–1990). Predictors of responsible behavior in members of three Wisconsin conservation organizations. *Journal of Environmental Education, 21*(2), 35–40.

68. See note 36.

69. See note 5.

70. Craik, K. H. (1970). Environmental psychology. In T. M. Newcomb (Ed.), *New directions in psychology.* New York: Holt, Rinehart and Winston.

71. McKechnie, G. E. (1977). The environmental response inventory in application. *Environment and Behavior, 9*, 255–276.

72. Bunting, T. E., & Cousins, L. R. (1985). Environmetal dispositions among school-age children: A preliminary report. *Environment and Behavior, 17*, 725–768.

73. Taylor, S. M., & Konrad, V. A. (1980). Scaling dispositions toward the past. *Environment and Behavior, 12*, 283–307.

74. See note 5.

75. Gifford, R. (1980). Environmental dispositions and the evaluation of architectural interiors. *Journal of Research in Personality, 14*, 386–399.

76. Kegel-Flom, P. (1976). Identifying the potential rural optometrist. *American Journal of Optometry and Physiological Optics, 53*, 479–482.

77. Kaplan, R. (1977). Patterns of environmental preference. *Environment and Behavior, 9*, 195–215.

78. Born, T. J., & Wieters, N. E. (1978). Non-reactive measurement of orientation toward the natural environment. *Journal of Environmental Education, 10*(1), 41–43.

79. See note 78.

80. See note 77.

81. Iwata, O. (1986). The relationship of personality to environmental vulnerabilty and proenvironmental orientation. *Progress in Experimental Personality Research, 14*, 165–203.

82. Mehrabian, A. (1976). *Manual for the questionaire measure of Stimulus Screening and Arousability.* Unpublished manuscript, University of California at Los Angeles.

83. Weinstein, N. D. (1978). Individual differences in reactions to noise: A longitudinal study in a college dormitory. *Journal of Applied Psychology, 63*, 456–466.

84. Weinstein, N. D. (1980). Individual differences in critical tendencies and noise annoyance. *Journal of Sound and Vibration, 68*, 241–248.

85. Mehrabian, A. (1978). Characteristic individual reactions to preferred and unpreferred environments. *Journal of Personality, 46*, 717–731.

86. Baum, A., Calesnick, L. E., Davis, G. E., & Gatchel, R. J. (1982). Individual differences in coping with crowding: Stimulus screening and social overload. *Journal of Personality and Social Psychology, 43*, 821–830.

87. Bhatia, P., & Muhar, I. (1988). Noise sensitivity and mental efficiency. *Psychologia: An International Journal of Psychology in the Orient, 31*, 163–169.

88. Jelinkova, Z., Picek, M., & Hyncica, V. (1988). Psychophysiological factors determining responses to noise load. 2nd European International Association for Interdisciplinary Study of Higher Nervous Functions Conference. *Activitas Nervosa Superior, 30*, 146–147.

89. Dornic, S., Laaksonen, T., & Ekehammer, B. (1990). Noise sensitivity: General self-report versus noise effect in laboratory situations. *Reports from the Department of Psychology*, No. 716.

90. See note 89.

91. Matsumura, Y., & Rylander, R. (1991). Noise sensitivity and road traffic annoyance in a population sample. *Journal of Sound and Vibration, 151*, 415–419.

92. See note 84.

93. Stansfeld, S. A., Clark, C. R., Jenkins, L. M., & Tarnopolsky, A. (1985). Sensitivity to noise in a community sample: I. Measurement of psychiatric disorder and personality. *Psychological Medicine, 15*, 243–254.

94. See note 83.

95. See note 87.

96. Weinstein, N. D. (1982). Community noise problems: Evidence against adaptation. *Journal of Environmental Psychology, 2*, 99–108.

97. Topf, M. (1985). Personal and environmental predictors of patient disturbance due to hospital noise. *Journal of Applied Psychology, 70*, 22–28.

98. Nivison, M. E., & Endresen, I. M. (1993). An analysis of relationships among environmental noise, annoyance and sensitivity to noise, and the consequences for health and sleep. *Journal of Behavioral Medicine, 16*, 257–276.

99. Jorgensen, D. O. (1978). Measurement of desire for control of the physical environment. *Psychological Reports, 42*, 603–608.

100. LeBrasseur, R., Blackford, K., & Whissell, C. (1988). The Leford Test of Tenant Locus of Control: Introducing an effective measure relating locus of control and housing satisfaction. *Environment and Behavior, 20*, 300–319.

101. Schmidt, F. N., & Gifford, R. (1989). A dispositional approach to hazard perception: Preliminary development of the Environmental Appraisal Inventory. *Journal of Environmental Psychology, 9*, 57–67.

102. Fridgen, C. (1994). Human disposition toward hazards: Testing the Environmental Appraisal Inventory. *Journal of Environmental Psychology, 14*, 101–111.

103. Levenson, H. (1973). Perception of environmental modifiability and involvement in antipollution activities. *Journal of Psychology, 84*, 237–239.

104. Smith-Sebasto, N. J. (1992). Design, development, and validation of an instrument to assess the relationship between locus-of-control of reinforcement and environmentally responsible behavior in university undergraduate students. *Dissertation Abstracts International, 53*(6–A), 1736.

105. Eso, S., & Gifford, R. (1994). *Survey of personal influence in common environments.* In preparation, Department of Psychology, University of Victoria.

106. See note 102.

107. Paciuk, M. T. (1990). The role of personal control of the environment in thermal comfort and satisfaction at the workplace. *Dissertation Abstracts International, 50*(8–A), 2709.

108. Craik, K. H. (1976). The personality research paradigm in environmental psychology. In S. Wapner, S. B. Cohen, & B. Kaplan (Eds.), *Experiencing the environment.* New York: Plenum.

Chapter 5

1. Sommer, R. (1969). *Personal space: The behavioral basis of design* (p. 26). Englewood Cliffs, NJ: Prentice-Hall.

2. See note 1.

3. Patterson, M. L. (1975). Personal space—Time to burst the bubble? *Man-Environment Systems, 5*, 67.

4. Knowles, E. S. (1980). An affiliative conflict theory of personal and group spatial behavior. In P. B. Paulus (Ed.), *Psychology of group influence.* Hillsdale, NJ: Erlbaum.

5. Howard, E. (1920). *Territory in bird life.* London: John Murray.

6. Hediger, H. (1950). *Wild animals in captivity.* London: Butterworth.

7. Hall, E. T. (1959). *The silent language.* Garden City, NY: Doubleday.

8. Hall, E. T. (1966). *The hidden dimension.* Garden City, NY: Doubleday.

9. See note 8, p. 113.

10. See note 7.

11. Patterson, M. (1968). Spatial factors in social interactions. *Human Relations, 21*, 351–361.

12. Evans, G. W., & Howard, R. E. (1973). Personal space. *Psychological Bulletin, 80*, 334–344.

13. Hayduk, L. A. (1978). Personal space: An evaluative and orienting overview. *Psychological Bulletin, 85*, 117–134.

14. Gifford, R., & Price, J. (1979). Personal space in nursery school children. *Canadian Journal of Behavioral Science, 11*, 318–326.

15. Gifford, R. (1983). The experience of personal space: Perception of interpersonal distance. *Journal of Nonverbal Behavior, 7*, 170–178.

16. Codol, J.-P., Jarymowicz, M., Kaminska-Feldman, M., & Szuster-Zarojewicz, A. (1989). Asymmetry in the estimation of interpersonal distance and identity affirmation. *European Journal of Social Psychology, 19*, 11–22.

17. Kaminska-Feldman, M. (1991). Self-salience and the autocentric versus allocentric asymmetry effect in interpersonal distance rating. *Cahiers de Psychologie Cognitive, 11*, 669–678.

18. Hayduk, L. A. (1983). Personal space: The conceptual and measurement implications of structural equation models. *Canadian Journal of Behavioral Science, 17*, 140–149.

19. See note 4.

20. See note 18.

21. Gifford, R., & Sacilotto, P. (1993). Social isolation and personal space: A field study. *Canadian Journal of Behavioral Science, 25*, 165–174.

22. Barnard, W. A., & Bell, P. B. (1982). An unobtrusive apparatus for measuring interpersonal distance. *Journal of General Psychology, 107*, 85–90.

23. Bell, P. A., Kline, L. M., & Barnard, W. A. (1988). Friendship and freedom of movement as moderators of sex differences in interpersonal distancing. *Journal of Social Psychology, 128*, 305–310.

24. Gifford, R. (1982). Projected interpersonal distances and orientation choices: Personality, sex, and social situation. *Social Psychology Quarterly, 45*, 145–152.

25. Lott, B. S., & Sommer, R. (1967). Seating arrangements and status. *Journal of Personality and Social Psychology, 7*, 90–95.

26. Pellegrini, R. J., & Empey, J. (1970). Interpersonal spatial orientation in dyads. *Journal of Psychology, 76*, 67–70.

27. See note 22.

28. Kuethe, J. L. (1962). Social schemas. *Journal of Abnormal and Social Psychology, 64*, 31–38.

29. Kuethe, J. L., & Weingartner, H. (1964). Male-female schemata of homosexual and non-homosexual penitentiary inmates. *Journal of Personality, 32*, 23–31.

30. Altman, I. (1975). *The environment and social behavior: Privacy, personal space, territoriality and crowding.* Monterey, CA: Brooks/Cole, p. 75.

31. Balogun, S. K. (1991). The influence of sex and religion on personal space among undergraduate students. *Indian Journal of Behaviour, 15*, 13–20.

32. Severy, L. J., Forsyth, D. R., & Wagner, P. J. (1979). A multimethod assessment of personal space development in female and male, black and white children. *Journal of Nonverbal Behavior, 4*, 68–86.

33. Greeno, C. (1990). Gender differences in children's proximity to adults. *Dissertation Abstracts International, 50*(11–B), 5345.

34. See note 18.

35. Castell, R. (1970). Effect of familiar and unfamiliar environments on proximity behavior of young children. *Journal of Experimental Child Psychology, 9*, 342–347.

36. See note 12.

37. Tennis, G. H., & Dabbs, J. M. (1975). Sex, setting and personal space: First grade through college. *Sociometry, 38*, 385–394.

38. Aiello, J. R., & Pagan, G. (1982). Development of personal space among Puerto Ricans. *Journal of Nonverbal Behavior, 7*, 59–80.

39. See note 13.

40. See note 30, p. 75.

41. Cook, M. (1970). Experiments on orientation and proxemics. *Human Relations, 23*, 61–76.

42. Mehrabian, A., & Diamond, S. G. (1971). The effects of furniture arrangement, props, and personality on social interaction. *Journal of Personality and Social Psychology, 20*, 18–30.

43. Patterson, M. L., & Holmes, D. S. (1966). Social interaction correlates of the MMPI extraversion-introversion scale. *American Psychologist, 21*, 18–30.

44. Kline, L. M., Bell, P. A., & Babcock, A. M. (1984). Field dependence and interpersonal distance. *Bulletin of of the Psychonomic Society, 2*, 421–422.

45. See note 24.

46. Andersen, P. A., & Sull, K. K. (1985). Out of touch, out of reach: Tactile predispositions as predictors of interpersonal distance. *Western Journal of Speech Communication, 49*, 57–72.

47. Karabenick, S., & Meisels, M. (1972). Effects of performance evaluation on interpersonal distance. *Journal of Personality, 40*, 275–286.

48. Luft, J. (1966). On nonverbal interaction. *Journal of Psychology, 63*, 261–268.

49. Patterson, M. L. (1973). Stability of nonverbal immediacy behaviors. *Journal of Experimental Social Psychology, 9*, 97–109.

50. Weinstein, L. (1968). The mother-child schema, anxiety, and academic achievement in elementary school boys. *Child Development, 39*, 257–264.

51. Strube, M. J., & Werner, C. (1984). Personal space claims as a function on interpersonal threat: The mediating role of need for control. *Journal of Nonverbal Behavior, 8*, 195–209.

52. Sommer, R. (1959). Studies in personal space. *Sociometry, 22*, 247–260.

53. Horowitz, M. J., Duff, D. F., & Stratton, L. O. (1964). Body-buffer zone: Exploration of personal space. *Archives of General Psychology, 11*, 651–656.

54. Srivastava, P., & Mandal, M. K. (1990). Proximal spacing to facial affect expressions in schizophrenia. *Comprehensive Psychiatry, 31*, 119–124.

55. Horowitz, M. J. (1968). Spatial behavior and psychopathology. *Journal of Nervous and Mental Diseases, 146*, 24–35.

56. Kinzel, A. S. (1970). Body buffer zone in violent prisoners. *American Journal of Psychiatry, 127*, 59–64.

57. Eastwood, L. (1985). Personality, intelligence, and personal space among violent and non-violent delinquents. *Personality and Individual Differences, 6*, 717–723.

58. Carifio, M. S. (1987). Personal space as a function of violence, race, and control. *Dissertation Abstracts International, 47*(7–B), 3100.

59. Jones, E. E. (1985). Interpersonal distancing behavior of hearing-impaired vs. normal-hearing children. *Volta Review, 87*, 223–330.

60. Pedersen, J., Livoir-Petersen, M. F., & Schelde, J. T. (1989). An ethological approach to autism: An analysis of visual behavior and interpersonal contact in a child versus adult interaction. *Acta Psychiatrica Scandinavica, 80*, 346–355.

61. Little, K. B. (1965). Personal space. *Journal of Experimental Social Psychology, 1*, 237–247.

62. Willis, F. N. (1966). Initial speaking distance as a function of the speakers' relationship. *Psychonomic Science, 5*, 221–222.

63. Edwards, D. J. (1972). Approaching the unfamiliar: A study of human interaction distances. *Journal of Behavioral Science, 1,* 249–250.

64. Aiello, J. R., & Cooper, R. E. (1972). The use of personal space as a function of social affect. *Proceedings of the Annual Convention of the American Psychological Association, 7,* 207–208.

65. Sinha, S. P., & Mukerjee, N. (1990). Marital adjustment and personal space orientation. *Journal of Social Psychology, 130,* 633–639.

66. King, M. G. (1966). Interpersonal relations in preschool children and average approach distance. *Journal of Genetic Psychology, 109,* 109–116.

67. Rosenfeld, H. M. (1965). Effect of an approval seeking induction on interpersonal proximity. *Psychological Reports, 17,* 120–122.

68. Smith, G. H. (1954). Personality scores and personal distance effect. *Journal of Social Psychology, 39,* 37–62.

69. Mandal, M. K., & Maitra, S. (1985). Perception of facial affect and physical proximity. *Perceptual and Motor Skills, 60,* 782.

70. Rivano-Fischer, M. (1984). Interactional space: Invasion as a function of the type of social interaction. *Psychological Research Bulletin, 24,* 15.

71. O'Neal, E. C., Brunault, M. S., Carifio, M. S., Troutwine, R., & Epstein, J. (1980). Effect of insult upon personal space preferences. *Journal of Nonverbal Behavior, 5,* 56–62.

72. Guardo, C. J., & Meisels, M. (1971). Child-parent spatial patterns under praise and reproof. *Developmental Psychology, 5,* 365.

73. Skorjanc, A. D. (1991). Differences in interpersonal distance among nonoffenders as a function of perceived violence of offenders. *Perceptual and Motor Skills, 73,* 659–662.

74. Aiken, J. (1991). Come closer—Stay back: Interpersonal space preferences. *Dissertation Abstracts International, 51*(9–B), 4639.

75. Kleck, R. E., Buck, P. L., Goller, W. C., London, R. S., Pfeiffer, J. R., & Vukcevic, D. P. (1968). Effect of stigmatizing conditions on the use of personal space. *Psychological Reports, 23,* 111–118.

76. Stephens, K. K., & Clark, D. W. (1987). A pilot study on the effect of visible physical stigma on personal space. *Journal of Applied Rehabilitation Counselling, 18,* 52–54.

77. Conigliaro, L., Cullerton, S., Flynn, K. E., & Roeder, S. (1989). Stigmatizing artifacts and their effect on personal space. *Psychological Reports, 65,* 897–898.

78. Wolfgang, J., & Wolfgang, A. (1971). Explanation of attitudes via physical interpersonal distance toward the obese, drug users, homosexuals, police, and other marginal figures. *Journal of Clinical Psychology, 27,* 510–512.

79. Worthington, M. (1974). Personal space as a function of the stigma effect. *Environmental and Behavior, 6,* 289–295.

80. See note 1.

81. See note 41.

82. Tedesco, J. F., & Fromme, D. K. (1974). Cooperation, competition, and personal space. *Sociometry, 37,* 116–121.

83. Rosenfeld, P., Giacalone, R. A., & Kennedy, J. G. (1987). Of status and suits: Personal space invasions in an administrative setting. *Social Behavior and Personality, 15,* 97–99.

84. See note 25.

85. Mehrabian, A. (1969). Significance of posture and position in the communication of attitude and status relationships. *Psychological Bulletin, 71,* 359–373.

86. See note 24.

87. Adams, L., & Zuckerman, D. (1991). The effect of lighting conditions on personal space requirements. *Journal of General Psychology, 118,* 335–340.

88. Daves, W. F., & Swaffer, P. W. (1971). Effect of room size on critical interpersonal distance. *Perceptual and Motor Skills, 33,* 926.

89. See note 37.

90. See note 61.

91. Savinar, J. (1975). The effect of ceiling height on personal space. *Man-Environment Systems, 5,* 321–324.

92. Cochran, C. D., Hale, W. D., & Hissam, C. P. (1984). Personal space requirements in indoor versus outdoor locations. *Journal of Psychology, 117,* 121–123.

93. Burgess, J. W., & Fordyce, W. K. (1989). Effects of preschool environments on nonverbal social behavior: Toddlers' interpersonal distances to teachers and classmates change with environmental density, classroom design, and parent-child interactions. *Journal of Child Psychology and Psychiatry and Allied Disciplines, 30,* 261–276.

94. Worchel, S. (1986). The influence of contextual variables on interpersonal spacing. *Journal of Nonverbal Behavior, 10,* 320–254.

95. See note 21.

96. Summit, J. E., Westfall, S. C., Sommer, R., & Harrison, A. A. (1992). Weightlessness and interaction distance: A simulation of interpersonal contact in outer space. *Environment and Behavior, 24,* 617–633.

97. See note 7, pp. 161–162.

98. Watson, O. M., & Graves, T. D. (1966). Quantitative research in proxemic behavior. *American Anthropologist, 68,* 971–985.

99. Mehrabian, A. (1966). Immediacy: An indicator of attitudes in linguistic communication. *Journal of Personality, 34,* 26–34.

100. Watson, O. M. (1970). *Proxemic behavior: A cross-cultural study.* The Hague: Mouton.

101. Forston, R. F., & Larson, C. U. (1968). The dynamics of space: An experimental study in proxemic behavior among Latin Americans and North Americans. *Journal of Communication, 18,* 109–116.

102. Mazur, A. (1977). Interpersonal spacing on public benches in "contact" and "noncontact" cultures. *Journal of Social Psychology, 101,* 53–58.

103. Shuter, R. (1976). Proxemics and tactility in Latin America. *Journal of Communication, 26,* 46–52.

104. Remland, M. S., Jones, T. S., & Brinkman, H. (1991). Proxemic and haptic behavior in three European countries. *Journal of Nonverbal Behavior, 15,* 215–232.

105. Scherer, S. E. (1974). Proxemic behavior of primary school children as a function of their socioeconomic class and subculture. *Journal of Personality and Social Psychology, 29,* 800–805.

106. Jones, S. E., & Aiello, J. R. (1973). Proxemic behavior of black and white first-, third-, and fifth-grade children. *Journal of Personality and Social Psychology, 25,* 21–27.

107. Sanders, J. L., Hakky, U. M., & Brizzolara, M. M. (1985). Personal space amongst Arabs and Americans. *International Journal of Psychology, 20,* 13–17.

108. Sussman, N. M., & Rosenfeld, H. M. (1982). Influence of culture, language, and sex on conversational distance. *Journal of Personality and Social Psychology, 42,* 66–74.

109. Balogun, S. K. (1991). Personal space as affected by religions of the approaching and approached people. *Indian Journal of Behaviour, 15,* 45–50.

110. Collett, D. (1971). Training Englishmen in the nonverbal behavior of Arabs. *International Journal of Psychology, 6,* 209–215.

111. Hern, W. (1991). Proxemics: The application of theory to conflict arising from antiabortion demonstrations. *Population and Environment: A Journal of Interdisciplinary Studies, 12,* 379–388.

112. Shaw, M. E. (1976). *Group dynamics: The psychology of small group behavior.* New York: McGraw-Hill.

113. See note 1.

114. Barash, D. P. (1973). Human ethology: Personal space reiterated. *Environment and Behavior, 5,* 67–73.

115. Young, A. E., & Guile, M. N. (1987). Departure latency to invasion of personal space: Effects of status and sex. *Perceptual and Motor Skills, 64,* 700–702.

116. Lombardo, J. P. (1986). Interaction of sex and sex role in response to violations of preferred seating arrangements. *Sex Roles, 15,* 173–183.

117. Baker, E., & Shaw, M. E. (1980). Reactions to interpersonal distance and topic intimacy: A comparison of strangers and friends. *Journal of Nonverbal Behavior, 5,* 80–91.

118. Ashton, N. L., Shaw, M. E., & Worsham, A. P. (1980). Affective reactions to interpersonal distances by friends and strangers. *Bulletin of the Psychonomic Society, 15,* 306–308.

119. Rustemli, A. (1988). The effects of personal space invasion on impressions and decisions. *Journal of Psychology, 122,* 113–118.

120. Hewitt, J., & Henley, R. (1987). Sex differences in reaction to spatial invasion. *Perceptual and Motor Skills, 64,* 809–810.

121. Fisher, J. D., & Byrne, D. (1975). Too close for comfort: Sex differences in response to invasions of personal space. *Journal of Personality and Social Psychology, 32,* 15–21.

122. Lane, P. L. (1989). Nurse-client perceptions: The double standard of touch. *Issues in Mental Health Nursing, 10,* 1–13.

123. See note 41.

124. O'Connor, B. P., & Gifford, R. (1988). A test among models of nonverbal immediacy reactions: Arousal labeling, discrepancy-arousal, and social cognition. *Journal of Nonverbal Behavior, 12,* 6–33.

125. Knowles, E. S. (1972). Boundaries around social space: Dyadic responses to an invader. *Environment and Behavior, 4,* 437–445.

126. Middlemist, R. D., Knowles, E. S., & Matter, C. F. (1976). Personal space invasions in the lavatory: Suggestive evidence for arousal. *Journal of Personality and Social Psychology, 33,* 541–546.

127. Mehrabian, A., & Williams, M. (1969). Nonverbal concomitants of perceived and intended persuasiveness. *Journal of Personality and Social Psychology, 13,* 37–58.

128. Knowles, E. S., & Brickner, M. A. (1981). Social cohesion effects on spatial cohesion. *Personality and Social Psychology Bulletin, 7,* 309–313.

129. See note 70.

130. Albert, S., & Dabbs, J. M., Jr. (1970). Physical distance and persuasion. *Journal of Personality, 15,* 265–270.

131. Burns, T. (1964, October). Nonverbal communication. *Discovery,* pp. 31–35.

132. Patterson, M. L., & Sechrest, L. B. (1970). Interpersonal distance and impression formation. *Journal of Personality, 38,* 161–166.

133. Aiello, J. R., & Thompson, D. E. (1980). When compensation fails: Mediating effects of sex and locus of control at extended interaction distances. *Basic and Applied Social Psychology, 1,* 65–82.

134. Winkel, F. W., Koppelaar, L., & Vrij, A. (1988). Creating suspects in police-citizen encounters: Two studies on personal space and being suspect. *Social Behavior, 3,* 307–318.

135. Kleck, R. (1969). Physical stigma and task oriented interactions. *Human Relations, 22,* 53–60.

136. Goldring, P. (1967). Role of distance and posture in the evaluation of interactions. *Proceedings of the 75th Annual Convention of the American Psychological Association.*

137. Haase, R. F., & Pepper, D. T., Jr. (1972). Nonverbal components of empathic communication. *Journal of Counselling Psychology, 19,* 417–424.

138. Konecni, V. J., Libuser, L., Morton, H., & Ebbesen, E. B. (1975). Effects of a violation of personal space on escape and helping response. *Journal of Experimental Social Psychology, 11,* 288–299.

139. DeBeer-Kelston, K., Mellon, L., & Solomon, L. Z. (1986). Helping behavior as a function of personal space invasion. *Journal of Social Psychology, 126,* 407–409.

140. Baron, R. A., & Bell, P. A. (1976). Physical distance and helping: Some unexpected benefits of "crowding in" on others. *Journals of Applied Social Psychology, 6,* 95–104.

141. Baron, R. A. (1978). Invasions of personal space and helping: Mediating effects of invader's apparent need. *Journal of Experimental Social Psychology, 14,* 304–312.

142. Buller, D. B. (1987). Communication apprehension and reactions to proxemic violations. *Journal of Nonverbal Behavior, 11,* 13–25.

143. Glick, P., DeMorest, J. A., & Hotze, C. A. (1988). Keeping your distance: Group membership, personal space, and requests for small favors. *Journal of Applied Social Psychology, 18,* 315–330.

144. See note 1.

145. Gardin, H., Kaplan, C. J., Firestone, I. J., & Cowan, G. A. (1973). Proxemic effects on cooperation, attitude, and approach-avoidance in prisoner's dilemma game. *Journal of Personality and Social Psychology, 27,* 13–19.

146. Seta, J. J., Paulus, P. B., & Schkade, J. K. (1976). Effects of group size and proximity under cooperative and competitive conditions. *Journal of Personality and Social Psychology, 34,* 47–53.

147. Edinger, J. A., & Patterson, M. L. (1983). Nonverbal involvement and social control. *Psychological Bulletin, 93,* 30–56.

148. Baxter, J. C. (1970). Interpersonal spacing in natural settings. *Sociometry, 33,* 444–456.

149. Duke, M. P., & Nowicki, S., Jr. (1972). A new measure and social learning model for interpersonal distance. *Journal of Experimental Research in Personality, 6,* 119–132.

150. Brown, S. R., Pipp, S., Martz, C., & Waring, R. (1993). Connection and separation in the mother-infant dyad: Patterns of touch and use of interpersonal space. *Infant Mental Health Journal, 14,* 317–329.

151. Lomranz, J., Shapira, A., Choresh, N., & Gilat, Y. (1975). Children's personal space as a function of age and sex. *Developmental Psychology, 11,* 541–545.

152. See note 14.

153. Isaacs, L. W., & Bearison, D. J. (1986). The development of children's prejudice against the aged. *International Journal of Aging and Human Development, 23,* 175–194.

154. Argyle, M., & Dean, J. (1965). Eye-contact, distance, and affiliation. *Sociometry, 28,* 289–304.

155. See note 49.

156. Ajdukovic, D. (1988). A contribution of the methodology of personal space research. *Psychologische Beitrage, 30,* 198–208.

157. Rosenfeld, H. M., Breck, B. E., Smith, S. H., & Kehoe, S. (1984). Intimacy mediators of the proximity-gaze compensation effect: Movement, conversational role, acquaintance, and gender. *Journal of Nonverbal Behavior, 8,* 235–249.

158. Cappella, J. N., & Green, J. O. (1984). The effects of distance and individual differences in arousability on nonverbal involvement: A test of discrepancy-arousal theory. *Journal of Nonverbal Behavior, 8,* 259–286.

159. Albas, D. C., & Albas, C. A. (1989). Meaning in context: The impact of eye contact and perception of threat on proximity. *Journal of Social Psychology, 129,* 525–531.

160. Hale, J. L., & Burgoon, J. K. (1984). Models of reactions to changes in nonverbal intimacy. *Journal of Nonverbal Behavior, 8,* 287–314.

161. Altman, I., & Taylor, D. A. (1973). *Social penetration: The development of interpersonal relationships.* New York: Holt, Rinehart and Winston.

162. Sundstrom, E., & Altman, I. (1976). Interpersonal relationships and personal space: Research review and theoretical model. *Human Ecology, 4,* 47–67.

163. Aiello, J. R. (1977). A further look at equilibrium theory: Visual interaction as a function of interpersonal distance. *Environmental Psychology and Nonverbal Behavior, 1,* 122–140.

164. Aiello, J. R., Thompson, D. E., & Baum, A. (1981). The symbiotic relationship between social psychology and environmental psychology: Implications from crowding, personal space, and intimacy regulation research. In J. H. Harvey (Ed.), *Cognition, social behavior, and the environment.* Hillsdale, NJ: Erlbaum.

165. Thompson, D. E., Aiello, J. R., & Epstein, Y. (1979). Interpersonal distance preferences. *Journal of Nonverbal Behavior, 4,* 113–118.

166. Aiello, J. R. (1972). A test of equilibrium theory: Visual interaction in relation to orientation, distance and sex of interactants. *Psychonomic Science, 27,* 335–336.

167. See note 163.

168. Aiello, J. R., & Thompson, D. E. (1980). When compensation fails: Mediating effects of sex and locus of control at extended interaction distances. *Basic and Applied Social Psychology, 1,* 65–82.

169. Knowles, E. S. (1980). An affiliative conflict theory of personal and group spatial behavior. In P. B. Paulus (Ed.), *Psychology of group influence.* Hillsdale, NJ: Erlbaum.

170. Knowles, E. S. (1989). Spatial behavior of individuals and groups. In P. B. Paulus (Ed.), *Psychology of group influence* (2nd ed.) Hillsdale, NJ: Erlbaum.

171. Sommer, R. (1974). Looking back at personal space. In J. Lang, C. Burnette, W. Moleski, & D. Vachon (Eds.), *Designing for human behavior: Architecture and behavioral sciences* (pp. 205–207). Stroudsburg, PA: Dowden, Hutchinson and Ross.

172. Osmond, H. (1957). Function as the basis of psychiatric ward design. *Mental Hospitals, 8,* 23–30.

173. Gifford, R. (1981). Sociability: Traits, settings, and interactions. *Journal of Personality and Social Psychology, 41,* 340–347.

174. Gifford, R., & Gallagher, T. M. B. (1985). Sociability: Personality, social context, and physical setting. *Journal of Personality and Social Psychology, 48,* 1015–1023.

175. Eastman, C. M., & Harper, J. (1971). A study of proxemic behavior. *Environment and Behavior, 3,* 418–437.

176. See note 41.

177. See note 1.

178. Winick, C., & Holt, H. (1961). Seating position as nonverbal communication in group analysis. *Psychiatry, 24,* 171–182.

179. Goodman, P. (1964). Seating arrangements: An elementary lecture in functional planning. *Utopian essays and practical proposals.* New York: Random House/Alfred A. Knopf.

Chapter 6

1. Kaplan, S., & Kaplan, R. (1978). *Humanscape: Environments for people.* North Scituate, MA: Duxbury Press, p. 264.

2. Edney, J. J. (1974). Human territoriality. *Psychological Bulletin, 81,* 959–975.

3. Taylor, R. B. (1988). *Human territorial functioning: An empirical, evolutionary perspective on individual and small group territorial cognitions, behaviors and consequences.* New York: Cambridge University Press.

4. See note 3.

5. Altman, I. (1975). *The environment and social behavior: Privacy, personal space, territoriality and crowding.* Monterey, CA: Brooks/Cole.

6. See note 5.

7. See note 5.

8. Lyman, S. M., & Scott, M. B. (1967). Territoriality: A neglected sociological dimension. *Social Problems, 15,* 235–249.

9. See note 8.

10. Kagehiro, D. K. (1990). Psycholegal research on the Fourth Amendment. *Psychological Science, 1,* 187–193.

11. Knapp, M. L. (1978). *Nonverbal communication in human interaction.* New York: Holt, Rinehart and Winston.

12. Jason, L. A., Reichler, A., & Rucker, W. (1981). Territorial behavior on beaches. *Journal of Social Psychology, 114,* 43–50.

13. Ruback, R. B., Pape, K. D., & Doriot, P. (1989). Waiting for a phone: Intrusion on callers leads to territorial defense. *Social Psychology Quarterly, 52,* 232–241.

14. Cashdan, E. (1983). Territoriality among human foragers: Ecological models and an application to four Bushman groups. *Current Anthropology, 24,* 47–66.

15. Taylor, R. B., & Lanni, J. C. (1981). Territorial dominance: The influence of the resident advantage in triadic decision making. *Journal of Personality and Social Psychology, 41,* 909–915.

16. Smith, H. W. (1981). Territorial spacing on a beach revisited: A cross-national exploration. *Social Psychology Quarterly, 44,* 132–137.

17. Sebba, R., & Churchman, A. (1983). Territories and territoriality in the home. *Environment and Behavior, 15,* 191–210.

18. Brower, S., Dockett, K., & Taylor, R. B. (1983). Residents' perceptions of territorial features and perceived local threat. *Environment and Behavior, 15,* 419–437.

19. Greenbaum, P. E., & Greenbaum, S. D. (1981). Territorial personalization: Group identity and social interaction in a Slavic-American neighborhood. *Environment and Behavior, 13,* 574–589.

20. See note 16.

21. Mercer, G. W., & Benjamin, M. L. (1980). Spatial behavior of university undergraduates in double occupancy residence rooms: An inventory of effects. *Journal of Applied Social Psychology, 10,* 32–44.

22. See note 17.

23. Wollman, N., Kelly, B. M., & Bordens, K. S. (1994). Environmental and intrapersonal predictors of reactions to potential territorial intrusions in the workplace. *Environment and Behavior, 26,* 179–194.

24. See note 21.

25. Kinney, J. M., Stephens, M. P., & Brockmann, A. M. (1987). Personal and environmental correlates of territoriality and use of space: An illustration in congregate housing for older adults. *Environment and Behavior, 19,* 722–737.

26. Taylor, R. B., Gottfredson, S. D., & Brower, S. (1981). Territorial cognitions and social climate in urban neighborhoods. *Basic and Applied Social Psychology, 2,* 289–303.

27. Marsh, P., & Collett, P. (1987). The car as a weapon. *Etc., 44,* 146–151.

28. See note 3.

29. See note 3.

30. See note 14.

31. See note 14.

32. See note 19.

33. See note 13.

34. Jacobs, J. (1961). *The death and life of great American cities.* New York: Vintage.

35. Newman, O. (1972). *Defensible space.* New York: Macmillan.

36. See note 3.

37. Brown, B. B., & Altman, I. (1983). Territoriality, defensible space, and residential burglary. *Journal of Environmental Psychology, 3,* 203–220.

38. Ley, D., & Cybriwsky, R. (1974). The spatial ecology of stripped cars. *Environment and Behavior, 6,* 53–68.

39. Sommer, R. (1987). Crime and vandalism in university residence halls: A confirmation of defensible space theory. *Journal of Environmental Psychology, 7,* 1–12.

40. D'Alessio, S., & Stolzenberg, L. (1990). A crime of convenience: The environment and convenience store robbery. *Environment and Behavior, 22,* 255–271.

41. Wise, J. A., & Wise, B. K. (ca. 1985). *Bank interiors and bank robberies: A design approach to environmental security.* Rolling Meadows, IL: Bank Administration Institute.

42. Macdonald, J. E., & Gifford, R. (1989). Territorial cues and defensible space theory: The burglar's point of view. *Journal of Environmental Psychology, 9,* 193–205.

43. Brown, B. B., & Bentley, D. L. (1993). Residential burglars judge risk: The role of territoriality. *Journal of Environmental Psychology, 13,* 51–61.

44. Newman, O. (1980). *Community of interest.* New York: Anchor Press/Doubleday.

45. Brown, B. B., & Werner, C. M. (1985). Social cohesiveness, territoriality, and holiday decorations: The influence of cul-de-sacs. *Environment and Behavior, 17,* 539–565.

46. Perkins, D. D., Wandersman, A. H., Rich, R. C., & Taylor, R. B. (1993). The physical environment of street crime: Defensible space, territoriality, and incivilities. *Journal of Environmental Psychology, 13,* 29–49.

47. See note 16.

48. Edney, J. J., & Jordan-Edney, N. L. (1974). Territorial spacing on a beach. *Sociometry, 37,* 92–104.

49. Worchel, S., & Lollis, M. (1982). Reactions to territorial contamination as a function of culture. *Personality and Social Psychology Bulletin, 8,* 370–375.

50. See note 19.

51. Campbell, A. C., Munce, S., & Galea, J. (1982). American gangs and British subcultures: A comparison. *International Journal of Offender Therapy and Comparative Criminology, 26,* 76–89.

52. Ruback, R. B., & Snow, J. J. (1993). Territoriality and nonconscious racism at water fountains: Intruders and drinkers (Blacks and Whites) are affected by race. *Environment and Behavior, 25,* 250–267.

53. Truscott, J. C., Parmelee, P., & Werner, C. (1977). Plate touching in restaurants: Preliminary observations of a food-related marking behavior in humans. *Personality and Social Psychology Bulletin, 3,* 425–428.

54. Werner, C., Brown, B., & Damron, G. (1981). Territorial marking in a game arcade. *Journal of Personality and Social Psychology, 41,* 1094–1104.

55. Ley, D., & Cybriwsky, R. (1974). Urban graffiti as territorial markers. *Annals of the Association of American Geographers, 64,* 491–505.

56. Becker, F. D. (1973). Study of spatial markers. *Journal of Personality and Social Psychology, 26,* 439–445.

57. Holahan, C. J. (1976). Environmental change in a psychiatric setting: A social systems analyze. *Human Relations, 29,* 153–166.

58. Vinsel, A., Brown, B. B., Altman, L., & Foss, C. (1980). Privacy regulation, territorial displays, and effectiveness of individual functioning. *Journal of Personality and Social Psychology, 39,* 1104–1115.

59. Edney, J. J. (1976). The psychological role of property rights in human behavior. *Environment and Planning: A, 8,* 811–822.

60. Edney, J. J. (1972). Property, possession and permanence: A field study in human territoriality. *Journal of Applied Social Psychology, 2,* 275–282.

61. See note 13.

62. Taylor, R. B., & Brooks, D. K. (1980). Temporary territories: Responses to intrusions in a public setting. *Population and Environment, 3,* 135–145.

63. See note 55.

64. Brown, B. B., & Harris, P. B. (1989). Residential burglary victimization: Reactions to the invasion of a primary territory. *Journal of Environmental Psychology, 9,* 119–132.

65. Edney, J. J. (1975). Territoriality and control: A field experiment. *Journal of Personality and Social Psychology, 6,* 1108–1115.

66. Esser, A. H. (1968). Dominance hierarchy and clinical course of psychiatrically hospitalized boys. *Child Development, 39,* 147–157.

67. Esser, A. H., Chamberlain, A. S., Chapple, E. D., & Kline, N. S. (1965). Territoriality of patients on a research ward. In J. Wortis (Ed.), *Recent advances in biological psychiatry.* New York: Plenum.

68. Paslawsky, L., & Ivinskis, A. (1980). Dominance, agonistic and territorial behavior in institutionalized mentally retarded patients. *Australian Journal of Developmental Disabilities, 6,* 17–24.

69. Sundstrom, E., & Altman, I. (1974). Field study of territorial behavior and dominance. *Journal of Personality and Social Psychology, 30,* 115–124.

70. See note 5.

71. See note 15.

72. Austin, W. T. (1982). Portrait of a courtroom: Social and ecological impressions of the adversary process. *Criminal Justice and Behavior, 9,* 286–302.

73. Harris, P. B., & McAndrew, F. T. (1986). Territoriality and compliance: The influence of gender and location on willingness to sign petitions. *Journal of Social Psychology, 126,* 657–662.

74. Schwartz, B., & Barsky, S. F. (1977). The home advantage. *Social Forces, 55,* 641–661.

75. Cornuneya, K. S., & Carron, A. V. (1992). The home advantage in sport competition: A literature review. *Journal of Sport and Exercise Psychology, 14*(1), 13–27.

76. Greer, D. L. (1983). Spectator booing and the home advantage: A study of social influence in the basketball arena. *Social Psychology Quarterly, 46,* 252–261.

77. Lehman, D. R., & Reifman, A. (1987). Spectator influence on basketball officiating. *Journal of Social Psychology, 127,* 673–675.

78. Agnew, G. A., & Carron, A. V. (1994). Crowd effects and the home advantage. *International Journal of Sport Psychology, 25,* 53–62.

79. Baumeister, R. F. (1985). The championship choke. *Psychology Today, 19*(4), 48–52.

80. James, B. (1984). A few words about the home field advantage. In B. James (Ed.), *The Bill James baseball abstract 1984.* New York: Ballantine.

81. Gifford, R. (1976). Environmental numbness in the classroom. *Journal of Experimental Education, 44,* 4–7.

82. Taylor, R. B., & Stough, R. R. (1978). Territorial cognition: Assessing Altman's typology. *Journal of Personality and Social Psychology, 36,* 418–423.

83. Schiavo, R. S., Kobashi, K. C., Quinn, C., Sefcsik, A., & Synn, L. (1990). *Territorial influences on permeability of group spatial boundaries.* Paper presented at the annual meetings of the American Psychological Association, Boston.

84. Ardrey, R. (1966). *The territorial imperative.* New York: Atheneum.

85. See note 3.

86. See note 59.

87. Barker, R. G. (1968). *Ecological psychology: Concepts and methods for studying the environment of human behavior.* Stanford, CA: Stanford University Press.

88. Willems, E. P., & Campbell, D. E. (1976). One path through the cafeteria. *Environment and Behavior, 8,* 125–140.

89. Wicker, A. W. (1979). *An introduction to ecological psychology.* Monterey, CA: Brooks/Cole.

90. See note 89.

91. Je, H. (1987). Urban residential streets: A study of street types and their territorial performances. *Dissertation Abstracts International, 47*(7-A), 2346.

92. Shumaker, S. A., & Reizenstein, J. E. (1982). Environmental factors affecting inpatient stress in acute care hospitals. In G. W. Evans (Ed.), *Environmental stress.* New York: Cambridge University Press.

93. Nelson, M. N., & Paluck, R. J. (1980). Territorial markings, self-concept, and the mental status of the institutionalized elderly. *Gerontologist, 20,* 96–98.

94. Sommer, R. (1969). *Personal space: The behavioral basis of design.* Englewood Cliffs, NJ: Prentice-Hall.

95. See note 92.

Chapter 7

1. Freedman, J. L. (1975). *Crowding and behavior.* San Francisco: Freeman.

2. China's Population Day marks 1.2–billionth birth. (1994, February 15). *Toronto Globe and Mail.*

3. Howard, G. S. (1993). On certain blindnesses in human beings: Psychology and world overpopulation. *Counseling Psychologist, 21,* 560–581.

4. Seligman, D. (1994, October 3). Keeping up. *Fortune Magazine,* pp. 155–156.

5. LeBon, G. (1903). *The crowd.* (Translated from Psychologie des Foules.) London: Allen and Unwin.

6. Allport, F. H. (1924). *Social psychology.* Boston: Houghton Mifflin.

7. LaPiere, R. T., & Farnsworth, P. R. (1942). *Social psychology.* New York: McGraw-Hill.

8. Lachman, S. J. (1993). Psychology and riots. *Psychology: A Journal of Human Behavior, 30,* 16–23.

9. Epstein, Y. M. (1982). Crowding stress and human behavior. In G. W. Evans (Ed.), *Environmental stress.* New York: Cambridge University Press.

10. James, J. (1951). A preliminary study of the size determinant in small group interaction. *American Sociological Review, 16,* 474–477.

11. Milgram, S., & Toch, H. (1969). Collective behavior: Crowds and social movements. In G. Lindzey & E. Aronson (Eds.), *The handbook of social psychology.* Reading, MA: Addison-Wesley.

12. Bruce, J. A. (1965). The pedestrian. In J. E. Baewald (Ed.), *Traffic engineering handbook.* Washington, DC: Institute of Traffic Engineers.

13. Weller, M. P. (1985). Crowds, mobs, and riots. *Medicine, Science, and the Law, 25,* 295–303.

14. Hovland, C. I., & Sears, R. R. (1940). Minor studies in aggression: VI. Correlation of lynchings with economic indices. *Journal of Psychology, 9,* 301–310.

15. Pickard, P. P. (1990). An investigation of crowd behaviors in selected Australian sports, with particular emphasis on violence, aggressive behavior and facilities. *Dissertation Abstracts International, 51–A,* 1547.

16. Stokols, D. (1972). On the distinction between density and crowding: Some implications for further research. *Psychological Review, 79,* 75–277.

17. Westover, T. N., & Collins, J. R. (1987). Perceived crowding in recreation settings: An urban case study. *Leisure Sciences, 9,* 87–99.

18. Gove, W. R., & Hughes, M. (1983). *Overcrowding in the household.* New York: Academic Press.

19. O'Brien, G. E., & Pembroke, M. (1982). Crowding, density and the job satisfaction of clerical employees. *Australian Journal of Psychology, 34,* 151–164.

20. Schaeffer, M. A., Baum, A., Paulus, P. B., & Gaess, G. G. (1988). Architecturally mediated effects of social density in prison. *Environment and Behavior, 20,* 3–19.

21. Rapoport, A. (1975). Toward a redefinition of density. *Environment and Behavior, 7,* 133–158.

22. West, P. C. (1982). Effects of user behavior on the perception of crowding in backcountry forest recreation. *Forest Science, 28,* 95–105.

23. Eroglu, S., & Harrell, G. D. (1986). Retail crowding: Theoretical and strategic implications. *Journal of Retailing, 62,* 346–363.

24. Eroglu, S., & Machleit, K. A. (1990). An empirical study of retail crowding: Antecedents and consequences. *Journal of Retailing, 66,* 201–221.

25. McGrew, P. L. (1970). Social and spatial density effects on spacing behavior in preschool children. *Journal of Child Psychology and Psychiatry, 11,* 197–205.

26. Schmitt, R. C. (1957). Density, delinquency and crime in Honolulu. *Sociology and Social Research, 41,* 274–276.

27. Zlutnick, S., & Altman, I. (1972). Crowding and human behavior. In J. Wohlwill & D. Carson (Eds.), *Environment and the social sciences: Perspectives and applications.* Washington, DC: American Psychological Association.

28. Knowles, E. (1979). The proximity of others: A critique of crowding research and integration with the social sciences. *Journal of Population, 2,* 3–17.

29. O'Brien, F. (1990). A crowding index for finite populations. *Perceptual and Motor Skills, 70,* 3–11.

30. O'Brien, F. (1992). Approximation methods in discrete spatial density analysis for finite populations. *Perceptual and Motor Skills, 74*(3, Part 1), 867–873.

31. Mielke, P. W., & Berry, K. J. (1992). Statistical inference for the population density index. *Perceptual and Motor Skills, 75*(2), 371–374.

32. O'Brien, F. (1993). Approximation formula unit lattice average distance in the population density index model. *Perceptual and Motor Skills, 76*(3, Part 2), 1071–1074.

33. O'Brien, F. (1993). Counting your M and N's. *Perceptual and Motor Skills, 76*(3, Part 2), 1153–1154.

34. Knowles, E. (1983). Social physics and the effects of others: Tests of the effects of audience size and distance on social judgments and behavior. *Journal of Personality and Social Psychology, 45,* 1263–1279.

35. Stokols, D. (1978). A typology of crowding experiences. In A. Baum & Y. M. Epstein (Eds.), *Human response to crowding.* Hillsdale, NJ: Erlbaum.

36. Sundstrom, E. (1978). Crowding as a sequential process: Review of research on the effects of population density on humans. In A. Baum & Y. M. Epstein (Eds), *Human response to crowding.* Hillsdale, NJ: Erlbaum.

37. Aiello, J. R., & Thompson, D. E. (1980). Personal space, crowding and spatial behavior in a cultural context. In I. Altman & J. F. Wohlwill (Eds.), *Environment and culture.* New York: Plenum.

38. Montano, D., & Adamopoulos, J. (1984). The perception of crowding in interpersonal situations: Affective and behavioral responses. *Environment and Behavior, 16,* 643–666.

39. See note 18.

40. Schmidt, D. E., & Keating, J. P. (1979). Human crowding and personal control: An integration of the research. *Psychological Bulletin, 86,* 680–700.

41. McCallum, R., Rusbalt, C. E., Hong, G. K., Walden, T. A., & Schopler, J. (1979). Effects of resource availability and importance of behavior on the experience of crowding. *Journal of Personality and Social Psychology, 37,* 1304–1313.

42. Walden, T. A., Nelson, P. A., & Smith, D. E. (1981). Crowding, privacy and coping. *Environment and Behavior, 13,* 205–224.

43. Aiello, J. R., Vautier, J. S., & Bernstein, M. D. (1983, August). *Crowding stress: Impact of social support, group formation and control.* Paper presented at the annual meeting of the American Psychological Association, Anaheim, CA.

44. Burger, J. M., Oakman, J. A., & Bullard, N. G. (1983). Desire for control and the perception of crowding. *Personality and Social Psychology Bulletin, 9,* 475–479.

45. Miller, S., & Nardini, R. M. (1977). Individual differences in the perception of crowding. *Environmental Psychology and Nonverbal Behavior, 2*, 3–13.

46. Miller, S., Rossbach, J., & Munson, R. (1981). Social density and affiliative tendency as determinants of dormitory residential outcomes. *Journal of Applied Social Psychology, 11*, 356–365.

47. Baum, A., Calesnick, L. E., Davis, G. E., & Gatchel, R. J. (1982). Individual differences in coping with crowding: Stimulus screening and social overload. *Journal of Personality and Social Psychology, 43*, 821–830.

48. Schreyer, R., & Roggenbuck, J. (1978). The influence of experience expectations on crowding perceptions and socio-psychological carrying capacities. *Leisure Sciences, 1*, 373–394.

49. Webb, B., Worchel, S., Riechers, L., Wayne, W. (1986). The influence of categorization on perceptions of crowding. *Personality and Social Psychology Bulletin, 12*, 539–546.

50. Kamal, P., & Gupta, I. D. (1988). Feeling of crowding and psychiatric disorders. *Indian Journal of Psychiatry, 30*, 85–89.

51. Womble, P., & Studebaker, S. (1981). Crowding in a national park campground: Katmai National Monument in Alaska. *Environment and Behavior, 13*, 557–573.

52. Shelby, B., Heberlein, T. A., Vaske, J. J., & Alfano, G. (1983). Expectations, preferences, and feeling crowded in recreation activities. *Leisure Sciences, 6*, 1–14.

53. Williams, D. R., Roggenbuck, J. W., & Bange, S. P. (1991). The effect of norm-encounter compatibility on crowding perceptions, experience, and behavior in river recreation settings. *Journal of Leisure Research, 23*, 154–172.

54. Baum, A., & Greenberg, C. I. (1975). Waiting for a crowd: The behavioral and perceptual effects of anticipated crowding. *Journal of Personality and Social Psychology, 32*, 671–679.

55. See note 36.

56. Baum, A., Fisher, J. D., & Solomon, S. K. (1981). Type of information, familiarity and the reduction of crowding stress. *Journal of Personality and Social Psychology, 40*, 11–23.

57. Rohe, W. M. (1982). The response to density in residential settings: The mediating effects of social and personal variables. *Journal of Applied Social Psychology, 12*, 292–303.

58. Manning, R. E. (1985). Crowding norms in backcountry settings: A review and synthesis. *Journal of Leisure Research, 17*, 75–89.

59. See note 35.

60. Booth, A. (1976). *Urban crowding and its consequences*. New York: Praeger.

61. Webb, W. M., & Worchel, S. (1993). Prior experience and expectation in the context of crowding. *Journal of Personality and Social Psychology, 65*, 512–521.

62. Aiello, J. R., Thompson, D. E., & Brodzinsky, D. M. (1983). How funny is crowding anyway? Effects of room size, group size and the introduction of humor. *Basic and Applied Social Psychology, 4*, 193–207.

63. Epstein, Y. M., & Karlin, R. A. (1975). Effects of acute experimental crowding. *Journal of Applied Social Psychology, 5*, 34–53.

64. Aiello, J. R., Epstein, Y. M., & Karlin, R. A. (1975). *Field experimental research on human crowding*. Paper presented at the annual meetings of the American Psychological Association, New York.

65. Aiello, J. R., Nicosia, G., & Thompson, D. E. (1979). Physiological, social and behavioral consequences of crowding on children and adolescents. *Child Development, 50*, 195–202.

66. Aiello, J. R., Baum, A., & Gormley, F. B. (1981). Social determinants of residential crowding stress. *Personality and Social Psychology Bulletin, 7*, 643–649.

67. See note 42.

68. Aiello, J. R., Thompson, D. E., & Baum, A. (1981). The symbiotic relationship between social psychology and environmental psychology: Implications from crowding, personal space, and intimacy regulation research. In J. H. Harvey (Ed.), *Cognition, social behavior, and the environment*. Hillsdale, NJ: Erlbaum.

69. Mueller, C. W. (1984). The effects of mood and type and timing of influence on the perception of crowding. *Journal of Psychology, 116*, 155–158.

70. Gurkaynak, M. R., & LeCompte, W. A. (1979). *Human consequences of crowding*. New York: Plenum.

71. Nasar, J. L., & Min, M. S. (1984). *Modifiers of perceived spaciousness and crowding: A cross-cultural study*. Paper presented at the annual meeting of the American Psychological Association, Toronto, Ontario.

72. Hall, E. T. (1966). *The hidden dimension*. Garden City, NY: Doubleday.

73. See note 40.

74. See note 42.

75. See note 34.

76. Six, B., Martin, P., & Pecher, M. (1983). A cultural comparison of perceived crowding and discomfort: The United States and West Germany. *The Journal of Psychology, 114*, 63–67.

77. Schiffenbauer, A. I. (1979). Designing for high-density living. In J. R. Aiello & A. Baum (Eds.), *Residential crowding and design*. New York: Plenum.

78. Hammitt, W. E., McDonald, C. D., & Noe, F. P. (1984). Use level and encounters: Important variables of perceived crowding among nonspecialized recreationists. *Journal of Leisure Research, 16*, 1–8.

79. Carron, A. V., Brawley, L. R., & Widmeyer, W. N. (1990). The impact of group size in an exercise setting. *Journal of Sport and Exercise Psychology, 12*, 376–387.

80. Andereck, K. L., & Becker, R. H. (1993). Perceptions of carry-over crowding in recreation environments. *Leisure Sciences, 15*, 25–35.

81. Nicosia, G. J., Hyman, D., Karlin, R. A., Epstein, Y. M., & Aiello, J. R. (1979). Effects of bodily contact on reactions to crowding. *Journal of Applied Social Psychology, 9*, 508–523.

82. See note 51.

83. See note 35.

84. Aiello, J. R., & Baum, A. (1979). *Residential crowding and design*. New York: Plenum.

85. Aiello, J. R., Epstein, Y. M., & Karlin, R. A. (1975, April). *Field experimental research on human crowding*. Paper presented at the annual meeting of the American Psychological Association, New York.

86. See note 43.

87. Baron, R. M., Mandel, D. R., Adams, C. A., & Griffin, L. M. (1976). Effects of social density in university residential environments. *Journal of Personality and Social Psychology, 34,* 434–446.

88. See note 42.

89. See note 66.

90. See note 43.

91. Gormley, F. P., & Aiello, J. R. (1982). Social density, interpersonal relationships and residential crowding stress. *Journal of Applied Social Psychology, 12,* 222–236.

92. Reddy, D. M., Baum, A., Fleming, R., & Aiello, J. R. (1981). Mediation on social density by coalition formation. *Journal of Applied Social Psychology, 11,* 529–537.

93. Baum, A., Shapiro, A., Murray, D., & Widerman, M. (1979). Interpersonal mediation of perceived crowding and control in residential dyads and triads. *Journal of Applied Social Psychology, 9,* 491–507.

94. See note 92.

95. Schaeffer, G. H., & Patterson, M. L. (1980). Intimacy, arousal and small group crowding. *Journal of Personal and Social Psychology, 38,* 283–290.

96. See note 58.

97. Fisher, J. D., & Baum, A. (1980). Situational and arousal-based messages and the reduction of crowding stress. *Journal of Applied Social Psychology, 10,* 191–201.

98. See note 56.

99. Osuna, E. E. (1985). The psychological cost of waiting. *Journal of Mathematical Psychology, 29,* 82–105.

100. See note 58.

101. Wener, R. E., & Kaminoff, R. D. (1983). Improving environmental information: Effects of signs on perceived crowding and behavior. *Environment and Behavior, 15,* 3–20.

102. Schmidt, D. E., Goldman, R. D., & Feimer, N. R. (1979). Perceptions of crowding: Predicting at the residence, neighborhood and city levels. *Environment and Behavior, 11,* 105–130.

103. Loo, C., & Ong, P. (1984). Crowding perceptions, attitudes, and consequences among the Chinese. *Environment and Behavior, 16,* 55–67.

104. Baum, A., Aiello, J. R., & Calesnick, L. E. (1978). Crowding and perceived control: Social density and the development of learned helplessness. *Journal of Personality and Social Psychology, 36,* 1000–1011.

105. Baum, A., Davis, G. E., & Valins, S. (1979). Generating behavioral data for the design process. In J. R. Aiello & A. Baum (Eds.), *Residential crowding and design.* New York: Plenum.

106. Baum, A., & Valins, S. (1977). *Architecture and social behavior: Psychological studies of social density.* Hillsdale, NJ: Erlbaum.

107. McCarthy, D., & Saegert, S. (1979). Residential density, social overload and social withdrawal. In J. R. Aiello & A. Baum (Eds.), *Residential crowding and design.* New York: Plenum.

108. See note 77.

109. See note 77.

110. See note 36.

111. See note 71.

112. Mandel, D. R., Baron, R. M., & Fisher, J. D. (1980). Room utilization and dimensions of density: Effects of height and view. *Environment and Behavior, 12,* 308–319.

113. See note 77.

114. See note 112.

115. See note 71.

116. See note 77.

117. Savinar, J. (1975). The effect of ceiling height on personal space. *Man-Environment Systems, 5,* 321–324.

118. Rotton, J. (1987). Hemmed in and hating it: Effects of shape of room on tolerance for crowding. *Perceptual and Motor Skills, 64,* 285–286.

119. Wener, R. (1977). Non-density factors in the perception of crowding. *Dissertation Abstracts International, 37B,* 3569–3570.

120. McConnell, K. E. (1977). Congestion and willingness to pay: A study of beach use. *Land Economics, 53,* 185–195.

121. Stankey, G. H. (1980). *A comparison of carrying capacity perceptions among visitors to two wildernesses* (Report INT-142). Ogden, UT: USDA Forest Service.

122. Vaske, J. J., Graefe, A. R., & Dempster, A. (1982). Social and environmental influences on perceived crowding. In *Proceedings of the wilderness psychology group conference* (pp. 211–227). Morgantown: West Virginia University.

123. Ruback, R. B., & Pandey, J. (1992). Very hot and really crowded: Quasi-experimental investigations of Indian "tempos." *Environment and Behavior, 24,* 527–554.

124. Wynne-Edwards, V. C. (1965). Self-regulating systems in populations of animals. *Science, 147,* 1543–1548.

125. Calhoun, J. B. (1971). Space and the strategy of life. In A. H. Esser (Ed.), *Behavior and environment: The use of space by animals and men.* New York: Plenum.

126. Wynne-Edwards, V. C. (1972). *Animal dispersion in relation to social behavior.* New York: Hafner.

127. Calhoun, J. B. (1962). Population density and social pathology. *Scientific American, 206,* 139–148.

128. Calhoun, J. B. (1966). The role of space in animal sociology. *Journal of Social Issues, 22*(4), 46–58.

129. See note 125.

130. Archer, J. (1970). Effects of population density on behavior in rodents. In J. H. Crook (Ed.), *Social behavior in birds and mammals.* New York: Academic Press.

131. Freedman, J. L. (1979). Reconciling apparent differences between the responses of human and other animals to crowding. *Psychological Review, 86,* 80–85.

132. See note 9.

133. D'Atri, D. A. (1975). Psychophysical responses to crowding. *Environment and Behavior, 7,* 237–252.

134. Epstein, Y. M., Woolfolk, R. L., & Lehrer, P. M. (1981). Physiological, cognitive and nonverbal responses to repeated exposure to crowding. *Journal of Applied Social Psychology, 11,* 1–13.

135. Evans, G. W. (1979). Crowding and human performance. *Journal of Applied Social Psychology, 9,* 27–46.

136. See note 65.

137. Cox, V. C., Paulus, P. B., McCain, G., & Schkade, J. K. (1979). Field research on the effects of crowding in persons and on off-

shore drilling platforms. In J. R. Aiello & A. Baum (Eds.), *Residential crowding and design*. New York: Plenum.

138. See note 81.

139. Fleming, I., Baum, A., & Weiss, L. (1987). Social density and perceived control as mediators of crowding stress in high-density residential neighborhoods. *Journal of Personality and Social Psychology, 52*, 899–906.

140. Cox, V. C., Paulus, P. B., & McCain, G. (1984). Prison crowding research: The relevance of prison housing standards and a general approach regarding crowding phenomena. *American Psychologist, 39*, 1148–1160.

141. McCain, G., Cox, V. C., & Paulus, P. B. (1976). The relationship between illness complaints and degree of crowding in a prison environment. *Environment and Behavior, 8*, 283–290.

142. Wener, R. E., & Keys, C. (1988). The effects of changes in jail population densities on crowding, sick call, and spatial behavior. *Journal of Applied Social Behavior, 18*, 852–866.

143. See note 1.

144. Levy, L., & Herzog, A. W. (1974). Effects of population density and crowding on health and social adaptation in the Netherlands. *Journal of Health and Social Behavior, 4*, 228–240.

145. Fuller, T. D., Edwards, J. N., Sermsri, S., & Vorakitphokatorn, S. (1993). Housing, stress, and physical well-being: Evidence from Thailand. *Social Science and Medicine, 36*, 1417–1428.

146. Aiello, J. R., DeRisi, D. T., Epstein, Y. M., & Karlin, R. A. (1977). Crowding, and the role of interpersonal distance preference. *Sociometry, 40*, 271–282.

147. Nianfeng, G. (1987). Social investigation and analysis of mental health problems. *International Journal of Mental Health, 16*, 43–50.

148. Marsella, A., Escudero, M., & Gordon, P. (1970). The effects of dwelling density on mental disorders in Filipino men. *Journal of Health and Social Behavior, 11*, 288–294.

149. Gabe, J., & Williams, P. (1986). Is space bad for your health? The relationship between crowding in the home and emotional distress in women. *Sociology of Health and Illness, 8*, 351–371.

150. Magaziner, J. (1988). Living density and psychopathology: A re-examination of the negative model. *Psychological Medicine, 18*, 419–431.

151. Lepore, S. J., Evans, G. W., & Palsane, M. N. (1991). Social hassles and psychological health in the context of chronic crowding. *Journal of Health and Social Behavior, 32*, 357–367.

152. Evans, G. W., Palsane, M. N., Lepore, S. J., & Martin, J. (1989). Residential density and psychological health: The mediating effects of social support. *Journal of Personality and Social Psychology, 57*, 994–999.

153. Lepore, S. J., Evans, G. W., & Schneider, M. L. (1992). Role of control and social support in explaining the stress of hassles and crowding. *Environment and Behavior, 24*, 795–811.

154. See note 152.

155. Sommer, R. (1965). The isolated drinker in the Edmonton beer parlor. *Quarterly Journal of Studies on Alcohol, 26*, 95–110.

156. Cutler, R. E., & Storm, T. (1975). Observational study of alcohol consumption in natural settings: The Vancouver beer parlor. *Journal of Studies on Alcohol, 36*, 1173–1183.

157. Graves, T. D., Graves, N. B., Semu, V. N., & Ah Sam, I. (1982). Patterns of public drinking in a multi-ethnic society: A systematic observational study. *Journal of Studies on Alcohol, 43*, 990–1009.

158. Donnelly, P. G. (1978). Alcohol problems and sales in the counties of Pennsylvania. A social area investigation. *Journal of Studies on Alcohol, 39*, 848–858.

159. Tryon, G. (1985). An exploratory study of the relationship between residence hall design and student alcohol consumption. *Journal of College Student Personnel, 20*, 372–373.

160. Foster, H. D. (1990). Population density and cirrhosis of the liver. Unpublished raw data, University of Victoria.

161. Hammer, T., & Vaglum, P. (1989). The increase in alcohol consumption among women: A phenomenon related to accessibility or stress? A general population study. *British Journal of Addiction, 84*, 767–775.

162. Dutton, D. B. (1985). Socioeconomic status and children's health. *Medical Care, 23*, 142–156.

163. Widmayer, S. M., Peterson, L. M., Larner, M., Carnahan, S., et al. (1990). Predictors of Haitian-American infant development at twelve months. *Child Development, 61*, 410–415.

164. Richter, L. M. (1989). Household density, family size and the growth and development of Black children: A cross-sectional study from infancy to middle childhood. *South African Journal of psychology, 19*, 191–198.

165. Maxwell, L. E. (1990). The effects of crowding on the social and cognitive development of young children. *Dissertation Abstracts International, 51*(6-B), 3187.

166. See note 135.

167. Nagar, D., Pandey, J., & Paulus, P. B. (1988). The effects of residential crowding experience on reactivity to laboratory crowding and noise. *Journal of Applied Social Psychology, 18*, 1423–1442.

168. Sinha, S. P., & Sinha, S. P. (1991). Personal space and density as factors in task performance and feeling of crowding. *Journal of Social Psychology, 131*, 831–837.

169. Heller, J. F., Groff, B. D., & Solomon, S. (1977). Toward an understanding of crowding: The role of physical interaction. *Journal of Personality and Social Psychology, 35*, 183–190.

170. See note 34.

171. Schkade, J. (1977). *The effects of expectancy set and crowding on task performance*. Doctoral dissertation, University of Texas at Arlington.

172. Klein, K., & Harris, B. (1979). Disruptive effects of disconfirmed expectancies about crowding. *Journal of Personality and Social Psychology, 37*, 769–777.

173. See note 167.

174. Kelley, K. (1985). Nine social indices as functions of population size or density. *Bulletin of the Psychonomic Society, 23*, 124–126.

175. Baum, A., & Koman, S. (1976). Differential response to anticipated crowding: Psychological effects of social and spatial density. *Journal of Personality and Social Psychology, 34*, 526–536.

176. Thalhofer, N. (1980). Violation of a spacing norm in high social density. *Journal of Applied Social Psychology, 10*, 175–183.

177. See note 140.

178. See note 140.

179. Palmstierna, T., Huitfeldt, B., & Wistedt, B. (1991). The relationship of crowding and aggressive behavior on a psychiatric intensive care unit. *Hospital and Community Psychiatry, 42,* 1237–1240.

180. Loo, C., & Kennelly, D. (1979). Social density: Its effects on behaviors and perceptions of preschoolers. *Environmental Psychology and Nonverbal Behavior, 3,* 131–146.

181. Loo, C. M. (1972). The effects of spatial density on the social behavior of children. *Journal of Applied Social Psychology, 4,* 372–381.

182. Smith, P., & Connolly, K. (1977). Social and aggressive behavior in preschool children as a function of crowding. *Social Science Information, 16,* 601–620.

183. Zuravin, S. J. (1986). Residential density and urban child mistreatment: An aggregate analysis. *Journal of Family Violence, 1,* 307–322.

184. Zeedyk-Ryan, J., & Smith, G. F. (1983). The effects of crowding on hostility, anxiety, and desire for social interaction. *Journal of Social Psychology, 120,* 245–252.

185. See note 54.

186. See note 65.

187. See note 134.

188. Liddell, C., & Kruger, P. (1987). Activity and social behavior in a South African township nursery: Some effects of crowding. *Merrill-Palmer Quarterly, 33,* 195–211.

189. Bickman, L., Teger, A., Gabriele, T., McLaughlin, C., & Sunaday, E. (1973). Dormitory density and helping behavior. *Environment and Behavior, 5,* 465–490.

190. Jorgenson, D. O., & Dukes, F. O. (1976). Deindividuation as a function of density and group membership. *Journal of Personality and Social Psychology, 34,* 24–39.

191. Levine, R. V., Martinez, T. S., Brase, G., & Sorenson, K. (1994). Helping in 36 U.S. cities. *Journal of Personality and Social Psychology, 67,* 69–82.

192. See note 36.

193. Sundstrom, E. (1975). An experimental study of crowding: Effects of room size, intrusion and goal blocking on nonverbal behavior, self disclosure and self-reported stress. *Journal of Personality and Social Psychology, 32,* 645–654.

194. See note 139.

195. See note 54.

196. See note 188.

197. Reichner, R. F. (1979). Differential responses to being ignored: The effects of architectural design and social density on interpersonal behavior. *Journal of Applied Social Psychology, 9,* 13–26.

198. Lakey, B. (1989). Personal and environmental antecedents of perceived social support developed at college. *American Journal of Community Psychology, 17,* 503–519.

199. Evans, G. W., & Lepore, S. J. (1993). Household crowding and social support: A quasi-experimental analysis. *Journal of Personality and Social Psychology, 65,* 308–316.

200. Jain, U. (1993). Concomitants of population density in India. *Journal of Social Psychology, 133,* 331–336.

201. See note 183.

202. Freedman, J. L., Birsky, J., & Cavoukian, A. (1980). Environmental determinants of behavioral contagion: Density and number. *Basic and Applied Social Psychology, 1,* 155–161.

203. See note 62.

204. See note 202.

205. See note 62.

206. Prerost, F. J. (1982). The development of the mood-inhibiting effects of crowding during adolescence. *Journal of Psychology, 110,* 197–202.

207. Prerost, F. J., & Brewer, R. K. (1980). The appreciation of humor by males and females during conditions of crowding experimentally induced. *Psychology: A Journal of Human Behavior, 17,* 15–17.

208. Burrus-Bammel, L. L., & Bammel, G. (1986). Visiting patterns and effects of density at a visitors' center. *Journal of Environmental Education, 18*(1), 7–10.

209. Fuhrer, U. (1987). Effects of social density and pre-knowledge on question-asking in a novel setting. *Journal of Environmental Psychology, 7,* 159–168.

210. Kuentzel, W. F., & Heberlein, T. A. (1992). Cognitive and behavioral adaptations to perceived crowding: A panel study of coping and displacement. *Journal of Leisure Research, 24,* 377–393.

211. See note 24.

212. Hui, M. K., & Bateson, J. E. (1991). Perceived control and the effects of crowding and consumer choice on the service experience. *Journal of Consumer Research, 18,* 174–184.

213. Langer, E. J., & Saegert, S. (1977). Crowding and cognitive control. *Journal of Personality and Social Psychology, 35,* 175–182.

214. Gillis, A. R., Richard, M. A., & Hagan, J. (1986). Ethnic susceptibility to crowding: An empirical analysis. *Environment and Behavior, 18,* 683–706.

215. Gifford, R., & Peacock, J. (1979). Crowding: More fearsome than crime-provoking? Comparison of an Asian city and a North American city. *Psychologia, 22,* 79–83.

216. Galle, O. R., & Gove, W. R. (1979). Crowding and behavior in Chicago, 1940–1970. In J. R. Aiello & A. Baum (Eds.), *Residential crowding and design.* New York: Plenum.

217. See note 144.

218. Draper, P. (1973). Crowding among hunter-gatherers: The Kung bushmen. *Science, 182,* 301–303.

219. Bagley, C. (1989). Urban crowding and the murder rate in Bombay, India. *Perceptual and Motor Skills, 69,* 1241–1242.

220. See note 216.

221. See note 18.

222. See note 218.

223. See note 37.

224. Sommer, R. (1969). *Personal space: The behavioral basis of design.* Englewood Cliffs, NJ: Prentice-Hall.

225. Anderson, E. N., Jr. (1972). Some Chinese methods in dealing with crowding. *Urban Anthropology, 1,* 141–150.

226. See note 37.

227. See note 103.

228. Munroe, R. L., & Munroe, R. H. (1972). Population density and affective relationships in three East African societies. *Journal of Social Psychology, 88,* 15–20.

229. Canter, D., & Canter, S. (1971). Closer together in Tokyo. *Design and Environment, 2,* 60–63.

230. Rapoport, A. (1977). *Human aspects of urban form: Towards a man-environment approach to human form and design.* New York: Pergamon.

231. Homma, M. (1990). A Japanese perspective on crowding: How well have the Japanese adjusted to high density? *Psychologia, 33,* 128–137.

232. Edney, J. J. (1977). Theories of human crowding: A review. *Environment and Planning: A, 9,* 1211–1232.

233. See note 36.

234. See note 140.

235. See note 1.

236. See note 1, p. 155.

237. See note 131.

238. See note 34.

239. See note 34.

240. Freimark, S., Werner, R., Phillips, D., & Korber, E. (1984). *Estimation of crowding, number and density for human and non-human stimuli.* Presentation at the annual meetings of the American Psychological Association, Toronto, Ontario.

241. Latane, B. (1981). The psychology of social impact. *American Psychologist, 36,* 343–356.

242. See note 58.

243. Barker, R. G. (1968). *Ecological psychology: Concepts and methods for studying the environment of human behavior.* Stanford, CA: Stanford University Press.

244. Wicker, A. W. (1979). *An introduction to ecological psychology.* Monterey, CA: Brooks/Cole.

245. Fischer, C. S. (1976). *The urban experience.* New York: Harcourt Brace Jovanovich.

246. See note 40.

247. See note 16.

248. Schopler, J., & Stockdale, J. E. (1977). An interference analysis of crowding. *Environmental Psychology and Nonverbal Behavior, 1,* 81–88.

249. Proshansky, H. M., Ittelson, W. H., & Rivlin, L. G. (1976). Freedom of choice and behavior in a physical setting. In H. M. Proshansky, W. H. Ittelson, & L. G. Rivlin (Eds.), *Environmental psychology: People and their physical settings.* New York: Holt, Rinehart and Winston.

250. Cohen, S. (1978). Environmental load and the allocation of attention. In A. Baum, J. E. Singer, & S. Valins (Eds.), *Advances in environmental psychology* ((Vol. 1). Hillsdale, NJ: Erlbaum.

251. Milgram, S. (1970). The experience of living in cities. *Science, 167,* 1461–1468.

252. Wirth, L. (1938). Urbanism as a way of life. *American Journal of Psychology, 44,* 9–14.

253. Simmel, G. (1957). The metropolis and mental life. In P. K. Hatt & A. J. Reiss, Jr. (Eds.), *Cities and societies: The revised reader in urban sociology.* New York: Free Press.

254. See note 40.

255. Helson, H. (1947). Adaptation level as a frame of reference for prediction of psychophysical data. *American Journal of Psychology, 60,* 1–29.

256. See note 140.

257. Bowerman, W. R. (1973). Ambulatory velocity in crowded and uncrowded conditions. *Perceptual and Motor Skills, 36,* 107–111.

258. Baron, R. M., & Rodin, J. (1978). Personal control as a mediator of crowding. In A. Baum, J. E. Singer, & S. Valins (Eds.), *Advances in environmental psychology* ((Vol. 1). Hillsdale, NJ: Erlbaum.

259. Brehm, J. W. (1966). *A theory of psychological reactance.* New York: Academic Press.

260. See note 251.

261. Freedman, J. L. (1979). Current status of work on crowding and suggestions for housing design. In J. R. Aiello & A. Baum (Eds.), *Residential crowding and design.* New York: Plenum.

262. Baum, A., & Davis, G. E. (1980). Reducing the stress of high-density living: An architectural intervention. *Journal of Personality and Social Psychology, 38,* 471–481.

263. Evans, G. W. (1979). Design implications of spatial research. In J. R. Aiello & A. Baum (Eds.), *Residential crowding and design.* New York: Plenum.

264. See note 21.

265. See note 244.

266. See note 22.

267. See note 140.

268. Jan, L. (1980). Overcrowding and inmate behavior: Some preliminary findings. *Criminal Justice and Behavior, 7,* 293–301.

269. Paulus, P. B. (1988). *Prison crowding: A psychological perspective.* New York: Springer-Verlag.

270. Ekland-Olson, S., Barrick, D. M., & Cohen, L. E. (1983). Prison overcrowding and disciplinary problems: An analysis of the Texas prison system. *Journal of Applied Behavioral Science, 19,* 163–176.

271. Bonta, J., & Gendreau, P. (1990). Reexamining the cruel and unusual punishment of prison life. *Law and Human Behavior, 14,* 347–372.

272. Anson, R. H., & Hancock, B. W. (1992). Crowding, proximity, inmate violence, and the Eighth Amendment. *Journal of Offender Rehabilitation, 17,* 123–132.

Chapter 8

1. Westin, A. F. (1967). *Privacy and freedom.* New York: Atheneum.

2. Altman, I. (1975). *The environment and social behavior: Privacy, personal space, territoriality and crowding.* Monterey, CA: Brooks/Cole, p. 18.

3. See note 2.

4. See note 2.

5. Weinstein, C. S. (1982). Privacy-seeking behavior in an elementary classroom. *Journal of Environmental Psychology, 2,* 23–35.

6. Walden, T. A., Nelson, P. A., & Smith, D. E. (1981). Crowding, privacy and coping. *Environment and Behavior, 13,* 205–224.

7. Melton, G. B. (1983). Toward "personhood" for adolescents: Autonomy and privacy as values in public policy. *American Psychologist, 38,* 99–103.

8. Smith, D. E. (1982). Privacy and corrections: A reexamination. *American Journal of Community Psychology, 10*, 207–224.

9. See note 1.

10. Marshall, N. J. (1972). Privacy and environment. *Human Ecology, 1*, 93–110.

11. Pedersen, D. M. (1979). Dimensions of privacy. *Perceptual and Motor Skills, 48*, 1291–1297.

12. Pedersen, D. M. (1982). Cross-validation of privacy factors. *Perceptual and Motor Skills, 55*, 57–58.

13. Hammitt, W. E., & Madden, M. A. (1989). Cognitive dimensions of wilderness privacy: A field test and further explanation. *Leisure Sciences, 11*, 293–301.

14. See note 10.

15. See note 6.

16. Rubin, Z., & Shenker, S. (1978). Friendship, proximity, and self-disclosure. *Journal of Personality, 46*, 1–22.

17. Firestone, I. J., Lichtman, C. M., & Evans, J. R. (1980). Privacy and solidarity: Effects of nursing home accommodation on environmental perception and sociability preferences. *International Journal of Aging and Human Development, 11*, 229–241.

18. McKechnie, G. E. (1974). *ERI manual: Environmental response inventory*. Berkeley, CA: Consulting Psychologists Press.

19. See note 14.

20. See note 12.

21. Stone, E. F., Gueutal, H. G., Gardner, D. G., & McClure, S. (1983). A field experiment comparing information-privacy values, beliefs, and attitudes across several types of organizations. *Journal of Applied Psychology, 68*, 459–468.

22. Tolchinsky, P. D., McCuddy, M. K., Adams, J., Ganster, D. C., Woodman, R. W., & Fromkin, H. C. (1981). Employee perceptions of invasion of privacy: A field simulation experiment. *Journal of Applied Psychology, 66*, 308–313.

23. Woodman, R. W., et al. (1982). A survey of employee perceptions of information privacy in organizations. *Academy of Management Journal, 25*, 647–663.

24. Fusilier, M. R., & Hoyer, W. D. (1980). Variables affecting perceptions of invasion of privacy in a personnel selection situation. *Journal of Applied Psychology, 65*, 623–626.

25. See note 10.

26. Altman, I., Vinsel, A., & Brown, B. B. (1981). Dialectic conceptions in social psychology: An application to social penetration and privacy regulation. *Advances in Experimental Social Psychology, 14*, 107–159.

27. Sundstrom, E., Herbert, R. K., & Brown, D. W. (1982). Privacy and communication in an open-plan office: A case study. *Environment and Behavior, 14*, 543–559.

28. Sundstrom, E., Town, J. P., Brown, D. W., Forman, A., & McGee, C. (1982). Physical enclosure, type of job, and privacy in the office. *Environment and Behavior, 14*, 554–559.

29. See note 10.

30. See note 10.

31. See note 8.

32. Chaikin, A. L., Derlega, V. J., & Miller, S. J. (1976). Effects of room environment on self-disclosure in a counseling analogue. *Journal of Counseling Psychology, 23*, 479–481.

33. Gifford, R. (1988). Light, decor, arousal, comfort, and communication. *Journal of Environmental Psychology, 8*, 177–189.

34. See note 16.

35. Patterson, A. H., & Chiswick, N. R. (1981). The role of the social and physical environment in privacy maintenance among the Iban of Borneo. *Journal of Environmental Psychology, 1*, 131–139.

36. Yoors, J. (1967). *The gypsies*. New York: Simon and Schuster.

37. See note 2.

38. See note 1.

39. See note 1.

40. See note 27.

41. See note 8.

42. Hammitt, W. E. (1982). Cognitive dimensions of wilderness solitude. *Environment and Behavior, 14*, 478–493.

43. Shumaker, S. A., & Reizenstein, J. E. (1982). Environmental factors affecting inpatient stress in acute care hospitals. In G. W. Evans (Ed.), *Environmental stress*. New York: Cambridge University Press.

44. Werner, C. M., Kelly, B. M., Haggard, L. M., & Gibson, B. (1990). *Environment behavior relationships: The case of privacy regulation*. Division 34 Presidential address at the annual meetings of the American Psychological Association, San Francisco.

45. Haggard, L. M., & Werner, C. M. (1990). Situational support, privacy regulation, and stress. *Basic and Applied Social Psychology, 11*, 313–337.

46. See note 1.

47. Foddy, W. H., & Finighan, W. R. (1980). The concept of privacy from a symbolic interaction perspective. *Journal for the Theory of Social Behavior, 10*, 1–17.

48. See note 1.

49. See note 7.

50. Wolfe, M. (1978). Childhood and privacy. In I. Altman & J. F. Wohlwill (Eds.), *Children and the environment*. New York: Plenum.

51. Parke, R. D., & Sawin, D. B. (1979). Children's privacy in the home: Developmental, ecological, and child-rearing determinants. *Environment and Behavior, 11*, 87–104.

52. Vinsel, A., Brown, B. B., Altman, I., & Foss, C. (1980). Privacy regulation, territorial displays, and effectiveness of individual functioning. *Journal of Personality and Social Psychology, 39*, 1104–1115.

53. See note 17.

54. Pastalan, L. A. (1970). Privacy as an expression of human territoriality. In L. A. Pastalan & D. H. Carson (Eds.), *Spatial behavior of older people*. Ann Arbor: University of Michigan Press.

55. Taylor, R. B., & Ferguson, G. (1980). Solitude and intimacy: Linking territoriality and privacy experiences. *Journal of Nonverbal Behavior, 4*, 227–239.

56. Edney, J. J., & Buda, M. A. (1976). Distinguishing territoriality and privacy: Two studies. *Human Ecology, 4*, 283–296.

57. Iwata, O. (1980). Territoriality orientation, privacy orientation and locus of control as determinants of the perception of crowding. *Japanese Psychological Research*, *22*, 13–21.

58. See note 47.

59. See note 2.

60. Altman, I. (1977). Privacy regulation: Culturally universal or culturally specific? *Journal of Social Issues*, *33*(3), 66–84.

61. See note 26.

62. Foddy, W. H. (1984). A critical examination of Altman's definition of privacy as a dialectical process. *Journal for the Theory of Social Behavior*, *14*, 297–307.

63. Margulis, S. T. (1977). Conceptions of privacy: Current status and next steps. *Journal of Social Issues*, *33*(3), 5–21.

64. See note 62.

65. See note 61, p. 143.

66. Laufer, R. S., & Wolfe, M. (1977). Privacy as a concept and a social issue: A multidimensional development theory. *Journal of Social Issues*, *33*(3), 22–42.

67. See note 7.

68. Sundstrom, E. (1986). *Workplaces: The psychology of the physical environment in offices and factories*. New York: Cambridge, pp. 309–311.

69. Archea, J. (1977). The place of architectural factors in behavioral theories of privacy. *Journal of Social Issues*, *33*(3), 116–137.

70. Harman, E., & Betak, J. F. (1974). *Some preliminary findings on the cognitive meaning of external privacy in housing*. Paper presented at the annual meetings of the Environmental Design Research Association, Milwaukee.

71. See note 10.

72. Finighan, W. R. (1980). Some environmental observations on the role of privacy in the residential environment. *Man-Environment Systems*, *10*, 153–159.

73. McCarthy, D., & Saegert, S. (1979). Residential density, social overload and social withdrawal. In J. R. Aiello & A. Baum (Eds.), *Residential crowding and design*. New York: Plenum.

74. Baum, A., Aiello, J. R., & Calesnick, L. E. (1979). Crowding and personal control: Social density and the development of learned helplessness. In J. R. Aiello & A. Baum (Eds.), *Residential crowding and design*. New York: Plenum.

75. Zeisel, J. (1975). *Sociology and architectural design*. New York: Russell Sage Foundation.

76. Vischer, J. C. (1986). The complexity of designing for social mix: An evaluation of site-planning principles. *Journal of Architectural and Planning Research*, *3*, 15–31.

77. Wineman, J. D. (1982). The office environment as a source of stress. In G. W. Evans (Ed.), *Environmental stress*. New York: Cambridge University Press.

78. Klitzman, S., & Stellman, J. (1989). The impact of the physical environment on the psychological well-being of office workers. *Social Science and Medicine*, *29*, 733–742.

79. Becker, F. D. (1981). *Workspace: Creating environments in organizations*. New York: Praeger.

80. Farrenkopf, T., & Roth, V. (1980). The university faculty office as an environment. *Environment and Behavior*, *12*, 467–477.

81. Justa, F. C., & Golan, M. B. (1977). Office design: Is privacy still a problem? *Journal of Architectural Research*, *6*(2), 5–12.

82. Block, L. K., & Stokes, G. S. (1989). Performance and satisfaction in private versus nonprivate working settings. *Environment and Behavior*, *21*, 277–297.

83. Cangelosi, V. E., & Lemoine, L. F. (1988). Effects of open versus closed physical environment on employee perception and attitude. *Social Behavior and Personality*, *16*, 71–77.

84. Ng, C. F., & Gifford, R. (1984). *Speech communication in the office: The effects of background sound level and conversational privacy*. Unpublished manuscript.

Chapter 9

1. Ruskin, J. (1865). *Sesame and lilies*. London: Smith and Elder.

2. Lawrence, R. J. (1987). What makes a house a home? *Environment and Behavior*, *19*, 154–168.

3. Altman, I., & Chemers, M. (1980). *Culture and environment*. Monterey, CA: Brooks/Cole.

4. Altman, I., & Gauvain, M. (1981). A cross-cultural and dialectical analysis of homes. In L. Liben, A. Patterson, & N. Newcombe (Eds.), *Spatial representation across the life span*. New York: Academic Press.

5. Rapoport, Am. (1969). *House form and culture*. Englewood Cliffs, NJ: Prentice Hall.

6. Rapoport, Am. (1985). Culture and the urban order. In J. A. Agnew, J. Mercer, & D. E. Sopher (Eds.), *The city in cultural context*. London: Allen and Unwin.

7. See note 3.

8. Hayward, D. G. (1975). Home as an environmental and psychological concept. *Landscape*, *20*(1), 2–9.

9. See note 8.

10. Dovey, K. (1985). Home and homelessness. In I. Altman & C. M. Werner (Eds.), *Home environments*. New York: Plenum.

11. Murray, A. (1990). Homelessness: The people. In G. Fallis & A. Murray (Eds.), *Housing and the homeless and poor*. Toronto: University of Toronto Press.

12. Smith, S. G. (1994). The essential qualities of a home. *Journal of Environmental Psychology*, *14*, 31–46.

13. Cooper, C. (1976). The house as a symbol of the self. In H. Proshansky, W. H. Ittelson, & L. G. Rivlin (Eds.), *Environmental psychology*. New York: Holt, Rinehart and Winston.

14. Stefanovic, I. L. (1992). The experience of place: Housing quality from a phenomenological perspective. *Canadian Journal of Urban Research*, *1*, 145–161.

15. See note 10.

16. Sixsmith, J. (1986). The meaning of home: An exploratory study of environmental experience. *Journal of Environmental Psychology*, *6*, 281–298.

17. Baumann, D. J., & Holahan, C. J. (1991). The community psychologist. In R. Gifford (Ed.), *Applied psychology: Variety and opportunity*. Boston: Allyn and Bacon.

18. Burn, S. (1991). Loss of control, attributions, and helplessness in the homeless. *Journal of Applied Social Psychology*, *22*, 1161–1174.

19. See note 17.

20. Macdonald, J. E., & Gifford, R. (1989). Territorial cues and defensible space theory: The burglar's point of view. *Journal of Environmental Psychology, 9,* 193–205.

21. Caldwell, B. M. (1967). Descriptive evaluations of development and of developmental settings. *Pediatrics, 40,* 46–54.

22. Elardo, E., Bradley, R., & Caldwell, B. M. (1975). The relations of infants' home environment to mental test performance from 6 to 36 months: A longitudinal analysis. *Child Development, 46,* 71–76.

23. Poresky, R. H. (1987). Environmental Assessment Index: Reliability, stability, and validity of the long and short forms. *Educational and Psychological Measurement, 47,* 969–975.

24. Casey, P. H., Bradley, R. H., & Nelson, J. Y. (1988). The clinical assessment of a child's social and physical environment during health visits. *Journal of Developmental and Behavioral Pediatrics, 9,* 333–338.

25. Shlay, A. B. (1985). Castles in the sky: Measuring housing and neighborhood ideology. *Environment and Behavior, 17,* 593–626.

26. Chapman, N. J., & Ritzdorf, M. (1986). A tradeoff method to assess housing location preferences. *Journal of Environmental Psychology, 6,* 345–358.

27. Lindberg, E., Garling, T., & Montgomery, H. (1986). Beliefs and values as determinants of residential preferences and choices. *Umea Psychological Reports,* No. 188.

28. Lindberg, E., Garling, T., & Montgomery, H. (1989). Preferences for and choices between verbally and numerically described housing alternatives. *Umea Psychological Reports,* No. 189.

29. Craik, K. H., & Zube, E. H. (Eds.). (1976). *Perceiving environmental quality.* New York: Plenum.

30. Canter, D. (1983). The purposive evaluation of places: A facet approach. *Environment and Behavior, 15,* 659–698.

31. See note 30.

32. Weidemann, S., Anderson, J. R., Butterfield, D. I., & O'Donnell, P. M. (1982). Residents' perception of satisfaction and safety: A basis for change in multifamily housing. *Environment and Behavior, 14,* 695–724.

33. Handal, P., Barling, P., & Morissy, E. (1981). Development of perceived and preferred measures of physical and social characteristics of the residential environment and their relationship to satisfaction. *Journal of Community Psychology, 9,* 118–124.

34. Paulus, P. B., Nagar, D., & Camacho, L. M. (1991). Environmental and psychological factors in reactions to apartments and mobile homes. *Journal of Environmental Psychology, 11,* 143–161.

35. Michelson, W. (1977). *Environmental choice, human behavior and residential satisfaction.* New York: Oxford University Press.

36. Nasar, J. L. (1981). Visual preferences of elderly public housing residents: Residential street scenes. *Journal of Environmental Psychology, 1,* 303–313.

37. Nasar, J. L. (1983). Adult viewers' preferences in residential scenes: A study of the relationship of environmental attributes to preference. *Environment and Behavior, 15,* 589–614.

38. See note 35.

39. Schiavo, R. S. (1990). Children's and adolescents' designs of ideal homes. *Children's Environments Quarterly, 7,* 37–46.

40. Filion, P., Wister, A. V., & Coblentz, E. J. (1992). Subjective dimensions of environmental adaptation among the elderly: A challenge to models of housing policy. *Journal of Housing for the Elderly, 10*(1–2), 3–32.

41. Golant, S. M. (1982). Individual differences underlying the dwelling satisfaction of the elderly. *Journal of Social Issues, 38*(3), 121–133.

42. Salling, M., & Harvey, M. E. (1981). Poverty, personality and sensitivity to residential stressors. *Environment and Behavior, 13,* 131–163.

43. See note 35.

44. Peatross, F. D., & Hasell, M. J. (1992). Changing lives/changing spaces: An investigation of the relationships between gender orientation and behaviors, and spatial preferences in residential kitchens. *Journal of Architectural and Planning Research, 9,* 239–257.

45. Hasell, M. J., Peatross, F. D., & Bono, C. A. (1993). Gender choice and domestic space: Preferences for kitchens in married households. *Journal of Architectural and Planning Research, 10,* 1–22.

46. Keeley, R. M., & Edney, J. J. (1983). Model house designs for privacy, security, and social interaction. *Journal of Social Psychology, 119,* 219–228.

47. Wiggins, J. S. (1975). *The relationship between personality characteristics and attitudes toward housing and related facilities in six Army posts.* Unpublished manuscript, University of Illinois.

48. Switzer, R., & Taylor, R. B. (1983). Sociability versus privacy of residential choice: Impacts of personality and local social ties. *Basic and Applied Social Psychology, 4,* 123–136.

49. See note 28.

50. Wiesenfeld, E. (1992). Public housing evaluation in Venezuela: A case study. *Journal of Environmental Psychology, 12,* 213–223.

51. See note 34.

52. Michelson, W. (1980). Long and short range criteria for housing choice and environmental behavior. *Journal of Social Issues, 36*(3), 135–149.

53. See note 34.

54. Popovics, A. J. (1990). Reasons for satisfaction and dissatisfaction with campus housing at an undergraduate school for women. *College Student Journal, 23,* 359–360.

55. Amerigo, M., & Aragones, J. I. (1990). Residential satisfaction in council housing. *Journal of Environmental Psychology, 10,* 313–325.

56. See note 55.

57. Weidemann, S., & Anderson, J. R. (1985). A conceptual framework for residential satisfaction. In I. Altman & C. M. Werner (Eds.), *Home environments.* New York: Plenum.

58. Wister, A. V. (1985). Living arrangement choices among the elderly. *Canadian Journal on Aging, 4,* 127–144.

59. See note 46.

60. Jelinkova, Z., & Picek, M. (1984). *Physical and psychological factors determining population responses to environment.* Presentation at the European C.I.A.N.S Conference, Olomouc, Czechoslovia.

61. Galster, G. C., & Hesser, G. W. (1981). Residential satisfaction: Compositional and contextual correlates. *Environment and Behavior, 13,* 735–758.

62. Widmar, R. (1984). Preferences for multiple-family housing: Some implications for public participation. *Journal of Architectural and Planning Research, 1,* 256–260.

63. See note 35.

64. Marans, R. W. (1976). Perceived quality of residential environments: Some methodological issues. In K. H. Craik & E. H. Zube (Eds.), *Perceiving environmental quality: Research and applications.* New York: Plenum.

65. Miller, S. I., & Evko, B. (1985). An ethnographic study of the influence of a mobile home community on suburban high school students. *Human Relations, 38,* 683–705.

66. Leger, J. M. (1985). The pre-fabricated house: Is it really a home? *Journal of Environmental Psychology, 5,* 345–354.

67. See note 34.

68. Nasar, J. (1989). Symbolic meanings of house styles. *Environment and Behavior, 21,* 235–257.

69. Baird, J. C., Cassidy, B., & Kurr, J. (1978). Room preference as a function of architectural design features and user activities. *Journal of Applied Psychology, 63,* 719–727.

70. Cunningham, M. R. (1977). Notes on the psychological basis of environmental design: The right-left dimension in apartment floor plans. *Environment and Behavior, 9,* 125–135.

71. Weisenthal, D. L., & Tubiana, J. H. (1981). Apartment design choices: A study of Israeli and Non-Israeli university students. *Environment and Behavior, 13,* 677–684.

72. Duffy, M., & Willson, V. L. (1984). The role of design factors of the residential environment in the physical and mental health of the elderly. *Journal of Housing for the Elderly, 2*(3), 37–45.

73. Mahnke, F. H., & Mahnke, R. H. (1987). *Color and light in man-made environments.* New York: Van Nostrand, 1987.

74. Kunishima, M., & Yanase, T. (1985). Visual effects of wall colors in living rooms. *Ergonomics, 28,* 869–882.

75. Levy-Leboyer, C., & Ratiu, E. (1993). The need for space and residential satisfaction. *Architecture et Comportment/Architecture and Behavior, 9,* 475–490.

76. Saarinen, T. F. (1988). Public perception of the desert in Tucson, Arizona. *Journal of Architectural and Planning Research, 5,* 197–207.

77. Kent, S. (1991). Partitioning space: Cross-cultural factors influencing domestic spatial segmentation. *Environment and Behavior, 23,* 438–473.

78. Lawrence, R. J. (1987). *Housing, dwellings, and homes: Design theory, research, and practice.* New York: Wiley.

79. Canter, D., & Thorne, R. (1972). Attitudes to housing: A cross cultural comparison. *Environment and Behavior, 4,* 3–32.

80. Groves, M., & Thorne, R. (1988). Aspects of housing preference: Revisiting a cross-cultural study with the hindsight of improved data analysis. *Journal of Environmental Psychology, 8,* 45–55.

81. Bonnes, M., Giuliani, M. V., Amoni, F., & Bernard, Y. (1987). Cross-cultural rules for the optimization of the living room. *Environment and Behavior, 19,* 204–227.

82. Amaturo, E., Costagliola, S., & Ragone, G. (1987). Furnishing and status attributes: A sociological study of the living room. *Environment and Behavior, 19,* 228–249.

83. Weisner, T. S., & Weibel, J. (1981). Home environments and family lifestyles in California. *Environment and Behavior, 13,* 417–460.

84. Ahrentzen, S., Levine, D. W., & Michelson, W. (1989). Space, time, and activity in the home: A gender analysis. *Journal of Environmental Psychology, 9,* 89–101.

85. Michelson, W. (1985). *From sun to sun: Daily obligations and community structure in the lives of employed women and their families.* Totowa, NJ: Rowman and Allanheld, pp. 89–101.

86. Parke, R. D., & Sawin, D. B. (1979). Children's privacy in the home: Developmental, ecological, and child-rearing determinants. *Environment and Behavior, 11,* 87–104.

87. Ashcraft, N., & Scheflen, A. (1976). *People space.* Garden City, NY: Anchor.

88. Becker, F. D. (1974). *Design for living: The residents' view of multi-family housing.* Ithaca, NY: Center for Urban Development Research.

89. Raviv, A., & Palgi, Y. (1985). The perception of social-environmental characteristics in kibbutz families with family-based and communal sleeping arrangements. *Journal of Personality and Social Psychology, 49,* 376–385.

90. Blood, R. (1953). A situational approach to the study of permissiveness in child rearing. *American Sociological Review, 18,* 84–87.

91. Kruusvall, J. (1988). Mass housing and psychological research in the Soviet Union. In D. Canter, M. Krampen, & D. Stea (Eds.), *Environmental policy, assessment, and communication.* Aldershot, UK: Avebury.

92. Pennartz, P. J. J. (1986). Atmosphere at home: A qualitative approach. *Journal of Environmental Psychology, 6,* 135–153.

93. Glyptis, S. A., & Chambers, D. A. (1982). No place like home. *Leisure Studies, 1,* 247–262.

94. McMillan, D. W., & Hiltonsmith, R. W. (1982). Adolescents at home: An exploratory study of the relationship between perception of family social climate, general well-being, and actual behavior in the home setting. *Journal of Youth and Adolescence, 11,* 301–315.

95. Goldstein, G., Novick, R., & Schaefer, M. (1990). Housing, health and well-being: An international perspective. *Journal of Sociology and Social Welfare, 17,* 161–181.

96. See note 95.

97. Priemus, H. (1986). Housing as a social adaptation process: A conceptual scheme. *Environment and Behavior, 18,* 31–52.

98. Kellett, J. (1989). Health and housing. *Journal of Psychosomatic Research, 33,* 255–268.

99. Norris-Baker, C., & Scheidt, R. J. (1989). Habituation theory and environment-aging research: Ennui to joie de vivre? *International Journal of Aging and Human Development, 29,* 241–257.

100. Zaborowski, C. A., Armstrong-Esther, F. M., & Sandilands, M. (1985). Environmental change as a factor in stress in the elderly. *Alberta Psychology, 14,* 10–11, 23–24.

101. Thompson, B. (1989). Preparing elderly people for life in a "home." *British Journal of Occupational Therapy, 52,* 103–104.

102. Lawton, M. P. (1990). Residential environment and self-directedness among older people. *American Psychologist, 45,* 638–640.

103. Fisher, S., & Hood, B. (1988). Vulnerability factors in the transition to university: Self-reported mobility history and sex differences as factors in psychological disturbance. *British Journal of Psychology, 79,* 309–320.

104. Stokols, D., Ohlig, W., & Resnick, S. M. (1979). Perceptions of residential crowding, classroom experiences, and student health. In J. R. Aiello & A. Baum (Eds.), *Residential crowding and design.* New York: Plenum.

105. Riemer, S. (1948). Maladjustment to the family home. *American Sociological Review, 10,* 642–648.

106. See note 98.

107. Evans, G. W., Palsane, M. N., Lepore, S. J., & Martin, J. (1989). Residential density and psychological health: The mediating effects of social support. *Journal of Personality and Social Psychology, 57,* 994–999.

108. Tryon, G. S. (1985). An exploratory study of the relationship between residence hall, design and student alcohol consumption. *Journal of College Student Personnel, 26,* 372–373.

109. Galle, O. R., & Gove, W. R. (1979). Crowding and behavior in Chicago, 1940–1970. In J. R. Aiello & A. Baum (Eds.), *Residential crowding and design.* New York: Plenum.

110. Lakey, B. (1989). Personal and environmental antecedents of perceived social support developed at college. *American Journal of Community Psychology, 17,* 503–517.

111. See note 107.

112. Stephan, E., Fath, M., & Lamm, H. (1988). Loneliness as related to various personality and environmental measures: Research with the German adaptation of the UCLA Loneliness Scale. *Social Behavior and Personality, 16,* 169–174.

113. Koller, K., & Gosden, S. (1984). On living alone, social isolation, and psychological disorder. *Australian and New Zealand Journal of Sociology, 20,* 81–92.

114. Wachs, T. D. (1979). Proximal experience and early cognitive-intellectual development: The physical environment. *Merrill-Palmer Quarterly, 25,* 3–41.

115. Heft, H. (1985). High residential density and perceptual-cognitive development: An examination of the effects of crowding and noise in the home. In J. F. Wohlwill & W. van Vliet (Eds.), *Habitats for children: The impacts of density.* Hillsdale, NJ: Erlbaum.

116. Gottfried, A. W., & Gottfried, A. E. (1984). Home environment and cognitive development in young children of middle-socioeconomic-status families. In A. W. Gottfried (Ed.), *Home environment and early cognitive development.* Orlando: Academic Press.

117. See note 116.

118. Wachs, T. D. (1988). Relevance of physical environment influences on toddler temperament. *Infant Behavior and Development, 11,* 431–445.

119. Bradley, R. H., & Caldwell, B. M. (1984). The HOME Inventory and family demographics. *Developmental Psychology, 20,* 315–320.

120. Bradley, R. H., & Caldwell, B. M. (1984). The relation of infants' home environments to achievement test performance in first grade: A follow-up study. *Child Development, 55,* 803–809.

121. Saegert, S. (1980, September). *The effect of residential density on low income children.* Paper presented at the annual meetings of the American Psychological Association, Montreal.

122. Booth, A., & Edwards, J. N. (1976). Crowding and family relations. *American Sociological Review, 41,* 308–321.

123. Booth, A., & Johnson, D. R. (1975). The effect of crowding on child health and development. *American Behavioral Scientist, 18,* 736–749.

124. See note 121.

125. Rodin, J. (1976). Density, perceived choice, and response to controllable and uncontrollable outcomes. *Journal of Experimental Social Psychology, 12,* 564–578.

126. See note 109.

127. Booth, A., & Welch, S. (1973). *The effects of crowding: A cross-national study.* Paper presented at the annual meetings of the American Psychological Association, Montreal.

128. Korosec-Serfaty, P., & Bollitt, D. (1986). Dwelling and the experience of burglary. *Journal of Environmental Psychology, 6,* 329–344.

129. Brown, B. B., & Harris, P. B. (1989). Residential burglary victimization: Reactions to the invasion of a primary territory. *Journal of Environmental Psychology, 9,* 119–132.

130. Normoyle, J. B., & Foley, J. M. (1988). The defensible space model of fear and elderly public housing residents. *Environment and Behavior, 20,* 50–74.

131. van Vliet, W. (1983). Families in apartment buildings: Sad storeys for children? *Environment and Behavior, 15,* 211–234.

132. McCarthy, D. P., & Saegert, S. (1978). Residential density, social overload, and social withdrawal. *Human Ecology, 6,* 253–272.

133. See note 88.

134. See note 72.

135. See note 116.

136. See note 114.

137. Oda, M., Taniguchi, K., Wen, M., & Higurashi, M. (1989). Effects of high-rise living on physical and mental development of children. *Journal of Human Ergology, 18,* 231–235.

138. See note 118.

139. Gaunt, L. (1980). Can children play at home? In P. F. Wilkinson (Ed.), *Innovation in play environments.* London: Croom Helm.

140. Golden, M., Rosenblath, L., Grossi, L., Policare, M., Freeman, Jr., H., & Brownlee, E. (1978). *The New York infant day care study.* New York: Medical and Health Research Association of New York City.

141. Dhillon, P. K., & Bhalla, M. (1988). The impact of built-living environment on behavior: An empirical study. *Journal of the Indian Academy of Applied Psychology, 14,* 16–25.

142. Stokols, D., Shumaker, S. A., & Martinez, J. (1983). Residential mobility and personal well-being. *Journal of Environmental Psychology, 3,* 5–19.

143. Rossi, P. H., & Shlay, A. B. (1982). Residential mobility and public policy issues: "Why Families Move" revisited. *Journal of Social Issues, 38*(3), 21–34.

144. Stokols, D., & Shumaker, S. A. (1982). The psychological context of residential mobility and well-being. *Journal of Social Issues, 38*(3), 149–171.

145. See note 142.

146. Newman, S. J., & Owen, M. S. (1982). Residential displacement: Extent, nature, and effects. *Journal of Social Issues, 38*(3), 135–148.

147. See note 142.

148. Masnick, G., & Bane, M. J. (1980). *The nation's families: 1960–1990.* Boston: Auburn House.

149. Ahrentzen, S. (1985). Residential fit and mobility among low-income, female-headed family households in the United States. In W. van Vliet, E. Huttman, & S. Fava (Eds.), *Housing needs and policy approaches: Trends in thirteen countries.* Durham, NC: Duke University Press.

150. Fisher, S., Murray, K., & Frazer, N. A. (1985). Homesickness, health, and efficiency in first year students. *Journal of Environmental Psychology, 5*, 181–195.

151. Clark, W. A. V. (1986). *Human migration.* Beverly Hills, CA: Sage.

152. Lindberg, E., Hartig, T., Garvill, J., & Garling, T. (1992). Residential-location preferences across the lifespan. *Journal of Environmental Psychology, 12*, 187–198.

153. Walker, P. R. (1992, August). *Residential relocation: Measuring the link between place and identity.* Paper presented at the annual meetings of the American Psychological Association, Washington, DC.

154. Anthony, K. H. (1991). Housing the single-parent family. In W. F. E. Preiser, J. C. Vischer, & E. T. White (Eds.), *Design intervention: Toward a more humane architecture.* New York: Van Nostrand Reinhold.

155. See note 78.

Chapter 10

1. Mumford, L. (1961). *The city in history: Its origins, its transformations, its prospects.* New York: Harcourt, Brace, and World.

2. Graham, C. (1993, January 14). We may have genetic need to live in smaller cities. *Victoria Times-Colonist*, p. A-4.

3. See note 2.

4. See note 2.

5. Fischer, D. (1994, December 22). Life more peaceful in the country, statistics say. *Vancouver Sun*, p. A-8.

6. Hall, S. (1989). Standing on those corners, watching all the folks go by. *Smithsonian Magazine, 19*(11), 119–131.

7. Taylor, R. B., Shumaker, S. A., & Gottfriedson, S. D. (1985). Neighborhood-level links between physical features and local sentiments: Deterioration, fear of crime, and confidence. *Journal of Architectural and Planning Research, 2*, 261–275.

8. Guest, A. M., & Lee, B. A. (1984). How urbanites define their neighborhoods. *Population & Environment: Behavioral & Social Issues, 7*, 32–56.

9. Feldman, R. M. (1986). Generic conceptions of place: The public views the city/suburb distinction. *Dissertation Abstracts International, 47*(9–B), 3942.

10. Rivlin, L. G. (1982). Group membership and place meanings in an urban neighborhood. *Journal of Social Issues, 38*(3), 75–93.

11. Unger, D. G., & Wandersman, A. (1985). The importance of neighbors: The social, cognitive, and affective components of neighboring. *American Journal of Community Psychology, 13*, 139–169.

12. Cherulnik, P. D., & Wilderman, S. K. (1986). Symbols of status in urban neighborhoods: Contemporary perceptions of nineteenth-century Boston. *Environment and Behavior, 18*, 604–622.

13. Varady, D. P. (1986). Neighborhood confidence: A critical factor in neighborhood revitalization? *Environment and Behavior, 18*, 480–501.

14. See note 11.

15. Fried, M. (1984). The structure and significance of community satisfaction. *Population & Environment: Behavioral and Social Issues, 7*, 61–86.

16. Lord, D. J., & Rent, G. S. (1987). Residential satisfaction in scattered-site public housing projects. *The Social Science Journal, 24*, 287–302.

17. Jirovec, R. L., Jirovec, M. M., & Bosse, R. (1985). Residential satisfaction as a function of micro and macro environmental conditions among urban elderly men. *Research on Aging, 7*, 601–616.

18. See note 16.

19. Cunningham, J. D. (1984). Egotism in prestige ratings of Sydney suburbs: Where I live is better than you think. *Australian Journal of Psychology, 36*, 429–438.

20. Geller, D. (1980). Responses to urban stimuli: A balanced approach. *Journal of Social Issues, 36*(3), 86–100.

21. Helson, H. (1964). *Adaptation-level theory.* New York: Harper and Row.

22. Michelson, W. (1977). *Environmental choice, human behavior and residential satisfaction.* New York: Oxford University Press.

23. Nasar, J. L. (1981). Visual preferences of elderly public housing residents: Residential street scenes. *Journal of Environmental Psychology, 1*, 303–313.

24. Taylor, R. B. (1982). Neighborhood physical environment and stress. In G. W. Evans (Ed.), *Environmental stress.* New York: Cambridge University Press.

25. See note 17.

26. Widgery, R. N. (1982). Satisfaction with the quality of urban life: A predictive model. *American Journal of Community Psychology, 10*, 37–48.

27. Hull, R. B., & Harvey, A. (1989). Explaining the emotion people experience in suburban parks. *Environment and Behavior, 21*, 323–345.

28. Nasar, J. L. (1983). Adult viewers' preferences in residential scenes: A study of the relationship of environmental attributes to preference. *Environment and Behavior, 15*, 589–614.

29. See note 16.

30. See note 16.

31. Regnier, V. (1985). Using outdoor space more effectively. *Generations, 9*, 22–24.

32. See note 22.

33. Llewellyn, L. G. (1981). The social cost of urban transportation. In I. Altman, J. Wohlwill, & P. B. Everett (Eds.), *Transportation and behavior.* New York: Plenum.

34. Levy-Leboyer, C. (1991). Neighborhood noise annoyance. *Journal of Environmental Psychology, 11,* 75–86.

35. Green, D. M., & Fidell, S. (1991). Variability in the criterion for reporting annoyance in community noise surveys. *Journal of the Acoustical Society of America, 89,* 234–243.

36. Moran, S. V., Gunn, W. J., & Loeb, M. (1981). Annoyance by aircraft noise and fear of overflying aircraft in relation to attitudes toward the environment and community. *The Journal of Auditory Research, 21,* 217–225.

37. Jue, G. M., Shumaker, S. A., & Evans, G. W. (1984). Community opinion concerning airport noise-abatement alternatives. *Journal of Environmental Psychology, 4,* 337–345.

38. Björkman, M. (1991). Community noise annoyance: Importance of noise levels and the number of noise events. *Journal of Sound and Vibration, 151,* 497–503.

39. Fidell, S., & Silvati, L. (1991). An assessment of the effect of residential acoustic insulation on prevalence of annoyance in an airport community. *Journal of the Acoustical Society of America, 89,* 244–247.

40. Weinstein, N. D. (1982). Community noise problems: Evidence against adaptation. *Journal of Environmental Psychology, 2,* 99–108.

41. Mehrabian, A. (1977). Individual differences in stimulus screening and arousability. *Journal of Personality, 45,* 237–250.

42. Jonah, B. A., Bradley, J. S., & Dawson, N. E. (1981). Predicting individual subjective responses and traffic noise. *Journal of Applied Psychology, 66,* 490–501.

43. Evans, G. W., Jacobs, S. V., & Frager, N. B. (1982). Adaptation to air pollution. *Journal of Environmental Psychology, 2,* 99–108.

44. Fried, M., & Gleicher, P. (1961). Some sources of satisfaction in an urban slum. *Journal of the American Institute of Planners, 27,* 305–315.

45. Fried, M. (1982). Residential attachment: Sources of residential and community satisfaction. *Journal of Social Issues, 38*(3), 107–119.

46. Handal, P., Barling, P., & Morrissy, E. (1981). Development of perceived and preferred measures of physical and social characteristics of the residential environment and their relationship to satisfaction. *Journal of Community Psychology, 9,* 118–124.

47. See note 16.

48. Garling, T., Svensson-Garling, A., & Valsiner, J. (1984). Parental concern about children's traffic safety in residential neighborhoods. *Journal of Environmental Psychology, 4,* 235–252.

49. Cook, C. C. (1988). Components of neighborhood satisfaction: Responses from urban and suburban single-parent women. *Environment and Behavior, 20,* 115–149.

50. Patterson, A. H. (1985). Fear of crime and other barriers to use of public transportation by the elderly. *Journal of Architectural and Planning Research, 2,* 277–288.

51. Hassinger, J. (1985). Fear of crime in public environments. *Journal of Architectural and Planning Research, 2,* 289–300.

52. Kirk, N. L. (1988). *Factors affecting perceptions of safety in a campus environment.* Nineteenth Annual Conference of the Environmental Design Research Association, Pomona, CA.

53. White, M., Kasl, S. V., Zahner, G. E., & Will, J. C. (1987). Perceived crime in the neighborhood and mental health of women and children. *Environment and Behavior, 19,* 588–613.

54. Gifford, R., & Peacock, J. (1979). Crowding: More fearsome than crime-provoking? Comparison of an Asian city and a North American city. *Psychologia, 22,* 79–83.

55. See note 24.

56. Newman, O. (1972). *Defensible space.* New York: Macmillan.

57. Tien, J., O'Donnell, V. F., Barnett, A., & Mirchandani, P. B. (1979). *Street lighting projects.* Washington, DC: U.S. Department of Justice.

58. Van der Wurff, A., & Stringer, P. (1989). Postvictimization fear of crime: Differences in the perceptions of people and places. *Journal of Interpersonal Violence, 4,* 469–481.

59. Baba, Y., & Austin, D. M. (1989). Neighborhood environmental satisfaction, victimization, and social participation as determinants of perceived neighborhood safety. *Environment and Behavior, 21,* 763–780.

60. See note 24.

61. See note 52.

62. Rapoport, Am. (1985). Culture and the urban order. In J. A. Agnew, J. Mercer, & D. E. Sopher (Eds.), *The city in cultural context.* Boston: Allen and Unwin.

63. See note 62.

64. Gifford, R. (1984–1985). Age, era and life perspective: Emotional connotations of the 1920s through the 1980s to individuals in their twenties through their eighties. *International Journal of Aging and Human Development, 20,* 33–40.

65. Rapoport, Am. (1982). *The meaning of the built environment: A nonverbal communication approach.* Beverly Hills, CA: Sage.

66. See note 10.

67. Loo, C. M., & Mar, D. (1982). Desired residential mobility in a low income ethnic community: A case study of Chinatown. *Journal of Social Issues, 38*(3), 95–106.

68. Demick, J., Hoffman, A., & Wapner, S. (1985). Residential context and environmental change as determinants of urban experience. *Children's Environments Quarterly, 2,* 44–54.

69. Carp, F. M., & Christensen, D. L. (1986). Older women living alone: Technical environment assessment of psychological well-being. *Research on Aging, 8,* 407–425.

70. Fried, M. (1982). Residential attachment: Sources of residential and community satisfaction. *Journal of Social Issues, 38*(3), 107–119.

71. Proshansky, H. M. (1978). The city and self-identity. *Environment and Behavior, 10,* 147–169.

72. Proshansky, H. M., Fabian, A. K., & Kaminoff, R. (1983). Place-identity: Physical world socialization of the self. *Journal of Environmental Psychology, 3,* 57–83.

73. Altman, I., & Low, S. M. (Eds.). (1992). *Place attachment.* New York: Plenum.

74. Taylor, R. B., Gottfredson, S. D., & Brower, S. (1985). Attachment to place: Discriminant validity and impacts of disorder and diversity. *American Journal of Community Psychology, 13,* 525–542.

75. Low, S. (1990). Cross-cultural place attachment: A preliminary typology. In Y. Yoshitake, R. B. Bechtel, T. Takahashi, & M. Asai (Eds.), *Current issues in environment-behavior research*. Tokyo: University of Tokyo.

76. Tuan, Y. F. (1980). Rootedness versus sense of place. *Landscape, 24*, 3–8.

77. Buttimer, A. (1980). Home, reach and a sense of place. In A. Buttimer & D. Seamon (Eds.), *The human experience of space and place*. London: Croom Helm.

78. Relph, E. (1976). *Place and placelessness*. London: Pion.

79. Davidson, W. B., & Cotter, P. R. (1986). Measurement of sense of community within the sphere of city. *Journal of Applied Social Psychology, 16*, 608–619.

80. See note 44.

81. Saegert, S., & Hart, R. (1978). The development of environmental competence in girls and boys. In M. Salter (Ed.), *Play: Anthropological perspectives*. Cornwall, NY: Leisure Press.

82. van Vliet, W. (1983). Exploring the fourth environment: An examination of the home range of city and suburban teenagers. *Environment and Behavior, 15*, 567–588.

83. McMillan, D. W., & Hiltonsmith, R. W. (1982). Adolescents at home: An exploratory study of the relationship between perception of family social climate, general well-being, and actual behavior in the home setting. *Journal of Youth and Adolescence, 11*, 301–315.

84. Stokols, D., Shumaker, S. A., & Martinez, J. (1983). Residential mobility and personal well-being. *Journal of Environmental Psychology, 3*, 5–19.

85. Goodman, A. C., & Hankin, J. R. (1984). Elderly Jews and happiness with locale. *Population and Environment: Behavioral and Social Issues, 7*, 87–102.

86. Kaplan, S. (1984). Affect and cognition in the context of home: The quest for intangibles. *Population and Environment: Behavioral and Social Issues, 7*, 126–133.

87. See note 85.

88. Sime, J. D., & Kimura, M. (1988). *Home gardens: Attachment to the natural environment and the experience of time from a Western and Japanese perspective*. Nineteenth Annual Conference of the Environmental Design Research Association, Pomona, CA.

89. See note 86.

90. See note 24.

91. Pinet, C. (1988). *A "sense of belonging" in the neighborhood: The effect of traffic on space appropriation*. Nineteenth Annual Conference of the Environmental Design Research Association, Pomona, CA.

92. Brown, B., & Werner, C. M. (1985). Social cohesiveness, territoriality, and holiday decorations: The influence of cul-de-sacs. *Environment and Behavior, 17*, 539–565.

93. Norris-Baker, C., & Scheidt, R. J. (1990). Place attachment among older residents of a "ghost town": A transactional approach. *Environmental Design Research Association, 21*, 333–340.

94. Kaplan, R. (1985). Nature at the doorstep: Residential satisfaction and the nearby environment. *Journal of Architecture and Planning Research, 2*, 115–127.

95. Nelson, T. M., & Loewen, L. J. (1993). Factors affecting perception of outdoor public environments. *Perceptual and Motor Skills, 76*, 139–146.

96. Habe, R. (1989). Community growth gaming: A survey method. *Environment and Behavior, 21*, 298–322.

97. Torrey, E. F., & Bowler, A. (1990). Geographical distribution of insanity in America: Evidence for an urban factor. *Schizophrenia Bulletin, 16*, 591–604.

98. Levine, R. V., Miyake, K., & Lee, M. (1989). Places rated revisited: Psycho-social pathology in metropolitan areas. *Environment and Behavior, 21*, 531–553.

99. Levine, R. (1988). City stress index: 25 best, 25 worst. *Psychology Today, 22*(11), 52–58.

100. Rohe, W. M. (1985). Urban planning and mental health. In A. Wandersman & R. Hess (Eds.), *Beyond the individual: Environmental approaches and prevention*. New York: Haworth.

101. Suarez de Balcaazar, Y., Fawcett, S. B., & Balcaazar, F. E. (1988). Effects of environmental design and police enforcement on violations of a handicapped parking ordinance. *Journal of Applied Behavior Analysis, 21*, 291–298.

102. Krupat, E., & Kubzansky, P. E. (1987). Designing to deter crime. *Psychology Today, 21*, 58–61.

103. Brantingham, P. S., & Brantingham, P. L. (1977). *A theoretical model of crime site selection*. Presentation at the American Society of Criminology Meetings, Atlanta.

104. Brown, B. B. (1980). *Territoriality, defensible space, and residential burglary*. Master's thesis, University of Utah.

105. Rand, G. (1984). Crime and the environment: A review of the literature and its implications for urban architecture and planning. *Journal of Architecture and Planning Research, 1*, 3–19.

106. See note 105.

107. Cose, E. (1994, July 11). Drawing up safer cities. *Newsweek*, p. 57.

108. See note 105.

109. Merry, S. E. (1981). *Urban danger: Life in a neighborhood of strangers*. Philadelphia: Temple University Press.

110. See note 105.

111. See note 102.

112. Archea, J. C. (1985). The use of architectural props in the conduct of criminal acts. *Journal of Architectural and Planning Research, 2*, 245–259.

113. MacDonald, J. E., & Gifford, R. (1989). Territorial cures and defensible space theory: The burglar's point of view. *Journal of Environmental Psychology, 9*, 193–205.

114. Jacobs, J. (1961). *The death and life of great American cities*. New York: Random House.

115. Fowler, E. P. (1987). Street management and city design. *Social Forces, 66*, 365–389.

116. van der Voordt, T. J. M., & van Wegen, H. B. (1990). Testing building plans for public safety: Usefulness of the Delft checklist. *Housing and Environmental Research, 5*, 129–154.

117. Sommer, R. (1972). *Design awareness*. New York: Holt, Rinehart and Winston.

118. Baron, R. M., & Fisher, J. D. (1984). The equity-control model of vandalism: A refinement. In C. Levy-Leboyer (Ed.), *Vandalism: Behavior and motivations*. Amsterdam: North Holland.

119. Baron, R. M. (1984, August). *A social-psychological perspective on environmental issues.* Paper presented at the annual meeting of the American Psychological Association, Toronto.

120. Harries, K., & Stadler, S. J. (1983). Determinism revisited: Assault and heat stress in Dallas, 1980. *Environment and Behavior, 15,* 235–256.

121. Bell, P. A., & Greene, T. C. (1982). Thermal stress: Physiological, comfort, performance and social effects of hot and cold environments. In G. W. Evans (Ed.), *Environmental stress.* New York: Cambridge University Press.

122. United States Riot Commission. (1968). *Report of the National Advisory Commission on Civil Disorders.* Bantam: New York.

123. Baron, R. A., & Ransberger, V. M. (1978). Ambient temperature and the occurrence of collective violence: The long hot summer revisited. *Journal of Personality and Social Psychology, 36,* 351–360.

124. Cohn, E. (1990). Weather and crime. *British Journal of Criminology, 30,* 51–64.

125. Byrne, G. (1988). Putting heat on the ball. *Science, 242,* 518.

126. Carlsmith, J. M., & Anderson, C. A. (1979). Ambient temperature and the occurrence of collective violence: A new analysis. *Journal of Personality and Social Psychology, 37,* 327–334.

127. Anderson, C. A., & Anderson, D. C. (1984). Ambient temperature and violent crime: Tests of the linear and curvilinear hypotheses. *Journal of Personality and Social Psychology, 46,* 91–97.

128. Rotton, J. L. (1982, August). *Temperature, humidity, and violent crime.* Paper presented at the annual convention of the American Psychological Association, Washington, DC.

129. Anderson. C. A. (1987). Temperature and aggression: Effects on quarterly, yearly and city rates of violent and nonviolent crime. *Journal of Personality and Social Psychology, 52,* 1161–1173.

130. Rotton, J. (1983). Affective and cognitive consequences of malodorous pollution. *Basic and Applied Social Psychology, 4,* 171–191.

131. Rotton, J., Frey, J., Barry, T., Milligan, M., & Fitzpatrick, M. (1979). The air pollution experience and physical aggression. *Journal of Applied Social Psychology, 9,* 397–412.

132. Rotton, J., & Frey, J. (1985). Psychological costs of air pollution: Atmospheric conditions, seasonal trends, and psychiatric emergencies. *Population and Environment, 7.*

133. Rotton, J., & Frey, J. (1985). Air pollution, weather, and violent crimes: Concomitant time-series analysis of archival data. *Journal of Personality and Social Psychology, 49,* 1207–1220.

134. Cunningham, M. R. (1979). Weather, mood, and helping behavior: Quasi-experiments with the sunshine samaritan. *Journal of Personality and Social Psychology, 37,* 1947–1956.

135. Korte, C., & Grant, R. (1980). Traffic noise, environmental awareness, and pedestrian behavior. *Environment and Behavior, 12,* 408–420.

136. Page, R. A. (1977). Noise and helping behavior. *Environment and Behavior, 9,* 311–334.

137. Mathews, K. E., Jr., & Canon, L. K. (1975). Environmental noise level as a determinant of helping behavior. *Journal of Personality and Social Psychology, 32,* 571–577.

138. Schneider, F. W., Lesko, W. A., & Garrett, W. A. (1980). Helping behavior in hot, comfortable and cold temperatures. *Environment and Behavior, 12,* 231–240.

139. Siegel, J. M., & Steele, C. M. (1980). Environmental distraction and interpersonal judgments. *British Journal of Social and Clinical Psychology, 19,* 23–32.

140. Latane, B., & Darley, J. M. (1970). *The unresponsive bystander: Why doesn't he help?* New York: Appleton-Century-Crofts.

141. Cohen, S., & Spacapan, S. (1978). The aftereffects of stress: An additional interpretation. *Environmental Psychology and Nonverbal Behavior, 3,* 43–57.

142. Kammann, R., Thomson, R., & Irwin, R. (1979). Unhelpful behavior in the street: City size or immediate pedestrian density? *Environment and Behavior, 11,* 245–250.

143. Levine, R. V., Martinez, T. S., Brase, G., & Sorenson, K. (1994). Helping in 36 U.S. cities. *Journal of Personality and Social Psychology, 67,* 69–82.

144. See note 141.

145. Weiner, F. H. (1976). Altruism, ambience, and action: The effects of rural and urban rearing on helping behavior. *Journal of Personality and Social Psychology, 34,* 112–124.

146. Milgram, S. (1970). The experience of living in cities. *Science, 167,* 1461–1468.

147. Franck, K. A. (1980). Friends and strangers: The social experience of living in urban and non-urban settings. *Journal of Social Issues, 36*(3), 52–71.

148. Korte, C. (1980). Urban-nonurban differences in social behavior and social psychological models of urban impact. *Journal of Social Issues, 36*(3), 29–51.

149. Amato, P. R. (1981). The effects of environmental complexity and pleasantness on prosocial behaviour: A field study. *Australian Journal of Psychology, 33,* 285–295.

150. Amato, P. R. (1981). The impact of the built environment on prosocial and affiliative behavior: A field study of the Townsville City mall. *Australian Journal of Psychology, 33,* 297–303.

151. Bennett, R., & Casey, D. (1989, August). *Ambient cigarette smoke and environmental load: Effects on prosocial behavior.* Paper presented at annual meetings of the American Psychological Association, New Orleans.

152. Appleyard, D. (1976). *Planning a pluralist city.* Cambridge, MA: MIT Press.

153. Hillman, J., Whyte, W. H., & Erickson, A. (1980). *The city as dwelling: Walking, sitting, shaping.* Center for Civic Leadership, University of Dallas, Texas, p. 3.

154. Fletcher, S., & Macauley, C. (1983). The shopping mall as a therapeutic arena. *Geriatric Nursing, 4*(2), 105–106.

155. Börnstein, M. H., & Börnstein, H. G. (1976). The pace of life. *Nature, 259,* 557–558.

156. Bornstein, M. H. (1979). The pace of life: Revisited. *International Journal of Psychology, 14,* 83–90.

157. Gifford, R., Ward, J., & Dahms, W. (1977). Pedestrian velocities: A multivariate study of social and environmental effects. *Journal of Human Movement Studies, 3,* 66–68.

158. Wirtz, P., & Ried, G. (1992). The pace of life—Reanalyzed: Why does walking speed of pedestrians correlate with city size? *Behaviour, 123*(1–2), 77–83.

159. Rotton, J., Shats, M., & Standers, R. (1990). Temperature and pedestrian tempo: Walking without awareness. *Environment and Behavior, 22,* 650–674.

160. Hill, M. R. (1984). Walking, crossing streets, and choosing pedestrian routes: A survey of recent insights from the social/behavioral sciences. *University of Nebraska Studies, New Series No. 66,* 1984.

161. See note 160.

162. McCauley, D., Coleman, G., & De Fusco, P. (1978). Commuters' eye contact with strangers in city and suburban train stations: Evidence of short-term adaptation to interpersonal overload in the city. *Environmental Psychology and Nonverbal Behavior, 2,* 215–225.

163. Lofland, L. (1973). *A world of strangers.* New York: Basic Books.

164. Wolff, M. (1973). Notes on the behavior of pedestrians. In A. Brienbaum & E. Sagarin (Eds.), *People in places: The sociology of the familiar.* New York: Praeger.

165. See note 82.

166. See note 82.

167. Owens, D. D. (1981). Ridesharing programs: Governmental response to urban transportation problems. *Environment and Behavior, 13,* 311–330.

168. Schiavo, S. R. (1988). Age differences in assessment and use of a suburban neighborhood among children and adolescents. *Children's Environments Quarterly, 5,* 4–9.

169. Gaster, S. (1991). Urban children's access to their neighborhood: Changes over three generations. *Environment and Behavior, 23,* 70–85.

170. Brown, D., Sijpkes, P., & MacLean, M. (1986). The community role of public indoor space. *Journal of Architecture and Planning Research, 3,* 161–172.

171. Smith, G. (1991). Grocery shopping patterns of the ambulatory urban elderly. *Environment and Behavior, 23,* 86–114.

172. Simon, S. L., Walsh, D. A., Regnier, V. A., & Krauss, I. K. (1992). Spatial cognition and neighborhood use: The relationship in older adults. *Psychology and Aging, 7,* 389–394.

173. Seattle stomps on vagrancy. (1994, May 24). *Victoria Times-Colonist,* p. A5.

174. Milgram, S. (1977). *The individual in a social world: Essays and experiments.* Reading, MA: Addison-Wesley.

175. Donovan, R. J., & Rossiter, J. R. (1982). Store atmosphere: An environmental psychology approach. *Journal of Retailing, 58,* 35–57.

176. Hawkins, D. I., Best, R. J., & Coney, K. A. (1983). *Consumer behavior: Implications for marketing strategy.* Plano, TX: Business Publications.

177. Williams, R. (1981, October–November). Outshopping: Problem or opportunity? *Arizona Business, 27,* 9.

178. See note 171.

179. Sommer, R., Herrick, J., & Sommer, T. R. (1981). The behavioral ecology of supermarkets and farmers' markets. *Journal of Environmental Psychology, 1,* 13–19.

180. May, F. E. (1969). Buying behavior: Some research findings. In J. U. McNeal (Ed.), *Dimensions of buying behavior.* New York: Appleton-Century-Crofts.

181. See note 175.

182. Jansen-Verbeke, M. (1987). Women, shopping and leisure. *Leisure Studies, 6,* 71–86.

183. Harrell, G., Hutt, M., & Anderson, J. (1980). Path analysis of buyer behavior under conditions of crowding. *Journal of Marketing Research, 17,* 45–51.

184. Segal, M. E., & McCauley, C. R. (1986). The sociability of commercial exchange in rural, suburban, and urban locations: A test of the urban overload hypothesis. *Basic and Applied Social Psychology, 7,* 115–135.

185. Cohen, P. (1981). *Consumer behavior.* New York: Random House.

186. Leed, T. W., & German, G. A. (1973). *Food merchandising: Principles and practices.* New York: Chain Store Age Books.

187. Patricios, N. N. (1979). Human aspects of planning shopping centers. *Environment and Behavior, 11,* 511–538.

188. Milliman, R. E. (1982). Using background music to affect the behavior of supermarket shoppers. *Journal of Marketing, 46,* 86–91.

189. Smith, P. C., & Curnow, R. (1966). Arousal hypotheses and the effects of music on purchasing behavior. *Journal of Applied Psychology, 50,* 255–256.

190. See note 188.

191. Roballey, T. C., McGreevy, C., Rongo, R. R., Schwantes, M. L., Steger, P. J., Wininger, M. A., & Gardiner, E. B. (1985). The effect of music on eating behavior. *Bulletin of the Psychonomic Society, 23,* 221–222.

192. Kohn, I. R., Franck, K. A., & Fox, A. S. (1975). *Defensible space modifications in row-house communities.* Report to the National Science Foundation. New York: Institute for Community Design Analysis.

193. Whyte, W. H. (1974). The best street life in the world. *New York Magazine, 15,* 26–33.

194. Whyte, W. H. (1980). *The social life of small urban spaces.* New York: The Conservation Foundation.

195. Nasar, J. L. (1990). Patterns of behavior in urban public spaces. *Journal of Architectural and Planning Research, 7,* 71–85.

196. Brower, S. (1988). *Design in familiar places: What makes home environments look good.* New York: Praeger.

197. Vis, A. A., Dijkstra, A., & Slop, M. (1992). Safety effects of 30 Km/H zones in the Netherlands. *Accident Analysis and Prevention, 24,* 75–86.

198. Zaidel, D., Hakkert, A. S., & Pistiner, A. H. (1992). The use of road humps for moderating speeds on urban streets. *Accident Analysis and Prevention, 24,* 45–56.

Chapter 11

1. Weinstein, C. (1979). The physical environment of school: A review of the research. *Review of Educational Research, 49,* 577–610.

2. Landers, S. (1987). Poll explores non-school learning. *American Psychological Association Monitor, 18*(2), 8–9.

3. Weinstein, C. S. (1982). Special issue on learning environments: An introduction. *Journal of Man-Environment Relations, 1*(3), 1–9.

4. Traub, R. E., & Weiss, J. (1974). Studying openness in education: An Ontario example. *Journal of Research and Development in Education, 8*, 47–59.

5. Weinstein, C. S. (1981). Classroom design as an external condition for learning. *Educational Technology, 21*, 12–19.

6. Gump, P. V., & Friesen, W. V. (1964). Participation in non-class settings. In R. G. Barker & P. V. Gump (Eds.), *Big school, small school: High school size and student behavior*. Stanford, CA: Stanford University Press.

7. Gump, P. V., & Friesen, W. V. (1964). Satisfactions derived from nonclass settings. In R. G. Barker & P. V. Gump (Eds.), *Big school, small school: High school size and student behavior*. Stanford, CA: Stanford University Press.

8. Baird, L. L. (1969). Big school, small school: A critical examination of the hypothesis. *Journal of Educational Psychology, 60*, 286–303.

9. Wicker, A. W. (1968). Undermanning, performance, and students' subjective experiences in behavior settings of large and small high schools. *Journal of Personality and Social Psychology, 10*, 255–261.

10. Prescott, E. (1970). The large day care center as a child rearing environment. *Voice for Child, 2*(4).

11. Myrick, R., & Marx, B. S. (1968), cited in R. H. Moos (1976). *The human context: Environmental determinants of behavior*. New York: Wiley.

12. Rittlemeyer, C. (1987). Meaning fields of the architecture of school buildings: An empirical study toward perception and evaluation of different school facades by students. *Psychologie in Erziehung und Unterricht, 34*, 171–177.

13. Piccigallo, P. R. (1989). Renovating urban schools is fundamental to improving them. *Phi Delta Kappan*, 402–406.

14. Decrepit schools linked to learning woes. (1993, October 6), *Victoria Times-Colonist*, p. A9.

15. Canter, D., & Stringer, P. (1975). *Environmental interaction: Psychological approaches to our physical surroundings*. London: Surrey University Press.

16. Ahrentzen, S. (1981). The environmental and social context of distraction in the classroom. In A. E. Osterberg, C. P. Tiernan, & R. A. Findlay (Eds.), *Design research interactions* (pp. 241–250). Ames, IA: Environmental Design Research Association.

17. Creekmore, W. N. (1987). Effective use of classroom walls. *Academic Therapy, 22*, 341–348.

18. Pellegrini, A. D. (1985). Social-cognitive aspects of children's play: The effects of age, gender, and activity centers. *Journal of Applied Developmental Psychology, 6*, 129–140.

19. Talton, E. L., & Simpson, R. D. (1987). Relationships of attitude toward classroom environment with attitude toward and achievement in science among tenth grade biology students. *Journal of Research in Science Teaching, 24*, 507–525.

20. Cohen, S., & Trostle, S. L. (1990). Young children's preferences for school-related physical-environmental setting characteristics. *Environment and Behavior, 22*, 753–766.

21. Dunn, R. (1987). Research on instructional environments: Implications for student achievement and attitudes. *Professional School Psychology, 2*, 43–52.

22. McGeoch, J. A. (1942). *The psychology of human learning*. New York: Longmans, Green, p. 501.

23. Abernathy, E. M. (1940). The effect of changed environmental conditions upon the result of college examinations. *Journal of Psychology, 10*, 293–301.

24. Godden, D. R., & Baddeley, A. D. (1975). Context-dependent memory in two natural environments: On land and underwater. *British Journal of Psychology, 66*, 325–331.

25. Weir, W., & May, R. B. (1988). Environmental context and student performance. *Canadian Journal of Education, 13*, 505–510.

26. Farnsworth, P. R. (1934). Examinations in familiar and unfamiliar surroundings. *Journal of Social Psychology, 4*, 128–129.

27. Cohen, R., Wetherford, D. L., Lomenick, T., & Koeller, K. (1979). Development of spatial representations: Role of task demands and familiarity with the environment. *Child Development, 50*, 1257–1260.

28. Smith S. M. (1986). Environmental context-dependent recognition memory using a short-term memory task for input. *Memory and Cognition, 14*, 347–354.

29. Eich, E. (1985). Context, memory, and integrated item/context imagery. *Journal of Experimental Psychology: Learning, Memory, and Cognition, 11*, 764–770.

30. Canas, J. J., & Nelson, D. L. (1986). Recognition and environmental context: The effect of testing by phone. *Bulletin of the Psychonomic Society, 24*, 407–409.

31. Nixon, S. J., & Kanak N. J. (1985). A theoretical account of the effects of environmental context upon cognitive processes. *Bulletin of the Psychomonic Society, 23*, 139–142.

32. Smith, S. M. (1979). Remembering in and out of context. *Journal of Experimental Psychology, 5*, 460–471.

33. Wilson, C. W., & Hopkins, B. L. (1973). The effects of contingent music on the intensity of noise in junior home economics classes. *Journal of Applied Behavior Analysis, 6*, 269–275.

34. Schmidt, G. W., & Ulrich, R. E. (1969). Effects of group contingent events upon classroom noise. *Journal of Applied Behavior Analysis, 2*, 171–179.

35. Strang, H. R., & George, J. R. (1975). Clowning around to stop clowning around: A brief report on an automated approach to monitor, record, and control classroom noise. *Journal of Applied Behavior Analysis, 8*, 471–474.

36. Hockey, G. R. J., & Hamilton, P. (1970). Arousal and information selection in short-term memory. *Nature, 226*, 866–867.

37. Bronzaft, A. L. (1981). The effect of a noise abatement program on reading ability. *Journal of Environmental Psychology, 1*, 215–222.

38. Hambrick-Dixon, P. J. (1988). The effect of elevated subway train noise over time on Black children's visual vigilance performance. *Journal of Environmental Psychology, 8*, 299–314.

39. Cohen, S., Evans, G. W., Krantz, D. S., Stokols, D., & Kelly, S. (1981). Aircraft noise and children: Longitudinal and cross-sectional evidence on adaptation to noise and the effectiveness of noise abatement. *Journal of Personality and Social Psychology, 40,* 331–345.

40. Madu, S. N. (1990). Effect of noise on memory and recall among Nigerian students. *Journal of African Psychology, 1,* 15–23.

41. Bell, P. A., Hess, S., Hill, E., Kukas, S., Richards, R. W., and Sargent, D. (1984). Noise and context-dependent memory. *Bulletin of the Psychonomic Society, 22,* 99–100.

42. Gulian, E., & Thomas, J. R. (1986). The effects of noise, cognitive set and gender on mental arithmetic performance. *British Journal of Psychology, 77,* 503–511.

43. Christie, D. J., & Glickman, C. D. (1980). The effects of classroom noise on children: Evidence for sex differences. *Psychology in the Schools, 17,* 405–408.

44. Hykin, S. (1984). *The effects of classroom noise on adults: Evidence for sex differences.* Unpublished master's thesis, University of Victoria, Victoria, BC.

45. Zentall, S. S. (1983). Learning environments: A review of physical and temporal factors. *EEQ: Exceptional Education Quarterly, 4,* 90–115.

46. Collins-Eiland, K., Dansereau, D. F., Brooks, L. W., & Holley, C. D. (1986). Effect of conversational noise, locus of control, and field dependence/independence on the performance of academic tasks. *Contemporary Educational Psychology, 11,* 139–149.

47. Edmonds, E. M., & Smith. L. R. (1985). Students' performance as a function of sex, noise, and intelligence. *Psychological Reports, 56,* 727–730.

48. Geen, R. G., McCown, E. J., & Broyles, J. W. (1985). Effects of noise on sensitivity of introverts and extraverts to signals in a vigilance task. *Personality and Individual Differences, 6,* 237–241.

49. Toplyn, G., & Maguire, W. (1991). The differential effect of noise on creative task performance. *Creativity Research Journal, 4,* 337–347.

50. See note 38.

51. Pizzo, J., Dunn, R., & Dunn, K. J. (1990). A sound approach to improving reading: Responding to students' learning styles. *Journal of Reading, Writing, and Learning Disabilities International, 6,* 249–260.

52. See note 45.

53. Breen-Lewis, K., & Wilding, J. (1984). Noise, time of day and test expectations in recall and recognition. *British Journal of Psychology, 75,* 51–63.

54. Hartley, L. R., Boultwood, B., & Dunne, M. P. (1987). Noise and verbal or spatial solutions of Rubik's cube. *Ergonomics, 30,* 503–509.

55. Salame, P., & Baddeley, A. (1987). Noise, unattended speech and short-term memory. *Ergonomics, 30,* 1185–1194.

56. Miller, G. M. (1988). Effects of a hearing protection device on cognitive and motor performance of students in noisy environments. *Dissertation Abstracts International, 47.*

57. Cohen, S., & Weinstein, N. (1982). Nonauditory effects of noise on behavior and health. In G. W. Evans (Ed.), *Environmental stress.* New York: Cambridge University Press.

58. Cohen, S., Glass, D. C., & Singer, J. E. (1973). Apartment noise, auditory discrimination and reading ability in children. *Journal of Experimental Social Psychology, 9,* 407–422.

59. Heft, H. (1979). Background and focal environmental conditions of the home and attention in young children. *Journal of Applied Social Psychology, 9,* 47–69.

60. See note 57.

61. Brunetti, F. (1972). Noise, distraction and privacy in conventional and open school environments. In W. J. Mitchell (Ed.), *Environmental design: Research and practice.* Los Angeles: University of California.

62. Ahrentzen, S., Jue, G. M., Skorpanich, M., & Evans, G. W. (1982). School environments and stress. In G. W. Evans (Ed.), *Environmental stress* (pp. 224–255). New York: Cambridge University Press.

63. Stein, C. (1975). School lighting re-evaluated. *American School and University, 48,* 70–78.

64. See note 63.

65. Mayron, L. W., Ott, J. N., Nations, R., & Mayron, E. L. (1974). Light, radiation, and academic behavior. *Academic Therapy, 10,* 441–448.

66. Fletcher, D. (1983). Effects of classroom lighting on the behavior of exceptional children. *EEQ: Exceptional Education Quarterly, 4,* 75–89.

67. Dalezman, Jones, Bevlig, Polf, & Keeny, cited in note 66.

68. Munson, P., & Ferguson, R. (1985). *The extra-visual effects of fluorescent illumination on the behavior of school children.* Manuscript in preparation, University of Victoria.

69. Riding, R. J., & Pugh, J. C. (1987). Dark-interval- threshold, illumination level and children's reading performance. *Journal of Research in Reading, 10,* 21–28.

70. Dunn, R. S., Krimsky, J. S., Murray, J. B., & Quinn, P. J. (1985). Light up their lives: A review of research on the effects of lighting on children's achievement and behavior. *Reading Teacher, 38,* 863–869.

71. Blue is beautiful. (1973, September). *Time,* p. 66.

72. Fehrman, K. R. (1987). The effects of interior pigment color on school task performance mediated by arousal. *Dissertation Abstracts International, 48*(4–A), 819.

73. Rosenstein, L. D. (1985). Effect of color of the environment on task performance and mood of males and females with high or low scores on the Scholastic Aptitude Test. *Perceptual and Motor Skills, 60,* 550.

74. Taylor, L. (1980, May 24). Improved lighting may make brighter work. *The Financial Post,* p. 25.

75. Veitch, J. A., Hine, D. W., & Gifford, R. (1993). End users' knowledge, beliefs, and preferences for lighting. *Journal of Interior Design, 19*(2), 15–26.

76. See note 66.

77. Ponte, L. (1981, February). How artificial light affects your health. *Reader's Digest,* pp. 131–134.

78. See note 66.

79. Colman, R., Frankel, F., Ritvo, E., & Freeman, B. (1976). The effects of fluorescent and incandescent illumination upon repetitive behavior in autistic children. *Journal of Autism and Childhood Schizophrenia, 6,* 157–162.

80. Painter, M. (1976–77). Fluorescent lights and hyperactivity in children: An experiment. *Academic Therapy, 12,* 181–184.

81. See note 66.

82. Mayron, L. W., Ott, J. N., Amontree, E. J., & Nations, R. (1975). Light, radiation and dental caries. *Academic Therapy, 10,* 33–47.

83. See note 66.

84. Kuller, R., & Lindsten, C. (1992). Health and behavior of children in classrooms with and without windows. *Journal of Environmental Psychology, 12,* 305–317.

85. See note 71.

86. See note 72.

87. Auliciems, A. (1969). Effects of weather on indoor thermal comfort. *International Journal of Biometerology, 13,* 147–162.

88. Flatt, D. L. (1975). The effects of high temperature upon performance of certain physical tasks by high school students. *Dissertation Abstracts International, 35,* 7678A.

89. Ryd, H., & Wyon, D. P. Methods of evaluating human stress due to climate. *National Swedish Institute for Building Research,* 1970, Document 6.

90. Pepler, R. (1971). Variations in students' performances and in classroom temperatures in climate controlled and non-climate controlled schools. *ASHRAE Transactions, 77,* 35–42.

91. Wyon, D. P. (1970). Studies of children under imposed noise and heat stress. *Ergonomics, 13,* 598–612.

92. Moos, R., & Sommers, P. (1976). The architectural environment: Physical space and building design. In R. Moos (Ed.), *The human context: Environmental determinants of behavior.* New York: Wiley.

93. See note 92.

94. See note 62.

95. Weldon, D. E., Loewy, J. H., Winer, J. I., & Elkin, D. J. (1981). Crowding and classroom learning. *Journal of Experimental Education, 49,* 160–177.

96. Glass, G. V., & Smith, M. L. (1978). *Meta-analysis of research on the relationship of class size and achievement.* San Francisco: The Far West Laboratory for Educational Research and Development.

97. Thomas, K. G. (1987). The effects of high and low social density on on-task behavior and correctness of work sheet completion of special education students. *Dissertation Abstracts International, 48,* 630–631.

98. Shapson, S. M. (1980). An experimental study of the effects of class size. *American Educational Research Journal, 17,* 141–152.

99. Heller, J. F., Groff, B. D., & Solomon, S. A. (1977). Toward an understanding of crowding: The role of physical interaction. *Journal of Personality and Social Psychology, 35,* 183–190.

100. See note 1.

101. See note 95.

102. Epstein, Y. M., & Karlin, R. A. (1975). Effects of acute experimental crowding. *Journal of Applied Social Psychology, 5,* 34–53.

103. Gochman, I. R., & Keating, J. P. (1976). *Perceived crowding as a function of unsuccessful goal attainment.* Paper presented at the annual meeting of the Western Psychological Association, Los Angeles.

104. Krantz, P. J., & Risley, T. R. (1977). Behavioral ecology in the classroom. In K. D. O'Leary & S. G. O'Leary (Eds.), *Classroom management: The successful use of behavior modification,* New York: Permagon Press.

105. Rohe, W., & Patterson, A. H. (1974). The effects of varied levels of resources and density on behavior in a day care center. In D. Carson (Ed.), *Man-environment interactions: Evaluations and applications.* Stroudsberg, PA: Dowden, Hutchinson and Ross.

106. Evans, G. W. (1978). Human spatial behavior: The arousal model. In A. Baum & Y. Epstein (Eds.), *Human response to crowding.* Hillsdale, NJ: Erlbaum.

107. Haines, L. L. (1985). *Density and territoriality: The effects on classroom performance.* Unpublished Honor's thesis, University of Victoria, Victoria, BC.

108. Smith, P., & Connolly, K. (1977). Social and aggressive behavior in preschool children as a function of crowding. *Social Science Information, 16,* 601–620.

109. McCain, G., Cox, V. C., Paulus, P. B., Luke, A., & Abadzi, H. (1985). Some effects of reduction of extra-classroom crowding in a school environment. *Journal of Applied Social Psychology, 15,* 503–515.

110. Ahrentzen, S. (1980). *Environment-behavior relations in the classroom setting: A multi-modal research perspective.* Unpublished master's thesis, University of California, Irvine.

111. See note 16.

112. See note 95.

113. Axelrod, S., Hall, R. V., & Tams, A. (1979). Comparison of two common classroom seating arrangements. *Academic Therapy, 15,* 29–36.

114. Wheldall, K., Morriss, M. Vaughan, P., & Ng, Y. (1981). Rows vs. tables: An example of the use of behavioral ecology in two classes of eleven-year-old children. *Educational Psychology, 1,* 171–184.

115. Wheldall, K., & Lam, Y. Y. (1987). Rows versus tables: II: The effects of two classroom seating arrangements on classroom disruption rate, on-task behavior and teacher behavior in three special school classes. *Educational Psychology, 7,* 303–312.

116. Rosenfield, P., Lambert, N. M., & Black, A. (1985). Desk arrangement effects on pupil classroom behavior. *Journal of Educational Psychology, 77,* 101–108.

117. Gill, W. M. (1977). A look at the change to open-plan schools in New Zealand. *New Zealand Journal of Educational Studies, 12,* 3–16.

118. Legendre, A., & Fontaine, A.-M. (1991). The effects of visual boundaries in two-year-olds' playrooms. *Children's Environments Quarterly, 8,* 2–16.

119. Zifferblatt, S. M. (1972). Architecture and human behavior: Toward increased understanding of a functional relationship. *Educational Technology, 12,* 54–57.

120. Weinstein, C. S. (1977). Modifying student behavior in an open classroom through changes in the physical design. *American Education Research Journal, 14,* 249–262.

121. Perkins, cited in note 5.

122. Nash, B. C. (1981). The effects of classroom spatial organization on four- and five-year-old children's learning. *British Journal of Educational Psychology, 51,* 144–155.

123. Trawick-Smith, J. (1992). A descriptive study of spatial arrangement in a family day care home. *Child and Youth Care Forum, 21,* 263–276.

124. Morrow, L. M. (1982). Relationships between literature programs, library corner designs, and children's use of literature. *Journal of Educational Research, 75,* 339–344.

125. Neill, S. R. St. J. (1982). Experimental alterations in playroom layout and their effect on staff and child behavior. *Educational Psychology, 2,* 103–119.

126. Porteous, C. (1972). *Learning as a function of molar environmental complexity.* Unpublished master's thesis, University of Victoria, Victoria, BC.

127. Santrock, J. W. (1976). Affect and facilitative self control: Influence of ecological setting, cognition, and social agent. *Journal of Educational Psychology, 68,* 529–535.

128. See note 62.

129. Griffith, C. R. (1921). A comment upon the psychology of the audience. *Psychological Monographs, 30*(136), 36–47.

130. Brooks, C. I., & Rebeta, J. L. (1991). College classroom ecology: The relation of sex of student to classroom performance and seating preference. *Environment and Behavior, 23,* 305–313.

131. Becker, F. D., Sommer, R., Bee, J., & Oxley, B. (1973). College classroom ecology. *Sociometry, 36,* 514–525.

132. Sommer (1967). Classroom ecology. *Journal of Applied Behavioral Science, 3,* 489–503.

133. Hillmann, R. B., Brooks, C. I., & O'Brien, J. P. (1991). Differences in self-esteem of college freshmen as a function of classroom seating-row preference. *Psychological Record, 41,* 315–320.

134. See note 133.

135. Schwebel, A. I., & Cherlin, D. L. (1972). Physical and social distancing in teacher-pupil relationships. *Journal of Educational Psychology, 63,* 543–550.

136. See note 133.

137. Buckalew, L. W., Daly, J. D., & Coffield, K. E. (1986). Relationship of initial class attendance and seating location to academic performance in psychology classes. *Bulletin of the Psychonomic Society, 24,* 63–64.

138. Walberg, H. (1969). Physical and psychological distance in the classroom. *School Review, 77,* 64–70.

139. Dykman, B. D., & Reis, H. T. (1979). Personality correlates of classroom seating position. *Journal of Educational Psychology, 71,* 346–354.

140. See note 133.

141. Morrison, T. L., & Thomas, M. D. (1975). Self-esteem and classroom participation. *Journal of Educational Research, 68,* 374–377.

142. See note 130.

143. MacPherson, J. C. (1984). Environments and interaction in row and column classrooms. *Environment and Behavior, 16,* 481–502.

144. Stires, L. (1980). Classroom seating location, student grades, and attitudes: Environment or self-selection? *Environment and Behavior, 12,* 241–254.

145. Knowles, E. S. (1982). A comment on the study of social ecology: A lament for the good old days. *Personality and Social Psychology Bulletin, 8,* 357–361.

146. Wulf, K. M. (1977). Relationship of assigned classroom seating area to achievement variables. *Educational Research Quarterly, 21,* 56–62.

147. Millard, R. J., & Stimpson, D. V. (1980). Enjoyment and productivity as a function of classroom seating location. *Perceptual and Motor Skills, 50,* 439–444.

148. Levine, D. W., O'Neal, E. C., Garwood, S. G. & McDonald, P. J. (1980). Classroom ecology: The effects of seating position on grades and participation. *Personality and Social Psychology Bulletin, 6,* 409–412.

149. Koneya, M. (1976). Location and interaction in row and column seating arrangements. *Environment and Behavior, 8,* 265–282.

150. Montello, D. R. (1988). Classroom seating location and its effect on course achievement, participation, and attitudes. *Journal of Environmental Psychology, 8,* 149–157.

151. Neill, S. R. St. J., & Denham, E. J. M. (1982). The effects of pre-school design. *Educational Research, 24,* 107–111.

152. Weinstein, C. S., & Weinstein, N. D. (1979). Noise and reading performance in an open space school. *Journal of Educational Research, 72,* 210–213.

153. Gump, P. V., & Ross, R. (1977). The fit of milieu and program in school environments. In H. McGurk (Ed.), *Ecological factors in human development.* New York: Elsevier North-Holland.

154. Ross, R. P. (1980). Modification of space in open plan schools: An examination of the press toward synomorphy. In R. R. Stough & A. Wandersman (Eds.), *Optimizing environments: Research, practice, and policy.* Washington, DC: Environmental Design Research Association.

155. Gump, P. V. (1978). School environments. In I. Altman & J. F. Wohlwill (Eds.), *Children and the environment.* New York: Plenum.

156. See note 155.

157. Reiss, S., & Dyhaldo, N. (1975). Persistence, achievement and open-space environments. *Journal of Educational Psychology, 67,* 506–513.

158. Cotterell, J. L. (1984). Effects of school architectural design on student and teacher anxiety. *Environment and Behavior, 16,* 455–479.

159. See note 155.

160. See note 62.

161. Bell, A. E., Switzer, F., & Zipursky, M. (1974). Open area education: An advantage or disadvantage for beginners? *Perceptual and Motor Skills, 39,* 407–416.

162. Grapko, M. F., cited in note 1.

163. See note 4.

164. See note 161.

165. Wright, R. J. (1975). The affective and cognitive consequences of an open education elementary school. *American Educational Research Journal, 12,* 449–468.

166. Gran, B., & Engquist, O. (1979). Cited in J. King, & R. W. Marans, *The physical environment and the learning process: A survey of recent research.* Ann Arbor, MI: Survey Research Center, Institute for Social Research, University of Michigan.

167. Evans, G. W., & Lovell, B. (1979). Design modification in an open plan school. *Journal of Educational Psychology, 71,* 41–49.

168. Solomon, D., & Kendall, A. J. (1976). Individual characteristics and children's performance in "open" and "traditional" classroom settings. *Journal of Educational Psychology, 68,* 613–625.

169. See note 155.

170. Sommer, R., & Becker, F. D. (1971). Room density and user satisfaction. *Environment and Behavior, 3,* 412–417.

171. See note 1.

172. Coles, R. (1969). Those places they call schools. *Harvard Educational Review: Architecture and Education, 39,* 46–57.

173. Hathaway, W. E. (1990). Planning schools for the 21st century. *The Canadian School Executive, 10,* 3–10.

174. Feitler, F. C., Weiner, W., & Blumberg, A. (1970). *The relationship between interpersonal relations orientations and preferred classroom physical settings.* Paper presented at the annual meeting of the American Educational Research Association, Minneapolis.

175. Ahrentzen, S., & Evans, G. W. (1984). Distraction, privacy, and classroom design. *Environment and Behavior, 16,* 437–454.

176. Traub, R., Weiss, J., & Fisher, C. (1977). *Openness in schools: An evaluation study.* Ottawa: Ontario Institute for Studies in Education.

177. Krovetz, M. L. (1977). Who needs what when: Design of pluralistic learning environments. In D. Stokols (Ed.), *Perspectives on environment and behavior: Theory, research and applications.* New York: Plenum.

178. See note 158.

179. See note 177.

180. See note 151.

181. Rothenberg, M., cited in note 177.

182. Chambers, J. A. (1963–1964). A study of attitudes and feelings toward windowless classrooms. *Dissertations Abstracts International, 24,* 4498.

183. See note 1.

184. Collins, B. L. (1965). Windows and people: Alternative survey. Psychological reactions to environments with and without windows. *National Bureau of Standards Building Science Series,* No. 70. Washington, DC: Institute for Applied Technology.

185. Karmel, L. J. (1965). Effects of windowless classroom environment on high school students. *Perceptual and Motor Skills, 20,* 277–278.

186. Weinstein, C. S., & Woolfolk, A. E. (1981). The classroom setting as a source of expectations about teachers and pupils. *Journal of Environmental Psychology, 1,* 117–129.

187. See note 1.

188. Rohe, W., & Patterson, A. H. (1974). The effects of varied levels of resources and density on behavior in a day care center. In D. Carson (Ed.), *Man-environment interactions: Evaluations and applications.* Stroudsberg, PA: Dowden, Hutchinson and Ross.

189. Rohe, W. M., & Nuffer, E. L. (1977). *The effects of density and partitioning on children's behavior.* Paper presented at the annual meetings of the American Psychological Association, San Francisco.

190. See note 189.

191. Fagot, B. I. (1977). Variations in density: Effect on task and social behaviors of pre-school children. *Developmental Psychology, 13,* 166–167.

192. See note 62.

193. See note 155.

194. Smith, P. K., & Connolly, K. J. (1980). *The ecology of preschool behaviour.* New York: Cambridge University Press.

195. McAfee, J. K. (1987). Classroom density and the aggressive behavior of handicapped children. *Education and Treatment of Children, 10,* 134–145.

196. Sherrill, A. A. (1986). Elementary classroom crowding and student aggressive behaviors. *Dissertation Abstracts International, 47,* 1146.

197. Banzinger, G. (1982). Teaching about crowding: Students as an independent variable. *Teaching of Psychology, 4,* 241–242.

198. See note 1.

199. Shapiro, S. (1975). Preschool ecology: A study of three environmental variables. *Reading Improvement, 12,* 236–241.

200. See note 194.

201. See note 189.

202. Weinstein, C. S. (1982). Privacy-seeking behavior in an elementary classroom. *Journal of Environmental Psychology, 2,* 23–35.

203. See note 175.

204. See note 1.

205. Stebbins, R. A. (1973). Physical context influences on behavior: The case of classroom disorderliness. *Environment and Behavior, 5,* 291–314.

206. Neill, S. R. St. J. (1982). Preschool design and child behavior. *Journal of Child Psychology and Psychiatry, 23,* 309–318.

207. See note 151.

208. Brunetti, F. (1972). Noise, distraction and privacy in conventional and open school environments. In W. J. Mitchell (Ed.), *Environmental design: Research and practice* (pp. 29–38). Los Angeles: University of California.

209. Wohlwill, J. F. (1966). The physical environment: A problem for a psychology of stimulation. *Journal of Social Issues, 22*(4), 29–30.

210. See note 45.

211. See note 45.

212. Steele, F. (1980). Defining and developing environmental competence. In C. P. Alderfer & C. L. Cooper (Eds.), *Advances in experimental social processes, 2,* 225–244.

213. See note 212.

214. Cornell, E. H., & Hay, D. H. (1984). Children's acquisition of a route via different media. *Environment and Behavior, 16,* 627–641.

215. Gifford, R., Hay, R., & Boros, K. (1982–83). Individual differences in environmental attitudes. *Journal of Environmental Education, 14*(2), 19–23.

216. Sommer, R. (1972). *Design awareness.* New York: Holt, Rinehart and Winston.

217. See note 212.

218. See note 212.

219. Stapp, W. B. (1971). An environmental education program (K–12) based on environmental encounters. *Environment and Behavior, 3,* 263–283.

220. Lingwood, D. A. (1971). Environmental education through information-seeking: The case of an "Environmental Teach-In." *Environment and Behavior, 3,* 230–262.

221. Robinson, B., & Wolfson, E. (1982). *Environmental education: A manual for elementary educators.* New York: Teachers College Press.

222. Martin, W. W., Falk, J. H., & Balling, J. D. (1981). Environmental effects on learning: The outdoor field trip. *Science Education, 65,* 301–309.

223. Schwab, K. E. (1982–1983). Instructional methods: Their use and effectiveness in environmental education. *Journal of Environmental Education, 14*(2), 8–12.

224. Ramsey, J. M., & Hungerford, H. R. (1989). The effects of issue investigation and action training on environmental behavior in seventh grade students. *Journal of Environmental Education, 20*(4), 29–34.

225. Jordan, J. R., Hungerford, H. R., & Tomera, A. N. (1986). Effects of two residential environmental workshops on high school students. *Journal of Environmental Education, 18*(1), 15–22.

226. Agee, J. K., Field, D. R., & Starkey, E. E. (1982–1983). Cooperative parks studies unit: University-based science programs in the national park service. *Journal of Environmental Education, 14*(2), 24–28.

227. van Wagenberg, D., Krasner, M., & Krasner, L. C. (1981). Children planning an ideal classroom: Environmental design in an elementary school. *Environment and Behavior, 13,* 349–359.

228. Powers, R. B. (1985–1986). The Commons Game: Teaching students about social dilemmas. *Journal of Environmental Education, 17*(2), 4–10.

229. Dresner, M. (1989–1990). Changing energy end-use patterns as a means of reducing global-warming trends. *Journal of Environmental Education, 21*(2), 41–46.

230. Carlander, M. (1988). Atomalderns barn: Att arbeta for fred, miljo och globalt medansvar med barn pa lag-och mellanstadiet. Nuclear-age children: Working for peace, the environment and global responsibility with children in grades 1–6. *Pedagogiska Hjalpmedel, 39,* 110.

231. Westphal, J. M., & Halverson, W. F. (1985–1986). Assessing the long-term effects of an environmental education program: A pragmatic approach. *Journal of Environmental Education, 17*(2), 26–30.

232. See note 216.

233. Kaplan, R. (1974). Some psychological benefits of an outdoor challenge program. *Environment and Behavior, 6,* 101–116.

234. Brockmeyer, F. M., Bowman, M., & Mullins, G. W. (1982–1983). Sensory versus non-sensory interpretation: A study of senior citizen's preferences. *Journal of Environmental Education, 14*(2), 3–7.

235. Morrow, L. M., & Weinstein, C. S. (1982). Increasing children's use of literature through program and physical design changes. *Elementary School Journal, 83,* 131–137.

236. Sommer, R., & Olsen, H. (1980). The soft classroom. *Environment and Behavior, 12,* 3–16.

237. Wollin, D. D., & Montagne, M. (1981). College classroom environment: Effects of sterility versus amiability on student and teacher performance. *Environment and Behavior, 13,* 707–716.

Chapter 12

1. Steele, F. I. (1973). *Physical settings and organization development.* Don Mills, ON: Addison-Wesley.

2. Roethlisberger, F. J., & Dickson, W. J. (1939). *Management and the worker.* Cambridge, MA: Harvard University Press.

3. Steele, F. I. (1973). *Physical settings and organization development.* Don Mills, ON: Addison-Wesley.

4. Davis, T. R. (1984). The influence of the physical environment in offices. *Academy of Management Review, 9,* 271–283.

5. Frone, M. R. (1989). Chronic occupational stressors, self-focused attention, and well-being: Testing a cybernetic model of stress. *Journal of Applied Psychology, 74,* 876–883.

6. Sutton, R. I., & Rafaeli, A. (1987). Characteristics of work stations as potential occupational stressors. *Academy of Management Journal, 30,* 260–276.

7. Wineman, J. D. (Ed.). (1986). *Behavioral issues in office design.* New York: Van Nostrand Reinhold.

8. See note 1.

9. Parsons, H. M. (1976). Work environments. In I. Altman & J. F. Wohlwill (Eds.), *Human behavior and environment* (Vol. 1). New York: Plenum.

10. Dunn, B. E. (1979). The noise environment of man. In H. W. Jones (Ed.), *Noise in the human environment* (Vol. 2). Edmonton, Alberta: Environmental Council of Alberta.

11. Moreland, J. B. (1988). Ambient noise measurements in open-plan offices. *Journal of the Acoustical Society of America, 83,* 1683–1685.

12. Park, M.-Y., & Casali, J. G. (1991). A controlled investigation of in-field attenuation performance of selected insert, earmuff, and canal cap hearing protectors. *Human Factors, 33,* 693–714.

13. See note 10.

14. Reif, Z. F., & Vermeulen, P. J. (1979). Noise from domestic appliances, construction, and industry. In H. W. Jones (Ed.), *Noise in the human environment* (Vol. 2). Edmonton, Alberta: Environmental Council of Alberta.

15. Workers' Compensation Board of British Columbia. (1979). *Industrial Health Safety Regulations.* Richmond, B.C.: Workers Compensation Board of British Columbia.

16. Broadbent, D. E. (1979). Human performance and noise. In C. M. Harris (Ed.), *Handbook of noise control.* New York: McGraw-Hill.

17. Miller, J. D. (1974). Effects of noise on people. *Journal of the Acoustical Society of America, 56,* 729–764.

18. Harrison, D. W. (1989). Age differences in cardiovascular and cognitive performance under noise conditions. *Perceptual & Motor Skills, 69,* 547–554.

19. Goldstein, J., & Dejoy, D. M. (1980). Behavioral and performance effects of noise: Perspectives for research. In J. V. Tobias, G. Jansen, & W. D. Ward (Eds.), *Proceedings of the third international congress on noise as a public health problem.* Rockville, MD: American Speech-Language-Hearing Association.

20. Baker, M. A., & Holding, D. H. (1993). The effects of noise and speech on cognitive task performance. *Journal of General Psychology, 120,* 339–355.

21. Weinstein, N. D. (1974). Effect of noise on intellectual performance. *Journal of Applied Psychology, 59*, 548–554.

22. See note 16.

23. Cohen, S., & Weinstein, N. (1982). Nonauditory effects of noise on behavior and health. In G. W. Evans (Ed.), *Environmental stress*. New York: Cambridge University Press.

24. Nagar, D., & Pandey, J. (1987). Affect and performance on cognitive task as a function of crowding and noise. *Journal of Applied Social Psychology, 17*, 147–157.

25. Reid, D. B., & Paulhus, D. L. (1987, June). *Aftereffects of noise on cognitive performance*. Poster presented at annual meetings of Canadian Psychological Association, Vancouver.

26. See note 16.

27. Albery, W. B. (1989). The effect of sustained acceleration and noise on workload in human operators. *Aviation, Space, & Environmental Medicine, 60*, 943–948.

28. Levy-Leboyer, C. (1989). Noise effects on two industrial tasks. *Work and Stress, 3*, 315–322.

29. Gulian, E., & Thomas, J. R. (1986). The effects of noise, cognitive set and gender on mental arithmetic performance. *British Journal of Psychology, 77*, 503–511.

30. Baker, M. A. (1984). Noise, sex and time of day effects in a mathematics task. *Ergonomics, 27*, 67–80.

31. Lahtela, K., Nieme, P., Kuusela, V., & Hypen, K. (1986). Noise and visual choice-reaction time: A large-scale population survey. *Scandinavian Journal of Psychology, 27*, 52–57.

32. Jennings, J. R., Nebes, R., & Brock, K. (1988). Memory retrieval in noise and psychophysiological response in the young and old. *Psychophysiology, 25*, 633–644.

33. Jennings, J. R., Brock, K., & Nebes, R. (1989). Aging but not arousal influences the effect of environmental noise on the span of attention. *Experimental Aging Research, 15*, 61–71.

34. Bhatia, P., Shipira, & Muhar, I. S. (1991). Effect of low and high intensity noise on work efficiency. *Psychologia: An International Journal of Psychology in the Orient, 34*, 259–265.

35. Ng, C. F. (1989). Office worker performance and satisfaction: The effects of office noise and individual characteristics. *Dissertation Abstracts International, 50*(5–B), 2190–2191.

36. Standing, L., Lynn, D., & Moxness, K. (1990). Effects of noise upon introverts and extroverts. *Bulletin of the Psychonomic Society, 28*, 138–140.

37. Eysenck, M. W., & Graydon, J. (1989). Susceptibility to distraction as a function of personality. *Personality and Individual Differences, 10*, 681–686.

38. Matthews, G. (1985). The effects of extraversion and arousal on intelligence test performance. *British Journal of Psychology, 76*, 479–493.

39. Veitch, J. (1990). Office noise and illumination effects on reading comprehension. *Journal of Environmental Psychology, 10*, 209–217.

40. Mehrabian, A. (1977). Individual differences in stimulus screening and arousability. *Journal of Personality, 45*, 237–250.

41. Toplyn, G. A. (1988). The differential effect of noise on creative task performance. *Dissertation Abstracts International, 48*, 3718.

42. See note 16.

43. Willner, P., & Neiva, J. (1986). Brief exposure to uncontrollable but not to controllable noise biases the retrieval of information from memory. *British Journal of Clinical Psychology, 25*, 93–100.

44. Smith, A. P. (1985). The effects of different types of noise on semantic processing and syntactic reasoning. *Acta Psychologica, 58*, 263–273.

45. See note 16.

46. Tafalla, R. J. (1990). Noise, physiology and human performance: The potential role of effort. *Dissertation Abstracts International, 51*(3-B), 1551.

47. Loewen, L. J., & Suedfeld, P. (1992). Cognitive and arousal effects of masking office noise. *Environment and Behavior, 24*, 381–395.

48. See note 35.

49. Srivastra, R. (1988). Adaptation with noise and its psychological consequences. *Perspectives in Psychological Researches, 11*, 1–27.

50. See note 43.

51. Champion, D. F. (1987). Some effects of combination of noise and vibration on the performance of a cognitive task. *Dissertation Abstracts International, 47*(10–B), 4296.

52. Glass, D. C., & Singer, J. E. (1972). *Urban stress: Experiments on noise and social stressors*. New York: Academic Press.

53. Agrawal, K. (1988). Dependence proneness as related to post-stress frustration-tolerance and performance. *Indian Journal of Current Psychological Research, 3*, 55–59.

54. Davidson, L. M., Hagmann, J., & Baum, A. (1990). An exploration of a possible physiological explanation for stressor aftereffects. *Journal of Applied Social Psychology, 20*, 869–880.

55. See note 25.

56. Klein, K., & Beith, B. (1985). Re-examination of residual arousal as an explanation of aftereffects: Frustration tolerance versus response speed. *Journal of Applied Psychology, 70*, 642–650.

57. Fox, J. G. (1983). Industrial music. In D. J. Oborne & M. M. Gruneberg (Eds.), *The physical environment at work*. New York: Wiley.

58. See note 57.

59. Harcum, E. R. (1987). Disturbance ratings for relevant and irrelevant noise during performance of a cognitive task. *Perceptual and Motor Skills, 65*, 333–334.

60. Harris, L., & associates. (1978). *The Steelcase national study of office environments: Do they work?* Grand Rapids, MI: Steelcase Inc.

61. Sundstrom, E., Burt, R., & Kamp, D. (1980). Privacy at work: Architectural correlates of job satisfaction and job performance. *Academy of Management Journal, 23*, 101–117.

62. de Barbenza, C. M., de Uhrlandt, M. S., & de Vila, N. C. (1985). Noise in the work environment. *Revista de Psicologia General Aplicada, 40*, 945–952.

63. Sundstrom, E., Town, J. P., Osborn, D., Rice, R. W., Konar, E., Mandel, D., & Brill, M. (1994). Office noise, satisfaction, and performance. *Environment and Behavior, 26*, 195–222.

64. See note 51.

65. Weinstein, N. D. (1977). Noise and intellectual performance: A confirmation and extension. *Journal of Applied Psychology, 62,* 104–126.

66. See note 60.

67. Welch, B. L. (1979, June). *Extra-auditory health effects of industrial noise: Survey of foreign literature.* Aerospace Medical Research Laboratory, Aerospace Medical Division, Airforce Systems Command, Wright-Patterson AFB.

68. Cohen, A. (1969). Effects of noise on psychological state. *Noise as a public health hazard.* Washington, DC: American Speech and Hearing Association.

69. Lewis, P., & O'Sullivan, P. (1974). Acoustic privacy in office design. *Journal of Architectural Research, 3,* 48–51.

70. Goodrich, R. (1982). Seven office evaluations: A review. *Environment and Behavior, 8,* 175–190.

71. Hedge, A. (1982). The open-plan office: A systematic investigation of employee reactions to their work environment. *Environment and Behavior, 14,* 519–542.

72. McDowell, K., & Carlson, K. (1984, June). *The effects of attributes of office environments on employee mood.* Paper presented at the annual meetings of the Canadian Psychological Association meeting, Ottawa.

73. See note 61.

74. Sundstrom, E., Herbert, R. K., & Brown, D. W. (1982). Privacy and communication in an open-plan office: A case study. *Environment and Behavior, 14,* 379–392.

75. Sundstrom, E., Town, J. P., Brown, D. W., Forman, A., & McGee, C. (1982). Physical enclosure, type of job, and privacy in the office. *Environment and Behavior, 14,* 543–559.

76. Mathews, K. E., Jr., & Canon, L. K. (1975). Environmental noise level as a determinant of helping behavior. *Journal of Personality and Social Psychology, 32,* 571–577.

77. Sauser, W. I., Jr., Arauz, C. G., & Chambers, R. M. (1978). Exploring the relationship between level of office noise and salary recommendations: A preliminary research note. *Journal of Management, 4,* 57–63.

78. Rohles, F. H., Jr., Konz, S., & Munson, D. (1980). Estimating occupant satisfaction from effective temperature. *Proceedings of the Human Factors Society, 24,* 223–227.

79. McCormick, E. J. (1976). *Human factors in engineering and design.* New York: McGraw-Hill.

80. Bell, P. A., & Greene, T. C. (1982). Thermal stress: Physiological, comfort, performance and social effects of hot and cold environments. In G. W. Evans (Ed.), *Environmental stress.* New York: Cambridge University Press.

81. See note 79.

82. Fox, W. F. (1967). Human performance in the cold. *Human Factors, 9,* 203–220.

83. Enander, A. (1987). Effects of moderate cold on performance of psychomotor and cognitive tasks. *Ergonomics, 30,* 1431–1445.

84. Nelson, T. M., Nilsson, T. H., & Hopkins, G. W. (1987). Thermal comfort: Advantages and deviations. *Ashrae Transactions, 93.*

85. Enander, A. E., & Hygge, S. (1990). Thermal stress and human performance. *Scandinavian Journal of Work, Environment, and Health, 16,* 44–50.

86. Vickroy, S. C., Shaw, J. B., & Fisher, C. D. (1982). Effects of temperature, clothing, and task complexity on task performance and satisfaction. *Journal of Applied Psychology, 67,* 97–102.

87. Markee White, N. L. (1987). Quantifications of factors influencing thermal comfort in an office environment: Implications for energy conservation. *Dissertation Abstracts International, 47*(12–B), 4843.

88. Rice, B. (1980). Cooling by deception. *Psychology Today, 14,* 20.

89. Stramler, C. S., Kleiss, J. A., & Howell, W. C. (1983). Thermal sensation shift induced by physical and psychological means. *Journal of Applied Psychology, 68,* 187–193.

90. Paciuk, M. (1989). The role of personal control of the environment in thermal comfort and satisfaction at the workplace. *Dissertation Abstracts International, 50*(8-A), 2276.

91. Nelson, T. M., Nilsson, T. H., & Johnson, M. (1984). Interaction of temperature illuminance and apparent time on sedentary work fatigue. *Ergonomics, 27,* 89–101.

92. LeBlanc, J. (1975). *Man in the cold.* Springfield, IL: Thomas.

93. Kristensen, T. S. (1989). Cardiovascular diseases and the work environment: A critical review of the epidemiologic literature on nonchemical factors. *Scandinavian Journal of Work, Environment and Health, 15,* 165–179.

94. See note 80.

95. Vickers, R. R., & Hervig, L. K. (1984). *Predictors of cold weather health behaviors.* San Diego, CA: U.S. Naval Health Research Center, Health Psychology Dept.

96. Rule, B. G., Taylor, B. R., & Dobbs, A. R. (1987). Priming effects of heat on aggressive thoughts. *Social Cognition, 5,* 131–142.

97. See note 80.

98. Schneider, F. W., Lesko, W. A., & Garrett, W. A. (1980). Helping behavior in hot, comfortable and cold temperatures. *Environment and Behavior, 12,* 231–240.

99. Moos, R. H. (1976). *The human context: Environmental determinants of behavior.* New York: Wiley.

100. National Academy of Sciences. (1977). *Medical and biological effects of environmental pollutants.* Washington, DC: National Academy of Sciences.

101. Evans, G. W., & Jacobs, S. V. (1982). Air pollution and human behavior. In G. W. Evans (Ed.), *Environmental stress.* New York: Cambridge University Press.

102. See note 101.

103. Rotton, J. (1983). Affective and cognitive consequences of malodorous pollution. *Basic and Applied Social Psychology, 4,* 171–191.

104. Hawkins, L. H. (1981). The influence of air ions, temperature, and humidity on subjective wellbeing and comfort. *Journal of Environmental Psychology, 1,* 279–292.

105. Hawkins, L. H., & Barker, T. (1978). Air ions and human performance. *Ergonomics, 21,* 273–278.

106. Tom, G., Poole, M. F., Galla, J., & Berrier, J. (1981). The influence of negative air ions on human performance and mood. *Human Factors, 23,* 633–636.

107. Farmer, E. W., & Bendix, A. (1982). Geophysical variables and behavior: V. Human performance in ionized air. *Perceptual and Motor Skills, 54*, 403–412.

108. Kozena, L., Frantik, E., & Lajcikova, A. (1988). Artificial air ionization doesn't compensate for deleterious effects of monotony in healthy young subjects. *Activitas Nervosa Superior, 30*, 255–258.

109. Charry, J. M., & Hawkenshire, F. B. W. (1981). Effects of atmospheric electricity on some substrates of disordered social behavior. *Journal of Personal and Social Psychology, 41*, 185–197.

110. Baron, R. A. (1987). Effects of negative ions on cognitive performance. *Journal of Applied Psychology, 72*, 131–137.

111. Baron, R. A., Russell, G. W., & Arms, R. L. (1985). Negative ions and behavior: Impact on mood, memory, and aggression among Type A and Type B persons. *Journal of Personality and Social Psychology, 48*, 746–754.

112. Baron, R. A. (1987). Effects of negative ions on interpersonal attraction: Evidence for intensification. *Journal of Personality and Social Psychology, 52*, 547–553.

113. Rotton, J., cited in note 101.

114. Warm, J. S., Dember, W. N., & Parasuraman, R. (1991). Effects of olfactory stimulation on performance and stress in a visual sustained attention task. *Journal of the Society of Cosmetic Chemists, 42*, 330–351.

115. Baron, R. A. (1994). The physical environment of work settings: Effects on task performance, interpersonal relations, and job satisfaction. *Research in Organizational Behavior, 16*, 1–46.

116. See note 60.

117. Rankin, R. E. (1969). Air pollution control and public apathy. *Journal of Air Pollution Control Association, 19*, 565–569.

118. Schultz, D. P. (1982). *Psychology and industry today.* New York: Macmillan.

119. Fanger, P. O., & Christenson, N. K. (1987). Prediction of draft. *ASHRAE Journal, 29*, 30–31.

120. Sterling, E. M. (1986). Indoor air quality—Total environment performance: Comfort and productivity issues in modern office buildings. *Resource—The Canadian Journal of Real Estate*, 21–25.

121. See note 104.

122. Buckalew, L. W., & Rizzuto, A. (1982). Subjective response to negative air ion exposure. *Aviation, Space, and Environmental Medicine, 53*, 822–823.

123. Baron, R. A. (1983). Sweet smell of success? The impact of pleasant artificial scents on evaluations of job applicants. *Journal of Applied Psychology, 68*, 709–713.

124. See note 101.

125. See note 115.

126. Hedge, A., Sterling, E. M., & Sterling, T. D. (1986). Building illness indices based on questionnaire responses. *Proceeding IAQ/86 Managing Indoor Air for Health and Energy conservation*, 31–43.

127. Adler, T. (1992). Chemicals just one part of indoor-air problems. *American Psychological Association Monitor, 23*(9), 35.

128. Ryan, C. M., & Morrow, L. A. (1992). Dysfunctional buildings or dysfunctional people: An examination of the sick building syndrome and allied disorders. *Journal of Clinical and Consulting Psychology, 60*, 220–224.

129. Bauer, R. M., Greve, K. W., Besch, E. L., Schramke, C. J., et al. (1992). The role of psychological factors in the report of building-related symptoms in sick building syndrome. *Journal of Clinical and Consulting Psychology, 60*.

130. Norback, D., Michel, I., & Widstrom, U. (1990). Indoor air quality and personal factors related to the sick building syndrome. *Scandinavian Journal of Work, Environment and Health, 16*, 121–128.

131. Turiel, I., Hollowell, C. D., Miksch, R. R., Rudy, J. V., & Young, R. A. (1983). The effects of reduced ventilation on indoor air quality in an office building. *Atmospheric Environment, 17*, 51–64.

132. See note 120.

133. Hawkins, L. H. (1982). Air ions and office health. *Occupational Health*, 116–124.

134. Bleda, P. R., & Sandman, P. H. (1977). In smoke's way: Socioemotional reaction to another's smoking. *Journal of Applied Psychology, 62*, 452–458.

135. Jones, J. W., & Bogat, A. G. (1978). Air pollution and human aggression. *Psychological Reports, 43*, 721–722.

136. Rotton, J., Barry, T., Frey, J., & Soler, E. (1978). Air pollution and interpersonal attraction. *Journal of Applied Social Psychology, 8*, 57–71.

137. Rotton, J., Frey, J., Barry, T., Milligan, M., & Fitzpatrick, M. (1979). The air pollution experience and interpersonal aggression. *Journal of Applied Social Psychology, 9*, 397–412.

138. Stone, J., Breidenbach, S., & Heimstra, N. (1979). Annoyance response of non-smokers to cigarette smoke. *Perceptual and Motor Skills, 49*, 907–916.

139. Barnaby, J. F. (1980). Lighting for productivity gains. *Lighting Design and Application*, 20–28.

140. Gifford, R., Hine, D. W., & Veitch, J. A. (in press). Meta-analysis for environment-behavior research, illuminated with a study of lighting level effects on office task performance. In G. T. Moore & R. W. Marans (Eds.), *Advances in environment, behavior, and design. Vol. 4: The integration of theory, research, and utilization.* New York: Plenum.

141. Boyce, P. R. (1981). *Human factors in lighting.* London: Applied Science Publishers.

142. Katzev, R. (1992). The impact of energy-efficient office lighting strategies on employee satisfaction and productivity. *Environment and Behavior, 24*, 759–778.

143. Boray, P. F., Gifford, R., & Rosenblood, L. (1989). Effects of warm white, cool white and full-spectrum fluorescent lighting on simple cognitive performance, mood and ratings of others. *Journal of Environmental Psychology, 9*, 297–307.

144. Veitch, J. A., Gifford, R., & Hine, D. W. (1991). Demand characteristics and full spectrum lighting effects on performance and mood. *Journal of Environmental Psychology, 11*, 87–95.

145. Campbell, S. S., & Dawson, D. (1990). Enhancement of nighttime alertness and performance with bright ambient light. *Physiology & Behavior, 48*, 317–320.

146. Czeisler, C. A., Johnson, M. P., Duffy, J. F., Brown, E. N,. et al. (1990). Exposure to bright light and darkness to treat physiologic maladaptation to night work. *New England Journal of Medicine, 322*, 1253–1259.

147. Boyce, P. R., Beckstead, J. W., Eklund, N. H., Stobel, R. W., & Rea, M. S. (1993). Lighting the graveyard shift: The influence of a daylight-simulating skylight on the task performance and mood of night-shift worker. *Bilaga*, 1–4.

148. Oldham, G. R., & Fried, Y. (1987). Employee reactions to workplace characteristics. *Journal of Applied Psychology, 72*, 75–80.

149. Veitch, J. A, & Gifford, R. (1992). *Personal control over workplace lighting.* Paper presented at the 100th Annual Convention of the American Psychological Association, Washington, DC.

150. Kwallek, N., Lewis, C. M., & Robbins, A. S. (1988). Effects of office interior color on workers' mood and productivity. *Perceptual and Motor Skills, 66*, 123–128.

151. Wineman, J. D. (1982). The office environment as a source of stress. In G. W. Evans (Ed.), *Environmental stress.* New York: Cambridge University Press.

152. Megaw, E. D., & Bellamy, L. J. (1983). Illumination at work. In D. J. Oborne & M. M. Gruneberg (Eds.), *The physical environment at work.* New York: Wiley.

153. Marans, R. W., & Yan, X. (1989). Lighting quality and environmental satisfaction in open and enclosed offices. *Journal of Architectural Planning and Research, 6*(2), 118–131.

154. See note 148.

155. Bhattacharya, S. K., Tripathi, S. R., & Kashyap, S. K. (1989). Evaluation of lighting conditions in relation to visual comfort in workplaces of weavers in a textile mill. *Journal of Human Ergology, 18*, 213–221.

156. Chao, A., & Bennett, C. A. (1981). Lamps for lighting people. *Proceedings of the Human Factors Society, 25*, 485–487.

157. Flynn, J. E., Hendrick, C., Spencer, T., & Martyniuk, D. (1979). The effects of light source color on user impression and satisfaction. *Journal of the Illuminating Engineering Society, 6*, 167–179.

158. See note 151.

159. Boubekri, M., Hull, R. B., & Boyer, L. L. (1991). Impact of window size and sunlight penetration on office workers' mood and satisfaction: A novel way of assessing sunlight. *Environment and Behavior, 23*, 474–493.

160. Farrenkopf, T., & Roth, V. (1980). The university faculty office as an environment. *Environment and Behavior, 12*, 467–477.

161. Stone, N. J., & Irvine, J. M. (1994). Direct or indirect window access, task type, and performance. *Journal of Environmental Psychology, 14*, 57–63.

162. Finnegan, M. C., & Solomon, L. Z. (1981). Work attitudes in windowed vs. windowless environments. *Journal of Social Psychology, 115*, 291–292.

163. Heerwagen, J. H., & Orians, G. H. (1986). Adaptations to windowlessness: A study of the use of visual decor in windowed and windowless offices. *Environment and Behavior, 18*, 623–639.

164. Biner, P. M., Butler, D. L., & Winsted, D. E. (1991). Inside windows: An alternative to conventional windows in offices and other settings. *Environment and Behavior, 23*, 359–382.

165. Butler, D. L., & Steuerwald, B. L. (1991). Effects of view and room size on window size preferences made in models. *Environment and Behavior, 23*, 334–358.

166. Kaye, S., & Larson, S. (1992). *Illumination levels and the perceived emotionality of literary passages.* Unpublished manuscript.

167. Weale, R. A. (1961). Retinal illumination and age. *Transactions of the Illumination Engineering Society, 26*, 95–100.

168. Briggs, R. P. (1986). Visual changes among older workers. *Proceedings of the Human Factors Society*, 801–803.

169. Kuller, R., & Wetterberg, L. (1993). Melatonin, cortisol, EEG, ECG and subjective comfort in healthy humans: Impact of two fluorescent lamp types at two light intensities. *Lighting Research and Technology, 25*, 71–81.

170. See note 120.

171. Bennett, C. A. (1974). Let's shed a little light. In D. H. Carson (Ed.), *Man-environment interactions: Evaluations and applications* (Part 2). Stroudsberg, PA: Dowden, Hutchinson and Ross.

172. See note 143.

173. Baron, R. A., Rea, M. S., & Daniels, S. G. (1992). Effects of indoor lighting (illuminance and spectral distribution) on the performance of cognitive tasks and interpersonal behaviors: The potential mediation role of positive affect. *Motivation and Emotion, 16*, 1–33.

174. Veitch, J. A., & Kaye, S. M. (1988). Illumination effects on conversational sound levels and job candidate evaluation. *Journal of Environmental Psychology, 8*, 223–233.

175. Gifford, R. (1988). Light, decor, arousal, comfort and communication. *Journal of Environmental Psychology, 8*, 177–189.

176. See note 173.

177. Becker, F. D. (1984). Loosely-coupled settings: A strategy for computer-aided work decentralization. In B. Staw & L. L. Cumming (Eds.), *Research in organizational behavior.* Greenwich, CT: JAI Press.

178. See note 177.

179. Swartz, J. (1986). Computer commuters busier and happier. *American Psychological Association Monitor, 17*(9), 8.

180. See note 79.

181. Simon, S. E. (1987). Productivity, efficiency and effectiveness: simple indicators of agency performance. *Journal of Rehabilitative Administration, 11*, 4–10.

182. See note 148.

183. Heller, J. F., Groff, B. D., & Solomon, S. A. (1977). Toward an understanding of crowding: The role of physical interaction. *Journal of Personality and Social Psychology, 35*, 183–190.

184. See note 148.

185. Oldham, G. R., Kulik, C. T., & Stepina, L. P. (1991). Physical environments and employee reactions: Effects of stimulus-screening skills and job complexity. *Academy of Management Journal, 34*, 929–938.

186. See note 151.

187. Becker, F., Gield, B., Gaylin, K., & Sayer, S. (1983). Office design in a community college: Effect on work and communication patterns. *Environment and Behavior, 15*, 699–726.

188. Ng, C. F., & Gifford, R. (1984). *Speech communication in the office: The effects of background sound level and conversational privacy.* University of Victoria.

189. Gifford, R. (1976). Environmental numbness in the classroom. *Journal of Experimental Education, 44*(3), 4–7.

190. Sutton, R. I., & Rafaeli, A. (1987). Characteristics of work stations as potential occupational stressors. *Academy of Management Journal, 30*, 260–276.

191. See note 188.

192. Posehn, K. (1984). *An environmental evaluation of open plan offices.* Paper presented at the Canadian Psychological Association annual meetings, Ottawa.

193. Zalesny, M. D., & Farace, R. V. (1987). Traditional versus open offices: A comparison of sociotechnical, social relation, and symbolic meaning perspectives. *Academy of Management Journal, 30,* 240–259.

194. Tausz, A. (1979, October 20). Landscape of the future. *The Financial Post,* p. S10.

195. Oldham, G. R., & Brass, D. J. (1979). Employee reactions to an open-plan office: A naturally occurring quasi-experiment. *Administrative Science Quarterly, 24,* 267–284.

196. Oldham, G. R., & Rotchford, N. R. (1983). Relationships between office characteristics and employee reactions. *Administrative Science Quarterly, 28,* 542–556.

197. Szilagyi, A., & Holland, W. (1980). Changes in social density: Relationships with functional interaction and perceptions of job characteristics, role stress, and work satisfaction. *Journal of Applied Psychology, 65,* 28–33.

198. Oldham, G. R. (1988). Effects of changes in workspace partitions and spatial density on employee reactions: A quasi-experiment. *Journal of Applied Psychology, 73,* 253–258.

199. Wineman, J. D. (1986). Current issues and future directions. In J. D. Wineman (Ed.), *Behavioral issues in office design.* New York: Van Nostrand Reinhold.

200. Oxley, D., & Barrera, M., Jr. (1984). Undermanning theory and the workplace: Implications of setting size for job satisfaction and social support. *Environment and Behavior, 16,* 211–234.

201. Barker, R. G. (1968). *Ecological psychology: Concepts and methods for studying the environment of human behavior.* Stanford, CA: Stanford University Press.

202. Wicker, A. W. (1979). *An introduction to ecological psychology.* Monterey, CA: Brooks/Cole.

203. See note 185.

204. See note 148.

205. Morrow, P. C., & McElroy, J. C. (1981). Interior office design and visitor response: A constructive replication. *Journal of Applied Psychology, 66,* 646–650.

206. Samuelson, D. J., & Lindauer, M. S. (1976). Perception, evaluation, and performance in a neat and messy room by high and low sensation seekers. *Environment and Behavior, 8,* 291–306.

207. Sitton, S. (1984). The messy desk effect: How tidiness affects the perception of others. *The Journal of Psychology, 117,* 263–267.

208. Becker, F. D., Gield, B., & Froggat, C. C. (1983). Seating positions and impression formation in an office setting. *Journal of Environmental Psychology, 3,* 253–261.

209. Ornstein, S. (1992). First impressions of the symbolic meaning connoted by reception area design. *Environment and Behavior, 24,* 85–110.

210. See note 209.

211. Fried, Y. (1990). Workspace characteristics, behavioral interferences, and screening ability as joint predictors of employee reactions: An examination of the intensification approach. *Journal of Organizational Behavior, 11,* 267–280.

212. Hedge, A. (1984). Evidence of a relationship between office design and self-reports of ill health among office workers in the United Kingdom. *Journal of Architectural and Planning Research, 1,* 163–174.

213. See note 151.

214. Sundstom, E., Herbert, R. K., & Brown, D. W. (1982). Privacy and communication in an open-plan office: A case study. *Environment and Behavior, 14,* 379–392.

215. Hatch, M. J. (1987). Physical barriers, task characteristics, and interaction activity in research and development firms. *Administrative Science Quarterly, 32,* 387–399.

216. Konar, E., Sundstrom, E., Brady, C., Mandel, D., & Rice, R. W. (1982). Status demarcation in the office. *Environment and Behavior, 4,* 561–580.

217. Mazumdar, S. (1992). "Sir, please do not take away my cubicle." The phenomenon of environmental deprivation. *Environment and Behavior, 24,* 691–722.

218. Werner, C. M., & Haggard, L. M. (1992). Avoiding intrusions at the office: Privacy regulation on typical and high solitude days. *Basic and Applied Social Psychology, 13,* 181–193.

219. Becker, F. D. (1981). *Workspace: Creating environments in organizations.* New York: Praeger.

220. Karasek, R. A., Jr. (1979). Job demands, job decision latitude and mental strain: Implications for job redesign. *Administrative Science Quarterly, 24,* 285–308.

221. Mercer, D. C. (1976). Motivational and social aspects of recreational behavior. In I. Altman & J. F. Wohlwill (Eds.), *Human behavior and environment* (Vol. 1). New York: Plenum.

222. Pearce, P. L. (1982). *The social psychology of tourist behavior.* Oxford: Pergamon.

223. Stringer, P. (1984). Studies in the socio-environmental psychology of tourism. *Annals of Tourism Research, 11,* 147–166.

224. Fridgen, J. D. (1984). Environmental psychology and tourism. *Annals of Tourism Research, 11,* 19–39.

225. Gifford, R. (1987). *The motivations of park users.* Victoria, BC: Ministry of Environment and Parks.

226. McArthur, D. (1984). Cashing in on the ultimate motivator: Incentive travel. *enRoute, 12*(8), 38, 40, 48, 50, 52.

227. Schreyer, R. (1986). *Motivation for participation in outdoor recreation and barriers to that participation—A commentary on salient issues.* Salt Lake City, UT: The President's Commission on Americans Outdoors.

228. Ellis, G. D., & Rademacher, C. *Barriers to recreation participation.* Salt Lake City, UT: The President's Commission on Americans Outdoors.

229. Pearce, P. L., & Moscardo, G. M. (1985). The relationship between travellers' career levels and the concept of authenticity. *Australian Journal of Psychology, 37,* 157–174.

230. President's Commission on Americans Outdoors. (1986). *Participation in outdoor recreation among American adults and the motivations which drive participation.* Market Opinion Research.

231. Germans now putting leisure ahead of jobs. (1984, January 8). *Victoria Times-Colonist,* p. C7.

232. Rubenstein, C. (1980). Survey report: How Americans view vacations. *Psychology Today, 13,* 62–66, 71–76.

233. Hirschman, E. C. (1984). Leisure motives and sex roles. *Journal of Leisure Research, 16,* 209–223.

234. Virden, R. J. (1986). The effects of recreation specialization and motivations on the environmental setting preferences of backcountry hikers. *Dissertation Abstracts International, 47*(6–A), 2314.

235. Iso-Ahola, S. E. (1983). Towards a social psychology of recreational travel. *Leisure Studies, 2,* 45–56.

236. See note 229.

237. See note 229.

238. Yuan, S. M. (1993). The relationship between tourism and timber harvesting: A social-psychological approach. *Dissertation Abstracts International, 53*(7–B), 3841.

239. Pearce, P. L. (1977). Mental souvenirs: A study of tourists and their city maps. *Australian Journal of Psychology, 29,* 203–210.

240. Pearce, P. L. (1980). Strangers, travellers, and Greyhound terminals: A study of small-scale helping behaviors. *Journal of Personality and Social Psychology, 38,* 935–940.

241. Gustke, L. D., & Hodgson, R. W. (1980). The rate of travel along an interpretive trail. *Environment and Behavior, 12,* 53–63.

242. Jackson, E. L. (1986). Outdoor recreation participation and attitudes to the environment. *Leisure Studies, 5,* 1–23.

243. Tinsley, H. E. A. (1986). *Motivations to participate in recreation: Their identification and measurement.* Carbondale, IL: The President's Commission on Americans Outdoors.

244. Hartig, T., Mang, M., & Evans, I. (1991). Restorative effects of natural environment experiences. *Environment and Behavior, 23,* 3–26.

245. Young, R. A., & Crandall, R. (1985, July). *Self-actualization and wilderness use: A panel story.* Paper presented at the National Wilderness Research Conference, Fort Collins, CO.

246. Talbot, J. F., & Kaplan, S. (1986). Perspectives on wilderness: Re-examining the value of extended wilderness experiences. *Journal of Environmental Psychology, 6,* 177–188.

247. Macdonald, J. E. (1994). *The restorative effects of a vacation from work: The role of novelty, positive affect, and nature.* Unpublished doctoral dissertation, University of Victoria.

248. Dorfman, P. W. (1979). Measurement and meaning of recreation satisfaction. *Environment and Behavior, 11,* 483–510.

249. Schreyer, R., & Beaulieu, J. T. (1986). Attribute preferences for wildland recreation settings. *Journal of Leisure Research, 18,* 231–247.

250. Applegate, J. E., & Clark, K. E. (1987). Satisfaction levels of birdwatchers: An observation on the consumptive-nonconsumptive continuum. *Leisure Sciences, 9,* 129–134.

251. Ditton, R. B., Fedler, A. J., & Graefe, A. R. (1983). Factors contributing to perceptions of recreational crowding. *Leisure Sciences, 5,* 273–288.

252. Hammitt, W. E., McDonald, C. D., & Noe, F. P. (1984). Use level and encounters: Important variables of perceived crowding among nonspecialized recreationists. *Journal of Leisure Research, 16,* 1–8.

253. See note 248.

254. Morris, P. A. (1982). The effect of pilgrimage on anxiety, depression, and religious attitude. *Psychological Medicine, 12,* 291–294.

255. Pearce, P. L. (1981). Environment shock: A study of tourists' reactions to two tropical islands. *Journal of Applied Social Psychology, 11,* 268–280.

256. Streltzer, J. (1979). Psychiatric emergencies in travellers to Hawaii. *Comprehensive Psychiatry, 20,* 463–468.

257. Ross, G. F. (1991). Tourist destination images of the wet tropical rainforests of North Queensland. *Austrailian Psychologist, 26,* 153–157.

258. Andressen, B. (1987). *Travel and geographic learning: A study of perception and attitude change in a Japanese tourist segment.* Unpublished doctoral dissertation, The University of Victoria, Victoria, B.C.

259. Walmsley, D. J., Boskovic, R. M., & Pigram, J. J. (1983). Tourism and crime: An Australian perspective. *Journal of Leisure Research, 15,* 136–155.

260. Walter, J. A. (1982). Social limits to tourism. *Leisure Studies, 1,* 295–304.

261. Pearce, P. L., & Moscardo, G. (1985). Tourist theme parks: Research practices and possibilities. *Australian Psychologist, 20,* 303–312.

262. Brill, M., Margulis, S., & Konar, E. (1984). *Using office design to increase productivity.* Buffalo, NY: Buffalo Organization for Social and Technological Innovation.

263. Gifford, R. (1992). *Performance and related outcomes of inadequate offices: An annotated bibliography.* Report to the British Columbia Buildings Corporation.

264. Becker, F. D. (1984). Loosely-coupled settings: A strategy for computer-aided work decentralization. In B. Staw & L. L. Cumming (Eds.), *Research in organizational behavior.* Greenwich, CT: JAI Press.

265. Hegvold, L. W. (1971). *Acoustical design of open-planned offices.* Ottawa, ON: National Research Council of Canada, Division of Building Research.

Chapter 13

1. Cited in Hartig, T., Mang, M., & Evans, G. W. (1991). Restorative effects of natural environment experiences. *Environment and Behavior, 23,* 3–26.

2. Friedman, H., Becker, R. O., & Bachman, C. H. (1965). Psychiatric ward behavior and geophysical parameters. *Nature, 205,* 1050–1052.

3. Gauquelin, M., Gauquelin, F., & Eysenck, S. B. G. (1979). Personality and position of the planets at birth: An empirical study. *British Journal of Social and Clinical Psychology, 18,* 71–75.

4. Cooke, D. J., & Coles, E. M. (1978). The concept of lunacy: A review. *Psychological Reports, 42,* 891–897.

5. Rotton, J., & Kelly, I. W. (1985). A scale for assessing belief in lunar effects: Reliability and concurrent validity. *Psychological Reports, 57,* 239–245.

6. Rotton, J., Kelly, I. W., & Elortegui, P. (1986). Assessing belief in lunar effects: Known-groups validation. *Psychological Reports, 59,* 171–174.

7. Garzino, S. J. (1982). Lunar effects on mental behavior: A defense of the empirical research. *Environment and Behavior, 14,* 395–417.

8. Campbell, D. E., & Beets, J. L. (1978). Lunacy and the moon. *Psychological Bulletin, 85,* 1123–1129.

9. See note 7.

10. Abel, E. L. (1976). *Moon madness.* Greenwich, CT: Fawcett.

11. Campbell, D. E. (1982). Lunar-lunacy research: When enough is enough. *Environment and Behavior, 14,* 418–424.

12. Culver, R., Rotton, J., & Kelly, I. W. (1988). Geophysical variables and behavior: XLIX. Moon mechanisms and myths: A critical appraisal of explanations of purported lunar effects on human behavior. *Psychological Reports, 62,* 683–710.

13. Rotton, J., & Kelly, I. W. (1985). Much ado about the full moon: A meta-analysis of lunar-lunacy research. *Psychological Bulletin, 97,* 286–306.

14. Dubitsky, S., Weber, R., & Rotton, J. (1993). Heat, hostility and immune function: The moderating effects of gender and demand characteristics. *Psychonomic Society, 31,* 534–536.

15. Schneider, F. W., & Whalley, A. M. (1980). Unpublished data, University of Windsor.

16. Cohn, E. G. (1990). Weather and crime. *British Journal of Criminology, 30,* 51–64.

17. See note 16.

18. Anderson, C. A. (1989). Temperature and aggression: Ubiquitous effects of heat on occurrence of human violence. *Psychological Bulletin, 106,* 74–96.

19. Kenrick, D. T., & MacFarlane, S. W. (1986). Ambient temperature and horn honking: A field study of the heat/aggression relationship. *Environment and Behavior, 18,* 179–191.

20. Rotton, J. (1986). Determinism redux: Climate and cultural correlates of violence. *Environment and Behavior, 18,* 346–368.

21. See note 18.

22. Bell, P. A. (1992). In defense of the negative affect escape model of heat and aggression. *Psychological Bulletin, 111,* 342–346.

23. Boyanowski cited in note number 16.

24. See note 16.

25. See note 16.

26. Sandilands, M. L., & Christman, G. (1987). *The effects of weather variables and month on frequency of call to a crisis line and visits to an emergency ward.* Paper presented at the annual convention of the Canadian Psychological Association, Vancouver.

27. Cunningham, M. R. (1979). Weather, mood, and helping behavior: Quasi experiments with the sunshine Samaritan. *Journal of Personality and Social Psychology, 37,* 1947–1956.

28. Carney, P. A., Fitzgerald, C. T., & Monaghan, C. E. (1988). Influence of climate on the prevalence of mania. *British Journal of Psychiatry, 152,* 820–823.

29. Ward-Smith, A. J. (1986). Altitude and wind effects on long jump performance with particular reference to the world record established by Bob Beamon. *Journal of Sports Sciences, 4,* 89–99.

30. Rotton, J., & Frey, J. (1985). Air pollution, weather, and violent crimes: Concomitant time-series analysis of archival data. *Journal of Personality and Social Psychology, 49,* 1207–1220.

31. Essa, E. L., Hilton, J. M., & Murray, C. I. (1990). The relationship between weather and preschoolers' behavior. *Children's Environments Quarterly, 7,* 32–36.

32. Campbell, D. E. & Beets, J. L. (1977). Meteorological variables and behavior: An annotated bibliography. *Catalog of Selected Documents in Psychology, 7,* 1.

33. Takei, N., Sham, P., O'Callaghan, E., Murray, G. K., Glover, G., & Murray, R. M. (1994). Prenatal exposure to influenza and the development of schizophrenia: Is the effect confined to females? *American Journal of Psychiatry, 151,* 117–119.

34. Kay, R. W. (1994). Geomagnetic storms: Association with incidence of depression as measured by hospital admission. *British Journal of Psychiatry, 164,* 403–409.

35. Gamberale, F. (1990). Physiological and psychological effects of exposure to extremely low-frequency electric and magnetic fields on humans. *Scandinavian Journal of Work, Environment and Health, 16,* 51–54.

36. O'Connor, M. E. (1993). Psychological studies in nonionizing electromagnetic energy research. *Journal of General Psychology, 120,* 33–47.

37. Furby, L., Slovic, P., Fischhoff, B., & Gregory, R. (1988). Public perceptions of electric power transmission lines. *Journal of Environmental Psychology, 8,* 19–43.

38. Ulrich, R. S., & Parsons, R. (1992). Influences of passive experiences with plants on individual well-being and health. In D. Relf (Ed.), *The role of horticulture in human well-being and social development.* Forest Grove, OR: Timber Press.

39. Outdoor Recreation Council of British Columbia. (1990). Surveys finds outdoor recreation very important to British Columbians. *The Outdoor Report, 4,* 2.

40. Environment Canada. (1989). *The importance of wildlife to Canadians in 1987: Highlights of a national survey.* Environment Canada, Canadian Wildlife Service.

41. Sandilands, M., & Cairns, J. (1988). *Hikers' attitudes towards bears and Zuckerman's thrill and adventure seeking scale.* Paper presented at the Canadian Psychological Association conference.

42. Ryzhikov, A. I. (1992). Nature and man: Psychological problems of alienation. *Journal of Russian & East European Psychology, 30,* 37–44.

43. Gifford, R. (1987). *The motivations of parks users.* Victoria, B.C.: Optimal Environments.

44. Haemoid, W. E. (1982). Cognitive dimensions of wilderness solitude. *Environment and Behavior, 14,* 478–493.

45. Fiedeldey, A. C. (1991). Experiencing nature on hiking trails: A psychological study. *Dissertation Abstracts International, 52*(12–B), 6698–6699.

46. Snyder, J. S. (1989). The experience of really feeling connected to nature. *Dissertation Abstracts International, 49*(9–B), 4025.

47. See note 45.

48. Scherl, L. M. (1989). Self in wilderness: Understanding the psychological benefits of individual-wilderness interaction through self-control. L*eisure Sciences, 11,* 123–135.

49. Ulrich, R. S. (1984). View through a window may influence recovery from surgery. *Science, 224,* 420–421.

50. Moore, E. O. (1982). A prison environment's effect on health care service demands. *Journal of Environmental Systems, 11,* 17–34.

51. West, M. J. (1985). University of Washington master's thesis. Reported in Ulrich (1993) (see note 62).

52. Ulrich, R. S., Simons, R. F., Losito, B. D., Fiorito, E., Miles, M. A., & Zelson, M. (1991). Stress recovery during exposure to natural and urban environments. *Journal of Environmental Psychology, 11,* 201–230.

53. O'Connor, B. P., Davidson, H., & Gifford, R. G. (1991). Window view, social exposure and nursing home adaptation. *Canadian Journal on Aging, 10,* 216–223.

54. See note 1.

55. Young, R. A., & Crandall, R. (1984). Wilderness use and self-actualization. *Journal of Leisure Research, 16,* 149–160.

56. Shin, W. S. (1993). Self-actualization and wilderness attitudes: A replication. *Journal of Social Behavior and Personality, 8,* 241–256.

57. Mehrabian, A., & Russell, J. A. (1974). *An approach to environmental psychology.* Cambridge, MA: MIT Press.

58. Cohen, S. (1978). Environmental load and the allocation of attention. In A. Baum, J. E. Singer, & S. Valins (Eds.), *Advances in environmental psychology* (Vol 1). Hillsdale, NJ: Lawrence Erlbaum.

59. Tuan, Y. F. (1974). *Topophilia: A study of environmental protection, attitudes, and values.* Englewood Cliffs, NJ: Prentice Hall.

60. Kaplan, R., & Kaplan, S. (1989). *The experience of nature: A psychological perspective.* New York: Cambridge University Press.

61. See note 52.

62. Ulrich, R. S. (1993). Biophilia, biophobia, and natural landscapes. In S. R. Kellert & E. O. Wilson (Eds.), *The biophilia hypothesis.* Washington, DC: Island Press/Shearwater Books.

63. Zajonc, R. B. (1980). Feeling and thinking: Preferences need no inferences. *American Psychologist, 35,* 151–175.

64. Burton, I., Kates, R. W., & White, G. F. (1978). *The environment as hazard.* New York: Oxford.

65. Baum, A., & Fleming, I. (1993). Implications of psychological research on stress and technological accidents. *American Psychologist, 48,* 665–672.

66. Florida strengthens its building codes. (1994, May). *Natural Hazards Observer, 18*(5), 3.

67. Gulaid, J. A., Sacks, J. J., & Sattin, R. W. (1988). Deaths from residential fires among older people, United States, 1984. *Journal of the American Geriatrics Society, 37,* 331–334.

68. Adeola, F. O. (1994). Environmental hazards, health, and racial inequity in hazardous waste distribution. *Environment and Behavior, 26,* 99–126.

69. Cvetkovich, G., & Earle, T. C. (1985). Classifying hazardous events. *Journal of Environmental Psychology, 5,* 5–53.

70. See note 69.

71. Baum, A., Fleming, R., & Davidson, L. M. (1983). Natural disaster and technological catastrophe. *Environment and Behavior, 15,* 333–354.

72. Foster, H. D. (1980). *Disaster planning: The preservation of life and property.* New York: Springer-Verlag.

73. Spreen, O., Tupper, D., Risser, A., Tuokko, H., & Edgell, D. (1984). *Human developmental neuropsychology.* New York: Oxford University Press.

74. Bord, R. J., & O'Connor, R. E. (1992). Determinants of risk perception of a hazardous waste site. *Risk Analysis, 12,* 411–416.

75. Levi, D. J., & Holder, E. E. (1988). Psychological factors in the nuclear power controversy. *Political Psychology, 9,* 445–457.

76. Sjoberg, L., & Drottz-Sjoberg, B. (1991). Knowledge and risk perception among nuclear power plant employees. *Risk Analysis, 11,* 607–618.

77. Pilisuk, M., & Acredolo, C. (1988). Fear of technological hazards: One concern or many? *Social Behavior, 3,* 17–24.

78. van der Plight, J. (1985). Public attitudes to nuclear energy: Salience and anxiety. *Journal of Environmental Psychology, 5,* 87–97.

79. Levi, D. J., & Holder, E. E. (1986). Nuclear power: The dynamics of acceptability. *Environment and Behavior, 18,* 385–395.

80. Eiser, J., Spears, R., Webley, P., & van der Plight, J. (1988). Local residents' attitudes to oil and nuclear developments. *Social Behavior, 3,* 237–253.

81. Schmidt, F. N., & Gifford, R. (1989). A dispositional approach to hazard perception: Preliminary development of the environmental appraisal inventory. *Journal of Environmental Psychology, 9,* 57–67.

82. Vari, A., Kemp, R., & Mumpower, J. L. (1991). Public concerns about LLRW facility siting. *Journal of Cross-Cultural Psychology, 22,* 83–102.

83. Baird, B. N. R. (1986). Tolerance for environmental health risks: The influence of knowledge, benefits, voluntariness, and environmental attitudes. *Risk Analysis, 6,* 425–435.

84. Vaughan, E. (1993). Chronic exposure to an environmental hazard: Risk perceptions and self-protective behavior. *Health Psychology, 12,* 74–85.

85. See note 77.

86. Kraus, N., Malmfors, T., & Slovic, P. (1992). Intuitive toxicology: Expert and lay judgements of chemical risks. *Risk Analysis, 12,* 215–232.

87. Brody, C. J. (1984). Differences by sex in support for nuclear power. *Social Forces, 63,* 209–228.

88. deMan, A., & Simpson-Housley, P. (1987). Factors in perception of tornado hazard: An exploratory study. *Social Behavior and Personality, 15,* 13–19.

89. Dooley, D., Catalano, R., Mishra, S., & Serxner, S. (1992). Earthquake preparedness: Predictors in a community survey. *Journal of Applied Social Psychology, 22,* 451–470.

90. Korol, M. (1990). *Psychological impact of chronic environmental stress in Fernald, Ohio.* Paper presented at the 98th annual convention of the American Psychological Association, Boston.

91. See note 89.

92. McClelland G. H., Schulz, W. D., & Hurd, B. (1990). The effects of risk beliefs on property values: A case study of a hazardous waste site. *Risk Analysis, 10,* 485–497.

93. See note 89.

94. See note 92.

95. See note 92.

96. Slovic, P., Fischhoff, B., & Lichtenstein, S. (1979). Rating the risks. *Environment, 21,* 14–20, 36–39.

97. van der Plight, J., Eiser, J. R., & Spears, R. (1987). Nuclear waste: Facts, fears, and attitudes. *Journal of Applied Social Psychology, 17,* 453–470.

98. Wober, M., & Gunter, B. (1985). Patterns of television viewing and of perceptions of hazards to life. *Journal of Environmental Psychology, 5,* 99–108.

99. Bochniak, S., & Lammers, H. B. (1991). Effect of numbers vs. pictures on perceived effectiveness of a public safety awareness advertisement. *Perceptual and Motor Skills, 73,* 77–78.

100. Kiser, L., Heston, J., Hickerson, S., & Millsap, P. (1993). Anticipatory stress in children and adolescents. *American Journal of Psychiatry, 150,* 87–92.

101. Spencer, J. W., Seydlitz, R., Laska, S., & Triche, E. (1992). The different influences of newspaper and television news reports of a natural hazard on response behavior. *Communication Research, 19,* 299–325.

102. van der Plight, J., Eiser, J. R., & Spears, R. (1986). Construction of a nuclear power station in one's locality: Attitudes and salience. *Basic & Applied Social Psychology, 7,* 1–15.

103. Wiegman, O., Boer, H., Gutteling, J. M., & Komilis, E. et al. (1992). The development of reactions of the public to warning and emergency situations in France, Greece, and the Netherlands. *Journal of Social Psychology, 132,* 101–116.

104. Stoffle, R. W., Traugott, M. W., Stone, J. V., McIntyre, P. D., et al. (1991). Risk perception mapping: Using ethnography to define the locally affected population for a low-level radioactive waste storage facility in Michigan. *American Anthropologist, 93,* 611–635.

105. Hostetler, A. J. (1987). Radon's origin alters perception of its risks. *American Psychological Association Monitor, 18,* 21.

106. Lehman, D. R., & Taylor, S. E. (1987). Date with an earthquake: Coping with a probable, unpredictable disaster. *Personality and Social Psychology Bulletin, 13,* 546–555.

107. Spielberg, W. E. (1986). Living with Indian Point: A study investigating the relationship between stress, time distortion, ideology, coping style and expressed vulnerability of high school students in close residence to a nuclear power plant. *Dissertation Abstracts International, 47*(9–B), 3971–3972.

108. Vaughan, E., & Nordenstam, B. (1989, August). *Farmworkers and pesticide exposure: Perceived risk, psychological distress, and health.* Paper presented at the 97th annual convention of American Psychological Association, New Orleans.

109. Stout-Wiegand, N., & Trent, R. B. (1984–85). Comparison of students' and non-student residents' attitudes toward local energy developments: Environmentalism versus economic interest. *Journal of Environmental Education, 16,* 29–35.

110. See note 83.

111. de Man, A., & Simpson-Housley, P. (1988). Correlates of responses to potential hazards. *Journal of Social Psychology, 128,* 385–391.

112. See note 89.

113. See note 102.

114. Lindell, M. K., & Perry, R. W. (1990). Effects of the Chernobyl accident on public perceptions of nuclear plant accident risks. *Risk Analysis, 10,* 393–399.

115. Hughey, J. B., & Sundstrom, E. (1988). Perceptions of Three Mile Island and acceptance of a nuclear power plant in a distant community. *Journal of Applied Social Psychology, 18,* 880–890.

116. Renn, O., Burns, W. J., Kasperson, J. X., Kasperson, R. E., et al. (1992). The social amplification of risk: Theoretical foundations and empirical applications. *Journal of Social Issues, 48*(4), 137–160.

117. van der Plight, J., van der Linden, J., & Ester, P. (1982). Attitudes to nuclear energy: Beliefs, values and false consensus. *Journal of Environmental Psychology, 2,* 221–231.

118. Baldwin, T. K. (1993). Response to an earthquake prediction in southeast Missouri: A study in pluralistic ignorance. *Dissertation Abstracts International, 53*(9–A), 3025–3026.

119. Larrain Navarro, P., Simpson-Housley, P., & de Man, A. F. (1987). Anxiety, locus of control and appraisal of air pollution. *Perceptual and Motor Skills, 64,* 811–814.

120. Krugman, M., & Yoder, C. Y. (1992, August). *Trust and anxiety influence the perception of environmental risks.* Poster presented at the American Psychological Association annual convention, Washington, DC.

121. Simpson-Housley, P., de Man, A. F., & Yachnin, R. (1986). Trait-anxiety and appraisal of flood hazard, a brief comment. *Psychological Reports, 58,* 509–510.

122. de Man, A. F., & Simpson-Housley, P. (1987). Factors in perception of earthquake hazard. *Perceptual and Motor Skills, 64,* 815–820.

123. de Man, A. F., Simpson-Housley, P., Curtis, F., & Smith, D. (1984). Trait anxiety and response to potential flood disaster. *Psychological Reports, 54,* 507–512.

124. See note 119.

125. See note 107.

126. Hallman, W. K. (1989). Coping with an environmental stressor: Perception of risk, attribution of responsibility and psychological distress in a community living near a hazardous waste facility. *Dissertation Abstracts International, 51*(1–B), 474–475.

127. Stallen, P. J. M., & Tomas, A. (1988). Public concern about industrial hazards. *Risk Analysis, 8,* 237–245.

128. See note 77.

129. See note 122.

130. Pilisuk, M., Parks, S. H., & Hawkes, G. (1987). Public perception of technological risk. *Social Science Journal, 24,* 403–413.

131. Lazarus, R. S. (1966). *Psychological stress and the coping process.* New York: McGraw-Hill.

132. See note 122.

133. See note 78.

134. See note 96.

135. Slovic, P., Fischhoff, B., & Lichtenstein, S. (1986). Regulation of risk: A psychological perspective. In R. Noll (Ed.), *Social science and regulatory policy.* Berkeley, CA: University of California Press.

136. Alhakami, A. S. (1992). A psychological study of the inverse relationship between perceived risk and perceived benefit of tech-

nological hazards. *Dissertation Abstracts International*, *52*(9–B), 5004.

137. Wandersman, A. H., & Hallman, W. K. (1993). Are people acting irrationally? Understanding public concerns about environmental threats. *American Psychologist*, *48*, 681–686.

138. Vaughan, E. (1993). Individual and cultural differences in adaptation to environmental risks. *American Psychologist*, *48*, 673–680.

139. Douglas, M., & Wildavsky, A. (1982). *Risk and culture*. Los Angeles: University of California Press.

140. Fiorino, D. J. (1989). Technical and democratic values in risk analysis. *Risk Analysis*, *9*, 293–299.

141. Eiser, J. R., Spears, R., & Webley, P. (1988). Predicting attitudes to oil and to nuclear energy. *Journal of Environmental Psychology*, *8*, 141–147.

142. See note 86.

143. Slovic, P., Kunreuther, H., & White, G. F. (1974). Decision processes, rationality, and adjustment to natural hazards. In G. F. White (Ed.), *Natural hazards: Local, national, global*. New York: Oxford University Press.

144. Slovic, P. (1978). The psychology of protective behavior. *Journal of Safety Research*, *10*, 58–68.

145. Kushnir, T. (1982). Skylab effects: Psychological reactions to a human-made environmental hazard. *Environment and Behavior*, *14*, 84–93.

146. Logsdon, T. (1983). The orbiting junkyard. *Technology Illustrated*, *3*, 30–34.

147. Maharik, M., & Fischhoff, B. (1992). The risks of using nuclear energy sources in space: Some lay activists' perceptions. *Risk Analysis*, *12*, 383–392.

148. Cvetkovich, G., & Earle, T. C. (1988). Judgement and hazard adaptation: A longitudinal study of responses to risks of water contamination. Eleventh conference on: Subjective probability, utility and decision making (1987, Cambridge, England). *Acta Psychologica*, *68*, 343–353.

149. Mulady, J. J. (1994). Building codes: They're not just hot air. *Natural Hazards Observer*, *18*(3), 4–5.

150. Lave, T. R., & Lave, L. B. (1991). Public perception of the risks of floods: Implications for communication. *Risk Analysis*, *11*, 255–267.

151. Bertness, J. E. (1986). Hazard perception research: A critique and proposal. *Dissertation Abstracts International*, *47*(9–A), 3528.

152. See note 138.

153. See note 143.

154. Jackson, E. L. (1981). Response to earthquake hazard: The west coast of North America. *Environment and Behavior*, *13*, 387–416.

155. See note 138.

156. Skov, T., Cordtz, T., Jensen, L. K., Saugman P., et al. (1991). Modifications of health behaviour in response to air pollution notifications in Copenhagen. *Social Science & Medicine*, *33*, 621–626.

157. See note 156.

158. Bachrach, K. M., & Zautra, A. J. (1985). Coping with a community stressor: The threat of a hazardous waste facility. *Journal of Health and Social Behavior*, *26*, 127–141.

159. Cook, J. R. (1983). Citizen response in a neighborhood under threat. *American Journal of Community Psychology*, *11*, 459–471.

160. Kaminstein, D. S. (1991). Toxic passivity: A study of the lack of protest in an environmentally threatened community. *Dissertation Abstracts International*, *52*(3-B), 1778–1779.

161. Hine, D. W., & Gifford, R. (1991). Fear appeals, individual differences, and environmental concern. *Journal of Environmental Education*, *23*(1), 36–41.

162. Sorenson, J. H. (1983). Knowing how to behave under the threat of disaster: Can it be explained? *Environment and Behavior*, *15*, 438–457.

163. Nasar, J. L., & Greenberg, M. L. (1984). The preparedness and reactions of citizens to warnings and crisis relocation for nuclear attack. *Journal of Applied Social Psychology*, *14*, 487–500.

164. Sims, J. H., & Baumann, D. D. (1983). The tornado threat: Coping styles of the North and South. *Science*, *176*, 1386–1391.

165. See note 164.

166. Mulilis, J., & Lippa, R. (1990). Behavioral change in earthquake preparedness due to negative threat appeals: A test of protection motivation theory. *Journal of Applied Social Psychology*, *20*, 619–638.

167. Hanson, S., Vitek, J. D., & Hanson, P. O. (1979). Natural disaster: Long-range impact on human responses to future disaster threats. *Environment and Behavior*, *11*, 268–284.

168. See note 72.

169. Quarantelli, E. L. (1976). *Human response in stress situations*. Laurel, MD: Johns Hopkins University Press.

170. Laska, S. B. (1990). Homeowner adaptation to flooding: An application of the general hazards coping theory. *Environment and Behavior*, *22*, 320–357.

171. Archea, J. (1990). Two earthquakes: Three human conditions. In Y. Yoshitake, R. B. Bechtel, T. Takahashi, & M. Asai (Eds.), *Current issues in environment-behavior research*. Tokyo: University of Tokyo.

172. Weinrich, S., Hardin, S. B., & Johnson, M. (1990). Nurses respond to hurricane Hugo victims' disaster stress. *Archives of Psychiatric Nursing*, *4*, 195–205.

173. Hansson, R. O., Noules, D., & Bellovich, S, J. (1982). Knowledge warning and stress: A study of comparative roles in an urban floodplain. *Environment and Behavior*, *14*, 171–185.

174. Chisholm, R. F., Kasl, S. V., & Eskenazi, B. (1983). The nature and predictors of job related tension in a crisis situation: Reactions of nuclear workers to the Three Mile Island accident. *Academy of Management Journal*, *26*, 385–405.

175. Sugiman, T., & Misumi, J. (1988). Development of a new evacuation method for emergencies: Control of collective behavior by emergent small groups. *Journal of Applied Psychology*, *73*, 3–10.

176. Sime, J. D. (1985). Movement toward the familiar: Person and place affiliation in a fire entrapment setting. *Environment and Behavior*, *17*, 697–724.

177. See note 175.

178. Cutter, S., & Barnes, K. (1982). Evacuation behavior and Three Mile Island. *Disasters*, *6*, 116–124.

179. Cuthbertson, B. H., & Nigg, J. M. (1987). Technological disaster and the nontherapeutic community: A question of true victimization. *Environment and Behavior, 19,* 462–483.

180. O'Riordan, T. (1984). Attitudes, behavior, and environmental policy issues. In I. Altman & J. F. Wohlwill (Eds.), *Human behavior and environment: Advances in theory and research* (Vol. 1). New York: Plenum.

181. Kaniasty, K. Z., Norris, F. H., & Murrell, S. A. (1990). Received and perceived social support following natural disaster. *Journal of Applied Social Psychology, 20,* 85–114.

182. MacGregor, D. (1991). Worry over technological activities and life concerns. *Risk Analysis, 11,* 315–324.

183. Mardberg, B., Carlstedt, L., Stalberg-Carlstedt, B., & Shalit, B. (1987). Sex differences in perception of threat from the Chernobyl accident. *Perceptual & Motor Skills, 65,* 228.

184. Burger, J., & Gochfeld, M. (1991). Fishing a Superfund site: Dissonance and risk perception of environmental hazards by fishermen in Puerto Rico. *Risk Analysis, 11,* 269–277.

185. Baron, J., Gowda, R., & Kunreuther, H. (1993). Attitudes toward managing hazardous waste: What should be cleaned up and who should pay for it? *Risk Analysis, 13,* 183–192.

186. deMan, A., Simpson-Housley, P., & Curtis, F. (1985). Assignment of responsibility and flood hazard in Catahoula County, Louisiana. *Environment and Behavior, 17,* 371–386.

187. Yates, S. (1992). Lay attributions about distress after a natural disaster. *Personality & Social Psychology Bulletin, 18,* 217–222.

188. Parker, S. D., Brewer, M. B., & Spencer, J. R. (1980). Natural disaster, perceived control and attributions to fate. *Personality & Social Psychology Bulletin, 6,* 454–459.

189. Arochova, O., Kontrova, J., Lipkova, V., & Liska, J. (1988). Effect of toxic atmosphere emissions on cognitive performance by children. *Studia Psychologica, 30,* 101–114.

190. Plous, S. (1991). Biases in the assimilation of technological breakdowns: Do accidents make us safer? *Journal of Applied Social Psychology, 21,* 1058–1082.

191. Shippee, G. E., Bradford, R., & Gregory, W. L. (1982). Community perceptions of natural disasters and post-disaster mental health services. *Journal of Community Psychology, 10,* 23–28.

192. Goldhaber, M. K., Houts, P. S., & DiSabella, R. (1984). Moving after the crisis: A prospective study of Three Mile Island area population mobility. *Environment and Behavior, 15,* 93–120.

193. Prince-Embury, S., & Rooney, J. F. (1989). A comparison of residents who moved versus those who remained prior to restart of Three Mile Island. *Journal of Applied Social Psychology, 19,* 959–975.

194. See note 192.

195. Rochford, E. B., Jr., & Blocker, T. J. (1991). Coping with "natural" hazards as stressors: The predictors of activism in a flood disaster. *Environment and Behavior, 23,* 171–194.

196. Edelstein, M. R., & Wandersman, A. (1987). Community dynamics in coping with toxic contaminants. In I. Altman & A. Wandersman (Eds.), *Neighborhood and community environments.* New York: Plenum.

197. Unger, D. G., Wandersman, A., & Hallman, W. (1992). Living near a hazardous waste facility: Coping with individual and family distress. *American Journal of Orthopsychiatry, 62,* 55–70.

198. Aguirre, B. E. (1982). The long term effects of major natural disasters on marriage and divorce: An ecological study. *Victimology: An International Journal, 5,* 298–307.

199. Chen, X., Dai, K., & Parnell, A. (1992). Disaster tradition and change: Remarriage and family reconstruction in a post-earthquake community in the People's Republic of China. *Journal of Comparative Family Studies, 23,* 115–132.

200. Horowitz, M. J., Stinson, C., & Field, N. (1991). Natural disasters and stress response syndromes. *Psychiatric Annals, 21,* 556–562.

201. Escobar, J. I., Canino, G., Rubio-Stipec, M., & Bravo, M. (1992). Somatic symptoms after a natural disaster: A prospective study. *American Journal of Psychiatry, 149,* 965–967.

202. Cohen, R. E. (1987). The Armero tragedy: Lessons for mental health professionals. *Hospital & Community Psychiatry, 38,* 1316–1321.

203. Adams, P. R., & Adams, G. R. (1984). Mount St. Helens ashfall: Evidence for a disaster stress reaction. *American Psychologist, 39,* 252–260.

204. Palinkas, L. A., Downs, M. A., Petterson, J. S., & Russell, J. (1993). Social, cultural, and psychological impacts of the Exxon Valdez oil spill. *Human Organization, 52,* 1–13.

205. McFarlane, A. C. (1987). Family functioning and overprotection following a natural disaster: The longitudinal effects of post-traumatic morbidity. *Australian & New Zealand Journal of Psychiatry, 21,* 210–218.

206. Wood, J. M., Bootzin, R. R., Rosenhan, D., Nolen-Hoeksema, S., et al. (1992). Effects of the 1989 San Francisco earthquake on frequency and content of nightmares. *Journal of Abnormal Psychology, 101,* 219–224.

207. Davidson, L. M., Baum, A., & Collins, D. L. (1982). Stress and control-related problems at Three Mile Island. *Journal of Applied Social Psychology, 12,* 349–359.

208. Schaeffer, M. A., & Baum, A. (1984). Adrenal cortical response to stress at Three Mile Island. *Psychosomatic Medicine, 46,* 227–237.

209. Rubonis, A. V., & Bickman, L. (1991). Psychological impairment in the wake of disaster: The disaster- psychopathology relationship. *Psychological Bulletin, 109,* 384–399.

210. Lima, B. R., & Pai, S. (1992–93). Responses to the psychological consequences of disasters in Latin America. *International Journal of Mental Health, 21,* 59–71.

211. Seroka, C. M., Knapp, C., Knight, S., Siemon, C. R., & Starbuck, S. (1986). A comprehensive program for postdisaster counseling. *The Journal of Contemporary Social Work, 67*(1), 37–44.

212. Bell, B. D. (1978). Disaster impact and response: Overcoming the thousand natural shocks. *The Gerontologist, 18,* 531–540.

213. Goldsteen, R., Schorr, J. K., & Goldsteen, K. S. (1989). Longitudinal study of appraisal at Three Mile Island: Implications for life event research. *Social Science and Medicine, 28,* 389–398.

214. Faupel, C. E., & Styles, S. P. (1993). Disaster education, household preparedness, and stress responses following Hurricane Hugo. *Environment and Behavior, 25,* 228–249.

215. Nolen-Hoeksema, S., & Morrow, J. (1991). A prospective study of depression and posttraumatic stress symptoms after a

natural disaster: The 1989 Loma Prieta earthquake. *Journal of Personality & Social Psychology, 61,* 115–121.

216. Norris, F. N., & Uhl, G. A. (1993). Chronic stress as a mediator of acute stress: The case of Hurricane Hugo. *Journal of Applied Social Psychology, 23,* 1263–1284.

217. Wasserstein, S. B., La Greca, A. M., & Silverman, W. K. (1994). *Hurricane Andrew: Parent conflict as a moderator of children's adjustment.* Presentation at the annual meetings of the American Psychological Association, Los Angeles.

218. Vincent, N. R., La Greca, A. M., & Silverman, W. K., Wasserstein, S. B., & Prinstein, M. J. (1994). *Predicting children's responses to natural disasters: role of academic achievement.* Presentation at the annual meetings of the American Psychological Association, Los Angeles.

219. Vitaliano, P. P., Maiuro, R. D., Bolton, P. A., & Armsden, G. C. (1987). A psychoepidemiologic approach to the study of disaster. *Journal of Community Psychology, 15,* 99–122.

220. See note 209.

221. Lima, B. R., Pai, S., Toledo, V., Caris, L., et al. (1993). Emotional stress in disaster victims: A follow-up study. *Journal of Nervous & Mental Disease, 181,* 388–393.

222. Zhang, H.-C., & Zhang, Y.-Z. (1991). Psychological consequences of earthquake disaster survivors. *International Journal of Psychology, 26,* 613–621.

223. Edelstein, M. R. (1986). Toxic exposure and the inversion of the home. *Journal of Architectural & Planning Research, 3,* 237–251.

224. Preston, V., Taylor, S. M., & Hodge, D. C. (1983). Adjustment to natural and technological hazards: A study of an urban residential community. *Environment and Behavior, 15,* 143–164.

225. Baum, A. (1988). Disasters, natural and otherwise. *Psychology Today, 22,* 57–60.

226. Baum, A., Fleming, R., & Davidson, L. M. (1983). Natural disaster and technological catastrophe. *Environment and Behavior, 15,* 333–354.

227. Baum, A., Fleming, I., Israel, A., & O'Keeffe, M. K. (1992). Symptoms of chronic stress following a natural disaster and discovery of a human-made hazard. *Environment and Behavior, 24,* 347–365.

228. See note 209.

229. See note 126.

230. See note 226.

231. Baum, A., Fleming, R., & Singer, J. E. (1983). Coping with victimization by technological disaster. *Journal of Social Issues, 39*(2), 117–138.

232. Collins, D. L., Baum, A., & Singer, J. E. (1983). Coping with chronic stress at Three Mile Island: Psychological and biochemical evidence. *Health Psychology, 2,* 149–166.

233. Prince-Embury, S., & Rooney, J. F. (1990). Life stage differences in resident coping with restart of the Three Mile Island nuclear generating facility. *Journal of Social Psychology, 130,* 771–779.

234. Palinkas, L. A., Russell, J., Downs, M. A., & Petterson, J. S. (1992). Ethnic differences in stress, coping, and depressive symptoms after the Exxon Valdez oil spill. *Journal of Nervous & Mental Disease, 180,* 287–295.

235. Fleming, R., Baum, A., Gisriel, M. M., & Gatchel, R. J. (1982). Mediating influences of social support on stress at Three Mile Island. *Journal of Human Stress, 8,* 14–22.

236. Solomon, Z. (1985). Stress, social support and affective disorders in mothers of pre-school children—A test of the stress-buffering effect of social support. *Social Psychiatry, 20,* 100–105.

237. Chisholm, R. F., Kasl, S. V., & Mueller, L. (1986). The effects of social support on nuclear workers response to the Three Mile Island accident. *Journal of Occupational Behaviour, 7,* 179–193.

238. Kaniasty, K., & Norris, F. H. (1993). A test of the social support deterioration model in the context of natural disaster. *Journal of Personality and Social Psychology, 64,* 395–408.

239. See also Solomon, S. D., Bravo, M., Rubio-Stipec, M., & Canino, G. J. (1993). Effect of family role on response to disaster. *Journal of Traumatic Stress, 6,* 255–269.

240. See also Jeney-Gammon, P., Daugherty, T. K., Finch, A. J., Belter, R. W., et al. (1993). Children's coping styles and report of depressive symptoms following a natural disaster. *Journal of Genetic Psychology, 154,* 259–267.

241. Pennebaker, J. W., & Harber, K. D. (1993). A social stage model of collective coping: The Loma Prieta earthquake and the Persian gulf. *Journal of Social Issues, 49*(4), 125–145.

242. Murphy, S. A. (1986). Perceptions of stress, coping, and recovery one and three years after a natural disaster. *Issues in Mental Health Nursing, 8,* 63–77.

243. McLeod, B. (1984). In the wake of disaster. *Psychology Today, 18,* 54–58.

244. Thaggard, S. L. (1991). The Huntsville tornado of 1989: A psychiatrist's perspective. *Psychiatric Annals, 21,* 553–555.

245. Ponton, L. E., & Bryant, E. C. (1991). After the earthquake: Organizing to respond to children and adolescents. *Psychiatric Annals, 21,* 539–546.

246. Berman, R., & Roel, G. (1993). Encounter with death and destruction: The 1985 Mexico City earthquake. Special section: In times of national crisis. *Group Analysis, 26,* 81–89.

247. McFarlane, A. C. (1989). The prevention and management of the psychiatric morbidity of natural disasters: An Australian experience. *Stress Medicine, 5,* 29–36.

248. Raphael, B., & Meldrum, L. (1993). The evolution of mental health responses and research in Australian disasters. *Journal of Traumatic Stress, 6,* 65–89.

249. DeAngelis, T. (1991). Psychologists bring disaster victims help. *Monitor, 22,* 24.

250. See note 249.

251. The importance of the social sciences to the International Decade for Natural Disaster Reduction. (1991). *Natural Hazards Observer, 15,* 3.

252. Michaelson, R. (1993). Flood volunteers build emotional levees. *Monitor, 24,* 30.

253. Burton, I., Kates R. W., & White, G. F. (1978). *The environment as hazard.* New York: Oxford.

254. Weinstein, N. D., Sandman, P. M., & Roberts, N. E. (1990). Determinants of self-protective behavior: Home radon testing. *Journal of Applied Social Psychology, 20,* 783–801.

255. McCallum, D. B., Hammond, S. L., & Covello, V. T. (1991). Communicating about environmental risks: How the public uses and perceives information sources. *Health Education Quarterly, 18*, 349–361.

256. deMarchi, B. (1991). The Seveso Directive: An Italian pilot study in enabling communication. *Risk Analysis, 11*, 207–215.

257. Ekker, K., Gifford, G., Leik, S. A., & Leik, R. K. (1988). Using microcomputer game-simulation experiments to study family responses to the Mt. St. Helens eruptions. Special issue: Computerized simulation in the social sciences. *Social Science Computer Review, 6*, 90–105.

258. Druckman, D. (1993). The situational levers of negotiating flexibility. *Journal of Conflict Resolution, 37*, 236–276.

259. Fischhoff, B. (1990). Psychology and public policy: Tool or toolmaker? *American Psychologist, 45*, 647–653.

260. Vaughan, E. (1993). Individual and cultural differences in adaptation to environmental risks. *American Psychologist, 48*, 673–680.

261. Kiecolt, K. J., & Nigg, J. M. (1982). Mobility and perceptions of a hazardous waste environment. *Environment and Behavior, 14*, 131–154.

262. See note 224.

263. Ives, S. M., & Furuseth, D. J. (1983). Immediate response to headwater flooding in Charlotte, North Carolina. *Environment and Behavior, 15*, 512–525.

264. Payne, R. J., & Pigram, J. J. (1981). Changing evaluations of flood plain hazard: The Hunter River Valley, Australia. *Environment and Behavior, 13*, 461–480.

265. Ruga, W. (1989). Designing for the six senses. *Journal of Health Care Interior Design, 1*, 29–34.

266. Ulrich, R. (1991). Effects of interior design on wellness: Theory and recent scientific research. *Journal of Health Care Interior Design, 3*, 97–109.

267. Davis, I. (1978). *Shelter after disaster.* Oxford: Oxford Polytechnic Press.

268. See note 267.

269. Rapoport, Am. (1969). *House form and culture.* Englewood Cliffs, NJ: Prentice Hall.

Chapter 14

1. Hardin, G. (1968). The tragedy of the commons. *Science, 162*, 1243–1248.

2. See note 1.

3. Lloyd, W. F. (1837/1968). *Lectures on population, value, poor laws and rent.* New York: August M. Kelley.

4. See note 1, p. 1244.

5. Mio, J. S., Thompson, S. C., & Givens, G. H. (1993). The commons dilemma as metaphor: Memory, influence, and implications for environmental conservation. *Metaphor and Symbolic Activity, 8*, 23–42.

6. Trees vanish 40% faster than in '83. (1993, March 10). *Victoria Times-Colonist,* p. A-8.

7. Edney, J. J., & Bell, P. A. (1984). Sharing scarce resources: Group-outcome orientation, external disaster, and stealing in a simulated commons. *Small Group Behavior, 15*, 87–108.

8. Coombs, C. H., Dawes, R. M., & Tversky, A. (1970). *Mathematical psychology: An elementary introduction.* Englewood Cliffs, NJ: Prentice-Hall.

9. Komorita, S. S. (1976). A model of the N-person dilemma-type game. *Journal of Experimental Social Psychology, 12*, 357–373.

10. Dawes, R. M. (1973). The commons dilemma game: An N-person mixed-motive game with a dominating strategy for defection. *ORI Research Bulletin, 13*, 1–12.

11. Platt, J. (1973). Social traps. *American Psychologist, 28*, 641–651.

12. Messick, D. M., & McClelland, C. L. (1983). Social traps and temporal traps. *Personality and Social Psychology Bulletin, 9*, 105–110.

13. Dawes, R. M. (1980). Social dilemmas. *Annual Review of Psychology, 31*, 169–193.

14. See note 13.

15. Edney, J. J., & Harper, C. S. (1978). The commons dilemma: A review of contributions from psychology. *Environmental Management, 2*, 491–507.

16. McClintock, C. G., Moskowitz, J. M., & McClintock, E. (1977). Variations in preferences for individualistic, competitive, and cooperative outcomes as a function of age, game class, and task in nursery school children. *Child Development, 48*, 1080–1085.

17. Mintz, A. (1951). Nonadaptive group behavior. *Journal of Abnormal Social Psychology, 46*, 150–159.

18. Rapoport, An., & Kahan, J. P. (1976). When three is not always two against one: Coalitions in experimental three person cooperative games. *Journal of Experimental Social Psychology, 12*, 253–273.

19. Chapman, J., Hu, L., & Mullen, B. (1986). GROUP1 and GROUP2: BASIC programs for laboratory research on the commons dilemma and group persuasion. *Behavior Research Methods, Instruments, and Computers, 18*, 466–467.

20. Powers, R. B. (1987). Bringing the commons into a large university classroom. *Simulation and Games, 18*, 443–457.

21. Gifford, R., & Wells, J. (1991). FISH: A commons dilemma simulation. *Behavior Research Methods, Intervention and Computers, 23*, 437–441.

22. Kirts, C. A., Tumeo, M. A., & Sinz, J. M. (1991). The COMMONS GAME: Its instructional value when used in a natural resources management context. *Simulation and Gaming, 22*, 5–18.

23. Fusco, M. E., Bell, P. A., Jorgenson, M. D., & Smith, J. M. (1991). Using a computer to study the commons dilemma. *Simulation and Gaming, 22*, 67–74.

24. Summers, C. (1993). *Natural resource management decisions: An interactive, animated simulation model.* Proceedings of the Society for Computer Simulation, San Diego.

25. Akimov, V., & Soutchanksi, M. (1994). Automata simulation of N-person social dilemma games. *Journal of Conflict Resolution, 38*, 138–148.

26. Tsai, Y.-M. (1993). Social conflict and social cooperation: Simulating "The Tragedy of the Commons." *Simulation and Gaming, 24*, 356–362.

27. See note 13.

28. Edney, J. J. (1979). The nuts game: A concise commons dilemma analog. *Environmental Psychology and Nonverbal Behavior, 3*, 252–254.

29. Dawes, R. M., McTavish, J., & Shaklee, H. (1977). Behavior communication and assumptions about other people's behavior in a common dilemma situation. *Journal of Personality and Social Psychology, 35*, 1–11.

30. Bonacich, P. (1976). Secrecy and solidarity. *Sociometry, 39*, 200–208.

31. Tindall, D. B., & O'Connor, B. (1987, June). *Attitudes, social identity, social values, and behavior in a commons dilemma.* Paper presented at the Canadian Psychological Association Conference, Vancouver, B.C.

32. Kelley, H. H., Condry, J. C., Jr., Dahlke, A. E., & Hill, A. H. (1965). Collective behavior in a simulated panic situation. *Journal of Experimental Social Psychology, 1*, 20–54.

33. See note 17.

34. Watzke, G. E., Dana, J. M., Doktor, R. H., & Rubenstein, F. D. (1972). An experimental study of individual vs. group interest. *Acta Sociologica, 15*, 366–370.

35. Rubenstein, F. D., Watzke, G., Doktor, R. H., & Dana, J. (1975). The effect of two incentive schemes upon the conservation of shared resource by five-person groups. *Organizational Behavior and Human Performance, 13*, 330–338.

36. Brechner, K. C. (1976). An experimental analysis of social traps. *Journal of Experimental Social Psychology, 13*, 552–564.

37. Brann, P., & Foddy, M. (1987). Trust and the consumption of a deteriorating common resource. *Journal of Conflict Resolution, 31*, 615–630.

38. Rutte, C. G., Wilke, H. A., & Messick, D. M. (1987). Scarcity or abundance caused by people or the environment as determinants of behavior in the resource dilemma. *Journal of Experimental Social Psychology, 23*, 208–216.

39. Samuelson, C. D., & Hannula, K. A. *Group identity and environmental uncertainty in a sequential resource dilemma.* Unpublished manuscript, Texas A & M University, Department of Psychology, College Station.

40. Budescu, D. V., Rapoport, A., & Suleiman, R. (1990). Resource dilemmas with environmental uncertainty and asymmetric players. *European Journal of Social Psychology, 20*, 475–487.

41. Hine, D. W., & Gifford, R. (1993). *Individual restraint and group efficiency in the commons: The effects of uncertainty in pool size and regeneration rate.* Manuscript submitted for publication.

42. See note 41.

43. Moore, S. F., Shaffer, L. S., Pollak, E. L., & Taylor-Lemke, P. (1987). The effects of interpersonal trust and prior commons problem experience on commons management. *Journal of Social Psychology, 127*, 19–29.

44. McClintock, C. G., Moskowitz, J. M., & McClintock, E. (1977). Variations in preferences for individualistic, competitive, and cooperative outcomes as a function of age, game class, and task in nursery school children. *Child Development, 48*, 1080–1085.

45. Gifford, R. (1982). Children and the commons dilemma. *Journal of Applied Social Psychology, 12*, 269–280.

46. See note 28.

47. Bixenstine, V. E., & Douglas, J. (1967). Effects of psychopathology on group consensus and cooperative choice in a six-person game. *Journal of Personality and Social Psychology, 5*, 32–37.

48. Vinacke, W. E., Mogy, R., Powers, W., Langan, C., & Beck, R. (1974). Accommodative strategy and communication in a three person matrix game. *Journal of Personality and Social Psychology, 29*, 509–525.

49. Caldwell, M. D. (1976). Communication and sex effects in a five-person prisoner dilemma game. *Journal of Personality and Social Psychology, 33*, 273–280.

50. Javine, D. L. (1986). *A gender comparison: Cooperation for the public good.* Unpublished doctoral dissertation, University of Nevada, Reno.

51. Rapoport, An., Chammah, A., Dwyer, J., and Gyr, J. (1962). Three-person non-zero-sum nonnegotiable games. *Behavioral Science, 7*, 38–58.

52. Meux, E. P. (1973). Concern for the common good in an N-person game. *Journal of Personality and Social Psychology, 28*, 414–418.

53. Liebrand, W. B. G., Jansen, R., Rijken, V. M., & Suhre, C. (1986). Might over morality: The interaction between social values and the intrepretation of decision-making in experimental games. *Journal of Experimental Social Psychology, 22*, 203–215.

54. Hine, D. W., & Gifford, R. (1991, June). *The commons dilemma: A quantitative review.* Paper presented at the annual convention of the Canadian Psychological Association, Calgary, Alberta.

55. Hine, D. W., & Gifford, R. (1996). Self-other attributions in commons dilemmas. *European Journal of Social Psychology, 26*.

56. Sattler, D. N., & Kerr, N. L. (1991). Might versus morality explored: motivational and cognitive bases for social motives. *Journal of Personality and Social Psychology, 60*, 756–765.

57. See note 31.

58. Allison, S. T., & Messick, D. M. (1985). Effects of experience in a replenishable resource trap. *Journal of Personality and Social Psychology, 49*, 943–948.

59. Hines, J. M., Hungerford, H. R., & Tomera, A. N. (1986–87). Analysis and synthesis of research on responsible environmental behavior: A meta-analysis. *Journal of Environmental Education, 18*(2), 1–8.

60. Messick, D. M., Wilke, H., Brewer, M. B., Kramer, R. M., Zemke, P. E., & Lui, L. (1983). Individual adaptations and structural change solutions to social dilemmas. *Journal of Personality and Social Psychology, 44*, 294–309.

61. Fleishman, J. A. (1988). The effects of decision framing and others' behavior on cooperation in a social dilemma. *Journal of Conflict Resolution, 32*, 162–180.

62. Smith, J. M., & Bell, P. A. (1994). Conformity as a determinant of behavior in a resource dilemma. *Journal of Social Psychology, 134*, 191–200.

63. See note 13.

64. Komorita, S. S., & Lapworth, C. W. (1982). Cooperative choice among individuals versus groups in an N-person dilemma situation. *Journal of Personality and Social Psychology, 42,* 487–496.

65. Edney, J. J. (1981). Paradoxes on the commons: Scarcity and the problem of equality. *Journal of Community Psychology, 9,* 3–34.

66. See note 65.

67. Sato, K. (1989). Trust and feedback in a social dilemma. *Japanese Journal of Experimental Social Psychology, 29,* 123–128.

68. Grzelak, J., & Tyska, T. (1974). Some preliminary experiments on cooperation in n-person games. *Polish Psychological Bulletin, 5,* 80–91.

69. See note 62.

70. See note 54.

71. See note 67.

72. See note 67.

73. See note 43.

74. See note 37.

75. See note 39.

76. See note 31.

77. Messick, D. M. (1984). Solving social dilemmas: Individual and collective approaches. *Representative Research in Social Psychology, 14,* 72–87.

78. Smith, J. M. (1989). The effects of others' behavior, punishment, and warning on behavior in a simulated commons dilemma. *Dissertation Abstracts International, 50*(3–B), 1140–1141.

79. See note 60.

80. See note 13.

81. Allison, S. T., & Messick, D. M. (1990). Social decision heuristics in the use of shared resources. *Journal of Behavioral Decision Making, 3,* 195–204.

82. Harvey, M. L., Bell, P. A., & Birjulin, A. A. (1993). Punishment and type of feedback in a simulated commons dilemma. *Psychological Reports, 73,* 447–450.

83. Komorita, S. S., & Barth, J. M. (1985). Components of reward in social dilemmas. *Journal of Personality and Social Psychology, 48,* 364–373.

84. Wit, A., & Wilke, H. A. (1990). The presentation of rewards and punishments in a simulated social dilemma. *Social Behavior, 5,* 231–245.

85. Bell, P. A., Petersen, T. R., & Hautaluoma, J. E. (1989). The effect of punishment probability on overconsumption and stealing in a simulated commons. *Journal of Applied Social Psychology, 19,* 1483–1495.

86. Kelley, H. H., & Grzelak, J. (1972). Conflict between individual and common interest in an n-person relationship. *Journal of Personality and Social Psychology, 21,* 190–197.

87. Edney, J. J., & Bell, P. A. (1983). The commons dilemma: Comparing altruism, the golden rule, perfect equality of outcomes, and territoriality. *Social Science Journal, 20,* 23–33.

88. Edney, J. J., & Bell, P. A. (1984). Sharing scarce resources: Group-outcome orientation, external disaster, and stealing in a simulated commons. *Small Group Behavior, 15,* 87–108.

89. See note 15.

90. Birjulin, A. A., & Smith, J. M. (1993). Monetary reward, verbal reinforcement and harvest strategy of others in the commons dilemma. *Journal of Social Psychology, 133,* 207–214.

91. Martichuski, D. K., & Bell, P. A. (1991). Reward, punishment, privatization, and moral suasion in a commons dilemma. *Journal of Applied Social Psychology, 21,* 1356–1369.

92. See note 49.

93. Ostrom, E., Walker, J. M., & Gardner, R. (1990, August–September). *Sanctioning by participants in collective action problems.* Paper presented at the 1990 Annual Meetings of the American Political Science Association, San Francisco.

94. See note 13.

95. See note 87.

96. See note 36.

97. See note 49.

98. See note 29.

99. See note 15.

100. See note 43.

101. Kerr, N. L., & Kaufman-Gilliland, C. M. (1994). Communication, commitment, and cooperation in social dilemma. *Journal of Personality and Social Psychology, 66,* 513–529.

102. Orbell, J. M., Van de Kragt, A. J., & Dawes, R. M. (1988). Explaining discussion-induced cooperation. *Journal of Personality and Social Psychology, 54,* 811–819.

103. Dawes, R. M., Orbell, J. M., & van de Kragt, A. J. C. (1985). *Doing well and doing good as ways of resolving social dilemma.* Manuscript in preparation.

104. Orbell, J. M., van de Kragt, A. J. C., & Dawes, R. M. (1985). *Moral order and the threshold of the room effect.* Manuscript in preparation.

105. Jerdee, T. H., & Rosen, B. (1974). Effects of opportunity to communicate and visibility of individual decisions on behavior in the common interest. *Journal of Applied Psychology, 59,* 712–716.

106. Levine, B. L. (1987). Community psychology of managing the commons: A simulation study comparing the effect of alternative social arrangements on groups' performance, perceptions, and values with special reference to sense of community. *Dissertation Abstracts International, 47*(11-B), 4701.

107. Bixenstine, V. E., & Douglas, J. (1967). Effects of psychopathology on group consensus and cooperative choice in a six-person game. *Journal of Personality and Social Psychology, 5,* 32–37.

108. See note 43.

109. Ostrom, E., & Walker, J. M. (1989, August–September). *Communication in a commons: Cooperation without external enforcement.* Paper presented at the American Political Science Association meetings, Atlanta.

110. Cass, R. C., & Edney, J. J. (1978). The commons dilemma: A simulation testing resource visibility and territorial division. *Human Ecology, 6,* 371–386.

111. Bixenstine, V. E., Levitt, C. A., & Wilson, K. R. (1966). Collaboration among six persons in a prisoner's dilemma game. *Journal of Conflict Resolution, 10,* 488–496.

112. See note 105.

113. Fox, J., & Guyer, M. (1978). Public choice and cooperation in an n-person prisoner's dilemma. *Journal of Conflict Resolution, 22,* 468–481.

114. See note 67.

115. Rapoport, A. (1988). Provision of step-level public goods: Effects of inequality in resources. *Journal of Personality and Social Psychology, 54,* 432–440.

116. Naseth, G. J. (1990). The effects of warning of impending resource depletion, resource control and environmental attitudes on behavior in a social dilemma. *Dissertation Abstracts International, 51*(3–B), 1549.

117. See note 85.

118. Acheson, J. M. (1975). The lobster fiefs: Economic and ecological effects of territoriality in the Maine lobster industry. *Human Ecology, 3,* 183–207.

119. See note 110.

120. See note 91.

121. Edney, J. J., & Bell, P. A. (1987). Freedom and equality in a simulated commons. *Political Psychology, 8,* 229–243.

122. Aquino, K., Steisel, V., & Kay, A. (1992). The effects of resource distribution, voice, and decision framing on the provision of public goods. *Journal of Conflict Resolution, 36,* 665–687.

123. See note 77.

124. See note 87.

125. Bennett, P. D., & Moore, N. K. (1981). Consumers' preferences for alternative energy conservation policies: A trade-off analysis. *Journal of Consumer Research, 8,* 313–321.

126. Sattler, D. N. (1991). Effects of group cohesion, beliefs of own deserving, and beliefs of other's deserving on cooperation in social dilemmas. *Dissertation Abstracts International, 52*(1–B), 575.

127. Samuelson, C. D., Messick, D. M., Rutte, C. G., & Wilke, H. (1984). Individual and structual solutions to resource dilemmas in two cultures. *Journal of Personality and Social Psychology, 47,* 94–104.

128. Samuelson, C. D., & Messick, D. M. (1986). Inequities in access to and use of shared resources in social dilemmas. *Journal of Personality and Social Psychology, 51,* 960–967.

129. Samuelson, C. D., & Messick, D. M. (1986). Alternative structural solutions to resource dilemmas. *Organizational Behavior & Human Decision Processes, 37,* 139–155.

130. Samuelson, C. D. (1991). Perceived task difficulty, causal attributions, and preferences for structural change in resource dilemmas. *Personality and Social Psychology Bulletin, 17,* 181–187.

131. Samuelson, C. D. (1993). *Evaluation of allocation systems in resource dilemmas: Effects of social values, perceived resource use, and outcome inequity.* Manuscript submitted for publication.

132. See note 129.

133. Wit, A., & Wilke, H. (1988). Subordinates' endorsement of an allocating leader in a commons dilemma: An equity theoretical approach. *Journal of Economic Psychology, 9,* 151–168.

134. Edney, J. J., & Harper, C. S. (1978). Heroism in a resource crisis: A simulation study. *Environmental Management, 2,* 523–527.

135. See note 1.

136. Edney, J. J. (1980). The commons problem: Alternative perspectives. *American Psychologist, 35,* 131–150.

137. Shippee, G. (1981). Energy policymaking and Edney's dilemma. *American Psychologist, 36,* 216–217.

138. See note 1.

139. Ophuls, W. (1973). Leviathan or oblivion? In H. E. Daly (Ed.), *Toward a steady state economy.* San Francisco: Freeman.

140. Fox, J. R. (1985). Psychology, ideology, utopia and the commons. *American Psychologist, 40,* 48–58.

141. See note 65.

142. Wiener, J. L., & Doescher, T. A. (1991). A framework for promoting cooperation. *Journal of Marketing, 55,* 38–47.

143. See note 136.

144. Wynne-Edwards, V. C. (1965). Self-regulating systems in populations of animals. *Science, 147,* 1543–1548.

145. Ardrey, R. (1970). *The social contract.* New York: Dell.

146. Dawkins, R. (1976). *The selfish gene.* New York: Oxford.

147. Calabresi, G., & Bobbitt, P.(1978). *Tragic choices.* New York: Norton.

148. See note 65.

149. See note 1.

150. See note 147.

151. See note 65.

152. See note 11.

153. Geller, E. S. (1989). Applied behavior analysis and social marketing: An integration for environmental preservation. *Journal of Social Issues, 45*(1), 17–36.

154. See note 65.

155. See note 1.

156. See note 13.

157. Yamagishi, T. (1986). The structural/goal expectation theory of cooperation in social dilemmas. In E. J. Lawler & B. Markovsky (Eds.), *Advances in group processes* (Vol. 3). Greenwich, CT: JAI Press.

158. See note 130.

159. See note 130.

160. See note 60.

161. Stewart, R., Baretta, E., Platte, L., Stewart, M. T., Kalbfleisch, J., Van Yserloo, B., and Rimm, A. (1974). Carboxyhemoglobin levels in American blood donors. *Journal of the American Medical Association, 229,* 1187–1195.

162. Wilson, G. (1987). Where there's smoke . . . . *Conserver Society Notes, 14,* 53–55.

163. Sommers, P., Van Dort, B., & Moos, R. (1976). Noise and air pollution. In R. Moos (Ed.), *The human context: Environmental determinants of behavior.* New York: Wiley.

164. Rose, E. F., & Rose, M. (1971). Carbon monoxide: A challenge to the physician. *Clinical Medicine, 78,* 12–19.

165. Schulte, J. H. (1963). Effects of mild carbon monoxide intoxication. *Archives of Environmental Health, 7,* 524–530.

166. Beard, R. R., & Wertheim, G. A. (1967). Behavioral impairment associated with small doses of carbon monoxide. *American Journal of Public Health, 57,* 2012–2022.

167. Horvath, S. M., Dahms, T. E., & O'Hanlon, J. F. (1971). Carbon monoxide and human vigilance: A deleterious effect of pre-

sent urban concentrations. *Archives of Environmental Health, 23,* 343–347.

168. See note 163.

169. Jones, J. W., & Bogat, A. G. (1978). Air pollution and human aggression. *Psychological Reports, 43,* 721–722.

170. Briere, J., Downes, A., & Spensley, J. (1983). Summer in the city: Weather conditions and psychiatric emergency-room visits. *Journal of Abnormal Psychology, 92,* 77–80.

171. Sommer, R. (1972). *Design awareness.* New York: Holt, Rinehart and Winston.

172. Evans, G. W., Jacobs, S. V., & Frager, N. B. (1982). Behavioral responses to air pollution. In A. Baum & J. E. Singer (Eds.), *Advances in environmental psychology.* Hillsdale, NJ: Erlbaum.

173. Wall, G. (1973). Public response to air pollution in South Yorkshire, England. *Environment and Behavior, 5,* 219–248.

174. Cone, J. D., & Hayes, S. C. (1980). *Environmental problems: Behavioral solutions.* Monterey, CA: Brooks/Cole.

175. Samuelson, C. D. (1990). Energy conservation: A social dilemma approach. *Social Behavior, 5,* 207–230.

176. Kempton, W., Darley, J. M., & Stern, P. C. (1992). Psychological research for the new energy problems: Strategies and opportunities. *American Psychologist, 47,* 1213–1223.

177. Stern, P. C. (1992). What psychology knows about energy conservation. *American Psychologist, 47,* 1224–1232.

178. Energy facts. (1993, March 18). *Victoria Times-Colonist,* p. D-1.

179. Stern, P. C., & Gardner, G. T. (1981). The place of behavior change in the management of environmental problems. *Journal Environmental Policy, 2,* 213–240.

180. Geller, E. S. (1983). The energy crisis and behavioral science: A conceptual framework for large-scale intervention. In A. W. Childs & G. B. Melton (Eds.), *Rural psychology.* New York: Plenum.

181. Socolow, R. H. (1978). *Saving energy in the home.* Cambridge, MA: Ballinger.

182. Geller, E. S., Winett, R. A., & Everett, P. B. (1982). *Preserving the environment.* New York: Pergamon Press.

183. Stern, P. C., & Aronson, E. (Eds.). (1984). *Energy use: The human dimension.* New York: Freeman.

184. Macey, S. M., & Brown, M. A. (1983). Residential energy conservation: The role of past experience in repetitive household behavior. *Environment and Behavior, 15,* 123–141.

185. Schulz, D. A. (1985). Self esteem and energy: Toward the internalization of a conservation ethic. *Marriage and Family Review, 9,* 67–80.

186. Ritchie, J. R. B., McDougall, G., & Claxton, J. D. (1981). Complexities of household energy consumption and conservation. *Journal of Consumer Research, 8,* 233–242.

187. Black, J. S., Stern, P. C., & Elworth, J. T. (1985). Personal and contextual influences on household energy adaptations. *Journal of Applied Psychology, 70,* 3–21.

188. Samuelson, C. D., & Biek, M. (1991). Attitudes toward energy conservation: A confirmatory factor analysis. *Journal of Applied Social Psychology, 21,* 549–568.

189. Becker, L. J., Seligman, C., Fazio, R. H., & Darley, J. M. (1981). Relating attitudes to residential energy use. *Environment and Behavior, 13,* 560–609.

190. Olsen, M. E. (1981). Consumers' attitudes toward energy conservation. *Journal of Social Issues, 37*(2), 108–131.

191. Neuman, K. (1986). Personal values and commitment to energy conservation. *Environment and Behavior, 18,* 53–74.

192. Simmons, D. A., Talbot, J. F., & Kaplan, R. (1984–85). Energy in daily activities: Muddling toward conservation. *Journal of Environmental Systems, 14,* 147–155.

193. Kantola, S. J., Syme, G. J., & Campbell, N. A. (1984). Cognitive dissonance and energy conservation. *Journal of Applied Psychology, 69,* 416–421.

194. Hirst, E., & Goeltz, R. (1985). Accuracy of self-reports: Energy conservation surveys. *Social Science Journal, 22,* 19–30.

195. Costanzo, M., Archer, D., Aronson, E., & Pettigrew, T. (1986). Energy conservation behavior: The difficult path from information to action. *American Psychologist, 41,* 521–528.

196. Baird, J. C., & Brier, J. M. (1981). Perceptual awareness of energy awareness of energy requirements of familiar objects. *Journal of Applied Psychology, 66,* 90–96.

197. Kempton, W. (1986). Two theories of home heat control. *Cognitive Science, 10,* 75–90.

198. See note 193.

199. Geller, E. S. (1981). Evaluating energy conservation programs: Is verbal report enough? *Journal of Consumer Research, 8,* 331–335.

200. Peters, J. S. (1989). Integrating psychological and economic perspectives on energy consumption: The determinants of thermostat setting behavior. *Dissertation Abstracts International, 51*(4–B), 2116–2117.

201. Belk, R., Painter, J., & Semenik, R. (1981). Preferred solutions to the energy crisis as a function of causal attributions. *Journal of Consumer Research, 8,* 306–312.

202. Jackson, E. L. (1985). Environmental attitudes and preferences for energy resource options. *Journal of Environmental Education, 17*(1), 23–30.

203. Taschian, R. O., & Slama, M. E. (1985). Survey data on attitudes and behaviors relevant to energy: Implications for policy. *Marriage & Family Review, 9,* 29–51.

204. Wentworth, W. R. (1988). Energy conservation attitudes, intentions, and behaviors of homeowners in Staten Island, New York. *Dissertation Abstracts International, 49*(8–B), 3505.

205. Marshall, M. J. (1987). Social-psychological correlates of household energy conservation activities. *Dissertation Abstracts International, 48*(1–B), 301–302.

206. Labay, D. G., & Kinnear, T. C. (1981). Exploring the consumer decision process in the adoption of solar energy systems. *Journal of Consumer Research, 8,* 271–278.

207. Griffin, R. J., Glynn, C. J., & McLeod, J. M. (1986). Energy and communication: Social status in a tale of two cities. *Man-Environment Systems, 16,* 34–44.

208. See note 205.

209. Leonard-Barton, D. (1981). Voluntary simplicity lifestyles and energy conservation. *Journal of Consumer Research, 8,* 243–252.

210. See note 190.

211. See note 200.

212. Macey, S. M. (1989). Hypothermia and energy conservation: A tradeoff for elderly persons? *International Journal of Aging and Human Development, 29,* 151–161.

213. See note 200.

214. Griffin, R. J. (1989). Communication and the adoption of energy conservation measures by the elderly. *Journal of Environmental Education, 20*(4), 19–28.

215. Luyben, P. D. (1982). Prompting thermostat setting behavior: Public response to a presidential appeal for conservation. *Environment and Behavior, 14,* 113–128.

216. Wodarski, J. B. (1982). National and state appeals for energy conservation: A behavioral analysis of effects. *Behavioral Engineering, 7,* 119–130.

217. Winkler, R. C., & Winett, R. A. (1982). Behavioral interventions in resource management: A systems approach based on behavioral economics. *American Psychologist, 37,* 421–435.

218. Walker, J. M. (1980). Voluntary response to energy conservation appeals. *Journal of Consumer Research, 7,* 88–92.

219. See note 174.

220. See note 182.

221. Zielinski, E. J., & Bethel, L. J. (1983). Winning the energy game. *The Science Teacher, 50,* 55–56.

222. Dresner, M. (1989–90). Changing energy end-use patterns as a means of reducing global-warming trends. *Journal of Environmental Education, 21*(2), 41–46.

223. Parthasarathy, R. (1989, Fall). Psychological or attitudinal factors which influence the introduction of energy conservation technologies. *Abhigyan,* pp. 36–47.

224. Seligman, C. (1985). Information and energy conservaiton. *Marriage and Family Review, 9,* 135–149.

225. Syme, G. J., Seligman, C., Kantola, S. J., & MacPherson, D. K. (1987). Evaluating a television campaign to promote petrol conservation. *Environment and Behavior, 19,* 444–461.

226. Pallak, M. S., & Cummings, W. (1976). Commitment and voluntary energy conservation. *Personality and Social Psychology Bulletin, 2,* 27–30.

227. Katzev, R., & Wang, T. (1994). Can commitment change behavior? A case study of environmental actions. *Journal of Social Behavior and Personality, 9,* 13–26.

228. Shippee, G., & Gregory, W. L. (1982). Public commitment and energy conservation. *American Journal of Community Psychology, 10,* 81–93.

229. Seligman, C., & Darley, J. M. (1977). Feedback as a means of decreasing residential energy consumption. *Journal of Applied Psychology, 62,* 363–368.

230. See note 182.

231. Siero, S., Boon, M., Kok, G., & Siero F. (1989). Modification of driving behavior in a large transport organization: A field experiment. *Journal of Applied Psychology, 74,* 417–423.

232. Sexton, R. J., Johnson, N. B., & Konakayama, A. (1987). Consumer response to continuous-display electricity-use monitors in a time-of-use pricing experiment. *Journal of Consumer Research, 14,* 55–62.

233. Becker, L. J. (1978). Joint effect of feedback and goal setting on performance: A field study of residential energy conservation. *Journal of Applied Psychology, 63,* 428–433.

234. Van Houwelingen, J. H., & Van Raaij, W. F. (1989). The effect of goal-setting and daily electronic feedback on in-home energy use. *Journal of Consumer Research, 16,* 98–105.

235. Aronson, E., & O'Leary, M. (1977). The relative effectiveness of models and prompts on energy conservation: A field experiment in a shower room. *Journal of Environmental Systems, 12,* 219–224.

236. Winett, R. A., Neale, M. S., & Grier, H. C. (1979). Effects of self-monitoring and feedback on residential electricity consumption. *Journal of Applied Behavior Analysis, 12,* 173–184.

237. Winett, R. A., Neale, M. S., Williams, K. R., Yokley, J., & Kauder, H. (1979). The effects of individual and group feedback on residential electricity consumption: Three replications. *Journal of Environmental Systems, 8,* 217–233.

238. Hollenbeck, B. G. (1984). Reducing residential energy consumption: The effects of government subsidies on energy conservation. *Dissertation Abstracts International, 47*(1–B), 376.

239. Gonzales, M. H., Aronson, E., & Costanzo, M. A. (1988). Using social cognition and persuasion to promote energy conservation: A quasi-experiment. *Journal of Applied Social Psychology, 18,* 1049–1066.

240. McDougall, G. H. G., Claxton, J. D., Ritchie, J. R. B., & Anderson, C. D. (1981). Consumer energy research: A review. *Journal of Consumer Research, 8,* 343–354.

241. See note 182.

242. Yates, S. M., & Aronson, E. (1983). A social psychological perspective on energy conservation in residential buildings. *American Psychologist, 38,* 435–444.

243. Stern, P. C. (Ed.). (1984). *Improving energy demand analysis.* Washington: National Academy Press.

244. See note 217.

245. Corbett, M. N. (1981). *A better place to live: New designs for tomorrow's communities.* Emmaus, PA: Rodale.

246. Sommer, R. (1983). *Social design: Creating buildings with people in mind.* Englewood Cliffs, NJ: Prentice-Hall.

247. See note 209.

248. Purcell, A. H. (1981, February). The world's trashiest people: Will they clean up their act or throw away their future? *The Futurist,* 51–59.

249. See note 182.

250. See note 182.

251. Blue box trees tallied. (1990, March). *Victoria Times-Colonist.*

252. Bailey, J. (1994, October 4). Curb recycling has little effect on trash in U.S. *Wall Street Journal,* p. A5.

253. Williams, E. (1991). College students and recycling: Their attitudes and behaviors. *Journal of College Student Development, 32,* 86–88.

254. Oskamp, S., Harrington, M. J., Edwards, T. C., Sherwood D. L., et al. (1991). Factors influencing household recycling behavior. *Environment and Behavior, 23,* 494–519.

255. McGuire, R. H. (1984). Recycling: Great expectations and garbage outcomes. Special Issue: household refuse analysis-theory, method, and applications in social science. *American Behavioral Scientist, 28*, 93–114.

256. Vining, J., & Ebreo, A. (1992). Predicting recycling behavior from global and specific environmental attitudes and changes in recycling opportunities. *Journal of Applied Social Psychology, 22*, 1580–1607.

257. Simmons, D., & Widmar, R. (1990). Motivations and barriers to recycling: Toward a strategy for public education. *Journal of Environmental Education, 22*(1), 13–18.

258. Lansana, F. M. (1992). Distinguishing potential recyclers from nonrecyclers: A basis for developing recycling strategies. *Journal of Environmental Education, 23*(2), 16–23.

259. Kallgren, C. A., & Wood, W. (1986). Access to attitude-relevant information in memory as a determinant of attitude-behavior consistency. *Journal of Experimental Social Psychology, 22*, 328–338.

260. See note 258.

261. See note 254.

262. Katsev, R., Blake, G., & Messer, B. (1993). Determinants of participation in multi-family recycling programs. *Journal of Applied Social Psychology, 23*, 374–385.

263. Howenstine, E. (1993). Market segmentation for recycling. *Environment and Behavior, 25*, 86–102.

264. Derksen, L., & Gartrell, J. (1993). The social context of recycling. *American Sociological Review, 58*, 434–442.

265. Gamba, R. J., & Oskamp, S. (1994). Factors influencing community residents' participation in commingled recycling programs. *Environment and Behavior, 26*, 587–612.

266. See note 262.

267. See note 259.

268. Hopper, J. R., & Nielson, J. M. (1991). Recycling as altruistic behavior: Normative and behavioral strategies to expand participation in a community recycling program. *Environment and Behavior, 23*, 195–220.

269. Burn, S. M., & Oskamp, S. (1986). Increasing community recycling with persuasive communication and public commitment. *Journal of Applied Social Psychology, 16*, 29–41.

270. de Young, R., Duncan, A., Frank, J., Gill, N., et al. (1993). Promoting source reduction behavior: The role of motivational information. *Environment and Behavior, 25*, 70–85.

271. Katzev, R., & Mishima, H. R. (1992). The use of posted feedback to promote recycling. *Psychological Reports, 71*, 259–264.

272. Diamond, W. D., & Loewy, B. Z. (1991). Effects of probabilistic rewards on recycling attitudes and behavior. *Journal of Applied Social Psychology, 21*, 1590–1607.

273. Lord, K. R. (1994). Motivating recycling behavior: A quasi-experimental investigation of message and source strategies. *Psychology and Marketing, 11*, 341–358.

274. Shrum, L. J., Lowrey, T. M., & McCarty, J. A. (1994). Recycling as a marketing problem: A framework for strategy development. *Psychology and Marketing, 11*, 393–416.

275. Witmer, J. F., & Geller, E. S. (1976). Facilitating paper recycling: Effects of prompts, raffles, and contests. *Journal of Applied Behavior Analysis, 9*, 315–322.

276. Austin, J., Hatfield, D. B., Grindle, A. C., & Bailey, J. S. (1993). Increasing recycling in office environments: The effects of specific, informative cues. *Journal of Applied Behavior Analysis, 26*, 247–253.

277. See note 217.

278. See note 272.

279. See note 268.

280. Burn, S. M. (1991). Social psychology and the stimulation of recycling behaviors: The block leader approach. *Journal of Applied Social Psychology, 21*, 611–629.

281. Kahle, L. R., & Beatty, S. E. (1987). Cognitive consequences of legislating postpurchase behavior: Growing up with the bottle bill. *Journal of Applied Social Psychology, 17*, 828–843.

282. See note 269.

283. Wang, T. H., & Katsev, R. D. (1990). Group commitment and resource conservation: Two field experiments on promoting recycling. *Journal of Applied Social Psychology, 20*, 265–272.

284. Goldenhar, L. M. (1991). Understanding, predicting, and influencing recycling behavior: The future generation. *Dissertation Abstracts International, 52*(3–B), 1379.

285. Crosby, L. A., & Taylor, J. R. (1982). Consumer satisfaction with Michigan's container deposit law—An ecological perspective. *Journal of Marketing, 46*, 47–60.

286. Trinkaus, J. (1984). A bottle law: An informal look. *Perceptual and Motor Skills, 59*, 806.

287. Wright, R. E. (1991). An investigation of the relative importance of factors influencing recycling behavior. *Dissertation Abstracts International, 52*(11–A), 4008–4009.

288. Lansana, F. (1992). Modelling household participation rates in recycling programs: An analysis of spatio-temporal variations. *Dissertation Abstracts International, 52*(7–A), 2673.

289. See note 257.

290. Humphrey, C. R., Bord, R. J., Hammond, M. M., & Mann, S. H. (1977). Attitudes and conditions for cooperation in a paper recycling program. *Environment and Behavior, 9*, 107–124.

291. Brothers, K. J., Krantz, P. J., & McClannahan, L. E. (1994). Office paper recycling: A function of container proximity. *Journal of Applied Behavior Analysis, 27*, 153–160.

292. See note 182.

293. Edney, J. J. (1984). Rationality and social justice. *Human Relations, 37*, 163–180.

Chapter 15

1. Izumi, K. (1970). LSD and architectural design. In B. Aaronson & H. Osmond (Eds.). *Psychedelics.* New York: Doubleday/Anchor.

2. Sommer, R. (1972). *Design awareness.* New York: Holt, Rinehart and Winston.

3. Sommer, R. (1983). *Social design.* Englewood Cliffs, NJ: Prentice-Hall.

4. See note 3, p. 7.

5. See note 3.

6. Slum surgery in St. Louis. (1951). *Architectural Forum, 94,* 128–136.

7. Devlin, K. (1990). An examination of architectural interpretation: Architects versus non-architects. *Journal of Architectural and Planning Research, 7,* 235–244.

8. Wilson, M. A., & Canter, D. V. (1990). The development of central concepts during professional education: An example of a multivariate model of the concept of architectural style. *Applied Psychology: An International Review, 39,* 431–455.

9. Goel, V., & Pirolli, P. (1992). The structure of design problem spaces. *Cognitive Science, 16,* 395–429.

10. Downing, F. (1992). The role of place and event imagery in the art of design. *Journal of Architectural and Planning Research, 9,* 64–80.

11. Ahrentzen, S., & Groat, L. N. (1992). Rethinking architectural education: Patriarchal convention and alternative visions from the perspectives of women faculty. *Journal of Architectural and Planning Research, 9,* 95–111.

12. Duffy, M., Bailey, S., Beck, B., & Barker, D. G. (1986). Preferences in nursing home design—A comparison of residents, administrators, and designers. *Environment and Behavior, 18,* 246–257.

13. Nasar, J. L., & Kang, J. (1989). A post-jury evaluation: The Ohio State University design competition for a center for the visual arts. *Environment and Behavior, 21,* 464–484.

14. Vischer, J. C., & Marcus, C. C. (1986). Evaluating evaluation: Analysis of a housing design awards program. *Places, 3,* 66–86.

15. Turner, J. F. C. (1987). The enabling practitioner and the recovery of creative work. *Journal of Architectural and Planning Research, 4,* 273–280.

16. Rabinowitz, H. Z., & Weisman, G. D. (1988). *The state of standards: Evaluating educational facilities.* Proceedings of the 19th annual meetings of the Environmental Design Research Association, pp. 237–241.

17. See note 3, p. 4.

18. See note 3.

19. Olwig, K. R. (1990). Designs upon children's special places? *Children's Environments Quarterly, 7,* 47–53.

20. Conway, D. (1973). *Social science and design: A process model for architect and social scientist collaboration.* Washington, DC: American Institute of Architects.

21. Sime, J. D. (1986). Creating places or designing spaces? *Journal of Environmental Psychology, 6,* 49–63.

22. Schneekloth, L. H., & Shibley, R. G. (1993). The practice of placemaking. *Architecture et Comportement/Architecture and Behavior, 9,* 121–144.

23. Stamps, A. (1989). Are environmental aesthetics worth studying? *Journal of Architectural and Planning Research, 6,* 344–356.

24. Dempsey, F. (1914). Nela Park: A novelty in the architectural grouping of industrial buildings. *Architectural Record, 35,* 472.

25. Wheeler, L. (1985). Behavior and design: A memoir. *Environment and Behavior, 17,* 133–144.

26. Rapoport, Am. (1969). *House form and culture.* Englewood Cliffs, NJ: Prentice Hall.

27. Holahan, C. J. (1983). Interventions to reduce stress: Enhancing social support and personal control. In E. Siedman (Ed.), *Handbook of social interventions.* Beverly Hills, CA: Sage.

28. See note 27.

29. Michelson, W. (1976). *Man and his urban environment: A sociological approach.* Don Mills, ON: Adison-Wesley.

30. Preiser, W. P. E., & Taylor, A. (1983). The habitability framework: Linking human behavior and physical environment in special education. *EEQ: Exceptional Education Quarterly, 4*(2), 1–15.

31. Lansing, J. B., & Marans, R. W. (1969). Evaluation of neighborhood quality. *Journal of the American Institute of Planners, 35,* 195–199.

32. Rule, B. G., Milke, D. L., & Dobbs, A. R. (1992). Design of institutions: Cognitive functioning and social interactions of the aged resident. *Journal of Applied Gerontology, 11,* 475–488.

33. Christenson, M. A. (1990). Aging in the designed environment. *Physical and Occupational Therapy in Geriatrics, 8,* 3–133.

34. Cohen, U., & Weisman, G. D. (1990). Experimental design to maximize autonomy for older adults with cognitive impairments. *Generations, 14*(Suppl.), 75–78.

35. Hunt, M. E. (1991). The design of supportive environments for older people. Special Issue: Congregate housing for the elderly: Theoretical, policy, and programmatic perspectives. *Journal of Housing for the Elderly, 9,* 127–140.

36. Osmond, H. (1957). Function as the basis of psychiatric ward design. *Mental Hospitals, 8,* 23–30.

37. Gulak, M. B. (1991). Architectural guidelines for state psychiatric hospitals. *Hospital and Community Psychiatry, 42,* 705–707.

38. Remen, S. (1991). Signs, symbols, and the psychiatric environment. *Psychiatric Hospital, 22,* 113–118.

39. Manoleas, P. (1991). Designing mental health facilities: An interactive process. *Hospital and Community Psychiatry, 42,* 305–308.

40. St. Clair, R. (1987). Psychiatric hospital design. *Psychiatric Hospital, 18,* 17–22.

41. Kennedy, D. (1991). The young child's experience of space and child care center design: A practical meditation. *Children's Environments Quarterly, 8,* 37–48.

42. Striniste, N. A., & Moore, R. C. (1989). Early childhood outdoors: A literature review related to the design of childcare environments. *Children's Environments Quarterly, 6,* 25–31.

43. Atlas, R. (1989). Reducing the opportunity for inmate suicide: A design guide. *Psychiatric Quarterly, 60,* 161–171.

44. Christenfeld, R., Wagner, J., Pastva, G., & Acrish, W. P. (1989). How physical settings affect chronic mental patients. *Psychiatric Quarterly, 60,* 253–264.

45. Hooper, J., & Reid, D. H. (1985). A simple environmental redesign for improving classroom performance of profoundly retarded students. *Education and Treatment of Children, 8,* 25–39.

46. See note 3.

47. van Hoogdalem, H., van der Voordt, T. J. M., & van Wegen, H. B. R. (1985). Comparative floorplan-analysis as a means to de-

velop design guidelines. *Journal of Environmental Psychology, 5,* 153–179.

48. Knight, R. C., & Campbell, D. E. (1980). Environmental evaluation research: Evaluator roles and inherent social commitments. *Environment and Behavior, 12,* 520–532.

49. Chapin, D., & Cooper Marcus, C. (1993). Design guidelines: Reflections of experiences passed. *Architecture and Behavior/Architecture et Comportement, 9,* 99–120.

50. Saegert, S. (1993). Charged contexts: Difference, emotion and power in environmental design research. *Architecture et Comportement/Architecture and Behavior, 9,* 69–84.

51. See note 3.

52. See note 3, p. 65.

53. Mirrer, S. B. (1987). Using anthropometric data in the design of children's health care environments. *Children's Environments Quarterly, 4,* 6–11.

54. Gutkowski, S., Ginath, Y., & Guttman, F. (1992). Improving psychiatric environments through minimal architectural change. *Hospital and Community Psychiatry, 43,* 920–923.

55. See note 27.

56. Moos, R. H. (1981). A social-ecological perspective on health. In G. Stone et al. (Eds.), *Health psychology.* San Francisco: Jossey-Bass.

57. Mehrabian, A., & Diamond, S. G. (1971). The effects of furniture arrangement, props and personality on social interaction. *Journal of Personality and Social Psychology, 20,* 18–30.

58. Holahan, C. J. (1972). Seating patterns and patient behavior in an experimental dayroom. *Journal of Abnormal Psychology, 80,* 115–124.

59. Refuerzo, B. J., & Verderber, S. (1990). Dimensions of person-environment relationships in shelters for victims of domestic violence. *Journal of Architectural and Planning Research, 7,* 33–52.

60. Hunt, M. E. (1985). Enhancing a building's imageability. *Journal of Architectural and Planning Research, 2,* 151–168.

61. See note 3.

62. Barrett, T. (1991, May 11). Thinking small. *Vancouver Sun,* pp. 1, 8–9.

63. Kira, A. (1976). *The bathroom.* New York: Viking.

64. Sommer, R. (1969). *Personal space: The behavioral basis of design.* Englewood Cliffs, NJ: Prentice-Hall.

65. Beal, G., & Keller, R. (1989). Group planning in a psychiatric facility: Problematic group reactions and lessons learned. *International Journal of Therapeutic Communities, 10,* 59–65.

66. Porteous, J. D. (1977). *Environment and behavior: Planning and everyday life.* Don Mills, ON: Addison-Wesley.

67. Shibley, R. G., & Schneekloth, L. H. (1988). Risking collaboration: Professional dilemmas in evaluation and design. *Journal of Architectural and Planning Research, 5,* 304–320.

68. Beck, W. C., & Meyer, R. H. (1982). *The health care environment: The user's viewpoint.* Boca Raton, FL: CRC Press.

69. See note 65.

70. See note 3.

71. Zimring, C. M., & Reitzenstein, J. E. (1981). A primer on post-occupancy evaluation. *AIA Journal, 70,* 52–58.

72. See note 3.

73. Wools, R. (1970). The effects of rooms on behavior. In D. Canter (Ed.), *Architectural psychology.* London: RIBA.

74. See note 71.

75. See note 3.

76. Reizenstein, J. E. (1982). Hospital design and human behavior: A review of the recent literature. In A. Baum & J. E. Singer (Eds.), *Advances in environmental psychology: Volume 4: Environment and health.* Hillsdale, NJ: Erlbaum.

77. Zeisel, J. (1975). *Sociology and architectural design.* New York: Russell Sage Foundation.

78. Wener, R., Frazier, F. W., & Farbstein, J. (1985). Three generations of evaluation and design of correctional facilities. *Environment and Behavior, 17,* 71–95.

79. Wener, R. E. (1988). Doing it right: Examples of successful applications of environment-behavior research. *Journal of Architectural and Planning Research, 5,* 284–303.

80. See note 2.

81. Sommer, R. (1976). *The end of imprisonment.* Englewood Cliffs, NJ: Prentice-Hall.

82. Al-Soliman, T. M. (1991). Societal values and their effect on the built environment in Saudi Arabia: A recent account. *Journal of Architectural and Planning Research, 8,* 235–254.

83. Kent, S. (1991). Partitioning space: Cross-cultural factors influencing domestic spatial segmentation. *Environment and Behavior, 23,* 438–473.

84. See note 77.

85. See note 3.

86. Kuller, R., & Mattsson, R. (1984). *The dining room at a geriatric hospital.* Paper presented at International Association for the Study of People and Their Surroundings, West Berlin.

87. Nasar, J. L., & Farokhpay, M. (1985). Assessment of activity priorities and design preferences of elderly residents in public housing: A case study. *Gerontologist, 25,* 251–257.

88. Butler, D. L., & Biner, P. M. (1987). Preferred lighting levels: Variability among settings, behaviors, and individuals. *Environment and Behavior, 19,* 695–721.

89. Butler, D. L., & Biner, P. M. (1989). Effects of setting on window preferences and factors associated with those preferences. *Environment and Behavior, 21,* 17–31.

90. See note 77.

91. Barkow, B. (1977). Public transit too often ignores people. *Notes from underground.* Long Island City, NY: Committee for Better Transit.

92. Hanlon, M. (1981, November 8). Psychologists used for pedestrian engineering. *Toronto Star,* p. E5.

93. Irvine, C. H., Snook, S. H., & Sparshatt, J. H. (1990). Stairway risers and treads: Acceptable and preferred dimensions. *Applied Ergonomics, 21,* 215–225.

94. Dalhoum, E. J., & Rydberg-Mitchell, B. (1992). Communicating with laypeople. *Architecture et Comportement/Architecture and Behavior, 8,* 241–251.

95. Martens, B. (1992). Tools for visual simulation of space and their use by students. *Architecture et Comportement/Architecture and Behavior, 8,* 265–272.

96. Rheingold, H. (1990). Travels in virtual reality. *Whole Earth Review, 67,* 80–86.

97. Campbell, D. E., & Schlecter, T. M. (1979). Library design influences on user behavior and satisfaction. *Library Quarterly, 49,* 26–41.

98. Ng, C. F., & Gifford, R. (1986). *Greater Victoria Public Library (Esquimalt Branch): A Post-occupancy report.* Report to the Greater Victoria Public Library Board.

99. See note 98.

100. See note 77.

101. See note 3.

102. Mueller, W. S. (1981). Translation of user requirements into house designs: A multi-dimensional scaling analysis. *Journal of Environmental Psychology, 1,* 97–116.

103. See note 2.

104. See note 3, p. 9.

105. Becker, F. D. (1983, July). Creating an office that works. *Xerox Learning Systems.*

106. Becker, F. D. (1980). Employees need role in design of work space. *Hospitals, 54,* 97–105.

107. van Wagenberg, D., Krasner, M., & Krasner, L. (1981). Children planning an ideal classroom: Environmental design in an elementary school. *Environment and Behavior, 13,* 211–234.

108. Kaplan, S. & Kaplan, R. (1982). *Cognition and environment: Functioning in an uncertain world.* New York: Praeger.

109. Breu, J. (1984, April 20). Patients, visitors getting chance to help design new hospital. *American Medical News,* pp. 10–11.

110. Lawrence, R. J. (1982). A psychological-spatial approach for architectural design and research. *Journal of Environmental Psychology, 2,* 37–51.

111. See note 96.

112. Davis, G., & Szigeti, F. (1982). Programming, space planning and office design. *Environment and Behavior, 14,* 299–317.

113. Becker, F. D. (1977). *Housing messages.* Stroudsberg, PA: Dowden, Hutchinson and Ross.

114. Carpman, J. R., Grant, M. A., & Simmons, D. A. (1986). *Design that cares: Planning health facilities for patients and visitors.* Chicago: American Hospital Publishing.

115. Busch-Rossnagel, N. A., Nasar, J. L., Campbell, J., & Danish, S. J. (1980). An interdisciplinary approach to designing environments for children. *Journal of Man-Environment Relations, 1,* 1–10.

116. Eisemon, T. (1975). Simulations and requirements for citizen participation in public housing: The Truax technique. *Environment and Behavior, 7,* 99–123.

117. Vischer, J. C. (1985). The adaptation and control model of user needs: A new direction for housing research. *Journal of Environmental Psychology, 5,* 287–296.

118. See note 76.

119. See note 76.

120. Mazumdar, S. (1992). How programming can be counterproductive: An analysis of approaches to programming. *Journal of Environmental Psychology, 12,* 65–91.

121. Steele, F. I. (1973). *Physical settings and organization development.* Don Mills, ON: Addison-Wesley.

122. See note 77.

123. See note 106.

124. Mackett-Stout, J., & Dewar, R. (1981). Evaluations of symbolic public information signs. *Human Factors, 23,* 139–151.

125. See note 77.

126. Olds, A. R. (1989). Psychological and physiological harmony in child care center design. *Children's Environments Quarterly, 6,* 8–16.

127. See note 106.

128. Hatch, C. R. (1984). *The scope of social architecture.* Toronto: Van Nostrand Reinhold.

129. See note 77.

130. Kaye, S. M. (1975). Psychology in relation to design: An overview. *Canadian Psychological Review, 16,* 104–110.

131. Zimring, C. M., & Reizenstein, J. E. (1980). Post-occupancy evaluation: An overview. *Environment and Behavior, 12,* 429–450.

132. See note 71.

133. Friedmann, A., Zimring, C., & Zube, E. (1978). *Environmental design evaluation.* New York: Plenum.

134. See note 133.

135. See note 131.

136. See note 71.

137. See note 77.

138. Webb, E. J., Campbell, D. T., Schwartz, R. D., & Sechrest, L. (1966). *Unobtrusive measures: Nonreactive research in the social sciences.* Chicago: Rand-McNally.

139. Zeisel, J. (1981). *Inquiry by design: Tools for environment-behavior research.* Monterey, CA: Brooks/Cole.

140. See note 2.

141. Zube, E. H. (1980). *Environmental evaluation: Perception and public policy.* Monterey, CA: Brooks/Cole.

142. Lemke, S., & Moos, R. H. (1985). Coping with an intrainstitutional relocation: Behavioral change as a function of residents' personal resources. *Journal of Environmental Psychology, 5,* 137–151.

143. Farbstein, J., & Wener, R. E. (1982). Evaluation of correctional environments. *Environment and Behavior, 14,* 671–694.

144. Gabb, B. S., Speicher, K., & Lodl, K. (1992). Environmental design for individuals with schizophrenia: An assessment tool. *Journal of Applied Rehabilitation Counseling, 23,* 35–40.

145. Davis, G., & Ventre, F. T. (Eds.). (1990). *Performance of buildings and serviceability of facilities.* Philadelphia: ASTM.

146. David, T. G. (1982). Evaluating school environments from a user perspective. *Journal of Man-Environment Relations, 1,* 79–89.

147. See note 44.

148. Devlin, A. S. (1992). Psychiatric ward renovation: Staff perception and patient behavior. *Environment and Behavior, 24,* 66–84.

149. Refuerzo, B. J., & Verderber, S. (1988). Creating a safe refuge: The functions of nature in the design of shelters for victims of domestic violence. EDRA: *Environmental Design Research Association, 19,* 63–69.

150. Becker, F. D., & Poe, D. B. (1980). The effects of user-generated design modifications in a general hospital. *Journal of Nonverbal Behavior, 4,* 195–218.

151. Marans, R. W., & Spreckelmeyer, K. F. (1982). Evaluating open and conventional office design. *Environment and Behavior, 14*, 333–351.

152. Marans, R. W., & Spreckelmeyer, K. F. (1982). Measuring overall architectural quality: A component of building evaluation. *Environment and Behavior, 14*, 652–670.

153. Gifford, R. (1976). *Personal and situational factors in judgements of typical architecture.* Unpublished doctoral dissertation, Simon Fraser University, Burnaby, British Columbia.

154. Weisman, G. D. (1983). Environmental programming and action research. *Environment and Behavior, 15*, 318–408.

Epilogue

1. Goerner, S. J. (1993). *The evolving ecological universe: A study in the science and human implications of a new world hypothesis.* Unpublished doctoral dissertation, Saybrook Institute.

2. Beringer, A. (1993). *The moral ideals of care and respect: A hermeneutic inquiry into adolescents' environmental ethics and moral functioning.* Unpublished doctoral dissertation, University of Michigan.

3. Berg, L. L. (1995, April 24). They always say it can't be done, and it always can. *Toronto Globe and Mail,* p. A-21.

4. Immen, W. (1995, April 22). Earth Day birthday cause for optimism. *Toronto Globe and Mail,* p. A-5.

5. Appleby, T. (1995, April 4). Smog rules green in more ways than one. *Toronto Globe and Mail,* p. B-26.

6. Wessan, L. (1994). "What's really bothering you, Lisa?" *The Ecopsychology Newsletter, 1*(2), 4.

NAME INDEX

SUBJECT INDEX

These pages constitute a continuation of the copyright page.